BRITISH RAILWAYS
LOCOMOTIVES & COACHING STOCK
2017

The Complete Guide to all Locomotives & Coaching Stock which operate on the National Rail network and Eurotunnel

Robert Pritchard & Peter Hall

Published by Platform 5 Publishing Ltd,
52 Broadfield Road, Sheffield, S8 0XJ, England.

Printed in England by The Lavenham Press, Lavenham, Suffolk.

ISBN 978 1 909431 36 2

CONTENTS

SECTION 1 – LOCOMOTIVES

SECTION 2 – LOCO-HAULED COACHING STOCK

SECTION 3 – DIESEL MULTIPLE UNITS

CONTENTS 3

SECTION 4 – ELECTRIC MULTIPLE UNITS

SECTION 5 – ON-TRACK MACHINES

SECTION 6 – CODES

COVER PHOTOGRAPHS

Front Cover: Great Western Railway Hitachi IEP 800 004 is seen at London Paddington on 30/06/16 as HST power car 43005, also in GWR green livery, arrives alongside.
Robert Pritchard

Back Cover: ScotRail-liveried 68007 "Valiant" arrives at Kinghorn with the 17.48 Glenrothes with Thornton–Edinburgh Waverley on 30/05/16 as 158 731 brings up the rear of the 17.48 Edinburgh–Glenrothes.
Ian Lothian

BRITAIN'S RAILWAY SYSTEM

INFRASTRUCTURE & OPERATION

Britain's national railway infrastructure is owned by a "not for dividend" company, Network Rail. In 2014 Network Rail was reclassified as a public sector company, being described by the Government as a "public sector arm's-length body of the Department for Transport".

Most stations and maintenance depots are leased to and operated by Train Operating Companies (TOCs), but some larger stations are controlled by Network Rail. The only exception is the infrastructure on the Isle of Wight: The Island Line franchise uniquely included maintenance of the infrastructure as well as the operation of passenger services. As Island Line is now part of the South West Trains franchise, both the infrastructure and trains are operated by South West Trains.

Trains are operated by TOCs over Network Rail tracks (the National Network), regulated by access agreements between the parties involved. In general, TOCs are responsible for the provision and maintenance of the locomotives, rolling stock and staff necessary for the direct operation of services, whilst Network Rail is responsible for the provision and maintenance of the infrastructure and also for staff to regulate the operation of services.

The Department for Transport (DfT) is the franchising authority for the national network, with Transport Scotland overseeing the award of the ScotRail franchise and the Welsh Government overseeing the Wales & Borders franchise.

A franchise is the right to run specified services within a specified area for a period of time, in return for the right to charge fares and, where appropriate, to receive financial support from the Government. Subsidy is payable in respect of socially necessary services. Service standards are monitored by the DfT throughout the duration of the franchise. Franchisees earn revenue primarily from fares and from subsidy. They generally lease stations from Network Rail and earn rental income by sub-letting parts of them, for example to retailers.

Franchisees' main costs are the track access charges they pay to Network Rail, the costs of leasing stations and rolling stock and of employing staff. Franchisees may do light maintenance work on rolling stock or contract it out to private companies. Heavy maintenance is normally carried out by the Rolling Stock Leasing Companies, according to contracts.

TOCs can take commercial risks, although some franchises are "management contracts", where ticket revenues pass directly to the DfT. Concessions (such as London Overground) see the operator paid a fee to run the service, usually within tightly specified guidelines. Operators running a concession would not normally take commercial risks, although there are usually penalties and rewards in the contract.

During 2012 the letting of new franchises was suspended pending a review of the franchise system. The process restarted in 2013 but it is taking a number of years to catch-up and in the meantime the Government has been negotiating directly with some incumbent operators which has seen some franchises extended as part of a "Direct Award".

Note that a railway "reporting period" is four weeks.

DOMESTIC PASSENGER TRAIN OPERATORS

The majority of passenger trains are operated by Train Operating Companies on fixed-term franchises or concessions. Franchise expiry dates are shown in the list below:

Franchise	*Franchisee*	*Trading Name*
Caledonian Sleeper	Serco (until 31 March 2030)	**Caledonian Sleeper**

This new franchise started in April 2015 when operation of the ScotRail and ScotRail Sleeper franchises was separated. Abellio won the ScotRail franchise and Serco the Caledonian Sleeper franchise. Caledonian Sleeper operates four trains nightly between London Euston and Scotland using locomotives hired from GBRf or Freightliner. New CAF rolling stock will be introduced from 2018 to replace the current Mark 2 and Mark 3 carriages that are used.

Chiltern	Arriva (Deutsche Bahn) (until 31 December 2021)	**Chiltern Railways**

There is an option to extend the franchise by 6 months to June 2022.

Chiltern Railways operates a frequent service between London Marylebone, Banbury and Birmingham Snow Hill, with some peak trains extending to Kidderminster. There are also regular services from Marylebone to Stratford-upon-Avon and to Aylesbury Vale Parkway via Amersham (along the London Underground Metropolitan Line). A new route to Oxford Parkway and then Oxford was added in 2015–16. The fleet consists of DMUs of Classes 121 (used on the Princes Risborough–Aylesbury route), 165, 168 and 172 plus a number of locomotive-hauled rakes used on some of the Birmingham route trains, worked by Class 68s hired from DRS.

Cross Country	Arriva (Deutsche Bahn) (until October 2019)	**CrossCountry**

CrossCountry operates a network of long distance services between Scotland, the North-East of England and Manchester to the South-West of England, Reading, Southampton, Bournemouth and Guildford, centred on Birmingham New Street. These trains are mainly formed of diesel Class 220/221 Voyagers, supplemented by a small number of HSTs on the NE–SW route. Inter-urban services also link Nottingham, Leicester and Stansted Airport with Birmingham and Cardiff. These trains use Class 170 DMUs.

Crossrail	MTR (until 30 May 2023)	**TfL Rail**

There is an option to extend the concession by 2 years to May 2025.

This is a new concession which started in May 2015. Initially Crossrail took over the Liverpool Street–Shenfield stopping service from Greater Anglia, using a fleet of Class 315 EMUs, with the service branded "TfL Rail". New Class 345 EMUs will be introduced on this route from May 2017 and then from 2018–19 Crossrail will operate through new tunnels beneath central London, from Shenfield and Abbey Wood in the east to Reading and Heathrow Airport in the west.

| **East Coast** | Stagecoach/Virgin Trains | **Virgin Trains East Coast** |
| | (until 31 March 2023) | |

There is an option to extend the franchise by 1 year to March 2024.

Virgin Trains East Coast operates frequent long distance trains on the East Coast Main Line between London King's Cross, Leeds, York, Newcastle and Edinburgh, with less frequent services to Bradford, Harrogate, Skipton, Hull, Lincoln, Glasgow, Aberdeen and Inverness. A mixed fleet of Class 91s and 30 Mark 4 sets, and 15 HST sets, are used on these trains.

| **East Midlands** | Stagecoach Group | **East Midlands Trains** |
| | (until 22 July 2018) | |

There is an option to extend the franchise by eight reporting periods to March 2019.

EMT operates a mix of long distance high speed services on the Midland Main Line (MML), from London St Pancras to Sheffield (to Leeds at peak times and with some extensions to York/Scarborough) and Nottingham (plus peak-hour trains to Lincoln), and local and regional services ranging from the Norwich–Liverpool route to Nottingham–Skegness, Newark–Mansfield–Worksop, Nottingham–Matlock and Derby–Crewe. It also operates local services in Lincolnshire. Trains on the MML are worked by a fleet of Class 222 DMUs and nine HSTs, whilst the local and regional fleet consists of DMU Classes 153, 156 and 158.

| **East Anglia** | Abellio (Netherlands Railways)/Mitsui Group* | **Greater Anglia** |
| | (until 15 October 2025) | |

There is an option to extend the franchise by 1 year to October 2026.
* In early 2017 Abellio sold a 40% stake of the franchise to Mitsui Group of Japan.

Greater Anglia operates main line trains between London Liverpool Street, Ipswich and Norwich and local trains across Norfolk, Suffolk and parts of Cambridgeshire. It also runs local and commuter services into Liverpool Street from the Great Eastern (including Southend, Braintree and Clacton) and West Anglia (including Cambridge and Stansted Airport) routes. It operates a varied fleet of Class 90s with locomotive-hauled Mark 3 sets, DMUs of Classes 153, 156 and 170 and EMUs of Classes 317, 321, 360 and 379. Two locomotive-hauled sets, using Class 37s and 68s, are currently hired for use on some trains between Norwich and Great Yarmouth/Lowestoft.

| **Essex Thameside** | National Express Group* | **c2c** |
| | (until 8 November 2029) | |

There is an option to extend the franchise by 6 months to May 2030.
* The acquisition of this franchise by Trenitalia, part of the FS Italiane Group, was being concluded as this book closed for press.

c2c operates an intensive, principally commuter, service from London Fenchurch Street to Southend and Shoeburyness via both Upminster and Tilbury. The fleet consists of 74 Class 357 EMUs, plus six Class 387s which arrived in late 2016. In 2014 c2c won the new 15-year franchise that promised to introduce 17 new 4-car EMUs from 2019.

| **Great Western** | First Group | **Great Western Railway** |
| | (until 1 April 2019) | |

There is an option to extend the franchise by 1 year to April 2020.

Great Western Railway (until September 2015 branded as First Great Western) operates long distance trains from London Paddington to South Wales, the West Country and Worcester and Hereford. In addition there are frequent trains along the Thames Valley corridor to Newbury/Bedwyn and Oxford, plus local and regional trains throughout the South-West including the Cornish, Devon and Thames Valley branches, the Reading–Gatwick North Downs Line and Cardiff–Portsmouth Harbour and Bristol–Weymouth regional routes. A fleet of 54 HSTs is used on the long-distance trains, with DMUs of Classes 165 and 166 used on the Thames Valley and

North Downs routes and Class 180s used alongside HSTs on the Cotswold Line to Worcester and Hereford. New Class 387 EMUs are now also being used on initial electric services from Paddington, firstly as far as Hayes & Harlington and then extending to Maidenhead in spring 2017. Classes 143, 150, 153 and 158 are used on local and regional trains in the South-West. A small fleet of Class 57s is maintained to principally work the overnight "Cornish Riviera" Sleeper service between London Paddington and Penzance.

| **London Rail** | Arriva (Deutsche Bahn) | **London Overground** |
| | (until May 2024) | |

This is a concession and is different from other rail franchises, as fares and service levels are set by Transport for London instead of by the DfT. There is an option to extend the concession by 2 years to May 2026.

London Overground operates services on the Richmond–Stratford North London Line and the Willesden Junction–Clapham Junction West London Line, plus the East London Line from Highbury & !slington to New Cross and New Cross Gate, with extensions to Clapham Junction (via Denmark Hill), Crystal Palace and West Croydon. It also runs services from London Euston to Watford Junction. These use Class 378 EMUs whilst Class 172 DMUs are used on the Gospel Oak–Barking route. London Overground also took over the operation of some suburban services from London Liverpool Street in 2015 – to Chingford, Enfield Town and Cheshunt. These use Class 315 and 317 EMUs, but will be replaced by new Bombardier Class 710s from 2018 – these will also be used on the Gospel Oak–Barking line, which is being electrified.

| **Merseyrail Electrics** | Serco/Abellio (Netherlands Railways) | **Merseyrail** |
| | (until 19 July 2028) | |

Under the control of Merseytravel PTE instead of the DfT. Franchise reviewed every five years to fit in with the Merseyside Local Transport Plan.

Merseyrail operates services between Liverpool and Southport, Ormskirk, Kirkby, Hunts Cross, New Brighton, West Kirby, Chester and Ellesmere Port, using Class 507 and 508 EMUs.

| **Northern** | Arriva (Deutsche Bahn) | **Northern** |
| | (until 31 March 2025) | |

There is an option to extend the franchise by 1 year to March 2026.

Northern operates a range of inter-urban, commuter and rural services throughout the North of England, including those around the cities of Leeds, Manchester, Sheffield, Liverpool and Newcastle. The network extends from Chathill in the north to Nottingham in the south, and Cleethorpes in the east to St Bees in the west. Long distance services include Leeds–Carlisle, Middlesbrough–Carlisle and York–Blackpool North. The operator uses a large fleet of DMUs of Classes 142, 144, 150, 153, 155, 156 and 158 plus EMU Classes 319, 321, 322, 323 and 333. Class 185s are hired from TransPennine Express for use on some services between Manchester Airport and Blackpool North/Barrow/Windermere. Two locomotive-hauled sets, with Class 37s, are hired from DRS for use on some trains between Carlisle and Barrow-in-Furness/Preston as part of a 4-year contract that started in May 2015.

| **ScotRail** | Abellio (Netherlands Railways) | **ScotRail** |
| | (until 31 March 2022) | |

There is an option to extend the franchise by 3 years to March 2025.

ScotRail provides almost all passenger services within Scotland and also trains from Glasgow to Carlisle via Dumfries, some of which extend to Newcastle (jointly operated with Northern). The company operates a large fleet of DMUs of Classes 156, 158 and 170 and EMU Classes 314, 318, 320, 334 and 380. Two locomotive-hauled rakes are also used on Fife Circle commuter trains, hauled by Class 68s hired from DRS.

| **South Eastern** | Govia (Go-Ahead/Keolis) (until 24 June 2018) | **Southeastern** |

There is an option to extend the franchise by 6 months to December 2018.

Southeastern operates all services in the South-East London suburbs, the whole of Kent and part of Sussex, which are primarily commuter services to London. It also operates domestic high speed trains on HS1 from London St Pancras to Ashford, Ramsgate, Dover and Faversham with additional peak services on other routes. EMUs of Classes 375, 376, 377, 465 and 466 are used, along with Class 395s on the High Speed trains.

| **South Western** | Stagecoach Group (until 20 August 2017) | **South West Trains** |

South West Trains operates trains from London Waterloo to destinations across the South and South-West including Woking, Basingstoke, Southampton, Portsmouth, Salisbury, Exeter, Reading and Weymouth as well as suburban services from Waterloo. SWT also runs services between Ryde and Shanklin on the Isle of Wight, using former London Underground 1938 stock (Class 483s). The rest of the fleet consists of DMU Classes 158 and 159 and EMU Classes 444, 450, 455, 456 and 458. Class 707s will be introduced in 2017.

| **Thameslink, Southern & Great Northern (TSGN)** | Govia (Go-Ahead/Keolis) (until 19 September 2021) | **Govia Thameslink Railway** |

There is an option to extend the franchise by 2 years to September 2023.

Govia operates this franchise, the largest in the UK, as a management contract. The former Southern franchise was combined with Thameslink/Great Northern in 2015. GTR uses four brands within the franchise: "Thameslink" for trains between Bedford and Brighton via central London and also on the Sutton/Wimbledon loop using Class 319, 377, 387 and new 700 EMUs (all Class 387s will transfer to Great Northern in early 2017). Some trains continue into Southeastern territory to Sevenoaks, Orpington and Ashford. "Great Northern" comprises services from London King's Cross and Moorgate to Welwyn Garden City, Hertford North, Peterborough, Cambridge and Kings Lynn using Class 313, 317, 321, 365 and 387 EMUs. "Southern" operates predominantly commuter services between London, Surrey and Sussex and "metro" services in South London, as well as services along the South Coast between Southampton, Brighton, Hastings and Ashford, plus the cross-London service from South Croydon to Milton Keynes. Class 171 DMUs are used on Brighton–Ashford and London Bridge–Uckfield services, whilst all other services are in the hands of Class 313, 377, 442 and 455 EMUs. Finally, the premium "Gatwick Express" operates non-stop trains between London Victoria, Gatwick Airport and Brighton using Class 387/2 EMUs.

| **Trans-Pennine Express** | First Group (until 31 March 2023) | **TransPennine Express** |

There is an option to extend the franchise by 2 years to March 2025.

TransPennine Express operates predominantly long distance inter-urban services linking major cities across the North of England, along with Edinburgh and Glasgow in Scotland. The main services are Manchester Airport/Manchester Piccadilly–Newcastle/Middlesbrough/ Hull plus Liverpool–Scarborough and Liverpool–Newcastle along the North Trans-Pennine route via Huddersfield, Leeds and York, and Manchester Airport–Cleethorpes along the South Trans-Pennine route via Sheffield. TPE also operates Manchester Airport–Edinburgh/ Glasgow. The fleet consists of Class 185 DMUs, plus Class 350 EMUs used on Manchester Airport–Scotland services.

Wales & Borders   Arriva (Deutsche Bahn)   **Arriva Trains Wales**
(until 14 October 2018)

There is an option to extend the franchise by 6 months to April 2019. The Welsh Government will be procuring the next Wales & Borders franchise.

Arriva Trains Wales operates a mix of long distance, regional and local services throughout Wales, including the Valley Lines network of lines around Cardiff, and also through services to the English border counties and to Manchester and Birmingham. The fleet consists of DMUs of Classes 142, 143, 150, 158 and 175 and two locomotive-hauled rakes: one used on a premium Welsh Government sponsored service on the Cardiff–Holyhead route, and one used between Manchester/Crewe and Holyhead (both are hauled by a Class 67).

West Coast   Virgin Rail Group (Virgin/Stagecoach Group)   **Virgin Trains**
(until 31 March 2019)

Virgin Trains operates long distance services along the West Coast Main Line from London Euston to Birmingham/Wolverhampton, Manchester, Liverpool and Glasgow using Class 390 Pendolino EMUs. It also operates Class 221 Voyagers on the Euston–Chester–Holyhead route, whilst a mixture of Class 221s and 390s are used on the Euston–Birmingham–Glasgow/Edinburgh route.

West Midlands   Govia (Go-Ahead/Keolis)   **London Midland**
(until 14 October 2017)

London Midland operates long distance and regional services from London Euston to Northampton and Birmingham/Crewe and also between Birmingham and Liverpool as well as local and regional services around Birmingham, including to Stratford-upon-Avon, Worcester, Hereford, Redditch and Shrewsbury. It also operates the Bedford–Bletchley and Watford Junction–St Albans Abbey branches. The fleet consists of DMU Classes 150, 153, 170 and 172 and EMU Classes 319, 323 and 350.

NON-FRANCHISED SERVICES

The following operators run non-franchised, or "open access" services (* special seasonal services):

Operator	Trading Name	Route
BAA	Heathrow Express	London Paddington–Heathrow Airport

Heathrow Express operates a frequent express passenger service between London Paddington and Heathrow Airport using Class 332 EMUs. A slower stopping service is operated jointly with Great Western Railway, and this uses Class 360 EMUs.

Hull Trains (part of First)	Hull Trains	London King's Cross–Hull

Hull Trains operates seven trains a day (weekdays) from Hull to London King's Cross via the East Coast Main Line using Class 180 DMUs. One train in each direction starts back from and extends to Beverley.

| Grand Central (part of Arriva) | Grand Central | London King's Cross–Sunderland/ Bradford Interchange |

Grand Central operates five trains a day from Sunderland and four trains a day from Bradford Interchange to London King's Cross. The Sunderland trains are a mix of HSTs and Class 180 DMUs, with Class 180s used on all the Bradford trains.

| North Yorkshire Moors Railway Enterprises | North Yorkshire Moors Railway | Pickering–Grosmont–Whitby/ Battersby |

The North Yorkshire Moors Railway operates services on the national network between Grosmont and Whitby or Grosmont and Battersby as an extension of its Pickering–Grosmont service.

| West Coast Railway Company | West Coast Railway Company | Birmingham–Stratford-upon-Avon* Fort William–Mallaig* York–Settle–Carlisle* |

West Coast Railway Company operates steam-hauled services on these routes on a seasonal basis.

INTERNATIONAL PASSENGER OPERATORS

Eurostar International operates passenger services between the UK and mainland Europe. The company, established in 2010, is jointly owned by SNCF (the national operator of France): 55%, SNCB (the national operator of Belgium): 5% and Patina Rail: 40%. Patina Rail is made up of Canadian-based Caisse de dépôt et placement du Québec (CDPG) and UK-based Hermes Infrastructure (owning 30% and 10% respectively). This 40% was previously owned by the UK Government until it was sold in 2015.

Eurostar uses mainly new Siemens Class 374 trains on its St Pancras–Paris route, with the original Class 373 sets used on the Brussels route. Eight of these sets are being retained and refurbished.

In addition, a service for the conveyance of accompanied road vehicles through the Channel Tunnel is provided by the tunnel operating company, Eurotunnel. All Eurotunnel services are operated in top-and-tail mode by the powerful Class 9 Bo-Bo-Bo locomotives.

FREIGHT TRAIN OPERATORS

The following operators operate freight services or empty passenger stock workings under "Open Access" arrangements:

Colas Rail: Colas Rail operates a number of On-Track Machines and also supplies infrastructure trains for Network Rail. It also operates a number of different freight flows, including steel, coal, oil and timber. Colas Rail has a small but varied fleet consisting of Class 37s, 47s, 56s, 60s, 66s, 67s and 70s.

DB Cargo (UK): Still the biggest freight operator in the country, DBC (EWS until bought by Deutsche Bahn, when it was initially called DB Schenker) provides a large number of infrastructure trains to Network Rail and also operates coal, steel, intermodal and aggregate trains nationwide. The core fleet is Class 66s. Of the original 250 ordered some have moved to DB's French and Polish operations, although some of the French locos do return to the UK when major maintenance is required. A fleet of around 15–20 Class 60s are also used on heavier trains.

DBC's six Class 59/2s are used alongside the Mendip Rail 59/0s and 59/1s on stone traffic from the Mendip quarries and around the South-East. DBC's fleet of Class 67s are used on passenger or standby duties for Arriva Trains Wales and Virgin Trains East Coast and also on excursions or special trains. Class 90s see some use on West Coast Main Line freight traffic and one is also hired to Virgin Trains East Coast for use on passenger trains. The Class 92s are mainly used on a limited number of overnight freights on High Speed 1.

DBC also operates the Class 325 EMUs for Royal Mail and a number of excursion trains.

Devon & Cornwall Railways (a subsidiary of British American Railway Services): DCRail specialises in short-term freight haulage contracts, mainly in the scrap, coal and aggregates markets, using its fleet of Class 56s. It also provides locomotives from its fleet of Class 31s or 56s for stock moves or to move On-Track Machines or other equipment.

Direct Rail Services: DRS has built on its original nuclear flask traffic to operate a number of different services. The main flows are intermodal plus the provision of crews and locomotives to Network Rail for autumn Railhead Treatment Trains and also NR infrastructure trains. Its Class 57s and 68s are used on excursion work.

DRS has a varied fleet of locomotives, with Class 20s, 37s, 57s and 66s working alongside new Class 68s that are currently being delivered and are hired to other TOCs such as Chiltern Railways for operating passenger trains. In early 2017 the first of the company's new Vossloh electric locomotives (Class 88s), that also feature a small diesel engine, will be delivered.

Freightliner: Freightliner has two divisions: Intermodal operates container trains from the main Ports at Southampton, Felixstowe, Tilbury and Thamesport to major cities including London, Manchester, Leeds and Birmingham. The Heavy Haul division covers the movement of coal, cement, infrastructure and aggregates nationwide. Most services are worked by Class 66s, with Class 70s mainly used on some of the heavier intermodal trains. A small fleet of Class 86 and 90 electrics are used on intermodal trains on the Great Eastern and West Coast Main Lines, the Class 86s mainly being used in pairs on the WCML between Crewe and Coatbridge. Class 90s are also hired to Caledonian Sleeper.

GB Railfreight: GBRf, now owned by the Hector Rail group, operates a mixture of traffic types, mainly using Class 66s together with a small fleet of Class 73s on infrastructure duties and test trains in the South-East. A growing fleet of Class 92s is also used on some intermodal flows to/from Dollands Moor or through the Channel Tunnel to Calais. Traffic includes coal, intermodal, biomass, aggregates and gypsum as well as infrastructure services for Network Rail and London Underground. GBRf also supplies locomotives to Caledonian Sleeper.

GBRf also operates some excursion trains, including those using the preserved Class 201 "Hastings" DEMU.

Rail Operations Group: This company mainly facilitates rolling stock movements by providing drivers or using locomotives hired from other companies or by using its own fleet of Class 47s. ROG also operates a small number of excursion trains.

West Coast Railway Company: WCRC has a freight licence but doesn't operate any freight as such – only empty stock movements. Its fleet of Class 47s, supplemented by a smaller number of Class 33s, 37s and 57s, is used on excursion work nationwide.

In addition, Amey, Balfour Beatty Rail, Harsco Rail, Loram (UK), South West Trains, Swietelsky Babcock Rail (SB Rail) and VolkerRail operate trains formed of On-Track Machines.

PROVISION OF INFORMATION

This book has been compiled with care to be as accurate as possible, but some information is not easily available and the publisher cannot be held responsible for any errors or omissions. We would like to thank the companies and individuals who have been helpful in supplying information to us. The authors of this series of books are always pleased to receive notification of any inaccuracies that may be found, to enhance future editions. Please send comments to:

Robert Pritchard, Platform 5 Publishing Ltd, 52 Broadfield Road, Sheffield, S8 0XJ, England.

e-mail: robert.pritchard@platform5.com   **Tel:** 0114 255 2625.

UPDATES

This book is updated to the start of January 2017. The Platform 5 railway magazine **"Today's Railways UK"** publishes Stock Changes every month to update this book. The magazine also contains news and rolling stock information on the railways of Great Britain and Ireland and is published on the second Monday of every month. For further details of **Today's Railways UK**, please contact Platform 5 Publishing Ltd.

UK LIGHT RAIL & METRO SYSTEMS

Platform 5 Publishing will be publishing a new book dedicated to the rolling stock of London Underground and the tramway and metro systems of the UK in spring 2017. As a result of this new publication, the fleet lists of the various tram and metro systems have been dropped from this book.

1. LOCOMOTIVES

INTRODUCTION

This section contains details of all locomotives which can run on Britain's national railway network, plus those of Eurotunnel.

Locomotives currently approved for use on the national railway network fall into the four broad types: passenger, freight, mixed traffic and shunting.

Passenger
The number of dedicated passenger locomotives has not changed significantly in recent years. However, the number is expected to decline in the future as new multiple unit stock replaces some of the remaining locomotive-hauled or propelled trains (although some companies, most notably TransPennine Express, is to introduce new locomotive-hauled passenger trains in the future). Classes 43 (HST) and 91 and some members of Classes 57, 67, 68, 73/9, 90 and 92 are dedicated to franchised and Open Access passenger operations. Excursion trains have a few dedicated locomotives but mainly use locomotives that are best described as mixed traffic.

Freight
By far the most numerous locomotives are those used solely for bulk commodity and intermodal freight. Since 1998 a large number of new Class 66 locomotives have replaced many former BR designs and in more recent years smaller numbers of Class 70s have also been introduced. There are however a significant number of BR era Class 20, 37, 47, 56, 60, 73/1, 86, 90 and 92 locomotives still in use; their number has increased slightly recently as some locomotives have been reinstated to cope with demand. In addition there is a small fleet of Class 59s acquired privately in the 1980s and 1990s and a small number of re-engined Class 57s in use.

Mixed Traffic
In addition to their use on passenger and commodity freight workings these locomotives are used for stock movements and specialist infrastructure and test trains. The majority, but not all, are fitted with Electric Train Supply. Locomotives from Classes 20, 31, 33, 37, 47, 57, 67, 68, 73/9, 88 and 90 fall into this category. Also included under this heading are preserved locomotives permitted to operate on the national railway network. Although these have in the past solely operated excursion trains they are increasingly seeing occasional use on other types of trains.

Shunting
Very few shunting locomotives are now permitted to operate freely on the National Railway network. The small number that are have to be fitted with a plethora of safety equipment in order to have engineering acceptance. They are mainly used for local workings such as trips between yards or stock movements between depots and stations. In the main section of this book all such shunting locomotives (Classes 08 and 09) in the fleets that have permitted locomotives are included. Otherwise, shunting locomotives are not permitted to venture from depots or yards onto the

National Railway network other than into defined limits within interface infrastructure. Generally such locomotives, which include an increasing number of remotely controlled driverless types, are not included in this book. However, those of BR pedigree, such as Class 08s, can be found in Section 1.4 – Former BR Locomotives in Industrial Service.

Locomotives which are owned by, for example, DB Cargo or Freightliner, which have been withdrawn from service and are awaiting disposal are listed in the main part of the book. Locomotives which are awaiting disposal at scrapyards are listed in the "Locomotives Awaiting Disposal" section.

Only preserved locomotives which are currently used on the National Railway network are included. Others, which may still be Network Rail registered but not at present certified for use, are not included, but can be found in the Platform 5 book, "Preserved Locomotives of British Railways".

LAYOUT OF INFORMATION

Locomotive classes are listed in numerical order of class. Principal details and dimensions are quoted for each class in metric and/or imperial units as considered appropriate bearing in mind common UK usage.

Where numbers actually carried are different from those officially allocated, these are noted in class headings where appropriate. Where locomotives have been recently renumbered, the most immediate previous number is shown in parentheses. Each locomotive entry is laid out as in the following example:

No.	Detail	Livery	Owner	Pool		Allocn.	Name
59206	*b	**DB**	DB	WDAM		MD	John F. Yeoman Rail Pioneer

Detail Differences. Only detail differences which currently affect the areas and types of train which locomotives may work are shown. All other detail differences are excluded. Where such differences occur within a class or part class, they are shown in the "Detail" column alongside the individual locomotive number.

Codes: Codes are used to denote the livery, owner, pool and depot of each locomotive. Details of these will be found in section 6 of this book.

Depot allocation codes for all locomotives are shown in this book (apart from shunting locomotives (Classes 08 & 09) where the actual location of each is shown). It should be noted that today much locomotive maintenance is undertaken away from these depots. This may be undertaken at fuelling points, berthing sidings or similar, or by mobile maintenance teams. Therefore locomotives in particular may not return to their "home" depots as often as in the past.

(S) denotes that the locomotive is stored (the actual location is shown).

Names: Only names carried with official sanction are listed. Names are shown in UPPER/lower case characters as actually shown on the name carried on the locomotive.

Builders: These are shown in class headings. More details and a full list of builders can be found in section 6.7.

GENERAL INFORMATION

CLASSIFICATION AND NUMBERING

All locomotives are classified and allocated numbers under the TOPS numbering system, introduced in 1972. This comprises a two-digit class number followed by a three-digit serial number.

For diesel locomotives, class numbers offer an indication of engine horsepower as shown in the table below.

Class No. Range	Engine hp
01–14	0–799
15–20	800–1000
21–31	1001–1499
32–39	1500–1999
40–54, 57	2000–2999
55–56, 58–70	3000+

For electric locomotives class numbers are allocated in ascending numerical order under the following scheme:

Class 71–80   Direct current and DC/diesel dual system locomotives.
Class 81 onwards Alternating current and AC/DC dual system locomotives.

Numbers in the 89xxx series are allocated to locomotives which have been deregistered but subsequently re-registered for use on the national railway network and whose original number has already been reused. 89xxx numbers are normally only carried inside locomotive cabs and are not carried externally in normal circumstances.

WHEEL ARRANGEMENT

For main line locomotives the number of driven axles on a bogie or frame is denoted by a letter (A = 1, B = 2, C = 3 etc) and the number of non-powered axles is denoted by a number. The use of the letter "o" after a letter indicates each axle is individually powered, whilst the "+" symbol indicates bogies are inter-coupled.

For shunting locomotives, the Whyte notation is used. In this notation the number of leading wheels are given, followed by the number of driving wheels and then the trailing wheels.

UNITS OF MEASUREMENT

All dimensions and weights are quoted for locomotives in an "as new" condition with all necessary supplies (eg oil, water and sand) on board. Dimensions are quoted in the order length x width. Lengths quoted are over buffers or couplers as appropriate. All widths quoted are maxima. Where two different wheel diameter dimensions are shown, the first refers to powered wheels and the second refers to non-powered wheels. All weights are shown as metric tonnes (t = tonnes).

HAULAGE CAPABILITY OF DIESEL LOCOMOTIVES

The haulage capability of a diesel locomotive depends upon three basic factors:

1. Adhesive weight. The greater the weight on the driving wheels, the greater the adhesion and more tractive power can be applied before wheelslip occurs.

2. The characteristics of its transmission. To start a train the locomotive has to exert a pull at standstill. A direct drive diesel engine cannot do this, hence the need for transmission. This may be mechanical, hydraulic or electric. The present British Standard for locomotives is electric transmission. Here the diesel engine drives a generator or alternator and the current produced is fed to the traction motors. The force produced by each driven wheel depends on the current in its traction motor. In other words, the larger the current, the harder it pulls. As the locomotive speed increases, the current in the traction motor falls, hence the *Maximum Tractive Effort* is the maximum force at its wheels the locomotive can exert at a standstill. The electrical equipment cannot take such high currents for long without overheating. Hence the *Continuous Tractive Effort* is quoted which represents the current which the equipment can take continuously.

3. The power of its engine. Not all power reaches the rail, as electrical machines are approximately 90% efficient. As the electrical energy passes through two such machines (the generator or alternator and the traction motors), the *Power at Rail* is approximately 81% (90% of 90%) of the engine power, less a further amount used for auxiliary equipment such as radiator fans, traction motor blowers, air compressors, battery charging, cab heating, Electric Train Supply (ETS) etc. The power of the locomotive is proportional to the tractive effort times the speed. Hence when on full power there is a speed corresponding to the continuous tractive effort.

HAULAGE CAPABILITY OF ELECTRIC LOCOMOTIVES

Unlike a diesel locomotive, an electric locomotive does not develop its power on board and its performance is determined only by two factors, namely its weight and the characteristics of its electrical equipment. Whereas a diesel locomotive tends to be a constant power machine, the power of an electric locomotive varies considerably. Up to a certain speed it can produce virtually a constant tractive effort. Hence power rises with speed according to the formula given in section three above, until a maximum speed is reached at which tractive effort falls, such that the power also falls. Hence the power at the speed corresponding to the maximum tractive effort is lower than the maximum speed.

BRAKE FORCE

Brake Force (also known as brake power) is a measure of the braking power of a locomotive. The Brake Force available is dependant on the adhesion between the rail and the wheels being braked and the normal reaction of the rail on the wheels being braked (and hence on the weight per braked wheel). A locomotive's Brake Force is shown on its data panels so operating staff can ensure sufficient brake power is available for specific trains.

ELECTRIC TRAIN SUPPLY (ETS)

A number of locomotives are equipped to provide a supply of electricity to the train being hauled to power auxiliaries such as heating, cooling fans, air conditioning and kitchen equipment. ETS is provided from the locomotive by means of a separate alternator (except Class 33 locomotives, which have a DC generator). The ETS index of a locomotive is a measure of the electrical power available for train supply. Class 55 locomotives provide an ETS directly from one of their traction generators into the train supply.

Similarly, most locomotive-hauled carriages also have an ETS index, which in this case is a measure of the power required to operate equipment mounted in the carriage. The sum of the ETS indices of all the hauled vehicles in a train must not exceed the ETS index of the locomotive.

ETS is commonly (but incorrectly) known as ETH (Electric Train Heating), which is a throwback to the days before locomotive-hauled carriages were equipped with electrically powered auxiliary equipment other than for train heating.

ROUTE AVAILABILITY (RA)

This is a measure of a railway vehicle's axle load. The higher the axle load of a vehicle, the higher the RA number on a scale from 1 to 10. Each Network Rail route has a RA number and in general no vehicle with a higher RA number may travel on that route without special clearance.

MULTIPLE WORKING

Multiple working between vehicles (ie two or more powered vehicles being driven from one cab) is facilitated by jumper cables connecting the vehicles. However, not all types of locomotive are compatible with each other, and a number of different systems are in use. Some are compatible with others, some are not. BR used "multiple working codes" to designate which locomotives were compatible. The list below shows which classes of locomotives are compatible with each other – the former BR multiple working code being shown in brackets. It should be noted that some locomotives have had the equipment removed or made inoperable.

With other classes:
Classes 20, 25, 31, 33, 37 40 & 73/1*. (Blue Star)
Classes 56 & 58. (Red Diamond; Colas Rail Class 56 Blue Star)
Classes 59, 66, 67, 68, 70 & 73/9.
* DRS has since adapted the systems so its Classes 20/3, 37, 47 & 57 can
work with each other only.

With other members of same class only:
Class 43, Class 47 (Green Circle), Class 50 (Orange Square), Class 60.

PUSH-PULL OPERATION

Some locomotives are modified to operate passenger and service (formed
of laboratory, test and inspection carriages) trains in "push-pull" mode –
which allows the train to be driven from either end – either with locomotives
at each end (both under power) or with a driving brake van at one end and
a locomotive at the other. Various different systems are now in use. Electric
locomotive Classes 86, 87, 90 & 91 use a time-division multiplex (TDM)
system for push-pull working which utilises the existing Railway Clearing
House (RCH) jumper cables fitted to carriages. Previously these cables had
only been used to control train lighting and public address systems.

More recently locomotives of Classes 67 and 68 have used the Association
of American Railroads (AAR) system.

ABBREVIATIONS

Standard abbreviations used in this book are:

a	Train air brake equipment only.
b	Drophead buckeye couplers.
c	Scharfenberg couplers.
d	Fitted with retractable Dellner couplers.
e	European Railway Traffic Management System (ERTMS) signalling equipment fitted.
k	Fitted with Swinghead Automatic "buckeye" combination couplers.
p	Train air, vacuum and electro-pneumatic brakes.
r	Radio Electric Token Block signalling equipment fitted.
s	Slow Speed Control equipment.
v	Train vacuum brake only.
x	Train air and vacuum brakes ("Dual brakes").
+	Additional fuel tank capacity.
§	Sandite laying equipment.

In all cases use of the above abbreviations indicates the equipment in
question is normally operable. The definition of non-standard abbreviations
and symbols is detailed in individual class headings.

1.1. DIESEL LOCOMOTIVES

CLASS 08   BR/ENGLISH ELECTRIC   0-6-0

Built: 1955–62 by BR at Crewe, Darlington, Derby Locomotive, Doncaster or Horwich Works.
Engine: English Electric 6KT of 298 kW (400 hp) at 680 rpm.
Main Generator: English Electric 801.
Traction Motors: Two English Electric 506.
Maximum Tractive Effort: 156 kN (35000 lbf).
Continuous Tractive Effort: 49 kN (11100 lbf) at 8.8 mph.

Power at Rail: 194 kW (260 hp).	**Train Brakes:** Air & vacuum.
Brake Force: 19 t.	**Dimensions:** 8.92 x 2.59 m.
Weight: 49.6–50.4 t.	**Wheel Diameter:** 1372 mm.
Design Speed: 20 mph.	**Maximum Speed:** 15 mph.
Fuel Capacity: 3037 litres.	**Route Availability:** 5.
Train Supply: Not equipped.	

† – Fitted with remote control equipment.

For shunting locomotives, instead of the two-letter depot code, actual locations at the time of publication are given.

Locomotives of Classes 08 and 09 that don't have current Network Rail engineering acceptance and are considered to be "in industrial service" can be found in section 1.4 of this book.

08850 has acceptance for use between Battersby and Whitby only, for rescue purposes.

Non-standard liveries/numbering:

08480   Yellow with a red bodyside band. Carries number "TOTON No 1".
08605   Carries the number "WIGAN2".
08616   Carries the number 3783.
08899   Crimson lake.

Class 08/0. Standard Design.

08405 a†	**E**	DB	WQAA	Crewe International Depot (S)
08410 a	**GW**	GW	EFSH	Penzance Long Rock depot
08417 a	**Y**	NR	QADD	Loram Derby
08428 ak	**E**	DB	WQDA	Warrington Yards (S)
08451	**B**	AM	ATLO	Glasgow Polmadie Depot
08454	**B**	AM	ATLO	Liverpool Edge Hill Depot
08472 a	**WA**	WA	RFSH	Edinburgh Craigentinny Depot
08480 a	**0**	DB	WQAB	Toton Depot (S)
08483 a	**K**	GW	EFSH	Old Oak Common HST Depot
08523	**RS**	RL	MRSO	Inverness Depot
08525	**ST**	EM	EMSL	Leeds Neville Hill Depot
08530	**FL**	P	DDIN	Felixstowe FLT
08531 a	**FH**	P	DDIN	LH Group, Barton-under-Needwood
08571 a	**WA**	WA	HBSH	Felixstowe FLT

08575	**FL**	P	DHLT	LH Group, Barton-under-Needwood (S)
08585	**FL**	P	DDIN	Trafford Park FLT
08596 at	**WA**	WA	HBSH	Edinburgh Craigentinny Depot
08605 †	**DB**	RV	RTSO	Wigan Springs Branch Depot
08611	**B**	AM	ATLO	Wembley Depot
08615	**WA**	WA	RFSH	LH Group, Barton-under-Needwood
08616	**LM**	LM	EJLO	Birmingham Tyseley Depot
08617	**B**	AM	ATLO	Arlington Fleet Services, Eastleigh Works
08623	**DB**	DB	WQBA	Bescot Yards (S)
08624	**FH**	P	DDIN	Felixstowe FLT
08632 †	**DB**	DB	WQDA	Mossend Yards (S)
08641	**B**	GW	EFSH	Plymouth Laira Depot
08644	**B**	GW	EFSH	Plymouth Laira Depot
08645	**DG**	GW	EFSH	Loram Derby
08663 a	**B**	GW	EFSH	Bristol St Philip's Marsh Depot
08669 a	**WA**	WA	RFSH	Wabtec Rail, Doncaster Works
08690	**ST**	EM	EMSL	Leeds Neville Hill Depot
08691	**FL**	FL	DDIN	LH Group, Barton-under-Needwood
08696 a	**B**	AM	ATLO	Wembley Depot
08703 a	**E**	DB	WQDA	Bescot Yards (S)
08706 †	**E**	DB	WQCA	Crewe International Depot (S)
08721	**B**	AM	ATLO	Manchester Longsight Depot
08724	**WA**	WA	HBSH	Wabtec Rail, Doncaster Works
08735 †	**E**	DB	WQCA	Eastleigh Yards (S)
08742 †	**RX**	DB	WQDA	Hinksey Yard (S)
08752 †	**E**	DB	WQDA	Bescot Yards (S)
08754	**B**	RL	MRSO	Norwich Crown Point Depot
08757 †	**RG**	DB	WQBA	Crewe International Depot (S)
08764	**B**	AM	ATLO	Glasgow Polmadie Depot
08782 at	**CU**	DB	WQBA	Doncaster Yards (S)
08785 a	**FL**	P	DDIN	Southampton Maritime FLT
08788	**K**	RL	MRSO	Tata Steel, Shotton Works
08790	**B**	AM	ATLO	Arlington Fleet Services, Eastleigh Works
08795	**K**	GW	EFSH	Swansea Landore Depot
08799 a	**E**	DB	WQAB	Westbury Yards (S)
08804 †	**E**	DB	WQBA	Crewe International Depot (S)
08805	**FO**	LM	EJLO	Birmingham Soho Depot
08822	**IC**	GW	EFSH	Bristol St Philip's Marsh Depot
08836	**GW**	GW	EFSH	Old Oak Common HST Depot
08847	**CD**	RL	MRSO	Norwich Crown Point Depot
08850	**B**	NY	MBDL	Grosmont Depot
08853 a	**WA**	WA	RFSH	Wabtec Rail, Doncaster Works
08874	**SL**	RL	MRSO	Tata Steel, Shotton Works
08887 a	**B**	AM	ATLO	Arlington Fleet Services, Eastleigh Works
08891	**FL**	P	DHLT	LH Group, Barton-under-Needwood (S)
08899	**O**	EM	EMSL	Derby Etches Park Depot
08904	**E**	DB	WQDA	Eastleigh Yards (S)
08908	**ST**	EM	EMSL	Leeds Neville Hill Depot
08925	**G**	GB	GBWM	March Whitemoor Yard
08934 a	**VP**	GB	GBWM	GBRf, Dagenham
08948 c	**EP**	EU	GPSS	Temple Mills Depot

| 08950 | **ST** EM EMSL | Leeds Neville Hill Depot |
| 08954 | **B** AM ATLO | Liverpool Edge Hill Depot |

Class 08 names:

08451	M.A. SMITH		08663	St. Silas
08483	NEIL / SCOUSEY		08669	Bob Machin
	Neil Morgan 1964–2014		08690	DAVID THIRKILL
	Team Leader O.O.C.		08691	Terri
08525	DUNCAN BEDFORD		08721	Longsight TMD
08585	Vicky		08799	FRED
08616	TYSELEY 100		08822	Dave Mills
08617	Steve Purser		08874	Catherine
08624	Rambo Paul Ramsey		08899	Midland Counties Railway
08644	Laira Diesel Depot			175 1839–2014
	50 Years 1962–2012		08908	IVAN STEPHENSON
08645	Mike Baggott		08950	DAVID LIGHTFOOT

CLASS 09   BR/ENGLISH ELECTRIC   0-6-0

Built: 1959–62 by BR at Darlington or Horwich Works.
Engine: English Electric 6KT of 298 kW (400 hp) at 680 rpm.
Main Generator: English Electric 801.
Traction Motors: English Electric 506.
Maximum Tractive Effort: 111 kN (25000 lbf).
Continuous Tractive Effort: 39 kN (8800 lbf) at 11.6 mph.
Power at Rail: 201 kW (269 hp).   **Train Brakes:** Air & vacuum.
Brake Force: 19 t.   **Dimensions:** 8.92 x 2.59 m.
Weight: 49 t.   **Wheel Diameter:** 1372 mm.
Design Speed: 27 mph.   **Maximum Speed:** 27 mph.
Fuel Capacity: 3037 litres.   **Route Availability:** 5.
Train Supply: Not equipped.

Class 09/0. Built as Class 09.

| 09002 | **G** GB GBWM | March Whitemoor Yard |
| 09009 | **G** GB GBWM | March Whitemoor Yard |

Class 09/1. Converted from Class 08 1992–93 by RFS Industries, Kilnhurst.

| 09106 (08759) | **DB** DB WQDA | Knottingley Depot (S) |

CLASS 20   ENGLISH ELECTRIC   Bo-Bo

Built: 1957–68 by English Electric at Vulcan Foundry, Newton-le-Willows or by Robert Stephenson & Hawthorns at Darlington.
Engine: English Electric 8SVT Mk II of 746 kW (1000 hp) at 850 rpm.
Main Generator: English Electric 819/3C.
Traction Motors: English Electric 526/5D or 526/8D.
Maximum Tractive Effort: 187 kN (42000 lbf).
Continuous Tractive Effort: 111 kN (25000 lbf) at 11 mph.
Power at Rail: 574 kW (770 hp).   **Train Brakes:** Air & vacuum.

Brake Force: 35 t.
Weight: 73.4–73.5 t.
Design Speed: 75 mph.
Fuel Capacity: 1727 litres.
Train Supply: Not equipped.

Dimensions: 14.25 x 2.67 m.
Wheel Diameter: 1092 mm.
Maximum Speed: 75 mph.
Route Availability: 5.

Class 20s that don't have current Network Rail engineering acceptance and are considered to be "in industrial service" can be found in section 1.4 of this book.

Non-standard liveries/numbering:

20088 RFS grey (carries No. 2017).
20142 LUL Maroon.
20227 White, red & blue with London Underground roundels.

Class 20/0. Standard Design.

20016	**B**	HN	HNRS	LM (S)	
20081	**B**	HN	HNRS	LM (S)	
20088	**0**	HN	HNRS	LM (S)	
20096	**B**	HN	GBEE	BH	
20107	**B**	HN	GBEE	BH	
20118	**FO**	HN	GBEE	BH	Saltburn-by-the-Sea
20132	**FO**	HN	GBEE	BH	Barrow Hill Depot
20142	**0**	20	MOLO	SK	SIR JOHN BETJEMAN
20189	**B**	20	MOLO	SK	
20205	**B**	2L	MOLO	SK	
20227	**0**	2L	MOLO	SK	

Class 20/3. Direct Rail Services refurbished locomotives. Details as Class 20/0 except:

Refurbished: 15 locomotives were refurbished 1995–96 by Brush Traction at Loughborough (20301–305) or 1997–98 by RFS(E) at Doncaster (20306–315). Disc indicators or headcode panels removed.
Train Brakes: Air.
Weight: 73 t (+ 76 t).
Brake Force: 35 t (+ 31 t).

Maximum Speed: 60 mph (+ 75 mph).
Fuel Capacity: 2909 (+ 4909) litres.
RA: 5 (+ 6).

20301	(20047)	r	**DS**	DR	XHSS	BH (S)	
20302	(20084)	r	**DS**	DR	XHSS	BH (S)	
20303	(20127)	r	**DS**	DR	XHSS	ZR (S)	Max Joule 1958–1999
20304	(20120)	r	**DS**	DR	XHSS	BH (S)	
20305	(20095)	r	**DS**	DR	XHSS	BH (S)	Gresty Bridge
20308	(20187)	r+	**DS**	DR	XHSS	ZA (S)	
20309	(20075)	r+	**DS**	DR	XHSS	BH (S)	
20311	(20102)	r+	**HN**	HN	GBEE	BH	
20312	(20042)	r+	**DS**	DR	XHSS	BH (S)	
20314	(20117)	r+	**HN**	HN	GBEE	BH	

Class 20/9. Harry Needle Railroad Company (former Hunslet-Barclay/ DRS) locomotives. Details as Class 20/0 except:

Refurbished: 1989 by Hunslet-Barclay at Kilmarnock.
Train Brakes: Air.
RA: 5 (+ 6).

Fuel Capacity: 1727 (+ 4727) litres.

20901	(20101)	**GB**	HN	GBEE	BH
20903	(20083) +	**DR**	HN	HNRS	BU (S)
20904	(20041)	**DR**	HN	HNRS	BU (S)
20905	(20225) +	**GB**	HN	GBEE	BH

CLASS 25   BR/BEYER PEACOCK/SULZER   Bo-Bo

Built: 1965 by Beyer Peacock at Gorton.
Engine: Sulzer 6LDA28-B of 930 kW (1250 hp) at 750 rpm.
Main Generator: AEI RTB15656.   **Traction Motors:** AEI 253AY.
Maximum Tractive Effort: 200 kN (45000 lbf).
Continuous Tractive Effort: 93 kN (20800 lbf) at 17.1 mph.
Power at Rail: 708 kW (949 hp).   **Train Brakes:** Air & vacuum.
Brake Force: 38 t.   **Dimensions:** 15.39 x 2.73 m.
Weight: 71.5 t.   **Wheel Diameter:** 1143 mm.
Design Speed: 90 mph.   **Maximum Speed:** 60 mph.
Fuel Capacity: 2270 litres.   **Route Availability:** 5.
Train Supply: Not equipped.

Carries original number D7628.

Only certified for use on Network Rail tracks between Whitby and Battersby, as an extension of North Yorkshire Moors Railway services.

25278	**GG**	NY	MBDL	NY	SYBILLA

CLASS 31   BRUSH/ENGLISH ELECTRIC   A1A-A1A

Built: 1958–62 by Brush Traction at Loughborough.
Engine: English Electric 12SVT of 1100 kW (1470 hp) at 850 rpm.
Main Generator: Brush TG160-48.   **Traction Motors:** Brush TM73-68.
Maximum Tractive Effort: 160 kN (35900 lbf).
Continuous Tractive Effort: 83 kN (18700 lbf) at 23.5 mph.
Power at Rail: 872 kW (1170 hp).   **Train Brakes:** Air & vacuum.
Brake Force: 49 t.   **Dimensions:** 17.30 x 2.67 m.
Weight: 106.7–111 t.   **Wheel Diameter:** 1092/1003 mm.
Design Speed: 90 mph.   **Maximum Speed:** 90 mph.
Fuel Capacity: 2409 litres.   **Route Availability:** 5 or 6.
Train Supply: Not equipped.

Non-standard liveries/numbering:

31190 Also carries the number D5613.
31452 DCR green.

Class 31/1. Standard Design. RA: 5.

31105		**Y**	NR	QADD	ZA
31106	a	**B**	HJ	RVLO	ZA (S)
31128		**B**	NS	NRLO	BU CHARYBDIS
31190		**G**	BA	HTLX	WH
31233	a	**Y**	NR	QADD	ZA
31285		**Y**	HN	HNRL	BU (S)

Class 31/4. Electric Train Supply equipment. RA: 6.
Train Supply: Electric, index 66.

31452	**O**	BA	HTLX	ZA	
31454	**IC**	BA	HTLX	WH (S)	
31459	**K**	HN	RVLO	ZA (S)	CERBERUS
31465	**Y**	HN	HNRL	ZA	
31468	**FR**	BA	RVLO	WO (S) HYDRA	

Class 31/6. ETS through wiring and controls. RA: 5.

31601	(31186)	**DC**	BA	HTLX	WH	Devon Diesel Society
31602	(31191)	**Y**	BA	HTLX	WO (S)	

CLASS 33   BRCW/SULZER   Bo-Bo

Built: 1960–62 by the Birmingham Railway Carriage & Wagon Company at Smethwick.
Engine: Sulzer 8LDA28 of 1160 kW (1550 hp) at 750 rpm.
Main Generator: Crompton Parkinson CG391B1.
Traction Motors: Crompton Parkinson C171C2.
Maximum Tractive Effort: 200 kN (45000 lbf).
Continuous Tractive Effort: 116 kN (26000 lbf) at 17.5 mph.

Power at Rail: 906 kW (1215 hp).	**Train Brakes:** Air & vacuum.
Brake Force: 35 t.	**Dimensions:** 15.47 x 2.82 (2.64 m 33/2).
Weight: 76-78 t.	**Wheel Diameter:** 1092 mm.
Design Speed: 85 mph.	**Maximum Speed:** 85 mph.
Fuel Capacity: 3410 litres.	**Route Availability:** 6.

Train Supply: Electric, index 48 (750 V DC only).

Non-standard numbering: 33012 Carries the number D6515.

Class 33/0. Standard Design.

33012	**G**	71	MBDL	SW	Lt Jenny Lewis RN
33025	**WC**	WC	AWCX	CS (S)	Glen Falloch
33029	**WC**	WC	AWCX	CS (S)	
33030	**DR**	WC	AWCX	CS (S)	

Class 33/2. Built to former Loading Gauge of Tonbridge–Battle Line.
Equipped with slow speed control.

33207	**WC**	WC	AWCA	CS	Jim Martin

CLASS 37   ENGLISH ELECTRIC   Co-Co

Built: 1960–66 by English Electric at Vulcan Foundry, Newton-le-Willows or by Robert Stephenson & Hawthorns at Darlington.
Engine: English Electric 12CSVT of 1300 kW (1750 hp) at 850 rpm.
Main Generator: English Electric 822/10G.
Traction Motors: English Electric 538/A.
Maximum Tractive Effort: 247 kN (55500 lbf).
Continuous Tractive Effort: 156 kN (35000 lbf) at 13.6 mph.
Power at Rail: 932 kW (1250 hp).   **Train Brakes:** Air & vacuum.
Brake Force: 50 t.   **Dimensions:** 18.75 x 2.74 m.
Weight: 102.8–108.4 t.   **Wheel Diameter:** 1092 mm.
Design Speed: 90 mph.   **Maximum Speed:** 80 mph.
Fuel Capacity: 4046 (+ 7683) litres.   **Route Availability:** 5 (§ 6).
Train Supply: Not equipped.

Non-standard numbering:

37057 Also carries original number D6757.
37424 Also carries the number 37558.
37703 Carries the number 37067.
37905 Also carries original number D6838.

Class 37/0. Standard Design.

37025	**BL**	37	COTS	BH	Inverness TMD
37038 a	**DI**	DR	XHNC	KM	
37057	**G**	CS	COTS	BH	
37059 ar+	**DI**	DR	XHNC	KM	
37069 ar+	**DI**	DR	XHNC	KM	
37099	**CS**	CS	COTS	BH	MERL EVANS 1947–2016
37116 +	**CS**	CS	COTS	BH	
37146	**CE**	CS	COLS	Leeming Bar (S)	
37165 a+	**CE**	WC	AWCX	CS (S)	
37175 a	**CS**	CS	COTS	BH	
37188	**F**	CS	COLS	BH (S)	
37198 +	**Y**	NR	MBDL	BU (S)	CHIEF ENGINEER
37207	**B**	CS	COLS	BH (S)	
37214	**WC**	WC	AWCX	CS (S)	
37218 ar+	**DI**	DR	XHNC	KM	
37219	**CS**	CS	COTS	BH	
37254	**IC**	CS	COTS	BH	
37259 ar	**DS**	DR	XHNC	KM	

Class 37/4. Refurbished with electric train supply equipment. Main generator replaced by alternator. Regeared (CP7) bogies. Details as Class 37/0 except:
Main Alternator: Brush BA1005A.   **Power At Rail:** 935 kW (1254 hp).
Traction Motors: English Electric 538/5A.
Maximum Tractive Effort: 256 kN (57440 lbf).
Continuous Tractive Effort: 184 kN (41250 lbf) at 11.4 mph.
Weight: 107 t.   **Design Speed:** 80 mph.
Fuel Capacity: 7683 litres.
Train Supply: Electric, index 30.

37401	ar	**BL**	DR	XHCC	KM	Mary Queen of Scots
37402	a	**BL**	DR	XHCC	KM	Stephen Middlemore 23.12.1954–8.6.2013
37403		**BL**	SP	XHAC	KM	Isle of Mull
37405	ar	**DS**	DR	XHAC	KM	
37407		**F**	DR	XHAC	KM	
37409	ar	**DS**	DR	XHCC	KM	Lord Hinton
37413		**E**	DR	XHSS	BH (S)	
37419	ar	**DS**	DR	XHAC	KM	Carl Haviland 1954–2012
37421		**CS**	CS	COTS	BH	
37422	ar	**DR**	DR	XHAC	KM	
37423	ar	**DI**	DR	XHCC	KM	Spirit of the Lakes
37424		**BL**	DR	XHAC	KM	Avro Vulcan XH558
37425	ar	**DS**	DR	XHAC	KM	Sir Robert McAlpine/Concrete Bob

Class 37/5. Refurbished without train supply equipment. Main generator replaced by alternator. Regeared (CP7) bogies. Details as Class 37/4 except:
Power At Rail: 932 kW (1250 hp).
Maximum Tractive Effort: 248 kN (55590 lbf).
Weight: 106.1–110.0 t.
Train Supply: Not equipped.

37503	r§	**E**	EP	EPUK	LR (S)	
37510	a	**DS**	EP	EPUK	LR (S)	
37516	s	**WC**	WC	AWCA	CS	Loch Laidon
37517	as	**LH**	WC	AWCX	CS (S)	
37518	ar	**WC**	WC	AWCA	CS	

Class 37/6. Originally refurbished for Nightstar services. Main generator replaced by alternator. UIC jumpers. Details as Class 37/5 except:
Maximum Speed: 90 mph.   **Train Brake:** Air.
Train Supply: Not equipped, but electric through wired.

37601	a	**DS**	DR	XHNC	KM	Class 37-'Fifty'
37602	ar	**DS**	DR	XHNC	KM	
37603	a	**DS**	DR	XHNC	KM	
37604	a	**DS**	DR	XHNC	KM	
37605	a	**DS**	DR	XHNC	KM	
37606	a	**DS**	DR	XHNC	KM	
37607	ar	**DS**	DR	XHNC	KM	
37608	ar	**EX**	EP	EPUK	LR	Andromeda
37609	a	**DI**	DR	XHNC	KM	
37610	ar	**DS**	DR	XHNC	KM	T.S.(Ted) Cassady 14.5.61–6.4.08
37611	a	**DR**	EP	EPUK	LR	
37612	a	**DS**	DR	XHNC	KM	

Class 37/5 continued.

37667	ars	**DS**	DR	XHNC	KM	
37668	e	**WC**	WC	AWCA	CS	
37669	e	**WC**	WC	AWCA	CS	
37670	r	**DB**	EP	EPUK	BH (S)	
37676	a	**WC**	WC	AWCA	CS (S)	Loch Rannoch
37685	a	**WC**	WC	AWCA	CS	Loch Arkaig
37688	ar	**DS**	DR	XHNC	KM	Kingmoor TMD

Class 37/7. Refurbished locomotives. Main generator replaced by alternator. Regeared (CP7) bogies. Ballast weights added. Details as Class 37/5 except:
Main Alternator: GEC G564AZ (37800) Brush BA1005A (others).
Maximum Tractive Effort: 276 kN (62000 lbf).
Weight: 120 t.   **Route Availability:** 7.

37703	**DR**	DR	XHHP	BO
37706	**WC**	WC	AWCA	CS
37710	**LH**	WC	AWCX	CS (S)
37712 a	**WC**	WC	AWCX	CS (S)
37716	**DI**	DR	XHNC	KM
37800 d	**EX**	EP	GROG	LR
37884 d	**EX**	EP	GROG	LR

Class 37/9. Refurbished locomotives. New power unit. Main generator replaced by alternator. Ballast weights added. Details as Class 37/4 except:
Engine: * Mirrlees 6MB275T of 1340 kW (1800 hp) or † Ruston 6RK270T of 1340 kW (1800 hp) at 900 rpm.
Main Alternator: Brush BA15005A.
Maximum Tractive Effort: 279 kN (62680 lbf).
Weight: 120 t.   **Route Availability:** 7.
Train Supply: Not equipped.

37901 *	**FO**	CS	COLS	SE (S)
37905 †	**G**	UR	UKRM	LR
37906 †	**FO**	UR	UKRM	LR (S)

Class 97/3. Class 37s refurbished for use on the Cambrian Lines which are signalled by ERTMS. Details as Class 37/0.

97301 (37100) e	**Y**	NR	QETS	ZA	
97302 (37170) e	**Y**	NR	QETS	ZA	
97303 (37178) e	**Y**	NR	QETS	ZA	
97304 (37217) e	**Y**	NR	QETS	ZA	John Tiley

CLASS 40   ENGLISH ELECTRIC   1Co-Co1

Built: 1961 by English Electric at Vulcan Foundry, Newton-le-Willows.
Engine: English Electric 16SVT Mk2 of 1492 kW (2000 hp) at 850 rpm.
Main Generator: English Electric 822/4C.
Traction Motors: English Electric 526/5D or EE526/7D.
Maximum Tractive Effort: 231 kN (52000 lbf).
Continuous Tractive Effort: 137 kN (30900 lbf) at 18.8 mph.
Power at Rail: 1160 kW (1550 hp).   **Train Brakes:** Air & vacuum.
Brake Force: 51 t.   **Dimensions:** 21.18 x 2.78 m.
Weight: 132 t.   **Wheel Diameter:** 914/1143 mm.
Design Speed: 90 mph.   **Maximum Speed:** 90 mph.
Fuel Capacity: 3250 litres.   **Route Availability:** 6.
Train Supply: Steam heating.

Carries original number 345.

40145	**B**	40	ELRD	BQ

CLASS 43   BREL/PAXMAN   Bo-Bo

Built: 1975–82 by BREL at Crewe Works.
Engine: MTU 16V4000 R41R of 1680kW (2250 hp) at 1500 rpm.
(* Paxman 12VP185 of 1565 kW (2100 hp) at 1500 rpm.)
Main Alternator: Brush BA1001B.
Traction Motors: Brush TMH68–46 or GEC G417AZ (43124–152); frame mounted.
Maximum Tractive Effort: 80 kN (17980 lbf).
Continuous Tractive Effort: 46 kN (10340 lbf) at 64.5 mph.
Power at Rail: 1320 kW (1770 hp).   **Train Brakes:** Air.
Brake Force: 35 t.   **Dimensions:** 17.79 x 2.74 m.
Weight: 70.25–75.0 t.   **Wheel Diameter:** 1020 mm.
Design Speed: 125 mph.   **Maximum Speed:** 125 mph.
Fuel Capacity: 4500 litres.   **Route Availability:** 5.
Train Supply: Three-phase electric.

† Buffer fitted.

43013, 43014 & 43062 are fitted with measuring apparatus & front-end cameras.

Power cars 43002, 43013, 43048, 43321 and 43423 carry small commemorative
plates to celebrate 40 years of the HST, reading "40 YEARS 1976–2016".

Non-standard and advertising liveries:

43002 Original HST BR blue & yellow.
43027 90 Glorious Years (blue).
43126 Bristol 2015 – European Green Capital (green & white).
43144 & 43146 Building a Greater West.
43163 Visit Plymouth (blue).
43172 We Shall Remember Them.
43238 National Railway Museum 40 Years.

43002	**0**	A	EFPC	LA	Sir Kenneth Grange
43003	**FB**	A	EFPC	LA	ISAMBARD KINGDOM BRUNEL
43004	**FB**	A	EFPC	LA	
43005	**GW**	A	EFPC	LA	
43009	**FB**	A	EFPC	LA	
43010	**FB**	A	EFPC	LA	
43012	**FB**	A	EFPC	LA	Exeter Panel Signal Box
					21st Anniversary 2009
43013 †	**Y**	P	QCAR	EC	
43014 †	**Y**	P	QCAR	EC	The Railway Observer
43015	**FB**	A	EFPC	LA	
43016	**FB**	A	EFPC	LA	
43017	**FB**	A	EFPC	LA	Hannahs discoverhannahs.org
43018	**FB**	A	EFPC	LA	
43020	**FB**	A	EFPC	LA	MTU Power. Passion. Partnership
43021	**FB**	A	EFPC	LA	David Austin – Cartoonist
43022	**FB**	A	EFPC	LA	The Duke of Edinburgh's Award
					Diamond Anniversary 1956–2016
43023	**FB**	A	EFPC	LA	SQN LDR HAROLD STARR
					ONE OF THE FEW

43024	**FB**	A	EFPC	LA	Great Western Society 1961–2011 Didcot Railway Centre
43025	**FB**	A	EFPC	LA	IRO The Institution of Railway Operators 2000–2010 TEN YEARS PROMOTING OPERATIONAL EXCELLENCE
43026	**FB**	A	EFPC	LA	Michael Eavis
43027	**AL**	A	EFPC	LA	
43028	**FB**	A	EFPC	LA	
43029	**FB**	A	EFPC	LA	
43030	**FB**	A	EFPC	LA	Christian Lewis Trust
43031	**FB**	A	EFPC	LA	
43032	**FB**	A	EFPC	LA	
43033	**FB**	A	EFPC	LA	Driver Brian Cooper 15 June 1947–5 October 1999
43034	**FB**	A	EFPC	LA	TravelWatch SouthWest
43035	**FB**	A	EFPC	LA	
43036	**FB**	A	EFPC	LA	
43037	**FB**	A	EFPC	LA	PENYDARREN
43040	**FB**	A	EFPC	LA	Bristol St. Philip's Marsh
43041	**GW**	A	EFPC	LE	Meningitis Trust Support for Life
43042	**FB**	A	EFPC	LE	
43043 *	**ST**	P	EMPC	NL	
43044 *	**ST**	P	EMPC	NL	
43045 *	**ST**	P	EMPC	NL	
43046 *	**ST**	P	EMPC	NL	
43047 *	**ST**	P	EMPC	NL	
43048 *	**ST**	P	EMPC	NL	T.C.B. Miller MBE
43049 *	**ST**	P	EMPC	NL	Neville Hill
43050 *	**ST**	P	EMPC	NL	
43052 *	**ST**	P	EMPC	NL	
43053	**FB**	P	EFPC	LE	University of Worcester
43054 *	**ST**	P	EMPC	NL	
43055 *	**ST**	P	EMPC	NL	The Sheffield Star 125 Years
43056	**FB**	P	EFPC	LE	The Royal British Legion
43058 *	**ST**	P	EMPC	NL	
43059 *	**ST**	P	EMPC	NL	
43060 *	**ST**	P	EMPC	NL	
43061 *	**ST**	P	EMPC	NL	The Fearless Foxes
43062	**Y**	P	QCAR	EC	John Armitt
43063	**FB**	P	EFPC	LE	
43064 *	**ST**	P	EMPC	NL	
43066 *	**ST**	P	EMPC	NL	
43069	**FB**	P	EFPC	LE	
43070	**FB**	P	EFPC	LE	The Corps of Royal Electrical and Mechanical Engineers
43071	**FB**	P	EFPC	LE	
43073 *	**ST**	P	EMPC	NL	
43075 *	**ST**	P	EMPC	NL	
43076 *	**ST**	P	EMPC	NL	IN SUPPORT OF HELP for HEROES
43078	**FB**	P	EFPC	LE	
43079	**FB**	P	EFPC	LE	

43081	*	**ST**	P	EMPC	NL
43082	*	**ST**	P	EMPC	NL
					RAILWAY children – THE VOICE FOR STREET CHILDREN WORLDWIDE
43083	*	**ST**	P	EMPC	NL
43086		**FB**	P	EFPC	LE
43087		**FB**	P	EFPC	LE
					11 Explosive Ordnance Disposal Regiment Royal Logistic Corps
43088		**FB**	P	EFPC	LE
43089	*	**ST**	P	EMPC	NL
43091		**FB**	P	EFPC	LE
43092		**FB**	FG	EFPC	LE
43093		**FB**	FG	EFPC	LE
43094		**FB**	FG	EFPC	LE
43097		**FB**	FG	EFPC	LE
					Environment Agency
43098		**FB**	FG	EFPC	LE
43122		**FB**	FG	EFPC	LE
43124		**FB**	A	EFPC	LE
43125		**FB**	A	EFPC	LE
43126		**AL**	A	EFPC	LE
43127		**FB**	A	EFPC	LE
					Sir Peter Parker 1924–2002 Cotswold Line 150
43128		**FB**	A	EFPC	LE
43129		**FB**	A	EFPC	LE
43130		**FB**	A	EFPC	LE
43131		**FB**	A	EFPC	LE
43132		**FB**	A	EFPC	LE
					We Save the Children – Will You?
43133		**FB**	A	EFPC	LE
43134		**FB**	A	EFPC	LE
43135		**FB**	A	EFPC	LE
43136		**FB**	A	EFPC	LE
43137		**FB**	A	EFPC	LE
					Newton Abbot 150
43138		**FB**	A	EFPC	LE
					Driver Stan Martin 25 June 1950 – 6 November 2004
43139		**FB**	A	EFPC	LE
					Landore Diesel Depot 1963 Celebrating 50 years 2013/ Depo Diesel Glandŵr 1963 Dathlu 50 Mlynedd 2013
43140		**FB**	A	EFPC	LE
43141		**FB**	A	EFPC	LE
					Cardiff Panel Signal Box 1966–2016/ Blwch Signalau Panel Caerdydd 1966–2016
43142		**FB**	A	EFPC	LE
					Reading Panel Signal Box 1965–2010
43143		**FB**	A	EFPC	LE
					Stroud 700
43144		**AL**	A	EFPC	LE
43145		**FB**	A	EFPC	LE
43146		**AL**	A	EFPC	LE
43147		**FB**	A	EFPC	LE
					Royal Marines Celebrating 350 Years
43148		**FB**	A	EFPC	LE
43149		**FB**	A	EFPC	LE
					University of Plymouth
43150		**FB**	A	EFPC	LE

43151	**FB**	A	EFPC	LE	
43152	**FB**	A	EFPC	LE	
43153	**FB**	FG	EFPC	OO	
43154	**FB**	FG	EFPC	OO	
43155	**FB**	FG	EFPC	OO	The Red Arrows
					50 Seasons of Excellence
43156	**FB**	P	EFPC	OO	Dartington International Summer School
43158	**FB**	FG	EFPC	OO	
43159	**FB**	P	EFPC	OO	
43160	**FB**	P	EFPC	OO	Sir Moir Lockhead OBE
43161	**FB**	P	EFPC	OO	
43162	**FB**	P	EFPC	OO	
43163	**AL**	A	EFPC	OO	
43164	**FB**	A	EFPC	OO	
43165	**FB**	A	EFPC	OO	Prince Michael of Kent
43168	**FB**	A	EFPC	OO	
43169	**FB**	A	EFPC	OO	THE NATIONAL TRUST
43170	**FB**	A	EFPC	OO	
43171	**FB**	A	EFPC	OO	
43172	**AL**	A	EFPC	OO	Harry Patch – The last survivor of
					the trenches
43174	**FB**	A	EFPC	OO	
43175	**FB**	A	EFPC	OO	GWR 175TH ANNIVERSARY
43176	**FB**	A	EFPC	OO	
43177	**FB**	A	EFPC	OO	
43179	**FB**	A	EFPC	OO	Pride of Laira
43180	**FB**	P	EFPC	OO	
43181	**FB**	A	EFPC	OO	
43182	**FB**	A	EFPC	OO	
43183	**FB**	A	EFPC	OO	
43185	**IC**	A	EFPC	OO	Great Western
43186	**FB**	A	EFPC	OO	
43187	**GW**	A	EFPC	OO	
43188	**GW**	A	EFPC	OO	
43189	**FB**	A	EFPC	OO	RAILWAY HERITAGE TRUST
43190	**FB**	A	EFPC	OO	
43191	**FB**	A	EFPC	OO	
43192	**FB**	A	EFPC	OO	
43193	**FB**	P	EFPC	OO	
43194	**FB**	FG	EFPC	OO	
43195	**FB**	P	EFPC	OO	
43196	**FB**	P	EFPC	OO	
43197	**FB**	P	EFPC	OO	
43198	**FB**	FG	EFPC	OO	Oxfordshire 2007

Class 43/2. Rebuilt Virgin Trains East Coast, CrossCountry and Grand Central power cars. Power cars have been renumbered by adding 200 to their original number or 400 to their original number (Grand Central), except 43123 which became 43423.

43206 (43006)	**VE**	A	IECP	EC
43207 (43007)	**XC**	A	EHPC	EC

43208 (43008)	**VE**	A	IECP	EC	Lincolnshire Echo
43238 (43038)	**AL**	A	IECP	EC	National Railway Museum
					40 Years 1975–2015
43239 (43039)	**VE**	A	IECP	EC	
43251 (43051)	**VE**	P	IECP	EC	
43257 (43057)	**VE**	P	IECP	EC	
43272 (43072)	**VE**	P	IECP	EC	
43274 (43074)	**VE**	P	IECP	EC	Spirit of Sunderland
43277 (43077)	**VE**	P	IECP	EC	
43285 (43085)	**XC**	P	EHPC	EC	
43290 (43090)	**VE**	P	IECP	EC	mtu fascination of power
43295 (43095)	**VE**	A	IECP	EC	
43296 (43096)	**VE**	A	IECP	EC	
43299 (43099)	**VE**	P	IECP	EC	
43300 (43100)	**VE**	P	IECP	EC	Craigentinny
					100 YEARS 1914–2014
43301 (43101)	**XC**	P	EHPC	EC	
43302 (43102)	**VE**	P	IECP	EC	
43303 (43103)	**XC**	P	EHPC	EC	
43304 (43104)	**XC**	A	EHPC	EC	
43305 (43105)	**VE**	A	IECP	EC	
43306 (43106)	**VE**	A	IECP	EC	
43307 (43107)	**VE**	A	IECP	EC	
43308 (43108)	**VE**	A	IECP	EC	HIGHLAND CHIEFTAIN
43309 (43109)	**VE**	A	IECP	EC	
43310 (43110)	**VE**	A	IECP	EC	
43311 (43111)	**VE**	A	IECP	EC	
43312 (43112)	**VE**	A	IECP	EC	
43313 (43113)	**VE**	A	IECP	EC	
43314 (43114)	**VE**	A	IECP	EC	
43315 (43115)	**VE**	A	IECP	EC	
43316 (43116)	**VE**	A	IECP	EC	
43317 (43117)	**VE**	A	IECP	EC	
43318 (43118)	**VE**	A	IECP	EC	
43319 (43119)	**VE**	A	IECP	EC	
43320 (43120)	**VE**	A	IECP	EC	
43321 (43121)	**XC**	P	EHPC	EC	
43357 (43157)	**XC**	P	EHPC	EC	
43366 (43166)	**XC**	A	EHPC	EC	
43367 (43167)	**VE**	A	IECP	EC	DELTIC 50 1955–2005
43378 (43178)	**XC**	A	EHPC	EC	
43384 (43184)	**XC**	A	EHPC	EC	
43423 (43123) †	**GC**	A	GCHP	HT	'VALENTA' 1972–2010
43465 (43065) †	**GC**	A	GCHP	HT	
43467 (43067) †	**GC**	A	GCHP	HT	
43468 (43068) †	**GC**	A	GCHP	HT	
43480 (43080) †	**GC**	A	GCHP	HT	
43484 (43084) †	**GC**	A	GCHP	HT	PETER FOX 1942–2011
					PLATFORM 5

CLASS 47   BR/BRUSH/SULZER   Co-Co

Built: 1963–67 by Brush Traction, at Loughborough or by BR at Crewe Works.
Engine: Sulzer 12LDA28C of 1920 kW (2580 hp) at 750 rpm.
Main Generator: Brush TG160-60 Mk4 or TM172-50 Mk1.
Traction Motors: Brush TM64-68 Mk1 or Mk1A.
Maximum Tractive Effort: 267 kN (60000 lbf).
Continuous Tractive Effort: 133 kN (30000 lbf) at 26 mph.
Power at Rail: 1550 kW (2080 hp).   **Train Brakes:** Air.
Brake Force: 61 t.   **Dimensions:** 19.38 x 2.79 m.
Weight: 111.5–120.6 t.   **Wheel Diameter:** 1143 mm.
Design Speed: 95 mph.   **Maximum Speed:** 95 mph.
Fuel Capacity: 3273 (+ 5887).   **Route Availability:** 6 or 7.
Train Supply: Not equipped.

Class 47s exported for use abroad are listed in section 1.6 of this book.

Non-standard liveries/numbering:

47270   Also carries original number 1971.
47501   Also carried original number D1944.
47773   Also carries original number D1755.
47798   Royal Train claret with Rail Express Systems markings.
47830   Also carries original number D1645.

Class 47/0. Standard Design. Built with train air and vacuum brakes.

47194 +	**F**	WC	AWCX	CS (S)	
47236 x+	**FE**	WC	AWCX	CS (S)	
47237 x+	**WC**	WC	AWCA	CS	
47245 x+	**WC**	WC	AWCA	CS	
47270 +	**B**	WC	AWCA	CS	SWIFT

Class 47/3. Built with train air and vacuum brakes. Details as Class 47/0 except: **Weight:** 113.7 t.

47355 a+	**K**	WC	AWCX	CS (S)
47368	**F**	WC	AWCX	CS (S)

Class 47/4. Electric Train Supply equipment.
Details as Class 47/0 except:

Weight: 120.4–125.1 t.   **Fuel Capacity:** 3273 (+ 5537) litres.
Train Supply: Electric, index 66. **Route Availability:** 7.

47492 x	**RX**	WC	AWCX	CS (S)	
47500 x	**WC**	WC	AWCX	CS (S)	
47501 x+	**GG**	LD	MBDL	CL	CRAFTSMAN
47526 x	**BL**	WC	AWCX	CS (S)	
47580 x	**BL**	47	MBDL	TM	County of Essex

Class 47/7. Former Railnet dedicated locomotives. Details as Class 47/0 except:
Fuel Capacity: 5887 litres.

47727	**CS**	CS	COLS	WH (S) Rebecca

47739	**CS**	CS	COFS	WH	Robin of Templecombe 1938–2013
47746	x	**WC**	WC	AWCA	CS	Chris Fudge 29.7.70 – 22.6.10
47749		**CS**	CS	COFS	WH	CITY OF TRURO
47760	x	**WC**	WC	AWCA	CS	
47768		**RX**	WC	AWCX	CS (S)	
47769		**V**	HN	HNRS	BH (S)	Resolve
47772	x	**RX**	WC	AWCX	CS (S)	
47773	x	**GG**	70	MBDL	TM	
47776	x	**RX**	WC	AWCX	CS (S)	
47786		**WC**	WC	AWCA	CS	Roy Castle OBE
47787		**WC**	WC	AWCX	CS (S)	Windsor Castle
47790		**VN**	LD	MBDL	CL	

Class 47/4 continued. Route Availability 6.

47798	x	**O**	NM	MBDL	YK	Prince William
47802	+	**WC**	WC	AWCA	CS	
47804	+	**WC**	WC	AWCA	CS	
47805	+	**DS**	LD	MBDL	CL	
47810	+	**DI**	AF	MBDL	ZG	
47811	+	**GL**	FL	DHLT	CB (S)	
47812	+	**RB**	RO	GROG	BU	
47813	+	**DS**	DR	XHSS	KM (S)	Solent
47815	+	**RB**	RO	GROG	BU	
47816	+	**GL**	FL	DHLT	CB (S)	
47818	+	**DS**	AF	MBDL	ZG	
47826	+	**WC**	WC	AWCA	CS	
47830	+	**GG**	FL	DFLH	CB	BEECHING'S LEGACY
47832	+	**WC**	WC	AWCA	CS	
47841	+	**DS**	LD	MBDL	ZG (S)	
47843	+	**RB**	RO	GROG	BU	
47847	+	**BL**	RO	GROG	BU	
47848	+	**RB**	RO	GROG	BU	
47851	+	**WC**	WC	AWCA	CS	
47853	+	**DR**	HN	GBHN	BH (S)	
47854	+	**WC**	WC	AWCA	CS	Diamond Jubilee

CLASS 50   ENGLISH ELECTRIC   Co-Co

Built: 1967–68 by English Electric at Vulcan Foundry, Newton-le-Willows.
Engine: English Electric 16CVST of 2010 kW (2700 hp) at 850 rpm.
Main Generator: English Electric 840/4B.
Traction Motors: English Electric 538/5A.
Maximum Tractive Effort: 216 kN (48500 lbf).
Continuous Tractive Effort: 147 kN (33000 lbf) at 23.5 mph.
Power at Rail: 1540 kW (2070 hp). **Train Brakes:** Air & vacuum.
Brake Force: 59 t. **Dimensions:** 20.88 x 2.78 m.
Weight: 116.9 t. **Wheel Diameter:** 1092 mm.
Design Speed: 105 mph. **Maximum Speed:** 90 mph.
Fuel Capacity: 4796 litres. **Route Availability:** 6.
Train Supply: Electric, index 61.

Non-standard numbering:

50050 Also carries original number D400.

50007	**B**	50	CFOL	KR	Hercules
50017	**N**	NB	MBDL	WH	Royal Oak
50044	**B**	50	CFOL	KR	Exeter
50049	**BL**	50	CFOL	KR	Defiance
50050	**B**	NB	MBDL	WH	Fearless

CLASS 52   BR/MAYBACH   C-C

Built: 1961–64 by BR at Swindon Works.
Engine: Two Maybach MD655 of 1007 kW (1350 hp) each at 1500 rpm.
Transmission: Hydraulic. Voith L630rV.
Maximum Tractive Effort: 297 kN (66700 lbf).
Continuous Tractive Effort: 201 kN (45200 lbf) at 14.5 mph.

Power at Rail: 1490 kW (2000 hp).	**Train Brakes:** Air & vacuum.
Brake Force: 83 t.	**Dimensions:** 20.70 m x 2.78 m.
Weight: 110 t.	**Wheel Diameter:** 1092 mm.
Design Speed: 90 mph.	**Maximum Speed:** 90 mph.
Fuel Capacity: 3900 litres.	**Route Availability:** 6.
Train Supply: Steam heating.	

Never allocated a number in the 1972 number series.

D1015	**M**	DT	MBDL	TM	WESTERN CHAMPION

CLASS 55   ENGLISH ELECTRIC   Co-Co

Built: 1961 by English Electric at Vulcan Foundry, Newton-le-Willows.
Engine: Two Napier-Deltic D18-25 of 1230 kW (1650 hp) each at 1500 rpm.
Main Generators: Two English Electric 829/1A.
Traction Motors: English Electric 538/A.
Maximum Tractive Effort: 222 kN (50000 lbf).
Continuous Tractive Effort: 136 kN (30500 lbf) at 32.5 mph.

Power at Rail: 1969 kW (2640 hp).	**Train Brakes:** Air & vacuum.
Brake Force: 51 t.	**Dimensions:** 21.18 x 2.68 m.
Weight: 100 t.	**Wheel Diameter:** 1092 mm.
Design Speed: 105 mph.	**Maximum Speed:** 100 mph.
Fuel Capacity: 3755 litres.	**Route Availability:** 5.
Train Supply: Electric, index 66.	

55002	**GG**	NM	MBDL	YK	THE KING'S OWN YORKSHIRE LIGHT INFANTRY
55009	**B**	DP	MBDL	BH	ALYCIDON
55022	**B**	MW	MBDL	NY	ROYAL SCOTS GREY

CLASS 56   BRUSH/BR/RUSTON   Co-Co

Built: 1976–84 by Electroputere at Craiova, Romania (as sub-contractors for Brush) or BREL at Doncaster or Crewe Works.
Engine: Ruston Paxman 16RK3CT of 2460 kW (3250 hp) at 900 rpm.
Main Alternator: Brush BA1101A.
Traction Motors: Brush TM73-62.
Maximum Tractive Effort: 275 kN (61800 lbf).
Continuous Tractive Effort: 240 kN (53950 lbf) at 16.8 mph.
Power at Rail: 1790 kW (2400 hp).   **Train Brakes:** Air.
Brake Force: 60 t.   **Dimensions:** 19.36 x 2.79 m.
Weight: 126 t.   **Wheel Diameter:** 1143 mm.
Design Speed: 80 mph.   **Maximum Speed:** 80 mph.
Fuel Capacity: 5228 litres.   **Route Availability:** 7.
Train Supply: Not equipped.

All equipped with Slow Speed Control.

Class 56s exported for use abroad are listed in section 1.6 of this book.

Non-standard liveries:

56009   All over blue.

56303   All over dark green.

56007	**B**	UR	UKRS	LR (S)	
56009	**O**	UR	UKRS	BL (S)	
56018	**FER**	UR	UKRS	LB (S)	
56031	**FER**	UR	UKRS	LR (S)	
56032	**FER**	UR	UKRS	LR (S)	
56037	**E**	UR	UKRS	LR (S)	
56038	**FER**	UR	UKRS	LR (S)	
56049	**CS**	CS	COLS	WH (S)	
56051	**CS**	CS	COLS	WH (S)	
56060	**FER**	UR	UKRS	LB (S)	
56065	**FER**	UR	UKRS	LR (S)	
56069	**FER**	UR	UKRS	LR (S)	
56077	**LH**	UR	UKRS	LR (S)	
56078	**CS**	CS	COFS	WH	
56081	**FO**	UR	UKRL	LR	
56087	**CS**	CS	COFS	WH	
56090	**CS**	CS	COLS	WH (S)	
56091	**FER**	BA	HTLX	WH	
56094	**CS**	CS	COFS	WH	
56096	**CS**	CS	COFS	WH	
56098	**FO**	UR	UKRL	LR	Lost Boys 68–88
56103	**FER**	BA	HTLX	WH	
56104	**FO**	UR	UKRL	LR	
56105	**CS**	CS	COFS	WH	
56106	**FER**	UR	UKRS	LR (S)	
56113	**CS**	CS	COFS	WH	
56128	**F**	BA	HTLX	WH (S)	

56301	(56045)	**FA**	56	UKRL	LR
56302	(56124)	**CS**	CS	COFS	WH	PECO The Railway Modeller 2016 40 Years
56303	(56125)	**0**	BA	HTLX	WH	
56311	(56057)	**DC**	BA	HTLX	WH	
56312	(56003)	**DC**	BA	HTLX	WH	Jeremiah Dixon Son of County Durham Surveyor of the Mason-Dixon Line U.S.A.

CLASS 57   BRUSH/GM   Co-Co

Built: 1964–65 by Brush Traction at Loughborough or BR at Crewe Works as Class 47. Rebuilt 1997–2004 by Brush Traction at Loughborough.
Engine: General Motors 12 645 E3 of 1860 kW (2500 hp) at 904 rpm.
Main Alternator: Brush BA1101D (recovered from Class 56).
Traction Motors: Brush TM64-68 Mark 1 or Mark 1A.
Maximum Tractive Effort: 244.5 kN (55000 lbf).
Continuous Tractive Effort: 140 kN (31500 lbf) at ?? mph.
Power at Rail: 1507 kW (2025 hp).   **Train Brakes:** Air.
Brake Force: 80 t.   **Dimensions:** 19.38 x 2.79 m.
Weight: 120.6 t.   **Wheel Diameter:** 1143 mm.
Design Speed: 75 mph.   **Maximum Speed:** 75 mph.
Fuel Capacity: 5550 litres.   **Route Availability:** 6
Train Supply: Not equipped.

Non-standard livery:

57604 Original Great Western Railway green.

Class 57/0. No Train Supply Equipment. Rebuilt 1997–2000.

57001	(47356)	**WC**	WC	AWCA	CS
57002	(47322)	**DI**	DR	XHCK	KM	RAIL EXPRESS
57003	(47317)	**DI**	DR	XHCK	KM	
57004	(47347)	**DS**	DR	XHSS	LW (S)
57005	(47350)	**AZ**	WC	AWCX	CS (S)
57006	(47187)	**WC**	WC	AWCX	CS (S)
57007	(47332)	**DI**	DR	XHCK	KM
57008	(47060)	**DS**	DR	XHSS	LW (S)
57009	(47079)	**DS**	DR	XHSS	LW (S)
57010	(47231)	**DI**	DR	XHSS	LW (S)
57011	(47329)	**DS**	DR	XHSS	ZG (S)
57012	(47204)	**DS**	DR	XHSS	LW (S)

Class 57/3. Electric Train Supply Equipment. Former Virgin Trains locomotives fitted with retractable Dellner couplers. Rebuilt 2002–04. Details as Class 57/0 except:

Engine: General Motors 12645F3B of 2050 kW (2750 hp) at 954 rpm.
Main Alternator: Brush BA1101F (recovered from Class 56) or Brush BA1101G.
Fuel Capacity: 5887 litres.   **Train Supply:** Electric, index 100.
Design Speed: 95 mph.   **Maximum Speed:** 95 mph.
Brake Force: 60 t.   **Weight:** 117 t.

57301	(47845)	d	DI	P	XHAC	KM	Goliath
57302	(47827)	d	DS	DR	XHVT	KM	Chad Varah
57303	(47705)	d	DI	P	XHAC	KM	Pride of Carlisle
57304	(47807)	d	DI	DR	XHVT	KM	Pride of Cheshire
57305	(47822)	d	VN	P	XHAC	KM	Northern Princess
57306	(47814)	d	DI	P	XHAC	KM	Her Majesty's Railway Inspectorate 175
57307	(47225)	d	DR	DR	XHVT	KM	LADY PENELOPE
57308	(47846)	d	DS	DR	XHVT	KM	County of Staffordshire
57309	(47806)	d	DI	DR	XHVT	KM	Pride of Crewe
57310	(47831)	d	DI	P	XHAC	KM	Pride of Cumbria
57311	(47817)	d	DS	DR	XHVT	KM	Thunderbird
57312	(47330)	d	VN	P	XHAC	KM	Solway Princess
57313	(47371)		WC	WC	AWCA	CS	
57314	(47372)		WC	WC	AWCA	CS	
57315	(47234)		WC	WC	AWCA	CS	
57316	(47290)		WC	WC	AWCA	CS	

Class 57/6. Electric Train Supply Equipment. Prototype ETS loco. Rebuilt 2001. Details as Class 57/0 except:

Main Alternator: Brush BA1101E.   **Fuel Capacity:** 3273 litres.
Train Supply: Electric, index 95.   **Weight:** 113t.
Design Speed: 95 mph.   **Maximum Speed:** 95 mph.
Brake Force: 60 t.

57601	(47825)	WC	WC	AWCA	CS	

Class 57/6. Electric Train Supply Equipment. Great Western Railway locomotives. Rebuilt 2004. Details as Class 57/3.

57602	(47337)	GW	P	EFOO	OO	Restormel Castle
57603	(47349)	GW	P	EFOO	OO	Tintagel Castle
57604	(47209)	0	P	EFOO	OO	PENDENNIS CASTLE
57605	(47206)	GW	P	EFOO	OO	Totnes Castle

CLASS 59   GENERAL MOTORS   Co-Co

Built: 1985 (59001–004) or 1989 (59005) by General Motors, La Grange, Illinois, USA or 1990 (59101–104), 1994 (59201) and 1995 (59202–206) by General Motors, London, Ontario, Canada.
Engine: General Motors 16-645E3C two stroke of 2460 kW (3300 hp) at 904 rpm.
Main Alternator: General Motors AR11 MLD-D14A.
Traction Motors: General Motors D77B.
Maximum Tractive Effort: 506 kN (113550 lbf).
Continuous Tractive Effort: 291 kN (65300 lbf) at 14.3 mph.
Power at Rail: 1889 kW (2533 hp).   **Train Brakes:** Air.
Brake Force: 69 t.   **Dimensions:** 21.35 x 2.65 m.
Weight: 121 t.   **Wheel Diameter:** 1067 mm.
Design Speed: 60 (* 75) mph.   **Maximum Speed:** 60 (* 75) mph.
Fuel Capacity: 4546 litres.   **Route Availability:** 7.
Train Supply: Not equipped.

Class 59/0. Owned by Aggregate Industries and GB Railfreight.

59001	**AI**	AI	XYPO	MD	YEOMAN ENDEAVOUR
59002	**AI**	AI	XYPO	MD	ALAN J DAY
59003	**GB**	GB	GBYH	RR	YEOMAN HIGHLANDER
59004	**FY**	AI	XYPO	MD	PAUL A HAMMOND
59005	**AI**	AI	XYPO	MD	KENNETH J PAINTER

Class 59/1. Owned by Hanson UK.

59101	**HA**	HA	XYPA	MD	Village of Whatley
59102	**HA**	HA	XYPA	MD	Village of Chantry
59103	**HA**	HA	XYPA	MD	Village of Mells
59104	**HA**	HA	XYPA	MD	Village of Great Elm

Class 59/2. Owned by DB Cargo.

59201	*	**DB**	DB	WDAM	MD	
59202	*	**DB**	DB	WDAM	MD	Alan Meddows Taylor
						MD Mendip Rail Limited
59203	*	**DB**	DB	WDAM	MD	
59204	*	**DB**	DB	WDAM	MD	
59205	*b	**DB**	DB	WDAM	MD	
59206	*b	**DB**	DB	WDAM	MD	John F. Yeoman Rail Pioneer

CLASS 60   BRUSH/MIRRLEES   Co-Co

Built: 1989–93 by Brush Traction at Loughborough.
Engine: Mirrlees 8MB275T of 2310 kW (3100 hp) at 1000 rpm.
Main Alternator: Brush BA1006A.
Traction Motors: Brush TM2161A.
Maximum Tractive Effort: 500 kN (106500 lbf).
Continuous Tractive Effort: 336 kN (71570 lbf) at 17.4 mph.
Power at Rail: 1800 kW (2415 hp).   **Train Brakes:** Air.
Brake Force: 74 t (+ 62 t).   **Dimensions:** 21.34 x 2.64 m.
Weight: 129 t (+ 131 t).   **Wheel Diameter:** 1118 mm.
Design Speed: 62 mph.   **Maximum Speed:** 60 mph.
Fuel Capacity: 4546 (+ 5225) litres.   **Route Availability:** 8.
Train Supply: Not equipped.

All equipped with Slow Speed Control.

* Refurbished locomotives.

60034, 60064, 60072, 60073, 60077, 60084 and 60090 carry their names on one side only.

60500 originally carried the number 60016.

Advertising liveries:

60066 Powering Drax (silver).
60099 Tata Steel (silver).

60001	*	**DB**	DB	WCAT	TO
60002	+*	**CS**	CS	COLO	TO

60003	+	**E**	DB	WQDA	TO (S)	FREIGHT TRANSPORT ASSOCIATION
60004	+	**E**	DB	WQDA	TO (S)	
60005	+	**E**	DB	WQDA	TO (S)	
60006		**CU**	DB	WQDA	TO (S)	
60007	+*	**DB**	DB	WCBT	TO	The Spirit of Tom Kendell
60008		**E**	DB	WQDA	TO (S)	Sir William McAlpine
60009	+	**E**	DB	WQBA	TO (S)	
60010	+*	**DB**	DB	WQAB	TO (S)	
60011		**DB**	DB	WQAB	TO (S)	
60012	+	**E**	DB	WQBA	TO (S)	
60013		**EG**	DB	WQDA	TO (S)	Robert Boyle
60014		**EG**	DB	WQDA	TO (S)	
60015	+*	**DB**	DB	WQAB	TO (S)	
60017	+*	**DB**	DB	WCBT	TO	
60018		**E**	DB	WQDA	TO (S)	
60019	*	**DB**	DB	WCAT	TO	Port of Grimsby & Immingham
60020	+*	**DB**	DB	WCBT	TO	The Willows
60021	+*	**CS**	CS	COLO	TO	
60022	+	**E**	DB	WQDA	TO (S)	
60023	+	**E**	DB	WQDA	TO (S)	
60024	*	**DB**	DB	WQAB	TO (S)	Clitheroe Castle
60025	+	**E**	DB	WQDA	TO (S)	
60026	+*	**CS**	CS	COLO	TO	
60027	+	**E**	DB	WQDA	TO (S)	
60028	+	**EG**	DB	WQCA	CE (S)	
60029		**E**	DB	WQCA	CE (S)	
60030	+	**E**	DB	WQDA	TO (S)	
60031		**E**	DB	WQDA	TO (S)	
60032		**F**	DB	WQDA	TO (S)	
60033	+	**CU**	DB	WQCA	TO (S)	Tees Steel Express
60034		**EG**	DB	WQBA	TO (S)	Carnedd Llewelyn
60035		**E**	DB	WQAB	TO (S)	
60036		**E**	DB	WQBA	TO (S)	GEFCO
60037	+	**E**	DB	WQDA	TO (S)	
60038	+	**E**	DB	WQCA	CE (S)	
60039	*	**DB**	DB	WCAT	TO	Dove Holes
60040	*	**DB**	DB	WCAT	TO	The Territorial Army Centenary
60041	+	**E**	DB	WQCA	TO (S)	
60042		**E**	DB	WQDA	TO (S)	
60043		**E**	DB	WQBA	TO (S)	
60044	*	**DB**	DB	WCAT	TO	Dowlow
60045		**E**	DB	WQAB	TO (S)	The Permanent Way Institution
60046	+	**EG**	DB	WQCA	CE (S)	
60047	*	**CS**	CS	COLO	TO	
60048		**E**	DB	WQCA	TO (S)	
60049		**E**	DB	WQAB	TO (S)	
60050		**E**	DB	WQDA	TO (S)	
60051	+	**E**	DB	WQDA	TO (S)	
60052	+	**E**	DB	WQDA	TO (S)	Glofa Twr – The last deep mine in Wales – Tower Colliery
60053		**E**	DB	WQBA	TO (S)	

60054 +*	**DB**	DB	WCBT	TO	
60055 +	**EG**	DB	WQCA	CE (S)	
60056 +*	**CS**	CS	COLO	TO	
60057	**EG**	DB	WQBA	TO (S)	Adam Smith
60058 +	**E**	DB	WQBA	TO (S)	
60059 +*	**DB**	DB	WCBT	TO	Swinden Dalesman
60060	**EG**	DB	WQBA	TO (S)	
60061	**F**	DB	WQCA	TO (S)	
60062 *	**DB**	DB	WQAB	TO (S)	Stainless Pioneer
60063 *	**DB**	DB	WCAT	TO	
60064 +	**EG**	DB	WQBA	TO (S)	Back Tor
60065	**E**	DB	WQAB	TO (S)	Spirit of JAGUAR
60066 *	**AL**	DB	WCAT	TO	
60067	**EG**	DB	WQBA	TO (S)	
60068	**EG**	DB	WQBA	TO (S)	
60069	**E**	DB	WQBA	TO (S)	Slioch
60070 +	**F**	DB	WQBA	TO (S)	John Loudon McAdam
60071 +	**E**	DB	WQAB	TO (S)	Ribblehead Viaduct
60072	**EG**	DB	WQBA	TO (S)	Cairn Toul
60073	**EG**	DB	WQBA	TO (S)	Cairn Gorm
60074 *	**DB**	DB	WCAT	TO	
60075	**E**	DB	WQBA	TO (S)	
60076 *	**CS**	CS	COLO	TO	Dunbar
60077 +	**EG**	DB	WQBA	TO (S)	Canisp
60078	**ML**	DB	WQBA	TO (S)	
60079 *	**DB**	DB	WQBA	TO (S)	
60080 +	**E**	DB	WQBA	TO (S)	
60081 +	**GW**	DB	WQBA	TO (S)	
60082	**EG**	DB	WQBA	CE (S)	
60083	**E**	DB	WQBA	TO (S)	
60084	**EG**	DB	WQBA	TO (S)	Cross Fell
60085 *	**CS**	CS	COLO	TO	
60086	**EG**	DB	WQBA	TO (S)	
60087 *	**CS**	CS	COLO	TO	CLIC Sargent www.clicsargent.co.uk
60088	**F**	DB	WQBA	TO (S)	
60089 +	**E**	DB	WQBA	TO (S)	
60090 +	**EG**	DB	WQBA	TO (S)	Quinag
60091 +*	**DB**	DB	WCBT	TO	Barry Needham
60092 +*	**DB**	DB	WCBT	TO	
60093	**E**	DB	WQBA	TO (S)	
60094	**E**	DB	WQBA	TO (S)	Rugby Flyer
60095 *	**CS**	CS	COLO	TO	
60096 +*	**CS**	CS	COLO	TO	
60097 +	**E**	DB	WQBA	TO (S)	
60098 +	**E**	DB	WQBA	TO (S)	
60099	**AL**	DB	WQAB	TO (S)	
60100 *	**DB**	DB	WCAT	TO	
60500	**E**	DB	WQBA	TO (S)	

CLASS 66   GENERAL MOTORS/EMD   Co-Co

Built: 1998–2008 by General Motors/EMD, London, Ontario, Canada (Model JT42CWR (low emission locomotives Model JT42CWRM)) or 2013–16 by EMD/Progress Rail, Muncie, Indiana (66752–779).
Engine: General Motors 12N-710G3B-EC two stroke of 2385 kW (3200 hp) at 904 rpm.
Main Alternator: General Motors AR8/CA6.
Traction Motors: General Motors D43TR.
Maximum Tractive Effort: 409 kN (92000 lbf).
Continuous Tractive Effort: 260 kN (58390 lbf) at 15.9 mph.
Power at Rail: 1850 kW (2480 hp).   **Train Brakes:** Air.
Brake Force: 68 t.   **Dimensions:** 21.35 x 2.64 m.
Weight: 127 t.   **Wheel Diameter:** 1120 mm.
Design Speed: 87.5 mph.   **Maximum Speed:** 75 mph.
Fuel Capacity: 6550 litres.   **Route Availability:** 7.
Train Supply: Not equipped.

All equipped with Slow Speed Control.

Class 66s previously used in the UK but now in use abroad are listed in section 1.6 of this book. Some of the DBC 66s moved to France return to Great Britain from time to time for maintenance or operational requirements.

Class 66 delivery dates. The Class 66 design and delivery evolved over an 18-year period, with more than 400 locomotives delivered. For clarity the delivery dates (by year) for each batch of locomotives is as follows:

66001–250	EWS (now DB Cargo). 1998–2000 (some now in use in France or Poland).
66301–305	Fastline. 2008. Now used by DRS.
66401–410	DRS. 2003. Now in use with GB Railfreight or Colas Rail and renumbered 66733–737 and 66742–746 (66734 since scrapped).
66411–420	DRS. 2006. Now leased by Freightliner (66411/412/417 exported to Poland).
66421–430	DRS. 2007
66431–434	DRS. 2008
66501–505	Freightliner. 1999
66506–520	Freightliner. 2000
66521–525	Freightliner. 2000 (66521 since scrapped).
66526–531	Freightliner. 2001
66532–537	Freightliner. 2001
66538–543	Freightliner. 2001
66544–553	Freightliner. 2001
66554	Freightliner. 2002†
66555–566	Freightliner. 2002
66567–574	Freightliner. 2003. 66573–574 now used by Colas Rail and renumbered 66846–847.
66575–577	Freightliner. 2004. Now used by Colas Rail and renumbered 66848–850.
66578–581	Freightliner. 2005. Now used by GBRf and renumbered 66738–741.
66582–594	Freightliner. 2007 (66582/583/584/586 exported to Poland).

66595–599	Freightliner. 2008
66601–606	Freightliner. 2000
66607–612	Freightliner. 2002 (66607/609/611/612 exported to Poland)
66613–618	Freightliner. 2003
66619–622	Freightliner. 2005
66623–625	Freightliner. 2007 (66624/625 exported to Poland).
66701–707	GB Railfreight. 2001
66708–712	GB Railfreight. 2002
66713–717	GB Railfreight. 2003
66718–722	GB Railfreight. 2006
66723–727	GB Railfreight. 2006
66728–732	GB Railfreight. 2008
66747–749	Built in 2008 as 20078968-004/006/007 (DE 6313/15/16) for Crossrail AG in the Netherlands but never used. Sold to GB Railfreight in 2012.
66750–751	Built in 2003 as 20038513-01/04 and have worked in the Netherlands, Germany and Poland. GBRf secured these two locomotives on lease in 2013.
66752–772	GB Railfreight. 2014.
66773–779	GB Railfreight. 2016.
66951–952	Freightliner. 2004
66953–957	Freightliner. 2008

† Replacement for 66521, written off in the Great Heck accident in 2001.

Advertising and non-standard liveries:

66522	Shanks Waste (one half of loco Freightliner green and one half Shanks' Waste light green).
66623	Bardon Aggregates blue.
66709	MSC – blue with images of a container ship.
66718	London Underground 150, (black).
66720	Day and night (various colours, different on each side).
66721	London Underground 150 (white with tube map images).
66727	Maritime (blue).
66779	BR dark green.

Class 66/0. DB Cargo-operated locomotives.

All fitted with Swinghead Automatic "Buckeye" Combination Couplers except 66001 and 66002.

† Fitted with additional lights and drawgear for Lickey banking duties.

t Fitted with tripcocks for working over London Underground tracks between Harrow-on-the-Hill and Amersham.

66001 t	**DB**	DB	WBAE	TO
66002	**E**	DB	WBAT	TO
66003	**E**	DB	WBAT	TO
66004	**E**	DB	WBAE	TO
66005	**E**	DB	WBAT	TO
66006	**E**	DB	WBAT	TO
66007	**E**	DB	WBAR	TO
66008	**E**	DB	WQAB	TO (S)

66009	E	DB	WBAE	TO	
66011	E	DB	WBAE	TO	
66012	E	DB	WBAT	TO	
66013	E	DB	WBAE	TO	
66014	E	DB	WBAE	TO	
66015	E	DB	WBAE	TO	
66016	E	DB	WBAE	TO	
66017 t	E	DB	WBAR	TO	
66018	E	DB	WBAE	TO	
66019 t	E	DB	WBAR	TO	
66020	E	DB	WBAT	TO	
66021	E	DB	WBAR	TO	
66023	E	DB	WBAT	TO	
66024	E	DB	WBAE	TO	
66025	E	DB	WBAE	TO	
66027	E	DB	WBAE	TO	
66030	E	DB	WBAR	TO	
66031	E	DB	WBAT	TO	
66034	E	DB	WBAE	TO	
66035	E	DB	WBAE	TO	
66037	E	DB	WBAR	TO	
66039	E	DB	WBAE	TO	
66040	E	DB	WBAR	TO	
66041	**DB**	DB	WBAT	TO	
66043	E	DB	WBAE	TO	
66044	E	DB	WBAE	TO	
66046	E	DB	WQAB	TO (S)	
66047	E	DB	WBAT	TO	
66050	E	DB	WBAE	TO	EWS Energy
66051	E	DB	WBAR	TO	
66053	E	DB	WBAE	TO	
66054	E	DB	WBAR	TO	
66055 †	**DB**	DB	WBAR	TO	Alain Thauvette
66056 †	E	DB	WBLT	TO	
66057 †	E	DB	WBLT	TO	
66058 †	**DB**	DB	WBLE	TO	Derek Clark
66059 †	E	DB	WBLE	TO	
66060	E	DB	WBAT	TO	
66061	E	DB	WBAE	TO	
66063	E	DB	WBAT	TO	
66065	E	DB	WBAR	TO	
66066	**DB**	DB	WBAR	TO	Geoff Spencer
66067	E	DB	WBAR	TO	
66068	E	DB	WBAT	TO	
66069	E	DB	WBAR	TO	
66070	E	DB	WBAT	TO	
66074	E	DB	WBAE	TO	
66075	E	DB	WBAT	TO	
66076	E	DB	WBAE	TO	
66077	E	DB	WBAE	TO	
66078	E	DB	WBAT	TO	

66079	E	DB	WBAR	TO	James Nightall G.C.
66080	E	DB	WBAE	TO	
66081	E	DB	WQAB	TO (S)	
66082	E	DB	WBAT	TO	
66083	E	DB	WBAR	TO	
66084	E	DB	WBAT	TO	
66085	E	DB	WBAR	TO	
66086	E	DB	WBAT	TO	
66087	E	DB	WBAT	TO	
66088	E	DB	WBAT	TO	
66089	E	DB	WBAR	TO	
66090	E	DB	WBAT	TO	
66091	E	DB	WBAE	TO	
66092	E	DB	WBAE	TO	
66093	E	DB	WBAE	TO	
66094	E	DB	WBAT	TO	
66095	E	DB	WBAE	TO	
66096	E	DB	WBAE	TO	
66097	DB	DB	WBAE	TO	
66098	E	DB	WQAA	TO (S)	
66099 r	E	DB	WBBE	TO	
66100 r	E	DB	WBBE	TO	
66101 r	DB	DB	WBBT	TO	
66102 r	E	DB	WBBE	TO	
66103 r	E	DB	WBBE	TO	
66104 r	E	DB	WBAR	TO	
66105 r	E	DB	WBBE	TO	
66106 r	E	DB	WBBE	TO	
66107 r	E	DB	WBAR	TO	
66108 r	E	DB	WBBT	TO	
66109	E	DB	WBAR	TO	
66110 r	E	DB	WBBE	TO	
66111 r	E	DB	WBBT	TO	
66112 r	E	DB	WBBE	TO	
66113 r	E	DB	WBBE	TO	
66114 r	DB	DB	WBBT	TO	
66115	E	DB	WBAT	TO	
66116	E	DB	WBAE	TO	
66117	E	DB	WBAE	TO	
66118	DB	DB	WBAE	TO	
66119	E	DB	WBAE	TO	
66120	E	DB	WBAE	TO	
66121	E	DB	WBAE	TO	
66122	E	DB	WBAE	TO	
66124	E	DB	WBAT	TO	
66125	E	DB	WBAE	TO	
66126	E	DB	WBAE	TO	
66127	E	DB	WBAT	TO	
66128	DB	DB	WBAE	TO	
66129	E	DB	WBAE	TO	
66130	E	DB	WBAT	TO	

66131	E	DB	WBAT	TO	
66132	E	DB	WBAE	TO	
66133	E	DB	WBAE	TO	
66134	E	DB	WBAE	TO	
66135	E	DB	WBAE	TO	
66136	DB	DB	WBAE	TO	
66137	E	DB	WBAE	TO	
66138	E	DB	WBAE	TO	
66139	E	DB	WBAE	TO	
66140	E	DB	WBAE	TO	
66141	E	DB	WQAB	TO (S)	
66142	E	DB	WBAR	TO	
66143	E	DB	WBAE	TO	
66144	E	DB	WBAR	TO	
66145	E	DB	WBAE	TO	
66147	E	DB	WBAT	TO	
66148	E	DB	WBAT	TO	
66149	DB	DB	WBAE	TO	
66150	DB	DB	WBAE	TO	
66151	E	DB	WBAE	TO	
66152	DB	DB	WBAE	TO	Derek Holmes Railway Operator
66154	E	DB	WBAE	TO	
66155	E	DB	WBAT	TO	
66156	E	DB	WBAE	TO	
66158	E	DB	WBAE	TO	
66160	E	DB	WBAE	TO	
66161	E	DB	WBAE	TO	
66162	E	DB	WBAE	TO	
66164	E	DB	WBAT	TO	
66165	E	DB	WBAR	TO	
66167	E	DB	WBAE	TO	
66168	E	DB	WBAR	TO	
66169	E	DB	WBAT	TO	
66170	E	DB	WBAT	TO	
66171	E	DB	WBAT	TO	
66172	E	DB	WBAT	TO	PAUL MELLENEY
66174	E	DB	WBAE	TO	
66175	E	DB	WBAE	TO	
66176	E	DB	WBAE	TO	
66177	E	DB	WBAT	TO	
66181	E	DB	WBAE	TO	
66182	E	DB	WBAT	TO	
66183	E	DB	WBAE	TO	
66184	E	DB	WBAT	TO	
66185	DB	DB	WBAE	TO	DP WORLD London Gateway
66186	E	DB	WBAT	TO	
66187	E	DB	WBAE	TO	
66188	E	DB	WBAR	TO	
66192	E	DB	WBAE	TO	
66194	E	DB	WBAR	TO	
66197	E	DB	WBAE	TO	

66198	**E**	DB	WBAR	TO
66199	**E**	DB	WBAE	TO
66200	**E**	DB	WBAE	TO
66206	**E**	DB	WBAR	TO
66207	**E**	DB	WBAE	TO
66221	**E**	DB	WBAT	TO
66230	**E**	DB	WBAT	TO
66238	**E**	DB	WBAR	TO
66250	**E**	DB	WQAB	TO (S)

**Class 66/3. Former Fastline-operated locomotives now operated by DRS.
Low emission**. Details as Class 66/0 except:

Engine: EMD 12N-710G3B-T2 two stroke of 2420 kW (3245 hp) at 904 rpm.
Traction Motors: General Motors D43TRC.
Fuel Capacity: 5150 litres.

66301	**DS**	BN	XHIM	KM
66302	**DR**	BN	XHIM	KM
66303	**DS**	BN	XHIM	KM
66304	**DS**	BN	XHIM	KM
66305	**DR**	BN	XHIM	KM

Class 66/4. Low emission. Macquarie Group-owned. Details as Class 66/3.

66413	**DS**	MQ	DFHJ	LD	
66414	**FH**	MQ	DFIN	LD	
66415	**DS**	MQ	DFHJ	LD	
66416	**FH**	MQ	DFIN	LD	
66418	**FH**	MQ	DFIN	LD	PATRIOT – IN MEMORY OF FALLEN RAILWAY EMPLOYEES
66419	**DS**	MQ	DFHJ	LD	
66420	**FH**	MQ	DFIN	LD	
66421	**DR**	MQ	XHIM	KM	
66422	**DR**	MQ	XHIM	KM	
66423	**DR**	MQ	XHIM	KM	
66424	**DR**	MQ	XHIM	KM	
66425	**DR**	MQ	XHIM	KM	
66426	**DR**	MQ	XHIM	KM	
66427	**DR**	MQ	XHIM	KM	
66428	**DS**	MQ	XHIM	ZN (S)	
66429	**DR**	MQ	XHIM	KM	
66430	**DR**	MQ	XHIM	KM	
66431	**DR**	MQ	XHIM	KM	
66432	**DR**	MQ	XHIM	KM	
66433	**DR**	MQ	XHIM	KM	
66434	**DR**	MQ	XHIM	KM	

Class 66/5. Standard design. Freightliner-operated locomotives. Details
as Class 66/0.

66501	**FL**	P	DFIM	LD	Japan 2001
66502	**FL**	P	DFIM	LD	Basford Hall Centenary 2001
66503	**FL**	P	DFIM	LD	The RAILWAY MAGAZINE

66504	**FH**	P	DFIM	LD	
66505	**FL**	P	DFIM	LD	
66506	**FL**	E	DFHH	LD	Crewe Regeneration
66507	**FL**	E	DFHJ	LD	
66508	**FL**	E	DFHJ	LD	
66509	**FL**	E	DFHH	LD	
66510	**FL**	E	DFHJ	LD	
66511	**FL**	E	DFHJ	LD	
66512	**FL**	E	DFHH	LD	
66513	**FL**	E	DFHJ	LD	
66514	**FL**	E	DFHJ	LD	
66515	**FL**	E	DFHJ	LD	
66516	**FL**	E	DFIM	LD	
66517	**FL**	E	DFIM	LD	
66518	**FL**	E	DFHJ	LD	
66519	**FL**	E	DFHH	LD	
66520	**FL**	E	DFHH	LD	
66522	**AL**	E	DFHH	LD	
66523	**FL**	E	DFHH	LD	
66524	**FL**	E	DFHJ	LD	
66525	**FL**	E	DFHJ	LD	
66526	**FL**	P	DFHJ	LD	Driver Steve Dunn (George)
66528	**FH**	P	DFHH	LD	Madge Elliot MBE
					Borders Railway Opening 2015
66529	**FL**	P	DFHH	LD	
66531	**FL**	P	DFHJ	LD	
66532	**FL**	P	DFIM	LD	P&O Nedlloyd Atlas
66533	**FL**	P	DFIM	LD	Hanjin Express/Senator Express
66534	**FL**	P	DFIM	LD	OOCL Express
66536	**FL**	P	DFHJ	LD	
66537	**FL**	P	DFIM	LD	
66538	**FL**	E	DFIM	LD	
66539	**FL**	E	DFHH	LD	
66540	**FL**	E	DFIM	LD	Ruby
66541	**FL**	E	DFIM	LD	
66542	**FL**	E	DFIM	LD	
66543	**FL**	E	DFIM	LD	
66544	**FL**	P	DFHJ	LD	
66545	**FL**	P	DFHH	LD	
66546	**FL**	P	DFHH	LD	
66547	**FL**	P	DFHH	LD	
66548	**FL**	P	DFHH	LD	
66549	**FL**	P	DFHH	LD	
66550	**FL**	P	DFHH	LD	
66551	**FL**	P	DFHJ	LD	
66552	**FL**	P	DFHH	LD	Maltby Raider
66553	**FL**	P	DFHH	LD	
66554	**FL**	E	DFHH	LD	
66555	**FL**	E	DFHH	LD	
66556	**FL**	E	DFIM	LD	
66557	**FL**	E	DFIM	LD	

66558	**FL**	E	DFIM	LD
66559	**FL**	E	DFHH	LD
66560	**FL**	E	DFHH	LD
66561	**FL**	E	DFHH	LD
66562	**FL**	E	DFHH	LD
66563	**FL**	E	DFHJ	LD
66564	**FL**	E	DFHJ	LD
66565	**FL**	E	DFIM	LD
66566	**FL**	E	DFIM	LD
66567	**FL**	E	DFIM	LD
66568	**FL**	E	DFIM	LD
66569	**FL**	E	DFIM	LD
66570	**FL**	E	DFIM	LD
66571	**FL**	E	DFIM	LD
66572	**FL**	E	DFIM	LD

Class 66/5. Freightliner-operated low emission locomotives. Details as Class 66/3.

66585	**FL**	MQ	DFHJ	LD	The Drax Flyer
66587	**FL**	MQ	DFIN	LD	
66588	**FL**	MQ	DFIN	LD	
66589	**FL**	MQ	DFIN	LD	
66590	**FL**	MQ	DFIN	LD	
66591	**FL**	MQ	DFIN	LD	
66592	**FL**	MQ	DFIN	LD	Johnson Stevens Agencies
66593	**FL**	MQ	DFIN	LD	3MG MERSEY MULTIMODAL GATEWAY
66594	**FL**	MQ	DFIN	LD	NYK Spirit of Kyoto
66595	**FL**	BN	DFHJ	LD	
66596	**FL**	BN	DFHJ	LD	
66597	**FL**	BN	DFHJ	LD	Viridor
66598	**FL**	BN	DFHG	LD	
66599	**FL**	BN	DFHG	LD	

Class 66/6. Freightliner-operated locomotives with modified gear ratios. Details as Class 66/0 except:

Maximum Tractive Effort: 467 kN (105080 lbf).
Continuous Tractive Effort: 296 kN (66630 lbf) at 14.0 mph.
Design Speed: 65 mph.   **Maximum Speed**: 65 mph.

66601	**FL**	P	DFHH	LD	The Hope Valley
66602	**FL**	P	DFHH	LD	
66603	**FL**	P	DFHH	LD	
66604	**FL**	P	DFHH	LD	
66605	**FL**	P	DFHH	LD	
66606	**FL**	P	DFHH	LD	
66607	**FL**	P	DFHH	LD	
66610	**FL**	P	DFHH	LD	
66613	**FL**	E	DFHH	LD	
66614	**FL**	E	DFHH	LD	1916 POPPY 2016
66615	**FL**	E	DFHH	LD	
66616	**FL**	E	DFHH	LD	

66617	**FL**	E	DFHH	LD	
66618	**FL**	E	DFHH	LD	
					Railways Illustrated Annual
					Photographic Awards Alan Barnes
66619	**FL**	E	DFHH	LD	Derek W. Johnson MBE
66620	**FL**	E	DFHH	LD	
66621	**FL**	E	DFHH	LD	
66622	**FL**	E	DFHH	LD	

Class 66/6. Freightliner-operated low emission locomotive with modified gear ratios. Details as Class 66/6 except:

Fuel Capacity: 5150 litres.

| 66623 | **0** | MQ | DFHG | LD | Bill Bolsover |

Class 66/7. Standard design. GB Railfreight-operated locomotives. Details as Class 66/0.

66701	**GB**	E	GBBT	RR	
66702	**GB**	E	GBBT	RR	Blue Lightning
66703	**GB**	E	GBBT	RR	Doncaster PSB 1981–2002
66704	**GB**	E	GBBT	RR	Colchester Power Signalbox
66705	**GB**	E	GBBT	RR	Golden Jubilee
66706	**GB**	E	GBBT	RR	Nene Valley
66707	**GB**	E	GBBT	RR	Sir Sam Fay GREAT CENTRAL RAILWAY
66708	**GB**	E	GBBT	RR	Jayne
66709	**AL**	E	GBBT	RR	Sorrento
66710	**GB**	E	GBBT	RR	Phil Packer BRIT
66711	**AI**	E	GBBT	RR	Sence
66712	**GB**	E	GBBT	RR	Peterborough Power Signalbox
66713	**GB**	E	GBBT	RR	Forest City
66714	**GB**	E	GBBT	RR	Cromer Lifeboat
66715	**GB**	E	GBBT	RR	VALOUR – IN MEMORY OF ALL RAILWAY EMPLOYEES WHO GAVE THEIR LIVES FOR THEIR COUNTRY
66716	**GB**	E	GBBT	RR	LOCOMOTIVE & CARRIAGE INSTITUTION CENTENARY 1911–2011
66717	**GB**	E	GBBT	RR	Good Old Boy

66718–751. GB Railfreight locomotives.

Details as Class 66/0 except 66718–732/747–749 as below:

Engine: EMD 12N-710G3B-T2 two stroke of 2420 kW (3245 hp) at 904 rpm.
Traction Motors: General Motors D43TRC.
Fuel Capacity: 5546 litres (66718–722) or 5150 litres (66723–732/747–749).

66747–749 were originally built for Crossrail AG in the Netherlands.

66750/751 were originally built for mainland Europe in 2003.

66718	**AL**	E	GBLT	RR	Sir Peter Hendy CBE
66719	**GB**	E	GBLT	RR	METRO-LAND
66720	**0**	E	GBLT	RR	
66721	**AL**	E	GBLT	RR	Harry Beck
66722	**GB**	E	GBLT	RR	Sir Edward Watkin

66723	**FS**	E	GBLT	RR	Chinook
66724	**FS**	E	GBLT	RR	Drax Power Station
66725	**FS**	E	GBLT	RR	SUNDERLAND
66726	**FS**	E	GBLT	RR	SHEFFIELD WEDNESDAY
66727	**AL**	E	GBLT	RR	Maritime One
66728	**GB**	P	GBLT	RR	Institution of Railway Operators
66729	**GB**	P	GBLT	RR	DERBY COUNTY
66730	**GB**	P	GBLT	RR	Whitemoor
66731	**GB**	P	GBLT	RR	interhub GB
66732	**GB**	P	GBLT	RR	GBRf The First Decade 1999–2009
					John Smith – MD

66733	(66401) r	**GB**	P	GBFM	RR	Cambridge PSB
66735	(66403)	**GB**	P	GBBT	RR	
66736	(66404) r	**GB**	P	GBFM	RR	WOLVERHAMPTON WANDERERS
66737	(66405) r	**GB**	P	GBFM	RR	Lesia
66738	(66578)	**GB**	BN	GBBT	RR	HUDDERSFIELD TOWN
66739	(66579)	**GB**	BN	GBFM	RR	Bluebell Railway
66740	(66580) r	**GB**	BN	GBFM	RR	Sarah
66741	(66581)	**GB**	BN	GBBT	RR	Swanage Railway

66742	(66406, 66841)	**GB**	BN	GBBT	RR	ABP Port of Immingham
						Centenary 1912–2012
66743	(66407, 66842) r	**M**	BN	GBFM	RR	
66744	(66408, 66843)	**GB**	BN	GBBT	RR	Crossrail
66745	(66409, 66844)	**GB**	BN	GBRT	RR	Modern Railways
						The first 50 years
66746	(66410, 66845) r	**M**	BN	GBFM	RR	
66747	(20078968-007)	**GB**	GB	GBEB	RR	
66748	(20078968-004)	**GB**	GB	GBEB	RR	West Burton 50
66749	(20078968-006)	**GB**	GB	GBEB	RR	
66750	(20038513-01)	**GB**	BN	GBEB	RR	Bristol Panel Signal Box
66751	(20038513-04) c	**GB**	BN	GBEB	RR	Inspirational Delivered
						Hitachi Rail Europe

66752–779. Low emission. New build locomotives. Details as Class 66/3.

66752	**GB**	GB	GBEL	RR	The Hoosier State
66753	**GB**	GB	GBEL	RR	EMD Roberts Road
66754	**GB**	GB	GBEL	RR	Northampton Saints
66755	**GB**	GB	GBEL	RR	
66756	**GB**	GB	GBEL	RR	
66757	**GB**	GB	GBEL	RR	West Somerset Railway
66758	**GB**	GB	GBEL	RR	
66759	**GB**	GB	GBEL	RR	Chippy
66760	**GB**	GB	GBEL	RR	David Gordon Harris
66761	**GB**	GB	GBEL	RR	Wensleydale Railway Association
					25 Years 1990–2015
66762	**GB**	GB	GBEL	RR	
66763	**GB**	GB	GBEL	RR	Severn Valley Railway
66764	**GB**	GB	GBEL	RR	
66765	**GB**	GB	GBEL	RR	

66766	**GB**	GB	GBEL	RR	
66767	**GB**	GB	GBEL	RR	
66768	**GB**	GB	GBEL	RR	
66769	**GB**	GB	GBEL	RR	
66770	**GB**	GB	GBEL	RR	
66771	**GB**	GB	GBEL	RR	
66772	**GB**	GB	GBEL	RR	
66773	**GB**	GB	GBNB	RR	
66774	**GB**	GB	GBNB	RR	
66775	**GB**	GB	GBNB	RR	
66776	**GB**	GB	GBNB	RR	
66777	**GB**	GB	GBNB	RR	
66778	**GB**	GB	GBNB	RR	
66779	**0**	GB	GBEL	RR	EVENING STAR

Class 66/8. Standard design. Colas Rail locomotives. Details as Class 66/0.

66846	(66573)	**CS**	CS	COLO	HJ	
66847	(66574)	**CS**	CS	COLO	HJ	
66848	(66575)	**CS**	CS	COLO	HJ	
66849	(66576)	**CS**	CS	COLO	HJ	Wylam Dilly
66850	(66577)	**CS**	CS	COLO	HJ	David Maidment OBE

Class 66/9. Freightliner locomotives. Low emission "demonstrator" locomotives. Details as Class 66/3.

* **Fuel Capacity:** 5905 litres.

| 66951 | * | **FL** | E | DFHG | LD | |
| 66952 | | **FL** | E | DFHG | LD | |

Class 66/5. Freightliner-operated low emission locomotives. Owing to the 665xx number range being full, subsequent deliveries of 66/5s were numbered from 66953 onwards. Details as Class 66/5 (low emission).

66953	**FL**	BN	DFHJ	LD	
66954	**FL**	BN	DFIN	LD	
66955	**FL**	BN	DFIN	LD	
66956	**FL**	BN	DFHG	LD	
66957	**FL**	BN	DFHG	LD	Stephenson Locomotive Society 1909–2009

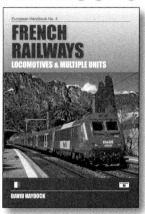

CLASS 67   ALSTOM/GENERAL MOTORS   Bo-Bo

Built: 1999–2000 by Alstom at Valencia, Spain, as sub-contractors for General Motors (General Motors model JT42 HW-HS).
Engine: GM 12N-710G3B-EC two stroke of 2385 kW (3200 hp) at 904 rpm.
Main Alternator: General Motors AR9A/HEP7/CA6C.
Traction Motors: General Motors D43FM.
Maximum Tractive Effort: 141 kN (31770 lbf).
Continuous Tractive Effort: 90 kN (20200 lbf) at 46.5 mph.
Power at Rail: 1860 kW.   **Train Brakes:** Air.
Brake Force: 78 t.   **Dimensions:** 19.74 x 2.72 m.
Weight: 90 t.   **Wheel Diameter:** 965 mm.
Design Speed: 125 mph.   **Maximum Speed:** 125 mph (* 80 mph).
Fuel Capacity: 4927 litres.   **Route Availability:** 8.
Train Supply: Electric, index 66.

All equipped with Slow Speed Control and Swinghead Automatic "Buckeye" Combination Couplers.

67001/002/003/014/022/029 have been modified to operate in push-pull mode on the Arriva Trains Wales locomotive-hauled sets.

67004, 67007, 67009 and 67011 were fitted with cast iron brake blocks for working the Fort William Sleeper.

Non-standard liveries:

67026 Diamond Jubilee silver.
67029 All over silver with DB logos.

67001	**AB**	DB	WQAA	CE (S)	
67002	**AB**	DB	WAAC	CE	
67003	**AB**	DB	WAAC	CE	
67004 r*	**CA**	DB	WQAB	CE (S)	Cairn Gorm
67005	**RZ**	DB	WAAC	CE	Queen's Messenger
67006	**RZ**	DB	WAAC	CE	Royal Sovereign
67007 r*	**E**	DB	WABC	CE	
67008	**E**	DB	WAWC	CE	
67009 r*	**E**	DB	WQAA	CE (S)	
67010	**DB**	DB	WAAC	CE	
67011 r*	**E**	DB	WQAB	CE (S)	
67012	**CM**	DB	WAWC	CE	
67013	**DB**	DB	WAAC	CE	
67014	**CM**	DB	WAAC	CE	
67015	**DB**	DB	WAWC	CE	
67016	**E**	DB	WAAC	CE	
67017	**E**	DB	WQAB	CE (S)	Arrow
67018	**DB**	DB	WAAC	CE	Keith Heller
67019	**E**	DB	WQBA	CE (S)	
67020	**E**	DB	WQAB	CE (S)	
67021	**E**	DB	WAAC	CE	
67022	**E**	DB	WAAC	CE	
67023	**E**	CS	COTS	RU	

67024	**E**	DB	WAAC	CE	
67025	**E**	DB	WQBA	CE (S)	Western Star
67026	**O**	DB	WQAB	CE (S)	Diamond Jubilee
67027	**DB**	CS	COTS	RU	
67028	**E**	DB	WAAC	CE	
67029	**O**	DB	WAAC	CE	Royal Diamond
67030 r	**E**	DB	WABC	CE	

CLASS 68   VOSSLOH/STADLER   Bo-Bo

New Vossloh/Stadler mixed-traffic locomotives currently being delivered to DRS. 68026–034 are on order for delivery in 2017.

Built: 2012–16 by Vossloh/Stadler, Valencia, Spain.
Engine: Caterpillar C175-16 of 2800 kW (3750 hp) at 1740 rpm.
Main Alternator: ABB WGX560.
Traction Motors: 4 x AC frame mounted ABB 4FRA6063.
Maximum Tractive Effort: 317 kN (71260 lbf).
Continuous Tractive Effort: 250 kN (56200 lbf) at 20.5 mph.

Power at Rail:	**Train Brakes:** Air.
Brake Force: 73 t.	**Dimensions:** 20.50 x 2.69 m.
Weight: 85 t.	**Wheel Diameter:** 1100 mm.
Design Speed: 100 mph.	**Maximum Speed:** 100 mph.
Fuel Capacity: 6000 litres.	**Route Availability:** 7.
Train Supply: Electric, index 96.	

68008–015 have been modified to operate in push-pull mode on the Chiltern Railways locomotive-hauled sets.

68001	**DI**	BN	XHVE	CR	Evolution
68002	**DI**	BN	XHVE	CR	Intrepid
68003	**DI**	BN	XHVE	CR	Astute
68004	**DI**	BN	XHVE	CR	Rapid
68005	**DI**	BN	XHVE	CR	Defiant
68006	**SR**	BN	XHVE	CR	Daring
68007	**SR**	BN	XHVE	CR	Valiant
68008	**DI**	BN	XHVE	CR	Avenger
68009	**DI**	BN	XHVE	CR	Titan
68010	**CM**	BN	XHCE	CR	Oxford Flyer
68011	**CM**	BN	XHCE	CR	
68012	**CM**	BN	XHCE	CR	
68013	**CM**	BN	XHCE	CR	
68014	**CM**	BN	XHCE	CR	
68015	**CM**	BN	XHCE	CR	
68016	**DI**	BN	XHVE	CR	Fearless
68017	**DI**	BN	XHVE	CR	Hornet
68018	**DI**	BN	XHVE	CR	Vigilant
68019	**DI**	BN	XHVE	CR	Brutus
68020	**DI**	BN	XHVE	CR	Reliance
68021	**DI**	BN	XHVE	CR	Tireless

68022	**DI**	BN	XHVE	CR	Resolution
68023	**DI**	BN	XHVE	CR	Achilles
68024	**DI**	BN	XHVE	CR	Centaur
68025	**DI**	BN	XHVE	CR	Superb
68026		BN			
68027		BN			
68028		BN			
68029		BN			
68030		BN			
68031		BN			
68032		BN			
68033		BN			
68034		BN			

CLASS 70   GENERAL ELECTRIC   Co-Co

New GE "PowerHaul" locomotives. 70012 was badly damaged whilst being unloaded in 2011 and was returned to Pennsylvania.

70801 (built as 70099) is a Turkish-built demonstrator that arrived in Britain in October 2012. Colas Rail leased this locomotive and then in 2013 ordered a further nine locomotives (70802–810) that were delivered in 2014.

70811–817 are on order for delivery in 2017.

Built: 2009–17 by General Electric, Erie, Pennsylvania, USA or by TÜLOMSAS, Eskişehir, Turkey (70801).
Engine: General Electric PowerHaul P616LDA1 of 2848 kW (3820 hp) at 1500 rpm.
Main Alternator: General Electric GTA series.
Traction Motors: AC-GE 5GEB30.
Maximum Tractive Effort: 544 kN (122000 lbf).
Continuous Tractive Effort: 427 kN (96000 lbf) at ?? mph.
Power at Rail:
Brake Force: 96.7 t.
Weight: 129 t.
Design Speed: 75 mph.
Fuel Capacity: 6000 litres.
Train Supply: Not equipped.
Train Brakes: Air.
Dimensions: 21.71 x 2.64 m.
Wheel Diameter: 1066 mm.
Maximum Speed: 75 mph.
Route Availability: 7.

Class 70/0. Freightliner locomotives.

70001	**FH**	MQ	DFGI	LD	PowerHaul
70002	**FH**	MQ	DFGH	LD	
70003	**FH**	MQ	DFGH	LD	
70004	**FH**	MQ	DFGI	LD	The Coal Industry Society
70005	**FH**	MQ	DFGH	LD	
70006	**FH**	MQ	DFGI	LD	
70007	**FH**	MQ	DFGI	LD	
70008	**FH**	MQ	DFGI	LD	
70009	**FH**	MQ	DFGI	LD	

70010	**FH**	MQ	DFGI	LD
70011	**FH**	MQ	DFGI	LD
70013	**FH**	MQ	DFGI	LD
70014	**FH**	MQ	DFGI	LD
70015	**FH**	MQ	DFGI	LD
70016	**FH**	MQ	DFGI	LD
70017	**FH**	MQ	DFGI	LD
70018	**FH**	MQ	DFGI	LD
70019	**FH**	MQ	DFGI	LD
70020	**FH**	MQ	DFGI	LD

Class 70/8. Colas Rail locomotives.

70801	**CS**	LF	COLO	CF
70802	**CS**	LF	COLO	CF
70803	**CS**	LF	COLS	LA (S)
70804	**CS**	LF	COLO	CF
70805	**CS**	LF	COLO	CF
70806	**CS**	LF	COLO	CF
70807	**CS**	LF	COLO	CF
70808	**CS**	LF	COLO	CF
70809	**CS**	LF	COLO	CF
70810	**CS**	LF	COLO	CF

70811
70812
70813
70814
70815
70816
70817

1.2. ELECTRO-DIESEL &
ELECTRIC LOCOMOTIVES

CLASS 73/1   BR/ENGLISH ELECTRIC   Bo-Bo

Electro-diesel locomotives which can operate either from a DC supply or using power from a diesel engine.

Built: 1965–67 by English Electric Co. at Vulcan Foundry, Newton-le-Willows.
Engine: English Electric 4SRKT of 447 kW (600 hp) at 850 rpm.
Main Generator: English Electric 824/5D.
Electric Supply System: 750 V DC from third rail.
Traction Motors: English Electric 546/1B.
Maximum Tractive Effort (Electric): 179 kN (40000 lbf).
Maximum Tractive Effort (Diesel): 160 kN (36000 lbf).
Continuous Rating (Electric): 1060 kW (1420 hp) giving a tractive effort of 35 kN (7800 lbf) at 68 mph.
Continuous Tractive Effort (Diesel): 60 kN (13600 lbf) at 11.5 mph.
Maximum Rail Power (Electric): 2350 kW (3150 hp) at 42 mph.
Train Brakes: Air, vacuum & electro-pneumatic († Air & electro-pneumatic).
Brake Force: 31 t.   **Dimensions:** 16.36 x 2.64 m.
Weight: 77 t.   **Wheel Diameter:** 1016 mm.
Design Speed: 90 mph.   **Maximum Speed:** 90 mph.
Fuel Capacity: 1409 litres.   **Route Availability:** 6.
Train Supply: Electric, index 66 (on electric power only).

Formerly numbered E6001–E6020/E6022–E6026/E6028–E6049 (not in order).

Locomotives numbered in the 732xx series are classed as 73/2 and were originally dedicated to Gatwick Express services.

There have been two separate Class 73 rebuild projects. For GB Railfreight 11 locomotives were rebuilt at Brush, Loughborough with a 1600 hp MTU engine (these were renumbered in the 73961–971 series). For Network Rail 73104/211 were rebuilt at RVEL Derby (now LORAM) with a pair of QSK19 750 hp engines (these have been renumbered 73951/952).

Non-standard liveries:

73128 Two-tone grey.
73139 Light blue & light grey.

73101	**PC**	LO	RVLO	ZA (S)	
73107	**GB**	GB	GBED	SE	Tracy
73109	**GB**	GB	GBED	SE	
73119	**GB**	GB	GBED	SE	Borough of Eastleigh
73128	**GB**	GB	GBED	SE	O.V.S. BULLEID C.B.E.
73133	**TT**	TT	MBED	BM	
73134	**IC**	GB	GBBR	LB (S)	Woking Homes 1885–1985
73136	**GB**	GB	GBED	SE	Mhairi
73138	**Y**	NR	QADD	ZA	

73139	**O**	LO	RVLO	ZA (S)	
73141	**GB**	GB	GBED	SE	Charlotte
73201 †	**B**	GB	GBED	SE	Broadlands
73202 †	**SN**	P	MBED	SL	Graham Stenning
73212 †	**GB**	GB	GBED	SE	Fiona
73213 †	**GB**	GB	GBED	SE	Rhodalyn
73235 †	**SD**	P	HYWD	BM	

CLASS 73/9 (RVEL)   BR/RVEL   Bo-Bo

The 7395x number series is reserved for rebuilt Network Rail locomotives.

Rebuilt: Re-engineered by RVEL Derby 2013–15.
Engine: 2 x QSK19 of 560 kW (750 hp) at 1800 rpm (total 1120 kw (1500 hp)).
Main Alternator: 2 x Marathon Magnaplus.
Electric Supply System: 750 V DC from third rail.
Traction Motors: English Electric 546/1B.
Maximum Tractive Effort (Electric): 179 kN (40000 lbf).
Maximum Tractive Effort (Diesel): 179 kN (40000 lbf).
Continuous Rating (Electric): 1060 kW (1420 hp) giving a tractive effort of 35 kN (7800 lbf) at 68 mph.
Continuous Tractive Effort (Diesel): 990 kW (1328 hp) giving a tractive effort of 33 kN (7420 lbf) at 68 mph.
Maximum Rail Power (Electric): 2350 kW (3150 hp) at 42 mph.

Train Brakes: Air.	**Brake Force:** 31 t.
Weight: 77 t.	**Dimensions:** 16.36 x 2.64 m.
Maximum Speed: 90 mph.	**Wheel Diameter:** 1016 mm.
Fuel Capacity: 2260 litres.	**Route Availability:** 6.
Train Supply: Not equipped.	

73951	(73104)	**Y**	LO	QADD	ZA	Malcolm Brinded
73952	(73211)	**Y**	LO	QADD	ZA	Janis Kong

CLASS 73/9 (GBRf)   BR/BRUSH   Bo-Bo

GBRf Class 73s rebuilt at Brush Loughborough. 73961–965 are normally used on Network Rail contracts and 73966–971 are used by Caledonian Sleeper.

Rebuilt: Re-engineered by Brush, Loughborough 2014– .
Engine: MTU 8V4000 R43L of 1195 kW (1600 hp) at 1800 rpm.
Main Alternator: Lechmotoren SDV 87.53-12.
Electric Supply System: 750 V DC from third rail (73961–965 only).
Traction Motors: English Electric 546/1B.
Maximum Tractive Effort (Electric): 179 kN (40000 lbf).
Maximum Tractive Effort (Diesel): 179 kN (40000 lbf).
Continuous Rating (Electric): 1060 kW (1420 hp) giving a tractive effort of 35 kN (7800 lbf) at 68 mph.
Continuous Tractive Effort (Diesel):
Maximum Rail Power (Electric): 2350 kW (3150 hp) at 42 mph.

Train Brakes: Air.	**Brake Force:** 31 t.
Weight: 77 t.	**Dimensions:** 16.36 x 2.64 m.

Maximum Speed: 90 mph.   **Wheel Diameter:** 1016 mm.
Fuel Capacity: 1409 litres.   **Route Availability:** 6.
Train Supply: Electric, index 38 (electric & diesel).

73961	(73209)	**GB**	GB	GBNR	SE	Alison
73962	(73204)	**GB**	GB	GBNR	SE	Dick Mabbutt
73963	(73206)	**GB**	GB	GBNR	SE	Janice
73964	(73205)	**GB**	GB	GBNR	SE	Jeanette
73965	(73208)	**GB**	GB	GBNR	SE	

73966–971 have been rebuilt for Caledonian Sleeper but their third rail electric capability has been retained. They have a higher Train Supply index and a slightly higher fuel capacity. Details as 73961–965 except:
Fuel Capacity: 1509 litres.   **Train Supply:** Electric, index 96.

73005 and 73006 were originally built at Eastleigh Works.

73966	(73005)	**CA**	GB	GBCS	EC
73967	(73006)	**CA**	GB	GBCS	EC
73968	(73117)	**CA**	GB	GBCS	EC
73969	(73105)	**CA**	GB	GBCS	EC
73970	(73103)	**CA**	GB	GBCS	EC
73971	(73207)	**CA**	GB	GBCS	EC

CLASS 86   BR/ENGLISH ELECTRIC   Bo-Bo

Built: 1965–66 by English Electric Co at Vulcan Foundry, Newton-le-Willows or by BR at Doncaster Works.
Electric Supply System: 25 kV AC 50 Hz overhead.
Traction Motors: AEI 282BZ axle hung.
Maximum Tractive Effort: 207 kN (46500 lbf).
Continuous Rating: 3010 kW (4040 hp) giving a tractive effort of 85kN (19200lbf) at 77.5mph.
Maximum Rail Power: 4550 kW (6100 hp) at 49.5 mph.
Train Brakes: Air.   **Brake Force:** 40 t.
Dimensions: 17.83 x 2.65 m.   **Weight:** 83–86.8 t.
Wheel Diameter: 1156 mm.   **Train Supply:** Electric, index 74.
Design Speed: 110–125 mph.   **Maximum Speed:** 100 mph.
Route Availability: 6.

Formerly numbered E3101–E3200 (not in order).

Class 86s exported for use abroad are listed in section 1.6 of this book.

Class 86/1. Class 87-type bogies & motors. Details as above except:

Traction Motors: GEC 412AZ frame mounted.
Maximum Tractive Effort: 258 kN (58000 lbf).
Continuous Rating: 3730 kW (5000 hp) giving a tractive effort of 95kN (21300lbf) at 87mph.
Maximum Rail Power: 5860 kW (7860 hp) at 50.8 mph.
Wheel Diameter: 1150 mm.
Design Speed: 110 mph.   **Maximum Speed:** 110 mph.

86101	**CA**	EL	GBCH	WN	Sir William A Stanier FRS

Class 86/2. Standard design rebuilt with resilient wheels & Flexicoil suspension. Details as in main class heading.

Non-standard livery:

86259 BR "Electric blue". Also carries number E3137.

86229	**V**	FL	EPEX	LM (S)	
86251	**V**	FL	EPEX	LM (S)	
86259 x	**0**	PP	GROG	WN	Les Ross

Class 86/4. Details as Class 86/2 except:

Traction Motors: AEI 282AZ axle hung.
Maximum Tractive Effort: 258 kN (58000 lbf).
Continuous Rating: 2680 kW (3600 hp) giving a tractive effort of 89 kN (20000 lbf) at 67 mph.
Maximum Rail Power: 4400 kW (5900 hp) at 38 mph.
Weight: 83–83.9 t.
Design Speed: 100 mph.   **Maximum Speed:** 100 mph.

86401	**CA**	EL	GBCH	WN	Mons Meg

Class 86/6. Freightliner-operated locomotives.

86608 was regeared and renumbered 86501 between 2000 and 2016.

Details as Class 86/4 except:

Maximum Speed: 75 mph.   **Train Supply:** Electric, isolated.

86604	**FL**	FL	DFNC	CB
86605	**FL**	FL	DFNC	CB
86607	**FL**	FL	DFNC	CB
86608	**FL**	FL	DFNC	CB
86609	**FL**	FL	DFNC	CB
86610	**FL**	FL	DFNC	CB
86612	**FL**	P	DFNC	CB
86613	**FL**	P	DFNC	CB
86614	**FL**	P	DFNC	CB
86622	**FH**	P	DFNC	CB
86627	**FL**	P	DFNC	CB
86628	**FL**	P	DFNC	CB
86632	**FL**	P	DFNC	CB
86637	**FH**	P	DFNC	CB
86638	**FL**	P	DFNC	CB
86639	**FL**	P	DFNC	CB

CLASS 87   BREL/GEC   Bo-Bo

Built: 1973–75 by BREL at Crewe Works.
Electric Supply System: 25 kV AC 50 Hz overhead.
Traction Motors: GEC G412AZ frame mounted.
Maximum Tractive Effort: 258 kN (58000 lbf).
Continuous Rating: 3730 kW (5000 hp) giving a tractive effort of 95 kN (21300 lbf) at 87 mph.
Maximum Rail Power: 5860 kW (7860 hp) at 50.8 mph.

Train Brakes: Air.	**Brake Force:** 40 t.
Dimensions: 17.83 x 2.65 m.	**Weight:** 83.3 t.
Wheel Diameter: 1150 mm.	**Train Supply:** Electric, index 95.
Design Speed: 110 mph.	**Maximum Speed:** 110 mph.
Route Availability: 6.	

Class 87s exported for use abroad are listed in section 1.6 of this book.

87002   **CA**   EL   GBCH   WN   Royal Sovereign

CLASS 88   VOSSLOH/STADLER   Bo-Bo

Ten new Vossloh/Stadler bi-mode locomotives for DRS, due for delivery in 2017.
Built: 2015–16 by Vossloh/Sladler, Valencia, Spain.
Electric Supply System: 25 kV AC 50 Hz overhead.
Engine: Caterpillar C27 12-cylinder 708 kW (950 hp) at 1750 rpm.
Main Alternator: ABB AMXL400.
Traction Motors: ABB AMXL400.
Maximum Tractive Effort (Electric): 317 kN (71 260 lbf).
Maximum Tractive Effort (Diesel): 317 kN (71 260 lbf).
Continuous Rating: 4000 kW (5360 hp) giving a tractive effort of 250 kN (56200 lbf) at 28 mph (electric) or 4.5 mph (diesel).
Maximum Rail Power:
Train Brakes: Air, regenerative & rheostatic.

Brake Force: 73 t.	**Dimensions:** 20.50 x 2.69 m.
Weight: 85 t.	**Wheel Diameter:** 1100 mm.
Fuel Capacity: 1800 litres.	**Train Supply:** Electric, index 96.
Design Speed: 100 mph.	**Maximum Speed:** 100 mph.
Route Availability: 7.	

88001	**DI**	BN	Revolution
88002	**DI**	BN	Prometheus
88003	**DI**	BN	
88004	**DI**	BN	
88005	**DI**	BN	
88006	**DI**	BN	
88007	**DI**	BN	
88008	**DI**	BN	
88009	**DI**	BN	
88010	**DI**	BN	

▲ GWR has painted its shunters into "retro" liveries. In InterCity livery, 08822 is seen at Bristol St Philip's Marsh depot on 02/05/16.

Robert Pritchard

▲ GBRf-liveried 20905 and BR Blue 20096 lead a train of London Underground S-Stock past Syston South Junction with 7X23 09.19 Derby–Old Dalby on 26/08/16. **Paul Biggs**

▼ DCR Green-liveried 31452 passes Alsager hauling preserved 47712 and 47192 from Barrow Hill to Crewe on 13/04/16. **Cliff Beeton**

▲ West Coast Railway Company Maroon-liveried 33207 and 47237 pass Chaloners Whin, south of York, with a return Scarborough–Carnforth railtour on 08/09/16.
Sean White

▼ Europhoenix-liveried 37884 is seen at Bristol St Philip's Marsh depot on 02/05/16. **Robert Pritchard**

▲ Revised Direct Rail Services-liveried 37405 and 37422 top-and-tail the 12.36 Norwich–Great Yarmouth at Stacey Arms on 18/07/16. **Dave Gommersall**

▲ Stagecoach East Midlands Trains-liveried 43043 is seen at Nottingham on 17/07/16. **Robert Pritchard**

▼ Grand Central-liveried 43423 leads the 08.30 Sunderland–London King's Cross at Colton on 19/09/15. **Andrew Mason**

▲ Colas Rail-liveried 47739 passes Besford with 5V47 09.00 Washwood Heath–Cardiff Canton (hauling vans 6364 and 6365) on 16/05/16. **Raymond Coates**

▼ BR Blue-liveried 50007 and 50050 pass Banbury with a Pathfinder railtour from Derby to Swanage on 11/06/16. **James Martin**

▲ BR Maroon-liveried D1015 passes South Brent with a railtour from London Paddington to Okehampton on 07/05/16 . **Tony Christie**

▼ Colas Rail-liveried 56105 and 56087 top-and-tail 6Z47 11.54 York–Kings Norton at Barrow-upon-Trent on 30/09/15. **Steve Madden**

▲ Original Great Western Railway Green-liveried 57604 awaits departure from Exeter St Davids with the 17.50 to Penzance on 13/08/16. **David Hunt**

▼ GB Railfreight-liveried 59003 stands in Heeley loop, Sheffield with 6M83 10.51 Tinsley–Bardon Hill empty aggregates train on 31/08/16. **Chris Booth**

▲ Colas Rail-liveried 60096 passes Loughborough with 6E38 13.54 Colnbrook–Lindsey discharged oil tanks on 12/08/16. **Paul Biggs**

▼ DB Cargo-liveried 66101 passes Cossington on the Midland Main Line with 6M45 14.17 Barham–Mountsorrel empty aggregates on 21/05/15. **Paul Biggs**

▲ GB Railfreight-liveried 66717 passes Enterkinfoot on the G&SW line with 6H97 12.35 Hunterston–Drax coal on 14/03/16.
Robin Ralston

▲ Royal Train-liveried 67006 is seen near Swanley with the 10.14 London Victoria–Folkestone West on 08/05/16. **Jamie Squibbs**

▼ Chiltern Mainline-liveried 68014 passes Neasden with the 17.15 London Marylebone–Kidderminster on 05/07/16. **Robert Pritchard**

▲ Colas Rail-liveried 70807 hauls 6C97 16.46 Westbury–St Austell on the approaches to Tiverton Parkway on 18/05/16. **Stephen Ginn**

▼ GBRf-liveried 73961 and 73964 are seen arriving at Great Yarmouth on the rear of the GB15 railtour on 09/09/16. **Dave Gommersall**

▲ Freightliner-liveried 86639 and 86605 haul 4S88 Felixstowe–Coatbridge north at Wandel on the WCML on 22/04/15. **Andi Walshaw**

▼ Caledonian Sleeper-liveried 87002 stands at Liverpool Lime Street after arrival with the "GB15" railtour from Edinburgh on 11/09/16. **Ian Beardsley**

▲ Brand new bi-mode 88002, in Direct Rail Services livery, stands outside Stadler Rail's Valencia factory in Spain in August 2016. DRS has ten of these locomotives on order. **Courtesy DRS**

▼ Abellio Greater Anglia-liveried 90001 passes Stratford on 14/08/16 with the 16.43 Ipswich–London Liverpool Street. **Robert Pritchard**

▲ Virgin Trains East Coast-liveried 91107 passes Colton with the 08.00 London King's Cross–Edinburgh on 19/09/15.
Andrew Mason

▲ Caledonian Sleeper-liveried 92038 is seen near Lanark Junction with 6S51 12.16 Carlisle–Mossend on 30/09/15. **Robin Ralston**

▼ Eurotunnel-liveried 9810 stands at Coquelles depot on 27 February 2014. **David Haydock**

CLASS 90 GEC Bo-Bo

Built: 1987–90 by BREL at Crewe Works (as sub-contractors for GEC).
Electric Supply System: 25 kV AC 50 Hz overhead.
Traction Motors: GEC G412CY frame mounted.
Maximum Tractive Effort: 258 kN (58000 lbf).
Continuous Rating: 3730 kW (5000 hp) giving a tractive effort of 95 kN (21300 lbf) at 87 mph.
Maximum Rail Power: 5860 kW (7860 hp) at 68.3 mph.
Train Brakes: Air.
Brake Force: 40 t.
Weight: 84.5 t.
Design Speed: 110 mph.
Train Supply: Electric, index 95.

Dimensions: 18.80 x 2.74 m.
Wheel Diameter: 1150 mm.
Maximum Speed: 110 mph.
Route Availability: 7.

Advertising livery:

90024 Malcolm Logistics (blue).

90001	b	**GA**	P	IANA	NC	Crown Point
90002	b	**GA**	P	IANA	NC	Eastern Daily Press 1870–2010 SERVING NORFOLK FOR 140 YEARS
90003	b	**GA**	P	IANA	NC	
90004	b	**GA**	P	IANA	NC	City of Chelmsford
90005	b	**GA**	P	IANA	NC	Vice-Admiral Lord Nelson
90006	b	**GA**	P	IANA	NC	Modern Railways Magazine/ Roger Ford
90007	b	**GA**	P	IANA	NC	Sir John Betjeman
90008	b	**GA**	P	IANA	NC	The East Anglian
90009	b	**GA**	P	IANA	NC	
90010	b	**GA**	P	IANA	NC	
90011	b	**GA**	P	IANA	NC	East Anglian Daily Times Suffolk & Proud
90012	b	**GA**	P	IANA	NC	Royal Anglian Regiment
90013	b	**GA**	P	IANA	NC	
90014	b	**GA**	P	IANA	NC	Norfolk and Norwich Festival
90015	b	**GA**	P	IANA	NC	Colchester Castle
90016		**FL**	P	DFLC	CB	
90017		**E**	DB	WQBA	CE (S)	
90018		**DB**	DB	WEAC	CE	The Pride of Bellshill
90019		**DB**	DB	WEAC	CE	Multimodal
90020		**E**	DB	WQAA	CE (S)	Collingwood
90021		**FS**	DB	WQAB	CE (S)	
90022		**EG**	DB	WQBA	CE (S)	Freightconnection
90023		**E**	DB	WQBA	CE (S)	
90024		**AL**	DB	WEAC	CE	
90025		**F**	DB	WQBA	CE (S)	
90026		**E**	DB	WQAB	CE (S)	
90027		**F**	DB	WQBA	CE (S)	Allerton T&RS Depot
90028		**E**	DB	WEAC	CE	
90029		**DB**	DB	WEAC	CE	
90030		**E**	DB	WQBA	CE (S)	

90031	**E**	DB	WQBA	CE (S)	The Railway Children Partnership
					Working For Street Children Worldwide
90032	**E**	DB	WQBA	CE (S)	
90033	**FE**	DB	WQBA	CE (S)	
90034	**DR**	DB	WEAC	CE	
90035	**E**	DB	WEAC	CE	
90036	**DB**	DB	WEAC	CE	Driver Jack Mills
90037	**E**	DB	WQAA	CE (S)	Spirit of Dagenham
90038	**FE**	DB	WQBA	CE (S)	
90039	**E**	DB	WEAC	CE	
90040	**DB**	DB	WEAC	CE	
90041	**FL**	P	DFLC	CB	
90042	**FH**	P	DFLC	CB	
90043	**FH**	P	DFLC	CB	
90044	**FF**	P	DFLC	CB	
90045	**FH**	P	DFLC	CB	
90046	**FL**	P	DFLC	CB	
90047	**FF**	P	DFLC	CB	
90048	**FF**	P	DFLC	CB	
90049	**FH**	P	DFLC	CB	
90050	**FF**	AV	DHLT	CB (S)	

CLASS 91   GEC   Bo-Bo

Built: 1988–91 by BREL at Crewe Works (as sub-contractors for GEC).
Electric Supply System: 25 kV AC 50 Hz overhead.
Traction Motors: GEC G426AZ.
Maximum Tractive Effort: 190 kN (43 000 lbf).
Continuous Rating: 4540 kW (6090 hp) giving a tractive effort of 170 kN at 96 mph.
Maximum Rail Power: 4700 kW (6300 hp) at ?? mph.
Train Brakes: Air.

Brake Force: 45 t.	**Dimensions:** 19.41 x 2.74 m.
Weight: 84 t.	**Wheel Diameter:** 1000 mm.
Design Speed: 140 mph.	**Maximum Speed:** 125 mph.
Train Supply: Electric, index 95.	**Route Availability:** 7.

Locomotives were originally numbered in the 910xx series, but were renumbered upon completion of overhauls at Bombardier, Doncaster by the addition of 100 to their original number. The exception to this rule was 91023 which was renumbered 91132.

91114 has been fitted with a second pantograph for evaluation purposes.

Advertising liveries:

91101 Flying Scotsman (red, white & purple).
91110 Battle of Britain (black and grey).
91111 For the fallen (various with poppy and Union Jack vinyls).

91101	**AL**	E	IECA	BN	FLYING SCOTSMAN
91102	**VE**	E	IECA	BN	City of York
91103	**VE**	E	IECA	BN	
91104	**VE**	E	IECA	BN	
91105	**VE**	E	IECA	BN	
91106	**VE**	E	IECA	BN	
91107	**VE**	E	IECA	BN	SKYFALL
91108	**VE**	E	IECA	BN	
91109	**VE**	E	IECA	BN	Sir Bobby Robson
91110	**AL**	E	IECA	BN	BATTLE OF BRITAIN MEMORIAL FLIGHT
91111	**AL**	E	IECA	BN	For the Fallen
91112	**VE**	E	IECA	BN	
91113	**VE**	E	IECA	BN	
91114	**VE**	E	IECA	BN	Durham Cathedral
91115	**VE**	E	IECA	BN	Blaydon Races
91116	**VE**	E	IECA	BN	
91117	**VE**	E	IECA	BN	WEST RIDING LIMITED
91118	**VE**	E	IECA	BN	
91119	**VE**	E	IECA	BN	
91120	**VE**	E	IECA	BN	
91121	**VE**	E	IECA	BN	
91122	**VE**	E	IECA	BN	
91124	**VE**	E	IECA	BN	
91125	**VE**	E	IECA	BN	
91126	**VE**	E	IECA	BN	
91127	**VE**	E	IECA	BN	
91128	**VE**	E	IECA	BN	INTERCITY 50
91129	**VE**	E	IECA	BN	
91130	**VE**	E	IECA	BN	Lord Mayor of Newcastle
91131	**VE**	E	IECA	BN	
91132	**VE**	E	IECA	BN	

CLASS 92   BRUSH   Co-Co

Built: 1993–96 by Brush Traction at Loughborough.
Electric Supply System: 25 kV AC 50 Hz overhead or 750 V DC third rail.
Traction Motors: Asea Brown Boveri design. Model 6FRA 7059B (Asynchronous 3-phase induction motors).
Maximum Tractive Effort: 400 kN (90 000 lbf).
Continuous Rating: 5040 kW (6760 hp) on AC, 4000 kW (5360 hp) on DC.

Maximum Rail Power:	**Train Brakes:** Air.
Brake Force: 63 t.	**Dimensions:** 21.34 x 2.67 m.
Weight: 126 t.	**Wheel Diameter:** 1070 mm.
Design Speed: 140 km/h (87 mph).	**Maximum Speed:** 145 km/h (90 mph).

Train Supply: Electric, index 108 (AC), 70 (DC).
Route Availability: 7.

* Fitted with TVM430 signalling equipment to operate on High Speed 1.

Class 92s exported for use abroad are listed in section 1.6 of this book.

Advertising livery:

92017 Stobart Rail (two-tone blue & white).

92003	**EG**	DB	WGEE	DM (S)	Beethoven
92004	**EG**	DB	WQBA	CE (S)	Jane Austen
92006	**EP**	GB	GBET	LB (S)	Louis Armand
92007	**EG**	DB	WQBA	CE (S)	Schubert
92008	**EG**	DB	WQBA	CE (S)	Jules Verne
92009 *	**DB**	DB	WQBA	CE (S)	Marco Polo
92010 *	**CA**	GB	GBST	WN	
92011 *	**EG**	DB	WFBC	CE	Handel
92013	**EG**	DB	WQAA	CE (S)	Puccini
92014	**CA**	GB	GBSL	WN	
92015 *	**DB**	DB	WFBC	CE	
92016 *	**DB**	DB	WFBC	CE	
92017	**AL**	DB	WQBA	CE (S)	Bart the Engine
92018 *	**CA**	GB	GBST	WN	
92019 *	**EG**	DB	WFBC	CE	Wagner
92020	**EP**	GB	GBET	LB (S)	Milton
92021	**EP**	GB	GBET	CO (S)	Purcell
92022	**EG**	DB	WGEE	DM (S)	Charles Dickens
92023 *	**CA**	GB	GBST	WN	
92026	**EG**	DB	WGEE	DM (S)	Britten
92028	**GB**	GB	GBSL	WN	
92029	**EG**	DB	WQBA	CE (S)	Dante
92031 *	**DB**	DB	WQAB	CE (S)	
92032 *	**GB**	GB	GBST	WN	IMechE Railway Division
92033	**CA**	GB	GBSL	WN	
92035	**EP**	DB	WQBA	CE (S)	Mendelssohn
92036 *	**EG**	DB	WFBC	CE	Bertolt Brecht
92037	**EG**	DB	WQAB	CE (S)	Sullivan
92038 *	**CA**	GB	GBST	WN	
92040	**EP**	GB	GBET	CO (S)	Goethe
92041 *	**EG**	DB	WQAA	CE (S)	Vaughan Williams
92042 *	**DB**	DB	WFBC	CE	
92043 *	**EP**	GB	GBST	WN	Debussy
92044 *	**EP**	GB	GBST	WN	Couperin
92045	**EP**	GB	GBET	LB (S)	Chaucer
92046	**EP**	GB	GBET	LB (S)	Sweelinck

1.3. EUROTUNNEL LOCOMOTIVES

DIESEL LOCOMOTIVES

0001–10 are registered on TOPS as 21901–910.

0001–0005   MaK   Bo-Bo

Channel Tunnel maintenance and rescue train locomotives.
Built: 1991–92 by MaK at Kiel, Germany (Model DE 1004).
Engine: MTU 12V396 TC 13 of 950 kW (1275 hp) at 1800 rpm.
Main Alternator: ABB.   **Traction Motors:** ABB.
Maximum Tractive Effort: 305 kN (68600 lbf).
Continuous Tractive Effort: 140 kN (31500 lbf) at 20 mph.
Power At Rail: 750 kW (1012 hp).   **Dimensions:** 14.40 x ?? m.
Brake Force: 120 kN.   **Wheel Diameter:** 1000 mm.
Train Brakes: Air.   **Weight:** 90 t.
Maximum Speed: 100 km/h.   **Design Speed:** 120 km/h.
Fuel Capacity: 3500 litres.   **Multiple Working:** Within class.
Train Supply: Not equipped.   **Signalling System:** TVM430 cab signalling.

0001	**GY**	ET	CO
0002	**GY**	ET	CO
0003	**GY**	ET	CO
0004	**GY**	ET	CO
0005	**GY**	ET	CO

0006–0010   MaK   Bo-Bo

Channel Tunnel maintenance and rescue train locomotives. Rebuilt from
Netherlands Railways/DB Cargo Nederland Class 6400. 0006/07 were
added to the Eurotunnel fleet in 2011, and 0008–10 in 2016. 0010 is deployed
for shunting at Coquelles.

Built: 1990–91 by MaK at Kiel, Germany (Model DE 6400).
Engine: MTU 12V396 TC 13 of 1180 kW (1580 hp) at 1800 rpm.
Main Alternator: ABB.   **Traction Motors:** ABB.
Maximum Tractive Effort: 290 kN (65200 lbf).
Continuous Tractive Effort: 140 kN (31500 lbf) at 20 mph.
Power At Rail: 750 kW (1012 hp).   **Dimensions:** 14.40 x ?? m.
Brake Force: 120 kN.   **Wheel Diameter:** 1000 mm.
Train Brakes: Air.   **Weight:** 80 t.
Maximum Speed: 120 km/h.   **Design Speed:** 120 km/h.
Fuel Capacity: 2900 litres.   **Multiple Working:** Within class.
Train Supply: Not equipped.

Not fitted with TVM 430 cab signalling so have to operate with another locomotive/s when used on HS1.

0006	(6456)	**GY**	ET	CO
0007	(6457)	**GY**	ET	CO
0008	(6450)	**GY**	ET	CO
0009	(6451)	**GY**	ET	CO
0010	(6447)	**EB**	ET	CO

0031–0042 HUNSLET/SCHÖMA 0-4-0

Built: 1989–90 by Hunslet Engine Company at Leeds as 900 mm gauge.
Rebuilt: 1993–94 by Schöma in Germany to 1435 mm gauge.
Engine: Deutz FL10L 413FW of 170 kW (230 hp) at 2300 rpm.
Transmission: Mechanical Clark 5000 series.
Maximum Tractive Effort:
Continuous Tractive Effort:
Power At Rail:
Brake Force: **Dimensions:** 6.63 x 2.69 m.
Weight: 26–28 t. **Wheel Diameter:**
Design Speed: 48 km/h. **Maximum Speed:** 50 km/h.
Fuel Capacity: **Train Brakes:** Air.
Train Supply: Not equipped. **Multiple Working:** Not equipped.

* Rebuilt with inspection platforms to check overhead catenary.

0031		**GY**	ET	CO	FRANCES
0032		**GY**	ET	CO	ELISABETH
0033		**GY**	ET	CO	SILKE
0034		**GY**	ET	CO	AMANDA
0035		**GY**	ET	CO	MARY
0036		**GY**	ET	CO	LAURENCE
0037		**GY**	ET	CO	LYDIE
0038		**GY**	ET	CO	JENNY
0039	*	**GY**	ET	CO	PACITA
0040		**GY**	ET	CO	JILL
0041	*	**GY**	ET	CO	KIM
0042		**GY**	ET	CO	NICOLE

ELECTRIC LOCOMOTIVES

9005–9840   BRUSH/ABB   Bo-Bo-Bo

Built: 1993–2002 by Brush Traction, Loughborough.
Electric Supply System: 25 kV AC 50 Hz overhead.
Traction Motors: Asea Brown Boveri design. Asynchronous 3-phase motors.
Model 6FHA 7059 (as built). Model 6FHA 7059C (7000 kW rated locos).
Maximum Tractive Effort: 400kN (90 000 lbf).
Continuous Rating: Class 9/0: 5760 kW (7725 hp). Class 9/7 and 9/8:
7000 kW (9387 hp).

Maximum Rail Power:	**Multiple Working:** TDM system.
Brake Force: 50 t.	**Dimensions:** 22.01 x 2.97 x 4.20 m.
Weight: 136 t.	**Wheel Diameter:** 1250 mm.
Maximum Speed: 100 mph.	**Design Speed:** 100 mph.
Train Supply: Electric.	**Train Brakes:** Air.

Class 9/0 Original build locos. Built 1993–94.

9005	**EB**	ET	CO	JESSYE NORMAN
9007	**EB**	ET	CO	DAME JOAN SUTHERLAND
9011	**EB**	ET	CO	JOSÉ VAN DAM
9013	**EB**	ET	CO	MARIA CALLAS
9015	**EB**	ET	CO	LÖTSCHBERG 1913
9018	**EB**	ET	CO	WILHELMENIA FERNANDEZ
9022	**EB**	ET	CO	DAME JANET BAKER
9024	**EB**	ET	CO	GOTTHARD 1882
9026	**EB**	ET	CO	FURKATUNNEL 1982
9029	**EB**	ET	CO	THOMAS ALLEN
9033	**EB**	ET	CO	MONTSERRAT CABALLE
9036	**EB**	ET	CO	ALAIN FONDARY
9037	**EB**	ET	CO	GABRIEL BACQUIER

Class 9/7. Increased power freight shuttle locos. Built 2001–02 (9711–23
built 1998–2001 as 9101–13 and rebuilt as 9711–23 2010–12).

9701	**EB**	ET	CO	
9702	**EB**	ET	CO	
9703	**EB**	ET	CO	
9704	**EB**	ET	CO	
9705	**EB**	ET	CO	
9706	**EB**	ET	CO	
9707	**EB**	ET	CO	
9711	(9101)	**EB**	ET	CO
9712	(9102)	**EB**	ET	CO
9713	(9103)	**EB**	ET	CO
9714	(9104)	**EB**	ET	CO
9715	(9105)	**EB**	ET	CO
9716	(9106)	**EB**	ET	CO
9717	(9107)	**EB**	ET	CO
9718	(9108)	**EB**	ET	CO

9719	(9109)	**EB**	ET	CO
9720	(9110)	**EB**	ET	CO
9721	(9111)	**EB**	ET	CO
9722	(9112)	**EB**	ET	CO
9723	(9113)	**EB**	ET	CO

Class 9/8 Locos rebuilt from Class 9/0 by adding 800 to the loco number. Uprated to 7000 kW.

9801	**EB**	ET	CO	LESLEY GARRETT
9802	**EB**	ET	CO	STUART BURROWS
9803	**EB**	ET	CO	BENJAMIN LUXON
9804	**EB**	ET	CO	VICTORIA DE LOS ANGELES
9806	**EB**	ET	CO	REGINE CRESPIN
9808	**EB**	ET	CO	ELISABETH SODERSTROM
9809	**EB**	ET	CO	FRANÇOISE POLLET
9810	**EB**	ET	CO	JEAN-PHILIPPE COURTIS
9812	**EB**	ET	CO	LUCIANO PAVAROTTI
9814	**EB**	ET	CO	LUCIA POPP
9816	**EB**	ET	CO	WILLARD WHITE
9817	**EB**	ET	CO (S)	JOSÉ CARRERAS
9819	**EB**	ET	CO	MARIA EWING
9820	**EB**	ET	CO	NICOLAI GHIAROV
9821	**EB**	ET	CO	TERESA BERGANZA
9823	**EB**	ET	CO	DAME ELISABETH LEGGE-SCHWARZKOPF
9825	**EB**	ET	CO	
9827	**EB**	ET	CO	BARBARA HENDRICKS
9828	**EB**	ET	CO	DAME KIRI TE KANAWA
9831	**EB**	ET	CO	
9832	**EB**	ET	CO	RENATA TEBALDI
9834	**EB**	ET	CO	MIRELLA FRENI
9835	**EB**	ET	CO	NICOLAI GEDDA
9838	**EB**	ET	CO	HILDEGARD BEHRENS
9840	**EB**	ET	CO	

1.4. FORMER BR MAIN LINE LOCOS IN INDUSTRIAL SERVICE

Former British Rail main line locomotives considered to be in "industrial use" are listed here. These locomotives do not currently have Network Rail engineering acceptance for operation on the national railway network.

Number Other no./name   Location

Class 03

03084	HELEN-LOUISE	West Coast Railway Company, Carnforth
03196	JOYCE/GLYNIS	West Coast Railway Company, Carnforth
D2381		West Coast Railway Company, Carnforth

Class 07

D2991	07007	Arlington Fleet Services, Eastleigh Works, Hampshire

Class 08

08220		EMD, Longport Works, Stoke-on-Trent, Staffordshire
		(on loan from Nottingham Transport Heritage Centre)
08308	23	PD Ports, Teesport, Grangetown, Middlesbrough
08331		Midland Railway-Butterley, Derbyshire
08375	21	Hanson Cement, Ketton Cement Works, nr Stamford
08389		Celsa Steel UK, Tremorfa Steelworks, Cardiff
08401		Hams Hall Distribution Park, Coleshill, Warwickshire
08411		RSS, Rye Farm, Wishaw, Sutton Coldfield
08418		West Coast Railway Company, Carnforth
08423	H011 14	PD Ports, Teesport, Grangetown, Middlesbrough
08441		Virgin Trains East Coast, Bounds Green Depot, London
08442		Arriva TrainCare, Eastleigh Depot, Hampshire
08445		Daventry International Railfreight Terminal, Crick
08447		John G Russell (Transport), Hillington, Glasgow
08460	SPIRIT OF THE OAK	Axiom Rail, Stoke-on-Trent Works, Staffordshire
08484	CAPTAIN NATHANIEL DARELL	Cemex UK, Washwood Heath, Birmingham
08485		West Coast Railway Company, Carnforth
08499	REDLIGHT	Colas Rail, Canton Depot, Cardiff
08500		Nemesis Rail, Burton-upon-Trent, Staffordshire
08502		GB Railfreight, Garston Car Terminal, Liverpool
08503		Barry Rail Centre, Vale of Glamorgan
08511		Chasewater Light Railway, Brownhills, Staffordshire
08516		Arriva TrainCare, Barton Hill Depot, Bristol
08527		GB Railfreight, Inter Terminals, Immingham East Dock
08536		Loram (UK), RTC Business Park, Derby
08567		Arlington Fleet Services, Eastleigh Works, Hampshire
08568	St. Rollox	Knorr-Bremse Rail UK, Springburn Depot, Glasgow
08573		Bombardier Transportation, Ilford Works, London
08578		Quinton Rail Technology Centre, Long Marston, Warks
08580		Colne Valley Railway, Halstead, Essex

08588		RMS Locotec, Washwood Heath, Birmingham
08593		RSS, Rye Farm, Wishaw, Sutton Coldfield
08598	H016 HERCULES	Chasewater Light Railway, Brownhills, Staffordshire
08600		AV Dawson, Ayrton Rail Terminal, Middlesbrough
08602	004	Bombardier Transportation, Derby Works
08613	H064	Celtic Energy, Onllwyn Coal & Distribution Centre, W Glamorgan
08622	H028 19	Weardale Railway, Wolsingham, County Durham
08629	Wolverton	Knorr-Bremse Rail UK, Wolverton Works, Milton Keynes
08630	CELSA 3	Celsa Steel UK, Tremorfa Steelworks, Cardiff
08643		Aggregate Industries, Merehead Rail Terminal
08648		Northern, Heaton Depot, Newcastle-upon-Tyne
08649	Bradwell	Knorr-Bremse Rail UK, Wolverton Works, Milton Keynes
08650	ISLE OF GRAIN	Hanson Aggregates, Whatley Quarry, near Frome
08652		Aggregate Industries, Merehead Rail Terminal
08653		Quinton Rail Technology Centre, Long Marston, Warks
08670		Virgin Trains East Coast, Bounds Green Depot, London
08676		East Kent Light Railway, Shepherdswell, Kent
08678	ARTILA	West Coast Railway Company, Carnforth
08682	Lionheart	Bombardier Transportation, Derby Works
08683		Bombardier Transportation, Derby Works
08685		East Kent Light Railway, Shepherdswell, Kent
08699		Weardale Railway, Wolsingham, County Durham
08700		Bombardier Transportation, Ilford Works, London
08701		Quinton Rail Technology Centre, Long Marston, Warks
08704		Nemesis Rail, Burton-upon-Trent, Staffordshire
08709		Colne Valley Railway, Halstead, Essex
08711		Tees Yard *(awaiting collection by HNRC)*
08714		Hope Construction Materials, Hope Cement Works, Derbyshire
08730	The Caley	Knorr-Bremse Rail UK, Springburn Depot, Glasgow
08738		Colne Valley Railway, Halstead, Essex
08743	Bryan Turner	SembCorp Utilities Teesside, Wilton, Middlesbrough
08750		Weardale Railway, Wolsingham, County Durham
08756		Tata Steel, Shotton Works, Deeside, Flintshire
08762		Loram (UK), RTC Business Park, Derby
08765		Barrow Hill Roundhouse, Chesterfield, Derbyshire
08774	ARTHUR VERNON DAWSON	AV Dawson, Ayrton Rail Terminal, Middlesbrough
08786		Barrow Hill Roundhouse, Chesterfield, Derbyshire
08787	"08296"	Hanson Aggregates, Machen Quarry, nr Newport
08802		RSS, Rye Farm, Wishaw, Sutton Coldfield
08807		AV Dawson, Ayrton Rail Terminal, Middlesbrough
08809	24	PD Ports, Teesport, Grangetown, Middlesbrough
08810	RICHARD J. WENHAM EASTLEIGH DEPOT	Arriva TrainCare, Eastleigh Depot, Hampshire
08818	MOLLY	Celsa Steel UK, Tremorfa Steelworks, Cardiff
08823	LIBBIE	Daventry International Railfreight Terminal, Crick
08824	IEMD 01	Barrow Hill Roundhouse, Chesterfield, Derbyshire
08834		Northern, Allerton Depot, Liverpool
08846	003	RSS, Rye Farm, Wishaw, Sutton Coldfield
08865		Barrow Hill Roundhouse, Chesterfield, Derbyshire
08868		Arriva TrainCare, Crewe Depot, Cheshire

08870	H024	Hanson Cement, Ketton Cement Works, nr Stamford
08871	H074	Tata Steel, Trostre Works, Llanelli, Carmarthenshire
08873		Maritime Freightliner Terminal, Southampton
08877		Barrow Hill Roundhouse, Chesterfield, Derbyshire
08879		Arlington Fleet Services, Eastleigh Works
08885	H042 18	Weardale Railway, Wolsingham, County Durham
08892		Bombardier Transportation, Old Dalby Test Centre, Asfordby
08903	John W Antill	SembCorp Utilities Teesside, Wilton, Middlesbrough
08905		Hope Construction Materials, Hope Cement Works, Derbyshire
08912		AV Dawson, Ayrton Rail Terminal, Middlesbrough
08913		LH Group, Barton-under-Needwood, Staffordshire
08918		Nemesis Rail, Burton-upon-Trent, Staffordshire
08924	CELSA 2	Celsa Steel UK, Tremorfa Steelworks, Cardiff
08927	D4157	EMD, Roberts Road Depot, Doncaster
08933		Aggregate Industries, Merehead Rail Terminal
08936		Weardale Railway, Wolsingham, County Durham
08937	D4167	Bardon Aggregates, Meldon Quarry, near Okehampton
08939		Colne Valley Railway, Halstead, Essex
08943		Bombardier Transportation, Central Rivers Depot, Barton-under-Needwood
08947		Hanson Aggregates, Whatley Quarry, near Frome
08956		Bombardier Transportation, Old Dalby Test Centre, Asfordby
08994		Nemesis Rail, Burton-upon-Trent, Staffordshire

Class 09

09006		Nemesis Rail, Burton-upon-Trent, Staffordshire
09007	D3671	London Overground, Willesden Depot, London
09014		Nemesis Rail, Burton-upon-Trent, Staffordshire
09022		Victoria Group, Port of Boston, Boston
09201		Hope Construction Materials, Hope Cement Works, Derbyshire
09204		Arriva TrainCare, Crewe Depot, Cheshire

Class 20

20056	81	British Steel, Appleby-Frodingham Works, Scunthorpe
20066	82	Hope Construction Materials, Hope Cement Works, Derbyshire
20110	D8110	East Lancashire Railway, Bury, Greater Manchester
20121		Barrow Hill Roundhouse, Chesterfield, Derbyshire
20166		Wensleydale Railway, Leeming Bar, North Yorkshire
20168	2 SIR GEORGE EARLE	Hope Construction Materials, Hope Cement Works, Derbyshire
20906	3	Hope Construction Materials, Hope Cement Works, Derbyshire

Class 47

| 47703 | | Wabtec Rail, Doncaster Works |
| 47714 | | Bombardier Transportation, Old Dalby Test Centre, Asfordby |

1.5. LOCOMOTIVES AWAITING DISPOSAL

Locomotives that are still extant but best classed as awaiting disposal are listed here.

Class 08

08783	European Metal Recycling, Kingsbury
08798	European Metal Recycling, Attercliffe
08872	European Metal Recycling, Attercliffe
08921	European Metal Recycling, Kingsbury

Class 09

09023	European Metal Recycling, Attercliffe
09107	European Metal Recycling, Kingsbury

Class 37

37194	CF Booth, Rotherham

Class 58

58012	Battlefield Line
58023	Battlefield Line

Class 66

66048	EMD, Longport Works

Class 86

86246	CF Booth, Rotherham
86901	CF Booth, Rotherham

1.6. LOCOMOTIVES EXPORTED FOR USE ABROAD

This section details former BR (plus privatisation era) diesel and electric locomotives that have been exported from the UK for use in industrial locations or by a main line operator abroad. Not included are locos that are "preserved" abroad, which are included in our "Preserved Locomotives of British Railways" publication. (S) denotes locomotives that are stored.

Number Other no./name   Location

Class 03

03156		Ferramenta Pugliese, Terlizzi, Bari, Italy

Class 04

D2289		Lonato SpA, Lonato Steelworks, Lonato, Brescia, Italy

Class 47

47375	92 70 00 47375-5	Continental Railway Solution, Hungary

Class 56

56101	92 55 0659 001-5	FLOYD, Hungary
56115	92 55 0659 002-3	FLOYD, Hungary
56117	92 55 0659 003-1	FLOYD, Hungary (S) Budapest Keleti

Class 58

58001		DB, France, (S) Alizay
58004		DB, France, (S) Alizay
58005		DB, France, (S) Alizay
58006		DB, France, (S) Alizay
58007		DB, France, (S) Alizay
58009		DB, France, (S) Alizay
58010		DB, France, (S) Alizay
58011		DB, France, (S) Alizay
58013		DB, France, (S) Alizay
58015	L54	Transfesa, Spain, Monforte del Cid, Alicante
58018		DB, France, (S) Alizay
58020	L43	Transfesa, Spain, Monforte del Cid, Alicante
58021		DB, France, (S) Alizay
58024	L42	Transfesa, Spain, Monforte del Cid, Alicante
58025		DB, Spain, (S) Albacete
58026		DB, France, (S) Alizay
58027	L52	DB, Spain, (S) Albacete
58029	L44	Transfesa, Spain, (S) Monforte del Cid, Alicante
58030	L46	Transfesa, Spain, Monforte del Cid, Alicante
58031	L45	Transfesa, Spain, Monforte del Cid, Alicante
58032		DB, France, (S) Alizay
58033		DB, France, (S) Alizay
58034		DB, France, (S) Alizay

58035		DB, France, (S) Alizay
58036		DB, France, (S) Alizay
58038		DB, France, (S) Alizay
58039		DB, France, (S) Alizay
58040		DB, France, (S) Alizay
58041	L36	Transfesa, Spain, (S) Albacete
58042		DB, France, (S) Alizay
58043	L37	Transfesa, Spain, Monforte del Cid, Alicante
58044		DB, France, (S) Woippy, Metz
58046		DB, France, (S) Alizay
58047	L51	Transfesa, Spain, Monforte del Cid, Alicante
58049		DB, France, (S) Alizay
58050	L53	DB, Spain, (S) Albacete

Class 66

66010	Euro Cargo Rail, France	66202	Euro Cargo Rail, France
66022	Euro Cargo Rail, France	66203	Euro Cargo Rail, France
66026	Euro Cargo Rail, France	66204	Euro Cargo Rail, France
66028	Euro Cargo Rail, France	66205	Euro Cargo Rail, France
66029	Euro Cargo Rail, France	66208	Euro Cargo Rail, France
66032	Euro Cargo Rail, France	66209	Euro Cargo Rail, France
66033	Euro Cargo Rail, France	66210	Euro Cargo Rail, France
66036	Euro Cargo Rail, France	66211	Euro Cargo Rail, France
66038	Euro Cargo Rail, France	66212	Euro Cargo Rail, France
66042	Euro Cargo Rail, France	66213	Euro Cargo Rail, France
66045	Euro Cargo Rail, France	66214	Euro Cargo Rail, France
66049	Euro Cargo Rail, France	66215	Euro Cargo Rail, France
66052	Euro Cargo Rail, France	66216	Euro Cargo Rail, France
66062	Euro Cargo Rail, France	66217	Euro Cargo Rail, France
66064	Euro Cargo Rail, France	66218	Euro Cargo Rail, France
66071	Euro Cargo Rail, France	66219	Euro Cargo Rail, France
66072	Euro Cargo Rail, France	66220	DB Cargo Polska, Poland
66073	Euro Cargo Rail, France	66222	Euro Cargo Rail, France
66123	Euro Cargo Rail, France	66223	Euro Cargo Rail, France
66146	DB Cargo Polska, Poland	66224	Euro Cargo Rail, France
66153	DB Cargo Polska, Poland	66225	Euro Cargo Rail, France
66157	DB Cargo Polska, Poland	66226	Euro Cargo Rail, France
66159	DB Cargo Polska, Poland	66227	DB Cargo Polska, Poland
66163	DB Cargo Polska, Poland	66228	Euro Cargo Rail, France
66166	DB Cargo Polska, Poland	66229	Euro Cargo Rail, France
66173	DB Cargo Polska, Poland	66231	Euro Cargo Rail, France
66178	DB Cargo Polska, Poland	66232	Euro Cargo Rail, France
66179	Euro Cargo Rail, France	66233	Euro Cargo Rail, France
66180	DB Cargo Polska, Poland	66234	Euro Cargo Rail, France
66189	DB Cargo Polska, Poland	66235	Euro Cargo Rail, France
66190	Euro Cargo Rail, France	66236	Euro Cargo Rail, France
66191	Euro Cargo Rail, France	66237	DB Cargo Polska, Poland
66193	Euro Cargo Rail, France	66239	Euro Cargo Rail, France
66195	Euro Cargo Rail, France	66240	Euro Cargo Rail, France
66196	DB Cargo Polska, Poland	66241	Euro Cargo Rail, France
66201	Euro Cargo Rail, France	66242	Euro Cargo Rail, France

66243		Euro Cargo Rail, France
66244		Euro Cargo Rail, France
66245		Euro Cargo Rail, France
66246		Euro Cargo Rail, France
66247		Euro Cargo Rail, France
66248		DB Cargo Polska, Poland
66249		Euro Cargo Rail, France
66411	66013	Freightliner, Poland
66412	66015	Freightliner, Poland
66417	66014	Freightliner, Poland
66527	66016	Freightliner, Poland
66530	66017	Freightliner, Poland
66535	66018	Freightliner, Poland
66582	66009	Freightliner, Poland
66583	66010	Freightliner, Poland
66584	66011	Freightliner, Poland
66586	66008	Freightliner, Poland
66608	66603	Freightliner, Poland
66609	66605	Freightliner, Poland
66611	66604	Freightliner, Poland
66612	66606	Freightliner, Poland
66624	66602	Freightliner, Poland
66625	66601	Freightliner, Poland

Class 86

86213	91 52 00 87703-2	Lancashire Witch	Bulmarket, Bulgaria
86215	91 55 0450 005-8		FLOYD, Hungary
86217	91 55 0450 006-6		FLOYD, Hungary
86218	91 55 0450 004-1		FLOYD, Hungary
86228	91 55 0450 007-4		FLOYD, Hungary
86231	91 52 00 87705-7		Bulmarket, Bulgaria
86232	91 55 0450 003-3		FLOYD, Hungary
86233			Bulmarket, Bulgaria (S) Ruse
86234			Bulmarket, Bulgaria (S) Ruse
86235	91 52 00 87704-0	Novelty	Bulmarket, Bulgaria
86242	91 55 0450 008-2		FLOYD, Hungary
86248	91 55 0450 001-7		FLOYD, Hungary
86250	91 55 0450 002-5		FLOYD, Hungary
86424	91 55 0450 009-0		FLOYD, Hungary (S) Budapest
86701	91 52 00 87701-6	Orion	Bulmarket, Bulgaria
86702	91 52 00 87702-4	Cassiopeia	Bulmarket, Bulgaria

Class 87

87003	91 52 00 87003-7		BZK, Bulgaria
87004	91 52 00 87004-5	Britannia	BZK, Bulgaria
87006	91 52 00 87006-0		BZK, Bulgaria
87007	91 52 00 87007-8		BZK, Bulgaria
87008	87008-9		BZK, Bulgaria (S) Ruse
87009	91 52 00 87009-4		Bulmarket, Bulgaria
87010	91 52 00 87010-2		BZK, Bulgaria
87012	91 52 00 87012-8		BZK, Bulgaria
87013	91 52 00 87013-6		BZK, Bulgaria
87014	87014-7		BZK, Bulgaria (S) Sofia
87017	91 52 00 87017-7	Iron Duke	Bulmarket, Bulgaria
87019	91 52 00 87019-3		BZK, Bulgaria
87020	91 52 00 87020-1		BZK, Bulgaria
87022	91 52 00 87022-7		BZK, Bulgaria
87023	91 52 00 87023-5	Velocity	Bulmarket, Bulgaria
87025	91 52 00 87025-0		Bulmarket, Bulgaria
87026	91 52 00 87026-8		BZK, Bulgaria
87028	91 52 00 87028-4		BZK, Bulgaria
87029	91 52 00 87029-2		BZK, Bulgaria

| 87033 | 91 52 00 87033-4 | | BZK, Bulgaria |
| 87034 | 91 52 00 87034-2 | | BZK, Bulgaria |

Class 92

Note: 92003, 92022 and 92026 are at Dollands Moor Yard awaiting export to mainland Europe. See Class 92 under section 1.2.

92001	91 53 0 472 002-1	Mircea Eliade	DB Cargo, Romania
92002	91 53 0 472 003-9	Lucian Blaga	DB Cargo, Romania
92005	91 53 0 472 005-4	Emil Cioran	DB Cargo, Romania
92012	91 53 0 472 001-3	Mihai Eminescu	DB Cargo, Romania
92024	91 53 0 472 004-7	Marin Preda	DB Cargo, Romania
92025	91 70 00 92025-1	Oscar Wilde	DB Cargo, Bulgaria
92027	91 70 00 92027-7	George Eliot	DB Cargo, Bulgaria
92030	91 70 00 92030-1	Ashford	DB Cargo, Bulgaria
92034	91 70 00 92034-3	Kipling	DB Cargo, Bulgaria
92039	91 53 0 472 006-2	Eugen Ionescu	DB Cargo, Romania

2. LOCO-HAULED COACHING STOCK

This section contains details of all locomotive-hauled or propelled coaching stock, often referred to as carriages, which can run on Britain's national railway network.

The number of locomotive-hauled or propelled carriages in use on the national railway network is much fewer than was once the case. Those that remain fall into two distinct groups.

Firstly, there are those used by franchised and open access operators for regular timetabled services. Most of these are formed in fixed or semi-fixed formations with either locomotives or a locomotive and Driving Brake Carriage at either end which allows for push-pull operation. There are also a small number of mainly overnight and peak-hour trains with variable formations that use conventional locomotive haulage.

Secondly there are those used for what can best be described as excursion trains. These include a wide range of carriage types ranging from luxurious saloons to those more suited to the "bucket and spade" seaside type of excursion. These are formed into sets to suit the requirements of the day. From time to time some see limited use with franchised and open access operators to cover for stock shortages and times of exceptional demand such as major sporting events.

In addition, there remain a small number of carriages referred to as "Service Stock" which are used internally within the railway industry and are not used to convey passengers.

FRANCHISED & OPEN ACCESS OPERATORS

For each operator regularly using locomotive-hauled carriages brief details are given here of the sphere of operation. For details of operators using HSTs see Section 2.

Arriva Trains Wales
The Monday–Friday Welsh Assembly Government sponsored train between Cardiff and Holyhead uses Mark 3 carriages in push-pull mode with a Class 67. A second similarly formed set is used for weekday trains between Crewe or Manchester and Chester/North Wales. These carriages are also used for relief trains, particularly in connection with sports fixtures at Cardiff and busy ferry sailings to/from Holyhead.

Caledonian Sleeper
This franchise, operated by Serco, started in 2015 when the Anglo-Scottish Sleeper operation was split from the ScotRail franchise. Caledonian Sleeper comprises seating and sleeping car services between London Euston and Scotland using sets of Mark 3 Sleeping Cars and Mark 2 seating and catering carriages. GBRf is contracted to supply the motive power for the Sleepers. Class 92s are intended to be used between London Euston and Edinburgh/Glasgow Central (although reliability problems with these locomotives has seen Class 90s substituting). Rebuilt Class 73/9s are used

between Edinburgh and Aberdeen, Inverness and Fort William, at the time of writing normally running with GBRf Class 66s.

Chiltern Railways
Chiltern operates four sets of Mark 3 carriages with Class 68 locomotives on its Mainline services between London Marylebone and Birmingham Moor Street/Kidderminster (plus one train to Oxford). Another set is used on a peak-hour commuter service between Marylebone and Banbury. All trains operate as push-pull sets.

Greater Anglia
The Inter-City service between London Liverpool Street and Norwich is operated using 12 sets of Mark 3 carriages with Class 90 locomotives in push-pull formations. In addition two sets of Mark 2 carriages supplied by DRS are used between Norwich and Great Yarmouth/Lowestoft, using Class 37s in push-pull mode or Class 68s.

Great Western Railway
The "Night Riviera" seating and sleeping car service between London Paddington and Penzance uses sets of Mark 3 carriages hauled by Class 57/6 locomotives. The seated carriages are also used in Devon and Cornwall for local services on summer Saturdays.

Northern
Northern operates two sets of Mark 2 carriages hired from DRS on the Cumbrian Coast route (between Carlisle and Barrow-in-Furness/Preston) with Class 37s in push-pull mode.

North Yorkshire Moors Railway
In addition to operating the North Yorkshire Moors Railway between Pickering and Grosmont the company operates through services to Whitby and occasionally Battersby. A fleet of Mark 1 passenger carriages and Pullman Cars are used for these services.

ScotRail
ScotRail operates two sets of Mark 2 carriages supplied by DRS on peak-hour services between Edinburgh and Fife using Class 68s.

Virgin Trains East Coast
VTEC operates 30 sets of Mark 4 carriages with Class 91 locomotives in push-pull formations on its Inter-City services between London King's Cross and Yorkshire, North-East England and Scotland.

EXCURSION TRAIN OPERATORS

Usually, three types of companies will be involved in the operation of an excursion train. There will be the promoter, the rolling stock provider and the train operator. In many cases two or more of these roles may be undertaken by the same or associated companies. Only a small number of Train Operating Companies facilitate the operation of excursion trains. This takes various forms ranging from the complete package of providing and operating the train, through offering a "hook up and haul" service, to operating the train for a third party rolling stock custodian.

DB Cargo UK
DBC currently operates its own luxurious train of Mark 3 carriages, called the Company Train. It also offers a hook up and haul service and regularly operates the Royal Train and the Belmond British Pullman as well as trains for Riviera Trains and Locomotives Services and their client promoters. An excursion train fleet of Mark 2 carriages is owned by DBC but these are currently not in use.

Direct Rail Services
DRS operates a fleet of Mark 2 carriages originally intended for use on excursion trains. These are currently hired to Greater Anglia, Northern and ScotRail for use on regular timetabled services. The company also offers a hook up and haul service operating the Belmond Northern Belle as well as trains for Riviera Trains and their client promoters.

GB Railfreight
GBRf initially operated excursion trains using the preserved Class 201 "Hastings" DEMU. It now also operates a small number of company excursions using hired carriages. The company also offers a hook up and haul service operating the Royal Scotsman luxury train, as well as trains for Riviera Trains and its client promoters.

Rail Operations Group
This company operates a small number of excursion trains using hired in carriages.

West Coast Railway Company
This vertically integrated company has its own fleet of steam and diesel locomotives as well as a full range of different carriage types. It operates its own regular trains, such as the "Jacobite" steam service between Fort William and Mallaig and numerous excursion trains for itself and client promoters. In addition, it offers a hook up and haul service operating trains for Vintage Trains, The Princess Royal Locomotive Trust, the Scottish Railway Preservation Society and the North Norfolk Railway.

LAYOUT OF INFORMATION

Carriages are listed in numerical order of painted number in batches according to type.

Where a carriage has been renumbered, the former number is shown in parentheses. If a carriage has been renumbered more than once, the original number is shown first in parentheses, followed by the most recent previous number.

Each carriage entry is laid out as in the following example (previous number(s) column may be omitted where not applicable):

No.	Prev. No.	Notes	Livery	Owner	Operator	Depot/Location
42346	(41053)	*h	**FD**	A	*GW*	LA

Codes: Codes are used to denote the livery, owner, operator and depot/location of each carriage. Details of codes used can be found in Section 6 of this book.

The owner is the responsible custodian of the carriage and this may not always be the legal owner. Actual ownership can be very complicated. Some vehicles are owned by finance/leasing companies. Others are owned by subsidiary companies of a holding company or by an associate company of the responsible custodian or operator.

The operator is the organisation which facilitates the use of the carriage and may not be the actual train operating company which runs the train. If no operator is shown the carriage is considered to be not in use.

The depot is the facility primarily responsible for the carriages maintenance. Light maintenance and heavy overhauls may be carried out elsewhere.

The location is where carriages not in use are currently being kept/stored.

GENERAL INFORMATION

CLASSIFICATION AND NUMBERING

Seven different numbering systems were in use on British Rail. These were the British Rail series, the four pre-nationalisation companies' series', the Pullman Car Company's series and the UIC (International Union of Railways) series. In this book BR number series carriages and former Pullman Car Company series are listed separately. There is also a separate listing of "Saloon" type carriages, that includes pre-nationalisation survivors, which are permitted to run on the national railway system, Locomotive Support Carriages and Service Stock. Please note the Mark 2 Pullman carriages were ordered after the Pullman Car Company had been nationalised and are therefore numbered in the British Rail series.

Also listed separately are the British Rail and Pullman Car Company number series carriages used on North Yorkshire Moors Railway and North Norfolk Railway services on the national railway system. This is due to their very restricted sphere of operation.

The BR number series grouped carriages of a particular type together in chronological order. Major modifications affecting type of accommodation resulted in renumbering into a more appropriate or new number series. Since privatisation such renumbering has not always taken place resulting in renumbering which has been more haphazard and greater variations within numbering groups.

With the introduction of the TOPS numbering system, coaching stock (including multiple unit vehicles) retained their original BR number unless this conflicted with a locomotive number. Carriages can be one–five digits, although no one or two digit examples remain in use on the national network. BR generally numbered "Service Stock" in a six-digit wagon number series.

UNITS OF MEASUREMENT

All dimensions and weights are quoted for carriages in an "as new" condition or after a major modification, such as fitting with new bogies etc. Dimensions are quoted in the order length x width. Lengths quoted are over buffers or couplers as appropriate. All widths quoted are maxima. All weights are shown as metric tonnes (t = tonnes).

DETAILED INFORMATION & CODES

Under each type heading, the following details are shown:

- "Mark" of carriage (see below).
- Descriptive text.
- Number of First Class seats, Standard Class seats, lavatory compartments and wheelchair spaces shown as F/S nT nW respectively. A number in brackets indicates tip-up seats (in addition to the regular seats).
- Bogie type (see below).
- Additional features.
- ETS Index.
- Weight: All weights are shown as metric tonnes (t = tonnes).

BOGIE TYPES

BR Mark 1 (BR1). Double bolster leaf spring bogie. Generally 90 mph, but Mark 1 bogies may be permitted to run at 100 mph with special maintenance. Weight: 6.1 t.

BR Mark 2 (BR2). Single bolster leaf-spring bogie used on certain types of non-passenger stock and suburban stock (all now withdrawn). Weight: 5.3 t.

COMMONWEALTH (C). Heavy, cast steel coil spring bogie. 100 mph. Weight: 6.75 t.

B4. Coil spring fabricated bogie. Generally 100 mph, but B4 bogies may be permitted to run at 110 mph with special maintenance. Weight: 5.2 t.

B5. Heavy duty version of B4. 100 mph. Weight: 5.3 t.

B5 (SR). A bogie originally used on Southern Region EMUs, similar in design to B5. Now also used on locomotive-hauled carriages. 100 mph.

BT10. A fabricated bogie designed for 125 mph. Air suspension.

T4. A 125 mph bogie designed by BREL (now Bombardier Transportation).

BT41. Fitted to Mark 4 carriages, designed by SIG in Switzerland. At present limited to 125 mph, but designed for 140 mph.

BRAKES

Air braking is now standard on British main line trains. Carriages with other equipment are denoted:

b   Air braked, through vacuum pipe.
v   Vacuum braked.
x   Dual braked (air and vacuum).

HEATING & VENTILATION

Electric heating and ventilation is now standard on British main-line trains. Certain carriages for use on excursion services may also have steam heating facilities, or be steam heated only. All carriages used on North Yorkshire Moors Railway trains have steam heating.

NOTES ON ELECTRIC TRAIN SUPPLY

The sum of ETS indices in a train must not be more than the ETS index of the locomotive or generator van. The normal voltage on British trains is 1000 V. Suffix "X" denotes 600 amp wiring instead of 400 amp. Trains whose ETS index is higher than 66 must be formed completely of 600 amp wired stock. Class 33 and 73/1 locomotives cannot provide a suitable electric train supply for Mark 2D, Mark 2E, Mark 2F, Mark 3, Mark 3A, Mark 3B or Mark 4 carriages. Class 55 locomotives provide an ETS directly from one of their traction generators into the train line. Consequently voltage fluctuations can result in motor-alternator flashover. Thus these locomotives are not suitable for use with Mark 2D, Mark 2E, Mark 2F, Mark 3, Mark 3A, Mark 3B or Mark 4 carriages unless modified motor-alternators are fitted. Such motor alternators were fitted to Mark 2D and 2F carriages used on the East Coast Main Line, but few remain fitted.

PUBLIC ADDRESS

It is assumed all carriages are now fitted with public address equipment, although certain stored carriages may not have this feature. In addition, it is assumed all carriages with a conductor's compartment have public address transmission facilities, as have catering carriages.

COOKING EQUIPMENT

It is assumed that Mark 1 catering carriages have gas powered cooking equipment, whilst Mark 2, 3 and 4 catering carriages have electric powered cooking equipment unless stated otherwise.

ADDITIONAL FEATURE CODES

d	Central Door Locking.
dg	Driver–Guard communication equipment.
f	Facelifted or fluorescent lighting.
h	"High density" seating
k	Composition brake blocks (instead of cast iron).
n	Day/night lighting.
pg	Public address transmission and driver-guard communication.
pt	Public address transmission facility.
q	Catering staff to shore telephone.
w	Wheelchair space.

BUILD DETAILS

Lot Numbers
Carriages ordered under the auspices of BR were allocated a lot (batch) number when ordered and these are quoted in class headings and sub-headings.

Builders
These are shown for each lot. More details and a full list of builders can be found in section 6.7.

Information on sub-contracting works which built parts of carriages eg the underframes etc is not shown.

In addition to the above, certain vintage Pullman cars were built or rebuilt at the following works:

Metropolitan Carriage & Wagon Company, Birmingham (later Alstom).
Midland Carriage & Wagon Company, Birmingham.
Pullman Car Company, Preston Park, Brighton.
Conversions have also been carried out at the Railway Technical Centre, Derby, LNWR Crewe and Blakes Fabrications, Edinburgh.

2.1. BR NUMBER SERIES COACHING STOCK

KITCHEN FIRST

Mark 1. Spent most of its life as a Royal Train vehicle and was numbered 2907 for a time. 24/–. B5 bogies. ETS 2.

Lot No. 30633 Swindon 1961. 41 t.

325	**VN**	BE	*NB*	CP	DUART

PULLMAN KITCHEN

Mark 2. Pressure Ventilated. Built with First Class seating but this has been replaced with a servery area. Gas cooking. 2T. B5 bogies. ETS 6.

Lot No. 30755 Derby 1966. 40 t.

504	**PC**	WC	*WC*	CS	ULLSWATER
506	**PC**	WC	*WC*	CS	WINDERMERE

PULLMAN OPEN FIRST

Mark 2. Pressure Ventilated. 36/– 2T. B4 bogies. ETS 5.

Lot No. 30754 Derby 1966. 35 t.

Non-standard livery: 546 Maroon & beige.

546	**0**	WC		CS	CITY OF MANCHESTER
548	**PC**	WC	*WC*	CS	GRASMERE
549	**PC**	WC	*WC*	CS	BASSENTHWAITE
550	**PC**	WC	*WC*	CS	RYDAL WATER
551	**PC**	WC	*WC*	CS	BUTTERMERE
552	**PC**	WC	*WC*	CS	ENNERDALE WATER
553	**PC**	WC	*WC*	CS	CRUMMOCK WATER

PULLMAN OPEN BRAKE FIRST

Mark 2. Pressure Ventilated. 30/– 2T. B4 bogies. ETS 4.

Lot No. 30753 Derby 1966. 35 t.

586	**PC**	WC	*WC*	CS	DERWENTWATER

BUFFET FIRST

Mark 2F. Air conditioned. Converted 1988–89/91 at BREL, Derby from Mark 2F Open Firsts. 1200/01/03/11/20/21 have Stones equipment, others have Temperature Ltd. 25/– 1T 1W. B4 bogies. d. ETS 6X.

1200/03/11/20. Lot No. 30845 Derby 1973. 33 t.
1201/07/10/12/21/54. Lot No. 30859 Derby 1973–74. 33 t.

1200	(3287, 6459)	**BG**	RV	RV	EH
1201	(3361, 6445)	**CH**	VT		TM
1203	(3291)	**IC**	RV	CA	PO
1207	(3328, 6422)	**V**	BE		ZG
1210	(3405, 6462)	**FS**	E	CA	PO
1211	(3305)	**PC**	LS		CL
1212	(3427, 6453)	**V**	RV	CA	PO
1220	(3315, 6432)	**FS**	E	CA	PO
1221	(3371)	**IC**	BE		ZG
1254	(3391)	**BG**	EP		LR

KITCHEN WITH BAR

Mark 1. Built with no seats but three Pullman-style seats now fitted in bar area. B5 bogies. ETS 1.

Lot No. 30624 Cravens 1960–61. 41 t.

| 1566 | **VN** | BE | NB | CP | CAERDYDD |

KITCHEN BUFFET UNCLASSIFIED

Mark 1. Built with 23 loose chairs. All remaining vehicles refurbished with 23 fixed polypropylene chairs and fluorescent lighting. 1683/91/92 were further refurbished with 21 chairs, wheelchair space and carpets. ETS 2 (* 2X).

Now used on excursion trains with the seating area adapted to various uses including servery and food preparation areas, with some or all seating removed.

1651–92. Lot No. 30628 Pressed Steel 1960–61. Commonwealth bogies. 39 t.
1730. Lot No. 30512 BRCW 1960–61. B5 bogies. 37 t.

1651		**CC**	RV	RV	EH	1683		**RB**	RV		BU
1657		**CH**	RV		ZG	1691		**CC**	RV	RV	EH
1659		**PC**	LS		CL	1692		**CH**	RV		WH
1666	x	**M**	RP	WC	CS	1730	x	**M**	SP	SP	BO
1671	x*	**CH**	RV	RV	EH						

BUFFET STANDARD

Mark 1. These carriages are basically an open standard with two full window spaces removed to accommodate a buffet counter, and four seats removed to allow for a stock cupboard. All remaining vehicles now have fluorescent lighting. –/44 2T. Commonwealth bogies. ETS 3.

1861 has had its toilets replaced with store cupboards.

1813–32. Lot No. 30520 Wolverton 1960. 38 t.
1840. Lot No. 30507 Wolverton 1960. 37 t.
1859–63. Lot No. 30670 Wolverton 1961–62. 38 t.
1882. Lot No. 30702 Wolverton 1962. 38 t.

1813	x	**CH**	RV	*RV*	EH	1860	x	**M**	WC	*WC*	CS
1832	x	**CC**	RV	*RV*	EH	1861	x	**M**	WC	*WC*	CS
1840	v	**M**	WC	*WC*	CS	1863	x	**CH**	LS		CL
1859	x	**M**	SP	*SP*	BO	1882	x	**M**	WC	*WC*	CS

KITCHEN UNCLASSIFIED

Mark 1. These carriages were built as Unclassified Restaurants. They were rebuilt with buffet counters and 23 fixed polypropylene chairs, then further refurbished by fitting fluorescent lighting. Further modified for use as servery vehicle with seating removed and kitchen extended. ETS 2X.

1953. Lot No. 30575 Swindon 1960. B4/B5 bogies. 36.5 t.
1961. Lot No. 30632 Swindon 1961. Commonwealth bogies. 39 t.

1953		**VN**	BE	*NB*	CP	1961	x	**M**	WC	*WC*	CS

HM THE QUEEN'S SALOON

Mark 3. Converted from an Open First built 1972. Consists of a lounge, bedroom and bathroom for HM The Queen, and a combined bedroom and bathroom for the Queen's dresser. One entrance vestibule has double doors. Air conditioned. BT10 bogies. ETS 9X.

Lot No. 30886 Wolverton 1977. 36 t.

2903	(11001)	**RP**	NR	*RT*		ZN

HRH THE DUKE OF EDINBURGH'S SALOON

Mark 3. Converted from an Open Standard built 1972. Consists of a combined lounge/dining room, a bedroom and a shower room for the Duke, a kitchen and a valet's bedroom and bathroom. Air conditioned. BT10 bogies. ETS 15X.

Lot No. 30887 Wolverton 1977. 36 t.

2904	(12001)	**RP**	NR	*RT*		ZN

ROYAL HOUSEHOLD SLEEPING CAR

Mark 3A. Built to similar specification as Sleeping Cars 10647–729. 12 sleeping compartments for use of Royal Household with a fixed lower berth and a hinged upper berth. 2T plus shower room. Air conditioned. BT10 bogies. ETS 11X.

Lot No. 31002 Derby/Wolverton 1985. 44 t.

| 2915 | | **RP** NR | *RT* | ZN |

HRH THE PRINCE OF WALES'S DINING CAR

Mark 3. Converted from HST TRUK (kitchen car) built 1976. Large kitchen retained, but dining area modified for Royal use seating up to 14 at central table(s). Air conditioned. BT10 bogies. ETS 13X.

Lot No. 31059 Wolverton 1988. 43 t.

| 2916 | (40512) | **RP** NR | *RT* | ZN |

ROYAL KITCHEN/HOUSEHOLD DINING CAR

Mark 3. Converted from HST TRUK built 1977. Large kitchen retained and dining area slightly modified with seating for 22 Royal Household members. Air conditioned. BT10 bogies. ETS 13X.

Lot No. 31084 Wolverton 1990. 43 t.

| 2917 | (40514) | **RP** NR | *RT* | ZN |

ROYAL HOUSEHOLD CARS

Mark 3. Converted from HST TRUKs built 1976/77. Air conditioned. BT10 bogies. ETS 10X.

Lot Nos. 31083 (* 31085) Wolverton 1989. 41.05 t.

| 2918 | (40515) | **RP** NR | ZN |
| 2919 | (40518) * | **RP** NR | ZN |

ROYAL HOUSEHOLD COUCHETTES

Mark 2B. Converted from Corridor Brake First built 1969. Consists of luggage accommodation, guard's compartment, workshop area, 350 kW diesel generator and staff sleeping accommodation. B5 bogies. ETS 2X (when generator not in use). ETS index ?? (when generator in use).

Lot No. 31044 Wolverton 1986. 48 t.

| 2920 | (14109, 17109) | **RP** NR | *RT* | ZN |

Mark 2B. Converted from Corridor Brake First built 1969. Consists of luggage accommodation, kitchen, brake control equipment and staff accommodation. B5 bogies. ETS 7X.

Lot No. 31086 Wolverton 1990. 41.5 t.

2921	(14107, 17107)	**RP**	NR	*RT*	ZN

HRH THE PRINCE OF WALES'S SLEEPING CAR

Mark 3B. Air conditioned. BT10 bogies. ETS 7X.

Lot No. 31035 Derby/Wolverton 1987.

2922	**RP**	NR	*RT*	ZN

ROYAL SALOON

Mark 3B. Air conditioned. BT10 bogies. ETS 6X.

Lot No. 31036 Derby/Wolverton 1987.

2923	**RP**	NR	*RT*	ZN

OPEN FIRST

Mark 1. 42/– 2T. ETS 3. Many now fitted with table lamps.

3058 was numbered DB 975313, 3068 was numbered DB 975606 and 3093 was numbered DB 977594 for a time when in departmental service for BR.

3058–69. Lot No. 30169 Doncaster 1955. B4 bogies. 33 t (* Commonwealth bogies 35 t).
3093. Lot No. 30472 BRCW 1959. B4 bogies. 33 t.
3096–3100. Lot No. 30576 BRCW 1959. B4 bogies. 33 t.

3058	*x **M**	WC	*WC*	CS	FLORENCE	3096	x **M**	SP	*SP*	BO
3066	**CC**	RV	*RV*	EH		3097	**CC**	RV	*RV*	EH
3068	**CC**	RV	*RV*	EH		3098	x **CH**	RV	*RV*	EH
3069	**CC**	RV	*RV*	EH		3100	x **CC**	LS	*LS*	CL
3093	x **M**	WC	*WC*	CS	FLORENCE					

Later design with fluorescent lighting, aluminium window frames and Commonwealth bogies.

3128/36/41/43/44/46/47/48 were renumbered 1058/60/63/65/66/68/69/70 when reclassified Restaurant Open First, then 3600/05/08/09/02/06/04/10 when declassified to Open Standard, but have since regained their original numbers. 3136 was numbered DB 977970 for a time when in use with Serco Railtest as a Brake Force Runner.

3105 has had its luggage racks removed and has tungsten lighting.

3105–28. Lot No. 30697 Swindon 1962–63. 36 t.
3130–50. Lot No. 30717 Swindon 1963. 36 t.

3105	x	**M**	WC	*WC*	CS
3106	x	**M**	WC	*WC*	CS
3107	x	**CH**	LS		CL
3110	x	**CH**	RV	*RV*	EH
3112	x	**CH**	LS		CL
3113	x	**M**	WC	*WC*	CS
3115	x	**M**	SP	*SP*	BO
3117	x	**M**	WC	*WC*	CS
3119		**CC**	RV	*RV*	EH
3120		**CC**	RV	*RV*	EH
3121		**CH**	RV	*RV*	EH
3122	x	**CH**	LS		CL
3123		**CC**	RV	*RV*	EH
3125	x	**CH**	LS		CL

3128	x	**M**	WC	*WC*	CS
3130	x	**M**	WC	*WC*	CS
3133	x	**M**	RV		WH
3136	x	**M**	WC	*WC*	CS
3140	x	**CH**	LS		CL
3141		**M**	RV		BU
3143	x	**M**	WC	*WC*	CS
3144	x	**M**	RV		BQ
3146		**M**	RV		EH
3147		**CH**	RV	*RV*	EH
3148		**CC**	LS	*LS*	CL
3149		**CH**	RV	*RV*	EH
3150		**M**	SP	*SP*	BO

Names:

3105	JULIA		3128	VICTORIA
3106	ALEXANDRA		3130	PAMELA
3113	JESSICA		3136	DIANA
3117	CHRISTINA		3143	PATRICIA

OPEN FIRST

Mark 2D. Air conditioned. Stones equipment. 42/– 2T. B4 bogies. ETS 5.

† Interior modified to Pullman Car standards with new seating, new panelling, tungsten lighting and table lights.

Lot No. 30821 Derby 1971–72. 34 t.

3174	†	**VN**	BE	*NB*	CP	GLAMIS
3182	†	**VN**	BE	*NB*	CP	WARWICK
3188		**PC**	LS		CL	CADAIR IDRIS

OPEN FIRST

Mark 2E. Air conditioned. Stones equipment. 42/– 2T (* 36/– 2T). B4 bogies. ETS 5.

r Refurbished with new seats.
† Interior modified to Pullman Car standards with new seating, new panelling, tungsten lighting and table lights.

Lot No. 30843 Derby 1972–73. 32.5 t. († 35.8 t).

3223		**RV**	LS		CL	DIAMOND
3231	*	**PC**	LS		CL	BEN CRUACHAN
3232	dr	**BG**	BE		CL	
3240		**RV**	LS		CL	SAPPHIRE
3247	†	**VN**	BE	*NB*	CP	CHATSWORTH
3267	†	**VN**	BE	*NB*	CP	BELVOIR
3273	†	**VN**	BE	*NB*	CP	ALNWICK
3275	†	**VN**	BE	*NB*	CP	HARLECH

OPEN FIRST

Mark 2F. Air conditioned. 3277–3318/3358–79 have Stones equipment, others have Temperature Ltd. All refurbished in the 1980s with power-operated vestibule doors, new panels and new seat trim. 42/– 2T. B4 bogies. d. ETS 5X.

r Further refurbished with table lamps and modified seats with burgundy seat trim.
u Fitted with power supply for Mark 1 Kitchen Buffet Unclassified.

3277–3318. Lot No. 30845 Derby 1973. 33.5 t.
3325–3426. Lot No. 30859 Derby 1973–74. 33.5 t.
3431–3438. Lot No. 30873 Derby 1974–75. 33.5 t.

3277		**AR**	RV		BU	3352	r	**M**	WC	*WC*	CS
3278	r	**BG**	RV	*RV*	EH	3356	r	**BG**	RV	*RV*	EH
3279	u	**M**	DB		ME	3358		**M**	DB		ME
3292		**M**	DB		ME	3359	r	**M**	WC	*WC*	CS
3295		**AR**	RV		BU	3360	r	**PC**	WC	*WC*	CS
3304	r	**V**	RV	*RV*	EH	3362	r	**PC**	WC	*WC*	CS
3312		**PC**	LS		CL	3364	r	**BG**	RV	*RV*	EH
3313	r	**M**	WC	*WC*	CS	3374		**BG**	EP		LR
3314	r	**V**	RV	*RV*	EH	3379	u	**AR**	RV		BU
3318		**M**	DB		ME	3384	r	**CC**	LS	*LS*	CL
3325	r	**V**	RV	*RV*	EH	3386	r	**BG**	RV	*RV*	EH
3326	r	**M**	WC	*WC*	CS	3390	r	**BG**	RV	*RV*	EH
3330	r	**CC**	LS	*LS*	CL	3392	r	**M**	WC	*WC*	CS
3331		**M**	DB		ME	3395	r	**M**	WC	*WC*	CS
3333	r	**BG**	RV	*RV*	EH	3397	r	**BG**	RV	*RV*	EH
3334		**AR**	RV		BU	3400		**M**	DB		ME
3336	u	**AR**	RV		BU	3417		**AR**	RV		BU
3340	r	**V**	RV	*RV*	EH	3424		**M**	DB		ME
3344	r	**V**	RV	*RV*	EH	3426	r	**RV**	LS		CL
3345	r	**BG**	RV	*RV*	EH	3431	r	**M**	WC	*WC*	CS
3348	r	**CC**	LS	*LS*	CL	3438	r	**PC**	LS		CL
3350	r	**M**	WC	*WC*	CS						
3351		**CH**	VT		TM						

Names:

3312	HELVELLYN	3438	BEN LOMOND
3426	ELGAR		

OPEN STANDARD

Mark 1. –/64 2T. ETS 4.

4831–36. Lot No. 30506 Wolverton 1959. Commonwealth bogies. 33 t.
4854/56. Lot No. 30525 Wolverton 1959–60. B4 bogies. 33 t.

4831	x	**M**	SP	*SP*	BO	4854	x	**M**	WC	*WC*	CS
4832	x	**M**	SP	*SP*	BO	4856	x	**M**	SP	*SP*	BO
4836	x	**M**	SP	*SP*	BO						

OPEN STANDARD

Mark 1. Commonwealth bogies. –/64 2T. ETS 4.

4905. Lot No. 30646 Wolverton 1961. 36 t.
4927–5044. Lot No. 30690 Wolverton 1961–62. 37 t.

4905	x	**M**	WC	*WC*	CS	4991		**CH**	RV	*RV*	EH
4927	x	**CC**	RV	*RV*	EH	4994	x	**M**	WC	*WC*	CS
4931	v	**M**	WC	*WC*	CS	4998		**CH**	RV	*RV*	EH
4940	x	**M**	WC	*WC*	CS	5007		**G**	RV		WH
4946	x	**CH**	RV	*RV*	EH	5009	x	**CH**	RV		EH
4949	x	**CH**	RV	*RV*	EH	5027		**G**	RV		BU
4951	x	**M**	WC	*WC*	CS	5028	x	**M**	SP	*SP*	BO
4954	v	**M**	WC	*WC*	CS	5032	x	**M**	WC	*WC*	CS
4959		**CH**	RV	*RV*	EH	5033	x	**M**	WC	*WC*	CS
4960	x	**M**	WC	*WC*	CS	5035	x	**M**	WC	*WC*	CS
4973	x	**M**	WC	*WC*	CS	5044	x	**M**	WC	*WC*	CS
4984	x	**M**	WC	*WC*	CS						

OPEN STANDARD

Mark 2. Pressure ventilated. –/64 2T. B4 bogies. ETS 4.

Lot No. 30751 Derby 1965–67. 32 t.

5157	v	**CH**	VT	*VT*	TM	5200	v	**M**	WC	*WC*	CS
5171	v	**M**	WC	*WC*	CS	5212	v	**CH**	VT	*VT*	TM
5177	v	**CH**	VT	*VT*	TM	5216	v	**M**	WC	*WC*	CS
5191	v	**CH**	VT	*VT*	TM	5222	v	**M**	WC	*WC*	CS
5198	v	**CH**	VT	*VT*	TM						

OPEN STANDARD

Mark 2. Pressure ventilated. –/48 2T. B4 bogies. ETS 4.

Lot No. 30752 Derby 1966. 32 t.

5229		**M**	WC	*WC*	CS	5239		**M**	WC	*WC*	CS
5236	v	**M**	WC	*WC*	CS	5249	v	**M**	WC	*WC*	CS
5237	v	**M**	WC	*WC*	CS						

OPEN STANDARD

Mark 2A. Pressure ventilated. –/64 2T (w –/62 2T). B4 bogies. ETS 4.

f Facelifted vehicles.

5278–5341. Lot No. 30776 Derby 1967–68. 32 t.
5366–5419. Lot No. 30787 Derby 1968. 32 t.

5278		**M**	WC	*WC*	CS	5366	f	**CH**	RV	*RV*	EH
5292	f	**CC**	RV	*RV*	EH	5419	w	**M**	WC	*WC*	CS
5341	f	**CC**	RV	*RV*	EH						

OPEN STANDARD

Mark 2B. Pressure ventilated. –/62. B4 bogies. ETS 4.

Lot No. 30791 Derby 1969. 32 t.

5487	**M**	WC	*WC*	CS

OPEN STANDARD

Mark 2D. Air conditioned. Stones equipment. Refurbished with new seats and end luggage stacks. –/58 2T. B4 bogies. d. ETS 5.

Lot No. 30822 Derby 1971. 33 t.

5631	**M**	DB		ME	5657	**M**	DB		ME
5632	**M**	DB		ME	5710	**FP**	DR		ZM

OPEN STANDARD

Mark 2E. Air conditioned. Stones equipment. Refurbished with new interior panelling. –/64 2T. B4 bogies. d. ETS 5.

s   Modified design of seat headrest and centre luggage stack. –/60 2T.
w   Fitted with one wheelchair space. –/62 2T 1W.

5787–97. Lot No. 30837 Derby 1972. 33.5 t.
5810. Lot No. 30844 Derby 1972–73. 33.5 t.

5787	s	**DS**	DR	*GA*	KM	5810	w	**DS**	DR	*NO*	KM
5797		**IC**	LS		CL						

OPEN STANDARD

Mark 2F. Air conditioned. Temperature Ltd equipment. InterCity 70 seats (* early Mark 2 style seats). All were refurbished in the 1980s with power-operated vestibule doors, new panels and seat trim. –/64 2T. B4 bogies. d. ETS 5X.

*   These vehicles have undergone a second refurbishment with carpets and new seat trim.
q   Fitted with two wheelchair spaces. –/60 2T 2W.
s   Fitted with centre luggage stack. –/60 2T.
t   Fitted with centre luggage stack and wheelchair space. –/58 2T 1W.
w   Fitted with one wheelchair space. –/62 2T 1W.

5910–55. Lot No. 30846 Derby 1973. 33 t.
5959–6158. Lot No. 30860 Derby 1973–74. 33 t.
6173–83. Lot No. 30874 Derby 1974–75. 33 t.

5910	q	**V**	RV		ZA	5922		**M**	DB		DR
5912		**PC**	LS		CL	5924		**M**	DB		DR
5919	s pt	**DS**	DR	*GA*	KM	5928		**CH**	VT		TM
5921		**AR**	RV	*RV*	EH	5929		**AR**	RV	*RV*	EH

5937		**DS**	DR	*GA*	KM	6024		**BG**	RV	*GA*	EH
5945		**SR**	RV	*SR*	ML	6027	q	**SR**	RV	*SR*	ML
5950		**AR**	RV	*RV*	EH	6036	*	**M**	DB		DR
5952		**SR**	RV	*SR*	ML	6042		**AR**	RV	*RV*	EH
5954		**M**	DB		ME	6046		**DS**	DR	*NO*	KM
5955		**SR**	RV	*SR*	ML	6051		**BG**	RV	*RV*	EH
5959	n	**M**	DB		DR	6054		**BG**	RV	*RV*	EH
5961	pt	**BG**	RV	*GA*	EH	6064	s	**DS**	DR	*NO*	KM
5964		**AR**	RV	*RV*	EH	6067	s pt	**V**	RV	*RV*	EH
5965	t	**SR**	RV	*SR*	ML	6103		**M**	WC	*WC*	CS
5971		**DS**	DR	*NO*	KM	6110		**M**	DB		ME
5976	t	**SR**	RV	*SR*	ML	6115	s	**M**	WC	*WC*	CS
5985		**AR**	RV	*RV*	EH	6117		**DS**	DR	*GA*	KM
5987		**SR**	RV	*SR*	ML	6122		**DS**	DR	*NO*	KM
5991		**PC**	LS		CL	6137	s pt	**SR**	RV	*SR*	ML
5995		**DS**	DR	*NO*	KM	6139	n*	**M**	DB		ME
5998		**AR**	RV	*RV*	EH	6141	q	**V**	DB		BU
6000	t	**M**	WC	*WC*	CS	6152	*	**M**	DB		DR
6001		**DS**	DR	*NO*	KM	6158		**V**	RV	*RV*	EH
6006		**AR**	RV		BU	6173	w	**DS**	DR	*NO*	KM
6008		**DS**	DR	*NO*	KM	6176	t	**SR**	RV	*SR*	ML
6012		**M**	WC	*WC*	CS	6177	s	**SR**	RV	*SR*	ML
6021		**M**	WC	*WC*	CS	6183	s	**SR**	RV	*SR*	ML
6022	s	**M**	WC	*WC*	CS						

BRAKE GENERATOR VAN

Mark 1. Renumbered 1989 from BR departmental series. Converted from Gangwayed Brake Van in 1973 to three-phase supply brake generator van for use with HST trailers. Modified 1999 for use with locomotive-hauled stock. B5 bogies. ETS index ??.

Lot No. 30400 Pressed Steel 1958.

6310	(81448, 975325)	**CH**	RV	*RV*	EH

GENERATOR VAN

Mark 1. Converted from Gangwayed Brake Vans in 1992. B4 (* B5) bogies. ETS index 75.

6311. Lot No. 30162 Pressed Steel 1958. 37.25 t.
6312. Lot No. 30224 Cravens 1956. 37.25 t.
6313. Lot No. 30484 Pressed Steel 1958. 37.25 t.

6311	(80903, 92911)		**B**	LS		CL
6312	(81023, 92925)		**M**	WC	*WC*	CS
6313	(81553, 92167)	*	**PC**	BE	*BP*	SL

BUFFET STANDARD

Mark 2C. Converted from Open Standard by removal of one seating bay and replacing this with a counter with a space for a trolley, now replaced with a more substantial buffet. Adjacent toilet removed and converted to steward's washing area/store. Pressure ventilated. –/55 1T. B4 bogies. ETS 4.

Lot No. 30795 Derby 1969–70. 32.5 t.

6528	(5592)	**M**	WC	*WC*	CS

SLEEPER RECEPTION CAR

Mark 2F. Converted from Open First. These vehicles consist of pantry, microwave cooking facilities, seating area for passengers (with loose chairs, staff toilet plus two bars). Now refurbished again with new "sofa" seating as well as the loose chairs. Converted at RTC, Derby (6700), Ilford (6701–05) and Derby (6706–08). Air conditioned. 6700/01/03/05–08 have Stones equipment and 6702/04 have Temperature Ltd equipment. The number of seats per coach can vary but typically is 25/– 1T (12 seats as "sofa" seating and 13 loose chairs). B4 bogies. d. ETS 5X.

6700–02/04/08. Lot No. 30859 Derby 1973–74. 33.5 t.
6703/05–07. Lot No. 30845 Derby 1973. 33.5 t.

6700	(3347)	**FS**	E	*CA*	PO
6701	(3346)	**CA**	E	*CA*	PO
6702	(3421)	**FS**	E	*CA*	PO
6703	(3308)	**FS**	E	*CA*	PO
6704	(3341)	**FS**	E	*CA*	PO
6705	(3310, 6430)	**FS**	E	*CA*	PO
6706	(3283, 6421)	**FS**	E	*CA*	PO
6707	(3276, 6418)	**FS**	E	*CA*	PO
6708	(3370)	**FS**	E	*CA*	PO

BUFFET FIRST

Mark 2D. Converted from Buffet Standard by the removal of another seating bay and fitting a more substantial buffet counter with boiler and microwave oven. Now converted to First Class with new seating and end luggage stacks. Air conditioned. Stones equipment. 30/– 1T. B4 bogies. d. ETS 5.
Lot No. 30822 Derby 1971. 33 t.

6722	(5736, 6661)	**FP**	E		LM
6723	(5641, 6662)	**M**	WC		CS
6724	(5721, 6665)	**M**	WC	*WC*	CS

OPEN BRAKE STANDARD WITH TROLLEY SPACE

Mark 2. This vehicle uses the same bodyshell as Mark 2 Corridor Brake Firsts and has First Class seat spacing and wider tables. Converted from Open Brake Standard by removal of one seating bay and replacing this with a counter with a space for a trolley. Adjacent toilet removed and converted to a steward's washing area/store. –/23. B4 bogies. ETS 4.

Lot No. 30757 Derby 1966. 31 t.

| 9101 | (9398) | v | **CH** | VT | *VT* | | TM |

OPEN BRAKE STANDARD

Mark 2. These vehicles use the same bodyshell as Mark 2 Corridor Brake Firsts and have First Class seat spacing and wider tables. Pressure ventilated. –/31 1T. B4 bogies. ETS 4.

9104 was originally numbered 9401. It was renumbered when converted to Open Brake Standard with trolley space. Now returned to original layout.

Lot No. 30757 Derby 1966. 31.5 t.

| 9104 | v | **M** | WC | *WC* | CS | | 9392 | v | **M** | WC | *WC* | CS |
| 9391 | | **M** | WC | *WC* | CS | | | | | | | |

OPEN BRAKE STANDARD

Mark 2D. Air conditioned. Stones Equipment. Refurbished with new seating –/22 1TD. B4 bogies. d. pg. ETS 5.

Lot No. 30824 Derby 1971. 33 t.

| 9488 | | **SR** | DR | *SR* | ML | | 9494 | | **M** | DB | | ME |
| 9493 | | **M** | WC | *WC* | CS | | | | | | | |

OPEN BRAKE STANDARD

Mark 2E. Air conditioned. Stones Equipment. Refurbished with new interior panelling. –/32 1T (* –/30 1T 1W). B4 bogies. d. pg. ETS 5.

Lot No. 30838 Derby 1972. 33 t.

Non-standard livery: 9502 Pullman umber & cream.

s Modified design of seat headrest.

9496		**M**	VT		TM		9507	s	**V**	RV	*CA*	PO
9502	s	**O**	BE	*BP*	SL		9508	s	**DR**	DR		ZM
9504	s*	**BG**	RV	*GA*	EH		9509	s	**AV**	RV		BU
9506	s	**BG**	DR		ZM							

OPEN BRAKE STANDARD

Mark 2F. Air conditioned. Temperature Ltd equipment. All were refurbished in the 1980s with power-operated vestibule doors, new panels and seat trim. All now further refurbished with carpets. –/32 1T. B4 bogies. d. pg. ETS 5X.

9537 has had all its seats removed for the purpose of carrying luggage.

Advertising livery: 9537 CruiseSaver Express (dark blue).

Lot No. 30861 Derby 1974. 34 t.

9520	n	**AR**	RV	*RV*	EH	9527	n	**SR**	RV	*SR*	ML
9521		**DS**	RV	*SR*	ML	9529	n	**M**	DB		DR
9522		**M**	DB		ME	9531		**M**	DB		DR
9525		**DS**	DR	*GA*	KM	9537	n	**AL**	RV		BU
9526	n	**IC**	RV	*CA*	PO	9539		**SR**	RV	*SR*	ML

DRIVING OPEN BRAKE STANDARD

Mark 2F. Air conditioned. Temperature Ltd equipment. Push & pull (tdm system). Converted from Open Brake Standard, these vehicles originally had half cabs at the brake end. They have since been refurbished and have had their cabs widened and the cab-end gangways removed. Five vehicles (9701–03/08/14) have been converted for use in Network Rail test trains and can be found in the Service Stock section of this book. –/30 1T 1W. B4 bogies. d. pg. Cowcatchers. ETS 5X.

9704–10. Lot No. 30861 Derby 1974. Converted Glasgow 1979. Disc brakes. 34 t.
9711. Lot No. 30861 Derby 1974. Converted Glasgow 1985. 34 t.

9704	(9512)	**DS**	DR	*NO*	KM	9709	(9515)	**DS**	DR	*NO*	KM
9705	(9519)	**DS**	DR	*NO*	KM	9710	(9518)	**DS**	DR	*NO*	KM
9707	(9511)	**DS**	DR	*NO*	KM	9711	(9532)	**AR**	VT		TM

OPEN BRAKE UNCLASSIFIED

Mark 2E. Converted from Open Standard with new seating by Railcare, Wolverton. Air conditioned. Stones equipment. –/31 2T. B4 bogies. d. ETS 4X.

9800–03. Lot No. 30837 Derby 1972. 33.5 t.
9804–10. Lot No. 30844 Derby 1972–73. 33.5 t.

9800	(5751)	**FS**	E	*CA*	PO	9806	(5840)	**FS**	E	*CA*	PO
9801	(5760)	**FS**	E	*CA*	PO	9807	(5851)	**FS**	E	*CA*	PO
9802	(5772)	**CA**	E	*CA*	PO	9808	(5871)	**FS**	E	*CA*	PO
9803	(5799)	**FS**	E	*CA*	PO	9809	(5890)	**FS**	E	*CA*	PO
9804	(5826)	**FS**	E	*CA*	PO	9810	(5892)	**FS**	E	*CA*	PO
9805	(5833)	**FS**	E	*CA*	PO						

KITCHEN BUFFET FIRST

Mark 3A. Air conditioned. Converted from HST catering vehicles and Mark 3 Open Firsts. Refurbished with table lamps and burgundy seat trim (except *). 18/– plus two seats for staff use (* 24/–, † 24/–, § 24/–, t 23/– 1T 1W). BT10 bogies. d. ETS 14X.

§ Great Western Railway Sleeper "day coaches" that have been fitted with former HST First Class seats to a 2+1 layout.

Non-standard livery: 10211 EWS dark maroon.

10202–211. Lot No. 30884 Derby 1977. 39.8 t.
10212–229. Lot No. 30878 Derby 1975–76. 39.8 t.
10232–259. Lot No. 30890 Derby 1979. 39.8 t.

10202	(40504)	†	**BG**	AV		LM	10233	(10013)		**V**	AV	LM
10211	(40510)		**O**	DB	*DB*	TO	10235	(10015)	†	**BG**	AV	LM
10212	(11049)		**VT**	P		LA	10237	(10022)		**DR**	AV	LM
10215	(11032)		**BG**	AV		LM	10241	(10009)	*	**1**	P	IL
10217	(11051)		**VT**	P		ZN	10242	(10002)		**BG**	AV	LM
10219	(11047)	§	**GW**	P	*GW*	PZ	10246	(10014)	†	**BG**	AV	LM
10222	(11063)		**BG**	AV		LM	10249	(10012)		**AW**	AV	*AW*	CF
10225	(11014)	§	**GW**	P	*GW*	PZ	10250	(10020)		**V**	AV	LM
10226	(11015)		**V**	AV		LM	10257	(10007)	†	**BG**	AV	LM
10229	(11059)	*	**GA**	P		LA	10259	(10025)	t	**AW**	AV	*AW*	CF
10232	(10027)	§	**FD**	P	*GW*	PZ						

KITCHEN BUFFET FIRST

Mark 3A. Air conditioned. Rebuilt 2011–12 and fitted with sliding plug doors. Interiors originally refurbished for Wrexham & Shropshire with Primarius seating, a new kitchen area and universal-access toilet. 30/– 1TD 1W. BT10 bogies. ETS 14X.

10271/273/274. Lot No. 30890 Derby 1979. 41.3 t.
10272. Lot No. 30884 Derby 1977. 41.3 t.

10271	(10018, 10236)	**CM**	AV	*CR*	AL
10272	(40517, 10208)	**CM**	AV	*CR*	AL
10273	(10021, 10230)	**CM**	AV	*CR*	AL
10274	(10010, 10255)	**CM**	AV	*CR*	AL

KITCHEN BUFFET STANDARD

Mark 4. Air conditioned. Rebuilt from First to Standard Class with bar adjacent to seating area instead of adjacent to end of coach. –/30 1T. BT41 bogies. ETS 6X.

Lot No. 31045 Metro-Cammell 1989–92. 43.2 t.

10300	**VE**	E	*VE*	BN	10303	**VE**	E	*VE*	BN
10301	**VE**	E	*VE*	BN	10304	**VE**	E	*VE*	BN
10302	**VE**	E	*VE*	BN	10305	**VE**	E	*VE*	BN

10306	**VE**	E	*VE*	BN	10320	**VE**	E	*VE*	BN
10307	**VE**	E	*VE*	BN	10321	**VE**	E	*VE*	BN
10308	**VE**	E	*VE*	BN	10323	**VE**	E	*VE*	BN
10309	**VE**	E	*VE*	BN	10324	**VE**	E	*VE*	BN
10310	**VE**	E	*VE*	BN	10325	**VE**	E	*VE*	BN
10311	**VE**	E	*VE*	BN	10326	**VE**	E	*VE*	BN
10312	**VE**	E	*VE*	BN	10328	**VE**	E	*VE*	BN
10313	**VE**	E	*VE*	BN	10329	**VE**	E	*VE*	BN
10315	**VE**	E	*VE*	BN	10330	**VE**	E	*VE*	BN
10317	**VE**	E	*VE*	BN	10331	**VE**	E	*VE*	BN
10318	**VE**	E	*VE*	BN	10332	**VE**	E	*VE*	BN
10319	**VE**	E	*VE*	BN	10333	**VE**	E	*VE*	BN

BUFFET STANDARD

Mark 3A. Air conditioned. Converted from Mark 3 Open Standard at Derby 2006. –/54. d. ETS 13X.

Lot No. 30877 Derby 1975–77. 37.8 t.

10401	(12168)	**GA**	P	*GA*	NC	10404	(12068)	**GA**	P	*GA*	NC
10402	(12010)	**GA**	P	*GA*	NC	10405	(12157)	**GA**	P	*GA*	NC
10403	(12135)	**GA**	P	*GA*	NC	10406	(12020)	**GA**	P	*GA*	NC

BUFFET STANDARD

Mark 3A. Air conditioned. Converted from Mark 3 Kitchen Buffet First 2015–16. –/54. BT10 bogies. d. ETS 13X.

10411–412. Lot No. 30884 Derby 1977. 37.8 t.
10413–416. Lot No. 30878 Derby 1975–76. 37.8 t.
10417. Lot No. 30890 Derby 1979. 37.8 t.

10411	(40519, 10200)	**GA**	P	*GA*	NC
10412	(40506, 10203)	**GA**	P	*GA*	NC
10413	(11034, 10214)	**GA**	P	*GA*	NC
10414	(11041, 10216)	**GA**	P	*GA*	NC
10415	(11043, 10223)	**GA**	P	*GA*	NC
10416	(11035, 10228)	**GA**	P	*GA*	NC
10417	(10011, 10247)	**GA**	P	*GA*	NC

SLEEPING CAR WITH PANTRY

Mark 3A. Air conditioned. Retention toilets. 12 compartments with a fixed lower berth and a hinged upper berth, plus an attendant's compartment. 2T. BT10 bogies. d. ETS 7X.

Non-standard livery: 10546 EWS dark maroon.

Lot No. 30960 Derby 1981–83. 41 t.

10501	**FS**	P	*CA*	PO	10506	**FS**	P	*CA*	PO
10502	**FS**	P	*CA*	PO	10507	**FS**	P	*CA*	PO
10504	**FS**	P	*CA*	PO	10508	**FS**	P	*CA*	PO

10513	**FS**	P	*CA*	PO		10563	**GW**	P	*GW*	PZ
10516	**FS**	P	*CA*	PO		10565	**FS**	P	*CA*	PO
10519	**FS**	P	*CA*	PO		10580	**CA**	P	*CA*	PO
10520	**FS**	P	*CA*	PO		10584	**GW**	P	*GW*	PZ
10522	**FS**	P	*CA*	PO		10589	**GW**	P	*GW*	PZ
10523	**FS**	P	*CA*	PO		10590	**GW**	P	*GW*	PZ
10526	**FS**	P	*CA*	PO		10594	**GW**	P	*GW*	PZ
10527	**FS**	P	*CA*	PO		10596	**GW**	P	*GW*	PZ
10529	**FS**	P	*CA*	PO		10597	**FS**	P	*CA*	PO
10531	**FS**	P	*CA*	PO		10598	**FS**	P	*CA*	PO
10532	**GW**	P	*GW*	PZ		10600	**FS**	P	*CA*	PO
10534	**GW**	P	*GW*	PZ		10601	**GW**	P	*GW*	PZ
10542	**FS**	P	*CA*	PO		10605	**FS**	P	*CA*	PO
10543	**FS**	P	*CA*	PO		10607	**FS**	P	*CA*	PO
10544	**FS**	P	*CA*	PO		10610	**FS**	P	*CA*	PO
10546	**0**	DB	*DB*	TO		10612	**GW**	P	*GW*	PZ
10548	**FS**	P	*CA*	PO		10613	**FS**	P	*CA*	PO
10551	**FS**	P	*CA*	PO		10614	**FS**	P	*CA*	PO
10553	**FS**	P	*CA*	PO		10616	**GW**	P	*GW*	PZ
10561	**FS**	P	*CA*	PO		10617	**FS**	P	*CA*	PO
10562	**FS**	P	*CA*	PO						

SLEEPING CAR

Mark 3A. Air conditioned. Retention toilets. 13 compartments with a fixed lower berth and a hinged upper berth (* 11 compartments with a fixed lower berth and a hinged upper berth + one compartment for a disabled person. 1TD). 2T. BT10 bogies. ETS 6X.

10734 was originally 2914 and used as a Royal Train staff sleeping car. It has 12 berths and a shower room and is ETS 11X.

10648–729. Lot No. 30961 Derby 1980–84. 43.5 t.
10734. Lot No. 31002 Derby/Wolverton 1985. 42.5 t.

10648	d*	**FS**	P	*CA*	PO		10699	d*	**FS**	P	*CA*	PO
10650	d*	**FS**	P	*CA*	PO		10703	d	**FS**	P	*CA*	PO
10666	d*	**FS**	P	*CA*	PO		10706	d*	**FS**	P	*CA*	PO
10675	d	**FS**	P	*CA*	PO		10714	d*	**FS**	P	*CA*	PO
10680	d*	**FS**	P	*CA*	PO		10718	d*	**FS**	P	*CA*	PO
10683	d	**FS**	P	*CA*	PO		10719	d*	**FS**	P	*CA*	PO
10688	d	**FS**	P	*CA*	PO		10722	d*	**FS**	P	*CA*	PO
10689	d*	**FS**	P	*CA*	PO		10723	d*	**FS**	P	*CA*	PO
10690	d	**FS**	P	*CA*	PO		10729		**VN**	BE	*NB*	CP
10693	d	**CA**	P	*CA*	PO		10734		**VN**	BE	*NB*	CP

Names:

10729	CREWE		10734	BALMORAL

OPEN FIRST

Mark 3A. Air conditioned. All refurbished with table lamps and new seat cushions and trim. 48/– 2T (* 48/– 1T 1TD). BT10 bogies. d. ETS 6X.

† Reseated with Standard Class seats: –/68 2T 2W.

11006/007 were open composites 11906/907 for a time.

Non-standard livery: 11039 EWS dark maroon.

Lot No. 30878 Derby 1975–76. 34.3 t.

11006	**V**	DR		BH	11029 †	**CM**	AV	*CR*	AL
11007	**VT**	P		LA	11031 †	**CM**	AV	*CR*	AL
11011 *	**V**	DR		BH	11033	**DR**	AV		LM
11018	**VT**	P		LA	11039	**0**	DB	*DB*	TO
11028	**V**	AV		ZB	11048	**VT**	P		LA

OPEN FIRST

Mark 3B. Air conditioned. InterCity 80 seats. All refurbished with table lamps and new seat cushions and trim. 48/– 2T (* 48/– 1T). BT10 bogies. d. ETS 6X.

† Fitted with disabled toilet and reduced seating, including three Compin Pegasus seats. 37/– 1TD 2W.

Lot No. 30982 Derby 1985. 36.5 t.

11066 *	**GA**	P	*GA*	NC	11085 †	**GA**	P	*GA*	NC
11067 *	**GA**	P	*GA*	NC	11087 †	**GA**	P	*GA*	NC
11068 *	**GA**	P	*GA*	NC	11088 †	**GA**	P	*GA*	NC
11069 *	**GA**	P	*GA*	NC	11090 †	**GA**	P	*GA*	NC
11070 *	**GA**	P	*GA*	NC	11091 *	**GA**	P	*GA*	NC
11072 *	**GA**	P	*GA*	NC	11092 †	**GA**	P	*GA*	NC
11073 *	**GA**	P	*GA*	NC	11093 †	**GA**	P	*GA*	NC
11075 *	**GA**	P	*GA*	NC	11094 †	**GA**	P	*GA*	NC
11076 *	**GA**	P	*GA*	NC	11095 †	**GA**	P	*GA*	NC
11077 *	**GA**	P	*GA*	NC	11096 †	**GA**	P	*GA*	NC
11078 †	**GA**	P	*GA*	NC	11097	**V**	AV		LM
11079	**V**	AV		LM	11098 †	**GA**	P	*GA*	NC
11080 *	**GA**	P	*GA*	NC	11099 †	**GA**	P	*GA*	NC
11081 *	**GA**	P	*GA*	NC	11100 †	**GA**	P	*GA*	NC
11082 *	**GA**	P	*GA*	NC	11101 †	**GA**	P	*GA*	NC

OPEN FIRST

Mark 4. Air conditioned. Rebuilt with new interior by Bombardier Wakefield 2003–05 (some converted from Standard Class vehicles) 41/– 1T (plus 2 seats for staff use). BT41 bogies. ETS 6X.

11201–11273. Lot No. 31046 Metro-Cammell 1989–92. 41.3 t.
11277–11299. Lot No. 31049 Metro-Cammell 1989–92. 41.3 t.

11201		**VE**	E	*VE*	BN		11284	(12487)	**VE**	E	*VE*	BN
11219		**VE**	E	*VE*	BN		11285	(12537)	**VE**	E	*VE*	BN
11229		**VE**	E	*VE*	BN		11286	(12482)	**VE**	E	*VE*	BN
11237		**VE**	E	*VE*	BN		11287	(12527)	**VE**	E	*VE*	BN
11241		**VE**	E	*VE*	BN		11288	(12517)	**VE**	E	*VE*	BN
11244		**VE**	E	*VE*	BN		11289	(12528)	**VE**	E	*VE*	BN
11273		**VE**	E	*VE*	BN		11290	(12530)	**VE**	E	*VE*	BN
11277	(12408)	**VE**	E	*VE*	BN		11291	(12535)	**VE**	E	*VE*	BN
11278	(12479)	**VE**	E	*VE*	BN		11292	(12451)	**VE**	E	*VE*	BN
11279	(12521)	**VE**	E	*VE*	BN		11293	(12536)	**VE**	E	*VE*	BN
11280	(12523)	**VE**	E	*VE*	BN		11294	(12529)	**VE**	E	*VE*	BN
11281	(12418)	**VE**	E	*VE*	BN		11295	(12475)	**VE**	E	*VE*	BN
11282	(12524)	**VE**	E	*VE*	BN		11298	(12416)	**VE**	E	*VE*	BN
11283	(12435)	**VE**	E	*VE*	BN		11299	(12532)	**VE**	E	*VE*	BN

OPEN FIRST (DISABLED)

Mark 4. Air conditioned. Rebuilt from Open First by Bombardier Wakefield 2003–05. 42/– 1TD 1W. BT41 bogies. ETS 6X.

Lot No. 31046 Metro-Cammell 1989–92. 40.7 t.

11301	(11215)	**VE**	E	*VE*	BN		11316	(11227)	**VE**	E	*VE*	BN
11302	(11203)	**VE**	E	*VE*	BN		11317	(11223)	**VE**	E	*VE*	BN
11303	(11211)	**VE**	E	*VE*	BN		11318	(11251)	**VE**	E	*VE*	BN
11304	(11257)	**VE**	E	*VE*	BN		11319	(11247)	**VE**	E	*VE*	BN
11305	(11261)	**VE**	E	*VE*	BN		11320	(11255)	**VE**	E	*VE*	BN
11306	(11276)	**VE**	E	*VE*	BN		11321	(11245)	**VE**	E	*VE*	BN
11307	(11217)	**VE**	E	*VE*	BN		11322	(11228)	**VE**	E	*VE*	BN
11308	(11263)	**VE**	E	*VE*	BN		11323	(11235)	**VE**	E	*VE*	BN
11309	(11259)	**VE**	E	*VE*	BN		11324	(11253)	**VE**	E	*VE*	BN
11310	(11272)	**VE**	E	*VE*	BN		11325	(11231)	**VE**	E	*VE*	BN
11311	(11221)	**VE**	E	*VE*	BN		11326	(11206)	**VE**	E	*VE*	BN
11312	(11225)	**VE**	E	*VE*	BN		11327	(11236)	**VE**	E	*VE*	BN
11313	(11210)	**VE**	E	*VE*	BN		11328	(11274)	**VE**	E	*VE*	BN
11314	(11207)	**VE**	E	*VE*	BN		11329	(11243)	**VE**	E	*VE*	BN
11315	(11238)	**VE**	E	*VE*	BN		11330	(11249)	**VE**	E	*VE*	BN

OPEN FIRST

Mark 4. Air conditioned. Rebuilt from Open First by Bombardier Wakefield 2003–05. Separate area for 7 smokers, although smoking is no longer allowed. 46/– 1TD 1W. BT41 bogies. ETS 6X.

Lot No. 31046 Metro-Cammell 1989–92. 42.1 t.

11401	(11214)	**VE**	E	*VE*	BN		11407	(11256)	**VE**	E	*VE*	BN
11402	(11216)	**VE**	E	*VE*	BN		11408	(11218)	**VE**	E	*VE*	BN
11403	(11258)	**VE**	E	*VE*	BN		11409	(11262)	**VE**	E	*VE*	BN
11404	(11202)	**VE**	E	*VE*	BN		11410	(11260)	**VE**	E	*VE*	BN
11405	(11204)	**VE**	E	*VE*	BN		11411	(11240)	**VE**	E	*VE*	BN
11406	(11205)	**VE**	E	*VE*	BN		11412	(11209)	**VE**	E	*VE*	BN

11413	(11212)	**VE**	E	*VE*	BN	11422	(11232)	**VE**	E	*VE*	BN
11414	(11246)	**VE**	E	*VE*	BN	11423	(11230)	**VE**	E	*VE*	BN
11415	(11208)	**VE**	E	*VE*	BN	11424	(11239)	**VE**	E	*VE*	BN
11416	(11254)	**VE**	E	*VE*	BN	11425	(11234)	**VE**	E	*VE*	BN
11417	(11226)	**VE**	E	*VE*	BN	11426	(11252)	**VE**	E	*VE*	BN
11418	(11222)	**VE**	E	*VE*	BN	11427	(11200)	**VE**	E	*VE*	BN
11419	(11250)	**VE**	E	*VE*	BN	11428	(11233)	**VE**	E	*VE*	BN
11420	(11242)	**VE**	E	*VE*	BN	11429	(11275)	**VE**	E	*VE*	BN
11421	(11220)	**VE**	E	*VE*	BN	11430	(11248)	**VE**	E	*VE*	BN

OPEN FIRST

Mark 4. Air conditioned. Converted from Kitchen Buffet Standard with new interior by Bombardier Wakefield 2005. 46/– 1T. BT41 bogies. ETS 6X.

Lot No. 31046 Metro-Cammell 1989–92. 41.3 t.

11998	(10314)	**VE**	E	*VE*	BN		11999	(10316)	**VE**	E	*VE*	BN

OPEN STANDARD

Mark 3A. Air conditioned. All refurbished with modified seat backs and new layout and further refurbished with new seat trim. –/76 2T († –/70 2T 1W, t –/72 2T, z –/70 1TD 1T 2W). BT10 bogies. d. ETS 6X.

*   Further refurbished with more unidirectional seating and one toilet removed. –/80 1T.

§   Sleeper day coaches fitted with former HST First Class seats to a 2+1 layout and effectively unclassified. –/45(+2) 2T 1W.

s   Refurbished Sleeper day coaches fitted with new Transcal seating to a 2+2 layout and a universal access toilet. –/65 1TD 1W.

12170/171 were converted from Open Composites 11909/910, formerly Open Firsts 11009/010.

12005–167. Lot No. 30877 Derby 1975–77. 34.3 t.
12170/171. Lot No. 30878 Derby 1975–76. 34.3 t.

12005	*	**GA**	P	*GA*	NC	12031	*	**GA**	P	*GA*	NC
12009	*	**GA**	P	*GA*	NC	12032	*	**GA**	P	*GA*	NC
12011		**VT**	P		LA	12034	*	**GA**	P	*GA*	NC
12012	*	**GA**	P	*GA*	NC	12035	*	**GA**	P	*GA*	NC
12013	*	**GA**	P	*GA*	NC	12036	†	**CM**	AV	*CR*	AL
12015	*	**GA**	P	*GA*	NC	12037	*	**GA**	P	*GA*	NC
12016	*	**GA**	P	*GA*	NC	12040	*	**GA**	P	*GA*	NC
12017	t	**CM**	AV	*CR*	AL	12041	*	**GA**	P	*GA*	NC
12019	*	**GA**	P	*GA*	NC	12042	*	**GA**	P	*GA*	NC
12021	*	**GA**	P	*GA*	NC	12043	†	**CM**	AV	*CR*	AL
12024	*	**GA**	P	*GA*	NC	12046	*	**GA**	P	*GA*	NC
12026	*	**GA**	P	*GA*	NC	12047	z	**V**	DR		BH
12027	*	**GA**	P	*GA*	NC	12049	*	**GA**	P	*GA*	NC
12030	*	**GA**	P	*GA*	NC	12051	*	**GA**	P	*GA*	NC

12054	†	**CM**	AV	*CR*	AL	12114	*	**GA**	P	*GA*	NC
12056	*	**GA**	P	*GA*	NC	12115	*	**GA**	P	*GA*	NC
12057	*	**GA**	P	*GA*	NC	12116	*	**GA**	P	*GA*	NC
12058		**V**	AV		LM	12118	*	**GA**	P	*GA*	NC
12060	*	**GA**	P	*GA*	NC	12119	t	**CM**	AV	*CR*	AL
12061	*	**GA**	P	*GA*	NC	12120	*	**GA**	P	*GA*	NC
12062	*	**GA**	P	*GA*	NC	12122	z	**VT**	P		LA
12063		**1**	DR		BH	12125	*	**GA**	P	*GA*	NC
12064	*	**GA**	P	*GA*	NC	12126	*	**GA**	P	*GA*	NC
12065		**1**	DR		BH	12129	*	**GA**	P	*GA*	NC
12066	*	**GA**	P	*GA*	NC	12130	*	**GA**	P	*GA*	NC
12067	*	**GA**	P	*GA*	NC	12132	*	**GA**	P	*GA*	NC
12073	*	**GA**	P	*GA*	NC	12133		**VT**	P		LA
12078		**VT**	P		LA	12134		**V**	DR		BH
12079	*	**GA**	P	*GA*	NC	12137	*	**GA**	P	*GA*	NC
12081	*	**GA**	P	*GA*	NC	12138		**VT**	P		LA
12082	*	**GA**	P	*GA*	NC	12139	*	**GA**	P	*GA*	NC
12084	*	**GA**	P	*GA*	NC	12141	*	**GA**	P	*GA*	NC
12087	†	**V**	DR		BH	12142	s	**GW**	P	*GW*	PZ
12089	*	**GA**	P	*GA*	NC	12143	*	**GA**	P	*GA*	NC
12090	*	**GA**	P	*GA*	NC	12146	*	**GA**	P	*GA*	NC
12091	*	**GA**	P	*GA*	NC	12147	*	**GA**	P	*GA*	NC
12093	*	**GA**	P	*GA*	NC	12148	*	**GA**	P	*GA*	NC
12094		**CM**	AV	*CR*	AL	12150	*	**GA**	P	*GA*	NC
12097	*	**GA**	P	*GA*	NC	12151	*	**GA**	P	*GA*	NC
12098	*	**GA**	P	*GA*	NC	12153	*	**GA**	P	*GA*	NC
12099	*	**GA**	P	*GA*	NC	12154	*	**GA**	P	*GA*	NC
12100	§	**FD**	P	*GW*	PZ	12159	*	**GA**	P	*GA*	NC
12103	*	**GA**	P	*GA*	NC	12161	§	**FD**	P	*GW*	PZ
12104		**V**	AV		LM	12164	*	**GA**	P	*GA*	NC
12105	*	**GA**	P	*GA*	NC	12165		**V**	AV		LM
12107	*	**GA**	P	*GA*	NC	12166	*	**GA**	P	*GA*	NC
12108	*	**GA**	P	*GA*	NC	12167	*	**GA**	P	*GA*	NC
12109	*	**GA**	P	*GA*	NC	12170	*	**GA**	P	*GA*	NC
12110	*	**GA**	P	*GA*	NC	12171	*	**GA**	P	*GA*	NC
12111	*	**GA**	P	*GA*	NC						

OPEN STANDARD

Mark 3A (†) or Mark 3B. Air conditioned. Converted from Mark 3A or 3B Open First. Fitted with new Grammer seating. –/70 2T 1W. BT10 bogies. d. ETS 6X.

12176–181/185. Mark 3B. Lot No. 30982 Derby 1985. 38.5 t.
12182–184. Mark 3A. Lot No. 30878 Derby 1975–76. 38.5 t.

12176	(11064)	**AW**	AV	*AW*	CF
12177	(11065)	**AW**	AV	*AW*	CF
12178	(11071)	**AW**	AV	*AW*	CF
12179	(11083)	**AW**	AV	*AW*	CF
12180	(11084)	**AW**	AV	*AW*	CF
12181	(11086)	**AW**	AV	*AW*	CF

12182 (11013)	†	**AW**	AV	*AW*	CF
12183 (11027)	†	**AW**	AV	*AW*	CF
12184 (11044)	†	**AW**	AV	*AW*	CF
12185 (11089)		**AW**	AV	*AW*	CF

OPEN STANDARD (END)

Mark 4. Air conditioned. Rebuilt with new interior by Bombardier Wakefield 2003–05. Separate area for 26 smokers, although smoking is no longer allowed. –/76 1T. BT41 bogies. ETS 6X.

12232 was converted from the original 12405.

12200–231. Lot No. 31047 Metro-Cammell 1989–91. 39.5 t.
12232. Lot No. 31049 Metro-Cammell 1989–92. 39.5 t.

12200	**VE**	E	*VE*	BN		12217	**VE**	E	*VE*	BN
12201	**VE**	E	*VE*	BN		12218	**VE**	E	*VE*	BN
12202	**VE**	E	*VE*	BN		12219	**VE**	E	*VE*	BN
12203	**VE**	E	*VE*	BN		12220	**VE**	E	*VE*	BN
12204	**VE**	E	*VE*	BN		12222	**VE**	E	*VE*	BN
12205	**VE**	E	*VE*	BN		12223	**VE**	E	*VE*	BN
12207	**VE**	E	*VE*	BN		12224	**VE**	E	*VE*	BN
12208	**VE**	E	*VE*	BN		12225	**VE**	E	*VE*	BN
12209	**VE**	E	*VE*	BN		12226	**VE**	E	*VE*	BN
12210	**VE**	E	*VE*	BN		12227	**VE**	E	*VE*	BN
12211	**VE**	E	*VE*	BN		12228	**VE**	E	*VE*	BN
12212	**VE**	E	*VE*	BN		12229	**VE**	E	*VE*	BN
12213	**VE**	E	*VE*	BN		12230	**VE**	E	*VE*	BN
12214	**VE**	E	*VE*	BN		12231	**VE**	E	*VE*	BN
12215	**VE**	E	*VE*	BN		12232	**VE**	E	*VE*	BN
12216	**VE**	E	*VE*	BN						

OPEN STANDARD (DISABLED)

Mark 4. Air conditioned. Rebuilt with new interior by Bombardier Wakefield 2003–05. –/68 2W 1TD. BT41 bogies. ETS 6X.

12331 was converted from Open Standard 12531.

12300–330. Lot No. 31048 Metro-Cammell 1989–91. 39.4 t.
12331. Lot No. 31049 Metro-Cammell 1989–92. 39.4 t.

12300	**VE**	E	*VE*	BN		12312	**VE**	E	*VE*	BN
12301	**VE**	E	*VE*	BN		12313	**VE**	E	*VE*	BN
12302	**VE**	E	*VE*	BN		12315	**VE**	E	*VE*	BN
12303	**VE**	E	*VE*	BN		12316	**VE**	E	*VE*	BN
12304	**VE**	E	*VE*	BN		12317	**VE**	E	*VE*	BN
12305	**VE**	E	*VE*	BN		12318	**VE**	E	*VE*	BN
12307	**VE**	E	*VE*	BN		12319	**VE**	E	*VE*	BN
12308	**VE**	E	*VE*	BN		12320	**VE**	E	*VE*	BN
12309	**VE**	E	*VE*	BN		12321	**VE**	E	*VE*	BN
12310	**VE**	E	*VE*	BN		12322	**VE**	E	*VE*	BN
12311	**VE**	E	*VE*	BN		12323	**VE**	E	*VE*	BN

12324	**VE**	E	*VE*	BN	12328	**VE**	E	*VE*	BN
12325	**VE**	E	*VE*	BN	12329	**VE**	E	*VE*	BN
12326	**VE**	E	*VE*	BN	12330	**VE**	E	*VE*	BN
12327	**VE**	E	*VE*	BN	12331	**VE**	E	*VE*	BN

OPEN STANDARD

Mark 4. Air conditioned. Rebuilt with new interior by Bombardier Wakefield 2003–05. –/76 1T. BT41 bogies. ETS 6X.

12405 is the second coach to carry that number. It was built from the bodyshell originally intended for 12221. The original 12405 is now 12232.

Lot No. 31049 Metro-Cammell 1989–92. 40.8 t.

12400	**VE**	E	*VE*	BN	12443	**VE**	E	*VE*	BN
12401	**VE**	E	*VE*	BN	12444	**VE**	E	*VE*	BN
12402	**VE**	E	*VE*	BN	12445	**VE**	E	*VE*	BN
12403	**VE**	E	*VE*	BN	12446	**VE**	E	*VE*	BN
12404	**VE**	E	*VE*	BN	12447	**VE**	E	*VE*	BN
12405	**VE**	E	*VE*	BN	12448	**VE**	E	*VE*	BN
12406	**VE**	E	*VE*	BN	12449	**VE**	E	*VE*	BN
12407	**VE**	E	*VE*	BN	12450	**VE**	E	*VE*	BN
12409	**VE**	E	*VE*	BN	12452	**VE**	E	*VE*	BN
12410	**VE**	E	*VE*	BN	12453	**VE**	E	*VE*	BN
12411	**VE**	E	*VE*	BN	12454	**VE**	E	*VE*	BN
12414	**VE**	E	*VE*	BN	12455	**VE**	E	*VE*	BN
12415	**VE**	E	*VE*	BN	12456	**VE**	E	*VE*	BN
12417	**VE**	E	*VE*	BN	12457	**VE**	E	*VE*	BN
12419	**VE**	E	*VE*	BN	12458	**VE**	E	*VE*	BN
12420	**VE**	E	*VE*	BN	12459	**VE**	E	*VE*	BN
12421	**VE**	E	*VE*	BN	12460	**VE**	E	*VE*	BN
12422	**VE**	E	*VE*	BN	12461	**VE**	E	*VE*	BN
12423	**VE**	E	*VE*	BN	12462	**VE**	E	*VE*	BN
12424	**VE**	E	*VE*	BN	12463	**VE**	E	*VE*	BN
12425	**VE**	E	*VE*	BN	12464	**VE**	E	*VE*	BN
12426	**VE**	E	*VE*	BN	12465	**VE**	E	*VE*	BN
12427	**VE**	E	*VE*	BN	12466	**VE**	E	*VE*	BN
12428	**VE**	E	*VE*	BN	12467	**VE**	E	*VE*	BN
12429	**VE**	E	*VE*	BN	12468	**VE**	E	*VE*	BN
12430	**VE**	E	*VE*	BN	12469	**VE**	E	*VE*	BN
12431	**VE**	E	*VE*	BN	12470	**VE**	E	*VE*	BN
12432	**VE**	E	*VE*	BN	12471	**VE**	E	*VE*	BN
12433	**VE**	E	*VE*	BN	12472	**VE**	E	*VE*	BN
12434	**VE**	E	*VE*	BN	12473	**VE**	E	*VE*	BN
12436	**VE**	E	*VE*	BN	12474	**VE**	E	*VE*	BN
12437	**VE**	E	*VE*	BN	12476	**VE**	E	*VE*	BN
12438	**VE**	E	*VE*	BN	12477	**VE**	E	*VE*	BN
12439	**VE**	E	*VE*	BN	12478	**VE**	E	*VE*	BN
12440	**VE**	E	*VE*	BN	12480	**VE**	E	*VE*	BN
12441	**VE**	E	*VE*	BN	12481	**VE**	E	*VE*	BN
12442	**VE**	E	*VE*	BN	12483	**VE**	E	*VE*	BN

12484	**VE**	E	*VE*	BN	12518	**VE**	E	*VE*	BN
12485	**VE**	E	*VE*	BN	12519	**VE**	E	*VE*	BN
12486	**VE**	E	*VE*	BN	12520	**VE**	E	*VE*	BN
12488	**VE**	E	*VE*	BN	12522	**VE**	E	*VE*	BN
12489	**VE**	E	*VE*	BN	12526	**VE**	E	*VE*	BN
12513	**VE**	E	*VE*	BN	12533	**VE**	E	*VE*	BN
12514	**VE**	E	*VE*	BN	12534	**VE**	E	*VE*	BN
12515	**VE**	E	*VE*	BN	12538	**VE**	E	*VE*	BN

OPEN STANDARD

Mark 3A. Air conditioned. Rebuilt 2011–13 and fitted with sliding plug doors and toilets with retention tanks. Original InterCity 70 seating retained but mainly arranged around tables. –/72(+6) or * –/69(+4) 1T. BT10 bogies. ETS 6X.

12602–609/614–616/618/620. Lot No. 30877 Derby 1975–77. 36.2 t (* 37.1 t).
12601/613/617–619/621/623/625/627. Lot No. 30878 Derby 1975–76. 36.2 t (* 37.1 t).

12602	(12072)			**CM**	AV	*CR*	AL
12603	(12053)	*	**CM**	AV	*CR*	AL
12604	(12131)		**CM**	AV	*CR*	AL
12605	(11040)	*	**CM**	AV	*CR*	AL
12606	(12048)		**CM**	AV	*CR*	AL
12607	(12038)	*	**CM**	AV	*CR*	AL
12608	(12069)		**CM**	AV	*CR*	AL
12609	(12014)	*	**CM**	AV	*CR*	AL
12610	(12117)		**CM**	AV	*CR*	AL
12613	(11042, 12173)	*	**CM**	AV	*CR*	AL
12614	(12145)		**CM**	AV	*CR*	AL
12615	(12059)	*	**CM**	AV	*CR*	AL
12616	(12127)		**CM**	AV	*CR*	AL
12617	(11052, 12174)	*	**CM**	AV	*CR*	AL
12618	(11008, 12169)		**CM**	AV	*CR*	AL
12619	(11058, 12175)	*	**CM**	AV	*CR*	AL
12620	(12124)		**CM**	AV	*CR*	AL
12621	(11046)	*	**CM**	AV	*CR*	AL
12623	(11019)	*	**CM**	AV	*CR*	AL
12625	(11030)	*	**CM**	AV	*CR*	AL
12627	(11054)	*	**CM**	AV	*CR*	AL

CORRIDOR FIRST

Mark 1. Seven compartments. 42/– 2T. B4 bogies. ETS 3.

Lot No. 30381 Swindon 1959. 33 t.

13227	x	**CH**	LS		CL	13230	xk	**M**	SP	*SP*	BO
13229	xk	**M**	SP	*SP*	BO						

OPEN FIRST

Mark 1 converted from Corridor First in 2013–14. 42/– 2T. Commonwealth bogies. ETS 3.

Lot No. 30667 Swindon 1962. 35 t.

13320 x   **M**   WC *WC*   CS   ANNA

CORRIDOR FIRST

Mark 2A. Seven compartments. Pressure ventilated. 42/– 2T. B4 bogies. ETS 4.

Lot No. 30774 Derby 1968. 33 t.

13440 v   **M**   WC *WC*   CS

SLEEPER SEATED CARRIAGE

Under construction by CAF for Caledonian Sleeper for delivery 2017–18. Full details awaited.

15001	CA	15007	CA
15002	CA	15008	CA
15003	CA	15009	CA
15004	CA	15010	CA
15005	CA	15011	CA
15006	CA		

SLEEPER LOUNGE CAR

Under construction by CAF for Caledonian Sleeper for delivery 2017–18. Full details awaited.

15101	CA	15106	CA
15102	CA	15107	CA
15103	CA	15108	CA
15104	CA	15109	CA
15105	CA	15110	CA

SLEEPING CAR (FULLY ACCESSIBLE)

Under construction by CAF for Caledonian Sleeper for delivery 2017–18. Full details awaited.

15201	CA	15208	CA
15202	CA	15209	CA
15203	CA	15210	CA
15204	CA	15211	CA
15205	CA	15212	CA
15206	CA	15213	CA
15207	CA	15214	CA

SLEEPING CAR

Under construction by CAF for Caledonian Sleeper for delivery 2017–18. Full details awaited.

15301	CA		15321	CA
15302	CA		15322	CA
15303	CA		15323	CA
15304	CA		15324	CA
15305	CA		15325	CA
15306	CA		15326	CA
15307	CA		15327	CA
15308	CA		15328	CA
15309	CA		15329	CA
15310	CA		15330	CA
15311	CA		15331	CA
15312	CA		15332	CA
15313	CA		15333	CA
15314	CA		15334	CA
15315	CA		15335	CA
15316	CA		15336	CA
15317	CA		15337	CA
15318	CA		15338	CA
15319	CA		15339	CA
15320	CA		15340	CA

CORRIDOR BRAKE FIRST

Mark 1. Four compartments. 24/– 1T. Commonwealth bogies. ETS 2.

Lot No. 30668 Swindon 1961. 36 t.

17018	(14018)	v	**CH**	VT	*VT*	TM	BOTAURUS

CORRIDOR BRAKE FIRST

Mark 2A. Four compartments. Pressure ventilated. 24/– 1T. B4 bogies. ETS 4.

17080/090 were numbered 35516/503 for a time when declassified.

17056. Lot No. 30775 Derby 1967–68. 32 t.
17080–102. Lot No. 30786 Derby 1968. 32 t.

17056	(14056)		**CC**	LS	*LS*	CL
17080	(14080)		**PC**	LS		CL
17090	(14090)	v	**CH**	VT		TM
17102	(14102)		**M**	WC	*WC*	CS

COUCHETTE/GENERATOR COACH

Mark 2B. Formerly part of Royal Train. Converted from Corridor Brake First built 1969. Consists of luggage accommodation, guard's compartment, 350 kW diesel generator and staff sleeping accommodation. Pressure ventilated. B5 bogies. ETS 5X (when generator not in use). ETS index ?? (when generator in use).

Lot No. 30888 Wolverton 1977. 46 t.

17105 (14105, 2905)		**RB**	RV	*RV*	EH

CORRIDOR BRAKE FIRST

Mark 2D. Four compartments. Air conditioned. Stones equipment. 24/– 1T. B4 Bogies. ETS 5.

Lot No. 30823 Derby 1971–72. 33.5 t.

17159 (14159)	d	**DS**	DR	*DR*	KM	
17167 (14167)		**VN**	BE	*NB*	CP	MOW COP

OPEN BRAKE UNCLASSIFIED

Mark 3B. Air conditioned. Fitted with hydraulic handbrake. Used as Sleeper day coaches. Fitted with former HST First Class seats to a 2+1 layout (effectively unclassified). 36/– 1T. BT10 bogies. pg. d. ETS 5X.

Lot No. 30990 Derby 1986. 35.81 t.

17173	**GW**	P	*GW*	PZ		17175	**GW**	P	*GW*	PZ
17174	**GW**	P	*GW*	PZ					

CORRIDOR STANDARD

Mark 1. –/48 2T. Eight Compartments. Commonwealth bogies. ETS 4.

Currently in use as part of the Harry Potter World exhibition at Leavesden, near Watford.

Lot No. 30685 Derby 1961–62. 36 t.

18756 (25756)	x	**M**	WC		SH

CORRIDOR BRAKE COMPOSITE

Mark 1. There are two variants depending upon whether the Standard Class compartments have armrests. Each vehicle has two First Class and three Standard Class compartments. 12/18 2T (* 12/24 2T). Commonwealth bogies. ETS 2.

21241–245. Lot No. 30669 Swindon 1961–62. 36 t.
21256. Lot No. 30731 Derby 1963. 37 t.
21266–272. Lot No. 30732 Derby 1964. 37 t.

21241	x	**M**	SP	*SP*	BO		21266	x*	**M**	WC	*WC*	CS
21245	x	**M**	RV	*RV*	EH		21269	*	**CC**	RV	*RV*	EH
21256	x	**M**	WC	*WC*	CS		21272	x*	**CH**	RV	*RV*	EH

CORRIDOR BRAKE STANDARD

Mark 1. Four compartments. –/24 1T. ETS 2.

35185. Lot No. 30427 Wolverton 1959. B4 bogies. 33 t.
35459. Lot No. 30721 Wolverton 1963. Commonwealth bogies. 37 t.

35185	x	**M**	SP	*SP*	BO
35459	x	**M**	WC	*WC*	CS

CORRIDOR BRAKE GENERATOR STANDARD

Mark 1. Four compartments. –/24 1T. Fitted with an ETS generator in the former luggage compartment. ETS 2 (when generator not in use). ETS index ?? (when generator in use).

Lot No. 30721 Wolverton 1963. Commonwealth bogies. 37 t.

35469	x	**CH**	RV	*RV*	EH

BRAKE/POWER KITCHEN

Mark 2C. Pressure ventilated. Converted from Corridor Brake First (declassified to Corridor Brake Standard) built 1970. Converted by West Coast Railway Company 2000–01. Consists of 60 kVA generator, guard's compartment and electric kitchen. B5 bogies. ETS ? (when generator not in use). ETS index ?? (when generator in use).

Non-standard livery: British Racing Green with gold lining.

Lot No. 30796 Derby 1969–70. 32.5 t.

35511	(14130, 17130)		**0**	LS		CL

KITCHEN CAR

Mark 1. Converted 1989/2006 from Kitchen Buffet Unclassified. Buffet and seating area replaced with additional kitchen and food preparation area. Fluorescent lighting. Commonwealth bogies. ETS 2X.

Lot No. 30628 Pressed Steel 1960–61. 39 t.

80041	(1690)	x	**M**	RV		EH
80042	(1646)		**BG**	RV	*RV*	EH

DRIVING BRAKE VAN (110 mph)

Mark 3B. Air conditioned. T4 bogies. dg. ETS 5X. Driving Brake Vans converted for use by Network Rail can be found in the Service Stock section of this book.

Non-standard livery: 82146 All over silver with DB logos.

Lot No. 31042 Derby 1988. 45.2 t.

82101	**V**	DR		ZA	82123	**V**	AV	LM
82102	**GA**	P	*GA*	NC	82126	**VT**	P		ZA
82103	**GA**	P	*GA*	NC	82127	**GA**	P	*GA*	NC
82105	**GA**	P	*GA*	NC	82132	**GA**	P	*GA*	NC
82106	**V**	AV		LB	82133	**GA**	P	*GA*	NC
82107	**GA**	P	*GA*	NC	82136	**GA**	P	*GA*	NC
82110	**V**	AV		LM	82137	**V**	AV		LM
82112	**GA**	P	*GA*	NC	82138	**V**	AV		LM
82113	**V**	AV		BO	82139	**GA**	P	*GA*	NC
82114	**GA**	P	*GA*	NC	82141	**V**	AV		LM
82115	**B**	NR		ZN	82143	**GA**	P	*GA*	NC
82116	**V**	AV		LM	82146	**0**	DB	*DB*	TO
82118	**GA**	P	*GA*	NC	82148	**V**	AV		LM
82120	**V**	AV		LM	82150	**V**	AV		LM
82121	**GA**	P	*GA*	NC	82152	**GA**	P	*GA*	NC
82122	**V**	AV		LM					

DRIVING BRAKE VAN (140 mph)

Mark 4. Air conditioned. Swiss-built (SIG) bogies. dg. ETS 6X.

Advertising livery: 82205 Flying Scotsman (red, white & purple).

Lot No. 31043 Metro-Cammell 1988. 43.5 t.

82200	**VE**	E	*VE*	BN	82216	**VE**	E	*VE*	BN
82201	**VE**	E	*VE*	BN	82217	**VE**	E	*VE*	BN
82202	**VE**	E	*VE*	BN	82218	**VE**	E	*VE*	BN
82203	**VE**	E	*VE*	BN	82219	**VE**	E	*VE*	BN
82204	**VE**	E	*VE*	BN	82220	**VE**	E	*VE*	BN
82205	**AL**	E	*VE*	BN	82222	**VE**	E	*VE*	BN
82206	**VE**	E	*VE*	BN	82223	**VE**	E	*VE*	BN
82207	**VE**	E	*VE*	BN	82224	**VE**	E	*VE*	BN
82208	**VE**	E	*VE*	BN	82225	**VE**	E	*VE*	BN
82209	**VE**	E	*VE*	BN	82226	**VE**	E	*VE*	BN
82210	**VE**	E	*VE*	BN	82227	**VE**	E	*VE*	BN
82211	**VE**	E	*VE*	BN	82228	**VE**	E	*VE*	BN
82212	**VE**	E	*VE*	BN	82229	**VE**	E	*VE*	BN
82213	**VE**	E	*VE*	BN	82230	**VE**	E	*VE*	BN
82214	**VE**	E	*VE*	BN	82231	**VE**	E	*VE*	BN
82215	**VE**	E	*VE*	BN					

DRIVING BRAKE VAN (110 mph)

Mark 3B. Air conditioned. T4 bogies. dg. ETS 6X.

82301–305 originally converted 2008. 82306–308 converted 2011–12. 82309 converted 2013.

g Fitted with a diesel generator for use while stabled in terminal stations or at depots. 48.5 t.

Lot No. 31042 Derby 1988. 45.2 t.

82301	(82117)	g	**CM**	AV	CR	AL
82302	(82151)	g	**CM**	AV	CR	AL
82303	(82135)	g	**CM**	AV	CR	AL
82304	(82130)	g	**CM**	AV	CR	AL
82305	(82134)	g	**CM**	AV	CR	AL
82306	(82144)		**AW**	AV	AW	CF
82307	(82131)		**AW**	AV	AW	CF
82308	(82108)		**AW**	AV	AW	CF
82309	(82104)	g	**CM**	AV	CR	AL

GANGWAYED BRAKE VAN (100 mph)

Mark 1. Short frame (57 ft). Load 10 t. Adapted 199? for use as Brake Luggage Van. Guard's compartment retained and former baggage area adapted for secure stowage of passengers' luggage. B4 bogies. 100 mph. ETS 1X.

Lot No. 30162 Pressed Steel 1956–57. 30.5 t.

92904	(80867, 99554)	**VN**	BE	NB	CP

HIGH SECURITY GENERAL UTILITY VAN

Mark 1. Short frame (57 ft). Load 14 t. Modified with new floors, three roller shutter doors per side and the end doors removed. Commonwealth bogies. ETS 0X.

Lot No. 30616 Pressed Steel 1959–60. 32 t.

94225	(86849, 93849)	**M**	WC	WC	CS

GENERAL UTILITY VAN (100 mph)

Mark 1. Short frame (57 ft). Load 14 t. Screw couplers. Adapted 2013/2010 for use as a water carrier with 3000 gallon capacity. ETS 0.

Non-standard livery: 96100 GWR Brown.

96100. Lot No. 30565 Pressed Steel 1959. 30 t. B5 bogies.
96175. Lot No. 30403 York/Glasgow 1958–60. 32 t. Commonwealth bogies.

96100	(86734, 93734)	x	**0**	VT	*VT*		TM
96175	(86628, 93628)	x	**M**	WC	*WC*		CS

KITCHEN CAR

Mark 1 converted from Corridor First in 2008 with staff accommodation. Commonwealth bogies. ETS 3.

Lot No. 30667 Swindon 1961. 35 t.

99316	(13321)	x	**M**	WC	*WC*		CS

BUFFET STANDARD

Mark 1 converted from Open Standard in 2013 by the removal of two seating bays and fitting of a buffet. –/48 2T. Commonwealth bogies. ETS 4.

Lot No. 30646 Wolverton 1961. 36 t.

99318	(4912)	x	**M**	WC	*WC*		CS

KITCHEN CAR

Mark 1 converted from Corridor Standard in 2011 with staff accommodation. Commonwealth bogies. ETS 3.

Lot No. 30685 Derby 1961–62. 34 t.

99712	(18893)	x	**M**	WC	*WC*		CS

OPEN STANDARD

Mark 1 Corridor Standard rebuilt in 1997 as Open Standard using components from 4936. –/64 2T. Commonwealth bogies. ETS 4.

Lot No. 30685 Derby 1961–62. 36 t.

99722	(25806, 18806)	x	**M**	WC	*WC*		CS

NNR REGISTERED CARRIAGES

These carriages are permitted to operate on the national railway network only between Sheringham and Cromer as an extension of North Norfolk Railway (NNR) "North Norfolkman" services. Only NNR coaches currently registered for use on the national railway network are listed.

KITCHEN BUFFET STANDARD

Mark 1. Built as Unclassified Restaurant. Rebuilt with Buffet Counter and seating reduced. –/23. Commonwealth bogies. Lot No. 30632 Swindon 1960–61. 39 t.

1969   v   **CC**   NN   *WC*   NO

OPEN FIRST

Mark 1. 42/–. Commonwealth bogies. Lot No. 30697 Swindon 1962–63. 36 t.

3116   v   **CC**   NN   *WC*   NO

OPEN STANDARD

Mark 1. –/48 2T. BR Mark 1 bogies. Lot No. 30121 Eastleigh 1953–55. 32 t.

4372   v   **CC**   NN   *WC*   NO

GANGWAYED BRAKE VAN

Mark 1. Short frame (57 ft). Now fitted with a kitchen. BR Mark 1 bogies. Lot No. 30224 Cravens 1955–56. 31.5 t.

81033   v   **CC**   NN   *WC*   NO

NYMR REGISTERED CARRIAGES

These carriages are permitted to operate on the national railway network but may only be used to convey fare-paying passengers between Middlesbrough and Whitby on the Esk Valley branch as an extension of North Yorkshire Moors Railway services between Pickering and Grosmont. Only NYMR coaches currently registered for use on the national railway network are listed.

RESTAURANT FIRST

Mark 1. 24/–. Commonwealth bogies. Lot No. 30633 Swindon 1961. 42.5 t.

324	x	**PC**	NY	*NY*	NY	JOS de CRAU

BUFFET STANDARD

Mark 1. –/44 2T. Commonwealth bogies.
Lot No. 30520 Wolverton 1960. 38 t.

1823	v	**M**	NY	*NY*	NY

OPEN STANDARD

Mark 1. –/64 2T (* –/60 2W 2T, † –/60 3W 1T). BR Mark 1 bogies.

3798/3801. Lot No. 30079 York 1953. 33 t.
3860/72. Lot No. 30080 York 1954. 33 t.
3948. Lot No. 30086 Eastleigh 1954–55. 33 t.
4198/4252. Lot No. 30172 York 1956. 33 t.
4286/90. Lot No. 30207 BRCW 1956. 33 t.
4455. Lot No. 30226 BRCW 1957. 33 t.

3798	v	**M**	NY	*NY*	NY		4198	v	**CC**	NY	*NY*	NY
3801	v	**CC**	NY	*NY*	NY		4252	v*	**CC**	NY	*NY*	NY
3860	v*	**M**	NY	*NY*	NY		4286	v	**CC**	NY	*NY*	NY
3872	v†	**BG**	NY	*NY*	NY		4290	v	**M**	NY	*NY*	NY
3948	v	**CC**	NY	*NY*	NY		4455	v	**CC**	NY	*NY*	NY

OPEN STANDARD

Mark 1. –/48 2T. BR Mark 1 bogies.

4786. Lot No. 30376 York 1957. 33 t.
4817. Lot No. 30473 BRCW 1959. 33 t.

4786	v	**CH**	NY	*NY*	NY		4817	v	**M**	NY	*NY*	NY

OPEN STANDARD

Mark 1. Later vehicles built with Commonwealth bogies. –/64 2T.
Lot No. 30690 Wolverton 1961–62. Aluminium window frames. 37 t.

4990	v	**M**	NY	*NY*	NY		5029	v	**CH**	NY	*NY*	NY
5000	v	**M**	NY	*NY*	NY								

OPEN BRAKE STANDARD

Mark 1. –/39 1T. BR Mark 1 bogies.

Lot No. 30170 Doncaster 1956. 34 t.

9225	v	**M**	NY	*NY*	NY	9274	v	**M**	NY	*NY*	NY
9267	v	**BG**	NY	*NY*	NY						

CORRIDOR COMPOSITE

Mark 1. 24/18 1T. BR Mark 1 bogies.

15745. Lot No. 30179 Metro Cammell 1956. 36 t.
16156. Lot No. 30665 Derby 1961. 36 t.

15745	v	**M**	NY	*NY*	NY	16156	v	**CC**	NY	*NY*	NY

CORRIDOR BRAKE COMPOSITE

Mark 1. Two First Class and three Standard Class compartments. 12/18 2T. BR Mark 1 bogies.

Lot No. 30185 Metro Cammell 1956. 36 t.

21100	v	**CC**	NY	*NY*	NY

CORRIDOR BRAKE STANDARD

Mark 1. –/24 1T. BR Mark 1 bogies.

Lot No. 30233 Gloucester 1957. 35 t.

35089	v	**CC**	NY	*NY*	NY

PULLMAN BRAKE THIRD

Built 1928 by Metropolitan Carriage & Wagon Company. –/30. Gresley bogies. 37.5 t.

232	v	**PC**	NY	*NY*	NY	CAR No. 79

PULLMAN KITCHEN FIRST

Built by Metro-Cammell 1960–61 for East Coast Main Line services. 20/– 2T. Commonwealth bogies. 41.2 t.

318	x	**PC**	NY	*NY*	NY	ROBIN

PULLMAN PARLOUR FIRST

Built by Metro-Cammell 1960–61 for East Coast Main Line services. 29/– 2T. Commonwealth bogies. 38.5 t.

328	x	**PC**	NY	*NY*	NY	OPAL

2.2. HIGH SPEED TRAIN TRAILER CARS

HSTs consist of a number of trailer cars (usually between six and nine) with a power car at each end. All trailers are classified Mark 3 and have BT10 bogies with disc brakes and central door locking. Heating is by a 415 V three-phase supply and vehicles have air conditioning. Maximum speed is 125 mph.

The trailer cars have one standard bodyshell for both First and Standard Class, thus facilitating easy conversion from one class to the other. As built all cars had facing seating around tables with Standard Class carriages having nine bays of seats per side which did not line up with the eight windows per side. This created a new unwelcome trend in British rolling stock of seats not lining up with windows.

All vehicles underwent a mid-life refurbishment in the 1980s with Standard Class seating layouts revised to incorporate unidirectional seating in addition to facing, in a somewhat higgledy-piggledy layout where seats did not line up either side of the aisle.

A further refurbishment programme was completed in November 2000, with each Train Operating Company having a different scheme as follows:

Great Western Trains (later First Great Western). Green seat covers and extra partitions between seat bays.

Great North Eastern Railway. New ceiling lighting panels and brown seat covers. First Class vehicles had table lamps and imitation walnut plastic end panels.

Virgin CrossCountry. Green seat covers. Standard Class vehicles had four seats in the centre of each carriage replaced with a luggage stack. All have now passed to other operators.

Midland Mainline. Grey seat covers, redesigned seat squabs, side carpeting and two seats in the centre of each Standard Class carriage and one in First Class carriages replaced with a luggage stack.

Since then the remaining three operators of HSTs embarked on separate, and very different, refurbishment projects:

Midland Mainline was first to refurbish its vehicles a second time during 2003–04. This involved fitting new fluorescent and halogen ceiling lighting, although the original seats were retained in First and Standard Class, but with blue upholstery.

London St Pancras–Sheffield/Leeds and Nottingham services are now operated by **East Midlands Trains** and in late 2009 this operator embarked on another, less radical, refurbishment which included retention of the original seats but with red upholstery in Standard Class and blue in First Class. This programme was completed in 2010.

First Great Western (now **Great Western Railway**) started a major rebuild of its HST sets in late 2006, with the programme completed in 2008. With an increased fleet of 54 sets the new interiors feature new lighting and seating throughout. First Class seats have leather upholstery, and are made by Primarius UK. Standard Class seats are of high-back design by Grammer. A number of sets operate without a full buffet or kitchen car, instead using one of 19 TS vehicles converted to include a "mini buffet" counter for use on shorter distance services. During 2012 15 402xx or 407xx buffet vehicles were converted to Trailer Standards to make the rakes formed as 7-cars up to 8-cars. During 2014–15 further changes to the FGW sets included the conversion of one First Class carriage from each set to Standard Class.

GNER modernised its buffet cars with new corner bars in 2004 and at the same time each HST set was made up to 9-cars with an extra Standard Class vehicle added with a disabled person's toilet.

At the end of 2006 **GNER** embarked on a major rebuild of its sets, with the work being carried out at Wabtec, Doncaster. All vehicles have similar interiors to the Mark 4 "Mallard" fleet, with new Primarius seats throughout. The refurbishment of the 13 sets was completed by **National Express East Coast** in late 2009, these trains are now operated by **Virgin Trains East Coast**. VTEC refurbished its sets in 2015–16, with the same seats retained but with new upholstery, and leather in First Class.

Ten sets ex-Virgin CrossCountry, and some spare vehicles, were temporarily allocated to Midland Mainline for the interim service to Manchester during 2003–04 and had a facelift. Buffet cars were converted from TSB to TFKB and renumbered in the 408xx series. Most of these vehicles are now in use with Great Western Railway.

Open access operator **Grand Central** started operation in December 2007 with a new service from Sunderland to London King's Cross. This operator has three sets mostly using stock converted from loco-hauled Mark 3s. The seats in Standard Class have First Class spacing and in most vehicles are all facing. Increases in the number of passengers on its services has seen rakes lengthened from 5-cars to 6-cars – they can run as 7-cars at busy times.

CrossCountry reintroduced HSTs to the Cross-Country network from 2008. Five sets were refurbished at Wabtec, Doncaster principally for use on the Plymouth–Edinburgh route. Three of these sets use stock mostly converted from loco-hauled Mark 3s and two are sets ex-Midland Mainline. The interiors are similar to refurbished East Coast sets, although the seating layout is different and one toilet per carriage has been removed in favour of a luggage stack.

Operator Codes

Operator codes are shown in the heading before each set of vehicles. The first letter is always "T" for HST carriages, denoting a Trailer vehicle. The second letter denotes the passenger accommodation in that vehicle, for example "F" for First. "GS" denotes Guards accommodation and Standard Class seating. This is followed by catering provision, with "B" for buffet, and "K" for a kitchen and buffet:

TC	Trailer Composite	TFKB	Trailer Kitchen Buffet First
TCK	Trailer Composite Kitchen	TSB	Trailer Buffet Standard
TF	Trailer First	TS	Trailer Standard
TFB	Trailer Buffet First	TGS	Trailer Guard's Standard

TRAILER BUFFET STANDARD   TSB

19 vehicles converted at Laira 2009–10 from HST TSs for First Great Western. Refurbished with Grammer seating.

40101–119. For Lot No. details see TS. –/70 1T. 35.5 t.

40101	(42170)	**FD**	P	*GW*	LA
40102	(42223)	**FD**	P	*GW*	LA
40103	(42316)	**FD**	P	*GW*	LA
40104	(42254)	**FD**	P	*GW*	LA
40105	(42084)	**FD**	P	*GW*	LA
40106	(42162)	**FD**	P	*GW*	LA
40107	(42334)	**FD**	P	*GW*	LA
40108	(42314)	**FD**	P	*GW*	LA
40109	(42262)	**FD**	P	*GW*	LA
40110	(42187)	**FD**	P	*GW*	LA
40111	(42248)	**FD**	P	*GW*	LA
40112	(42336)	**FD**	P	*GW*	LA
40113	(42309)	**FD**	P	*GW*	LA
40114	(42086)	**FD**	P	*GW*	LA
40115	(42320)	**FD**	P	*GW*	LA
40116	(42147)	**FD**	P	*GW*	LA
40117	(42249)	**FD**	P	*GW*	LA
40118	(42338)	**FD**	P	*GW*	LA
40119	(42090)	**FD**	P	*GW*	LA

TRAILER BUFFET FIRST   TFB

Converted from TSB by fitting First Class seats. Renumbered from 404xx series by subtracting 200. All refurbished by First Great Western and fitted with Primarius leather seating. 23/–.

40204–221. Lot No. 30883 Derby 1976–77. 36.12 t.
40231. Lot No. 30899 Derby 1978–79. 36.12 t.

40204	**FD**	A	*GW*	LA		40210	**FD**	A	*GW*	LA
40205	**FD**	A	*GW*	LA		40221	**FD**	A	*GW*	LA
40207	**FD**	A	*GW*	LA		40231	**FD**	A	*GW*	LA

TRAILER BUFFET STANDARD   TSB

Renumbered from 400xx series by adding 400. –/33 1W.

40433 was numbered 40233 for a time when fitted with 23 First Class seats.

40402–426. Lot No. 30883 Derby 1976–77. 36.12 t.
40433. Lot No. 30899 Derby 1978–79. 36.12 t.

40402	**V**	AV		LM		40426	**GC**	A	*GC*	HT
40419	**V**	AV		LM		40433	**GC**	A	*GC*	HT
40424	**GC**	A	*GC*	HT						

TRAILER KITCHEN BUFFET FIRST TFKB

These vehicles have larger kitchens than the 402xx and 404xx series vehicles, and are used in trains where a full meal service is required. They were renumbered from the 403xx series (in which the seats were unclassified) by adding 400 to the previous number. 17/–.

* Refurbished Great Western Railway vehicles. Primarius leather seating.
m Refurbished Virgin Trains East Coast vehicles with Primarius seating.

40700–721. Lot No. 30921 Derby 1978–79. 38.16 t.
40722–735. Lot No. 30940 Derby 1979–80. 38.16 t.
40737–753. Lot No. 30948 Derby 1980–81. 38.16 t.
40754–757. Lot No. 30966 Derby 1982. 38.16 t.

40700		**ST**	P	*EM*	NL	40732		**VE**	P	*VE*	EC
40701	m	**VE**	P	*VE*	EC	40733	*	**FD**	A	*GW*	LA
40702	m	**VE**	P	*VE*	EC	40734	*	**FD**	A	*GW*	LA
40703	*	**FD**	A	*GW*	LA	40735	m	**VE**	A	*VE*	EC
40704	m	**VE**	A	*VE*	EC	40737	m	**VE**	A	*VE*	EC
40705	m	**VE**	A	*VE*	EC	40739	*	**FD**	A	*GW*	LA
40706	m	**VE**	A	*VE*	EC	40740	m	**VE**	A	*VE*	EC
40707	*	**FD**	A	*GW*	LA	40741		**ST**	P	*EM*	NL
40708	m	**VE**	P	*VE*	EC	40742	m	**VE**	A	*VE*	EC
40710	*	**FD**	A	*GW*	LA	40743	*	**GW**	A	*GW*	LA
40711	m	**VE**	A	*VE*	EC	40746		**ST**	P	*EM*	NL
40713	*	**FD**	A	*GW*	LA	40748	m	**VE**	A	*VE*	EC
40715	*	**GW**	A	*GW*	LA	40749		**ST**	P	*EM*	NL
40716	*	**FD**	A	*GW*	LA	40750	m	**VE**	A	*VE*	EC
40718	*	**FD**	A	*GW*	LA	40751		**VE**	P	*VE*	NL
40720	m	**VE**	A	*VE*	EC	40752	*	**FD**	A	*GW*	LA
40721	*	**FD**	A	*GW*	LA	40753		**ST**	P	*EM*	NL
40722	*	**FD**	A	*GW*	LA	40754		**ST**	P	*EM*	NL
40727	*	**FD**	A	*GW*	LA	40755	*	**FD**	A	*GW*	LA
40728		**ST**	P	*EM*	NL	40756		**ST**	P	*EM*	NL
40730		**ST**	P	*EM*	NL	40757	*	**FD**	A	*GW*	LA

TRAILER KITCHEN BUFFET FIRST TFKB

These vehicles have been converted from TSBs in the 404xx series to be similar to the 407xx series vehicles. 17/–.

40802/804/811 were numbered 40212/232/211 for a time when fitted with 23 First Class seats.

* Refurbished Great Western Railway vehicles. Primarius leather seating.
m Refurbished Virgin Trains East Coast vehicle with Primarius seating.

40801–803/805/808/809/811. Lot No. 30883 Derby 1976–77. 38.16 t.
40804/806/807/810. Lot No. 30899 Derby 1978–79. 38.16 t.

40801	(40027, 40427)	*	**FD**	P	*GW*	LA
40802	(40012, 40412)	*	**FD**	P	*GW*	LA

40803	(40018, 40418)	*	**FD**	P	*GW*	LA
40804	(40032, 40432)	*	**FD**	P	*GW*	LA
40805	(40020, 40420)	m	**VE**	P	*VE*	EC
40806	(40029, 40429)	*	**FD**	P	*GW*	LA
40807	(40035, 40435)	*	**FD**	P	*GW*	LA
40808	(40015, 40415)	*	**FD**	P	*GW*	LA
40809	(40014, 40414)	*	**FD**	P	*GW*	LA
40810	(40030, 40430)	*	**FD**	P	*GW*	LA
40811	(40011, 40411)	*	**FD**	P	*GW*	LA

TRAILER BUFFET FIRST   TFB

Converted from TSB by First Great Western. Refurbished with Primarius leather seating. 23/–.

40900/902/904. Lot No. 30883 Derby 1976–77. 36.12 t.
40901/903. Lot No. 30899 Derby 1978–79. 36.12 t.

40900	(40022, 40422)	**FD**	FG	*GW*	LA
40901	(40036, 40436)	**FD**	FG	*GW*	LA
40902	(40023, 40423)	**FD**	FG	*GW*	LA
40903	(40037, 40437)	**FD**	FG	*GW*	LA
40904	(40001, 40401)	**FD**	FG	*GW*	LA

TRAILER FIRST   TF

As built and m 48/– 2T (m† 48/– 1T – one toilet removed for trolley space).
* Refurbished Great Western Railway vehicles. Primarius leather seating.
c Refurbished CrossCountry vehicles with Primarius seating and 2 tip-up seats. One toilet removed. 40/– 1TD 1W.
m Refurbished Virgin Trains East Coast vehicles with Primarius seating.
s Fitted with centre luggage stack, disabled toilet and wheelchair space. 46/– 1T 1TD 1W.
w Wheelchair space. 47/– 2T 1W. (41154 47/– 1TD 1T 1W).
x Toilet removed for trolley space (FGW). 48/– 1T.

41004–056. Lot No. 30881 Derby 1976–77. 33.66 t.
41057–120. Lot No. 30896 Derby 1977–78. 33.66 t.
41122–146. Lot No. 30938 Derby 1979–80. 33.66 t.
41149–166. Lot No. 30947 Derby 1980. 33.66 t.
41167/169. Lot No. 30963 Derby 1982. 33.66 t.
41170. Lot No. 30967 Derby 1982. Former prototype vehicle. 33.66 t.
41176. Lot No. 30897 Derby 1977. 33.66 t.
41180. Lot No. 30884 Derby 1976–77. 33.66 t.
41182/183/189. Lot No. 30939 Derby 1979–80. 33.66 t.
41185–187. Lot No. 30969 Derby 1982. 33.66 t.
41190. Lot No. 30882 Derby 1976–77. 33.60 t.
41192. Lot No. 30897 Derby 1977–79. 33.60 t.
41193–195/201–206. Lot No. 30878 Derby 1975–76. 34.3 t. Converted from Mark 3A Open First.

41004	*x	**FD**	A	*GW*	LA	41095	mw	**VE**	P	*VE*	EC
41006	*w	**FD**	A	*GW*	LA	41097	m†	**VE**	A	*VE*	EC
41008	*w	**FD**	A	*GW*	LA	41098	mw	**VE**	A	*VE*	EC
41010	*w	**FD**	A	*GW*	LA	41099	m†	**VE**	A	*VE*	EC
41012	*w	**FD**	A	*GW*	LA	41100	mw	**VE**	A	*VE*	EC
41016	*w	**FD**	A	*GW*	LA	41102	*w	**FD**	A	*GW*	LA
41018	*w	**FD**	A	*GW*	LA	41103	*x	**FD**	A	*GW*	LA
41020	*w	**FD**	A	*GW*	LA	41104	*w	**FD**	A	*GW*	LA
41022	*w	**FD**	A	*GW*	LA	41106	*w	**FD**	A	*GW*	LA
41024	*w	**FD**	A	*GW*	LA	41108	*w	**FD**	P	*GW*	LA
41026	c	**XC**	A	*XC*	EC	41110	*w	**FD**	A	*GW*	LA
41028	*w	**FD**	A	*GW*	LA	41111		**ST**	P	*EM*	NL
41030	*w	**FD**	A	*GW*	LA	41112		**VE**	P	*VE*	NL
41032	*w	**FD**	A	*GW*	LA	41113	s	**ST**	P	*EM*	NL
41034	*w	**FD**	A	*GW*	LA	41115	m†	**VE**	P	*VE*	EC
41035	c	**XC**	A	*XC*	EC	41116	*x	**FD**	A	*GW*	LA
41038	*w	**FD**	A	*GW*	LA	41117		**ST**	P	*EM*	NL
41039	m†	**VE**	A	*VE*	EC	41118	mw	**VE**	A	*VE*	EC
41040	mw	**VE**	A	*VE*	EC	41120	m†	**VE**	A	*VE*	EC
41041	s	**ST**	P	*EM*	NL	41122	*w	**FD**	A	*GW*	LA
41044	mw	**VE**	A	*VE*	EC	41124	*w	**FD**	A	*GW*	LA
41046	s	**ST**	P	*EM*	NL	41126	*w	**FD**	A	*GW*	LA
41052	*w	**FD**	A	*GW*	LA	41128	*w	**FD**	A	*GW*	LA
41056	*w	**FD**	A	*GW*	LA	41130	*w	**FD**	A	*GW*	LA
41057		**ST**	P	*EM*	NL	41132	*w	**FD**	A	*GW*	LA
41059	*w	**FD**	FG	*GW*	LA	41134	*w	**FD**	A	*GW*	LA
41061	w	**ST**	P	*EM*	NL	41135	*w	**FD**	A	*GW*	LA
41062		**VE**	P	*VE*	EC	41136	*w	**FD**	A	*GW*	LA
41063		**ST**	P	*EM*	NL	41137	*x	**FD**	A	*GW*	LA
41064	s	**ST**	P	*EM*	NL	41138	*w	**FD**	A	*GW*	LA
41066	m†	**VE**	A	*VE*	EC	41140	*w	**FD**	A	*GW*	LA
41067	s	**ST**	P	*EM*	NL	41142	*w	**FD**	A	*GW*	LA
41068	w	**VE**	P	*VE*	NL	41144	*w	**FD**	A	*GW*	LA
41069	s	**ST**	P	*EM*	NL	41146	*w	**GW**	A	*GW*	LA
41070	s	**ST**	P	*EM*	NL	41149	*w	**FD**	P	*GW*	LA
41071		**ST**	P	*EM*	NL	41150	mw	**VE**	A	*VE*	EC
41072	s	**ST**	P	*EM*	NL	41151	m†	**VE**	A	*VE*	EC
41075		**ST**	P	*EM*	NL	41152	mw	**VE**	A	*VE*	EC
41076	s	**ST**	P	*EM*	NL	41154	w	**VE**	P	*VE*	EC
41077		**ST**	P	*EM*	NL	41156		**ST**	P	*EM*	NL
41079		**ST**	P	*EM*	NL	41158	*w	**GW**	A	*GW*	LA
41083	mw	**VE**	P	*VE*	EC	41159	m†	**VE**	P	*VE*	EC
41084	s	**ST**	P	*EM*	NL	41160	*w	**FD**	FG	*GW*	LA
41087	m†	**VE**	A	*VE*	EC	41161	*w	**FD**	P	*GW*	LA
41088	mw	**VE**	A	*VE*	EC	41162	*w	**FD**	FG	*GW*	LA
41089	*w	**FD**	A	*GW*	LA	41164	mw	**VE**	A	*VE*	EC
41090	m†	**VE**	A	*VE*	EC	41165	mw	**VE**	P	*VE*	EC
41091	m†	**VE**	A	*VE*	EC	41166	*w	**FD**	FG	*GW*	LA
41092	mw	**VE**	A	*VE*	EC	41167	*w	**FD**	FG	*GW*	LA
41094	*w	**FD**	A	*GW*	LA	41169	*w	**FD**	P	*GW*	LA

41170	(41001)	m†	**VE**	A	*VE*	EC
41176	(42142, 42352)	*w	**FD**	P	*GW*	LA
41180	(40511)	*w	**FD**	A	*GW*	LA
41182	(42278)	*w	**FD**	P	*GW*	LA
41183	(42274)	*w	**FD**	P	*GW*	LA
41185	(42313)	m†	**VE**	P	*VE*	EC
41186	(42312)	*w	**FD**	P	*GW*	LA
41187	(42311)	*w	**FD**	P	*GW*	LA
41189	(42298)	*w	**FD**	P	*GW*	LA
41190	(42088)	m†	**VE**	P	*VE*	EC
41192	(42246)	*w	**FD**	P	*GW*	LA

The following carriages have been converted from loco-hauled Mark 3 vehicles for CrossCountry or Grand Central.

41193	(11060)	c	**XC**	P	*XC*	EC
41194	(11016)	c	**XC**	P	*XC*	EC
41195	(11020)	c	**XC**	P	*XC*	EC
41201	(11045)		**GC**	A	*GC*	HT
41202	(11017)		**GC**	A	*GC*	HT
41203	(11038)		**GC**	A	*GC*	HT
41204	(11023)		**GC**	A	*GC*	HT
41205	(11036)		**GC**	A	*GC*	HT
41206	(11055)		**GC**	A	*GC*	HT

TRAILER STANDARD   TS

42158 was numbered 41177 for a time when fitted with First Class seats.
42310 was numbered 41188 for a time when fitted with First Class seats.

Standard seating and m –/76 2T.
* Refurbished Great Western Railway vehicles. Grammer seating. –/80 2T (unless h – high density).
c Refurbished CrossCountry vehicles with Primarius seating. One toilet removed. –/82 1T.
§c Refurbished CrossCountry vehicles with Primarius seating and 2 tip-up seats. One toilet removed. –/66 1TD 2W. 42379/380 are –/71 1TD 1T 2W.
d Great Western Railway vehicles with disabled persons toilet and 5, 6 or 7 tip-up seats. –/68 1T 1TD 2W.
h "High density" Great Western Railway vehicles. –/84 2T.
k "High density" Great Western Railway refurbished vehicle with disabled persons toilet and 5, 6 or 7 tip-up seats. –/72 1T 1TD 2W.
m Refurbished Virgin Trains East Coast vehicles with Primarius seating.
u Centre luggage stack (EMT) –/74 2T.
w Centre luggage stack and wheelchair space (EMT) –72 2T 1W.
† Disabled persons toilet (VTEC) –/62 1T 1TD 1W.

▲ Pullman Car Company-liveried Mark 2 Pullman Open Brake First 586 is seen at Stirling on 12/09/15. **Robert Pritchard**

▼ Belmond Northern Belle-liveried Mark 1 Kitchen with Bar 1566 is seen at Bletchley on 16/04/16. **Mark Beal**

▲ West Coast Railway Company Maroon-liveried Mark 1 Open First 3106 (99122) near Carstairs on 19/03/16. **Robin Ralston**

▼ Pullman Car Company-liveried Mark 2E Open First 3231 at Ravenglass on 25/07/15. **Andrew Mason**

▲ Carmine & Cream-liveried Mark 1 Open Standard 4927 stands in Worcester Shrub Hill Yard on 14/06/16. **Steve Widdowson**

▼ West Coast Railway Company Maroon-liveried Mark 2 Open Standard 5249 at Maidstone East on 29/08/15. **Robert Pritchard**

▲ West Coast Railway Company Maroon-liveried Mark 2F Open Standard 6000 at York on 28/05/16. **Robert Pritchard**

▼ Revised Direct Rail Services-liveried Mark 2F Open Standard 6046 is seen at Acle on 18/07/16. **Dave Gommersall**

▲ ScotRail Saltire-liveried Mark 2F Open Brake Standard 9539 at Edinburgh Waverley on 11/09/15. **Robert Pritchard**

▼ Revised DRS-liveried Driving Open Brake Standard 9704 brings up the rear of the 08.45 Barrow-in-Furness–Carlisle at Parton on 06/08/16. **Tom McAtee**

▲ First Group-liveried Mark 2E Open Brake Unclassified 9805 at Old Linslade on 18/07/15.　**Andrew Mason**

▼ Arriva Trains Wales-liveried Mark 3A Kitchen Buffet First 10259 at Cardiff Central on 14/06/16.　**Robert Pritchard**

▲ Newly converted Abellio Greater Anglia-liveried Mark 3A Buffet Standard 10416 at Ipswich on 14/06/16. **Robert Pritchard**

▼ Caledonian Sleeper-liveried Mark 3A Sleeping Car 10693 at Old Linslade on 18/07/15. **Andrew Mason**

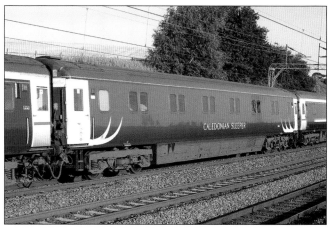

▲ Virgin Trains East Coast-liveried Mark 4 Open First (Disabled) 11311 at Doncaster on 22/09/15. **Robert Pritchard**

▼ Chiltern Railways Mainline-liveried Mark 3A Open Standard 12623 is seen at Neasden on 05/07/16. **Robert Pritchard**

▲ Riviera blue-liveried Mark 2B Couchette/Generator Coach 17105 is seen near Sheffield on 10/04/16. **Robert Pritchard**

▼ Great Western Railway green-liveried Open Brake Unclassified 17174 is seen at Plymouth on 13/06/16. **Robert Pritchard**

▲ Virgin Trains East Coast-liveried Mark 4 Driving Brake Van 82201 is seen at Doncaster on 22/09/15. **Robert Pritchard**

▼ Stagecoach East Midlands Trains-liveried HST Trailer Standard 42121 is seen at Nottingham on 17/07/16. **Robert Pritchard**

▲ In the Great Western Railway green livery applied to two HST sets, Trailer Guard's Standard 44040 is seen at St Germans on 16/08/16. **Tony Christie**

▼ CrossCountry-liveried HST Trailer Composite Kitchen 45003 at Plymouth on 16/08/16. **Tony Christie**

▲ Royal Scotsman Maroon-liveried Observation Car 319 (99965) at Falkirk Grahamston on 21/04/16.　　**Ian Lothian**

▼ Pullman Car Company-liveried Pullman Kitchen First 245 "IBIS" at Ashford on 16/06/16.　　**Robert Pritchard**

▲ Pullman Parlour Second 348 "TOPAZ" on Dainton bank on 07/08/16.
Tony Christie

▼ BR Maroon-liveried Mark 1 Corridor Brake Composite Support Coach 21232 (99040) at Woodhouse on 17/08/16.
Andrew Wills

▲ Arlington Fleet Services EMU Translator Vehicle 64664 at Eastleigh Works on 25/10/14. **Mark Beal**

▼ Network Rail Yellow-liveried Mark 1 Generator Van 6263 at Worcester Shrub Hill on 15/08/16. **Steve Widdowson**

▲ Network Rail Ultrasonic Test Coach 62287 (a former Class 421 EMU MBSO) at Worcester Shrub Hill on 15/08/16. **Steve Widdowson**

▼ BR Green-liveried Network Rail Inspection Saloon 975025 "CAROLINE" is propelled through Narborough by 47818 on 03/07/15. **Paul Biggs**

▲ Network Rail New Measurement Train Overhead Line Equipment Test Coach 977993 at Newton Abbot on 03/06/16. **Tony Christie**

▼ One of several Internal User vehicles across the UK, Mark 2D Open Standard 5636 is used as an Instruction Coach by Great Western Railway at Bristol St Philip's Marsh depot. It is seen there on 02/05/16. **Andy Barclay**

42003–089/362. Lot No. 30882 Derby 1976–77. 33.6 t.
42091–250. Lot No. 30897 Derby 1977–79. 33.6 t.
42251–305. Lot No. 30939 Derby 1979–80. 33.6 t.
42306–322. Lot No. 30969 Derby 1982. 33.6 t.
42323–341. Lot No. 30983 Derby 1984–85. 33.6 t.
42342/360. Lot No. 30949 Derby 1982. 33.47 t. Converted from TGS.
42343/345. Lot No. 30970 Derby 1982. 33.47 t. Converted from TGS.
42344/361. Lot No. 30964 Derby 1982. 33.47 t. Converted from TGS.
42346/347/350/351/379/380/551–564. Lot No. 30881 Derby 1976–77. 33.66 t. Converted from TF.
42248/349/363–365/381/565–570. Lot No. 30896 Derby 1977–78. 33.66 t. Converted from TF.
42354. Lot No. 30897 Derby 1977. Was TF from 1983 to 1992. 33.66 t.
42353/355–357. Lot No. 30967 Derby 1982. Ex-prototype vehicles. 33.66 t.
42366–378/382/383/401–409. Lot No. 30877 Derby 1975–77. 34.3 t. Converted from Mark 3A Open Standard.
42384. Lot No. 30896 Derby 1977–78. 33.66 t. Converted from TF.
42501/509/513/515/517. Lot No. 30948 Derby 1980–81. 34.8 t. Converted from TFKB.
42502/506/508/514/516. Lot No. 30940 Derby 1979–80. 34.8 t. Converted from TFKB.
42503/504/510/511. Lot No. 30921 Derby 1978–79. 34.8 t. Converted from TFKB.
42505/507/512/518/519. Lot No. 30883 Derby 1976–77. 34.8 t. Converted from TSB.
42520. Lot No. 30899 Derby 1978–79. 34.8 t. Converted from TSB.
42251–579. Lot No. 30938 Derby 1979–80. 33.66 t. Converted from TF.
42580–583. Lot No. 30947 Derby 1980. 33.66 t. Converted from TF.

42003	*h	**FD**	A	*GW*	LA	42031	*h	**FD**	A	*GW*	LA
42004	*d	**FD**	A	*GW*	LA	42032	*h	**FD**	A	*GW*	LA
42005	*h	**FD**	A	*GW*	LA	42033	*	**FD**	A	*GW*	LA
42006	*h	**FD**	A	*GW*	LA	42034	*	**FD**	A	*GW*	LA
42007	*d	**FD**	A	*GW*	LA	42035	*	**FD**	A	*GW*	LA
42008	*k	**FD**	A	*GW*	LA	42036	c	**XC**	A	*XC*	EC
42009	*h	**FD**	A	*GW*	LA	42037	c	**XC**	A	*XC*	EC
42010	*h	**FD**	A	*GW*	LA	42038	c	**XC**	A	*XC*	EC
42012	*k	**FD**	A	*GW*	LA	42039	*h	**FD**	A	*GW*	LA
42013	*h	**FD**	A	*GW*	LA	42040	*h	**FD**	A	*GW*	LA
42014	*h	**FD**	A	*GW*	LA	42041	*h	**FD**	A	*GW*	LA
42015	*k	**FD**	A	*GW*	LA	42042	*h	**FD**	A	*GW*	LA
42016	*h	**FD**	A	*GW*	LA	42043	*h	**FD**	A	*GW*	LA
42019	*	**FD**	A	*GW*	LA	42044	*h	**FD**	A	*GW*	LA
42021	*k	**FD**	A	*GW*	LA	42045	*	**FD**	A	*GW*	LA
42023	*h	**FD**	A	*GW*	LA	42046	*	**FD**	A	*GW*	LA
42024	*k	**FD**	A	*GW*	LA	42047	*	**FD**	A	*GW*	LA
42025	*h	**FD**	A	*GW*	LA	42048	*h	**FD**	A	*GW*	LA
42026	*h	**FD**	A	*GW*	LA	42049	*h	**FD**	A	*GW*	LA
42027	*h	**FD**	A	*GW*	LA	42050	*h	**FD**	A	*GW*	LA
42028	*h	**FD**	A	*GW*	LA	42051	c	**XC**	A	*XC*	EC
42029	*h	**FD**	A	*GW*	LA	42052	c	**XC**	A	*XC*	EC
42030	*k	**FD**	A	*GW*	LA	42053	c	**XC**	A	*XC*	EC

No.						No.					
42054	*	**FD**	A	*GW*	LA	42110	m	**VE**	P	*VE*	EC
42055	*	**FD**	A	*GW*	LA	42111	u	**ST**	P	*EM*	NL
42056	*	**FD**	A	*GW*	LA	42112	u	**ST**	P	*EM*	NL
42057	m	**VE**	A	*VE*	EC	42113	u	**ST**	P	*EM*	NL
42058	m	**VE**	A	*VE*	EC	42115	*h	**FD**	P	*GW*	LA
42059	m	**VE**	A	*VE*	EC	42116	m†	**VE**	A	*VE*	EC
42060	*h	**FD**	A	*GW*	LA	42117	m	**VE**	P	*VE*	EC
42061	*h	**FD**	A	*GW*	LA	42118	*h	**FD**	A	*GW*	LA
42062	*k	**FD**	A	*GW*	LA	42119	u	**ST**	P	*EM*	NL
42063	m	**VE**	A	*VE*	EC	42120	u	**ST**	P	*EM*	NL
42064	m	**VE**	A	*VE*	EC	42121	u	**ST**	P	*EM*	NL
42065	m	**VE**	A	*VE*	EC	42122	m	**VE**	A	*VE*	EC
42066	*k	**FD**	A	*GW*	LA	42123		**VE**	P	*VE*	EC
42067	*h	**FD**	A	*GW*	LA	42124	u	**ST**	P	*EM*	NL
42068	*h	**FD**	A	*GW*	LA	42125		**VE**	P	*VE*	EC
42069	*k	**FD**	A	*GW*	LA	42126	*h	**FD**	A	*GW*	LA
42070	*h	**FD**	A	*GW*	LA	42127	m†	**VE**	A	*VE*	EC
42071	*h	**FD**	A	*GW*	LA	42128	m†	**VE**	A	*VE*	EC
42072	*	**FD**	A	*GW*	LA	42129	*	**GW**	A	*GW*	LA
42073	*h	**FD**	A	*GW*	LA	42130	m	**VE**	P	*VE*	EC
42074	*h	**FD**	A	*GW*	LA	42131	u	**ST**	P	*EM*	NL
42075	*	**FD**	A	*GW*	LA	42132	w	**ST**	P	*EM*	NL
42076	*	**FD**	A	*GW*	LA	42133	u	**ST**	P	*EM*	NL
42077	*	**FD**	A	*GW*	LA	42134	m	**VE**	A	*VE*	EC
42078	*	**FD**	A	*GW*	LA	42135	u	**ST**	P	*EM*	NL
42079	*h	**FD**	A	*GW*	LA	42136	u	**ST**	P	*EM*	NL
42080	*h	**FD**	A	*GW*	LA	42137	u	**ST**	P	*EM*	NL
42081	*k	**FD**	A	*GW*	LA	42138	*k	**FD**	A	*GW*	LA
42083	*h	**FD**	A	*GW*	LA	42139	u	**ST**	P	*EM*	NL
42085	*h	**FD**	P	*GW*	LA	42140	u	**ST**	P	*EM*	NL
42087	*h	**FD**	P	*GW*	LA	42141	u	**ST**	P	*EM*	NL
42089	*h	**FD**	A	*GW*	LA	42143	*	**FD**	A	*GW*	LA
42091	m†	**VE**	A	*VE*	EC	42144	*	**FD**	A	*GW*	LA
42092	*k	**FD**	FG	*GW*	LA	42145	*	**FD**	A	*GW*	LA
42093	*h	**FD**	FG	*GW*	LA	42146	m	**VE**	A	*VE*	EC
42094	*h	**FD**	FG	*GW*	LA	42148	u	**ST**	P	*EM*	NL
42095	*	**FD**	FG	*GW*	LA	42149	u	**ST**	P	*EM*	NL
42096	*h	**FD**	FG	*GW*	LA	42150	m	**VE**	A	*VE*	EC
42097	c	**XC**	A	*XC*	EC	42151	w	**ST**	P	*EM*	NL
42098	*h	**FD**	A	*GW*	LA	42152	u	**ST**	P	*EM*	NL
42099	*h	**FD**	A	*GW*	LA	42153	u	**ST**	P	*EM*	NL
42100	u	**ST**	P	*EM*	NL	42154	m	**VE**	A	*VE*	EC
42101	*h	**FD**	P	*GW*	LA	42155	w	**ST**	P	*EM*	NL
42102	*h	**FD**	P	*GW*	LA	42156	u	**ST**	P	*EM*	NL
42103	*k	**FD**	FG	*GW*	LA	42157	u	**ST**	P	*EM*	NL
42104	m	**VE**	A	*VE*	EC	42158	m	**VE**	A	*VE*	EC
42105	*k	**FD**	FG	*GW*	LA	42159	m†	**VE**	P	*VE*	EC
42106	m	**VE**	A	*VE*	EC	42160	m	**VE**	P	*VE*	EC
42107	*	**FD**	A	*GW*	LA	42161	m†	**VE**	A	*VE*	EC
42108	*h	**FD**	FG	*GW*	LA	42163	m	**VE**	P	*VE*	EC
42109	m	**VE**	P	*VE*	EC	42164		**ST**	P	*EM*	NL

42165	**ST** P	*EM*	NL
42166 *h	**FD** P	*GW*	LA
42167 *h	**FD** FG	*GW*	LA
42168 *h	**FD** FG	*GW*	LA
42169 *h	**FD** FG	*GW*	LA
42171 m	**VE** A	*VE*	EC
42172 m	**VE** A	*VE*	EC
42173 *k	**FD** P	*GW*	LA
42174 *k	**FD** P	*GW*	LA
42175 *h	**FD** FG	*GW*	LA
42176 *h	**FD** FG	*GW*	LA
42177 *h	**FD** FG	*GW*	LA
42178 *h	**FD** P	*GW*	LA
42179 m	**VE** A	*VE*	EC
42180	**VE** A	*VE*	EC
42181 m	**VE** A	*VE*	EC
42182 m	**VE** A	*VE*	EC
42183 *d	**FD** A	*GW*	LA
42184 *	**FD** A	*GW*	LA
42185 *	**FD** A	*GW*	LA
42186 m	**VE** A	*VE*	EC
42188 m†	**VE** A	*VE*	EC
42189 m†	**VE** A	*VE*	EC
42190 m	**VE** A	*VE*	EC
42191 m	**VE** A	*VE*	EC
42192 m	**VE** A	*VE*	EC
42193 m	**VE** A	*VE*	EC
42194 u	**VE** P	*VE*	NL
42195 *k	**FD** P	*GW*	LA
42196 *h	**FD** A	*GW*	LA
42197 *h	**FD** A	*GW*	LA
42198 m	**VE** A	*VE*	EC
42199 m	**VE** A	*VE*	EC
42200 *d	**GW** A	*GW*	LA
42201 *k	**FD** A	*GW*	LA
42202 *k	**FD** A	*GW*	LA
42203 *h	**FD** A	*GW*	LA
42204 *h	**FD** A	*GW*	LA
42205	**VE** P	*VE*	EC
42206 *d	**FD** A	*GW*	LA
42207 *d	**FD** A	*GW*	LA
42208 *	**FD** A	*GW*	LA
42209 *	**FD** A	*GW*	LA
42210	**VE** P	*VE*	EC
42211 *k	**FD** A	*GW*	LA
42212 *h	**FD** A	*GW*	LA
42213 *h	**FD** A	*GW*	LA
42214 *h	**FD** A	*GW*	LA
42215 m	**VE** A	*VE*	EC
42216 *h	**FD** A	*GW*	LA
42217 *k	**FD** P	*GW*	LA
42218 *k	**FD** P	*GW*	LA
42219 m	**VE** A	*VE*	EC
42220 w	**ST** P	*EM*	NL
42221 *h	**FD** A	*GW*	LA
42222 *h	**FD** P	*GW*	LA
42224 *k	**FD** P	*GW*	LA
42225	**VE** P	*VE*	NL
42226 m	**VE** A	*VE*	EC
42227	**VE** P	*VE*	NL
42228 m	**VE** P	*VE*	EC
42229	**VE** P	*VE*	NL
42230 u	**ST** P	*EM*	NL
42231 *h	**FD** FG	*GW*	LA
42232 *h	**FD** FG	*GW*	LA
42233 *h	**FD** FG	*GW*	LA
42234 c	**XC** P	*XC*	EC
42235 m	**VE** A	*VE*	EC
42236 *h	**FD** A	*GW*	LA
42237 m	**VE** P	*VE*	EC
42238 m†	**VE** A	*VE*	EC
42239 m†	**VE** A	*VE*	EC
42240 m	**VE** A	*VE*	EC
42241 m	**VE** A	*VE*	EC
42242 m	**VE** A	*VE*	EC
42243 m	**VE** A	*VE*	EC
42244 m	**VE** A	*VE*	EC
42245 *	**GW** A	*GW*	LA
42247 *h	**FD** P	*GW*	LA
42250 *	**GW** A	*GW*	LA
42251 *k	**FD** A	*GW*	LA
42252 *	**FD** A	*GW*	LA
42253 *	**FD** A	*GW*	LA
42255 *d	**FD** A	*GW*	LA
42256 *	**FD** A	*GW*	LA
42257 *	**FD** A	*GW*	LA
42258 *h	**FD** P	*GW*	LA
42259 *k	**FD** A	*GW*	LA
42260 *h	**FD** A	*GW*	LA
42261 *h	**FD** A	*GW*	LA
42263 *	**FD** A	*GW*	LA
42264 *k	**FD** A	*GW*	LA
42265 *	**FD** A	*GW*	LA
42266 *k	**FD** P	*GW*	LA
42267 *d	**FD** A	*GW*	LA
42268 *d	**FD** A	*GW*	LA
42269 *	**FD** A	*GW*	LA
42271 *k	**FD** A	*GW*	LA
42272 *h	**FD** A	*GW*	LA
42273 *h	**FD** A	*GW*	LA
42275 *d	**FD** A	*GW*	LA
42276 *	**FD** A	*GW*	LA

42277	*	**FD**	A	*GW*	LA
42279	*d	**FD**	A	*GW*	LA
42280	*	**FD**	A	*GW*	LA
42281	*	**FD**	A	*GW*	LA
42283	*h	**FD**	A	*GW*	LA
42284	*h	**FD**	A	*GW*	LA
42285	*h	**FD**	A	*GW*	LA
42286	mt	**VE**	P	*VE*	EC
42287	*k	**FD**	A	*GW*	LA
42288	*h	**FD**	A	*GW*	LA
42289	*h	**FD**	A	*GW*	LA
42290	c	**XC**	P	*XC*	EC
42291	*d	**FD**	A	*GW*	LA
42292	*d	**FD**	A	*GW*	LA
42293	*	**FD**	A	*GW*	LA
42294	*	**FD**	P	*GW*	LA
42295	*d	**FD**	A	*GW*	LA
42296	*	**FD**	A	*GW*	LA
42297	*	**FD**	A	*GW*	LA
42299	*d	**GW**	A	*GW*	LA
42300	*	**GW**	A	*GW*	LA
42301	*	**GW**	A	*GW*	LA
42302	*k	**FD**	FG	*GW*	LA
42303	*h	**FD**	FG	*GW*	LA
42304	*h	**FD**	FG	*GW*	LA
42305	*h	**FD**	FG	*GW*	LA
42306	m	**VE**	P	*VE*	EC
42307	m	**VE**	P	*VE*	EC
42308	*h	**FD**	P	*GW*	LA
42310	*k	**FD**	P	*GW*	LA
42315	*h	**FD**	P	*GW*	LA
42317	*k	**FD**	P	*GW*	LA
42319	*h	**FD**	P	*GW*	LA
42321	*h	**FD**	P	*GW*	LA
42322	m	**VE**	P	*VE*	EC
42323	m	**VE**	A	*VE*	EC
42325	*	**FD**	A	*GW*	LA
42326	m	**VE**	P	*VE*	EC
42327	w	**ST**	P	*EM*	NL
42328	w	**ST**	P	*EM*	NL
42329	w	**ST**	P	*EM*	NL
42330	m	**VE**	P	*VE*	EC
42331	u	**ST**	P	*EM*	NL
42332	*	**FD**	A	*GW*	LA
42333	*	**FD**	A	*GW*	LA
42335	w	**VE**	P	*VE*	EC
42337	w	**ST**	P	*EM*	NL
42339	w	**ST**	P	*EM*	NL
42340	m	**VE**	A	*VE*	EC
42341	u	**ST**	P	*EM*	NL

42342	(44082)	c	**XC**	A	*XC*	EC
42343	(44095)	*	**FD**	A	*GW*	LA
42344	(44092)	*k	**FD**	A	*GW*	LA
42345	(44096)	*d	**FD**	A	*GW*	LA
42346	(41053)	*h	**FD**	A	*GW*	LA
42347	(41054)	*k	**FD**	A	*GW*	LA
42348	(41073)	*k	**FD**	A	*GW*	LA
42349	(41074)	*h	**FD**	A	*GW*	LA
42350	(41047)	*	**FD**	A	*GW*	LA
42351	(41048)		**GW**	A	*GW*	LA
42353	(42001, 41171)	*k	**FD**	FG	*GW*	LA
42354	(42114, 41175)	m	**VE**	A	*VE*	EC
42355	(42000, 41172)	m	**VE**	A	*VE*	EC
42356	(42002, 41173)	*k	**FD**	A	*GW*	LA
42357	(41002, 41174)	m	**VE**	A	*VE*	EC
42360	(44084, 45084)	*h	**FD**	A	*GW*	LA
42361	(44099, 42000)	*h	**FD**	A	*GW*	LA
42362	(42011, 41178)	*h	**FD**	A	*GW*	LA
42363	(41082)	mt	**VE**	A	*VE*	EC
42364	(41080)	*k	**FD**	P	*GW*	LA
42365	(41107)	*h	**FD**	P	*GW*	LA

42366–378 were converted from loco-hauled Mark 3 vehicles for CrossCountry and 42382/383 for First Great Western.

42366	(12007)	§c	**XC**	P	*XC*	EC

42367	(12025)	c	**XC**	P	*XC*	EC
42368	(12028)	c	**XC**	P	*XC*	EC
42369	(12050)	c	**XC**	P	*XC*	EC
42370	(12086)	c	**XC**	P	*XC*	EC
42371	(12052)	§c	**XC**	P	*XC*	EC
42372	(12055)	c	**XC**	P	*XC*	EC
42373	(12071)	c	**XC**	P	*XC*	EC
42374	(12075)	c	**XC**	P	*XC*	EC
42375	(12113)	c	**XC**	P	*XC*	EC
42376	(12085)	§c	**XC**	P	*XC*	EC
42377	(12102)	c	**XC**	P	*XC*	EC
42378	(12123)	c	**XC**	P	*XC*	EC
42379	(41036)	§c	**XC**	A	*XC*	EC
42380	(41025)	§c	**XC**	A	*XC*	EC
42381	(41058)	*k	**FD**	P	*GW*	LA
42382	(12128)	*h	**FD**	P	*GW*	LA
42383	(12172)	*h	**FD**	P	*GW*	LA
42384	(41078)	w	**ST**	P	*EM*	NL

The following carriages have been converted from loco-hauled Mark 3 vehicles for Grand Central. They have a lower density seating layout (most seats arranged around tables). –/64 2T († –/60 1TD 1T 2W).

42401	(12149)		**GC**	A	*GC*	HT
42402	(12155)		**GC**	A	*GC*	HT
42403	(12033)	†	**GC**	A	*GC*	HT
42404	(12152)		**GC**	A	*GC*	HT
42405	(12136)		**GC**	A	*GC*	HT
42406	(12112)	†	**GC**	A	*GC*	HT
42407	(12044)		**GC**	A	*GC*	HT
42408	(12121)		**GC**	A	*GC*	HT
42409	(12088)	†	**GC**	A	*GC*	HT

These carriages have been converted from TFKB or TSB buffet cars to TS vehicles in 2011–12 (42501–515) and 2013–14 (42516–520) at Wabtec Kilmarnock for FGW. Refurbished with Grammer seating. –/84 1T. 34.8 t.

42501	(40344, 40744)	**FD**	A	*GW*	LA
42502	(40331, 40731)	**FD**	A	*GW*	LA
42503	(40312, 40712)	**FD**	A	*GW*	LA
42504	(40314, 40714)	**FD**	A	*GW*	LA
42505	(40428, 40228)	**FD**	A	*GW*	LA
42506	(40324, 40724)	**FD**	A	*GW*	LA
42507	(40409, 40209)	**FD**	A	*GW*	LA
42508	(40325, 40725)	**FD**	A	*GW*	LA
42509	(40336, 40736)	**FD**	A	*GW*	LA
42510	(40317, 40717)	**FD**	A	*GW*	LA
42511	(40309, 40709)	**FD**	A	*GW*	LA
42512	(40408, 40208)	**FD**	A	*GW*	LA
42513	(40338, 40738)	**FD**	A	*GW*	LA
42514	(40326, 40726)	**FD**	A	*GW*	LA
42515	(40347, 40747)	**FD**	A	*GW*	LA
42516	(40323, 40723)	**FD**	A	*GW*	LA

42517	(40345, 40745)	**FD**	A	*GW*	LA
42518	(40003, 40403)	**FD**	P	*GW*	LA
42519	(40016, 40416)	**FD**	P	*GW*	LA
42520	(40234, 40434)	**FD**	P	*GW*	LA

These carriages have been converted from TF to TS vehicles in 2014 at Wabtec Kilmarnock for FGW. Refurbished with Grammer seating. –/80 1T. 35.5 t.

42551	(41003)	**FD**	A	*GW*	LA
42552	(41007)	**FD**	A	*GW*	LA
42553	(41009)	**FD**	A	*GW*	LA
42554	(41011)	**FD**	A	*GW*	LA
42555	(41015)	**FD**	A	*GW*	LA
42556	(41017)	**FD**	A	*GW*	LA
42557	(41019)	**FD**	A	*GW*	LA
42558	(41021)	**FD**	A	*GW*	LA
42559	(41023)	**FD**	A	*GW*	LA
42560	(41027)	**FD**	A	*GW*	LA
42561	(41031)	**FD**	A	*GW*	LA
42562	(41037)	**FD**	A	*GW*	LA
42563	(41045)	**FD**	FG	*GW*	LA
42564	(41051)	**FD**	A	*GW*	LA
42565	(41085)	**FD**	FG	*GW*	LA
42566	(41086)	**FD**	FG	*GW*	LA
42567	(41093)	**FD**	A	*GW*	LA
42568	(41101)	**FD**	A	*GW*	LA
42569	(41105)	**FD**	A	*GW*	LA
42570	(41114)	**FD**	FG	*GW*	LA
42571	(41121)	**FD**	A	*GW*	LA
42572	(41123)	**FD**	A	*GW*	LA
42573	(41127)	**FD**	A	*GW*	LA
42574	(41129)	**FD**	A	*GW*	LA
42575	(41131)	**FD**	A	*GW*	LA
42576	(41133)	**FD**	A	*GW*	LA
42577	(41141)	**FD**	A	*GW*	LA
42578	(41143)	**FD**	A	*GW*	LA
42579	(41145)	**GW**	A	*GW*	LA
42580	(41155)	**FD**	P	*GW*	LA
42581	(41157)	**GW**	A	*GW*	LA
42582	(41163)	**FD**	FG	*GW*	LA
42583	(41153, 42385)	**FD**	P	*GW*	LA

TRAILER GUARD'S STANDARD   TGS

As built and m –/65 1T.
* Refurbished Great Western Railway vehicles. Grammer seating and toilet removed for trolley store. –/67 (unless h).
c Refurbished CrossCountry vehicles with Primarius seating. –/67 1T.
h "High density" Great Western Railway vehicles. –/71.
m Refurbished Virgin Trains East Coast vehicles with Primarius seating.
s Fitted with centre luggage stack (EMT) –/63 1T. 44027 is –/64 1T.
t Fitted with centre luggage stack –/61 1T.

44000. Lot No. 30953 Derby 1980. 33.47 t.
44001–090. Lot No. 30949 Derby 1980–82. 33.47 t.
44091–094. Lot No. 30964 Derby 1982. 33.47 t.
44097–101. Lot No. 30970 Derby 1982. 33.47 t.

44000	*h	**FD**	P	*GW*	LA	44047	s	**ST**	P	*EM*	NL
44001	*	**FD**	A	*GW*	LA	44048	s	**ST**	P	*EM*	NL
44002	*h	**FD**	A	*GW*	LA	44049	*	**FD**	A	*GW*	LA
44003	*h	**FD**	A	*GW*	LA	44050	m	**VE**	P	*VE*	EC
44004	*h	**FD**	A	*GW*	LA	44051	s	**ST**	P	*EM*	NL
44005	*h	**FD**	A	*GW*	LA	44052	c	**XC**	P	*XC*	EC
44007	*h	**FD**	A	*GW*	LA	44054	s	**ST**	P	*EM*	NL
44008	*h	**FD**	A	*GW*	LA	44055	*h	**FD**	FG	*GW*	LA
44009	*h	**FD**	A	*GW*	LA	44056	m	**VE**	A	*VE*	EC
44010	*h	**FD**	A	*GW*	LA	44057	m	**VE**	P	*VE*	EC
44011	*	**FD**	A	*GW*	LA	44058	m	**VE**	A	*VE*	EC
44012	c	**XC**	A	*XC*	EC	44059	*	**FD**	A	*GW*	LA
44013	*h	**FD**	A	*GW*	LA	44060	*h	**FD**	P	*GW*	LA
44014	*h	**FD**	A	*GW*	LA	44061	m	**VE**	A	*VE*	EC
44015	*	**FD**	A	*GW*	LA	44063	m	**VE**	A	*VE*	EC
44016	*h	**FD**	A	*GW*	LA	44064	*h	**FD**	A	*GW*	LA
44017	c	**XC**	A	*XC*	EC	44065	t	**V**	AV		LM
44018	*	**FD**	A	*GW*	LA	44066	*	**FD**	A	*GW*	LA
44019	m	**VE**	A	*VE*	EC	44067	*h	**FD**	A	*GW*	LA
44020	*h	**FD**	A	*GW*	LA	44068	*h	**FD**	FG	*GW*	LA
44021	c	**XC**	P	*XC*	EC	44069	*h	**FD**	P	*GW*	LA
44022	*h	**FD**	A	*GW*	LA	44070	s	**ST**	P	*EM*	NL
44023	*h	**FD**	A	*GW*	LA	44071	s	**ST**	P	*EM*	NL
44024	*h	**FD**	A	*GW*	OO	44072	c	**XC**	P	*XC*	EC
44025	*	**FD**	A	*GW*	LA	44073	†	**VE**	P	*VE*	EC
44026	*h	**FD**	A	*GW*	LA	44074	*h	**FD**	FG	*GW*	LA
44027	s	**VE**	P	*VE*	NL	44075	m	**VE**	P	*VE*	EC
44028	*	**FD**	A	*GW*	LA	44076	*h	**FD**	FG	*GW*	LA
44029	*	**FD**	A	*GW*	LA	44077	m	**VE**	A	*VE*	EC
44030	*h	**FD**	A	*GW*	LA	44078	*h	**FD**	P	*GW*	LA
44031	m	**VE**	A	*VE*	EC	44079	*h	**FD**	P	*GW*	LA
44032	*	**FD**	A	*GW*	LA	44080	m	**VE**	A	*VE*	EC
44033	*h	**FD**	A	*GW*	LA	44081	*h	**FD**	FG	*GW*	LA
44034	*h	**FD**	A	*GW*	LA	44083	*h	**FD**	P	*GW*	LA
44035	*	**FD**	A	*GW*	LA	44085	s	**ST**	P	*EM*	NL
44036	*h	**FD**	A	*GW*	LA	44086	*	**GW**	A	*GW*	LA
44037	*h	**FD**	A	*GW*	LA	44089	t	**V**	AV		LM
44038	*	**FD**	A	*GW*	LA	44090	*h	**FD**	P	*GW*	LA
44039	*	**FD**	A	*GW*	LA	44091	*h	**FD**	P	*GW*	LA
44040	*	**GW**	A	*GW*	LA	44093	*h	**FD**	A	*GW*	LA
44041	s	**ST**	P	*EM*	NL	44094	m	**VE**	A	*VE*	EC
44042	*h	**FD**	P	*GW*	LA	44097	*h	**FD**	P	*GW*	LA
44043	*h	**FD**	A	*GW*	LA	44098	m	**VE**	A	*VE*	EC
44044	s	**ST**	P	*EM*	NL	44100	*h	**FD**	FG	*GW*	PM
44045	m	**VE**	A	*VE*	EC	44101	*h	**FD**	P	*GW*	LA
44046	s	**ST**	P	*EM*	NL						

TRAILER COMPOSITE KITCHEN   TCK

Converted from Mark 3A Open Standard. Refurbished CrossCountry vehicles with Primarius seating. Small kitchen for the preparation of hot food and stowage space for two trolleys between First and Standard Class. One toilet removed. 30/10 1T.

45001–005. Lot No. 30877 Derby 1975–77. 34.3 t.

45001	(12004)	**XC**	P	*XC*	EC
45002	(12106)	**XC**	P	*XC*	EC
45003	(12076)	**XC**	P	*XC*	EC
45004	(12077)	**XC**	P	*XC*	EC
45005	(12080)	**XC**	P	*XC*	EC

TRAILER COMPOSITE   TC

Converted from TF for First Great Western 2014–15. Refurbished with Grammer seating. 24/39 1T.

46001–004. Lot No. 30881 Derby 1976–77. 35.6 t. Converted from TF.
46005–009. Lot No. 30896 Derby 1977–78. 35.6 t. Converted from TF.
46010–013. Lot No. 30938 Derby 1979–80. 35.6 t. Converted from TF.
46014. Lot No. 30963 Derby 1982. 35.6 t. Converted from TF.
46015. Lot No. 30884 Derby 1976–77. 35.6 t. Converted from TF.
46016/017. Lot No. 30939 Derby 1979–80. 35.6 t. Converted from TF.
46018. Lot No. 30969 Derby 1982. 35.6 t. Converted from TF.

46001	(41005)	**FD**	A	*GW*	LA
46002	(41029)	**FD**	A	*GW*	LA
46003	(41033)	**FD**	A	*GW*	LA
46004	(41055)	**FD**	A	*GW*	LA
46005	(41065)	**FD**	A	*GW*	LA
46006	(41081)	**FD**	P	*GW*	LA
46007	(41096)	**FD**	P	*GW*	LA
46008	(41109)	**FD**	P	*GW*	LA
46009	(41119)	**FD**	P	*GW*	LA
46010	(41125)	**FD**	A	*GW*	LA
46011	(41139)	**FD**	A	*GW*	LA
46012	(41147)	**FD**	P	*GW*	LA
46013	(41148)	**FD**	P	*GW*	LA
46014	(41168)	**FD**	P	*GW*	LA
46015	(40505, 41179)	**FD**	A	*GW*	LA
46016	(42282, 41181)	**FD**	P	*GW*	LA
46017	(42270, 41184)	**FD**	P	*GW*	LA
46018	(42318, 41191)	**FD**	P	*GW*	LA

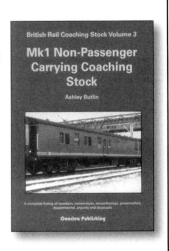

2.3. HST SET FORMATIONS

GREAT WESTERN RAILWAY

The largest operator of HSTs is Great Western Railway with 54 sets to cover 49 diagrams (of these one is a "hot spare" at Old Oak Common and one a "hot spare" at Bristol St Philip's Marsh).

The sets are split into three types, as shown below. These are 16 "low density" sets mainly used on West Country services, 20 "high density" sets with a full kitchen or buffet vehicle and 18 "super high density" sets including a TSB vehicle (with just a small corner buffet counter).

Although some sets are prefixed "OC" for Old Oak Common, for maintenance purposes all trailers are now based at Laira apart from two spare vehicles.

By summer 2015 all GWR HSTs were 8-car rakes with one full First Class carriage and either a First Class buffet car or one of the newly converted Composite vehicles – essentially both providing 1½ coaches of First Class.

Number of sets: 54.
Maximum number of daily diagrams: 49.
Formations: 8-cars.
Allocation: Laira (Plymouth).
Other maintenance and servicing depots: Landore (Swansea), St Philip's Marsh (Bristol), Long Rock (Penzance).
Operation: London Paddington–Exeter/Paignton/Plymouth/(Newquay in the summer)/Penzance, Bristol, Cardiff/Swansea/West Wales, Oxford/Hereford/Great Malvern/Cheltenham Spa.

Set	L	K	F	E	D	C	B	A	density
LA01	41024	40755	42034	42559	42033	42007	42035	44011	L
LA02	41032	40727	42046	42561	42045	42207	42047	44015	L
LA03	41038	40757	42055	42562	42343	42292	42056	44018	L
LA04	41052	40710	42077	42564	42076	42004	42078	44025	L
LA05	41094	40707	42185	42567	42184	42183	42107	44001	L
LA06	41104	40713	42208	42511	42054	42206	42209	44066	L
LA07	41122	40722	42252	42571	42019	42345	42253	44028	L
LA08	41124	40739	42256	42572	42263	42255	42257	44029	L
LA09	41130	40716	42072	42574	42325	42267	42269	44032	L
LA10	41134	40721	42276	42576	42332	42275	42277	44034	L
LA11	41135	40703	42280	42502	42265	42279	42281	44035	L
LA12	41136	40752	42144	42551	42143	42268	42145	44049	L
LA13	41142	40734	42333	42577	42075	42291	42293	44038	L
LA14	41144	40733	42296	42578	42350	42295	42297	44039	L
LA15	41146	40715	42300	42579	42351	42299	42301	44040	L
LA16	41158	40743	42245	42581	42129	42200	42250	44086	L
OC30	41008	40807	42079	42552	42236	42251	42080	44026	H
OC31	41038	40804	42060	42573	42197	42347	42061	44020	H
OC32	41018	40801	42025	42556	42362	42024	42026	44008	H
OC33	41028	40806	42040	42560	42039	42348	42041	44013	H

OC34	41102	40803	42203	42568	42027	42201	42204	44064	H
OC35	41106	40808	42213	42569	42212	42211	42214	44067	H
OC36	41110	40809	42346	42517	42349	42138	42089	44003	H
OC37	41132	40802	42272	42575	42073	42271	42273	44033	H
OC38	41138	40810	42284	42505	42003	42202	42285	44036	H
LA60	41162	40900	42231	42570	42232	42353	42233	44074	H
LA61	41160	40901	42304	42566	42303	42302	42305	44068	H
LA62	41167	40902	42167	42565	42168	42103	42169	44055	H
LA63	41059	40903	42175	42563	42176	42105	42177	44081	H
LA64	41166	40904	42094	42582	42093	42092	42108	44076	H
LA71	41010	40204	42013	42553	42360	42012	42014	44004	H
LA72	41012	40205	42016	42554	42005	42015	42361	44005	H
LA73	41016	40207	42006	42555	42096	42021	42023	44007	H
LA74	41020	40221	42028	42557	42009	42259	42029	44009	H
LA75	41022	40210	42031	42558	42010	42030	42032	44010	H
LA80	41137	40718	42083	42095	42102	42356	42049	44083	H

Set	L	K	F	E	D	C	B	A	density
OC40	41149	46016	40106	42580	42166	42218	42071	44079	SH
OC41	41182	46008	40107	42520	42222	42224	42382	44101	SH
OC42	41183	46014	40108	42519	42315	42317	42383	44090	SH
OC43	41186	46012	40109	42515	42258	42266	42365	44000	SH
OC44	41192	46018	40110	42514	42115	42174	42288	44097	SH
OC45	41187	46009	40111	42501	42247	42173	42260	44078	SH
OC46	41161	46007	40112	42512	42178	42195	42043	44042	SH
OC47	41108	46006	40113	42509	42308	42217	42067	44060	SH
OC48	41189	46017	40114	42518	42085	42310	42087	44069	SH
OC49	41169	46013	40115	42583	42319	42364	42321	44091	SH
OC50	41108	46015	40101	42516	42098	42264	42283	44093	SH
OC51	41006	46001	40103	42513	42070	42069	42118	44023	SH
OC52	41030	46002	40102	42510	42042	42008	42044	44014	SH
OC53	41034	46003	40118	42506	42048	42066	42050	44016	SH
OC54	41056	46004	40117	42503	42074	42081	42126	44043	SH
OC55	41089	46005	40104	42504	42221	42062	42068	44022	SH
OC56	41126	46010	40116	42508	42216	42344	42261	44030	SH
OC57	41140	46011	40105	42507	42099	42287	42289	44037	SH

L = Low density; H = High density; SH = Super High density.

Spares:

LA:	40119	40231	40811	41004	41103	41116	41176	42101	42196
	42294	42381	44002	44059					
OO:	44024								
PM:	44100								

VIRGIN TRAINS EAST COAST

Virgin Trains East Coast operates 15 HST sets on the ECML. As well as serving non-electrified destinations such as Hull and Inverness the VTEC HSTs also work alongside Class 91s and Mark 4 sets on services to Leeds, Newcastle and Edinburgh. Set EC64 (ex-NL05) transferred from East Midlands Trains in 2011 and set NL65 (ex-NL02) as an 8-car followed in 2015.

Number of sets: 15.
Maximum number of daily diagrams: 14.
Formations: 9-cars.
Allocation: Craigentinny (Edinburgh).
Other maintenance depot: Neville Hill (Leeds).
Operation: London King's Cross–Leeds/Harrogate/Skipton/Hull/Lincoln/ Newcastle/Edinburgh/Aberdeen/Inverness.

Set	M	L	J	G	F	E	D	C	B
EC51	41120	41150	40748	42215	42091	42146	42150	42154	44094
EC52	41039	41040	40735	42323	42189	42057	42058	42059	44019
EC53	41090	41044	40737	42340	42127	42063	42064	42065	44045
EC54	41087	41088	40706	42104	42161	42171	42172	42219	44056
EC55	41091	41092	40704	42179	42188	42180	42181	42106	44058
EC56	41170	41118	40720	42241	42363	42242	42243	42244	44098
EC57	41151	41152	40740	42226	42128	42182	42186	42190	44080
EC58	41097	41098	40750	42158	42238	42191	42192	42193	44061
EC59	41099	41100	40711	42235	42239	42240	42198	42199	44063
EC60	41066	41164	40742	42122	42116	42357	42134	42355	44031
EC61	41115	41165	40702	42117	42159	42160	42109	42110	44057
EC62	41185	41095	40701	42306	42326	42330	42237	42307	44075
EC63	41159	41083	40708	42163	42286	42228	42130	42322	44050
EC64	41062	41154	40732	42125	42335	42123	42205	42210	44073
NL65	41112	41068	40751	42194	42229	42227	42225		44027

Spares:

EC: 40705   40805   41190   42354   44077

GRAND CENTRAL

GC operates HSTs between Sunderland and King's Cross. Formations are flexible: there are enough vehicles to form three 6-car sets or one set can be disbanded to enable two sets to run as 7-cars at times of high demand.

Number of sets: 3.
Maximum number of daily diagrams: 2.
Formations: 6-cars or 7-cars.
Allocation: Heaton (Newcastle).
Operation: London King's Cross–Sunderland.

Set	TF	TSB	TS	TS	TS	TF*
GC01	41201	40424	42403	42402	42401	41204
GC02	41202	40426	42406	42405	42404	41205
GC03	41203	40433	42409	42408	42407	41206

* declassified.

EAST MIDLANDS TRAINS

East Midlands Trains HSTs are concentrated on the St Pancras–Nottingham corridor during the day, with early morning and evening services to Leeds for servicing at Neville Hill.

Number of sets: 9.
Maximum number of daily diagrams: 8.
Formations: 8-cars.
Allocation: Neville Hill (Leeds).
Other maintenance depot: Derby Etches Park.
Operation: London St Pancras–Nottingham, Sheffield/Leeds.

Set	J	G	F	E	D	C	B	A
NL01	41057	41084	40730	42327	42111	42112	42113	44041
NL03	41061	41067	40741	42337	42119	42120	42121	44054
NL04	41077	41064	40749	42151	42164	42165	42153	44047
NL06	41156	41041	40746	42132	42131	42331	42133	44046
NL07	41111	41070	40754	42339	42135	42136	42137	44044
NL08	41071	41072	40753	42329	42139	42140	42141	44048
NL10	41075	41076	40756	42328	42341	42148	42149	44051
NL11	41117	41046	40728	42220	42100	42230	42124	44085
NL12	41079	41069	40700	42155	42156	42157	42152	44070

Spares:

NL:	41063	41113	42384	44071

CROSSCOUNTRY

CrossCountry reintroduced regular HST diagrams on its services from the December 2008 timetable. Trains run in 7-car formation with the spare TS coaches regularly used in traffic as coaches "C", "D" or "E".

Number of sets: 5.
Maximum number of daily diagrams: 4.
Formations: 7-cars.
Allocation: Craigentinny (Edinburgh).
Other maintenance depots: Laira (Plymouth) or Neville Hill (Leeds).
Operation: Edinburgh–Leeds–Plymouth is the core route with some services extending to Dundee or Penzance.

Set	A	B	C	D	E	F	G
XC01	41193	45001	42368	42374	42367	42366	44021
XC02	41194	45002	42375	42373	42372	42371	44072
XC03	41195	45003	42369	42378	42377	42376	44052
XC04	41026	45004	42038	42037	42036	42380	44012
XC05	41035	45005	42051	42053	42052	42379	44017

Spares:

EC:	42097	42234	42290	42342	42370

2.4. SALOONS

Several specialist passenger carrying carriages, normally referred to as saloons are permitted to run on the national railway system. Many of these are to pre-nationalisation designs.

WCJS FIRST CLASS SALOON

Built 1892 by LNWR, Wolverton. Originally dining saloon mounted on six-wheel bogies. Rebuilt with new underframe with four-wheel bogies in 1927. Rebuilt 1960 as observation saloon with DMU end. Gangwayed at other end. The interior has a saloon, kitchen, guards vestibule and observation lounge. 19/– 1T. Gresley bogies. 28.5 t. 75 mph. ETS x.

41   (484, 45018) x   **M**   WC *WC*   CS

LNWR DINING SALOON

Built 1890 by LNWR, Wolverton. Mounted on the underframe of LMS General Utility Van 37908 in the 1980s. Contains kitchen and dining area seating 12 at tables for two. 12/–. Gresley bogies. 75 mph. 25.4 t. ETS x.

159   (5159)   x   **M**   WC *WC*   CS

GNR FIRST CLASS SALOON

Built 1912 by GNR, Doncaster. Contains entrance vestibule, lavatory, two separate saloons, library and luggage space. 19/– 1T. Gresley bogies. 75 mph. 29.4 t. ETS x.

Non-standard livery: Teak.

807   (4807)   x   **O**   WC *WC*   CS

LNER GENERAL MANAGERS SALOON

Built 1945 by LNER, York. Gangwayed at one end with a veranda at the other. The interior has a dining saloon seating 12, kitchen, toilet, office and nine seat lounge. 21/– 1T. B4 bogies. 75 mph. 35.7 t. ETS 3.

1999   (902260)   **M**   WC   CS   DINING CAR No. 2

GENERAL MANAGER'S SALOON

Renumbered 1989 from London Midland Region departmental series. Formerly the LMR General Manager's saloon. Rebuilt from LMS period 1 Corridor Brake First M5033M to dia 1654 and mounted on the underframe of BR suburban Brake Standard M43232. Screw couplings have been removed. B4 bogies. 100 mph. ETS 2X.

LMS Lot No. 326 Derby 1927. 27.5 t.

6320   (5033, DM 395707)   x   **M**   PR   *PR*   SK

BELMOND BRITISH PULLMAN SUPPORT CAR

Converted 199? from Courier vehicle converted from Mark 1 Corridor Brake Standard 1986–87. Toilet retained and former compartment area replaced with train manager's office, crew locker room, linen store and dry goods store. The former luggage area has been adapted for use as an engineers' compartment and workshop. B5 bogies. 100 mph. ETS 2.

Lot No. 30721 Wolverton 1963. 35.5 t.

99545 (35466, 80207)   **PC**   BE   *BP*   SL   BAGGAGE CAR No. 11

SERVICE CAR

Converted from BR Mark 1 Corridor Brake Standard. Commonwealth bogies. 100 mph. ETS 2.

Lot No. 30721 Wolverton 1963.

99886 (35407)   x   **M** WC   *WC* CS   86 SERVICE CAR No. 1

ROYAL SCOTSMAN SALOONS

Built 1960 by Metro-Cammell as Pullman Kitchen Second for East Coast Main Line Services. Rebuilt 2016 as a Spa Car with two large bedrooms with bathroom/spa areas. Commonwealth bogies. xx t. ETS ?.

99337 (CAR No. 337)   **M** BE   *RS*   ZG   SPA STATEROOM

Built 1960 by Metro-Cammell as Pullman Kitchen First for East Coast Main Line services. Rebuilt 2013 as dining car. Commonwealth bogies. 38.5 t. ETS ?.

99960 (321 SWIFT)   **M** BE   *RS*   ZG   DINING CAR No. 2

Built 1960 by Metro-Cammell as Pullman Parlour First (§ Pullman Kitchen First) for East Coast Main Line services. Rebuilt 1990 as sleeping cars with four twin sleeping rooms (*§ three twin sleeping rooms and two single sleeping rooms at each end). Commonwealth bogies. 38.5 t. ETS ?.

99961	(324 AMBER) *	M	BE	*RS*	ZG	STATE CAR 1
99962	(329 PEARL)	M	BE	*RS*	ZG	STATE CAR 2
99963	(331 TOPAZ)	M	BE	*RS*	ZG	STATE CAR 3
99964	(313 FINCH) §	M	BE	*RS*	ZG	STATE CAR 4

Built 1960 by Metro-Cammell as Pullman Kitchen First for East Coast Main Line services. Rebuilt 1993 as observation car with open verandah seating 32. B4 bogies. 36.95 t. ETS ?.

| 99965 | (319 SNIPE) | M | BE | *RS* | ZG | OBSERVATION CAR |

Built 1960 by Metro-Cammell as Pullman Kitchen First for East Coast Main Line services. Rebuilt 1993 as dining car. Commonwealth bogies. 38.5 t. ETS ?.

| 99967 | (317 RAVEN) | M | BE | *RS* | ZG | DINING CAR No. 1 |

Mark 3A. Converted 1997 from a Sleeping Car at Carnforth Railway Restoration & Engineering Services. BT10 bogies. Attendant's and adjacent two sleeping compartments converted to generator room containing a 160 kW Volvo unit. In 99968 four sleeping compartments remain for staff use with another converted for use as a staff shower and toilet. The remaining five sleeping compartments have been replaced by two passenger cabins. In 99969 seven sleeping compartments remain for staff use. A further sleeping compartment, along with one toilet, have been converted to store rooms. The other two sleeping compartments have been combined to form a crew mess. 41.5 t. 99968 ETS index ?. 99969 ETS 7X (when generator not in use). ETS index ?? (when generator in use).

Lot No. 30960 Derby 1981–83.

| 99968 | (10541) | M | BE | *RS* | ZG | STATE CAR 5 |
| 99969 | (10556) | M | BE | *RS* | ZG | SERVICE CAR |

"LMS CLUB CAR"

Converted from BR Mark 1 Open Standard at Carnforth Railway Restoration & Engineering Services in 1994. Contains kitchen, pantry and two dining saloons. 20/– 1T. Commonwealth bogies. 100 mph. ETS 4.

Lot No. 30724 York 1963. 37 t.

| 99993 | (5067) | x | M | LS | | CL | LMS CLUB CAR |

BR INSPECTION SALOON

Mark 1. Short frames. Non-gangwayed. Observation windows at each end. The interior layout consists of two saloons interspersed by a central lavatory/kitchen/guards/luggage section. 90 mph. ETS x.

BR Wagon Lot No. 3095 Swindon 1957. B4 bogies. 30.5 t.

| 999506 | | | M | WC | *WC* | CS | |

2.5. PULLMAN CAR COMPANY SERIES

Pullman cars have never generally been numbered as such, although many have carried numbers, instead they have carried titles. However, a scheme of schedule numbers exists which generally lists cars in chronological order. In this section those numbers are shown followed by the car's title. Cars described as "kitchen" contain a kitchen in addition to passenger accommodation and have gas cooking unless otherwise stated. Cars described as "parlour" consist entirely of passenger accommodation. Cars described as "brake" contain a compartment for the use of the guard and a luggage compartment in addition to passenger accommodation.

PULLMAN PARLOUR FIRST

Built 1927 by Midland Carriage & Wagon Company. 26/– 2T. Gresley bogies. 41 t. ETS 2.

| 213 | MINERVA | **PC** | BE | *BP* | SL |

PULLMAN KITCHEN FIRST

Built 1928 by Metropolitan Carriage & Wagon Company. 20/– 1T. Gresley bogies. 42 t. ETS 4.

| 238 | PHYLISS | **PC** | BE | | SL |

PULLMAN PARLOUR FIRST

Built 1928 by Metropolitan Carriage & Wagon Company. 24/– 2T. Gresley bogies. 40 t. ETS 4.

| 239 | AGATHA | **PC** | BE | | SL |
| 243 | LUCILLE | **PC** | BE | *BP* | SL |

PULLMAN KITCHEN FIRST

Built 1925 by BRCW. Rebuilt by Midland Carriage & Wagon Company in 1928. 20/– 1T. Gresley bogies. 41 t. ETS 4.

| 245 | IBIS | **PC** | BE | *BP* | SL |

PULLMAN PARLOUR FIRST

Built 1928 by Metropolitan Carriage & Wagon Company. 24/– 2T. Gresley bogies. ETS 4.

| 254 | ZENA | **PC** | BE | *BP* | SL |

PULLMAN KITCHEN FIRST

Built 1928 by Metropolitan Carriage & Wagon Company. 20/– 1T. Gresley bogies. 42 t. ETS 4.

255   IONE   **PC**   BE   *BP*   SL

PULLMAN KITCHEN COMPOSITE

Built 1932 by Metropolitan Carriage & Wagon Company. Originally included in 6-Pul EMU. Electric cooking. 12/16 1T. EMU bogies. ETS x.

264   RUTH   **PC**   BE   SL

PULLMAN KITCHEN FIRST

Built 1932 by Metropolitan Carriage & Wagon Company. Originally included in "Brighton Belle" EMUs but now used as hauled stock. Electric cooking. 20/– 1T. B5 (SR) bogies (§ EMU bogies). 44 t. ETS 2.

280   AUDREY   **PC**   BE   *BP*   SL
281   GWEN   **PC**   BE   *BP*   SL
283   MONA   §   **PC**   BE   SL
284   VERA   **PC**   BE   *BP*   SL

PULLMAN PARLOUR THIRD

Built 1932 by Metropolitan Carriage & Wagon Company. Originally included in "Brighton Belle" EMUs. –/56 2T. EMU bogies. ETS x.

Non-standard livery: BR Revised Pullman (blue & white lined out in white).

286   CAR No. 86   **0**   BE   SL

PULLMAN BRAKE THIRD

Built 1932 by Metropolitan Carriage & Wagon Company. Originally driving motor cars in "Brighton Belle" EMUs. Traction and control equipment removed for use as hauled stock. –/48 1T. EMU bogies. ETS x.

292   CAR No. 92   **PC**   BE   SL
293   CAR No. 93   **PC**   BE   SL

PULLMAN PARLOUR FIRST

Built 1951 by Birmingham Railway Carriage & Wagon Company. 32/– 2T. Gresley bogies. 39 t. ETS 3.

301   PERSEUS   **PC**   BE   *BP*   SL

Built 1952 by Pullman Car Company, Preston Park using underframe and bogies from 176 RAINBOW, the body of which had been destroyed by fire. 26/– 2T. Gresley bogies. 38 t. ETS 4.

302   PHOENIX   **PC**   BE   *BP*   SL

PULLMAN PARLOUR FIRST

Built 1951 by Birmingham Railway Carriage & Wagon Company. 32/– 2T.
Gresley bogies. 39 t. ETS 3.

308   CYGNUS   **PC**   BE   *BP*   SL

PULLMAN BAR FIRST

Built 1951 by Birmingham Railway Carriage & Wagon Company. Rebuilt
1999 by Blake Fabrications, Edinburgh with original timber-framed body
replaced by a new fabricated steel body. Contains kitchen, bar, dining
saloon and coupé. Electric cooking. 14/– 1T. Gresley bogies. ETS 3.

310   PEGASUS   x   **PC**   LS   *LS*   CL

Also carries "THE TRIANON BAR" branding.

PULLMAN PARLOUR FIRST

Built 1960–61 by Metro-Cammell for East Coast Main Line services. –/36 2T.
Commonwealth bogies. 38.5 t. ETS x.

326   EMERALD   x   **PC**   WC   *WC*   CS

PULLMAN KITCHEN SECOND

Built 1960–61 by Metro-Cammell for East Coast Main Line services.
Commonwealth bogies. –/30 1T. 40 t. ETS x.

335   CAR No. 335   x   **PC**   VT   *VT*   TM

PULLMAN PARLOUR SECOND

Built 1960–61 by Metro-Cammell for East Coast Main Line services. 347, 348
and 350 are used as Open Firsts. –/42 2T. Commonwealth bogies. 38.5 t. ETS x.

347	CAR No. 347	x	**M**	WC	*WC*	CS	
348	CAR No. 348	x	**PC**	WC	*WC*	CS	TOPAZ
349	CAR No. 349	x	**PC**	VT	*VT*	TM	
350	CAR No. 350	x	**M**	WC	*WC*	CS	
351	CAR No. 351	x	**PC**	WC	*WC*	CS	SAPPHIRE
352	CAR No. 352	x	**PC**	WC	*WC*	CS	AMETHYST
353	CAR No. 353	x	**PC**	VT	*VT*	TM	

PULLMAN SECOND BAR

Built 1960–61 by Metro-Cammell for East Coast Main Line services.
–/24+17 bar seats. Commonwealth bogies. 38.5 t. ETS x.

354   THE HADRIAN BAR x   **PC**   WC   *WC*   CS

2.6.LOCOMOTIVESUPPORTCARRIAGES

These carriages have been adapted from Mark 1s and Mark 2s for use as support carriages for heritage steam and diesel locomotives. Some seating is retained for the use of personnel supporting the locomotives operation with the remainder of the carriage adapted for storage, workshop, dormitory and catering purposes. These carriages can spend considerable periods of time off the national railway system when the locomotives they support are not being used on that system. No owner or operator details are included in this section. After the depot code, the locomotive(s) each carriage is usually used to support is given.

CORRIDOR BRAKE FIRST

Mark 1. Commonwealth bogies. ETS 2.

14007. Lot No. 30382 Swindon 1959. 35 t.
17015. Lot No. 30668 Swindon 1961. 36 t.
17025. Lot No. 30718 Swindon 1963. Metal window frames. 36 t.

14007 (14007, 17007)	x	**M**	NY	LNER 61264
17015 (14015)	x	**CC**	TM	Tyseley Locomotive Works-based locos
17025 (14025)	v	**M**	CS	LMS 45690

CORRIDOR BRAKE FIRST

Mark 2A. Pressure ventilated. B4 bogies. ETS 4.

14064. Lot No. 30775 Derby 1967–68. 32 t.
14099/17096. Lot No. 30786 Derby 1968. 32 t.

14064 (14064, 17064)	x	**M**	CS	LMS 45305/BR 70013	
14099 (14099, 17099)	v	**M**	CS	LMS 45305/BR 70013	
17096 (14096)		**PC**	SL	SR 35028	MERCATOR

CORRIDOR BRAKE COMPOSITE

Mark 1. ETS 2.

21096. Lot No. 30185 Metro-Cammell 1956. BR Mark 1 bogies. 32.5 t.
21232. Lot No. 30574 GRCW 1960. B4 bogies. 34 t.
21249. Lot No. 30669 Swindon 1961–62. Commonwealth bogies. 36 t.

21096	x	**M**	NY	LNER 60007
21232	x	**M**	SK	LMS 46201
21249	x	**CC**	SL	New Build 60163

CORRIDOR BRAKE STANDARD

Mark 1. Metal window frames and melamine interior panelling. ETS 2.

35317–322. Lot No. 30699 Wolverton 1962–63. Commonwealth bogies. 37 t.
35449. Lot No. 30728 Wolverton 1963. Commonwealth bogies. 37 t.
35451–486. Lot No. 30721 Wolverton 1963. Commonwealth bogies. 37 t.

35317	x	**CC**	SH	LMS 46100
35322	x	**M**	CS	WCRC Carnforth-based locomotives
35449	x	**M**	CS	LMS 45231
35451	x	**CC**	SH	SR 34046
35461	x	**CH**	CL	GWR 5029
35463	v	**M**	CS	WCRC Carnforth-based locomotives
35465	x	**CC**	SH	BR 70000
35468	x	**M**	YK	National Railway Museum locomotives
35470	v	**CH**	TM	Tyseley Locomotive Works-based locos
35476	x	**M**	SK	LMS 46233
35479	v	**M**	SH	LNER 61306
35486	x	**M**	TN	LNER 60009/61994

CORRIDOR BRAKE FIRST

Mark 2C. Pressure ventilated. Renumbered when declassified. B4 bogies. ETS 4.

Lot No. 30796 Derby 1969–70. 32.5 t.

35508	(14128, 17128)	**M**	BQ	LMS 44871/45407

CORRIDOR BRAKE FIRST

Mark 2A. Pressure ventilated. Renumbered when declassified. B4 bogies. ETS 4.

Lot No. 30786 Derby 1968. 32 t.

35517	(14088, 17088)	b	**M**	BQ	LMS 44871/45407
35518	(14097, 17097)	b	**G**	SH	SR 34067

COURIER VEHICLE

Mark 1. Converted 1986–87 from Corridor Brake Standards. ETS 2.

80204/217. Lot No. 30699 Wolverton 1962. Commonwealth bogies. 37 t.
80220. Lot No. 30573 Gloucester 1960. B4 bogies. 33 t.

80204	(35297)	**M**	CS	WCRC Carnforth-based locomotives
80217	(35299)	**M**	CS	WCRC Carnforth-based locomotives
80220	(35276)	**M**	NY	LNER 62005

2.7. 95xxx & 99xxx RANGE NUMBER CONVERSION TABLE

The following table is presented to help readers identify carriages which may still carry numbers in the 95xxx and 99xxx number ranges of the former private owner number series, which is no longer in general use.

9xxxx	BR No.	9xxxx	BR No.	9xxxx	BR No.
95402	Pullman 326	99350	Pullman 350	99673	550
99035	35322	99351	Pullman 351	99674	551
99040	21232	99352	Pullman 352	99675	552
99041	35476	99353	Pullman 353	99676	553
99052	Saloon 41	99354	Pullman 354	99677	586
99121	3105	99361	Pullman 335	99678	504
99122	3106	99371	3128	99679	506
99125	3113	99405	35486	99680	17102
99127	3117	99530	Pullman 301	99710	18767
99128	3130	99531	Pullman 302	99716 *	18808
99131	Saloon 1999	99532	Pullman 308	99718	18862
99241	35449	99534	Pullman 245	99721	18756
99302	13323	99535	Pullman 213	99723	35459
99304	21256	99536	Pullman 254	99880	Saloon 159
99311	1882	99537	Pullman 280	99881	Saloon 807
99312	35463	99539	Pullman 255	99883	2108
99319	17168	99541	Pullman 243	99885	2110
99326	4954	99543	Pullman 284	99887	2127
99327	5044	99546	Pullman 281	99953	35468
99328	5033	99547	Pullman 292	99966	34525
99329	4931	99548	Pullman 293	99970	Pullman 232
99347	Pullman 347	99670	546	99972	Pullman 318
99348	Pullman 348	99671	548	99973	324
99349	Pullman 349	99672	549	99974	Pullman 328

* The number 99716 has also been applied to 3416 for filming purposes.

2.8. SET FORMATIONS

VIRGIN TRAINS EAST COAST MARK 4 SET FORMATIONS

The Virgin Trains East Coast Mark 4 sets generally run in fixed formations since their refurbishment at Bombardier, Wakefield in 2003–05. These rakes are listed below. Class 91 locomotives are positioned next to Coach B.

Set	B	C	D	E	F	H	K	L	M	DVT
BN01	12207	12417	12415	12414	12307	10307	11298	11301	11401	82207
BN02	12232	12402	12450	12448	12302	10302	11299	11302	11402	82202
BN03	12201	12401	12459	12478	12301	10320	11277	11303	11403	82219
BN04	12202	12480	12421	12518	12327	10303	11278	11304	11404	82209
BN05	12209	12486	12520	12522	12300	10326	11219	11305	11405	82210
BN06	12208	12406	12420	12422	12313	10309	11279	11306	11406	82208
BN07	12231	12411	12405	12489	12329	10323	11280	11307	11407	82204
BN08	12205	12481	12485	12407	12328	10300	11229	11308	11408	82211
BN09	12230	12513	12483	12514	12308	10304	11281	11309	11409	82215
BN10	12214	12419	12488	12443	12305	10331	11282	11310	11410	82205
BN11	12203	12437	12436	12484	12315	10308	11283	11311	11411	82218
BN12	12212	12431	12404	12426	12330	10333	11284	11312	11412	82212
BN13	12228	12469	12430	12424	12311	10313	11285	11313	11413	82213
BN14	12229	12410	12526	12423	12312	10332	11201	11314	11414	82206
BN15	12226	12442	12409	12515	12309	10306	11286	11315	11415	82214
BN16	12213	12428	12445	12433	12304	10315	11287	11316	11416	82222
BN17	12223	12444	12427	12432	12303	10324	11288	11317	11417	82225
BN18	12215	12453	12468	12467	12324	10305	11289	11318	11418	82220
BN19	12211	12434	12400	12470	12310	10318	11290	11319	11419	82201
BN20	12224	12477	12439	12440	12326	10321	11241	11320	11420	82200
BN21	12222	12461	12441	12476	12323	10330	11244	11321	11421	82227
BN22	12210	12452	12460	12473	12316	10301	11291	11322	11422	82230
BN23	12225	12454	12456	12455	12318	10325	11292	11323	11423	82226
BN24	12219	12447	12425	12403	12319	10328	11293	11324	11424	82229
BN25	12217	12446	12519	12464	12322	10312	11294	11325	11425	82216
BN26	12220	12474	12465	12429	12325	10311	11295	11326	11426	82223
BN27	12216	12449	12466	12538	12317	10319	11237	11327	11427	82228
BN28	12218	12458	12463	12533	12320	10310	11273	11328	11428	82217
BN29	12204	12462	12457	12438	12321	10317	11998	11329	11429	82231
BN30	12227	12471	12534	12472	12331	10329	11999	11330	11430	82203
Spare	12200									82224

2.9. SERVICE STOCK

Carriages in this section are used for internal purposes within the railway industry, ie they do not generate revenue from outside the industry. Most are numbered in the former BR departmental number series.

BARRIER, ESCORT & TRANSLATOR VEHICLES

These vehicles are used to move multiple unit, HST and other vehicles around the national railway system.

HST Barrier Vehicles. Mark 1/2A. Renumbered from BR departmental series, or converted from various types. B4 bogies (* Commonwealth bogies).

Non-standard livery: 6340, 6344, 6346 All over dark blue.

6330. Mark 2A. Lot No. 30786 Derby 1968.
6336/38/44. Mark 1. Lot No. 30715 Gloucester 1962.
6340. Mark 1. Lot No. 30669 Swindon 1962.
6346. Mark 2A. Lot No. 30777 Derby 1967.
6348. Mark 1. Lot No. 30163 Pressed Steel 1957.

6330	(14084, 975629)		**FB**	A	*GW*	LA
6336	(81591, 92185)		**FB**	A	*GW*	LA
6338	(81581, 92180)		**FB**	A	*GW*	LA
6340	(21251, 975678)	*	**0**	A	*VE*	EC
6344	(81263, 92080)		**0**	A	*VE*	EC
6346	(9422)		**0**	A	*VE*	EC
6348	(81233, 92963)		**FB**	A	*GW*	LA

Mark 4 Barrier Vehicles. Mark 2A/2C. Converted from Corridor First (*) or Open Brake Standard. B4 bogies.

Non-standard livery: 6358 All over dark blue.

6352/53. Mark 2A. Lot No. 30774 Derby 1968.
6354/55. Mark 2C. Lot No. 30820 Derby 1970.
6358/59. Mark 2A. Lot No. 30788 Derby 1968.

6352	(13465, 19465)	*	**HB**	E	*VE*	BN
6353	(13478, 19478)	*	**HB**	E	*VE*	BN
6354	(9459)		**GN**	DR		LW
6355	(9477)		**GN**	DR		LW
6358	(9432)		**0**	DR		LW
6359	(9429)		**GN**	DR		LW

EMU Translator Vehicles. Mark 1. Converted 1980 from Restaurant Unclassified Opens. 6376/77 have Tightlock couplers and 6378/79 Dellner couplers. Commonwealth bogies.

Lot No. 30647 Wolverton 1959–61.

6376	(1021, 975973)	**PB**	P	*DB*	TO *(works with 6377)*
6377	(1042, 975975)	**PB**	P	*DB*	TO *(works with 6376)*
6378	(1054, 975971)	**PB**	P	*DB*	TO *(works with 6379)*
6379	(1059, 975972)	**PB**	P	*DB*	TO *(works with 6378)*

HST Barrier Vehicles. Mark 1. Converted from Gangwayed Brake Vans in 1994–95. B4 bogies.

6392. Lot No. 30715 Gloucester 1962.
6393/97. Lot No. 30716 Gloucester 1962.
6394. Lot No. 30162 Pressed Steel 1956–57.
6398/99. Lot No. 30400 Pressed Steel 1957–58.

6392	(81588, 92183)	**PB**	P		LM
6393	(81609, 92196)	**PB**	P	*VE*	EC
6394	(80878, 92906)	**PB**	P	*VE*	EC
6397	(81600, 92190)	**PB**	P		LM
6398	(81471, 92126)	**PB**	EM	*EM*	NL
6399	(81367, 92994)	**PB**	EM	*EM*	NL

Escort Coaches. Converted from Mark 2A Open Brake Standards. These vehicles use the same bodyshell as the Mark 2A Corridor Brake First. B4 bogies.

9419. Lot No.30777 Derby 1970.
9428. Lot No.30820 Derby 1970.

9419	**DS**	DR	*DR*	KM
9428	**DS**	DR	*DR*	KM

EMU Translator Vehicles. Converted from Class 508 driving cars.

64664. Lot No. 30979 York 1979–80.
64707. Lot No. 30981 York 1979–80.

64664	**AG**	A	*GB*	ZG	Liwet	*(works with 64707)*
64707	**AG**	A	*GB*	ZG	Labezerin	*(works with 64664)*

Eurostar Barrier Vehicles. Mark 1. Converted from General Utility Vans with bodies removed. Fitted with B4 bogies for use as Eurostar barrier vehicles.

96380/381. Lot No. 30417 Pressed Steel 1958–59.
96383. Lot No. 30565 Pressed Steel 1959.
96384. Lot No. 30616 Pressed Steel 1959–60.

96380	(86386, 6380)	**B**	EU	*EU*	TI
96381	(86187, 6381)	**B**	EU	*EU*	TI
96383	(86664, 6383)	**B**	EU	*EU*	TI
96384	(86955, 6384)	**B**	EU	*EU*	TI

Brake Force Runners. Converted from Motorail vans built 1998–99 by Marcroft Engineering using underframe and running gear from Motorail General Utility Vans. B5 bogies.

Lot No. 30417 Pressed Steel 1958–59.

96604	(86337, 96156)	**Y**	CS	*CS*	ZA
96606	(86324, 96213)	**Y**	CS	*CS*	ZA
96608	(86385, 96216)	**Y**	CS	*CS*	ZA
96609	(86327, 96217)	**Y**	CS	*CS*	ZA

EMU Translator Vehicles. Converted from various Mark 1s.

Non-standard livery: All over blue.

975864. Lot No. 30054 Eastleigh 1951–54. Commonwealth bogies.
975867. Lot No. 30014 York 1950–51. Commonwealth bogies.
975875. Lot No. 30143 Charles Roberts 1954–55. Commonwealth bogies.
975974/978. Lot No. 30647 Wolverton 1959–61. B4 bogies.
977087. Lot No. 30229 Metro–Cammell 1955–57. Commonwealth bogies.

975864	(3849)	**HB**	E	*GB*	ZH		*(works with 975867)*
975867	(1006)	**HB**	E	*GB*	ZH		*(works with 975864)*
975875	(34643)	**0**	E	*RG*	WH		*(works with 977087)*
975974	(1030)	**AG**	A	*GB*	ZG	Paschar	*(works with 975978)*
975978	(1025)	**AG**	A	*GB*	ZG	Perpetiel	*(works with 975974)*
977087	(34971)	**0**	E	*RG*	WH		*(works with 975875)*

LABORATORY, TESTING & INSPECTION COACHES

These coaches are used for research, development, testing and inspection on the national railway system. Many are fitted with sophisticated technical equipment.

Plain Line Pattern Recognition Coaches. Converted from BR Mark 2F Buffet First (*) or Open Standard. B4 bogies.

1256. Lot No. 30845 Derby 1973.
5981. Lot No. 30860 Derby 1973–74.

1256	(3296)	*	**Y**	NR	*CS*	ZA
5981			**Y**	NR	*CS*	ZA

Generator Vans. Mark 1. Converted from BR Mark 1 Gangwayed Brake Vans. B5 bogies.

6260. Lot No. 30400 Pressed Steel 1957–58.
6261. Lot No. 30323 Pressed Steel 1957.
6262. Lot No. 30228 Metro-Cammell 1957–58.
6263. Lot No. 30163 Pressed Steel 1957.
6264. Lot No. 30173 York 1956.

6260	(81450, 92116)	**Y**	NR	*CS*	ZA
6261	(81284, 92988)	**Y**	NR	*CS*	ZA
6262	(81064, 92928)	**Y**	NR	*CS*	ZA
6263	(81231, 92961)	**Y**	NR	*CS*	ZA
6264	(80971, 92923)	**Y**	NR	*CS*	ZA

Staff Coach. Mark 2D. Converted from BR Mark 2D Open Brake Standard. Lot No. 30824 Derby 1971. B4 bogies.

9481	**Y**	NR	*CS*	ZA

Test Train Brake Force Runners. Mark 2F. Converted from BR Mark 2F Open Brake Standard. Lot No. 30861 Derby 1974. B4 bogies.

9516	**Y**	NR	*CS*	ZA
9523	**Y**	NR	*CS*	ZA

Driving Trailer Coaches. Converted 2008 at Serco, Derby from Mark 2F Driving Open Brake Standards. Fitted with generator. Disc brakes. B4 bogies.

9701–08. Lot No. 30861 Derby 1974. Converted to Driving Open Brake Standard Glasgow 1974.
9714. Lot No. 30861 Derby 1974. Converted to Driving Open Brake Standard Glasgow 1986.

9701	(9528)	**Y**	NR	*CS*	ZA
9702	(9510)	**Y**	NR	*CS*	ZA
9703	(9517)	**Y**	NR	*CS*	ZA
9708	(9530)	**Y**	NR	*CS*	ZA
9714	(9536)	**Y**	NR	*CS*	ZA

Ultrasonic Test Coach. Converted from Class 421 EMU MBSO.

62287. Lot No. 30808. York 1970. SR Mark 6 bogies.
62384. Lot No. 30816. York 1970. SR Mark 6 bogies.

62287	**Y**	NR	*CS*	ZA
62384	**Y**	NR	*CS*	ZA

Test Train Brake Force Runners. Converted from Mark 2F Open Standard converted to Class 488/3 EMU TSOLH. These vehicles are included in test trains to provide brake force and are not used for any other purposes. Lot No. 30860 Derby 1973–74. B4 bogies.

72612	(6156)	**Y**	NR	*CS*	ZA
72616	(6007)	**Y**	NR	*CS*	ZA

Structure Gauging Train Coach. Converted from Mark 2F Open Standard converted to Class 488/3 EMU TSOLH. Lot No. 30860 Derby 1973–74. B4 bogies.

72630	(6094)	**Y**	NR	*CS*	ZA *(works with 99666)*

Plain Line Pattern Recognition Coaches. Converted from BR Mark 2F Open Standard converted to Class 488/3 EMU TSOLH. Lot No. 30860 Derby 1973–74. B4 bogies.

72631	(6096)	**Y**	NR	*CS*	ZA
72639	(6070)	**Y**	NR	*CS*	ZA

Driving Trailer Coaches. Converted from Mark 3B 110 mph Driving Brake Vans. Fitted with diesel generator. Lot No. 31042 Derby 1988.

82111	**Y**	NR	ZA
82124	**Y**	NR	ZA
82129	**Y**	NR	ZA
82145	**Y**	NR	ZA

Structure Gauging Train Coach. Converted from BR Mark 2E Open First then converted to exhibition van. Lot No. 30843 Derby 1972–73. B4 bogies.

99666	(3250)	**Y**	NR	*CS*	ZA *(works with 72630)*

Inspection Saloon. Converted from Class 202 DEMU TRB at Stewarts Lane for use as a BR Southern Region General Manager's Saloon. Overhauled at FM Rail, Derby 2004–05 for use as a New Trains Project Saloon. Can be used in push-pull mode with suitably equipped locomotives. Eastleigh 1958. SR Mark 4 bogies.

975025 (60755)   **G**   NR   *CS*   ZA   CAROLINE

Overhead Line Equipment Test Coach ("MENTOR"). Converted from BR Mark 1 Corridor Brake Standard. Lot No. 30142 Gloucester 1954–55. Fitted with pantograph. B4 bogies.

975091 (34615)   **Y**   NR   *CS*   ZA

New Measurement Train Conference Coach. Converted from prototype HST TF Lot No. 30848 Derby 1972. BT10 bogies.

975814 (11000, 41000)   **Y**   NR   *CS*   EC

New Measurement Train Lecture Coach. Converted from prototype HST catering vehicle. Lot No. 30849 Derby 1972–73. BT10 bogies.

975984 (10000, 40000)   **Y**   NR   *CS*   EC

Radio Survey Coach. Converted from BR Mark 2E Open Standard. Lot No. 30844 Derby 1972–73. B4 bogies.

977868 (5846)   **Y**   NR   *CS*   ZA

Staff Coach. Converted from Royal Household couchette Lot No. 30889, which in turn had been converted from BR Mark 2B Corridor Brake First. Lot No. 30790 Derby 1969. B5 bogies.

977969 (14112, 2906)   **Y**   NR   *CS*   ZA

Track Inspection Train Coach. Converted from BR Mark 2E Open Standard. Lot No. 30844 Derby 1972–73. B4 bogies.

977974 (5854)   **Y**   NR   *CS*   ZA

Electrification Measurement Coach. Converted from BR Mark 2F Open First converted to Class 488/2 EMU TFOH. Lot No. 30859 Derby 1973–74. B4 bogies.

977983 (3407, 72503)   **Y**   NR   *CS*   ZA

New Measurement Train Staff Coach. Converted from HST catering vehicle. Lot No. 30884 Derby 1976–77. BT10 bogies.

977984 (40501)   **Y**   P   *CS*   EC

Structure Gauging Train Coaches. Converted from Mark 2F Open Standard converted to Class 488/3 EMU TSOLH or from BR Mark 2D Open First subsequently declassified to Open Standard and then converted to exhibition van. B4 bogies.

977985. Lot No. 30860 Derby 1973–74.
977986. Lot No. 30821 Derby 1971.

977985 (6019, 72715)   **Y**   NR   *CS*   ZA *(works with 977986)*
977986 (3189, 99664)   **Y**   NR   *CS*   ZA *(works with 977985)*

New Measurement Train Overhead Line Equipment Test Coach. Converted from HST TGS. Lot No. 30949 Derby 1982. Fitted with pantograph. BT10 bogies.

977993 (44053)   **Y**   P   *CS*   EC

New Measurement Train Track Recording Coach. Converted from HST TGS. Lot No. 30949 Derby 1982. BT10 bogies.

977994	(44087)	**Y**	P	*CS*	EC

New Measurement Train Coach. Converted from HST catering vehicle. Lot No. 30921 Derby 1978–79. BT10 bogies. Fitted with generator.

977995	(40719, 40619)	**Y**	P	*CS*	EC

Radio Survey Coach. Converted from Mark 2F Open Standard converted to Class 488/3 EMU TSOLH. Lot No. 30860 Derby 1973–74.

977997	(72613, 6126)	**Y**	NR	*CS*	ZA

Track Recording Coach. Purpose built Mark 2. B4 bogies.

999550		**Y**	NR	*CS*	ZA

Ultrasonic Test Coaches. Converted from Class 421 EMU MBSO and Class 432 EMU MSO.

999602/605. Lot No. 30862 York 1974. SR Mk 6 bogies.
999606. Lot No. 30816. York 1970. SR Mk 6 bogies.

999602	(62483)	**Y**	NR	*CS*	ZA
999605	(62482)	**Y**	NR	*CS*	ZA
999606	(62356)	**Y**	NR	*CS*	ZA

BREAKDOWN TRAIN COACHES

These coaches are formed in trains used for the recovery of derailed railway vehicles and were converted from BR Mark 1 Corridor Brake Standard and General Utility Van. The current use of each vehicle is given.

971001/003/004. Lot No. 30403 York/Glasgow 1958–60. Commonwealth bogies.
971002. Lot No. 30417 Pressed Steel 1958–59. Commonwealth bogies.
975087. Lot No. 30032 Wolverton 1951–52. BR Mark 1 bogies.
975464. Lot No. 30386 Charles Roberts 1956–58. Commonwealth bogies.
975471. Lot No. 30095 Wolverton 1953–55. Commonwealth bogies.
975477. Lot No. 30233 GRCW 1955–57. BR Mark 1 bogies.
975486. Lot No. 30025 Wolverton 1950–52. Commonwealth bogies.

971001	(86560, 94150)	**Y**	NR	*DB*	BS	Tool & Generator Van
971002	(86624, 94190)	**Y**	NR	*DB*	SP	Tool Van
971003	(86596, 94191)	**Y**	NR	*DB*	BS	Tool Van
971004	(86194, 94168)	**Y**	NR	*DB*	SP	Tool Van
975087	(34289)	**Y**	NR	*DB*	SP	Tool & Generator Van
975464	(35171)	**Y**	NR	*DB*	SP	Staff Coach
975471	(34543)	**Y**	NR	*DB*	BS	Staff Coach
975477	(35108)	**Y**	NR	*DB*	SP	Staff Coach
975486	(34100)	**Y**	NR	*DB*	SP	Tool & Generator Van

INFRASTRUCTURE MAINTENANCE COACHES

De-Icing Coaches

These coaches are used for removing ice from the conductor rail of DC lines. They were converted from Class 489 DMLVs that had originally been Class 414/3 DMBSOs.

Lot No. 30452 Ashford/Eastleigh 1959. Mk 4 bogies.

68501	(61281)	**Y**	NR	*GB*	ZG
68504	(61286)	**Y**	NR	*GB*	ZG
68505	(61299)	**Y**	NR	*GB*	ZG

Winterisation Train Coach. Converted from BR Mark 2E Open Standard. Lot No. 30844 Derby 1972–73. B4 bogies.

977869	(5858)	**Y**	NR	*DR*	Perth CS

INTERNAL USER VEHICLES

These vehicles are confined to yards and depots or do not normally move. Details are given of the internal user number (if allocated), type, former identity, current use and location. Many no longer see regular use. * = Grounded body.

975403 carries its original number 4598.

024787*	BR GUV 93219	Stores Van	Nottingham Eastcroft Depot
041474*	BR SPV 975418	Stores Van	Worksop Up Yard
041947	BR GUV 93425	Stores van	Ilford Depot (London)
041989*	BR SPV 975423	Stores Van	Toton Depot
042154	BR GUV 93975	Stores Van	Ipswich Upper Yard
061202*	BR GUV 93498	Stores Van	Laira Depot (Plymouth)
083602	BR CCT 94494	Stores Van	Three Bridges Station
083637	BR NW 99203	Stores Van	Stewarts Lane Depot
083644	BR Ferry Van 889201	Stores van	Eastleigh Depot
083664	BR Ferry Van 889203	Stores van	Eastleigh Depot
–	BR Open Standard 5636	Instruction Coach	St Philip's Marsh Depot
–	BR BV 6360	Barrier vehicle	Neville Hill Depot, Leeds
–	BR BV 6396	Stores van	Longsight Depot (Manchester)
–	BR RFKB 10256	Instruction Coach	Yoker Depot
–	BR RFKB 10260	Instruction Coach	Yoker Depot
–	BR SPV 88045*	Stores Van	Thames Haven Yard
–	BR BG 92901	Stores van	Wembley Depot (London)
–	BR NL 94003	Stores van	Old Oak Common HST Depot
–	BR NL 94006	Stores van	Old Oak Common HST Depot
–	BR NK 94121	Stores van	Toton Depot
–	BR NB 94438	Stores van	Toton Depot
–	BR CCT 94663*	Stores Van	Mossend Up Yard
–	BR GUV 96139	Stores van	Longsight Depot (Manchester)
–	BR Ferry Van 889200	Stores van	Stewarts Lane Depot
–	BR Ferry Van 889202	Stores van	Stewarts Lane Depot
–	BR Open Standard 975403	Cinema Coach	St Philip's Marsh Depot

| – | SR PMV 977045* | Stores Van | EMD, Longport Works |
| – | SR CCT 2516* | Stores Van | Eastleigh Depot |

Abbreviations:
BG = Gangwayed Brake Van
BV = Barrier Vehicle
CCT = Covered Carriage Truck (a 4-wheeled van similar to a GUV)
GUV = General Utility Van (bogied van with side and end doors)
NB = High Security Brake Van (converted from BG, gangways removed)
NK = High Security General Utility Van (end doors removed)
NL = Newspaper Van (converted from a GUV)
NW = Bullion Van (converted from a Corridor Brake Standard)
PMV = Parcels & Miscellaneous Van (a 4-wheeled van similar to a CCT but without end doors)
RFKB = Kitchen Buffet First
SPV = Special Parcels Van (a 4-wheeled van converted from a Fish Van)

2.10. COACHING STOCK AWAITING DISPOSAL

This list shows the locations of carriages awaiting disposal. The definition of which vehicles are awaiting disposal is somewhat vague, but often these are vehicles of types not now in normal service, those not expected to see further use or that have originated from preservationists as a source of spares or possible future use or carriages which have been damaged by fire, vandalism or collision.

1252	SH	3060	CL	5186	TM	6029	SH
1253	SH	3091	CL	5193	TM	6041	CS
1258	CS	3241	CS	5194	TM	6045	SH
1644	CS	3229	BU	5221	TM	6050	CS
1650	CS	3255	FA	5331	FA	6073	SH
1652	CS	3303	TO	5386	FA	6134	SH
1655	CS	3309	TM	5420	TM	6151	SH
1658	CL	3368	FA	5453	CS	6154	SH
1663	CS	3388	FA	5463	CS	6175	CS
1670	CS	3399	FA	5478	CS	6179	CS
1679	CL	3408	CS	5491	CS	6324	CP
1680	CL	3416	TM	5569	CS	6351	BU
1696	CL	4362	BU	5737	CS	6361	NL
1800	SH	4796	BU	5740	CS	6364	Barry
2108	CS	4799	BU	5756	CS	6365	Barry
2110	CS	4849	CS	5815	SH	6412	CL
2127	CS	4860	CS	5876	SH	6720	FA
2131	CS	4932	CS	5888	SH	7931	BU
2833	CS	4997	CS	5925	SH	9440	SH
2834	EH	5054	CL	5943	CS	9479	BU
2909	CS	5148	TM	5958	SH	9489	CS
3045	CL	5179	TM	5978	SH	9490	BU
3051	CL	5183	TM	6009	SH	10201	LM

10245	CS	94106	BU	94431	CS	96170	CS
10530	ZH	94116	BU	94434	CL	96178	CS
10578	ZN	94153	WE	94435	TO	96182	CS
10588	ZH	94166	BS	94445	WE	96191	CS
10656	ZN	94170	CL	94450	WE	96192	CS
10682	LM	94176	BS	94451	WE	96371	LB
11005	LM	94177	TO	94470	TO	96372	LM
11021	LM	94195	BS	94479	TO	96373	LM
12008	LM	94196	CS	94482	CS	96374	ZB
12029	LM	94197	BS	94488	BU	96375	LM
12095	LM	94207	TO	94490	BU	96602	Barry
12096	ZN	94208	TO	94492	WE	96603	CF
12101	LM	94214	CS	94495	Hellifield	96605	Barry
12144	LM	94222	CS	94498	CS	96607	Barry
12156	LM	94227	HM	94501	TO	99019	CS
12160	LM	94229	CL	94504	Hellifield	99884	CL
12163	LM	94302	Hellifield	94512	CS	889400	ZA
13306	CS	94303	Hellifield	94515	**	975081	ZA
13323	CS	94304	MH	94517	BU	975280	ZA
13508	CL	94306	Hellifield	94520	BU	975454	TO
16204	CL	94308	CS	94522	CL	975484	CS
17168	CS	94310	WE	94525	CS	975639	CS
18767	SH	94311	WE	94526	CS	975681	Portobello
18808	SH	94313	WE	94527	Hellifield	975682	Portobello
18862	CS	94316	TO	94530	CS	975685	Portobello
21268	CL	94317	TO	94531	BU	975686	Portobello
34525	CS	94322	CS	94538	CY	975687	Portobello
35333	CL	94323	Hellifield	94539	CS	975688	Portobello
35467	CL	94326	Hellifield	94540	TJ	975920	Portobello
40729	NL	94332	CS	94542	CS	977077	**
41043	LB	94333	Hellifield	94545	HM	977085	BU
80212	CS	94335	CL	94546	Hellifield	977095	CS
80374	BU	94336	CL	94547	CS	977111	**
80403	CS	94337	WE	94548	CS	977112	**
80404	CS	94338	WE	95300	CS	977169	CL
80414	SL	94344	TO	95410	CS	977241	BU
82125	LM	94401	CS	95727	WE	977618	BY
92114	ZA	94406	CS	95754	CS	999509	CL
92159	CS	94408	CS	95761	WE		
92303	BU	94410	WE	95763	BS	083439	BU
92908	CS	94420	CS	96110	CS		
92936	BU	94422	TO	96132	CS	DS 70220	**
93723	BY	94423	BS	96135	CS		
94058	BU	94427	WE	96164	CS	Pullman 315	CS
94101	CS	94428	CS	96165	CS	Pullman 316	CS
94104	TO	94429	HM			Pullman 325	CS

** Other locations:

94515	Eastleigh East Yard	977112	Ripple Lane Yard
977077	Ripple Lane Yard	DS 70220	Western Trading Estate
977111	Ripple Lane Yard		Siding, North Acton

3. DIESEL MULTIPLE UNITS

INTRODUCTION

This section contains details of all Diesel Multiple Units, usually referred to as DMUs, which can run on Britain's national railway network.

The number of DMUs used on the national railway network has increased dramatically since the 1980s as they have replaced more traditional locomotive-hauled trains on many routes. DMUs today work a wide variety of services, from long distance Intercity to inter-urban and suburban duties.

LAYOUT OF INFORMATION

DMUs are listed in numerical order of set – using current numbers as allocated by the RSL. Individual "loose" vehicles are listed in numerical order after vehicles formed into fixed formations. Where sets or vehicles have been renumbered in recent years, former numbering detail is shown in parentheses. Each entry is laid out as in the following example:

Set No.	Detail	Livery	Owner	Operator	Depot	Formation	Name
153 309	cr	**GA**	P	*GA*	NC	52309	GERALD FIENNES

Codes: Codes are used to denote the livery, owner, operator and depot allocation of each Diesel Multiple Unit. Details of these can be found in section 6 of this book. Where a unit or spare car is off-lease, the operator column is left blank.

Detail Differences: Detail differences which currently affect the areas and types of train which vehicles may work are shown, plus differences in interior layout. Where such differences occur within a class, these are shown either in the heading information or alongside the individual set or vehicle number. The following standard abbreviations are used:

e   European Railway Traffic Management System (ERTMS) signalling equipment fitted.
r   Radio Electric Token Block signalling equipment fitted.

Use of the above abbreviations indicates the equipment fitted is normally operable. Meaning of non-standard abbreviations is detailed in individual class headings.

Set Formations: Regular set formations are shown where these are normally maintained. Readers should note set formations might be temporarily varied from time to time to suit maintenance and/or operational requirements. Vehicles shown as "Spare" are not formed in any regular set formation.

Names: Only names carried with official sanction are listed. Names are shown in UPPER/lower case characters as actually shown on the name carried on the vehicle(s). Unless otherwise shown, complete units are regarded as named rather than just the individual car(s) which carry the name.

GENERAL INFORMATION

CLASSIFICATION AND NUMBERING

DMU Classes are listed in class number order.

First generation ("Heritage") DMUs were classified in the series 100–139.
Parry People Movers (not actually technically DMUs) are classified in the series 139.
Second generation DMUs are classified in the series 140–199.
Diesel Electric Multiple Units are classified in the series 200–249.
Service units are classified in the series 930–999.

First and second generation individual cars are numbered in the series 50000–59999 and 79000–79999.

Parry People Mover cars are numbered in the 39000 series.

DEMU individual cars are numbered in the series 60000–60999, except for a few former EMU vehicles which retain their EMU numbers.

The Class 230 D-Train DEMU individual cars are numbered in the 300xxx series.

Service Stock individual cars are numbered in the series 975000–975999 and 977000–977999, although this series is not exclusively used for DMU vehicles.

UNITS OF MEASUREMENT

Principal details and dimensions are quoted for each class in metric and/or imperial units as considered appropriate bearing in mind common usage in the UK.

All dimensions and weights are quoted for vehicles in an "as new" condition with all necessary supplies (eg oil, water, sand) on board. Dimensions are quoted in the order Length – Width. All lengths quoted are over buffers or couplers as appropriate. Where two lengths are quoted, the first refers to outer vehicles in a set and the second to inner vehicles. All width dimensions quoted are maxima. All weights are shown as metric tonnes (t = tonnes).

OPERATING CODES

These codes are used by train operating company staff to describe the various different types of vehicles and normally appear on data panels on the inner (ie non driving) ends of vehicles.

The first part of the code describes whether the car has a motor or a driving cab as follows:

DM	Driving motor	M	Motor
DT	Driving trailer	T	Trailer

The next letter is a "B" for cars with a brake compartment.
This is followed by the saloon details:

F	First	L	denotes a vehicle with a toilet.
S	Standard	W	denotes a Wheelchair space.
C	Composite		

Finally vehicles with a buffet or kitchen area are suffixed RB or RMB for a miniature buffet counter.

Where two vehicles of the same type are formed within the same unit, the above codes may be suffixed by (A) and (B) to differentiate between the vehicles.

A composite is a vehicle containing both First and Standard Class accommodation, whilst a brake vehicle is a vehicle containing separate specific accommodation for the conductor.

Where vehicles have been declassified, the correct operating code which describes the actual vehicle layout is quoted in this publication.

BUILD DETAILS

Lot Numbers

Vehicles ordered under the auspices of BR were allocated a Lot (batch) number when ordered and these are quoted in class headings and sub-headings. Vehicles ordered since 1995 have no Lot Numbers, but the manufacturer and location that they were built is given.

Builders

These are shown for each lot. More details and a full list of builders can be found in section 6.7.

Information on sub-contracting works which built parts of carriages eg the underframes etc is not shown.

ACCOMMODATION

The information given in class headings and sub-headings is in the form F/S nT (or TD) nW. For example 12/54 1T 1W denotes 12 First Class and 54 Standard Class seats, one toilet and one space for a wheelchair. A number in brackets (ie (+2)) denotes tip-up seats (in addition to the fixed seats). Tip-up seats in vestibules do not count. The seating layout of open saloons is shown as 2+1, 2+2 or 3+2 as the case may be. Where units have First Class accommodation as well as Standard Class and the layout is different for each class then these are shown separately prefixed by "1:" and "2:". TD denotes a "universal access" toilet suitable for use by a disabled person.

NEW DMUS ON ORDER

Northern has a fleet of new DMUs on order, but the unit number and vehicle number series' had not been confirmed when this book went to press. The units on order are summarised here:

Class	Manufacturer	Operator	Quantity	Delivery dates
195	CAF	Northern	25 x 2-car	2018–19
			30 x 2-car	2018–19

3.1. DIESEL MECHANICAL & DIESEL HYDRAULIC UNITS

3.1.1 FIRST GENERATION UNITS

CLASS 121   PRESSED STEEL SUBURBAN

First generation units. One set is used on weekdays by Chiltern Railways on peak-hour Aylesbury–Princes Risborough services.
Construction: Steel.
Engines: Two Leyland 1595 of 112 kW (150 hp) at 1800 rpm.
Transmission: Mechanical. Cardan shaft and freewheel to a four-speed epicyclic gearbox and final drive.
Bogies: DD10.
Brakes: Vacuum.
Couplers: Screw.
Dimensions: 20.45 x 2.82 m.
Gangways: Non gangwayed single cars with cabs at each end.
Wheel arrangement: 1-A + A-1.
Doors: Manually-operated slam.
Maximum Speed: 70 mph.
Seating Layout: 3+2 facing.
Multiple Working: "Blue Square" coupling code. First Generation vehicles cannot be coupled to Second Generation units.

Fitted with central door locking.

121 020 formerly in departmental use as unit 960 002 (977722).

121 034 returned to service with Chiltern Railways in 2011. Formerly in departmental use as 977828.

Non-standard livery: 121 020 All over Chiltern blue with a silver stripe.

DMBS. Lot No. 30518 1960–61. –/65. 38.0 t.

121 020	**O**	CR	*CR*	AL	55020
121 034	**G**	CR	*CR*	AL	55034

3.1.2 PARRY PEOPLE MOVERS

CLASS 139   PPM-60

Gas/flywheel hybrid drive Railcars used on the Stourbridge Junction–Stourbridge Town branch.
Body construction: Stainless steel framework.
Chassis construction: Welded mild steel box section.
Primary Drive: Ford MVH420 2.3 litre 64 kW (86 hp) LPG fuel engine driving through Newage marine gearbox, Tandler bevel box and 4 "V" belt driver to flywheel.
Flywheel Energy Store: 500 kg, 1 m diameter, normal operational speed range 1000–1500 rpm.
Final transmission: 4 "V" belt driver from flywheel to Tandler bevel box, Linde hydrostatic transmission and spiral bevel gearbox at No. 2 end axle.
Braking: Normal service braking by regeneration to flywheel (1 m/s/s); emergency/parking braking by sprung-on, air-off disc brakes (3 m/s/s).
Maximum Speed: 45 mph.
Dimensions: 8.7 x 2.4 m.
Doors: Deans powered doors, double-leaf folding (one per side).
Seating Layout: 1+1 unidirectional/facing.
Multiple Working: Not applicable.

39001–002. DMS. Main Road Sheet Metal, Leyland 2007–08. –/17(+4) 1W. 12.5 t.

139 001	**LM** P	*LM*	SJ	39001
139 002	**LM** P	*LM*	SJ	39002

3.1.3 SECOND GENERATION UNITS

All units in this section have air brakes and are equipped with public address, with transmission equipment on driving vehicles and flexible diaphragm gangways. Except where otherwise stated, transmission is Voith 211r hydraulic with a cardan shaft to a Gmeinder GM190 final drive.

CLASS 142   PACER   BREL DERBY/LEYLAND

DMS–DMSL.

Construction: Steel underframe, rivetted steel body and roof. Built from Leyland National bus parts on Leyland Bus four-wheeled underframes.
Engines: One Cummins LT10-R of 165 kW (225 hp) at 1950 rpm.
Couplers: BSI at outer ends, bar within unit.
Dimensions: 15.55 x 2.80 m.
Gangways: Within unit only.   **Wheel Arrangement:** 1-A + A-1.
Doors: Twin-leaf inward pivoting.   **Maximum Speed:** 75 mph.
Seating Layout: 3+2 mainly unidirectional bus/bench style unless stated.
Multiple Working: Within class and with Classes 143, 144, 150, 153, 155, 156, 158 and 159.

c Refurbished Arriva Trains Wales units. Fitted with 2+2 individual Chapman seating.
s Fitted with 2+2 individual high-back seating.
t Former First North Western facelifted units – DMS fitted with a luggage/bicycle rack and wheelchair space.
u Merseytravel units – Fitted with 3+2 individual low-back seating.

55542–591. DMS. Lot No. 31003 1985–86. –/62 (c –/46(+6) 2W, s –/56, t –/53 or 55 1W, u –/52 or 54 1W). 24.5 t.
55592–641. DMSL. Lot No. 31004 1985–86. –/59 1T (c –/44(+6) 1T 2W, s –/50 1T, u –/60 1T). 25.0 t.
55701–746. DMS. Lot No. 31013 1986–87. –/62 (c –/46(+6) 2W, s –/56, t –/53 or 55 1W, u –/52 or 54 1W). 24.5 t.
55747–792. DMSL. Lot No. 31014 1986–87. –/59 1T (c –/44(+6) 1T 2W, s –/50 1T, u –/60 1T). 25.0 t.

142 001	t	**NO**	A	*NO*	NH	55542	55592
142 002	c	**AV**	A	*AW*	CF	55543	55593
142 003		**NO**	A	*NO*	NH	55544	55594
142 004	t	**NO**	A	*NO*	NH	55545	55595
142 005	t	**NO**	A	*NO*	NH	55546	55596
142 006	c	**AV**	A	*AW*	CF	55547	55597
142 007	t	**NO**	A	*NO*	NH	55548	55598
142 009	t	**NO**	A	*NO*	HT	55550	55600
142 010	c	**AV**	A	*AW*	CF	55551	55601
142 011	t	**NO**	A	*NO*	NH	55552	55602
142 012	t	**NO**	A	*NO*	NH	55553	55603
142 013		**NO**	A	*NO*	NH	55554	55604
142 014	t	**NO**	A	*NO*	NH	55555	55605
142 015	s	**NO**	A	*NO*	HT	55556	55606
142 016	s	**NO**	A	*NO*	HT	55557	55607
142 017	s	**NO**	A	*NO*	HT	55558	55608
142 018	s	**NO**	A	*NO*	HT	55559	55609
142 019	s	**NO**	A	*NO*	HT	55560	55610
142 020	s	**NO**	A	*NO*	HT	55561	55611
142 021	s	**NO**	A	*NO*	HT	55562	55612
142 022	s	**NO**	A	*NO*	HT	55563	55613
142 023	t	**NO**	A	*NO*	HT	55564	55614
142 024	t	**NO**	A	*NO*	HT	55565	55615
142 025	s	**NO**	A	*NO*	HT	55566	55616
142 026	s	**NO**	A	*NO*	HT	55567	55617
142 027	t	**NO**	A	*NO*	NH	55568	55618
142 028	t	**NO**	A	*NO*	NH	55569	55619
142 029		**NO**	A	*NO*	NH	55570	55620
142 030		**NO**	A	*NO*	NH	55571	55621
142 031	t	**NO**	A	*NO*	NH	55572	55622
142 032	t	**NO**	A	*NO*	NH	55573	55623
142 033	t	**NO**	A	*NO*	NH	55574	55624
142 034	t	**NO**	A	*NO*	NH	55575	55625
142 035	t	**NO**	A	*NO*	NH	55576	55626
142 036	t	**NO**	A	*NO*	NH	55577	55627
142 037	t	**NO**	A	*NO*	NH	55578	55628

142 038	t	NO	A	NO	NH	55579	55629
142 039	t	NO	A	NO	NH	55580	55630
142 040	t	NO	A	NO	NH	55581	55631
142 041	u	NO	A	NO	NH	55582	55632
142 042	u	NO	A	NO	NH	55583	55633
142 043	u	NO	A	NO	NH	55584	55634
142 044	u	NO	A	NO	NH	55585	55635
142 045	u	NO	A	NO	NH	55586	55636
142 046	u	NO	A	NO	NH	55587	55637
142 047	u	NO	A	NO	NH	55588	55638
142 048	u	NO	A	NO	NH	55589	55639
142 049	u	NO	A	NO	NH	55590	55640
142 050	s	NO	A	NO	HT	55591	55641
142 051	u	NO	A	NO	NH	55701	55747
142 052	u	NO	A	NO	NH	55702	55748
142 053	u	NO	A	NO	NH	55703	55749
142 054	u	NO	A	NO	NH	55704	55750
142 055	u	NO	A	NO	NH	55705	55751
142 056	u	NO	A	NO	NH	55706	55752
142 057	u	NO	A	NO	NH	55707	55753
142 058	u	NO	A	NO	NH	55708	55754
142 060	t	NO	A	NO	NH	55710	55756
142 061	t	NO	A	NO	NH	55711	55757
142 062	t	NO	A	NO	NH	55712	55758
142 063	t	NO	A	NO	NH	55713	55759
142 064	t	NO	A	NO	HT	55714	55760
142 065	s	NO	A	NO	HT	55715	55761
142 066	s	NO	A	NO	HT	55716	55762
142 067		NO	A	NO	HT	55717	55763
142 068	t	NO	A	NO	HT	55718	55764
142 069	c	AV	A	AW	CF	55719	55765
142 070	t	NO	A	NO	HT	55720	55766
142 071	s	NO	A	NO	HT	55721	55767
142 072	c	AV	A	AW	CF	55722	55768
142 073	c	AV	A	AW	CF	55723	55769
142 074	c	AV	A	AW	CF	55724	55770
142 075	c	AV	A	AW	CF	55725	55771
142 076	c	AV	A	AW	CF	55726	55772
142 077	c	AV	A	AW	CF	55727	55773
142 078	s	NO	A	NO	HT	55728	55774
142 079	s	NO	A	NO	HT	55729	55775
142 080	c	AV	A	AW	CF	55730	55776
142 081	c	AV	A	AW	CF	55731	55777
142 082	c	AV	A	AW	CF	55732	55778
142 083	c	AV	A	AW	CF	55733	55779
142 084	s	NO	A	NO	HT	55734	55780
142 085	c	AV	A	AW	CF	55735	55781
142 086	s	NO	A	NO	HT	55736	55782
142 087	s	NO	A	NO	HT	55737	55783
142 088	s	NO	A	NO	HT	55738	55784
142 089	s	NO	A	NO	HT	55739	55785

142 090	s	**NO**	A	*NO*	HT	55740	55786
142 091	s	**NO**	A	*NO*	HT	55741	55787
142 092	s	**NO**	A	*NO*	HT	55742	55788
142 093	s	**NO**	A	*NO*	HT	55743	55789
142 094	s	**NO**	A	*NO*	HT	55744	55790
142 095	s	**NO**	A	*NO*	HT	55745	55791
142 096	s	**NO**	A	*NO*	HT	55746	55792

CLASS 143   PACER   ALEXANDER/BARCLAY

DMS–DMSL. Similar design to Class 142, but bodies built by W Alexander with Barclay underframes.

Construction: Steel underframe, aluminium alloy body and roof. Alexander bus bodywork on four-wheeled underframes.
Engines: One Cummins LT10-R of 165 kW (225 hp) at 1950 rpm.
Couplers: BSI at outer ends, bar within unit.
Dimensions: 15.45 x 2.80 m.
Gangways: Within unit only.   **Wheel Arrangement:** 1-A + A-1.
Doors: Twin-leaf inward pivoting.   **Maximum Speed:** 75 mph.
Seating Layout: 2+2 high-back Chapman seating, mainly unidirectional.
Multiple Working: Within class and with Classes 142, 144, 150, 153, 155, 156, 158 and 159.

DMS. Lot No. 31005 Andrew Barclay 1985–86. –/48(+6) 2W. 24.0 t.
DMSL. Lot No. 31006 Andrew Barclay 1985–86. –/44(+6) 1T 2W. 24.5 t.

143 601	**AV**	MG	*AW*	CF	55642	55667	
143 602	**AW**	P	*AW*	CF	55651	55668	
143 603	**FI**	P	*GW*	EX	55658	55669	
143 604	**AW**	P	*AW*	CF	55645	55670	
143 605	**AW**	P	*AW*	CF	55646	55671	
143 606	**AW**	P	*AW*	CF	55647	55672	
143 607	**AW**	P	*AW*	CF	55648	55673	
143 608	**AW**	P	*AW*	CF	55649	55674	
143 609	**AV**	SG	*AW*	CF	55650	55675	Sir Tom Jones
143 610	**AV**	MG	*AW*	CF	55643	55676	
143 611	**FI**	P	*GW*	EX	55652	55677	
143 612	**FI**	P	*GW*	EX	55653	55678	
143 614	**AV**	MG	*AW*	CF	55655	55680	
143 616	**AW**	P	*AW*	CF	55657	55682	
143 617	**FI**	GW	*GW*	EX	55644	55683	
143 618	**FI**	GW	*GW*	EX	55659	55684	
143 619	**FI**	GW	*GW*	EX	55660	55685	
143 620	**FI**	P	*GW*	EX	55661	55686	
143 621	**FI**	P	*GW*	EX	55662	55687	
143 622	**AW**	P	*AW*	CF	55663	55688	
143 623	**AW**	P	*AW*	CF	55664	55689	
143 624	**AW**	P	*AW*	CF	55665	55690	
143 625	**AW**	P	*AW*	CF	55666	55691	

CLASS 144   PACER   ALEXANDER/BREL DERBY

DMS–DMSL or DMS–MS–DMSL. As Class 143, but underframes built by BREL.

Construction: Steel underframe, aluminium alloy body and roof. Alexander bus bodywork on four-wheeled underframes.
Engines: One Cummins LT10-R of 165 kW (225 hp) at 1950 rpm.
Couplers: BSI at outer ends, bar within unit.
Dimensions: 15.45/15.43 x 2.80 m.
Gangways: Within unit only.   **Wheel Arrangement:** 1-A + A-1.
Doors: Twin-leaf inward pivoting.   **Maximum Speed:** 75 mph.
Seating Layout: 2+2 high-back Richmond seating, mainly unidirectional.
Multiple Working: Within class and with Classes 142, 143, 150, 153, 155, 156, 158 and 159.

† Prototype demonstrator unit, refurbished by RVEL for Porterbrook as a trial, with new Fainsa seating and a universal access toilet to meet the 2020 accessibility regulations. Details are as follows:
DMS 55812: Lot No. 31015 BREL Derby 1986–87. –/43(+3). 27.2 t.
DMSL 55835: Lot No. 31016 BREL Derby 1986–87. –/35 1TD 2W. 28.0 t.

Non-standard livery: 144 012 144evolution (blue & purple).

DMS. Lot No. 31015 BREL Derby 1986–87. –/45(+3) 1W 24.0 t.
MS. Lot No. 31037 BREL Derby 1987. –/58. 23.5 t.
DMSL. Lot No. 31016 BREL Derby 1986–87. –/41(+3) 1T. 24.5 t.

144 001		**NO**	P	*NO*	NL	55801		55824
144 002		**NO**	P	*NO*	NL	55802		55825
144 003		**NO**	P	*NO*	NL	55803		55826
144 004		**NO**	P	*NO*	NL	55804		55827
144 005		**NO**	P	*NO*	NL	55805		55828
144 006		**NO**	P	*NO*	NL	55806		55829
144 007		**NO**	P	*NO*	NL	55807		55830
144 008		**NO**	P	*NO*	NL	55808		55831
144 009		**NO**	P	*NO*	NL	55809		55832
144 010		**NO**	P	*NO*	NL	55810		55833
144 011		**NO**	P	*NO*	NL	55811		55834
144 012	†	**0**	P	*NO*	NL	55812		55835
144 013		**NO**	P	*NO*	NL	55813		55836
144 014		**NO**	P	*NO*	NL	55814	55850	55837
144 015		**NO**	P	*NO*	NL	55815	55851	55838
144 016		**NO**	P	*NO*	NL	55816	55852	55839
144 017		**NO**	P	*NO*	NL	55817	55853	55840
144 018		**NO**	P	*NO*	NL	55818	55854	55841
144 019		**NO**	P	*NO*	NL	55819	55855	55842
144 020		**NO**	P	*NO*	NL	55820	55856	55843
144 021		**NO**	P	*NO*	NL	55821	55857	55844
144 022		**NO**	P	*NO*	NL	55822	55858	55845
144 023		**NO**	P	*NO*	NL	55823	55859	55846

Name: 144 001 THE PENISTONE LINE PARTNERSHIP

CLASS 150/0   SPRINTER   BREL YORK

DMSL–MS–DMS. Prototype Sprinter.

Construction: Steel.
Engines: One Cummins NT855R5 of 213 kW (285 hp) at 2100 rpm.
Bogies: BX8P (powered), BX8T (non-powered).
Couplers: BSI at outer end of driving vehicles, bar non-driving ends.
Dimensions: 19.93/19.92 x 2.73 m.
Gangways: Within unit only.   **Wheel Arrangement:** 2-B + 2-B + B-2.
Doors: Twin-leaf sliding.   **Maximum Speed:** 75 mph.
Seating Layout: 3+2 (mainly unidirectional).
Multiple Working: Within class and with Classes 142, 143, 144, 153, 155, 156, 158, 159, 170 and 172.

DMSL. Lot No. 30984 1984. –/72 1T. 35.4 t.
MS. Lot No. 30986 1984. –/92. 35.0 t.
DMS. Lot No. 30985 1984. –/69(+6). 34.7 t.

150 001	**GW**	A	*GW*	RG	55200	55400	55300
150 002	**GW**	A	*GW*	RG	55201	55401	55301

CLASS 150/1   SPRINTER   BREL YORK

DMSL–DMS.

Construction: Steel.
Engines: One Cummins NT855R5 of 213 kW (285 hp) at 2100 rpm.
Bogies: BP38 (powered), BT38 (non-powered).
Couplers: BSI.
Dimensions: 19.74 x 2.82 m.
Gangways: Within unit only.   **Wheel Arrangement:** 2-B (+ 2-B) + B-2.
Doors: Twin-leaf sliding.   **Maximum Speed:** 75 mph.
Seating Layout: 3+2 facing as built but Centro units were reseated with mainly unidirectional seating.
Multiple Working: Within class and with Classes 142, 143, 144, 153, 155, 156, 158, 159, 170 and 172.

c 3+2 Chapman seating.

DMSL. Lot No. 31011 1985–86. –/72 1T (c –/59 1TD (except 52144 –/62 1TD), t –/71 1T, u –/71 1T). 38.3 t.
DMS. Lot No. 31012 1985–86. –/76 (c –/65, t –/73, u –/70(+6)). 38.1 t.

150 101	u	**FB**	A	*GW*	PM	52101 57101
150 102	u	**FB**	A	*GW*	PM	52102 57102
150 103	u	**NO**	A	*NO*	NH	52103 57103
150 104	u	**FB**	A	*GW*	PM	52104 57104
150 105	u	**LM**	A	*LM*	TS	52105 57105
150 106	u	**FB**	A	*GW*	PM	52106 57106
150 107	u	**LM**	A	*LM*	TS	52107 57107
150 108	u	**FB**	A	*GW*	PM	52108 57108
150 109	u	**LM**	A	*LM*	TS	52109 57109
150 110	u	**NO**	A	*NO*	NH	52110 57110

150 111	u	**N0**	A	*NO*	NH	52111	57111
150 112	u	**N0**	A	*NO*	NH	52112	57112
150 113	u	**N0**	A	*NO*	NH	52113	57113
150 114	u	**N0**	A	*NO*	NH	52114	57114
150 115	u	**N0**	A	*NO*	NH	52115	57115
150 116	u	**N0**	A	*NO*	NH	52116	57116
150 117	u	**N0**	A	*NO*	NH	52117	57117
150 118	u	**N0**	A	*NO*	NH	52118	57118
150 119	u	**N0**	A	*NO*	NH	52119	57119
150 120	t	**FB**	A	*GW*	EX	52120	57120
150 121	u	**FB**	A	*GW*	EX	52121	57121
150 122	u	**FB**	A	*GW*	PM	52122	57122
150 123	t	**FB**	A	*GW*	EX	52123	57123
150 124	u	**FB**	A	*GW*	PM	52124	57124
150 127	u	**FB**	A	*GW*	EX	52127	57127
150 128	t	**FB**	A	*GW*	EX	52128	57128
150 129	t	**FB**	A	*GW*	EX	52129	57129
150 130	t	**FB**	A	*GW*	EX	52130	57130
150 131	t	**FB**	A	*GW*	EX	52131	57131
150 132	u	**N0**	A	*NO*	NH	52132	57132
150 133	c	**N0**	A	*NO*	NH	52133	57133
150 134	c	**N0**	A	*NO*	NH	52134	57134
150 135	c	**N0**	A	*NO*	NH	52135	57135
150 136	c	**N0**	A	*NO*	NH	52136	57136
150 137	c	**N0**	A	*NO*	NH	52137	57137
150 138	c	**N0**	A	*NO*	NH	52138	57138
150 139	c	**N0**	A	*NO*	NH	52139	57139
150 140	c	**N0**	A	*NO*	NH	52140	57140
150 141	c	**N0**	A	*NO*	NH	52141	57141
150 142	c	**N0**	A	*NO*	NH	52142	57142
150 143	c	**N0**	A	*NO*	NH	52143	57143
150 144	c	**N0**	A	*NO*	NH	52144	57144
150 145	c	**N0**	A	*NO*	NH	52145	57145
150 146	c	**N0**	A	*NO*	NH	52146	57146
150 147	c	**N0**	A	*NO*	NH	52147	57147
150 148	c	**N0**	A	*NO*	NH	52148	57148
150 149	c	**N0**	A	*NO*	NH	52149	57149
150 150	c	**N0**	A	*NO*	NH	52150	57150

Names:

| 150 129 | Devon & Cornwall RAIL PARTNERSHIP |
| 150 130 | Severnside Community Rail Partnership |

CLASS 150/2   SPRINTER   BREL YORK

DMSL–DMS.

Construction: Steel.
Engines: One Cummins NT855R5 of 213 kW (285 hp) at 2100 rpm.
Bogies: BP38 (powered), BT38 (non-powered).
Couplers: BSI.

Dimensions: 19.74 x 2.82 m.
Gangways: Throughout.   **Wheel Arrangement:** 2-B + B-2.
Doors: Twin-leaf sliding.   **Maximum Speed:** 75 mph.
Seating Layout: 3+2 mainly unidirectional seating as built, but most units have now been refurbished with new 2+2 seating.
Multiple Working: Within class and with Classes 142, 143, 144, 153, 155, 156, 158, 159, 170 and 172.

c Former First North Western units with 3+2 Chapman seating.
p Refurbished Arriva Trains Wales units with 2+2 Primarius seating.
v Units refurbished for Valley Lines with 2+2 Chapman seating.
w Units refurbished for First Great Western with 2+2 Chapman seating.
* Refurbished units for Great Western Railway with 2+2 Chapman seating and a new universal access toilet to meet the 2020 accessibility regulations.
† Refurbished units for Northern with a new universal access toilet to meet the 2020 accessibility regulations. 3+2 Chapman seating.

Northern promotional vinyls:

150 203/205/207/211/215/218/222/223/225/228/268–271/273–277 Welcome to Yorkshire.
150 272 R&B Festival week, Colne.

DMSL. Lot No. 31017 1986–87. * –/50(+4) 1TD 2W, † –/58(+3) 1TD 2W, c –/62 1TD, p –/60(+4) 1T, s –/68 1T 1W, u –/71 1T), v –/60(+8) 1T, w –/60(+8) 1T. 37.5 t (* 35.8 t, † 38.1 t).
DMS. Lot No. 31018 1986–87. * –/58(10), † –/70(+6), c –/70, p –/56(+10) 1W, s –/71(+3), †u –/70(+6), v –/56(+15) 2W, w –/56(+17) 2W. 36.5 t.

150 201	c	**NO**	A	*NO*	NH	52201	57201
150 202	u	**FB**	A	*GW*	PM	52202	57202
150 203	c	**NO**	A	*NO*	NH	52203	57203
150 204	†	**NO**	A	*NO*	NH	52204	57204
150 205	c	**NO**	A	*NO*	NH	52205	57205
150 206	†	**NO**	A	*NO*	NH	52206	57206
150 207	c	**NO**	A	*NO*	NH	52207	57207
150 208	p	**AV**	P	*AW*	CF	52208	57208
150 210	u	**NO**	A	*NO*	NH	52210	57210
150 211	c	**NO**	A	*NO*	NH	52211	57211
150 213	p	**AW**	P	*AW*	CF	52213	57213
150 214	u	**NO**	A	*NO*	NH	52214	57214
150 215	c	**NO**	A	*NO*	NH	52215	57215
150 216	u	**FB**	A	*GW*	PM	52216	57216
150 217	p	**AW**	P	*AW*	CF	52217	57217
150 218	c	**NO**	A	*NO*	NH	52218	57218
150 219	*	**FB**	P	*GW*	PM	52219	57219
150 220	†	**NO**	A	*NO*	NH	52220	57220
150 221	w	**FI**	P	*GW*	PM	52221	57221
150 222	†	**NO**	A	*NO*	NH	52222	57222
150 223	c	**NO**	A	*NO*	NH	52223	57223
150 224	c	**NO**	A	*NO*	NH	52224	57224
150 225	c	**NO**	A	*NO*	NH	52225	57225
150 226	u	**NO**	A	*NO*	NH	52226	57226

150 227	p	**AW**	P	*AW*	CF	52227	57227
150 228	s	**N0**	P	*NO*	NH	52228	57228
150 229	p	**AW**	P	*AW*	CF	52229	57229
150 230	w	**AW**	P	*AW*	CF	52230	57230
150 231	p	**AW**	P	*AW*	CF	52231	57231
150 232	*	**GW**	P	*GW*	PM	52232	57232
150 233	*	**GW**	P	*GW*	PM	52233	57233
150 234	*	**GW**	P	*GW*	PM	52234	57234
150 235	p	**AW**	P	*AW*	CF	52235	57235
150 236	w	**AW**	P	*AW*	CF	52236	57236
150 237	p	**AW**	P	*AW*	CF	52237	57237
150 238	*	**FB**	P	*GW*	PM	52238	57238
150 239	w	**FI**	P	*GW*	PM	52239	57239
150 240	w	**AW**	P	*AW*	CF	52240	57240
150 241	w	**AW**	P	*AW*	CF	52241	57241
150 242	w	**AW**	P	*AW*	CF	52242	57242
150 243	w	**FI**	P	*GW*	PM	52243	57243
150 244	w	**FI**	P	*GW*	PM	52244	57244
150 245	p	**AV**	P	*AW*	CF	52245	57245
150 246	*	**GW**	P	*GW*	PM	52246	57246
150 247	*	**GW**	P	*GW*	PM	52247	57247
150 248	*	**GW**	P	*GW*	PM	52248	57248
150 249	w	**FI**	P	*GW*	PM	52249	57249
150 250	p	**AW**	P	*AW*	CF	52250	57250
150 251	w	**AW**	P	*AW*	CF	52251	57251
150 252	p	**AV**	P	*AW*	CF	52252	57252
150 253	w	**AW**	P	*AW*	CF	52253	57253
150 254	w	**AW**	P	*AW*	CF	52254	57254
150 255	p	**AW**	P	*AW*	CF	52255	57255
150 256	p	**AV**	P	*AW*	CF	52256	57256
150 257	p	**AW**	P	*AW*	CF	52257	57257
150 258	p	**AV**	P	*AW*	CF	52258	57258
150 259	p	**AV**	P	*AW*	CF	52259	57259
150 260	p	**AV**	P	*AW*	CF	52260	57260
150 261	w	**FB**	P	*GW*	PM	52261	57261
150 262	p	**AV**	P	*AW*	CF	52262	57262
150 263	*	**GW**	P	*GW*	PM	52263	57263
150 264	p	**AV**	P	*AW*	CF	52264	57264
150 265	w	**FI**	P	*GW*	PM	52265	57265
150 266	*	**GW**	P	*GW*	PM	52266	57266
150 267	v	**AW**	P	*AW*	CF	52267	57267
150 268	s	**N0**	P	*NO*	NH	52268	57268
150 269	s	**N0**	P	*NO*	NH	52269	57269
150 270	s	**N0**	P	*NO*	NH	52270	57270
150 271	s	**N0**	P	*NO*	NH	52271	57271
150 272	s	**N0**	P	*NO*	NH	52272	5/272
150 273	s	**N0**	P	*NO*	NH	52273	57273
150 274	s	**N0**	P	*NO*	NH	52274	57274
150 275	s	**NR**	P	*NO*	NH	52275	57275
150 276	s	**N0**	P	*NO*	NH	52276	57276
150 277	s	**N0**	P	*NO*	NH	52277	57277

150 278	v	**AW**	P	*AW*	CF	52278	57278
150 279	v	**AW**	P	*AW*	CF	52279	57279
150 280	v	**AW**	P	*AW*	CF	52280	57280
150 281	v	**AW**	P	*AW*	CF	52281	57281
150 282	v	**AW**	P	*AW*	CF	52282	57282
150 283	p	**AV**	P	*AW*	CF	52283	57283
150 284	p	**AV**	P	*AW*	CF	52284	57284
150 285	p	**AV**	P	*AW*	CF	52285	57285

Name:

150 261   THE TARKA LINE THE FIRST 25 YEARS 1989–2014

CLASS 150/9   SPRINTER   BREL YORK

3-car Great Western Railway hybrids formed of a Class 150/1 with a 150/2 centre vehicle. DMSL–DMS–DMS. For details see Class 150/1 or Class 150/2.

150 925	u	**FB**	A	*GW*	PM	52125	57209	57125
150 926	u	**FB**	A	*GW*	PM	52126	57212	57126

Name:

150 925   THE HEART OF WESSEX LINE

CLASS 153   SUPER SPRINTER   LEYLAND BUS

DMSL. Converted by Hunslet-Barclay, Kilmarnock from Class 155 2-car units.

Construction: Steel underframe, rivetted steel body and roof. Built from Leyland National bus parts on Leyland Bus bogied underframes.
Engine: One Cummins NT855R5 of 213 kW (285 hp) at 2100 rpm.
Bogies: One P3-10 (powered) and one BT38 (non-powered).
Couplers: BSI.
Dimensions: 23.21 x 2.70 m.
Gangways: Throughout.   **Wheel Arrangement:** 2-B.
Doors: Single-leaf sliding plug.   **Maximum Speed:** 75 mph.
Seating Layout: 2+2 facing/unidirectional.
Multiple Working: Within class and with Classes 142, 143, 144, 150, 155, 156, 158, 159, 170 and 172.

Cars numbered in the 573xx series were renumbered by adding 50 to their original number so that the last two digits correspond with the set number.

c   Chapman seating.
d   Richmond seating.

Advertising liveries:

153 325   Citizens Rail (pink).
153 333   Visit South Devon by train (dark blue).

52301–52335. DMSL. Lot No. 31026 1987–88. Converted under Lot No. 31115 1991–92. –/72(+3) 1T 1W. (s –/72 1T 1W, t –/72(+2) 1T 1W). 41.2 t.
57301–57335. DMSL. Lot No. 31027 1987–88. Converted under Lot No. 31115 1991–92. –/72(+3) 1T 1W (s –/72 1T 1W). 41.2 t.

153 301	d	NO	A	NO	NL	52301	
153 302	c	EM	A	EM	NM	52302	
153 303	c	AW	A	AW	CF	52303	
153 304	ds	NO	A	NO	NL	52304	
153 305	d	FI	A	GW	EX	52305	
153 306	cr	GA	P	GA	NC	52306	
153 307	d	NO	A	NO	NL	52307	
153 308	c	EM	A	EM	NM	52308	
153 309	cr	GA	P	GA	NC	52309	GERARD FIENNES
153 310	c	EM	P	EM	NM	52310	
153 311	c	EM	P	EM	NM	52311	
153 312	s	AW	A	AW	CF	52312	
153 313	cs	EM	P	EM	NM	52313	
153 314	cr	GA	P	GA	NC	52314	
153 315	ds	NO	A	NO	NL	52315	
153 316	c	NO	P	NO	NL	52316	John "Longitude" Harrison Inventor of the Marine Chronometer
153 317	ds	NO	A	NO	NL	52317	
153 318	d	FI	A	GW	EX	52318	
153 319	c	EM	A	EM	NM	52319	
153 320	c	AV	P	AW	CF	52320	
153 321	ct	EM	P	EM	NM	52321	
153 322	cr	GA	P	GA	NC	52322	BENJAMIN BRITTEN
153 323	c	AV	P	AW	CF	52323	
153 324	c	NO	P	NO	NL	52324	
153 325	c	AL	P	GW	EX	52325	
153 326	c	EM	P	EM	NM	52326	
153 327	c	AW	A	AW	CF	52327	
153 328	ds	NO	A	NO	NL	52328	
153 329	c	FB	P	GW	EX	52329	
153 330	cs	NO	P	NO	NL	52330	
153 331	d	NO	A	NO	NL	52331	
153 332	c	NO	P	NO	NL	52332	
153 333	cs	AL	P	GW	EX	52333	
153 334	ct	LM	P	LM	TS	52334	
153 335	cr	GA	P	GA	NC	52335	MICHAEL PALIN
153 351	d	NO	A	NO	NL	57351	
153 352	ds	NO	A	NO	NL	57352	
153 353	c	AW	A	AW	CF	57353	
153 354	c	LM	P	LM	TS	57354	
153 355	c	EM	A	EM	NM	57355	
153 356	c	LM	P	LM	TS	57356	
153 357	c	EM	A	EM	NM	57357	
153 358	c	NO	P	NO	NL	57358	
153 359	c	NO	P	NO	NL	57359	
153 360	c	NO	P	NO	NL	57360	
153 361	cs	FB	P	GW	EX	57361	
153 362	cs	AW	A	AW	CF	57362	
153 363	cs	NO	P	NO	NL	57363	
153 364	c	LM	P	LM	TS	57364	
153 365	c	LM	P	LM	TS	57365	

153 366	c	**LM**	P	*LM*	TS	57366	
153 367	cs	**AV**	P	*AW*	CF	57367	
153 368	d	**FI**	A	*GW*	EX	57368	
153 369	c	**FB**	P	*GW*	EX	57369	
153 370	d	**FI**	A	*GW*	EX	57370	
153 371	c	**LM**	P	*LM*	TS	57371	
153 372	d	**FI**	A	*GW*	EX	57372	
153 373	d	**FI**	A	*GW*	EX	57373	
153 374	c	**EM**	A	*EM*	NM	57374	
153 375	c	**LM**	P	*LM*	TS	57375	
153 376	c	**EM**	P	*EM*	NM	57376	X24-EXPEDITIOUS
153 377	d	**FI**	A	*GW*	EX	57377	
153 378	d	**NO**	A	*NO*	NL	57378	
153 379	c	**EM**	P	*EM*	NM	57379	
153 380	d	**FI**	A	*GW*	EX	57380	
153 381	c	**EM**	P	*EM*	NM	57381	
153 382	d	**FI**	A	*GW*	EX	57382	
153 383	c	**EM**	P	*EM*	NM	57383	
153 384	c	**EM**	P	*EM*	NM	57384	
153 385	c	**EM**	P	*EM*	NM	57385	

CLASS 155   SUPER SPRINTER   LEYLAND BUS

DMSL–DMS.

Construction: Steel underframe, rivetted steel body and roof. Built from Leyland National bus parts on Leyland Bus bogied underframes.
Engines: One Cummins NT855R5 of 213 kW (285 hp) at 2100 rpm.
Bogies: One P3-10 (powered) and one BT38 (non-powered).
Couplers: BSI.
Dimensions: 23.21 x 2.70 m.

Gangways: Throughout.	**Wheel Arrangement:** 2-B + B-2.
Doors: Single-leaf sliding plug.	**Maximum Speed:** 75 mph.

Seating Layout: 2+2 facing/unidirectional Chapman seating.
Multiple Working: Within class and with Classes 142, 143, 144, 150, 153, 156, 158, 159, 170 and 172.

Northern promotional vinyls:

155 341–347 Leeds–Bradford–Manchester route (the "Calder Valley").

DMSL. Lot No. 31057 1988. –/76 1TD 1W. 39.0 t.
DMS. Lot No. 31058 1988. –/80. 38.6 t.

155 341	**NO**	P	*NO*	NL	52341	57341
155 342	**NO**	P	*NO*	NL	52342	57342
155 343	**NO**	P	*NO*	NL	52343	57343
155 344	**NO**	P	*NO*	NL	52344	57344
155 345	**NO**	P	*NO*	NL	52345	57345
155 346	**NO**	P	*NO*	NL	52346	57346
155 347	**NO**	P	*NO*	NL	52347	57347

CLASS 156   SUPER SPRINTER   METRO-CAMMELL

DMSL–DMS.

Construction: Steel.
Engines: One Cummins NT855R5 of 213 kW (285 hp) at 2100 rpm.
Bogies: One P3-10 (powered) and one BT38 (non-powered).
Couplers: BSI.
Dimensions: 23.03 x 2.73 m.
Gangways: Throughout.   **Wheel Arrangement:** 2-B + B-2.
Doors: Single-leaf sliding.   **Maximum Speed:** 75 mph.
Seating Layout: 2+2 facing/unidirectional.
Multiple Working: Within class and with Classes 142, 143, 144, 150, 153, 155, 158, 159, 170 and 172.

† Greater Anglia units fitted with a new universal access toilet to meet the 2020 accessibility regulations.
* Angel-owned Northern units fitted with a new universal access toilet to meet the 2020 accessibility regulations.
b Refurbished as a demonstrator unit by Brodies, Kilmarnock with a new universal access toilet to meet the 2020 accessibility regulations. Full details awaited.
c Chapman seating.
d Richmond seating.
v ScotRail units fitted with a new universal access toilet to meet the 2020 accessibility regulations. Full details awaited.

Northern promotional vinyls:

156441 Manchester and Liverpool
156443/454/472 We Are Northern
156461 Ravenglass & Eskdale Railway
156464 Lancashire DalesRail
156484 Settle & Carlisle line

DMSL. Lot No. 31028 1988–89. –/74 1TD 1W († –/62 1TD 2W, * –/64(+2) 1TD 2W, c –/70, s –/72, t –/68 1W, u –/68,). 38.6 t.
DMS. Lot No. 31029 1987–89. –/76 († –/74, *–/76, d –/78 , t & u –/72). 36.1 t.

156 401	cs **EM**	P	*EM*	DY	52401	57401
156 402	†cr **GA**	P	*GA*	NC	52402	57402
156 403	cs **EM**	P	*EM*	DY	52403	57403
156 404	cs **EM**	P	*EM*	DY	52404	57404
156 405	cs **EM**	P	*EM*	DY	52405	57405
156 406	cs **EM**	P	*EM*	DY	52406	57406
156 407	†cr **GA**	P	*GA*	NC	52407	57407
156 408	cs **EM**	P	*EM*	DY	52408	57408
156 409	†cr **GA**	P	*GA*	NC	52409	57409
156 410	cs **EM**	P	*EM*	DY	52410	57410
156 411	cs **EM**	P	*EM*	DY	52411	57411
156 412	†cr **GA**	P	*GA*	NC	52412	57412
156 413	cs **EM**	P	*EM*	DY	52413	57413
156 414	cs **EM**	P	*EM*	DY	52414	57414

156 415	cs	**EM**	P	*EM*	DY	52415	57415
156 416	†cr	**GA**	P	*GA*	NC	52416	57416
156 417	†cr	**GA**	P	*GA*	NC	52417	57417
156 418	†cr	**GA**	P	*GA*	NC	52418	57418
156 419	†cr	**GA**	P	*GA*	NC	52419	57419
156 420	c	**NO**	P	*NO*	AN	52420	57420
156 421	c	**NO**	P	*NO*	AN	52421	57421
156 422	†cr	**GA**	P	*GA*	NC	52422	57422
156 423	c	**NO**	P	*NO*	AN	52423	57423
156 424	c	**NO**	P	*NO*	AN	52424	57424
156 425	c	**NO**	P	*NO*	AN	52425	57425
156 426	c	**NO**	P	*NO*	AN	52426	57426
156 427	c	**NO**	P	*NO*	AN	52427	57427
156 428	c	**NO**	P	*NO*	AN	52428	57428
156 429	c	**NO**	P	*NO*	AN	52429	57429
156 430	t	**SR**	A	*SR*	CK	52430	57430
156 431	t	**SR**	A	*SR*	CK	52431	57431
156 432	t	**SR**	A	*SR*	CK	52432	57432
156 433	t	**SR**	A	*SR*	CK	52433	57433
156 434	t	**SR**	A	*SR*	CK	52434	57434
156 435	t	**SR**	A	*SR*	CK	52435	57435
156 436	†	**SR**	A	*SR*	CK	52436	57436
156 437	t	**SR**	A	*SR*	CK	52437	57437
156 438	d	**NO**	A	*NO*	HT	52438	57438
156 439	t	**SR**	A	*SR*	CK	52439	57439
156 440	c	**NO**	P	*NO*	AN	52440	57440
156 441	c	**NO**	P	*NO*	AN	52441	57441
156 442	t	**SR**	A	*SR*	CK	52442	57442
156 443	*d	**NO**	A	*NO*	HT	52443	57443
156 444	*d	**NO**	A	*NO*	HT	52444	57444
156 445	ru	**SR**	A	*SR*	CK	52445	57445
156 446	t	**FS**	A	*SR*	CK	52446	57446
156 447	ru	**FS**	A	*SR*	CK	52447	57447
156 448	*d	**NO**	A	*NO*	HT	52448	57448
156 449	u	**FS**	A	*SR*	CK	52449	57449
156 450	ru	**FS**	A	*SR*	CK	52450	57450
156 451	*d	**NO**	A	*NO*	HT	52451	57451
156 452	c	**NO**	P	*NO*	AN	52452	57452
156 453	ru	**FS**	A	*SR*	CK	52453	57453
156 454	*d	**NO**	A	*NO*	HT	52454	57454
156 455	c	**NO**	P	*NO*	AN	52455	57455
156 456	rt	**FS**	A	*SR*	CK	52456	57456
156 457	rt	**FS**	A	*SR*	CK	52457	57457
156 458	rt	**FS**	A	*SR*	CK	52458	57458
156 459	c	**NO**	P	*NO*	AN	52459	57459
156 460	c	**NO**	P	*NO*	AN	52460	57460
156 461	c	**NO**	P	*NO*	AN	52461	57461
156 462		**FS**	A	*SR*	CK	52462	57462
156 463	*d	**NO**	A	*NO*	HT	52463	57463
156 464	c	**NO**	P	*NO*	AN	52464	57464
156 465	ru	**FS**	A	*SR*	CK	52465	57465

156 466	c	**NO**	P	*NO*	AN	52466	57466
156 467	r	**FS**	A	*SR*	CK	52467	57467
156 468	d	**NO**	A	*NO*	AN	52468	57468
156 469	d	**NO**	A	*NO*	HT	52469	57469
156 470	c	**EM**	A	*EM*	DY	52470	57470
156 471	*d	**NO**	A	*NO*	AN	52471	57471
156 472	*d	**NO**	A	*NO*	AN	52472	57472
156 473	c	**EM**	A	*EM*	DY	52473	57473
156 474	rt	**FS**	A	*SR*	CK	52474	57474
156 475	*d	**NO**	A	*NO*	HT	52475	57475
156 476	rt	**FS**	A	*SR*	CK	52476	57476
156 477	t	**FS**	A	*SR*	CK	52477	57477
156 478	b	**SR**	BR	*SR*	CK	52478	57478
156 479	d	**NO**	A	*NO*	HT	52479	57479
156 480	*d	**NO**	A	*NO*	HT	52480	57480
156 481	d	**NO**	A	*NO*	HT	52481	57481
156 482	*d	**NO**	A	*NO*	AN	52482	57482
156 483	*d	**NO**	A	*NO*	AN	52483	57483
156 484	d	**NO**	A	*NO*	HT	52484	57484
156 485	ru	**FS**	A	*SR*	CK	52485	57485
156 486	d	**NO**	A	*NO*	AN	52486	57486
156 487	*d	**NO**	A	*NO*	AN	52487	57487
156 488	d	**NO**	A	*NO*	AN	52488	57488
156 489	d	**NO**	A	*NO*	AN	52489	57489
156 490	d	**NO**	A	*NO*	HT	52490	57490
156 491	d	**NO**	A	*NO*	AN	52491	57491
156 492	rs	**SR**	A	*SR*	CK	52492	57492
156 493	rt	**FS**	A	*SR*	CK	52493	57493
156 494	u	**SR**	A	*SR*	CK	52494	57494
156 495	u	**SR**	A	*SR*	CK	52495	57495
156 496	u	**FS**	A	*SR*	CK	52496	57496
156 497	c	**EM**	A	*EM*	DY	52497	57497
156 498	c	**EM**	A	*EM*	DY	52498	57498
156 499	rt	**SR**	A	*SR*	CK	52499	57499
156 500	ru	**SR**	A	*SR*	CK	52500	57500
156 501		**SR**	A	*SR*	CK	52501	57501
156 502	v	**SR**	A	*SR*	CK	52502	57502
156 503	v	**SR**	A	*SR*	CK	52503	57503
156 504		**SR**	A	*SR*	CK	52504	57504
156 505		**SR**	A	*SR*	CK	52505	57505
156 506		**SR**	A	*SR*	CK	52506	57506
156 507		**SR**	A	*SR*	CK	52507	57507
156 508		**SR**	A	*SR*	CK	52508	57508
156 509	v	**SR**	A	*SR*	CK	52509	57509
156 510		**SR**	A	*SR*	CK	52510	57510
156 511		**SR**	A	*SR*	CK	52511	b/511
156 512		**SR**	A	*SR*	CK	52512	57512
156 513		**SR**	A	*SR*	CK	52513	57513
156 514		**SR**	A	*SR*	CK	52514	57514

Names:

156 416	Saint Edmund
156 418	ESTA 1965–2015
156 420	LA' AL RATTY Ravenglass & Eskdale Railway
156 438	Timothy Hackworth
156 440	George Bradshaw
156 441	William Huskisson MP
156 444	Councillor Bill Cameron
156 448	Bram Stoker Creator of Dracula
156 459	Benny Rothman – The Manchester Rambler
156 460	Driver John Axon G.C.
156 464	Lancashire DalesRail
156 466	Gracie Fields
156 469	The Royal Northumberland Fusiliers (The Fighting Fifth)
156 482	Elizabeth Gaskell
156 490	Captain James Cook Master Mariner

CLASS 158/0   BREL

DMSL(B)–DMSL(A) or DMCL–DMSL or DMSL–MSL–DMSL.

Construction: Welded aluminium.
Engines: 158 701–813/158 880–890/158 950–961: One Cummins NTA855R1 of 260 kW (350 hp) at 2100 rpm.
158 815–862: One Perkins 2006-TWH of 260 kW (350 hp) at 2100 rpm.
158 863–872: One Cummins NTA855R3 of 300 kW (400 hp) at 1900 rpm.
Bogies: One BREL P4 (powered) and one BREL T4 (non-powered) per car.
Couplers: BSI.   **Dimensions:** 22.57 x 2.70 m.
Gangways: Throughout.   **Wheel Arrangement:** 2-B + B-2.
Doors: Twin-leaf swing plug.   **Maximum Speed:** 90 mph.
Seating Layout: 2+2 facing/unidirectional in all Standard and First Class except 2+1 in South West Trains First Class.
Multiple Working: Within class and with Classes 142, 143, 144, 150, 153, 155, 156, 159, 170 and 172.

ScotRail 158s 158 701–736/738–741 are "fitted" for RETB. When a unit arrives at Inverness the cab display unit is clipped on and plugged in.

Arriva Trains Wales units have ERTMS plugged in at Shrewsbury for working the Cambrian Lines.

*   Refurbished ScotRail units fitted with Grammer seating, additional luggage racks and cycle stowage areas.
      ScotRail units 158 726–736/738–741 are fitted with Richmond seating.
†   Refurbished East Midlands Trains units with Grammer seating.
c   Chapman seating.
s   Refurbished Arriva Trains Wales units with Grammer seating.
u   Refurbished former South West Trains units with Class 159-style interiors, including First Class seating.
w   Refurbished First Great Western units. Units 158 745–749/751/762/767 (now formed into 3-car sets) are fitted with Richmond seating.

Advertising livery:

158 798   Springboard Opportunity Group (light blue).

Northern promotional vinyls:

158 784 PTEG: 40 years.
158 787, 158 792–796: Sheffield–Leeds fast service.
158 790/842/843/844/845/848/849/850/853/855: We Are Northern.
158 860: Keighley & Brontë Country.
158 901–910: Leeds–Bradford–Manchester route (the "Calder Valley").

DMSL(B). Lot No. 31051 BREL Derby 1989–92. –/68 1TD 1W. († –/72 1TD 1W, c, w –/66 1TD 1W, s –/64(+4) 1TD 1W, t –/62 1TD 2W). 38.5 t.
MSL. Lot No. 31050 BREL Derby 1991. –/66(+3) 1T. 38.5 t.
DMSL(A). Lot No. 31052 BREL Derby 1989–92. –/70 1T († –/74, c, t, w –/68 1T, * –/64(+2) 1T plus cycle stowage area, s –/70 1T). 38.5 t.

The above details refer to the "as built" condition. The following DMSL(B) have now been converted to DMCL as follows:
52701–736/738–741 (ScotRail). 15/53 1TD 1W (* refurbished sets –/60(+6) 1TD 1W plus cycle stowage area).
52786/789 (Former South West Trains units). 13/44 1TD 1W.

158 701	*	**SR**	P	*SR*	IS	52701 57701
158 702	*	**SR**	P	*SR*	IS	52702 57702
158 703	*	**FS**	P	*SR*	IS	52703 57703
158 704	*	**SR**	P	*SR*	IS	52704 57704
158 705	*	**FS**	P	*SR*	IS	52705 57705
158 706	*	**SR**	P	*SR*	IS	52706 57706
158 707	*	**FS**	P	*SR*	IS	52707 57707
158 708	*	**FS**	P	*SR*	IS	52708 57708
158 709	*	**SR**	P	*SR*	IS	52709 57709
158 710	*	**FS**	P	*SR*	IS	52710 57710
158 711	*	**SR**	P	*SR*	IS	52711 57711
158 712	*	**SR**	P	*SR*	IS	52712 57712
158 713	*	**SR**	P	*SR*	IS	52713 57713
158 714	*	**SR**	P	*SR*	IS	52714 57714
158 715	*	**SR**	P	*SR*	IS	52715 57715
158 716	*	**SR**	P	*SR*	IS	52716 57716
158 717	*	**SR**	P	*SR*	IS	52717 57717
158 718	*	**FS**	P	*SR*	IS	52718 57718
158 719	*	**SR**	P	*SR*	IS	52719 57719
158 720	*	**FS**	P	*SR*	IS	52720 57720
158 721	*	**SR**	P	*SR*	IS	52721 57721
158 722	*	**SR**	P	*SR*	IS	52722 57722
158 723	*	**SR**	P	*SR*	IS	52723 57723
158 724	*	**SR**	P	*SR*	IS	52724 57724
158 725	*	**FS**	P	*SR*	IS	52725 57725
158 726		**FS**	P	*SR*	HA	52726 57726
158 727		**FS**	P	*SR*	HA	52727 57727
158 728		**FS**	P	*SR*	HA	52728 57728
158 729		**FS**	P	*SR*	HA	52729 57729
158 730		**FS**	P	*SR*	HA	52730 57730

158 731		FS	P	SR	HA	52731	57731	
158 732		FS	P	SR	HA	52732	57732	
158 733		FS	P	SR	HA	52733	57733	
158 734		FS	P	SR	HA	52734	57734	
158 735		FS	P	SR	HA	52735	57735	
158 736		FS	P	SR	HA	52736	57736	
158 738		FS	P	SR	HA	52738	57738	
158 739		FS	P	SR	HA	52739	57739	
158 740		FS	P	SR	HA	52740	57740	
158 741		FS	P	SR	HA	52741	57741	
158 752		NR	P	NO	NL	52752	58716	57752
158 753		NO	P	NO	NL	52753	58710	57753
158 754		NO	P	NO	NL	52754	58708	57754
158 755		NO	P	NO	NL	52755	58702	57755
158 756		NR	P	NO	NL	52756	58712	57756
158 757		NO	P	NO	NL	52757	58706	57757
158 758		NO	P	NO	NL	52758	58714	57758
158 759		NO	P	NO	NL	52759	58713	57759
158 763	w	FI	P	GW	PM	52763	57763	
158 766	w	FI	P	GW	PM	52766	57766	
158 770	†	ST	P	EM	NM	52770	57770	
158 773	†	ST	P	EM	NM	52773	57773	
158 774	†	ST	P	EM	NM	52774	57774	
158 777	†	ST	P	EM	NM	52777	57777	
158 780	†	ST	A	EM	NM	52780	57780	
158 782		SR	A	SR	HA	52782	57782	
158 783	†	ST	A	EM	NM	52783	57783	
158 784		NO	A	NO	NL	52784	57784	
158 785	†	ST	A	EM	NM	52785	57785	
158 786	u	SR	A	SR	HA	52786	57786	
158 787		NO	A	NO	NL	52787	57787	
158 788	†	ST	A	EM	NM	52788	57788	
158 789	u	SR	A	SR	HA	52789	57789	
158 790		NO	A	NO	NL	52790	57790	
158 791		NO	A	NO	NL	52791	57791	
158 792		NO	A	NO	NL	52792	57792	
158 793		NO	A	NO	NL	52793	57793	
158 794		NO	A	NO	NL	52794	57794	
158 795		NO	A	NO	NL	52795	57795	
158 796		NO	A	NO	NL	52796	57796	
158 797		NO	A	NO	NL	52797	57797	
158 798	w	AL	P	GW	PM	52798	58715	57798
158 799	†	ST	P	EM	NM	52799	57799	
158 806	†	ST	P	EM	NM	52806	57806	
158 810	†	ST	P	EM	NM	52810	57810	
158 812	†	ST	P	EM	NM	52812	57812	
158 813	†	ST	P	EM	NM	52813	57813	
158 815	c	NO	A	NO	NL	52815	57815	
158 816	c	NO	A	NO	NL	52816	57816	
158 817	c	NO	A	NO	NL	52817	57817	
158 818	es	AW	A	AW	MN	52818	57818	

158 819	es	**AW**	A	*AW*	MN	52819	57819
158 820	es	**AW**	A	*AW*	MN	52820	57820
158 821	es	**AW**	A	*AW*	MN	52821	57821
158 822	es	**AW**	A	*AW*	MN	52822	57822
158 823	es	**AW**	A	*AW*	MN	52823	57823
158 824	es	**AW**	A	*AW*	MN	52824	57824
158 825	es	**AW**	A	*AW*	MN	52825	57825
158 826	es	**AW**	A	*AW*	MN	52826	57826
158 827	es	**AW**	A	*AW*	MN	52827	57827
158 828	es	**AW**	A	*AW*	MN	52828	57828
158 829	es	**AW**	A	*AW*	MN	52829	57829
158 830	es	**AW**	A	*AW*	MN	52830	57830
158 831	es	**AW**	A	*AW*	MN	52831	57831
158 832	es	**AW**	A	*AW*	MN	52832	57832
158 833	es	**AW**	A	*AW*	MN	52833	57833
158 834	es	**AW**	A	*AW*	MN	52834	57834
158 835	es	**AW**	A	*AW*	MN	52835	57835
158 836	es	**AW**	A	*AW*	MN	52836	57836
158 837	es	**AW**	A	*AW*	MN	52837	57837
158 838	es	**AW**	A	*AW*	MN	52838	57838
158 839	es	**AW**	A	*AW*	MN	52839	57839
158 840	es	**AW**	A	*AW*	MN	52840	57840
158 841	es	**AW**	A	*AW*	MN	52841	57841
158 842	c	**NO**	A	*NO*	NL	52842	57842
158 843	c	**NO**	A	*NO*	NL	52843	57843
158 844		**NO**	A	*NO*	NL	52844	57844
158 845		**NO**	A	*NO*	NL	52845	57845
158 846	†	**ST**	A	*EM*	NM	52846	57846
158 847	†	**ST**	A	*EM*	NM	52847	57847
158 848		**NO**	A	*NO*	NL	52848	57848
158 849		**NO**	A	*NO*	NL	52849	57849
158 850		**NO**	A	*NO*	NL	52850	57850
158 851		**NO**	A	*NO*	NL	52851	57851
158 852	†	**ST**	A	*EM*	NM	52852	57852
158 853		**NO**	A	*NO*	NL	52853	57853
158 854	†	**ST**	A	*EM*	NM	52854	57854
158 855		**NO**	A	*NO*	NL	52855	57855
158 856	†	**ST**	A	*EM*	NM	52856	57856
158 857	†	**ST**	A	*EM*	NM	52857	57857
158 858	†	**ST**	A	*EM*	NM	52858	57858
158 859		**NO**	A	*NO*	NL	52859	57859
158 860		**NO**	A	*NO*	NL	52860	57860
158 861		**NO**	A	*NO*	NL	52861	57861
158 862	†	**ST**	A	*EM*	NM	52862	57862
158 863	†	**ST**	A	*FM*	NM	52863	57863
158 864	†	**ST**	A	*EM*	NM	52864	57864
158 865	†	**ST**	A	*EM*	NM	52865	57865
158 866	†	**ST**	A	*EM*	NM	52866	57866
158 867	c	**SR**	A	*SR*	HA	52867	57867
158 868	c	**SR**	A	*SR*	HA	52868	57868
158 869	c	**SR**	A	*SR*	HA	52869	57869

158 870	c	**SR**	A	*SR*	HA	52870	57870
158 871	c	**SR**	A	*SR*	HA	52871	57871
158 872	c	**NO**	A	*NO*	NL	52872	57872

Names (ScotRail units carry their names on the unit ends):

158 707	Far North Line 125th ANNIVERSARY
158 720	Inverness & Nairn Railway – 150 years
158 773	EASTCROFT DEPOT
158 784	Barbara Castle
158 791	County of Nottinghamshire
158 796	Fred Trueman Cricketing Legend
158 797	Jane Tomlinson
158 847	Lincoln Castle Explorer
158 860	Ian Dewhirst
158 861	Magna Carta 800 Lincoln 2015

Class 158/8. Refurbished South West Trains and East Midlands Trains units. Converted from former TransPennine Express units at Wabtec, Doncaster in 2007. 2+1 seating in First Class.

158 885 has been fitted with new ZF transmission as a trial.

Details as Class 158/0 except:

DMCL. Lot No. 31051 BREL Derby 1989–92. 13/44 1TD 1W. 38.5 t.
DMSL. Lot No. 31052 BREL Derby 1989–92. –/70 1T. 38.5 t.

158 880	(158 737)	**ST**	P	*SW*	SA	52737	57737
158 881	(158 742)	**ST**	P	*SW*	SA	52742	57742
158 882	(158 743)	**ST**	P	*SW*	SA	52743	57743
158 883	(158 744)	**ST**	P	*SW*	SA	52744	57744
158 884	(158 772)	**ST**	P	*SW*	SA	52772	57772
158 885	(158 775)	**ST**	P	*SW*	SA	52775	57775
158 886	(158 779)	**ST**	P	*SW*	SA	52779	57779
158 887	(158 781)	**ST**	P	*SW*	SA	52781	57781
158 888	(158 802)	**ST**	P	*SW*	SA	52802	57802
158 889	(158 808)	**ST**	P	*EM*	NM	52808	57808
158 890	(158 814)	**ST**	P	*SW*	SA	52814	57814

CLASS 158/9   BREL

DMSL–DMS. Units leased by West Yorkshire PTE but managed by Eversholt Rail. Details as Class 158/0 except for seating and toilets.

DMSL. Lot No. 31051 BREL Derby 1990–92. –/70 1TD 1W. 38.5 t.
DMS. Lot No. 31052 BREL Derby 1990–92. –/72 and parcels area. 38.5 t.

158 901	**NO**	E	*NO*	NL	52901	57901
158 902	**NO**	E	*NO*	NL	52902	57902
158 903	**NO**	E	*NO*	NL	52903	57903
158 904	**NO**	E	*NO*	NL	52904	57904
158 905	**NO**	E	*NO*	NL	52905	57905
158 906	**NO**	E	*NO*	NL	52906	57906
158 907	**NO**	E	*NO*	NL	52907	57907

158 908	**NO**	E	*NO*	NL	52908	57908	
158 909	**NO**	E	*NO*	NL	52909	57909	
158 910	**NO**	E	*NO*	NL	52910	57910	William Wilberforce

CLASS 158/0   BREL

DMSL(A)–DMSL(B)–DMSL(A). Units reformed as 3-car hybrid sets for Great Western Railway, mainly used between Cardiff and Portsmouth. For vehicle details see above. Formations can be flexible depending on when unit exams become due.

t – refurbished Great Western Railway units with modifications to comply with the 2020 accessibility regulations.

158 950	w	**FI**	P	*GW*	PM	57751	52761	57761
158 951	w	**FI**	P	*GW*	PM	52751	52764	57764
158 952	w	**FI**	P	*GW*	PM	57745	52762	57762
158 953	w	**FI**	P	*GW*	PM	52745	52750	57750
158 954	w	**FI**	P	*GW*	PM	57747	52760	57760
158 955	w	**FI**	P	*GW*	PM	52747	52765	57765
158 956	t	**GW**	P	*GW*	PM	52748	52768	57768
158 957	t	**GW**	P	*GW*	PM	52748	52771	57771
158 958	w	**FI**	P	*GW*	PM	57746	52776	57776
158 959	w	**FI**	P	*GW*	PM	52746	52778	57778
158 960	w	**FI**	P	*GW*	PM	57749	52769	57769
158 961	w	**FI**	P	*GW*	PM	52749	52767	57767

CLASS 159/0   BREL

DMCL–MSL–DMSL. Built as Class 158. Converted before entering passenger service to Class 159 by Rosyth Dockyard.

Construction: Welded aluminium.
Engines: One Cummins NTA855R3 of 300 kW (400 hp) at 1900 rpm.
Bogies: One BREL P4 (powered) and one BREL T4 (non-powered) per car.
Couplers: BSI.   **Dimensions:** 22.16 x 2.70 m.
Gangways: Throughout.   **Wheel Arrangement:** 2-B + B-2 + B-2.
Doors: Twin-leaf swing plug.   **Maximum Speed:** 90 mph.
Seating Layout: 1: 2+1 facing, 2: 2+2 facing/unidirectional.
Multiple Working: Within class and with Classes 142, 143, 144, 150, 153, 155, 156, 158 and 170.

DMCL. Lot No. 31051 BREL Derby 1992–93. 23/28 1TD 1W. 38.5 t.
MSL. Lot No. 31050 BREL Derby 1992–93. –/70(+6) 1T. 38.5 t.
DMSL. Lot No. 31052 BREL Derby 1992–93. –/72 1T. 38.5 t.

159 001	**ST**	P	*SW*	SA	52873	58718	57873	CITY OF EXETER
159 002	**ST**	P	*SW*	SA	52874	58719	57874	CITY OF SALISBURY
159 003	**ST**	P	*SW*	SA	52875	58720	57875	TEMPLECOMBE
159 004	**ST**	P	*SW*	SA	52876	58721	57876	BASINGSTOKE AND DEANE
159 005	**ST**	P	*SW*	SA	52877	58722	57877	WEST OF ENGLAND LINE

159 006	**ST**	P	*SW*	SA	52878	58723	57878	THE SEATON TRAMWAY
								Seaton–Colyford–Colyton
159 007	**ST**	P	*SW*	SA	52879	58724	57879	
159 008	**ST**	P	*SW*	SA	52880	58725	57880	
159 009	**ST**	P	*SW*	SA	52881	58726	57881	
159 010	**ST**	P	*SW*	SA	52882	58727	57882	
159 011	**ST**	P	*SW*	SA	52883	58728	57883	
159 012	**ST**	P	*SW*	SA	52884	58729	57884	
159 013	**ST**	P	*SW*	SA	52885	58730	57885	
159 014	**ST**	P	*SW*	SA	52886	58731	57886	
159 015	**ST**	P	*SW*	SA	52887	58732	57887	
159 016	**ST**	P	*SW*	SA	52888	58733	57888	
159 017	**ST**	P	*SW*	SA	52889	58734	57889	
159 018	**ST**	P	*SW*	SA	52890	58735	57890	
159 019	**ST**	P	*SW*	SA	52891	58736	57891	
159 020	**ST**	P	*SW*	SA	52892	58737	57892	
159 021	**ST**	P	*SW*	SA	52893	58738	57893	
159 022	**ST**	P	*SW*	SA	52894	58739	57894	

CLASS 159/1   BREL

DMCL–MSL–DMSL. Units converted from Class 158s at Wabtec, Doncaster in 2006–07 for South West Trains.

Details as Class 158/0 except:
Seating Layout: 1: 2+1 facing, 2: 2+2 facing/unidirectional.

DMCL. Lot No. 31051 BREL Derby 1989–92. 24/24(+2) 1TD 2W. 38.5 t.
MSL. Lot No. 31050 BREL Derby 1989–92. –/70 1T. 38.5 t.
DMSL. Lot No. 31052 BREL Derby 1989–92. –/72 1T. 38.5 t.

159 101	(158 800)	**ST**	P	*SW*	SA	52800	58717	57800
159 102	(158 803)	**ST**	P	*SW*	SA	52803	58703	57803
159 103	(158 804)	**ST**	P	*SW*	SA	52804	58704	57804
159 104	(158 805)	**ST**	P	*SW*	SA	52805	58705	57805
159 105	(158 807)	**ST**	P	*SW*	SA	52807	58707	57807
159 106	(158 809)	**ST**	P	*SW*	SA	52809	58709	57809
159 107	(158 811)	**ST**	P	*SW*	SA	52811	58711	57811
159 108	(158 801)	**ST**	P	*SW*	SA	52801	58701	57801

CLASS 165/0   NETWORK TURBO   BREL

DMSL–DMS and DMSL–MS–DMS. Chiltern Railways units. Refurbished 2003–05 with First Class seats removed and air conditioning fitted.
Construction: Welded aluminium.
Engines: One Perkins 2006-TWH of 260 kW (350 hp) at 2100 rpm.
Bogies: BREL P3-17 (powered), BREL T3-17 (non-powered).
Couplers: BSI.
Dimensions: 23.50/23.25 x 2.81 m.
Gangways: Within unit only.   **Wheel Arrangement:** 2-B (+ B-2) + B-2.

Doors: Twin-leaf swing plug. **Maximum Speed:** 75 mph.
Seating Layout: 2+2/3+2 facing/unidirectional.
Multiple Working: Within class and with Classes 166, 168, 170 and 172.

Fitted with tripcocks for working over London Underground tracks between Harrow-on-the-Hill and Amersham.

* Refurbished with a new universal access toilet to comply with the 2020 accessibility regulations.

58801–822/58873–878. DMSL. Lot No. 31087 BREL York 1990. –/82(+7) 1T 2W (* –/77(+7) 1TD 2W). 42.1 t.
58823–833. DMSL. Lot No. 31089 BREL York 1991–92. –/82(+7) 1T 2W (* –/77(+7) 1TD 2W). 40.1 t.
MS. Lot No. 31090 BREL York 1991–92. –/106. 37.0 t.
DMS. Lot No. 31088 BREL York 1991–92. –/94. 41.5 t.

165 001		**CR**	A	*CR*	AL	58801		58834
165 002		**CR**	A	*CR*	AL	58802		58835
165 003		**CR**	A	*CR*	AL	58803		58836
165 004		**CR**	A	*CR*	AL	58804		58837
165 005		**CR**	A	*CR*	AL	58805		58838
165 006		**CR**	A	*CR*	AL	58806		58839
165 007		**CR**	A	*CR*	AL	58807		58840
165 008		**CR**	A	*CR*	AL	58808		58841
165 009		**CR**	A	*CR*	AL	58809		58842
165 010		**CR**	A	*CR*	AL	58810		58843
165 011		**CR**	A	*CR*	AL	58811		58844
165 012		**CR**	A	*CR*	AL	58812		58845
165 013		**CR**	A	*CR*	AL	58813		58846
165 014		**CR**	A	*CR*	AL	58814		58847
165 015	*	**CR**	A	*CR*	AL	58815		58848
165 016	*	**CR**	A	*CR*	AL	58816		58849
165 017		**CR**	A	*CR*	AL	58817		58850
165 018	*	**CR**	A	*CR*	AL	58818		58851
165 019		**CR**	A	*CR*	AL	58819		58852
165 020	*	**CR**	A	*CR*	AL	58820		58853
165 021		**CR**	A	*CR*	AL	58821		58854
165 022		**CR**	A	*CR*	AL	58822		58855
165 023		**CR**	A	*CR*	AL	58873		58867
165 024	*	**CR**	A	*CR*	AL	58874		58868
165 025		**CR**	A	*CR*	AL	58875		58869
165 026	*	**CR**	A	*CR*	AL	58876		58870
165 027		**CR**	A	*CR*	AL	58877		58871
165 028		**CR**	A	*CR*	AL	58878		58872
165 029	*	**CR**	A	*CR*	AL	58823	55404	58856
165 030		**CR**	A	*CR*	AL	58824	55405	58857
165 031		**CR**	A	*CR*	AL	58825	55406	58858
165 032	*	**CR**	A	*CR*	AL	58826	55407	58859
165 033		**CR**	A	*CR*	AL	58827	55408	58860
165 034	*	**CR**	A	*CR*	AL	58828	55409	58861
165 035		**CR**	A	*CR*	AL	58829	55410	58862
165 036	*	**CR**	A	*CR*	AL	58830	55411	58863

165 037	**CR**	A	*CR*	AL	58831	55412	58864
165 038	**CR**	A	*CR*	AL	58832	55413	58865
165 039	**CR**	A	*CR*	AL	58833	55414	58866

CLASS 165/1   NETWORK TURBO   BREL

Great Western Railway units. DMSL–MS–DMS or DMSL–DMS. In 2015 GWR removed First Class from all its Class 165s – which are all now Standard Class only.

Construction: Welded aluminium.
Engines: One Perkins 2006-TWH of 260 kW (350 hp) at 2100 rpm.
Bogies: BREL P3-17 (powered), BREL T3-17 (non-powered).
Couplers: BSI.
Dimensions: 23.50/23.25 x 2.81 m.
Gangways: Within unit only.   **Wheel Arrangement:** 2-B (+ B-2) + B-2.
Doors: Twin-leaf swing plug.   **Maximum Speed:** 90 mph.
Seating Layout: 3+2/2+2 facing/unidirectional.
Multiple Working: Within class and with Classes 166, 168, 170 and 172.

* Refurbished with a new universal access toilet to comply with the 2020 accessibility regulations. Full details awaited.

58953–969. DMSL. Lot No. 31098 BREL York 1992. –/82 1T. 38.0 t.
58879–898. DMSL. Lot No. 31096 BREL York 1992. –/88 1T. 38.0 t.
MS. Lot No. 31099 BREL 1992. –/106. 37.0 t.
DMS. Lot No. 31097 BREL 1992. –/98. 37.0 t.

165 101		**GW**	A	*GW*	RG	58953	55415	58916
165 102		**GW**	A	*GW*	RG	58954	55416	58917
165 103		**GW**	A	*GW*	RG	58955	55417	58918
165 104	*	**GW**	A	*GW*	RG	58956	55418	58919
165 105	*	**GW**	A	*GW*	RG	58957	55419	58920
165 106		**FD**	A	*GW*	RG	58958	55420	58921
165 107		**FD**	A	*GW*	RG	58959	55421	58922
165 108		**FD**	A	*GW*	RG	58960	55422	58923
165 109		**FD**	A	*GW*	RG	58961	55423	58924
165 110		**FD**	A	*GW*	RG	58962	55424	58925
165 111		**FD**	A	*GW*	RG	58963	55425	58926
165 112		**FD**	A	*GW*	RG	58964	55426	58927
165 113		**FD**	A	*GW*	RG	58965	55427	58928
165 114		**FD**	A	*GW*	RG	58966	55428	58929
165 116		**FD**	A	*GW*	RG	58968	55430	58931
165 117		**FD**	A	*GW*	RG	58969	55431	58932
165 118		**FD**	A	*GW*	RG	58879		58933
165 119		**FD**	A	*GW*	RG	58880		58934
165 120		**FD**	A	*GW*	RG	58881		58935
165 121		**FD**	A	*GW*	RG	58882		58936
165 122		**FD**	A	*GW*	RG	58883		58937
165 123		**FD**	A	*GW*	RG	58884		58938
165 124		**FD**	A	*GW*	RG	58885		58939
165 125		**FD**	A	*GW*	RG	58886		58940

165 126	**FD**	A	*GW*	RG	58887	58941
165 127	**FD**	A	*GW*	RG	58888	58942
165 128	**FD**	A	*GW*	RG	58889	58943
165 129	**FD**	A	*GW*	RG	58890	58944
165 130	**FD**	A	*GW*	RG	58891	58945
165 131	**FD**	A	*GW*	RG	58892	58946
165 132	**FD**	A	*GW*	RG	58893	58947
165 133	**FD**	A	*GW*	RG	58894	58948
165 134	**FD**	A	*GW*	RG	58895	58949
165 135	**FD**	A	*GW*	RG	58896	58950
165 136	**FD**	A	*GW*	RG	58897	58951
165 137	**FD**	A	*GW*	RG	58898	58952

CLASS 166   NETWORK EXPRESS TURBO   ABB

DMCL–MS–DMSL. Great Western Railway units, built for Paddington–Oxford/Newbury services. Air conditioned and with additional luggage space compared to the Class 165s. The DMSL vehicles have had their 16 First Class seats declassified. Refurbished with a new universal access toilet to comply with the 2020 accessibility regulations.

Construction: Welded aluminium.
Engines: One Perkins 2006-TWH of 260 kW (350 hp) at 2100 rpm.
Bogies: BREL P3-17 (powered), BREL T3-17 (non-powered).
Couplers: BSI.
Dimensions: 23.50 x 2.81 m.
Gangways: Within unit only.   **Wheel Arrangement:** 2-B + B-2 + B-2.
Doors: Twin-leaf swing plug.   **Maximum Speed:** 90 mph.
Seating Layout: 1: 2+2 facing, 2: 2+2/3+2 facing/unidirectional.
Multiple Working: Within class and with Classes 165, 168, 170 and 172.

DMCL. Lot No. 31116 ABB York 1992–93. 16/53 1TD 2W. 41.2 t.
MS. Lot No. 31117 ABB York 1992–93. –/91. 38.0 t.
DMSL. Lot No. 31116 ABB York 1992–93. –/84 1T. 39.6 t.

166 201	**FB**	A	*GW*	RG	58101	58601	58122
166 202	**FB**	A	*GW*	RG	58102	58602	58123
166 203	**FB**	A	*GW*	RG	58103	58603	58124
166 204	**GW**	A	*GW*	RG	58104	58604	58125
166 205	**GW**	A	*GW*	RG	58105	58605	58126
166 206	**GW**	A	*GW*	RG	58106	58606	58127
166 207	**FB**	A	*GW*	RG	58107	58607	58128
166 208	**GW**	A	*GW*	RG	58108	58608	58129
166 209	**FB**	A	*GW*	RG	58109	58609	58130
166 210	**GW**	A	*GW*	RG	58110	58610	58131
166 211	**FB**	A	*GW*	RG	58111	58611	58132
166 212	**GW**	A	*GW*	RG	58112	58612	58133
166 213	**GW**	A	*GW*	RG	58113	58613	58134
166 214	**GW**	A	*GW*	RG	58114	58614	58135
166 215	**FB**	A	*GW*	RG	58115	58615	58136
166 216	**GW**	A	*GW*	RG	58116	58616	58137
166 217	**GW**	A	*GW*	RG	58117	58617	58138

166 218	**GW**	A	*GW*	RG	58118	58618	58139
166 219	**GW**	A	*GW*	RG	58119	58619	58140
166 220	**GW**	A	*GW*	RG	58120	58620	58141
166 221	**FB**	A	*GW*	RG	58121	58621	58142

Names:

166 204   Norman Topsom MBE
166 221   Reading Train Care Depot/READING TRAIN CARE DEPOT *(alt sides)*

CLASS 168   CLUBMAN   ADTRANZ/BOMBARDIER

Air conditioned.

Construction: Welded aluminium bodies with bolt-on steel ends.
Engines: One MTU 6R183TD13H of 315 kW (422 hp) at 1900 rpm.
Transmission: Hydraulic. Voith T211rzze to ZF final drive.
Bogies: One Adtranz P3–23 and one BREL T3–23 per car.
Couplers: BSI at outer ends, bar within unit.
Dimensions: Class 168/0: 24.10/23.61 x 2.69 m. Others: 23.62/23.61 x 2.69 m.
Gangways: Within unit only.   **Wheel Arrangement:** 2-B (+ B-2 + B-2) + B-2.
Doors: Twin-leaf swing plug.   **Maximum Speed:** 100 mph.
Seating Layout: 2+2 facing/unidirectional.
Multiple Working: Within class and with Classes 165 and 166.

Fitted with tripcocks for working over London Underground tracks between Harrow-on-the-Hill and Amersham.

Class 168/0. Original Design. DMSL(A)–MS–MSL–DMSL(B) or DMSL(A)–MSL–MS–DMSL(B).

58451–455 were numbered 58656–660 for a time when used in 168 106–110.

58151–155. DMSL(A). Adtranz Derby 1997–98. –/57 1TD 1W. 44.0 t.
58651–655. MSL. Adtranz Derby 1998. –/73 1T. 41.0 t.
58451–455. MS. Adtranz Derby 1998. –/77. 41.0 t.
58251–255. DMSL(B). Adtranz Derby 1998. –/68 1T. 43.6 t.

168 001	**CL**	P	*CR*	AL	58151	58651	58451	58251
168 002	**CL**	P	*CR*	AL	58152	58652	58452	58252
168 003	**CL**	P	*CR*	AL	58153	58453	58653	58253
168 004	**CL**	P	*CR*	AL	58154	58654	58454	58254
168 005	**CL**	P	*CR*	AL	58155	58455	58655	58255

Class 168/1. These units are effectively Class 170s. DMSL(A)–MSL–MS–DMSL(B) or DMSL(A)–MS–DMSL(B).

58461–463 have been renumbered from 58661–663.

58156–163. DMSL(A). Adtranz Derby 2000. –/57 1TD 2W. 45.2 t.
58456–460. MS. Bombardier Derby 2002. –/76. 41.8 t.
58756–757. MSL. Bombardier Derby 2002. –/73 1T. 42.9 t.
58461–463. MS. Adtranz Derby 2000. –/76. 42.4 t.
58256–263. DMSL(B). Adtranz Derby 2000. –/69 1T. 45.2 t.

| 168 106 | **CL** | P | *CR* | AL | 58156 | 58756 | 58456 | 58256 |
| 168 107 | **CL** | P | *CR* | AL | 58157 | 58757 | 58457 | 58257 |

168 108	**CL**	P	*CR*	AL	58158		58458	58258
168 109	**CL**	P	*CR*	AL	58159		58459	58259
168 110	**CL**	P	*CR*	AL	58160		58460	58260
168 111	**CL**	E	*CR*	AL	58161		58461	58261
168 112	**CL**	E	*CR*	AL	58162		58462	58262
168 113	**CL**	E	*CR*	AL	58163		58463	58263

Class 168/2. These units are effectively Class 170s. DMSL(A)–(MS)–MS–DMSL(B).

58164–169. DMSL(A). Bombardier Derby 2003–04. –/57 1TD 2W. 45.4 t.
58365–367. MS. Bombardier Derby 2006. –/76. 43.3 t.
58444/468/469. MS. Bombardier Derby 2003–04. –/76. 44.0 t.
58445–467. MS. Bombardier Derby 2006. –/76. 43.3 t.
58264–269. DMSL(B). Bombardier Derby 2003–04. –/69 1T. 45.5 t.

168 214	**CL**	P	*CR*	AL	58164			58464	58264
168 215	**CL**	P	*CR*	AL	58165	58365		58465	58265
168 216	**CL**	P	*CR*	AL	58166	58466	58366		58266
168 217	**CL**	P	*CR*	AL	58167	58367		58467	58267
168 218	**CL**	P	*CR*	AL	58168			58468	58268
168 219	**CL**	P	*CR*	AL	58169			58469	58269

Class 168/3. Former South West Trains/TransPennine Express Class 170s taken on by Chiltern Railways in 2015–16 and renumbered in the 168 3xx series. 170 309 was originally numbered 170 399. DMSL(A)–DMSL(B).

50301–308/399. DMCL. Adtranz Derby 2000–01. –/59 1TD 2W. 45.8 t.
79301–308/399. DMSL. Adtranz Derby 2000–01. –/69 1T. 45.8 t.

168 321	(170 301)	**CL**	P	*CR*	AL	50301	79301
168 322	(170 302)	**CL**	P	*CR*	AL	50302	79302
168 323	(170 303)	**CL**	P	*CR*	AL	50303	79303
168 324	(170 304)	**CL**	P	*CR*	AL	50304	79304
168 325	(170 305)	**CL**	P	*CR*	AL	50305	79305
168 326	(170 306)	**CL**	P	*CR*	AL	50306	79306
168 327	(170 307)	**CL**	P	*CR*	AL	50307	79307
168 328	(170 308)	**CL**	P	*CR*	AL	50308	79308
168 329	(170 309)	**CL**	P	*CR*	AL	50399	79399

CLASS 170   TURBOSTAR   ADTRANZ/BOMBARDIER

Various formations. Air conditioned.

Construction: Welded aluminium bodies with bolt-on steel ends.
Engines: One MTU 6R183TD13H of 315 kW (422 hp) at 1900 rpm.
Transmission: Hydraulic. Voith T211rzze to ZF final drive.
Bogies: One Adtranz P3–23 and one BREL T3–23 per car.
Couplers: BSI at outer ends, bar within later build units.
Dimensions: 23.62/23.61 x 2.69 m.
Gangways: Within unit only.   **Wheel Arrangement:** 2-B (+ B-2) + B-2.
Doors: Twin-leaf sliding plug.   **Maximum Speed:** 100 mph.
Seating Layout: 1: 2+1 facing/unidirectional. 2: 2+2 unidirectional/facing.

Multiple Working: Within class and with Classes 150, 153, 155, 156, 158, 159 and 172.

Class 170/1. CrossCountry (former Midland Mainline) units. Lazareni seating. DMSL–MS–DMCL/DMSL–DMCL.

DMSL. Adtranz Derby 1998–99. –/59 1TD 2W. 45.0 t.
MS. Adtranz Derby 2001. –/80. 43.0 t.
DMCL. Adtranz Derby 1998–99. 9/52 1T. 44.8 t

170 101	**XC**	P	*XC*	TS	50101	55101	79101
170 102	**XC**	P	*XC*	TS	50102	55102	79102
170 103	**XC**	P	*XC*	TS	50103	55103	79103
170 104	**XC**	P	*XC*	TS	50104	55104	79104
170 105	**XC**	P	*XC*	TS	50105	55105	79105
170 106	**XC**	P	*XC*	TS	50106	55106	79106
170 107	**XC**	P	*XC*	TS	50107	55107	79107
170 108	**XC**	P	*XC*	TS	50108	55108	79108
170 109	**XC**	P	*XC*	TS	50109	55109	79109
170 110	**XC**	P	*XC*	TS	50110	55110	79110
170 111	**XC**	P	*XC*	TS	50111		79111
170 112	**XC**	P	*XC*	TS	50112		79112
170 113	**XC**	P	*XC*	TS	50113		79113
170 114	**XC**	P	*XC*	TS	50114		79114
170 115	**XC**	P	*XC*	TS	50115		79115
170 116	**XC**	P	*XC*	TS	50116		79116
170 117	**XC**	P	*XC*	TS	50117		79117

Class 170/2. Greater Anglia 3-car units. Chapman seating. DMCL–MSL–DMSL.

Advertising livery: 170 208 Breckland Line (Norwich–Cambridge).

DMCL. Adtranz Derby 1999. 7/39 1TD 2W. 45.0 t.
MSL. Adtranz Derby 1999. –/68 1T. Guard's office. 45.3 t.
DMSL. Adtranz Derby 1999. –/66 1T. 43.4 t.

170 201	r	**1**	P	*GA*	NC	50201	56201	79201
170 202	r	**1**	P	*GA*	NC	50202	56202	79202
170 203	r	**1**	P	*GA*	NC	50203	56203	79203
170 204	r	**1**	P	*GA*	NC	50204	56204	79204
170 205	r	**1**	P	*GA*	NC	50205	56205	79205
170 206	r	**1**	P	*GA*	NC	50206	56206	79206
170 207	r	**1**	P	*GA*	NC	50207	56207	79207
170 208	r	**AL**	P	*GA*	NC	50208	56208	79208

Class 170/2. Greater Anglia 2-car units. Chapman seating. DMSL–DMCL.

DMSL. Bombardier Derby 2002. –/57 1TD 2W. 45.7 t.
DMCL. Bombardier Derby 2002. 9/53 1T. 45.7 t.

170 270	r	**1**	P	*GA*	NC	50270	79270
170 271	r	**AN**	P	*GA*	NC	50271	79271
170 272	r	**AN**	P	*GA*	NC	50272	79272
170 273	r	**AN**	P	*GA*	NC	50273	79273

▲ Chiltern Railways BR green-liveried "bubble car" 121 034 is seen at North Lee shortly after departure from Aylesbury with the 08.49 to Princes Risborough on 04/07/16. **Jamie Squibbs**

▼ London Midland-liveried Parry People Mover 139 001 arrives at Stourbridge Town with the 13.15 shuttle from Stourbridge Jn on 26/09/15. **Robert Pritchard**

▲ Northern-liveried 142 019 and 144 013 pass Rotherham Parkgate with the 18.26 Doncaster–Sheffield on 16/08/16. **Robert Pritchard**

▼ First Great Western "Local Lines"-liveried 143 612 runs along the Dawlish sea wall with the 08.30 Paignton–Exmouth on 18/07/16. **David Hunt**

▲ Rebuilt Northern 144evolution demonstrator 144 012 leaves Sheffield with the 08.27 Lincoln–Adwick on 02/11/15. **Robert Pritchard**

▼ London Midland-liveried 150 109 arrives at Millbrook with the 18.26 Bedford–Bletchley on 13/05/15. **Nigel Gibbs**

▲ Carrying a bright pink advertising livery for citizenrail.org, 153 325 leads 150 131 away from Torre with the 13.24 Exmouth–Paignton on 29/05/16.　**Tony Christie**

▼ Northern-liveried 155 346 and 153 358 stand at Harrogate with a Leeds–York service on 02/09/15.　**Tony Christie**

▲ East Midlands Trains-liveried 156 406 leads a Class 153 at Longton with the 13.07 Crewe–Derby on 06/04/15. **Cliff Beeton**

▼ ScotRail Saltire-liveried 158 867 leaves Gorebridge with the 12.59 Tweedbank–Edinburgh Waverley Borders Railway service on 10/09/15. **Robert Pritchard**

▲ South West Trains-liveried 159 008 arrives at Pinhoe with the 11.25 Exeter St Davids–London Waterloo on 02/06/16. **David Hunt**

▼ Chiltern Railways-liveried 165 013 and 165 028 pass Neasden with the 16.54 High Wycombe–London Marylebone on 05/07/16. **Robert Pritchard**

▲ Great Western Railway Green-liveried 166 213 passes Southall with the 08.32 Didcot Parkway–London Paddington on 06/08/16. **Chris Wilson**

▼ Chiltern Railways Mainline-liveried 168 325 passes Wembley Stadium with the 14.47 Oxford Parkway–London Marylebone on 05/07/16. **Robert Pritchard**

▲ CrossCountry-liveried 170 519 arrives at Derby with the 13.19 Birmingham New Street–Nottingham on 12/08/16. **Robert Pritchard**

▼ ScotRail Saltire-liveried 170 472 leaves Stirling with the 15.18 Glasgow Queen Street–Alloa on 12/09/15. **Robert Pritchard**

▲ London Midland-liveried 172 341 arrives at Worcester Shrub Hill with the 09.24 Birmingham Moor Street–Great Malvern on 26/09/15. **Robert Pritchard**

▼ Arriva Trains-liveried 175 105 passes Longport with a diverted Manchester Piccadilly–Crewe service on 29/05/16. **Cliff Beeton**

▲ Hull Trains-liveried 180 109 leaves Doncaster with the 09.48 London King's Cross–Hull on 02/09/15. **Tony Christie**

▼ In the new TransPennine Express livery, 185 108 stands at Manchester Piccadilly on 01/04/16. **Robert Pritchard**

▲ CrossCountry-liveried 220 016 leaves Sheffield on with the 15.05 Newcastle–Reading on 24/09/15. **Robert Pritchard**

▼ Virgin Trains-liveried 221 113 approaches New Cumnock with the diverted 13.00 Carlisle–Glasgow Central on 14/02/16. **Robin Ralston**

▲ East Midlands Trains-liveried 222 013 and 222 009 pass Woodseats Road, Sheffield with the 12.33 Sheffield–Derby empty stock on 10/04/16. **Robert Pritchard**

▼ The prototype Vivarail unit, 230 001, was expected to enter service with London Midland on the Coventry–Nuneaton route in late 2016. The completed unit is seen here at Long Marston. **Courtesy Vivarail**

▲ BR Green-liveried "Hastings" unit 1001 passes East Goscote, near Melton Mowbray, with a 06.37 Hastings–Ruddington railtour on 19/09/15. **Bill Atkinson**

▼ Swietelsky Babcock Rail Plasser & Theurer 09-3X-RT Tamper DR 73110 passes Cossington on the Midland Main Line with a 14.02 Leagrave–Grantham on 13/03/14. **Paul Biggs**

▲ Colas Rail Matisa B 41 UE Tamper DR 75407 passes Totnes working a 10.30 Westbury–Truro on 28/08/16. **Tony Christie**

▼ Railcare UK 16000-480-UK RailVac OTM 99 70 9515 004-8 is seen being hauled west near Dainton by 70804 on 14/10/15. **Tony Christie**

▲ Colas Rail Plasser & Theurer USP 5000C Regulator DR 77327 passes Dawlish with a 09.30 Tavistock Junction–Taunton on 03/12/15. **David Hunt**

▼ Network Rail Harsco Track Technologies RGH20C Rail Grinding Train DR 79271/261 passes Stenson Junction with a 13.10 Chaddesden Sidings–Swindon on 12/12/14. **Paul Biggs**

▲ Network Rail General Purpose Vehicle Windhoff MPV DR 98008 passes Castlethorpe on the WCML working a 08.35 Rugby–Rugby on 23/04/16. **Mark Beal**

▼ The piling equipment section of the Network Rail Electrification Train formation consisting of 99 70 9131 005-9 "DR 76905" (leading) , 99 70 9131 003-4 "DR 76903" (centre) and 99 70 9131 001-8 "DR 76901" (tailing) passes Great Bedwyn heading west on 25/09/15. **Tony Bartlett**

Class 170/3. Units built for Hull Trains, now in use with ScotRail. Chapman seating. DMSL–MSLRB–DMSL.

DMSL(A). Bombardier Derby 2004. –/55 1TD 2W. 46.5 t.
MSLRB. Bombardier Derby 2004. –/57 1T. Buffet and guard's office 44.7 t.
DMSL(B). Bombardier Derby 2004. –/67 1T. 47.0 t.

170 393	**SR**	P	*SR*	HA	50393	56393	79393
170 394	**SR**	P	*SR*	HA	50394	56394	79394
170 395	**SR**	P	*SR*	HA	50395	56395	79395
170 396	**SR**	P	*SR*	HA	50396	56396	79396

Class 170/3. CrossCountry units. Lazareni seating. DMSL–MS–DMCL.

DMSL. Bombardier Derby 2002. –/59 1TD 2W. 45.4 t.
MS. Bombardier Derby 2002. –/80. 43.0 t.
DMCL. Bombardier Derby 2002. 9/52 1T. 45.8 t.

170 397	**XC**	P	*XC*	TS	50397	56397	79397
170 398	**XC**	P	*XC*	TS	50398	56398	79398

Class 170/4. ScotRail "express" units. Chapman seating. DMCL–MS–DMCL.

170 416–420 are sub-leased from Southern to ScotRail.

170 421–424 have been renumbered as Southern 171 201/202 and 170 401/402.

Non-standard/Advertising liveries:

170 407	BTP text number 61016 (blue).
170 414	Borders Railway (green & blue).
170 416	Unbranded Saltire blue with grey doors.

DMCL(A). Adtranz Derby 1999–2001. 9/43 1TD 2W. 45.2 t.
MS. Adtranz Derby 1999–2001. –/76. 42.5 t.
DMCL(B). Adtranz Derby 1999–2001. 9/49 1T. 45.2 t.

170 401	**SR**	P	*SR*	HA	50401	56401	79401
170 402	**SR**	P	*SR*	HA	50402	56402	79402
170 403	**SR**	P	*SR*	HA	50403	56403	79403
170 404	**SR**	P	*SR*	HA	50404	56404	79404
170 405	**SR**	P	*SR*	HA	50405	56405	79405
170 406	**SR**	P	*SR*	HA	50406	56406	79406
170 407	**AL**	P	*SR*	HA	50407	56407	79407
170 408	**SR**	P	*SR*	HA	50408	56408	79408
170 409	**SR**	P	*SR*	HA	50409	56409	79409
170 410	**SR**	P	*SR*	HA	50410	56410	79410
170 411	**FS**	P	*SR*	HA	50411	56411	79411
170 412	**SR**	P	*SR*	HA	50412	56412	79412
170 413	**FS**	P	*SR*	HA	50413	56413	79413
170 414	**AL**	P	*SR*	HA	50414	56414	79414
170 415	**SR**	P	*SR*	HA	50415	56415	79415
170 416	**O**	E	*SR*	HA	50416	56416	79416
170 417	**FS**	E	*SR*	HA	50417	56417	79417
170 418	**SR**	E	*SR*	HA	50418	56418	79418
170 419	**FS**	E	*SR*	HA	50419	56419	79419
170 420	**FS**	E	*SR*	HA	50420	56420	79420

Class 170/4. ScotRail "express" units. Chapman seating. DMCL–MS–DMCL.

DMCL. Bombardier Derby 2003–05. 9/43 1TD 2W. 46.8 t.
MS. Bombardier Derby 2003–05. –/76. 43.7 t.
DMCL. Bombardier Derby 2003–05. 9/49 1T. 46.5 t.

170 425	**SR**	P	*SR*	HA	50425	56425	79425
170 426	**SR**	P	*SR*	HA	50426	56426	79426
170 427	**SR**	P	*SR*	HA	50427	56427	79427
170 428	**SR**	P	*SR*	HA	50428	56428	79428
170 429	**SR**	P	*SR*	HA	50429	56429	79429
170 430	**SR**	P	*SR*	HA	50430	56430	79430
170 431	**SR**	P	*SR*	HA	50431	56431	79431
170 432	**SR**	P	*SR*	HA	50432	56432	79432
170 433	**SR**	P	*SR*	HA	50433	56433	79433
170 434	**SR**	P	*SR*	HA	50434	56434	79434

Class 170/4. ScotRail units. Originally built as Standard Class only units. 170 450–457 have been retro-fitted with First Class. Chapman seating. DMSL–MS–DMSL or † DMCL–MS–DMCL.

DMSL. Bombardier Derby 2004–05. –/55 1TD 2W († 9/47 1TD 2W). 46.3 t.
MS. Bombardier Derby 2004–05. –/76. 43.4 t.
DMSL. Bombardier Derby 2004–05. –/67 1T († 9/49 1T 1W). 46.4 t.

170 450	†	**SR**	P	*SR*	HA	50450	56450	79450
170 451	†	**SR**	P	*SR*	HA	50451	56451	79451
170 452	†	**SR**	P	*SR*	HA	50452	56452	79452
170 453	†	**SR**	P	*SR*	HA	50453	56453	79453
170 454	†	**SR**	P	*SR*	HA	50454	56454	79454
170 455	†	**SR**	P	*SR*	HA	50455	56455	79455
170 456	†	**SR**	P	*SR*	HA	50456	56456	79456
170 457	†	**SR**	P	*SR*	HA	50457	56457	79457
170 458		**SR**	P	*SR*	HA	50458	56458	79458
170 459		**SR**	P	*SR*	HA	50459	56459	79459
170 460		**SR**	P	*SR*	HA	50460	56460	79460
170 461		**SR**	P	*SR*	HA	50461	56461	79461

Class 170/4. ScotRail units. Standard Class only units. Chapman seating. DMSL–MS–DMSL.

50470–471. DMSL(A). Adtranz Derby 2001. –/55 1TD 2W. 45.1 t.
50472–478. DMSL(A). Bombardier Derby 2004–05. –/57 1TD 2W. 46.3 t.
56470–471. MS. Adtranz Derby 2001. –/76. 42.4 t.
56472–478. MS. Bombardier Derby 2004–05. –/76. 43.4 t.
79470–471. DMSL(B). Adtranz Derby 2001. –/67 1T. 45.1 t.
79472–478. DMSL(B). Bombardier Derby 2004–05. –/67 1T. 46.4 t.

170 470	**SR**	P	*SR*	HA	50470	56470	79470
170 471	**SR**	P	*SR*	HA	50471	56471	79471
170 472	**SR**	P	*SR*	HA	50472	56472	79472
170 473	**SR**	P	*SR*	HA	50473	56473	79473
170 474	**SR**	P	*SR*	HA	50474	56474	79474
170 475	**SR**	P	*SR*	HA	50475	56475	79475
170 476	**SR**	P	*SR*	HA	50476	56476	79476

| 170 477 | **SR** | P | *SR* | HA | 50477 | 56477 | 79477 |
| 170 478 | **SR** | P | *SR* | HA | 50478 | 56478 | 79478 |

Class 170/5. London Midland and CrossCountry 2-car units. Lazareni seating. DMSL–DMSL or * DMSL–DMCL (CrossCountry).

DMSL(A). Adtranz Derby 1999–2000. –/55 1TD 2W (* –/59 1TD 2W). 45.8 t.
DMSL(B). Adtranz Derby 1999–2000. –/67 1T (* DMCL 9/52 1T). 45.9 t.

170 501		**LM**	P	*LM*	TS	50501	79501
170 502		**LM**	P	*LM*	TS	50502	79502
170 503		**LM**	P	*LM*	TS	50503	79503
170 504		**LM**	P	*LM*	TS	50504	79504
170 505		**LM**	P	*LM*	TS	50505	79505
170 506		**LM**	P	*LM*	TS	50506	79506
170 507		**LM**	P	*LM*	TS	50507	79507
170 508		**LM**	P	*LM*	TS	50508	79508
170 509		**LM**	P	*LM*	TS	50509	79509
170 510		**LM**	P	*LM*	TS	50510	79510
170 511		**LM**	P	*LM*	TS	50511	79511
170 512		**LM**	P	*LM*	TS	50512	79512
170 513		**LM**	P	*LM*	TS	50513	79513
170 514		**LM**	P	*LM*	TS	50514	79514
170 515		**LM**	P	*LM*	TS	50515	79515
170 516		**LM**	P	*LM*	TS	50516	79516
170 517		**LM**	P	*LM*	TS	50517	79517
170 518	*	**XC**	P	*XC*	TS	50518	79518
170 519	*	**XC**	P	*XC*	TS	50519	79519
170 520	*	**XC**	P	*XC*	TS	50520	79520
170 521	*	**XC**	P	*XC*	TS	50521	79521
170 522	*	**XC**	P	*XC*	TS	50522	79522
170 523	*	**XC**	P	*XC*	TS	50523	79523

Class 170/6. London Midland and CrossCountry 3-car units. Lazareni seating. DMSL–MS–DMSL or * DMSL–MS–DMCL (CrossCountry).

DMSL(A). Adtranz Derby 2000. –/55 1TD 2W (* –/59 1TD 2W). 45.8 t.
MS. Adtranz Derby 2000. –/74 (* –/80). 42.4 t.
DMSL(B). Adtranz Derby 2000. –/67 1T (* DMCL 9/52 1T). 45.9 t.

170 630		**LM**	P	*LM*	TS	50630	56630	79630
170 631		**LM**	P	*LM*	TS	50631	56631	79631
170 632		**LM**	P	*LM*	TS	50632	56632	79632
170 633		**LM**	P	*LM*	TS	50633	56633	79633
170 634		**LM**	P	*LM*	TS	50634	56634	79634
170 635		**LM**	P	*LM*	TS	50635	56635	79635
170 636	*	**XC**	P	*XC*	TS	50636	56636	79636
170 637	*	**XC**	P	*XC*	TS	50637	56637	79637
170 638	*	**XC**	P	*XC*	TS	50638	56638	79638
170 639	*	**XC**	P	*XC*	TS	50639	56639	79639

CLASS 171   TURBOSTAR   BOMBARDIER

DMCL–DMSL or DMCL–MS–MS–DMCL. Southern units. Air conditioned. Chapman seating.

Construction: Welded aluminium bodies with bolt-on steel ends.
Engines: One MTU 6R183TD13H of 315 kW (422 hp) at 1900 rpm.
Transmission: Hydraulic. Voith T211rzze to ZF final drive.
Bogies: One Adtranz P3–23 and one BREL T3–23 per car.
Couplers: Dellner 12 at outer ends, bar within unit (Class 171/8).
Dimensions: 23.62/23.61 x 2.69 m.
Gangways: Within unit only.   **Wheel Arrangement:** 2-B (+ B-2 + B-2) + B-2.
Doors: Twin-leaf swing plug.   **Maximum Speed:** 100 mph.
Seating Layout: 1: 2+1 facing/unidirectional. 2: 2+2 facing/unidirectional.
Multiple Working: Within class and with EMU Classes 375 and 377 in an emergency.

Class 171/2. 2-car units rebuilt from ScotRail Class 170s. Full details awaited. DMCL–DMSL.

Originally built as 3-car units 170 421/423, but renumbered as Class 171 on fitting with Dellner couplers.

DMCL. Adtranz Derby 1999–2001.
DMSL. Adtranz Derby 1999–2001.

171 201	**SN**	E	*SN*	SU	50421	79421
171 202	**SN**	E	*SN*	SU	50423	79423

Class 171/4. 4-car units rebuilt from ScotRail Class 170s. Full details awaited. DMCL(A)–MS–MS–DMCL(B).

Reformed and renumbered Class 171s in 2016 using vehicles from ScotRail 3-car Class 170s 170 421–424.

DMCL(A). Adtranz Derby 1999–2001.
MS. Adtranz Derby 1999–2001.
DMCL(B). Adtranz Derby 1999–2001.

171 401	**SN**	E	*SN*	SU	50422	56421	56422	79422
171 402	**SN**	E	*SN*	SU	50424	56423	56424	79424

Class 171/7. 2-car units. DMCL–DMSL.

171 721–726 were built as Class 170s (170 721–726), but renumbered as Class 171 on fitting with Dellner couplers.

171 730 was formerly South West Trains unit 170 392, before transferring to Southern in 2007.

50721–726. DMCL. Bombardier Derby 2003. 9/43 1TD 2W. 47.6 t.
50727–729. DMCL. Bombardier Derby 2005. 9/43 1TD 2W. 46.3 t.
50392. DMCL. Bombardier Derby 2003. 9/43 1TD 2W. 46.6 t.
79721–726. DMSL. Bombardier Derby 2003. –/64 1T. 47.8 t.
79727–729. DMSL. Bombardier Derby 2005. –/64 1T. 46.2 t.
79392. DMSL. Bombardier Derby 2003. –/64 1T. 46.5 t.

171 721	**SN**	P	*SN*	SU	50721	79721
171 722	**SN**	P	*SN*	SU	50722	79722
171 723	**SN**	P	*SN*	SU	50723	79723
171 724	**SN**	P	*SN*	SU	50724	79724
171 725	**SN**	P	*SN*	SU	50725	79725
171 726	**SN**	P	*SN*	SU	50726	79726
171 727	**SN**	P	*SN*	SU	50727	79727
171 728	**SN**	P	*SN*	SU	50728	79728
171 729	**SN**	P	*SN*	SU	50729	79729
171 730	**SN**	P	*SN*	SU	50392	79392

Class 171/8. 4-car units. DMCL(A)–MS–MS–DMCL(B).

DMCL(A). Bombardier Derby 2004. 9/43 1TD 2W. 46.5 t.
MS. Bombardier Derby 2004. –/74. 43.7 t.
DMCL(B). Bombardier Derby 2004. 9/50 1T. 46.5 t.

171 801	**SN**	P	*SN*	SU	50801	54801	56801	79801
171 802	**SN**	P	*SN*	SU	50802	54802	56802	79802
171 803	**SN**	P	*SN*	SU	50803	54803	56803	79803
171 804	**SN**	P	*SN*	SU	50804	54804	56804	79804
171 805	**SN**	P	*SN*	SU	50805	54805	56805	79805
171 806	**SN**	P	*SN*	SU	50806	54806	56806	79806

CLASS 172   TURBOSTAR   BOMBARDIER

New generation London Overground, Chiltern Railways and London Midland Turbostars. Air conditioned.

Construction: Welded aluminium bodies with bolt-on steel ends.
Engines: One MTU 6H1800R83 of 360 kW (483 hp) at 1800 rpm.
Transmission: Mechanical. Supplied by ZF, Germany.
Bogies: B5006 type "lightweight" bogies.
Couplers: BSI at outer ends, bar within unit.
Dimensions: 23.62/23.0 x 2.69 m.
Gangways: London Overground & Chiltern units: Within unit only. London Midland units: Throughout.
Wheel Arrangement: 2-B (+ B-2) + B-2.
Doors: Twin-leaf sliding plug.
Maximum Speed: 100 mph (London Overground units 75 mph).
Seating Layout: 2+2 facing/unidirectional.
Multiple Working: Within class and with Classes 150, 153, 155, 156, 158, 159, 165, 166 and 170.

Class 172/0. London Overground units. Used on the Gospel Oak–Barking line. DMS–DMS.

59311–318. DMS(W). Bombardier Derby 2009–10. –/60 2W. 41.6 t.
59411–418. DMS. Bombardier Derby 2009–10. –/64. 41.5 t.

172 001	**LO**	A	*LO*	WN	59311	59411
172 002	**LO**	A	*LO*	WN	59312	59412
172 003	**LO**	A	*LO*	WN	59313	59413
172 004	**LO**	A	*LO*	WN	59314	59414

172 005	**LO**	A	*LO*	WN	59315	59415
172 006	**LO**	A	*LO*	WN	59316	59416
172 007	**LO**	A	*LO*	WN	59317	59417
172 008	**LO**	A	*LO*	WN	59318	59418

Class 172/1. Chiltern Railways units. DMSL–DMS.

59111–114. DMSL. Bombardier Derby 2009–10. –/60(+5) 1TD 2W. 42.4 t.
59211–214. DMS. Bombardier Derby 2009–10. –/80. 41.8 t.

172 101	**CR**	A	*CR*	AL	59111	59211
172 102	**CR**	A	*CR*	AL	59112	59212
172 103	**CR**	A	*CR*	AL	59113	59213
172 104	**CR**	A	*CR*	AL	59114	59214

Class 172/2. London Midland 2-car units. DMSL–DMS. Used on local services via Birmingham Snow Hill.

50211–222. DMSL. Bombardier Derby 2010–11. –/52(+11) 1TD 2W. 42.5 t.
79211–222. DMS. Bombardier Derby 2010–11. –/68(+8). 41.9 t.

172 211	**LM**	P	*LM*	TS	50211	79211
172 212	**LM**	P	*LM*	TS	50212	79212
172 213	**LM**	P	*LM*	TS	50213	79213
172 214	**LM**	P	*LM*	TS	50214	79214
172 215	**LM**	P	*LM*	TS	50215	79215
172 216	**LM**	P	*LM*	TS	50216	79216
172 217	**LM**	P	*LM*	TS	50217	79217
172 218	**LM**	P	*LM*	TS	50218	79218
172 219	**LM**	P	*LM*	TS	50219	79219
172 220	**LM**	P	*LM*	TS	50220	79220
172 221	**LM**	P	*LM*	TS	50221	79221
172 222	**LM**	P	*LM*	TS	50222	79222

Class 172/3. London Midland 3-car units. DMSL–MS–DMS. Used on local services via Birmingham Snow Hill.

50331–345. DMSL. Bombardier Derby 2010–11. –/52(+11) 1TD 2W. 42.5 t.
56331–345. MS. Bombardier Derby 2010–11. –/72(+8). 38.8 t.
79331–345. DMS. Bombardier Derby 2010–11. –/68(+8). 41.9 t.

172 331	**LM**	P	*LM*	TS	50331	56331	79331
172 332	**LM**	P	*LM*	TS	50332	56332	79332
172 333	**LM**	P	*LM*	TS	50333	56333	79333
172 334	**LM**	P	*LM*	TS	50334	56334	79334
172 335	**LM**	P	*LM*	TS	50335	56335	79335
172 336	**LM**	P	*LM*	TS	50336	56336	79336
172 337	**LM**	P	*LM*	TS	50337	56337	79337
172 338	**LM**	P	*LM*	TS	50338	56338	79338
172 339	**LM**	P	*LM*	TS	50339	56339	79339
172 340	**LM**	P	*LM*	TS	50340	56340	79340
172 341	**LM**	P	*LM*	TS	50341	56341	79341
172 342	**LM**	P	*LM*	TS	50342	56342	79342
172 343	**LM**	P	*LM*	TS	50343	56343	79343
172 344	**LM**	P	*LM*	TS	50344	56344	79344
172 345	**LM**	P	*LM*	TS	50345	56345	79345

CLASS 175   CORADIA 1000   ALSTOM

Air conditioned.

Construction: Steel.
Engines: One Cummins N14 of 335 kW (450 hp).
Transmission: Hydraulic. Voith T211rzze to ZF Voith final drive.
Bogies: ACR (Alstom FBO) – LTB-MBS1, TB-MB1, MBS1-LTB.
Couplers: Scharfenberg outer ends and bar within unit (Class 175/1).
Dimensions: 23.7 x 2.73 m.

Gangways: Within unit only.
Doors: Single-leaf swing plug.
Wheel Arrangement: 2-B (+ B-2) + B-2.
Maximum Speed: 100 mph.
Seating Layout: 2+2 facing/unidirectional.
Multiple Working: Within class and with Class 180.

Class **175/0**. DMSL–DMSL. 2-car units.

DMSL(A). Alstom Birmingham 1999–2000. –/54 1TD 2W. 48.8 t.
DMSL(B). Alstom Birmingham 1999–2000. –/64 1T. 50.7 t.

175 001	**AV**	A	*AW*	CH	50701	79701
175 002	**AV**	A	*AW*	CH	50702	79702
175 003	**AV**	A	*AW*	CH	50703	79703
175 004	**AV**	A	*AW*	CH	50704	79704
175 005	**AV**	A	*AW*	CH	50705	79705
175 006	**AV**	A	*AW*	CH	50706	79706
175 007	**AV**	A	*AW*	CH	50707	79707
175 008	**AV**	A	*AW*	CH	50708	79708
175 009	**AV**	A	*AW*	CH	50709	79709
175 010	**AV**	A	*AW*	CH	50710	79710
175 011	**AV**	A	*AW*	CH	50711	79711

Class **175/1**. DMSL–MSL–DMSL. 3-car units.

DMSL(A). Alstom Birmingham 1999–2001. –/54 1TD 2W. 50.7 t.
MSL. Alstom Birmingham 1999–2001. –/68 1T. 47.5 t.
DMSL(B). Alstom Birmingham 1999–2001. –/64 1T. 49.5 t.

175 101	**AV**	A	*AW*	CH	50751	56751	79751
175 102	**AV**	A	*AW*	CH	50752	56752	79752
175 103	**AV**	A	*AW*	CH	50753	56753	79753
175 104	**AV**	A	*AW*	CH	50754	56754	79754
175 105	**AV**	A	*AW*	CH	50755	56755	79755
175 106	**AV**	A	*AW*	CH	50756	56756	79756
175 107	**AV**	A	*AW*	CH	50757	56757	79757
175 108	**AV**	A	*AW*	CH	50758	56758	79758
175 109	**AV**	A	*AW*	CH	50759	56759	79759
175 110	**AV**	A	*AW*	CH	50760	56760	79760
175 111	**AV**	A	*AW*	CH	50761	56761	79761
175 112	**AV**	A	*AW*	CH	50762	56762	79762
175 113	**AV**	A	*AW*	CH	50763	56763	79763
175 114	**AV**	A	*AW*	CH	50764	56764	79764
175 115	**AV**	A	*AW*	CH	50765	56765	79765
175 116	**AV**	A	*AW*	CH	50766	56766	79766

CLASS 180   ADELANTE   ALSTOM

Air conditioned.

Construction: Steel.
Engines: One Cummins QSK19 of 560 kW (750 hp) at 2100 rpm.
Transmission: Hydraulic. Voith T312br to Voith final drive.
Bogies: ACR (Alstom FBO): LTB1-MBS2, TB1-MB2, TB1-MB2, TB2-MB2, MBS2-LTB1.
Couplers: Scharfenberg outer ends, bar within unit.
Dimensions: 23.71/23.03 x 2.73 m.
Gangways: Within unit only.
Wheel Arrangement: 2-B + B-2 + B-2 + B-2 + B-2.
Doors: Single-leaf swing plug.   **Maximum Speed:** 125 mph.
Seating Layout: 1: 2+1 facing/unidirectional, 2: 2+2 facing/unidirectional.
Multiple Working: Within class and with Class 175.

DMSL(A). Alstom Birmingham 2000–01. –/46 2W 1TD. 51.7 t.
MFL. Alstom Birmingham 2000–01. 42/– 1T 1W + catering point. 49.6 t.
MSL. Alstom Birmingham 2000–01. –/68 1T. 49.5 t.
MSLRB. Alstom Birmingham 2000–01. –/56 1T. 50.3 t.
DMSL(B). Alstom Birmingham 2000–01. –/56 1T. 51.4 t.

180 101	**GC**	A	*GC*	HT	50901	54901	55901	56901	59901
180 102	**FD**	A	*GW*	OO	50902	54902	55902	56902	59902
180 103	**FD**	A	*GW*	OO	50903	54903	55903	56903	59903
180 104	**FD**	A	*GW*	OO	50904	54904	55904	56904	59904
180 105	**GC**	A	*GC*	HT	50905	54905	55905	56905	59905
180 106	**FD**	A	*GW*	OO	50906	54906	55906	56906	59906
180 107	**GC**	A	*GC*	HT	50907	54907	55907	56907	59907
180 108	**FD**	A	*GW*	OO	50908	54908	55908	56908	59908
180 109	**FD**	A	*HT*	OO	50909	54909	55909	56909	59909
180 110	**FD**	A	*HT*	OO	50910	54910	55910	56910	59910
180 111	**FD**	A	*HT*	OO	50911	54911	55911	56911	59911
180 112	**GC**	A	*GC*	HT	50912	54912	55912	56912	59912
180 113	**FD**	A	*HT*	OO	50913	54913	55913	56913	59913
180 114	**GC**	A	*GC*	HT	50914	54914	55914	56914	59914

Names (carried on DMSL(A):

180 105	THE YORKSHIRE ARTIST ASHLEY JACKSON
180 107	HART OF THE NORTH
180 112	JAMES HERRIOT

CLASS 185   DESIRO UK   SIEMENS

Air conditioned. Grammer seating.

Construction: Aluminium.
Engines: One Cummins QSK19 of 560 kW (750 hp) at 2100 rpm.
Transmission: Voith.
Bogies: Siemens.
Couplers: Dellner 12.   **Dimensions:** 23.76/23.75 x 2.66 m.

Gangways: Within unit only.   **Wheel Arrangement:** 2-B + 2-B + B-2.
Doors: Double-leaf sliding plug.   **Maximum Speed:** 100 mph.
Seating Layout: 1: 2+1 facing/unidirectional, 2: 2+2 facing/unidirectional.
Multiple Working: Within class only.

DMCL. Siemens Krefeld 2005–06. 15/18(+8) 2W 1TD + catering point. 55.4 t.
MSL. Siemens Krefeld 2005–06. –/72 1T. 52.7 t.
DMS. Siemens Krefeld 2005–06. –/64(4). 54.9 t.

185 101	**FT**	E	*TP*	AK	51101	53101	54101
185 102	**FT**	E	*TP*	AK	51102	53102	54102
185 103	**FT**	E	*TP*	AK	51103	53103	54103
185 104	**FT**	E	*TP*	AK	51104	53104	54104
185 105	**FT**	E	*TP*	AK	51105	53105	54105
185 106	**FT**	E	*TP*	AK	51106	53106	54106
185 107	**FT**	E	*TP*	AK	51107	53107	54107
185 108	**TP**	E	*TP*	AK	51108	53108	54108
185 109	**FT**	E	*TP*	AK	51109	53109	54109
185 110	**FT**	E	*TP*	AK	51110	53110	54110
185 111	**FT**	E	*TP*	AK	51111	53111	54111
185 112	**FT**	E	*TP*	AK	51112	53112	54112
185 113	**FT**	E	*TP*	AK	51113	53113	54113
185 114	**TP**	E	*TP*	AK	51114	53114	54114
185 115	**TP**	E	*TP*	AK	51115	53115	54115
185 116	**FT**	E	*TP*	AK	51116	53116	54116
185 117	**FT**	E	*TP*	AK	51117	53117	54117
185 118	**FT**	E	*TP*	AK	51118	53118	54118
185 119	**FT**	E	*TP*	AK	51119	53119	54119
185 120	**FT**	E	*TP*	AK	51120	53120	54120
185 121	**FT**	E	*TP*	AK	51121	53121	54121
185 122	**FT**	E	*TP*	AK	51122	53122	54122
185 123	**TP**	E	*TP*	AK	51123	53123	54123
185 124	**FT**	E	*TP*	AK	51124	53124	54124
185 125	**FT**	E	*TP*	AK	51125	53125	54125
185 126	**FT**	E	*TP*	AK	51126	53126	54126
185 127	**TP**	E	*TP*	AK	51127	53127	54127
185 128	**FT**	E	*TP*	AK	51128	53128	54128
185 129	**FT**	E	*TP*	AK	51129	53129	54129
185 130	**FT**	E	*TP*	AK	51130	53130	54130
185 131	**TP**	E	*TP*	AK	51131	53131	54131
185 132	**FT**	E	*TP*	AK	51132	53132	54132
185 133	**FT**	E	*TP*	AK	51133	53133	54133
185 134	**FT**	E	*TP*	AK	51134	53134	54134
185 135	**TP**	E	*TP*	AK	51135	53135	54135
185 136	**FT**	E	*TP*	AK	51136	53136	54136
185 137	**FT**	E	*TP*	AK	51137	53137	54137
185 138	**TP**	E	*TP*	AK	51138	53138	54138
185 139	**TP**	E	*TP*	AK	51139	53139	54139
185 140	**FT**	E	*TP*	AK	51140	53140	54140
185 141	**FT**	E	*TP*	AK	51141	53141	54141
185 142	**FT**	E	*TP*	AK	51142	53142	54142
185 143	**FT**	E	*TP*	AK	51143	53143	54143

185 144	**TP**	E	*TP*	AK	51144	53144	54144
185 145	**FT**	E	*TP*	AK	51145	53145	54145
185 146	**FT**	E	*TP*	AK	51146	53146	54146
185 147	**FT**	E	*TP*	AK	51147	53147	54147
185 148	**FT**	E	*TP*	AK	51148	53148	54148
185 149	**FT**	E	*TP*	AK	51149	53149	54149
185 150	**TP**	E	*TP*	AK	51150	53150	54150
185 151	**FT**	E	*TP*	AK	51151	53151	54151

3.2. DIESEL ELECTRIC UNITS

CLASS 201/202   PRESERVED "HASTINGS" UNIT   BR

DMBS–TSL–TSL–TSRB–TSL–DMBS.

Preserved unit made up from two Class 201 short-frame cars and three Class 202 long-frame cars. The "Hastings" units were made with narrow body-profiles for use on the section between Tonbridge and Battle which had tunnels of restricted loading gauge. These tunnels were converted to single track operation in the 1980s thus allowing standard loading gauge stock to be used. The set also contains a Class 411 EMU trailer (not Hastings line gauge) and a Class 422 EMU buffet car.

Construction: Steel.
Engine: One English Electric 4SRKT Mk. 2 of 450 kW (600 hp) at 850 rpm.
Main Generator: English Electric EE824.
Traction Motors: Two English Electric EE507 mounted on the inner bogie.
Bogies: SR Mk 4. (Former EMU TSL vehicles have Commonwealth bogies).
Couplers: Drophead buckeye.
Dimensions: 18.40 x 2.50 m (60000), 20.35 x 2.50 m (60116/118/529), 18.36 x 2.50 m (60501), 20.35 x 2.82 (69337), 20.30 x 2.82 (70262).
Gangways: Within unit only.   **Doors:** Manually operated slam.
Brakes: Electro-pneumatic and automatic air.
Maximum Speed: 75 mph.   **Seating Layout:** 2+2 facing.
Multiple Working: Other ex-BR Southern Region DEMU vehicles.

60000. DMBS. Lot No. 30329 Eastleigh 1957. –/22. 55.0 t.
60116. DMBS. Lot No. 30395 Eastleigh 1957. –/31. 56.0 t.
60118. DMBS. Lot No. 30395 Eastleigh 1957. –/30. 56.0 t.
60501. TSL. Lot No. 30331 Eastleigh 1957. –/52 2T. 29.5 t.
60529. TSL. Lot No. 30397 Eastleigh 1957. –/60 2T. 30.5 t.
69337. TSRB (ex-Class 422 EMU). Lot No. 30805 York 1970. –/40. 35.0 t.
70262. TSL (ex-Class 411/5 EMU). Lot No. 30455 Eastleigh 1958. –/64 2T. 31.5 t.

| 201 001 | **G** | HD | *HD* | SE | 60116 | 60529 | 70262 | 69337 | 60501 | 60118 |
| Spare | **G** | HD | *HD* | SE | 60000 | | | | | |

Names:

60000	Hastings
60116	Mountfield
60118	Tunbridge Wells

CLASS 220 VOYAGER BOMBARDIER

DMS–MS–MS–DMF. All engines have been derated from 750 hp to 700 hp.

Construction: Steel.
Engine: Cummins QSK19 of 520 kW (700 hp) at 1800 rpm.
Transmission: Two Alstom Onix 800 three-phase traction motors of 275 kW.
Braking: Rheostatic and electro-pneumatic.
Bogies: Bombardier B5005.
Couplers: Dellner 12 at outer ends, bar within unit.
Dimensions: 23.85/23.00 (602xx) x 2.73 m.
Gangways: Within unit only.
Wheel Arrangement: 1A-A1 + 1A-A1 + 1A-A1 + 1A-A1.
Doors: Single-leaf swing plug.
Maximum Speed: 125 m.p.h.
Seating Layout: 1: 2+1 facing/unidirectional, 2: 2+2 mainly unidirectional.
Multiple Working: Within class and with Classes 221 and 222 (in an emergency). Also can be controlled from Class 57/3 locomotives.

DMS. Bombardier Bruges/Wakefield 2000–01. –/42 1TD 1W. 51.1 t.
MS(A). Bombardier Bruges/Wakefield 2000–01. –/66. 45.9 t.
MS(B). Bombardier Bruges/Wakefield 2000–01. –/66 1TD. 46.7 t.
DMF. Bombardier Bruges/Wakefield 2000–01. 26/– 1TD 1W. 50.9 t.

220 001	**XC**	VL	*XC*	CZ	60301	60701	60201	60401
220 002	**XC**	VL	*XC*	CZ	60302	60702	60202	60402
220 003	**XC**	VL	*XC*	CZ	60303	60703	60203	60403
220 004	**XC**	VL	*XC*	CZ	60304	60704	60204	60404
220 005	**XC**	VL	*XC*	CZ	60305	60705	60205	60405
220 006	**XC**	VL	*XC*	CZ	60306	60706	60206	60406
220 007	**XC**	VL	*XC*	CZ	60307	60707	60207	60407
220 008	**XC**	VL	*XC*	CZ	60308	60708	60208	60408
220 009	**XC**	VL	*XC*	CZ	60309	60709	60209	60409
220 010	**XC**	VL	*XC*	CZ	60310	60710	60210	60410
220 011	**XC**	VL	*XC*	CZ	60311	60711	60211	60411
220 012	**XC**	VL	*XC*	CZ	60312	60712	60212	60412
220 013	**XC**	VL	*XC*	CZ	60313	60713	60213	60413
220 014	**XC**	VL	*XC*	CZ	60314	60714	60214	60414
220 015	**XC**	VL	*XC*	CZ	60315	60715	60215	60415
220 016	**XC**	VL	*XC*	CZ	60316	60716	60216	60416
220 017	**XC**	VL	*XC*	CZ	60317	60717	60217	60417
220 018	**XC**	VL	*XC*	CZ	60318	60718	60218	60418
220 019	**XC**	VL	*XC*	CZ	60319	60719	60219	60419
220 020	**XC**	VL	*XC*	CZ	60320	60720	60220	60420
220 021	**XC**	VL	*XC*	CZ	60321	60721	60221	60421
220 022	**XC**	VL	*XC*	CZ	60322	60722	60222	60422
220 023	**XC**	VL	*XC*	CZ	60323	60723	60223	60423
220 024	**XC**	VL	*XC*	CZ	60324	60724	60224	60424
220 025	**XC**	VL	*XC*	CZ	60325	60725	60225	60425
220 026	**XC**	VL	*XC*	CZ	60326	60726	60226	60426
220 027	**XC**	VL	*XC*	CZ	60327	60727	60227	60427
220 028	**XC**	VL	*XC*	CZ	60328	60728	60228	60428

220 029	**XC**	VL	*XC*	CZ	60329	60729	60229	60429
220 030	**XC**	VL	*XC*	CZ	60330	60730	60230	60430
220 031	**XC**	VL	*XC*	CZ	60331	60731	60231	60431
220 032	**XC**	VL	*XC*	CZ	60332	60732	60232	60432
220 033	**XC**	VL	*XC*	CZ	60333	60733	60233	60433
220 034	**XC**	VL	*XC*	CZ	60334	60734	60234	60434

CLASS 221   SUPER VOYAGER   BOMBARDIER

* DMS–MS–MS–MSRMB–DMF (Virgin Trains units) or DMS–MS–MS–MS–DMF (CrossCountry units). Built as tilting units but tilt now isolated on CrossCountry sets. All engines have been derated from 750 hp to 700 hp.

Construction: Steel.
Engine: Cummins QSK19 of 520 kW (700 hp) at 1800 rpm.
Transmission: Two Alstom Onix 800 three-phase traction motors of 275 kW.
Braking: Rheostatic and electro-pneumatic.
Bogies: Bombardier HVP.
Couplers: Dellner 12 at outer ends, bar within unit.
Dimensions: 23.67 x 2.73 m.
Gangways: Within unit only.
Wheel Arrangement: 1A-A1 + 1A-A1 + 1A-A1 (+ 1A-A1) + 1A-A1.
Doors: Single-leaf swing plug.
Maximum Speed: 125 mph.
Seating Layout: 1: 2+1 facing/unidirectional, 2: 2+2 mainly unidirectional.
Multiple Working: Within class and with Classes 220 and 222 (in an emergency). Also can be controlled from Class 57/3 locomotives.

* Virgin Trains units. MSRMB moved adjacent to the DMF. The seating in this vehicle (2+2 facing) can be used by First or Standard Class passengers depending on demand.
Advertising livery: 221 115 Dark grey Bombardier branding on end vehicles.

DMS. Bombardier Bruges/Wakefield 2001–02. –/42 1TD 1W. 58.5 t (* 58.9 t.)
60751–794 MS (* MSRMB). Bombardier Bruges/Wakefield 2001–02. –/66 (* –/52). 54.1 t (* 55.9 t.)
60951–994. MS. Bombardier Bruges/Wakefield 2001–02. –/66 1TD (* –/68 1TD). 54.8 t (* 54.3 t.)
60851–890. MS. Bombardier Bruges/Wakefield 2001–02. –/62 1TD (* –/68 1TD). 54.4 t (* 55.0 t.)
DMF. Bombardier Bruges/Wakefield 2001–02. 26/– 1TD 1W. 58.9 t (* 59.1 t.)

221 101	*	**VT**	VL	*VW*	CZ	60351	60951	60851	60751	60451
221 102	*	**VT**	VL	*VW*	CZ	60352	60952	60852	60752	60452
221 103	*	**VT**	VL	*VW*	CZ	60353	60953	60853	60753	60453
221 104	*	**VT**	VL	*VW*	CZ	60354	60954	60854	60754	60454
221 105	*	**VT**	VL	*VW*	CZ	60355	60955	60855	60755	60455
221 106	*	**VT**	VL	*VW*	CZ	60356	60956	60856	60756	60456
221 107	*	**VT**	VL	*VW*	CZ	60357	60957	60857	60757	60457
221 108	*	**VT**	VL	*VW*	CZ	60358	60958	60858	60758	60458
221 109	*	**VT**	VL	*VW*	CZ	60359	60959	60859	60759	60459
221 110	*	**VT**	VL	*VW*	CZ	60360	60960	60860	60760	60460

221 111	*	**VT**	VL	*VW*	CZ	60361	60961	60861	60761	60461
221 112	*	**VT**	VL	*VW*	CZ	60362	60962	60862	60762	60462
221 113	*	**VT**	VL	*VW*	CZ	60363	60963	60863	60763	60463
221 114	*	**VT**	VL	*VW*	CZ	60364	60964	60864	60764	60464
221 115	*	**AL**	VL	*VW*	CZ	60365	60965	60865	60765	60465
221 116	*	**VT**	VL	*VW*	CZ	60366	60966	60866	60766	60466
221 117	*	**VT**	VL	*VW*	CZ	60367	60967	60867	60767	60467
221 118	*	**VT**	VL	*VW*	CZ	60368	60968	60868	60768	60468
221 119		**XC**	VL	*XC*	CZ	60369	60769	60969	60869	60469
221 120		**XC**	VL	*XC*	CZ	60370	60770	60970	60870	60470
221 121		**XC**	VL	*XC*	CZ	60371	60771	60971	60871	60471
221 122		**XC**	VL	*XC*	CZ	60372	60772	60972	60872	60472
221 123		**XC**	VL	*XC*	CZ	60373	60773	60973	60873	60473
221 124		**XC**	VL	*XC*	CZ	60374	60774	60974	60874	60474
221 125		**XC**	VL	*XC*	CZ	60375	60775	60975	60875	60475
221 126		**XC**	VL	*XC*	CZ	60376	60776	60976	60876	60476
221 127		**XC**	VL	*XC*	CZ	60377	60777	60977	60877	60477
221 128		**XC**	VL	*XC*	CZ	60378	60778	60978	60878	60478
221 129		**XC**	VL	*XC*	CZ	60379	60779	60979	60879	60479
221 130		**XC**	VL	*XC*	CZ	60380	60780	60980	60880	60480
221 131		**XC**	VL	*XC*	CZ	60381	60781	60981	60881	60481
221 132		**XC**	VL	*XC*	CZ	60382	60782	60982	60882	60482
221 133		**XC**	VL	*XC*	CZ	60383	60783	60983	60883	60483
221 134		**XC**	VL	*XC*	CZ	60384	60784	60984	60884	60484
221 135		**XC**	VL	*XC*	CZ	60385	60785	60985	60885	60485
221 136		**XC**	VL	*XC*	CZ	60386	60786	60986	60886	60486
221 137		**XC**	VL	*XC*	CZ	60387	60787	60987	60887	60487
221 138		**XC**	VL	*XC*	CZ	60388	60788	60988	60888	60488
221 139		**XC**	VL	*XC*	CZ	60389	60789	60989	60889	60489
221 140		**XC**	VL	*XC*	CZ	60390	60790	60990	60890	60490
221 141		**XC**	VL	*XC*	CZ	60391	60791	60991		60491
221 142	*	**VT**	VL	*VW*	CZ	60392	60992	60994	60792	60492
221 143	*	**VT**	VL	*VW*	CZ	60393	60993	60794	60793	60493
Spare	*	**VT**	VL		CZ	60394				60494

Names (carried on MS No. 609xx):

221 101	Louis Bleriot		221 110	James Cook
221 102	John Cabot		221 111	Roald Amundsen
221 103	Christopher Columbus		221 112	Ferdinand Magellan
221 104	Sir John Franklin		221 113	Sir Walter Raleigh
221 105	William Baffin		221 115	Polmadie Depot
221 106	Willem Barents		221 117	The Wrekin Giant
221 107	Sir Martin Frobisher		221 142	BOMBARDIER Voyager
221 108	Sir Ernest Shackleton		221 143	Auguste Picard
221 109	Marco Polo			

CLASS 222   MERIDIAN   BOMBARDIER

Construction: Steel.
Engine: Cummins QSK19 of 560 kW (750 hp) at 1800 rpm.
Transmission: Two Alstom Onix 800 three-phase traction motors of 275 kW.
Braking: Rheostatic and electro-pneumatic.
Bogies: Bombardier B5005.   **Dimensions:** 23.85/23.00 x 2.73 m.
Couplers: Dellner at outer ends, bar within unit.
Gangways: Within unit only.   **Wheel Arrangement:** All cars 1A-A1.
Doors: Single-leaf swing plug.   **Maximum Speed:** 125 mph.
Seating Layout: 1: 2+1, 2: 2+2 facing/unidirectional.
Multiple Working: Within class and with Classes 220 and 221 (in an emergency).

222 001–006. 7-car units. DMF–MF–MF–MSRMB–MS–MS–DMS.

The 7-car units were built as 9-car units, before being reduced to 8-car sets
and then later to 7-car sets to strengthen all 4-car units to 5-cars. 222 007
was built as a 9-car unit but later reduced to a 5-car unit.

DMRF. Bombardier Bruges 2004–05. 22/– 1TD 1W. 52.8 t.
MF. Bombardier Bruges 2004–05. 42/– 1T. 46.8 t.
MSRMB. Bombardier Bruges 2004–05. –/62. 48.0 t.
MS. Bombardier Bruges 2004–05. –/68 1T. 47.0 t.
DMS. Bombardier Bruges 2004–05. –/38 1TD 1W. 49.4 t.

222 001	**ST**	E	*EM*	DY	60241	60445	60341	60621
					60561	60551	60161	
222 002	**ST**	E	*EM*	DY	60242	60346	60342	60622
					60562	60552	60162	
222 003	**ST**	E	*EM*	DY	60243	60446	60343	60623
					60563	60553	60163	
222 004	**ST**	E	*EM*	DY	60244	60345	60344	60624
					60564	60554	60164	
222 005	**ST**	E	*EM*	DY	60245	60347	60443	60625
					60555	60565	60165	
222 006	**ST**	E	*EM*	DY	60246	60447	60441	60626
					60566	60556	60166	

Names (carried on MSRMB or DMS (222 003)):

222 001 THE ENTREPRENEUR EXPRESS
222 002 THE CUTLERS' COMPANY
222 003 TORNADO
222 004 CHILDREN'S HOSPITAL SHEFFIELD
222 006 THE CARBON CUTTER

222 007–023. 5-car units. DMF–MC–MSRMB–MS–DMS.

DMRF. Bombardier Bruges 2003–04. 22/– 1TD 1W. 52.8 t.
MC. Bombardier Bruges 2003–04. 28/22 1T. 48.6 t.
MSRMB. Bombardier Bruges 2003–04. –/62. 49.6 t.
MS. Bombardier Bruges 2004–05. –/68 1T. 47.0 t.
DMS. Bombardier Bruges 2003–04. –/40 1TD 1W. 51.0 t.

222 007	**ST**	E	*EM*	DY	60247	60442	60627	60567	60167
222 008	**ST**	E	*EM*	DY	60248	60918	60628	60545	60168
222 009	**ST**	E	*EM*	DY	60249	60919	60629	60557	60169
222 010	**ST**	E	*EM*	DY	60250	60920	60630	60546	60170
222 011	**ST**	E	*EM*	DY	60251	60921	60631	60531	60171
222 012	**ST**	E	*EM*	DY	60252	60922	60632	60532	60172
222 013	**ST**	E	*EM*	DY	60253	60923	60633	60533	60173
222 014	**ST**	E	*EM*	DY	60254	60924	60634	60534	60174
222 015	**ST**	E	*EM*	DY	60255	60925	60635	60535	60175
222 016	**ST**	E	*EM*	DY	60256	60926	60636	60536	60176
222 017	**ST**	E	*EM*	DY	60257	60927	60637	60537	60177
222 018	**ST**	E	*EM*	DY	60258	60928	60638	60444	60178
222 019	**ST**	E	*EM*	DY	60259	60929	60639	60547	60179
222 020	**ST**	E	*EM*	DY	60260	60930	60640	60543	60180
222 021	**ST**	E	*EM*	DY	60261	60931	60641	60552	60181
222 022	**ST**	E	*EM*	DY	60262	60932	60642	60542	60182
222 023	**ST**	E	*EM*	DY	60263	60933	60643	60541	60183

Names (carried on MSRMB or DMS):

222 008 Derby Etches Park
222 011 Sheffield City Battalion 1914–1918
222 015 175 YEARS OF DERBY'S RAILWAYS 1839–2014
222 022 INVEST IN NOTTINGHAM

222 101–104. 4-car former Hull Trains units. DMF–MC–MSRMB–DMS.

DMRF. Bombardier Bruges 2005. 22/– 1TD 1W. 52.8 t.
MC. Bombardier Bruges 2005. 11/46 1T. 47.1 t.
MSRMB. Bombardier Bruges 2005. –/62. 48.0 t.
DMS. Bombardier Bruges 2005. –/40 1TD 1W. 49.4 t.

222 101	**ST**	E	*EM*	DY	60271	60571	60681	60191
222 102	**ST**	E	*EM*	DY	60272	60572	60682	60192
222 103	**ST**	E	*EM*	DY	60273	60573	60683	60193
222 104	**ST**	E	*EM*	DY	60274	60574	60684	60194

CLASS 230 D-TRAIN METRO-CAMMELL/VIVARAIL

The Class 230 D-Train is a prototype 3-car DEMU rebuilt from former London Underground D78 Stock by Vivarail at Long Marston. The D-Train uses the bodyshells, bogies and electric traction motors of D78 Stock. Instead of being powered by electricity the motors are instead powered by new underfloor-mounted diesel engines – two per driving car. Modern IGBT electronic controls replace the previous mechanical camshaft controllers, incorporating the latest automotive stop-start technology and dynamic braking.

The prototype was due to commence trial operation on the Coventry–Nuneaton line in 2017, but following fire damage sustained during test running in December 2016 this trial has been cancelled. Full interior details are awaited but include a mix of seating layouts and a universal access toilet in the TSO.

Vivarail has acquired more than 200 redundant D78 Stock vehicles that are stored at Long Marston and it is hoped that orders for further conversions will be forthcoming.

Construction: Aluminium.
Engine: 2 x Ford Duratorq 3.2 litre engines of 150 kw (200 hp).
Control System: IGBT Inverter.   **Braking:** Rheostatic & Dynamic.
Bogies: Bombardier flexible-frame.   **Dimensions:** 18.37/18.12 x 2.85 m.
Couplers: LUL automatic wedgelock. **Gangways:** Within unit only.
Wheel Arrangement: Bo-Bo + 2-2 + Bo-Bo.
Doors: Sliding.   **Maximum Speed:** 60 mph.
Seating Layout: Longitudinal or 2+2 facing.
Multiple Working: Within class.

Rebuilt from former London Underground D78 Stock:
300001 rebuilt from Driving Motor 7058; redesignated DMSO(A).
300101 rebuilt from Driving Motor 7511; redesignated DMSO(B).
300201 rebuilt from Trailer 17128; redesignated TSO.

DMSO(A). Metro-Cammell Birmingham 1979–83. 28 t.
TSO. Metro-Cammell Birmingham 1979–83. 20 t.
DMSO(B). Metro-Cammell Birmingham 1979–83. 28 t.

| 230 001 | **VI** VI | LM | 300001 | 300201 | 300101 |

4. ELECTRIC MULTIPLE UNITS

INTRODUCTION

This section contains details of all Electric Multiple Units, usually referred to as EMUs, which can run on Britain's national railway network.

The number of EMUs in operation has been steadily increasing in recent years as both more lines have been opened or have been electrified and as the number of passengers travelling on the network has increased. EMUs work a wide variety of services, from long distance Intercity (such as the Class 390 Pendolinos) to inter-urban and suburban duties.

LAYOUT OF INFORMATION

25 kV AC 50 Hz overhead EMUs and dual voltage EMUs are listed in numerical order of set numbers. Individual "loose" vehicles are listed in numerical order after vehicles formed into fixed formations.

750 V DC third rail EMUs are listed in numerical order of class number, then in numerical order of set number. Some of these use the former Southern Region four-digit set numbers. These are derived from theoretical six digit set numbers which are the four-digit set number prefixed by the first two numbers of the class.

Where sets or vehicles have been renumbered in recent years, former numbering detail is shown alongside current detail. Each entry is laid out as in the following example:

Set No.	Detail	Livery	Owner	Operator	Allocation	Formation
5912	†	**SS**	P	*SW*	WD	77835 62837 67400 77836

Codes: Codes are used to denote the livery, owner, operator and depot allocation of each Electric Multiple Unit. Details of these can be found in section 6 of this book. Where a unit or spare car is off-lease, the operator column is left blank.

Detail Differences: Detail differences which currently affect the areas and types of train which vehicles may work are shown, plus differences in interior layout. Where such differences occur within a class, these are shown either in the heading information or alongside the individual set or vehicle number.

Set Formations: Regular set formations are shown where these are normally maintained. Readers should note set formations might be temporarily varied from time to time to suit maintenance and/or operational requirements. Vehicles shown as "Spare" are not formed in any regular set formation.

Names: Only names carried with official sanction are listed. Names are shown in UPPER/lower case characters as actually shown on the name carried on the vehicle(s). Unless otherwise shown, complete units are regarded as named rather than just the individual car(s) which carry the name.

GENERAL INFORMATION

CLASSIFICATION AND NUMBERING

25 kV AC 50 Hz overhead and "Versatile" EMUs are classified in the series 300–399. 750 V DC third rail EMUs are classified in the series 400–599. More recently dual-voltage units have been numbered in the 700–710 series and Hitachi InterCity Express Programme (IEP) units are numbered in the 800–802 series. Classes 800 and 802 are bi-mode units which can operate under both diesel or electric power.

Until 2014 EMU individual cars were numbered in the series 61000–78999, except for vehicles used on the Isle of Wight – which are numbered in a separate series, and the Class 378s, 380s and 395s, which took up the 38xxx and 39xxx series'.

For all new EMU vehicles allocated by the Rolling Stock Library since 2014 6-digit vehicle numbers are being used.

Any vehicle constructed or converted to replace another vehicle following accident damage and carrying the same number as the original vehicle is denoted by the suffix[II] in this publication.

UNITS OF MEASUREMENT

Principal details and dimensions are quoted for each class in metric and/or imperial units as considered appropriate bearing in mind common UK usage.

All dimensions and weights are quoted for vehicles in an "as new" condition with all necessary supplies (eg oil, water, sand) on board. Dimensions are quoted in the order Length – Width. All lengths quoted are over buffers or couplers as appropriate. Where two lengths are quoted, the first refers to outer vehicles in a set and the second to inner vehicles. All width dimensions quoted are maxima. All weights are shown as metric tonnes (t = tonnes).

Bogie Types are quoted in the format motored/non-motored (eg BP20/BT13 denotes BP20 motored bogies and BT non-motored bogies).

Unless noted to the contrary, all vehicles listed have bar couplers at non-driving ends.

Traction motors power details refer to each motored car per unit.

Vehicles ordered under the auspices of BR were allocated a Lot (batch) number when ordered and these are quoted in class headings and sub-headings. Vehicles ordered since 1995 have no Lot Numbers, but the manufacturer and location that they were built is given.

OPERATING CODES

These codes are used by train operating company staff to describe the various different types of vehicles and normally appear on data panels on the inner (ie non driving) ends of vehicles.

A "B" prefix indicates a battery vehicle.
A "P" prefix indicates a trailer vehicle on which is mounted the pantograph, instead of the default case where the pantograph is mounted on a motor vehicle.

The first part of the code describes whether or not the car has a motor or a driving cab as follows:

DM Driving motor   M   Motor   T Trailer
DT Driving trailer

The next letter is a "B" for cars with a brake compartment.

This is followed by the saloon details:

F   First   S   Standard   C Composite

The next letter denotes the style of accommodation, which is "O" for Open for all EMU vehicles still in service.

Finally vehicles with a buffet or kitchen area are suffixed RB or RMB for a miniature buffet counter.

Where two vehicles of the same type are formed within the same unit, the above codes may be suffixed by (A) and (B) to differentiate between vehicles.

A composite is a vehicle containing both First and Standard Class accommodation, whilst a brake vehicle is a vehicle containing separate specific accommodation for the conductor.

ACCOMMODATION

The information given in class headings and sub-headings is in the form F/S nT (or TD) nW. For example 12/54 1T 1W denotes 12 First Class and 54 Standard Class seats, one toilet and one space for a wheelchair. A number in brackets (ie (+2)) denotes tip-up seats (in addition to the fixed seats). Tip-up seats in vestibules do not count. The seating layout of open saloons is shown as 2+1, 2+2 or 3+2 as the case may be. Where units have First Class accommodation as well as Standard Class and the layout is different for each class then these are shown separately prefixed by "1:" and "2:". TD denotes a universal access toilet suitable for use by a disabled person.

NEW EMUS ON ORDER

Where possible all EMUs for which firm orders have been placed are listed in this book. However there are now a large number of new EMUs that are on order but for which the unit number and/or vehicle number series' have not yet been confirmed. EMUs or bi-mode units that are on order but <u>are not shown in this book</u> are summarised in the table below:

Class	Manufacturer	Operator	Quantity	Delivery dates
331	CAF	Northern	31 x 3-car	2018–19
331	CAF	Northern	12 x 4-car	2018–19
397	CAF	TransPennine Express	12 x 5-car	2019
717	Siemens	Govia Thameslink (GN)	25 x 6-car	2018
802/0	Hitachi	GWR (bi-mode)	22 x 5-car[1]	2018
802/1	Hitachi	GWR (bi-mode)	14 x 9-car[1]	2018
802/2	Hitachi	TP Express (bi-mode)	19 x 5-car	2019–20
802/3	Hitachi	Hull Trains (bi-mode)	5 x 5-car	2019
tbc	Stadler	Greater Anglia	20 x 12-car	2019
tbc	Stadler	Greater Anglia (bi-mode)	14 x 3-car	2019
tbc	Stadler	Greater Anglia (bi-mode)	24 x 4-car	2019
tbc	Bombardier	Greater Anglia	22 x 10-car	2020
tbc	Bombardier	Greater Anglia	89 x 5-car	2020
tbc	Stadler	Merseyrail	52 x 4-car	2019–20

[1] There is an option for up to 87 more vehicles.

4.1. 25 kV AC 50 Hz OVERHEAD & DUAL VOLTAGE UNITS

Except where otherwise stated, all units in this section operate on 25 kV AC 50 Hz overhead only.

CLASS 313   BREL YORK

Inner suburban units.

Formation: DMSO–PTSO–BDMSO or DMSO–TSO–BDMSO.
Systems: 25 kV AC overhead/750 V DC third rail.
Construction: Steel underframe, aluminium alloy body and roof.
Traction Motors: Four GEC G310AZ of 82.125 kW.
Wheel Arrangement: Bo-Bo + 2-2 + Bo-Bo.
Braking: Disc & rheostatic.   **Dimensions:** 20.33/20.18 x 2.82 m.
Bogies: BX1.   **Couplers:** Tightlock.
Gangways: Within unit + end doors.   **Control System:** Camshaft.
Doors: Sliding.   **Maximum Speed:** 75 mph.
Seating Layout: Various, see sub-class headings.
Multiple Working: Within class.

DMSO. Lot No. 30879 1976–77. –/74. 36.0 t.
PTSO. Lot No. 30880 1976–77. –/83. 31.0 t.
BDMSO. Lot No. 30885 1976–77. –/74. 37.5 t.

Class 313/0. Standard Design. Refurbished with high-back seating (3+2 facing). Fitted with tripcocks for operating between Moorgate and Drayton Park.

313018	**FU**	E	*GN*	HE	62546	71230	62610
313024	**FU**	E	*GN*	HE	62552	71236	62616
313025	**FU**	E	*GN*	HE	62553	71237	62617
313026	**FU**	E	*GN*	HE	62554	71238	62618
313027	**FU**	E	*GN*	HE	62555	71239	62619
313028	**FU**	E	*GN*	HE	62556	71240	62620
313029	**FU**	E	*GN*	HE	62557	71241	62621
313030	**FU**	E	*GN*	HE	62558	71242	62622
313031	**FU**	E	*GN*	HE	62559	71243	62623
313032	**FU**	E	*GN*	HE	62560	71244	62643
313033	**FU**	E	*GN*	HE	62561	71245	62625
313035	**FU**	E	*GN*	HE	62563	71247	62627
313036	**FU**	E	*GN*	HE	62564	71248	62628
313037	**FU**	E	*GN*	HE	62565	71249	62629
313038	**FU**	E	*GN*	HE	62566	71250	62630
313039	**FU**	E	*GN*	HE	62567	71251	62631
313040	**FU**	E	*GN*	HE	62568	71252	62632
313041	**FU**	E	*GN*	HE	62569	71253	62633
313042	**FU**	E	*GN*	HE	62570	71254	62634
313043	**FU**	E	*GN*	HE	62571	71255	62635
313044	**FU**	E	*GN*	HE	62572	71256	62636
313045	**FU**	E	*GN*	HE	62573	71257	62637

313046	**FU**	E	*GN*	HE	62574	71258	62638
313047	**FU**	E	*GN*	HE	62575	71259	62639
313048	**FU**	E	*GN*	HE	62576	71260	62640
313049	**FU**	E	*GN*	HE	62577	71261	62641
313050	**FU**	E	*GN*	HE	62578	71262	62649
313051	**FU**	E	*GN*	HE	62579	71263	62624
313052	**FU**	E	*GN*	HE	62580	71264	62644
313053	**FU**	E	*GN*	HE	62581	71265	62645
313054	**FU**	E	*GN*	HE	62582	71266	62646
313055	**FU**	E	*GN*	HE	62583	71267	62647
313056	**FU**	E	*GN*	HE	62584	71268	62648
313057	**FU**	E	*GN*	HE	62585	71269	62642
313058	**FU**	E	*GN*	HE	62586	71270	62650
313059	**FU**	E	*GN*	HE	62587	71271	62651
313060	**FU**	E	*GN*	HE	62588	71272	62652
313061	**FU**	E	*GN*	HE	62589	71273	62653
313062	**FU**	E	*GN*	HE	62590	71274	62654
313063	**FU**	E	*GN*	HE	62591	71275	62655
313064	**FU**	E	*GN*	HE	62592	71276	62656

Name (carried on PTSO): 313054   Captain William Leefe Robinson V.C.

Class 313/1. Former London Overground units. Original low back seating (3+2 facing). Fitted with tripcocks for operating between Moorgate and Drayton Park. Details as Class 313/0.

313122	**FU**	E	*GN*	HE	62550	71234	62614
313123	**FU**	E	*GN*	HE	62551	71235	62615
313134	**FU**	E	*GN*	HE	62562	71246	62626

Names (carried on PTSO):

313122   Eric Roberts 1946–2012 "The Flying Nottsman"
313134   City of London

Class 313/2. Southern units. Units refurbished for Brighton Coastway services. Fitted with 2+2 mainly facing high-back seating. 750 V DC only (pantographs removed).

DMSO. Lot No. 30879 1976–77. –/64. 37.0 t.
TSO. Lot No. 30880 1976–77. –/64(+2). 31.0 t.
BDMSO. Lot No. 30885 1976–77. –/64. 37.0 t.

313201	(313101)	**SN**	BN	*SN*	BI	62529	71213	62593
313202	(313102)	**SN**	BN	*SN*	BI	62530	71214	62594
313203	(313103)	**SN**	BN	*SN*	BI	62531	71215	62595
313204	(313104)	**SN**	BN	*SN*	BI	62532	71216	62596
313205	(313105)	**SN**	BN	*SN*	BI	62533	71217	62597
313206	(313106)	**SN**	BN	*SN*	BI	62534	71218	62598
313207	(313107)	**SN**	BN	*SN*	BI	62535	71219	62599
313208	(313108)	**SN**	BN	*SN*	BI	62536	71220	62600
313209	(313109)	**SN**	BN	*SN*	BI	62537	71221	62601
313210	(313110)	**SN**	BN	*SN*	BI	62538	71222	62602
313211	(313111)	**SN**	BN	*SN*	BI	62539	71223	62603
313212	(313112)	**SN**	BN	*SN*	BI	62540	71224	62604

313213	(313113)	**SN**	BN	*SN*	BI	62541	71225	62605
313214	(313114)	**SN**	BN	*SN*	BI	62542	71226	62606
313215	(313115)	**SN**	BN	*SN*	BI	62543	71227	62607
313216	(313116)	**SN**	BN	*SN*	BI	62544	71228	62608
313217	(313117)	**SN**	BN	*SN*	BI	62545	71229	62609
313219	(313119)	**SN**	BN	*SN*	BI	62547	71231	62611
313220	(313120)	**SN**	BN	*SN*	BI	62548	71232	62612

CLASS 314   BREL YORK

Inner suburban units.

Formation: DMSO–PTSO–DMSO.
Construction: Steel underframe, aluminium alloy body and roof.
Traction Motors: Four GEC G310AZ (* Brush TM61-53) of 82.125 kW.
Wheel Arrangement: Bo-Bo + 2-2 + Bo-Bo.
Braking: Disc & rheostatic.   **Dimensions:** 20.33/20.18 x 2.82 m.
Bogies: BX1.   **Couplers:** Tightlock.
Gangways: Within unit + end doors. **Control System:** Thyristor.
Doors: Sliding.   **Maximum Speed:** 70 mph.
Seating Layout: 3+2 low-back facing.
Multiple Working: Within class and with Class 315.

DMSO. Lot No. 30912 1979. –/68. 34.5 t.
64588II. DMSO. Lot No. 30908 1978–80. Rebuilt Railcare Glasgow 1996 from Class 507 No. 64426. The original 64588 was scrapped. –/74. 34.5 t.
PTSO. Lot No. 30913 1979. –/76. 33.0 t.

314201	*	**SC**	A	*SR*	GW	64583	71450	64584
314202	*	**SC**	A	*SR*	GW	64585	71451	64586
314203	*	**SR**	A	*SR*	GW	64587	71452	64588II
314204	*	**SR**	A	*SR*	GW	64589	71453	64590
314205	*	**SC**	A	*SR*	GW	64591	71454	64592
314206	*	**SC**	A	*SR*	GW	64593	71455	64594
314207		**SC**	A	*SR*	GW	64595	71456	64596
314208		**SR**	A	*SR*	GW	64597	71457	64598
314209		**SR**	A	*SR*	GW	64599	71458	64600
314210		**SC**	A	*SR*	GW	64601	71459	64602
314211		**SR**	A	*SR*	GW	64603	71460	64604
314212		**SR**	A	*SR*	GW	64605	71461	64606
314213		**SC**	A	*SR*	GW	64607	71462	64608
314214		**SR**	A	*SR*	GW	64609	71463	64610
314215		**SC**	A	*SR*	GW	64611	71464	64612
314216		**SC**	A	*SR*	GW	64613	71465	64614

CLASS 315   BREL YORK

Inner suburban units.

Formation: DMSO–TSO–PTSO–DMSO.
Construction: Steel underframe, aluminium alloy body and roof.
Traction Motors: Four Brush TM61-53 (* GEC G310AZ) of 82.125 kW.

Wheel Arrangement: Bo-Bo + 2-2 + 2-2 + Bo-Bo.
Braking: Disc & rheostatic.   **Dimensions:** 20.18 x 2.82 m.
Bogies: BX1.   **Couplers:** Tightlock.
Gangways: Within unit + end doors. **Control System:** Thyristor.
Doors: Sliding.   **Maximum Speed:** 75 mph.
Seating Layout: 3+2 low-back facing.
Multiple Working: Within class and with Class 314.

DMSO. Lot No. 30902 1980–81. –/74. 38.2 t.
TSO. Lot No. 30904 1980–81. –/86. 27.4 t.
PTSO. Lot No. 30903 1980–81. –/75(+7) 2W. 33.8 t.

315801	**LO**	E	*LO*	IL	64461	71281	71389	64462
315802	**LO**	E	*LO*	IL	64463	71282	71390	64464
315803	**LO**	E	*LO*	IL	64465	71283	71391	64466
315804	**LO**	E	*LO*	IL	64467	71284	71392	64468
315805	**LO**	E	*LO*	IL	64469	71285	71393	64470
315806	**LO**	E	*LO*	IL	64471	71286	71394	64472
315807	**LO**	E	*LO*	IL	64473	71287	71395	64474
315808	**LO**	E	*LO*	IL	64475	71288	71396	64476
315809	**LO**	E	*LO*	IL	64477	71289	71397	64478
315810	**LO**	E	*LO*	IL	64479	71290	71398	64480
315811	**LO**	E	*LO*	IL	64481	71291	71399	64482
315812	**LO**	E	*LO*	IL	64483	71292	71400	64484
315813	**LO**	E	*LO*	IL	64485	71293	71401	64486
315814	**LO**	E	*LO*	IL	64487	71294	71402	64488
315815	**LO**	E	*LO*	IL	64489	71295	71403	64490
315816	**LO**	E	*LO*	IL	64491	71296	71404	64492
315817	**LO**	E	*LO*	IL	64493	71297	71405	64494
315818	**TF**	E	*XR*	IL	64495	71298	71406	64496
315819	**TF**	E	*XR*	IL	64497	71299	71407	64498
315820	**TF**	E	*XR*	IL	64499	71300	71408	64500
315821	**TF**	E	*XR*	IL	64501	71301	71409	64502
315822	**TF**	E	*XR*	IL	64503	71302	71410	64504
315823	**TF**	E	*XR*	IL	64505	71303	71411	64506
315824	**TF**	E	*XR*	IL	64507	71304	71412	64508
315825	**TF**	E	*XR*	IL	64509	71305	71413	64510
315826	**TF**	E	*XR*	IL	64511	71306	71414	64512
315827	**TF**	E	*XR*	IL	64513	71307	71415	64514
315828	**TF**	E	*XR*	IL	64515	71308	71416	64516
315829	**TF**	E	*XR*	IL	64517	71309	71417	64518
315830	**TF**	E	*XR*	IL	64519	71310	71418	64520
315831	**TF**	E	*XR*	IL	64521	71311	71419	64522
315832	**TF**	E	*XR*	IL	64523	71312	71420	64524
315833	**TF**	E	*XR*	IL	64525	71313	71421	64526
315834	**TF**	E	*XR*	IL	64527	71314	71422	64528
315835	**TF**	E	*XR*	IL	64529	71315	71423	64530
315836	**TF**	E	*XR*	IL	64531	71316	71424	64532
315837	**TF**	E	*XR*	IL	64533	71317	71425	64534
315838	**TF**	E	*XR*	IL	64535	71318	71426	64536
315839	**TF**	E	*XR*	IL	64537	71319	71427	64538
315840	**TF**	E	*XR*	IL	64539	71320	71428	64540

315841		**TF**	E	*XR*	IL	64541	71321	71429	64542
315842	*	**TF**	E	*XR*	IL	64543	71322	71430	64544
315843	*	**TF**	E	*XR*	IL	64545	71323	71431	64546
315844	*	**TF**	E	*XR*	IL	64547	71324	71432	64548
315845	*	**TF**	E	*XR*	IL	64549	71325	71433	64550
315846	*	**TF**	E	*XR*	IL	64551	71326	71434	64552
315847	*	**TF**	E	*XR*	IL	64553	71327	71435	64554
315848	*	**TF**	E	*XR*	IL	64555	71328	71436	64556
315849	*	**TF**	E	*XR*	IL	64557	71329	71437	64558
315850	*	**TF**	E	*XR*	IL	64559	71330	71438	64560
315851	*	**TF**	E	*XR*	IL	64561	71331	71439	64562
315852	*	**TF**	E	*XR*	IL	64563	71332	71440	64564
315853	*	**TF**	E	*XR*	IL	64565	71333	71441	64566
315854	*	**TF**	E	*XR*	IL	64567	71334	71442	64568
315855	*	**TF**	E	*XR*	IL	64569	71335	71443	64570
315856	*	**TF**	E	*XR*	IL	64571	71336	71444	64572
315857	*	**TF**	E	*XR*	IL	64573	71337	71445	64574
315858	*	**TF**	E	*XR*	IL	64575	71338	71446	64576
315859	*	**TF**	E	*XR*	IL	64577	71339	71447	64578
315860	*	**TF**	E	*XR*	IL	64579	71340	71448	64580
315861	*	**TF**	E	*XR*	IL	64581	71341	71449	64582

Names (carried on DMSO):

315817	Transport for London
315829	London Borough of Havering Celebrating 40 years
315845	Herbie Woodward

CLASS 317   BREL YORK/DERBY

Outer suburban units.

Formation: Various, see sub-class headings.
Construction: Steel.
Traction Motors: Four GEC G315BZ of 247.5 kW (except 317 722, see below).
Wheel Arrangement: 2-2 + Bo-Bo + 2-2 + 2-2.
Braking: Disc.   **Dimensions:** 19.83/20.18 x 2.82 m.
Bogies: BP20 (MSO), BT13 (others).   **Couplers:** Tightlock.
Gangways: Throughout   **Control System:** Thyristor.
Doors: Sliding.   **Maximum Speed:** 100 mph.
Seating Layout: Various, see sub-class headings.
Multiple Working: Within class & with Classes 318, 319, 320, 321, 322 and 323.

Class 317/1. Pressure ventilated.

Formation: DTSO–MSO–TCO–DTSO.
Seating Layout: 1: 2+2 facing, 2: 3+2 facing.

DTSO(A) Lot No. 30955 York 1981–82. –/74. 29.5 t.
MSO. Lot No. 30958 York 1981–82. –/79. 49.0 t.
TCO. Lot No. 30957 Derby 1981–82. 22/46 2T. 29.0 t.
DTSO(B) Lot No. 30956 York 1981–82. –/71. 29.5 t.

317337	**TL**	A	*GN*	HE	77036	62671	71613	77084
317338	**TL**	A	*GN*	HE	77037	62698	71614	77085
317339	**TL**	A	*GN*	HE	77038	62699	71615	77086
317340	**TL**	A	*GN*	HE	77039	62700	71616	77087
317341	**TL**	A	*GN*	HE	77040	62701	71617	77088
317342	**TL**	A	*GN*	HE	77041	62702	71618	77089
317343	**TL**	A	*GN*	HE	77042	62703	71619	77090
317344	**FU**	A	*GN*	HE	77029	62690	71620	77091
317345	**FU**	A	*GN*	HE	77044	62705	71621	77092
317346	**FU**	A	*GN*	HE	77045	62706	71622	77093
317347	**FU**	A	*GN*	HE	77046	62707	71623	77094
317348	**FU**	A	*GN*	HE	77047	62708	71624	77095

Names (carried on TCO):

317345 Driver John Webb | 317348 Richard A Jenner

Class 317/5. Pressure ventilated. Units renumbered from Class 317/1 in 2005 for West Anglia Metro services. Refurbished with new upholstery and Passenger Information Systems. Details as Class 317/1.

The original DTSO 77048 was written off after the Cricklewood accident of 1983. A replacement vehicle was built (at Wolverton) in 1987 and given the same number.

317501	**GA**	A	*GA*	IL	77024	62661	71577	77048ᴵᴵ
317502	**GA**	A	*GA*	IL	77001	62662	71578	77049
317503	**GA**	A	*GA*	IL	77002	62663	71579	77050
317504	**GA**	A	*GA*	IL	77003	62664	71580	77051
317505	**GA**	A	*GA*	IL	77004	62665	71581	77052
317506	**GA**	A	*GA*	IL	77005	62666	71582	77053
317507	**GA**	A	*GA*	IL	77006	62667	71583	77054
317508	**GA**	A	*GA*	IL	77010	62697	71587	77058
317509	**GA**	A	*GA*	IL	77011	62672	71588	77059
317510	**GA**	A	*GA*	IL	77012	62673	71589	77060
317511	**NC**	A	*GA*	IL	77014	62675	71591	77062
317512	**GA**	A	*GA*	IL	77015	62676	71592	77063
317513	**GA**	A	*GA*	IL	77016	62677	71593	77064
317514	**GA**	A	*GA*	IL	77017	62678	71594	77065
317515	**GA**	A	*GA*	IL	77019	62680	71596	77067

Name (carried on TCO):

317507 University of Cambridge 800 Years 1209–2009

Class 317/6. Convection heating. Units converted from Class 317/2 by Railcare, Wolverton 1998–99 with Chapman seating.

Formation: DTSO–MSO–TSO–DTCO.
Seating Layout: 2+2 facing.

77200–219. DTSO. Lot No. 30994 York 1985–86. –/64. 29.5 t.
77280–283. DTSO. Lot No. 31007 York 1987. –/64. 29.5 t.
62846–865. MSO. Lot No. 30996 York 1985–86. –/71. 49.0 t.
62886–889. MSO. Lot No. 31009 York 1987. –/71. 49.0 t.
71734–753. TSO. Lot No. 30997 York 1985–86. –/60(+3) 2T. 29.0 t.

71762–765. TSO. Lot No. 31010 York 1987. –/60(+3) 2T. 29.0 t.
77220–239. DTCO. Lot No. 30995 York 1985–86. 24/36. 29.5 t.
77284–287. DTCO. Lot No. 31008 York 1987. 24/36. 29.5 t.

317649	**NC**	A	*GA*	IL	77200	62846	71734	77220
317650	**NC**	A	*GA*	IL	77201	62847	71735	77221
317651	**NC**	A	*GA*	IL	77202	62848	71736	77222
317652	**NC**	A	*GA*	IL	77203	62849	71739	77223
317653	**NC**	A	*GA*	IL	77204	62850	71738	77224
317654	**NC**	A	*GA*	IL	77205	62851	71737	77225
317655	**GA**	A	*GA*	IL	77206	62852	71740	77226
317656	**NC**	A	*GA*	IL	77207	62853	71742	77227
317657	**NC**	A	*GA*	IL	77208	62854	71741	77228
317658	**GA**	A	*GA*	IL	77209	62855	71743	77229
317659	**GA**	A	*GA*	IL	77210	62856	71744	77230
317660	**GA**	A	*GA*	IL	77211	62857	71745	77231
317661	**GA**	A	*GA*	IL	77212	62858	71746	77232
317662	**GA**	A	*GA*	IL	77213	62859	71747	77233
317663	**GA**	A	*GA*	IL	77214	62860	71748	77234
317664	**GA**	A	*GA*	IL	77215	62861	71749	77235
317665	**GA**	A	*GA*	IL	77216	62862	71750	77236
317666	**NC**	A	*GA*	IL	77217	62863	71752	77237
317667	**GA**	A	*GA*	IL	77218	62864	71751	77238
317668	**GA**	A	*GA*	IL	77219	62865	71753	77239
317669	**NC**	A	*GA*	IL	77280	62886	71762	77284
317670	**GA**	A	*GA*	IL	77281	62887	71763	77285
317671	**NC**	A	*GA*	IL	77282	62888	71764	77286
317672	**GA**	A	*GA*	IL	77283	62889	71765	77287

Name (carried on DTCO): 317654   Richard Wells

Class 317/7. Units converted from Class 317/1 by Railcare, Wolverton 2000 for Stansted Express services between London Liverpool Street and Stansted. Air conditioning. Fitted with luggage stacks. Displaced from Stansted services in 2011 by Class 379s – most units are now operated by London Overground.

* 317722 has received new Bombardier MJA 280-8 AC traction motors as part of an Angel trial. Two vehicles (77021 and 62682, now in **GA** livery) have also received an interior refurbishment with new Fainsa seating whilst the other two vehicles have been left in their former Stansted Express condition (and still in **NX** livery). Leased to Greater Anglia as a demonstrator unit.

Formation: DTSO–MSO–TSO–DTCO.
Seating Layout: 1: 2+1 facing, 2: 2+2 facing.

DTSO. Lot No. 30955 York 1981–82. –/52 + catering point. 31.4 t.
MSO. Lot No. 30958 York 1981–82. –/62 (* –/64). 51.3 t.
TSO. Lot No. 30957 Derby 1981–82. –/42(+5) 1W 1T 1TD. 30.2 t.
DTCO Lot No. 30956 York 1981–82. 22/16 + catering point. 31.6 t.

317708	**LO**	A	*LO*	IL	77007	62668	71584	77055
317709	**LO**	A	*LO*	IL	77008	62669	71585	77056
317710	**LO**	A	*LO*	IL	77009	62670	71586	77057

317714	**LO**	A	*LO*	IL	77013	62674	71590	77061
317719	**LO**	A	*LO*	IL	77018	62679	71595	77066
317722	* **GA/NX**	A	*GA*	IL	77021	62682	71598	77069
317723	**LO**	A	*LO*	IL	77022	62683	71599	77070
317729	**LO**	A	*LO*	IL	77028	62689	71605	77076
317732	**LO**	A	*LO*	IL	77031	62692	71608	77079

Class 317/8. Pressure Ventilated. Units refurbished and renumbered from Class 317/1 in 2005–06 at Wabtec, Doncaster for use on Stansted Express services. Displaced from Stansted services in 2011.

Formation: DTSO–MSO–TCO–DTSO.
Seating Layout: 1: 2+2 facing, 2: 3+2 facing.

DTSO(A) Lot No. 30955 York 1981–82. –/66. 29.5 t.
MSO. Lot No. 30958 York 1981–82. –/71. 49.0 t.
TCO. Lot No. 30957 Derby 1981–82. 20/42 2T († –/62 2T). 29.0 t.
DTSO(B) Lot No. 30956 York 1981–82. –/66. 29.5 t.

317881		**GA**	A	*GA*	IL	77020	62681	71597	77068	
317882		**NC**	A	*GA*	IL	77023	62684	71600	77071	
317883		**NC**	A	*GA*	IL	77000	62685	71601	77072	
317884		**NC**	A	*GA*	IL	77025	62686	71602	77073	
317885		**NC**	A	*GA*	IL	77026	62687	71603	77074	
317886		**NC**	A	*GA*	IL	77027	62688	71604	77075	
317887	†	**NX**	A	*LO*	IL	77043	62704	71606	77077	
317888	†	**LO**	A	*LO*	IL	77030	62691	71607	77078	
317889	†	**LO**	A	*LO*	IL	77032	62693	71609	77080	
317890	†	**NX**	A	*LO*	IL	77033	62694	71610	77081	
317891	†	**NX**	A	*LO*	IL	77034	62695	71611	77082	
317892	†	**NX**	A	*LO*	IL	77035	62696	71612	77083	Ilford Depot

CLASS 318   BREL YORK

Outer suburban units. A refurbishment programme is underway that involves fitted a new universal access toilet to comply with the 2020 accessibility regulations (units in **SR** livery).

Formation: DTSO–MSO–DTSO.
Construction: Steel.
Traction Motors: Four Brush TM 2141 of 268 kW.
Wheel Arrangement: 2-2 + Bo-Bo + 2-2.
Braking: Disc.   **Dimensions:** 19.83/19.92 x 2.82 m.
Bogies: BP20 (MSO), BT13 (others).   **Couplers:** Tightlock.
Gangways: Within unit.   **Control System:** Thyristor.
Doors: Sliding.   **Maximum Speed:** 90 mph.
Seating Layout: 3+2 facing.
Multiple Working: Within class & with Classes 317, 319, 320, 321, 322 and 323.

77240–259. DTSO. Lot No. 30999 1985–86. –/64 1T (–/55 1TD 2W). 30.0 t (* 32.0 t).
77288. DTSO. Lot No. 31020 1987. –/55 1TD 2W. 32.0 t.
62866–885. MSO. Lot No. 30998 1985–86. –/77 (* –/79). 50.9 t (* 53.0 t).
62890. MSO. Lot No. 31019 1987. –/79. 53.0 t.

77260–279. DTSO. Lot No. 31000 1985–86. –/72 (* –/74). 29.6 t (* 31.6 t).
77289. DTSO. Lot No. 31021 1987. –/74. 31.6 t.

318 250		**SC**	E	*SR*	GW	77240	62866	77260
318 251	*	**SR**	E	*SR*	GW	77241	62867	77261
318 252	*	**SR**	E	*SR*	GW	77242	62868	77262
318 253	*	**SR**	E	*SR*	GW	77243	62869	77263
318 254	*	**SR**	E	*SR*	GW	77244	62870	77264
318 255	*	**SR**	E	*SR*	GW	77245	62871	77265
318 256		**SC**	E	*SR*	GW	77246	62872	77266
318 257	*	**SR**	E	*SR*	GW	77247	62873	77267
318 258	*	**SR**	E	*SR*	GW	77248	62874	77268
318 259	*	**SR**	E	*SR*	GW	77249	62875	77269
318 260		**SC**	E	*SR*	GW	77250	62876	77270
318 261		**SC**	E	*SR*	GW	77251	62877	77271
318 262	*	**SR**	E	*SR*	GW	77252	62878	77272
318 263	*	**SR**	E	*SR*	GW	77253	62879	77273
318 264	*	**SR**	E	*SR*	GW	77254	62880	77274
318 265	*	**SR**	E	*SR*	GW	77255	62881	77275
318 266	*	**SR**	E	*SR*	GW	77256	62882	77276
318 267		**SC**	E	*SR*	GW	77257	62883	77277
318 268		**SC**	E	*SR*	GW	77258	62884	77278
318 269	*	**SR**	E	*SR*	GW	77259	62885	77279
318 270	*	**SR**	E	*SR*	GW	77288	62890	77289

CLASS 319   BREL YORK

Express and outer suburban units. A refurbishment programme is underway that involves fitting a new universal access toilet to comply with the 2020 accessibility regulations (units shown *).

Formation: Various, see sub-class headings.
Systems: 25 kV AC overhead/750 V DC third rail.
Construction: Steel.
Traction Motors: Four GEC G315BZ of 268 kW.
Wheel Arrangement: 2-2 + Bo-Bo + 2-2 + 2-2.
Braking: Disc.   **Dimensions:** 20.17/20.16 x 2.82 m.
Bogies: P7-4 (MSO), T3-7 (others). **Couplers:** Tightlock.
Gangways: Within unit + end doors. **Control System:** GTO chopper.
Doors: Sliding.   **Maximum Speed:** 100 mph.
Seating Layout: Various, see sub-class headings.
Multiple Working: Within class & with Classes 317, 318, 320, 321, 322 and 323.

Class 319/0. DTSO–MSO–TSO–DTSO.

319 004/005 are due to transfer to Northern in 2017.

Seating Layout: 3+2 facing.

DTSO(A). Lot No. 31022 (odd nos.) 1987–88. –/82 (* –/79). 28.2 t (* 30.7 t).
MSO. Lot No. 31023 1987–88. –/82 (* –/81). 49.2 t (* 50.9 t)..
TSO. Lot No. 31024 1987–88. –/77 2T (* –/63 1TD 2W). 31.0 t (* 32.5 t)..
DTSO(B). Lot No. 31025 (even nos.) 1987–88. –/78 (* –/79). 28.1 t (* 30.0 t).

319001		**TL**	P	*TL*	BF	77291	62891	71772	77290
319002	*	**TL**	P	*TL*	BF	77293	62892	71773	77292
319003	*	**TL**	P	*TL*	BF	77295	62893	71774	77294
319004		**TL**	P		ZN	77297	62894	71775	77296
319005	*	**TL**	P		ZN	77299	62895	71776	77298
319006	*	**TL**	P	*TL*	BF	77301	62896	71777	77300
319007	*	**TL**	P	*TL*	BF	77303	62897	71778	77302
319008	*	**TL**	P	*TL*	BF	77305	62898	71779	77304
319009		**TL**	P	*TL*	BF	77307	62899	71780	77306
319010		**TL**	P	*TL*	BF	77309	62900	71781	77308
319011		**TL**	P	*TL*	BF	77311	62901	71782	77310
319012	*	**TL**	P	*TL*	BF	77313	62902	71783	77312
319013		**LM**	P	*LM*	NN	77315	62903	71784	77314

Names (carried on TSO):

319001 Driver Mick Winnett	319009 Coquelles
319008 Cheriton	319011 John Ruskin College

Class 319/2. DTSO–MSO–TSO–DTCO. Units converted from Class 319/0.

Seating Layout: 1: 2+1 facing, 2: 2+2/3+2 facing.

DTSO. Lot No. 31022 (odd nos.) 1987–88. –/64. 30.0 t.
MSO. Lot No. 31023 1987–88. –/73. 51.0 t.
TSO. Lot No. 31024 1987–88. –/52 1T 1TD. 31.0 t.
DTCO. Lot No. 31025 (even nos.) 1987–88. 18/36. 30.0 t.

319214	*	**TL**	P	*TL*	BF	77317	62904	71785	77316	
319215	*	**TL**	P	*TL*	BF	77319	62905	71786	77318	
319216	*	**LM**	P	*LM*	NN	77321	62906	71787	77320	
319217	*	**TL**	P	*TL*	BF	77323	62907	71788	77322	Brighton
319218	*	**TL**	P	*NO*	AN	77325	62908	71789	77324	
319219	*	**TL**	P	*NO*	AN	77327	62909	71790	77326	
319220	*	**TL**	P	*TL*	BF	77329	62910	71791	77328	

Class 319/3. DTSO–MSO–TSO–DTSO. Converted from Class 319/1 by replacing First Class seats with Standard Class seats.

Seating Layout: 3+2 facing.

DTSO(A). Lot No. 31063 1990. –/72. 29.0 t.
MSO. Lot No. 31064 1990. –/79. 50.6 t.
TSO. Lot No. 31065 1990. –/74 2T. 31.0 t.
DTSO(B). Lot No. 31066 1990. –/77 2W. 29.7 t.

319361	**NP**	P	*NO*	AN	77459	63043	71929	77458
319362	**NP**	P	*NO*	AN	77461	63044	71930	77460
319363	**NP**	P	*NO*	AN	77463	63045	71931	77462
319364	**NP**	P	*NO*	AN	77465	63046	71932	77464
319365	**NP**	P	*NO*	AN	77467	63047	71933	77466
319366	**NP**	P	*NO*	AN	77469	63048	71934	77468
319367	**NP**	P	*NO*	AN	77471	63049	71935	77470
319368	**NP**	P	*NO*	AN	77473	63050	71936	77472
319369	**NP**	P	*NO*	AN	77475	63051	71937	77474
319370	**FU**	P		ZN	77477	63052	71938	77476

319371		**NP**	P	*NO*	AN	77479	63053	71939	77478
319372	*	**TL**	P	*TL*	BF	77481	63054	71940	77480
319373		**TL**	P	*TL*	BF	77483	63055	71941	77482
319374		**NP**	P	*NO*	AN	77485	63056	71942	77484
319375		**NP**	P	*NO*	AN	77487	63057	71943	77486
319376		**NP**	P	*NO*	AN	77489	63058	71944	77488
319377		**NP**	P	*NO*	AN	77491	63059	71945	77490
319378		**NP**	P	*NO*	AN	77493	63060	71946	77492
319379		**NP**	P	*NO*	AN	77495	63061	71947	77494
319380		**NP**	P	*NO*	AN	77497	63062	71948	77496
319381		**FU**	P		ZN	77973	63093	71979	77974
319382		**NP**	P	*NO*	AN	77975	63094	71980	77976
319383		**NP**	P	*NO*	AN	77977	63095	71981	77978
319384		**FU**	P		ZN	77979	63096	71982	77980
319385		**FU**	P	*TL*	BF	77981	63097	71983	77982
319386		**NP**	P	*NO*	AN	77983	63098	71984	77984

Name (carried on TSO): 319362   Northern Powerhouse

Class 319/4. DTCO–MSO–TSO–DTSO. Converted from Class 319/0. Refurbished with carpets. DTSO(A) converted to composite.

319427 is at Brush, Loughborough as part of a trial conversion to a bi-mode unit, with diesel engines fitted.

319 424/431/434/442/448/450/456/458 are due to transfer to Northern in 2017.

Seating Layout: 1: 2+1 facing 2: 2+2/3+2 facing.

77331–381. DTCO. Lot No. 31022 (odd nos.) 1987–88. 12/51 (* 12/50). 30.0t (* 31.0t).
77431–457. DTCO. Lot No. 31038 (odd nos.) 1988. 12/51 (* 12/50). 30.0t (* 31.0t).
62911–936. MSO. Lot No. 31023 1987–88. –/74 (* –/75). 49.2t (* 52.4t).
62961–974. MSO. Lot No. 31039 1988. –/74 (* –/75). 49.2t (* 52.4t).
71792–817. TSO. Lot No. 31024 1987–88. –/67 2T (* –/58 1TD 2W). 31.0t (* 33.7t).
71866–879. TSO. Lot No. 31040 1988. –/67 2T (* –/58 1TD 2W). 31.0t (* 33.7t).
77330–380. DTSO. Lot No. 31025 (even nos.) 1987–88. –/71 1W (* –/73). 28.1t (* 30.7t).
77430–456. DTSO. Lot No. 31041 (even nos.) 1988. –/71 1W (* –/73). 28.1t (* 30.7t).

319421	*	**TL**	P	*TL*	BF	77331	62911	71792	77330
319422	*	**TL**	P	*TL*	BF	77333	62912	71793	77332
319423	*	**TL**	P	*TL*	BF	77335	62913	71794	77334
319424	*	**TL**	P		ZN	77337	62914	71795	77336
319425	*	**TL**	P	*TL*	BF	77339	62915	71796	77338
319426	*	**TL**	P	*TL*	BF	77341	62916	71797	77340
319427	*	**TL**	P		LB	77343	62917	71798	77342
319428	*	**TL**	P	*TL*	BF	77345	62918	71799	77344
319429		**LM**	P	*LM*	NN	77347	62919	71800	77346
319430	*	**TL**	P	*TL*	BF	77349	62920	71801	77348
319431	*	**TL**	P		ZN	77351	62921	71802	77350
319432	*	**TL**	P	*TL*	BF	77353	62922	71803	77352
319433	*	**TL**	P	*TL*	BF	77355	62923	71804	77354
319434	*	**TL**	P		ZN	77357	62924	71805	77356
319435	*	**TL**	P	*TL*	BF	77359	62925	71806	77358
319436	*	**TL**	P	*TL*	BF	77361	62926	71807	77360

319437	*	TL	P	TL	BF	77363	62927	71808	77362
319438	*	TL	P	TL	BF	77365	62928	71809	77364
319439	*	TL	P	TL	BF	77367	62929	71810	77366
319440	*	TL	P	TL	BF	77369	62930	71811	77368
319441	*	LM	P	LM	NN	77371	62931	71812	77370
319442		FU	P		ZN	77373	62932	71813	77372
319443	*	TL	P	TL	BF	77375	62933	71814	77374
319444	*	TL	P	TL	BF	77377	62934	71815	77376
319445	*	TL	P	TL	BF	77379	62935	71816	77378
319446	*	TL	P	TL	BF	77381	62936	71817	77380
319447	*	TL	P	TL	BF	77431	62961	71866	77430
319448		FU	P		ZN	77433	62962	71867	77432
319449	*	TL	P	TL	BF	77435	62963	71868	77434
319450	*	NR	P	TL	BF	77437	62964	71869	77436
319451		FU	P		BF	77439	62965	71870	77438
319452	*	TL	P	TL	BF	77441	62966	71871	77440
319453		FU	P	TL	BF	77443	62967	71872	77442
319454		FU	P	TL	BF	77445	62968	71873	77444
319455		LM	P	LM	NN	77447	62969	71874	77446
319456	*	TL	P		ZN	77449	62970	71875	77448
319457		LM	P	LM	NN	77451	62971	71876	77450
319458	*	TL	P		ZN	77453	62972	71877	77452
319459	*	TL	P	TL	BF	77455	62973	71878	77454
319460		LM	P	LM	NN	77457	62974	71879	77456

Name (carried on TSO): 319444 City of St Albans

CLASS 320   **BREL YORK**

Suburban units. All 320/3s refurbished 2011–13 and fitted with a new universal access toilet to comply with the 2020 accessibility regulations. In 2016 ScotRail received 320411–417 (ex-321411–417), reformed as 3-cars and also refurbished with a new universal access toilet.

Formation: DTSO–MSO–DTSO.
Construction: Steel
Traction Motors: Four Brush TM2141B of 268 kW.
Wheel Arrangement: 2-2 + Bo-Bo + 2-2.
Braking: Disc.   **Dimensions:** 19.95 x 2.82 m.
Bogies: P7-4 (MSO), T3-7 (others).   **Couplers:** Tightlock.
Gangways: Within unit.   **Control System:** Thyristor.
Doors: Sliding.   **Maximum Speed:** 90 mph.
Seating Layout: 3+2 facing.
Multiple Working: Within class & with Classes 317, 318, 319, 321, 322 and 323.

Class 320/3. Original build.

DTSO (A). Lot No. 31060 1990. –/51(+4) 1TD 2W. 31.7 t.
MSO. Lot No. 31062 1990. –/78. 52.6 t.
DTSO (B). Lot No. 31061 1990. –/77. 31.6 t.

| 320301 | SR | E | SR | GW | 77899 | 63021 | 77921 |
| 320302 | SR | E | SR | GW | 77900 | 63022 | 77922 |

320303	**SR**	E	*SR*	GW	77901	63023	77923
320304	**SR**	E	*SR*	GW	77902	63024	77924
320305	**SR**	E	*SR*	GW	77903	63025	77925
320306	**SR**	E	*SR*	GW	77904	63026	77926
320307	**SR**	E	*SR*	GW	77905	63027	77927
320308	**SR**	E	*SR*	GW	77906	63028	77928
320309	**SR**	E	*SR*	GW	77907	63029	77929
320310	**SR**	E	*SR*	GW	77908	63030	77930
320311	**SR**	E	*SR*	GW	77909	63031	77931
320312	**SR**	E	*SR*	GW	77910	63032	77932
320313	**SR**	E	*SR*	GW	77911	63033	77933
320314	**SR**	E	*SR*	GW	77912	63034	77934
320315	**SR**	E	*SR*	GW	77913	63035	77935
320316	**SR**	E	*SR*	GW	77914	63036	77936
320317	**SR**	E	*SR*	GW	77915	63037	77937
320318	**SR**	E	*SR*	GW	77916	63038	77938
320319	**SR**	E	*SR*	GW	77917	63039	77939
320320	**SR**	E	*SR*	GW	77918	63040	77940
320321	**SR**	E	*SR*	GW	77919	63041	77941
320322	**SR**	E	*SR*	GW	77920	63042	77942

Class 320/4. Former London Midland Class 321s reduced to 3-car formation and refurbished as Class 320/4s by Wabtec Doncaster 2015–16. Full details awaited.

DTSO (A). Lot No. 31060 1990.   .   t.
MSO. Lot No. 31062 1990.   .   t.
DTSO (B). Lot No. 31061 1990.   .   t.

320411	(321411)	**SR**	E	*SR*	GW	78105	63073	77953
320412	(321412)	**SR**	E	*SR*	GW	78106	63074	77954
320413	(321413)	**SR**	E	*SR*	GW	78107	63075	77955
320414	(321414)	**SR**	E	*SR*	GW	78108	63076	77956
320415	(321415)	**SR**	E	*SR*	GW	78109	63077	77957
320416	(321416)	**SR**	E	*SR*	GW	78110	63078	77958
320417	(321417)	**SR**	E	*SR*	GW	78111	63079	77959

CLASS 321   BREL YORK

Outer suburban units.

Formation: DTCO (DTSO on Class 321/9)–MSO–TSO–DTSO.
Construction: Steel.
Traction Motors: Four Brush TM2141C of 268 kW († Four TSA010163 AC motors of 300 kW).
Wheel Arrangement: 2-2 + Bo-Bo + 2-2 + 2-2.
Braking: Disc († and regenerative).   **Dimensions:** 19.95 x 2.82 m.
Bogies: P7-4 (MSO), T3-7 (others).   **Couplers:** Tightlock.
Gangways: Within unit.
Control System: Thyristor († IGBT Inverter).
Doors: Sliding.   **Maximum Speed:** 100 mph.
Seating Layout: 1: 2+2 facing, 2: 3+2 facing.

Multiple Working: Within class & with Classes 317, 318, 319, 320, 322 and 323.

Class 321/3.

* "Renatus" rebuilt units with completely new interiors and Quantum seating, still arranged to a 3+2 layout in Standard Class. 30 Class 321/3 units will be refurbished by summer 2018.

† "Renatus" rebuilt units also fitted with new TSA AC traction motors.

DTCO. Lot No. 31053 1988–90. 16/57 (321 347–366 16/56) (* 16/31(+4) 1TD 2W. 29.7 t.
MSO. Lot No. 31054 1988–90. –/82 (* –/80). 51.5 t.
TSO. Lot No. 31055 1988–90. –/75 2T (* –/78 1T). 29.1 t.
DTSO. Lot No. 31056 1988–90. –/78 (* –/76). 29.7 t.

321 301	**NX**	E	*GA*	IL	78049	62975	71880	77853
321 302	**NX**	E	*GA*	IL	78050	62976	71881	77854
321 303	*† **GA**	E	*GA*	IL	78051	62977	71882	77855
321 304	* **GA**	E	*GA*	IL	78052	62978	71883	77856
321 305	**NX**	E	*GA*	IL	78053	62979	71884	77857
321 306	**NX**	E	*GA*	IL	78054	62980	71885	77858
321 307	**NX**	E	*GA*	IL	78055	62981	71886	77859
321 308	**NX**	E	*GA*	IL	78056	62982	71887	77860
321 309	**NX**	E	*GA*	IL	78057	62983	71888	77861
321 310	**NX**	E	*GA*	IL	78058	62984	71889	77862
321 311	**NX**	E	*GA*	IL	78059	62985	71890	77863
321 312	**NX**	E	*GA*	IL	78060	62986	71891	77864
321 313	**NX**	E	*GA*	IL	78061	62987	71892	77865
321 314	**NX**	E	*GA*	IL	78062	62988	71893	77866
321 315	**NX**	E	*GA*	IL	78063	62989	71894	77867
321 316	**NX**	E	*GA*	IL	78064	62990	71895	77868
321 317	**NX**	E	*GA*	IL	78065	62991	71896	77869
321 318	**NX**	E	*GA*	IL	78066	62992	71897	77870
321 319	**NX**	E	*GA*	IL	78067	62993	71898	77871
321 320	**NX**	E	*GA*	IL	78068	62994	71899	77872
321 321	* **GA**	E	*GA*	IL	78069	62995	71900	77873
321 322	**NX**	E	*GA*	IL	78070	62996	71901	77874
321 323	**NX**	E	*GA*	IL	78071	62997	71902	77875
321 324	**NX**	E	*GA*	IL	78072	62998	71903	77876
321 325	**NX**	E	*GA*	IL	78073	62999	71904	77877
321 326	**NX**	E	*GA*	IL	78074	63000	71905	77878
321 327	**NC**	E	*GA*	IL	78075	63001	71906	77879
321 328	**NX**	E	*GA*	IL	78076	63002	71907	77880
321 329	**NX**	E	*GA*	IL	78077	63003	71908	77881
321 330	**NC**	E	*GA*	IL	78078	63004	71909	77882
321 331	**NC**	E	*GA*	IL	78079	63005	71910	77883
321 332	**NC**	E	*GA*	IL	78080	63006	71911	77884
321 333	**NC**	E	*GA*	IL	78081	63007	71912	77885
321 334	**NC**	E	*GA*	IL	78082	63008	71913	77886
321 335	**NC**	E	*GA*	IL	78083	63009	71914	77887
321 336	**NC**	E	*GA*	IL	78084	63010	71915	77888
321 337	**NC**	E	*GA*	IL	78085	63011	71916	77889

321338	NC	E	GA	IL	78086	63012	71917	77890
321339	NC	E	GA	IL	78087	63013	71918	77891
321340	NC	E	GA	IL	78088	63014	71919	77892
321341	NC	E	GA	IL	78089	63015	71920	77893
321342	NC	E	GA	IL	78090	63016	71921	77894
321343	NC	E	GA	IL	78091	63017	71922	77895
321344	NC	E	GA	IL	78092	63018	71923	77896
321345	NC	E	GA	IL	78093	63019	71924	77897
321346	NC	E	GA	IL	78094	63020	71925	77898
321347	NC	E	GA	IL	78131	63105	71991	78280
321348	NC	E	GA	IL	78132	63106	71992	78281
321349	NC	E	GA	IL	78133	63107	71993	78282
321350	NC	E	GA	IL	78134	63108	71994	78283
321351	NC	E	GA	IL	78135	63109	71995	78284
321352	NC	E	GA	IL	78136	63110	71996	78285
321353	NC	E	GA	IL	78137	63111	71997	78286
321354	NC	E	GA	IL	78138	63112	71998	78287
321355	NC	E	GA	IL	78139	63113	71999	78288
321356	NC	E	GA	IL	78140	63114	72000	78289
321357	NC	E	GA	IL	78141	63115	72001	78290
321358	NC	E	GA	IL	78142	63116	72002	78291
321359	GA	E	GA	IL	78143	63117	72003	78292
321360	NC	E	GA	IL	78144	63118	72004	78293
321361	GA	E	GA	IL	78145	63119	72005	78294
321362	GA	E	GA	IL	78146	63120	72006	78295
321363	GA	E	GA	IL	78147	63121	72007	78296
321364	GA	E	GA	IL	78148	63122	72008	78297
321365	GA	E	GA	IL	78149	63123	72009	78298
321366	GA	E	GA	IL	78150	63124	72010	78299

Names (carried on TSO):

321312 Southend-on-Sea
321313 University of Essex
321321 NSPCC ESSEX FULL STOP
321334 Amsterdam
321336 GEOFFREY FREEMAN ALLEN
321342 R. Barnes
321343 RSA RAILWAY STUDY ASSOCIATION
321351 London Southend Airport
321361 Phoenix

Class 321/4.

The original vehicles 71966 and 77960 from 321418 and 78114 and 63082 from 321420 were written off after the Watford Junction accident in 1996. The undamaged vehicles were formed together as 321418 whilst four new vehicles were built in 1997, taking the same numbers as the scrapped vehicles, and these became the second 321420.

The DTCOs of 321421–437 have had 12 First Class seats declassified.

Units 321 411–417 have been refurbished as Class 320/4 3-car units for ScotRail (their TSO vehicles are stored).

In 2017 321401/403/404 are due to transfer to ScotRail.

† 321448 received an interior refurbishment as an Eversholt demonstrator unit. Fitted with two different types of interior using seats supplied by Quantum it acted as the pilot unit for the "Renatus" work being carried out on the Class 321/3s. 78130 and 63104 have a "suburban" interior with a 3+2 seating layout and 78279 and 71990 have a "metro" interior with 2+2 seating. It is also fitted with the new TSA AC traction motors.

Non-standard livery: 321448 Eversholt demonstrator (silver with blue doors and multi-coloured stripes).

DTCO. Lot No. 31067 1989–90. 28/40 (321 421–437 16/52, 321 438–447 16/56). 29.8 t. († 16/30(+4) 1TD 2W 33.9 t).
MSO. Lot No. 31068 1989–90. –/79 (321 438–447 –/82). 51.6 t († –/82. 54.0 t).
TSO. Lot No. 31069 1989–90. –/74 2T (321 438–447 –/75 2T). 29.2 t († –/62 1T. 31.7 t).
DTSO. Lot No. 31070 1989–90. –/78. 29.8 t. († –/58. 33.2 t).

321401	**FU**	E	*GN*	HE	78095	63063	71949	77943
321402	**FU**	E	*GA*	IL	78096	63064	71950	77944
321403	**FU**	E	*GN*	HE	78097	63065	71951	77945
321404	**FU**	E	*GN*	HE	78098	63066	71952	77946
321405	**FU**	E	*GA*	IL	78099	63067	71953	77947
321406	**FU**	E	*GA*	IL	78100	63068	71954	77948
321407	**FU**	E	*GA*	IL	78101	63069	71955	77949
321408	**FU**	E	*GA*	IL	78102	63070	71956	77950
321409	**FU**	E	*GA*	IL	78103	63071	71957	77951
321410	**FU**	E	*GA*	IL	78104	63072	71958	77952
321418	**FU**	E	*GA*	IL	78112	63080	71968	77962
321419	**FU**	E	*GA*	IL	78113	63081	71967	77961
321420	**FU**	E	*GA*	IL	78114‖	63082‖	71966‖	77960‖
321421	**NC**	E	*GA*	IL	78115	63083	71969	77963
321422	**NC**	E	*GA*	IL	78116	63084	71970	77964
321423	**NC**	E	*GA*	IL	78117	63085	71971	77965
321424	**NX**	E	*GA*	IL	78118	63086	71972	77966
321425	**NC**	E	*GA*	IL	78119	63087	71973	77967
321426	**NX**	E	*GA*	IL	78120	63088	71974	77968
321427	**NX**	E	*GA*	IL	78121	63089	71975	77969
321428	**NX**	E	*GA*	IL	78122	63090	71976	77970
321429	**NX**	E	*GA*	IL	78123	63091	71977	77971
321430	**NX**	E	*GA*	IL	78124	63092	71978	77972
321431	**NX**	E	*GA*	IL	78151	63125	72011	78300
321432	**NC**	E	*GA*	IL	78152	63126	72012	78301
321433	**NC**	E	*GA*	IL	78153	63127	72013	78302
321434	**NC**	E	*GA*	IL	78154	63128	72014	78303
321435	**NC**	E	*GA*	IL	78155	63129	72015	78304
321436	**NC**	E	*GA*	IL	78156	63130	72016	78305
321437	**NC**	E	*GA*	IL	78157	63131	72017	78306
321438	**GA**	E	*GA*	IL	78158	63132	72018	78307
321439	**GA**	E	*GA*	IL	78159	63133	72019	78308
321440	**GA**	E	*GA*	IL	78160	63134	72020	78309
321441	**GA**	E	*GA*	IL	78161	63135	72021	78310
321442	**GA**	E	*GA*	IL	78162	63136	72022	78311

321443	**GA**	E	*GA*	IL	78125	63099	71985	78274
321444	**NC**	E	*GA*	IL	78126	63100	71986	78275
321445	**NC**	E	*GA*	IL	78127	63101	71987	78276
321446	**NC**	E	*GA*	IL	78128	63102	71988	78277
321447	**GA**	E	*GA*	IL	78129	63103	71989	78278
321448 †	**O**	E	*GA*	IL	78130	63104	71990	78279
Spare	**LM**	E		ZB (S)	71959	71960	71963	71964
					71965			
Spare	**LO**	E		ZB (S)	71961	71962		

Names (carried on TSO):

321403	Stewart Fleming Signalman King's Cross
321428	The Essex Commuter
321442	Crouch Valley 1889–2014
321444	Essex Lifeboats
321446	George Mullings

Class 321/9. DTSO(A)–MSO–TSO–DTSO(B).

Refurbished 2015 with a new universal access toilet to comply with the 2020 accessibility regulations.

DTSO(A). Lot No. 31108 1991. –/45(+6) 1TD 2W. 31.7 t.
MSO. Lot No. 31109 1991. –/79. 52.1 t.
TSO. Lot No. 31110 1991. –/78. 30.6 t.
DTSO(B). Lot No. 31111 1991. –/79. 30.6 t.

321901	**NB**	E	*NO*	NL	77990	63153	72128	77993
321902	**NB**	E	*NO*	NL	77991	63154	72129	77994
321903	**NB**	E	*NO*	NL	77992	63155	72130	77995

CLASS 322   BREL YORK

Units built for use on Stansted Airport services, used for a number of years with ScotRail before transfer to Northern. Refurbished 2014–15 with a universal access toilet to comply with the 2020 accessibility regulations.

Formation: DTSO–MSO–TSO–DTSO.
Construction: Steel.
Traction Motors: Four Brush TM2141C of 268 kW.
Wheel Arrangement: 2-2 + Bo-Bo + 2-2 + 2-2.
Braking: Disc.   **Dimensions:** 19.95/19.92 x 2.82 m.
Bogies: P7-4 (MSO), T3-7 (others).   **Couplers:** Tightlock.
Gangways: Within unit.   **Control System:** Thyristor.
Doors: Sliding.   **Maximum Speed:** 100 mph.
Seating Layout: 3+2 facing.
Multiple Working: Within class & with Classes 317, 318, 319, 320, 321 and 323.

DTSO(A). Lot No. 31094 1990. –/54(+4) 1TD 2W. 31.7 t.
MSO. Lot No. 31092 1990. –/83. 52.1 t.
TSO. Lot No. 31093 1990. –/80 1T. 30.6 t.
DTSO(B). Lot No. 31091 1990. –/79. 30.6 t.

322 481	**NB**	E	*NO*	NL	78163	63137	72023	77985
322 482	**NB**	E	*NO*	NL	78164	63138	72024	77986
322 483	**NB**	E	*NO*	NL	78165	63139	72025	77987
322 484	**NB**	E	*NO*	NL	78166	63140	72026	77988
322 485	**NB**	E	*NO*	NL	78167	63141	72027	77989

CLASS 323 HUNSLET TRANSPORTATION PROJECTS

Suburban units.

Formation: DMSO–PTSO–DMSO.
Construction: Welded aluminium alloy.
Traction Motors: Four Holec DMKT 52/24 asynchronous of 146 kW.
Wheel Arrangement: Bo-Bo + 2-2 + Bo-Bo.
Braking: Disc.   **Dimensions:** 23.37/23.44 x 2.80 m.
Bogies: SRP BP62 (DMSO), BT52 (PTSO).   **Couplers:** Tightlock.
Gangways: Within unit.   **Control System:** IGBT Inverter.
Doors: Sliding plug.   **Maximum Speed:** 90 mph.
Seating Layout: 3+2 facing/unidirectional.
Multiple Working: Within class & with Classes 317, 318, 319, 320, 321 and 322.

DMSO(A). Lot No. 31112 Hunslet 1992–93. –/98 († –/82). 41.0 t.
TSO. Lot No. 31113 Hunslet 1992–93. –/88(+5) 1T 2W. († –/80(+5) 1T 2W). 39.4 t.
DMSO(B). Lot No. 31114 Hunslet 1992–93. –/98 († –/82). 41.0 t.

323 201		**LM**	P	*LM*	SO	64001	72201	65001
323 202		**LM**	P	*LM*	SO	64002	72202	65002
323 203		**LM**	P	*LM*	SO	64003	72203	65003
323 204		**LM**	P	*LM*	SO	64004	72204	65004
323 205		**LM**	P	*LM*	SO	64005	72205	65005
323 206		**LM**	P	*LM*	SO	64006	72206	65006
323 207		**LM**	P	*LM*	SO	64007	72207	65007
323 208		**LM**	P	*LM*	SO	64008	72208	65008
323 209		**LM**	P	*LM*	SO	64009	72209	65009
323 210		**LM**	P	*LM*	SO	64010	72210	65010
323 211		**LM**	P	*LM*	SO	64011	72211	65011
323 212		**LM**	P	*LM*	SO	64012	72212	65012
323 213		**LM**	P	*LM*	SO	64013	72213	65013
323 214		**LM**	P	*LM*	SO	64014	72214	65014
323 215		**LM**	P	*LM*	SO	64015	72215	65015
323 216		**LM**	P	*LM*	SO	64016	72216	65016
323 217		**LM**	P	*LM*	SO	64017	72217	65017
323 218		**LM**	P	*LM*	SO	64018	72218	65018
323 219		**LM**	P	*LM*	SO	64019	72219	65019
323 220		**LM**	P	*LM*	SO	64020	72220	65020
323 221		**LM**	P	*LM*	SO	64021	72221	65021
323 222		**LM**	P	*LM*	SO	64022	72222	65022
323 223	†	**NO**	P	*NO*	LG	64023	72223	65023
323 224	†	**NO**	P	*NO*	LG	64024	72224	65024
323 225	†	**NO**	P	*NO*	LG	64025	72225	65025

323 226	**NO**	P	*NO*	LG	64026	72226	65026
323 227	**NO**	P	*NO*	LG	64027	72227	65027
323 228	**NO**	P	*NO*	LG	64028	72228	65028
323 229	**NO**	P	*NO*	LG	64029	72229	65029
323 230	**NO**	P	*NO*	LG	64030	72230	65030
323 231	**NO**	P	*NO*	LG	64031	72231	65031
323 232	**NO**	P	*NO*	LG	64032	72232	65032
323 233	**NO**	P	*NO*	LG	64033	72233	65033
323 234	**NO**	P	*NO*	LG	64034	72234	65034
323 235	**NO**	P	*NO*	LG	64035	72235	65035
323 236	**NO**	P	*NO*	LG	64036	72236	65036
323 237	**NO**	P	*NO*	LG	64037	72237	65037
323 238	**NO**	P	*NO*	LG	64038	72238	65038
323 239	**NO**	P	*NO*	LG	64039	72239	65039
323 240	**LM**	P	*LM*	SO	64040	72340	65040
323 241	**LM**	P	*LM*	SO	64041	72341	65041
323 242	**LM**	P	*LM*	SO	64042	72342	65042
323 243	**LM**	P	*LM*	SO	64043	72343	65043

CLASS 325   ABB DERBY

Postal units based on Class 319s. Compatible with diesel or electric locomotive haulage. Built for dual voltage use, but 750 V DC third rail equipment has been removed as it is not required on current duties.

Formation: DTPMV–MPMV–TPMV–DTPMV.
System: 25 kV AC overhead.
Construction: Steel.
Traction Motors: Four GEC G315BZ of 268 kW.
Wheel Arrangement: 2-2 + Bo-Bo + 2-2 + 2-2.
Braking: Disc.   **Dimensions:** 19.33 x 2.82 m.
Bogies: P7-4 (MSO), T3-7 (others).   **Couplers:** Drop-head buckeye.
Gangways: None.   **Control System:** GTO Chopper.
Doors: Roller shutter.   **Maximum Speed:** 100 mph.
Multiple Working: Within class.

DTPMV. Lot No. 31144 1995. 29.1 t.
MPMV. Lot No. 31145 1995. 49.5 t.
TPMV. Lot No. 31146 1995. 30.7 t.

325001	**RL**	RM	*DB*	CE	68300	68340	68360	68301
325002	**RL**	RM	*DB*	CE	68302	68341	68361	68303
325003	**RL**	RM	*DB*	CE	68304	68342	68362	68305
325004	**RL**	RM	*DB*	CE	68306	68343	68363	68307
325005	**RM**	RM	*DB*	CE	68308	68344	68364	68309
325006	**RM**	RM	*DB*	CE	68310	68345	68365	68311
325007	**RM**	RM	*DB*	CE	68312	68346	68366	68313
325008	**RM**	RM	*DB*	CE	68314	68347	68367	68315
325009	**RL**	RM	*DB*	CE	68316	68349	68368	68317
325011	**RL**	RM	*DB*	CE	68320	68350	68370	68321
325012	**RL**	RM	*DB*	CE	68322	68351	68371	68323
325013	**RL**	RM	*DB*	CE	68324	68352	68372	68325

325014	**RL**	RM	*DB*	CE	68326	68353	68373	68327
325015	**RL**	RM	*DB*	CE	68328	68354	68374	68329
325016	**RM**	RM	*DB*	CE	68330	68355	68375	68331

Names (carried on one side of each DTPMV):

325002 Royal Mail North Wales & North West
325006 John Grierson
325008 Peter Howarth CBE

CLASS 332   HEATHROW EXPRESS CAF/SIEMENS

Dedicated Heathrow Express units. Five units were increased from 4-car to 5-car in 2002. Usually operate in coupled pairs.

Formations: DMSO–TSO–PTSO–(TSO)–DMFO.
Construction: Steel.
Traction Motors: Two Siemens monomotors asynchronous of 350 kW.
Wheel Arrangement: B-B + 2-2 + 2-2 (+ 2-2) + B-B.
Braking: Disc.   **Dimensions:** 23.74/23.35/23.14 x 2.75 m.
Bogies: CAF.   **Couplers:** Scharfenberg 10L.
Gangways: Within unit.   **Control System:** IGBT Inverter.
Doors: Sliding plug.   **Maximum Speed:** 100 mph.
Heating & ventilation: Air conditioning.
Seating: 1: 1+1 facing/unidirectional, 2: 2+2 mainly unidirectional.
Multiple Working: Within class.

Advertising livery: Tata Communications (blue).

DMSO. CAF 1997–98. –/43(+8). 49.9 t.
72400–413. TSO. CAF 1997–98. –/64(+11). 38.4 t.
72414–418. TSO. CAF 2002. –/56 35.8 t.
PTSO. CAF 1997–98. –/39(+11) 1TD 2W. 47.6 t.
DMFO. CAF 1997–98. 20/–. 49.5 t.

332001	**AL**	HE	*HE*	OH	78400	72412	63400		78401
332002	**AL**	HE	*HE*	OH	78402	72409	63406		78403
332003	**AL**	HE	*HE*	OH	78404	72407	63402		78405
332004	**AL**	HE	*HE*	OH	78406	72405	63403		78407
332005	**AL**	HE	*HE*	OH	78408	72411	63404	72417	78409
332006	**AL**	HE	*HE*	OH	78410	72410	63405	72415	78411
332007	**AL**	HE	*HE*	OH	78412	72401	63401	72414	78413
332008	**AL**	HE	*HE*	OH	78414	72413	63407	72416	78415
332009	**AL**	HE	*HE*	OH	78416	72400	63408	72416	78417
332010	**AL**	HE	*HE*	OH	78418	72402	63409		78419
332011	**AL**	HE	*HE*	OH	78420	72403	63410		78421
332012	**AL**	HE	*HE*	OH	78422	72404	63411		78423
332013	**AL**	HE	*HE*	OH	78424	72408	63412		78425
332014	**AL**	HE	*HE*	OH	78426	72406	63413		78427

CLASS 333   CAF/SIEMENS

West Yorkshire area suburban units.

Formation: DMSO–PTSO–TSO–DMSO.
Construction: Steel.
Traction Motors: Two Siemens monomotors asynchronous of 350 kW.
Wheel Arrangement: B-B + 2-2 + 2-2 + B-B.
Braking: Disc.
Dimensions: 23.74 (outer ends)/23.35 (TSO) x 2.75 m.
Bogies: CAF.   **Couplers:** Dellner 10L.
Gangways: Within unit.   **Control System:** IGBT Inverter.
Doors: Sliding plug.   **Maximum Speed:** 100 mph.
Heating & ventilation: Air conditioning.**Multiple Working:** Within class.
Seating layout: 3+2 facing/unidirectional.

333001–008 were made up to 4-car units from 3-car units in 2002.

333009–016 were made up to 4-car units from 3-car units in 2003.

DMSO(A). (Odd Nos.) CAF 2001. –/90. 50.0 t.
PTSO. CAF 2001. –/73(+7) 1TD 2W. 46.0 t.
TSO. CAF 2002–03. –/100. 38.5 t.
DMSO(B). (Even Nos.) CAF 2001. –/90. 50.0 t.

333001	**YR**	A	*NO*	NL	78451	74461	74477	78452
333002	**YR**	A	*NO*	NL	78453	74462	74478	78454
333003	**YR**	A	*NO*	NL	78455	74463	74479	78456
333004	**YR**	A	*NO*	NL	78457	74464	74480	78458
333005	**YR**	A	*NO*	NL	78459	74465	74481	78460
333006	**YR**	A	*NO*	NL	78461	74466	74482	78462
333007	**YR**	A	*NO*	NL	78463	74467	74483	78464
333008	**YR**	A	*NO*	NL	78465	74468	74484	78466
333009	**YR**	A	*NO*	NL	78467	74469	74485	78468
333010	**YR**	A	*NO*	NL	78469	74470	74486	78470
333011	**YR**	A	*NO*	NL	78471	74471	74487	78472
333012	**YR**	A	*NO*	NL	78473	74472	74488	78474
333013	**YR**	A	*NO*	NL	78475	74473	74489	78476
333014	**YR**	A	*NO*	NL	78477	74474	74490	78478
333015	**YR**	A	*NO*	NL	78479	74475	74491	78480
333016	**YR**	A	*NO*	NL	78481	74476	74492	78482

Names (carried on end cars):

333007 Alderman J Arthur Godwin First Lord Mayor of Bradford 1907
333011 Olicana Ilkley's Roman Fort

CLASS 334   JUNIPER   ALSTOM BIRMINGHAM

Outer suburban units.

Formation: DMSO–PTSO–DMSO.
Construction: Steel.
Traction Motors: Two Alstom ONIX 800 asynchronous of 270 kW.
Wheel Arrangement: 2-Bo + 2-2 + Bo-2.

Braking: Disc.
Bogies: Alstom LTB3/TBP3.
Gangways: Within unit.
Doors: Sliding plug.
Heating & ventilation: Pressure heating and ventilation.
Seating Layout: 2+2 facing/unidirectional (3+2 in PTSO).
Multiple Working: Within class.

Dimensions: 21.01/19.94 x 2.80 m.
Couplers: Dellner.
Control System: IGBT Inverter.
Maximum Speed: 90 mph.

DMSO(A). Alstom Birmingham 1999–2001. –/64. 42.6 t.
PTSO. Alstom Birmingham 1999–2001. –/55 1TD 1W. 39.4 t.
DMSO(B). Alstom Birmingham 1999–2001. –/64. 42.6 t.

334 001	**SR**	E	*SR*	GW	64101	74301	65101
334 002	**SR**	E	*SR*	GW	64102	74302	65102
334 003	**SR**	E	*SR*	GW	64103	74303	65103
334 004	**SR**	E	*SR*	GW	64104	74304	65104
334 005	**SR**	E	*SR*	GW	64105	74305	65105
334 006	**SR**	E	*SR*	GW	64106	74306	65106
334 007	**SR**	E	*SR*	GW	64107	74307	65107
334 008	**SR**	E	*SR*	GW	64108	74308	65108
334 009	**SR**	E	*SR*	GW	64109	74309	65109
334 010	**SR**	E	*SR*	GW	64110	74310	65110
334 011	**SR**	E	*SR*	GW	64111	74311	65111
334 012	**SR**	E	*SR*	GW	64112	74312	65112
334 013	**SR**	E	*SR*	GW	64113	74313	65113
334 014	**SR**	E	*SR*	GW	64114	74314	65114
334 015	**SR**	E	*SR*	GW	64115	74315	65115
334 016	**SR**	E	*SR*	GW	64116	74316	65116
334 017	**SR**	E	*SR*	GW	64117	74317	65117
334 018	**SR**	E	*SR*	GW	64118	74318	65118
334 019	**SR**	E	*SR*	GW	64119	74319	65119
334 020	**SR**	E	*SR*	GW	64120	74320	65120
334 021	**SR**	E	*SR*	GW	64121	74321	65121
334 022	**SR**	E	*SR*	GW	64122	74322	65122
334 023	**SR**	E	*SR*	GW	64123	74323	65123
334 024	**SR**	E	*SR*	GW	64124	74324	65124
334 025	**SR**	E	*SR*	GW	64125	74325	65125
334 026	**SR**	E	*SR*	GW	64126	74326	65126
334 027	**SR**	E	*SR*	GW	64127	74327	65127
334 028	**SR**	E	*SR*	GW	64128	74328	65128
334 029	**SR**	E	*SR*	GW	64129	74329	65129
334 030	**SR**	E	*SR*	GW	64130	74330	65130
334 031	**SR**	E	*SR*	GW	64131	74331	65131
334 032	**SR**	E	*SR*	GW	64132	74332	65132
334 033	**SR**	E	*SR*	GW	64133	74333	65133
334 034	**SR**	E	*SR*	GW	64134	74334	65134
334 035	**SR**	E	*SR*	GW	64135	74335	65135
334 036	**SR**	E	*SR*	GW	64136	74336	65136
334 037	**SR**	E	*SR*	GW	64137	74337	65137
334 038	**SR**	E	*SR*	GW	64138	74338	65138
334 039	**SR**	E	*SR*	GW	64139	74339	65139
334 040	**SR**	E	*SR*	GW	64140	74340	65140

CLASS 345   AVENTRA   BOMBARDIER DERBY

9-car units currently under construction for London's Crossrail. The first 15 units will enter traffic in May 2017 (initially as 7-car units) on Liverpool Street–Shenfield services, and then on the cross-London new Crossrail services from December 2018. The design is marketed as "Aventra" by Bombardier and is a development on the successful Electrostar design. There is an option for a further 17 9-car units. Full details awaited.

Formations: DMSO–PMSO–MSO–MSO*–TSO–MSO*–MSO–PMSO–DMSO.
* Initially these MSO vehicles will be missing from units 345 001–015.
Systems: 25 kV AC overhead.
Construction: Aluminium.
Traction Motors: Two Bombardier asynchronous of 250 kW.
Wheel Arrangement: 2-Bo + Bo-2 + Bo-Bo (+ Bo-2) + 2-2 (+ 2-Bo) + Bo-Bo + 2-Bo + Bo-2.
Braking: Disc & regenerative.
Bogies: Inside-frame.
Gangways: Within unit.
Doors: Sliding plug.
Heating & ventilation: Air conditioning.
Seating Layout: Longitudinal/2+2 facing.
Multiple Working: Within class.

Dimensions:
Couplers: Dellner.
Control System: IGBT Inverter.
Maximum Speed: 90 mph.

DMSO(A). Bombardier Derby 2015–18.
PMSO(A). Bombardier Derby 2015–18.
MSO(A). Bombardier Derby 2015–18.
MSO(B). Bombardier Derby 2015–18.
TSO. Bombardier Derby 2015–18.
MSO(C). Bombardier Derby 2015–18.
MSO(D). Bombardier Derby 2015–18.
PMSO(B). Bombardier Derby 2015–18.
DMSO(B). Bombardier Derby 2015–18.

345 001	**XR**	XR		340101	340201	340301	*340401*	340501
				340601	340701	340801	340901	
345 002	**XR**	XR	IL	340102	340202	340302	*340402*	340502
				340602	340702	340802	340902	
345 003		XR		340103	340203	340303	*340403*	340503
				340603	340703	340803	340903	
345 004		XR		340104	340204	340304	*340404*	340504
				340604	340704	340804	340904	
345 005		XR		340105	340205	340305	*340405*	340505
				340605	340705	340805	340905	
345 006		XR		340106	340206	340306	*340406*	340506
				340606	340706	340806	340906	
345 007		XR		340107	340207	340307	*340407*	340507
				340607	340707	340807	340907	
345 008		XR		340108	340208	340308	*340408*	340508
				340608	340708	340808	340908	
345 009		XR		340109	340209	340309	*340409*	340509
				340609	340709	340809	340909	

345 010	XR	340110	340210	340310	*340410*	340510
		340610	340710	340810	340910	
345 011	XR	340111	340211	340311	*340411*	340511
		340611	340711	340811	340911	
345 012	XR	340112	340212	340312	*340412*	340512
		340612	340712	340812	340912	
345 013	XR	340113	340213	340313	*340413*	340513
		340613	340713	340813	340913	
345 014	XR	340114	340214	340314	*340414*	340514
		340614	340714	340814	340914	
345 015	XR	340115	340215	340315	*340415*	340515
		340615	340715	340815	340915	
345 016	XR	340116	340216	340316	340416	340516
		340616	340716	340816	340916	
345 017	XR	340117	340217	340317	340417	340517
		340617	340717	340817	340917	
345 018	XR	340118	340218	340318	340418	340518
		340618	340718	340818	340918	
345 019	XR	340119	340219	340319	340419	340519
		340619	340719	340819	340919	
345 020	XR	340120	340220	340320	340420	340520
		340620	340720	340820	340920	
345 021	XR	340121	340221	340321	340421	340521
		340621	340721	340821	340921	
345 022	XR	340122	340222	340322	340422	340522
		340622	340722	340822	340922	
345 023	XR	340123	340223	340323	340423	340523
		340623	340723	340823	340923	
345 024	XR	340124	340224	340324	340424	340524
		340624	340724	340824	340924	
345 025	XR	340125	340225	340325	340425	340525
		340625	340725	340825	340925	
345 026	XR	340126	340226	340326	340426	340526
		340626	340726	340826	340926	
345 027	XR	340127	340227	340327	340427	340527
		340627	340727	340827	340927	
345 028	XR	340128	340228	340328	340428	340528
		340628	340728	340828	340928	
345 029	XR	340129	340229	340329	340429	340529
		340629	340729	340829	340929	
345 030	XR	340130	340230	340330	340430	340530
		340630	340730	340830	340930	
345 031	XR	340131	340231	340331	340431	340531
		340631	340731	340831	340931	
345 032	XR	340132	340232	340332	340432	340532
		340632	340732	340832	340932	
345 033	XR	340133	340233	340333	340433	340533
		340633	340733	340833	340933	
345 034	XR	340134	340234	340334	340434	340534
		340634	340734	340834	340934	

345035	XR	340135	340235	340335	340435	340535
		340635	340735	340835	340935	
345036	XR	340136	340236	340336	340436	340536
		340636	340736	340836	340936	
345037	XR	340137	340237	340337	340437	340537
		340637	340737	340837	340937	
345038	XR	340138	340238	340338	340438	340538
		340638	340738	340838	340938	
345039	XR	340139	340239	340339	340439	340539
		340639	340739	340839	340939	
345040	XR	340140	340240	340340	340440	340540
		340640	340740	340840	340940	
345041	XR	340141	340241	340341	340441	340541
		340641	340741	340841	340941	
345042	XR	340142	340242	340342	340442	340542
		340642	340742	340842	340942	
345043	XR	340143	340243	340343	340443	340543
		340643	340743	340843	340943	
345044	XR	340144	340244	340344	340444	340544
		340644	340744	340844	340944	
345045	XR	340145	340245	340345	340445	340545
		340645	340745	340845	340945	
345046	XR	340146	340246	340346	340446	340546
		340646	340746	340846	340946	
345047	XR	340147	340247	340347	340447	340547
		340647	340747	340847	340947	
345048	XR	340148	340248	340348	340448	340548
		340648	340748	340848	340948	
345049	XR	340149	340249	340349	340449	340549
		340649	340749	340849	340949	
345050	XR	340150	340250	340350	340450	340550
		340650	340750	340850	340950	
345051	XR	340151	340251	340351	340451	340551
		340651	340751	340851	340951	
345052	XR	340152	340252	340352	340452	340552
		340652	340752	340852	340952	
345053	XR	340153	340253	340353	340453	340553
		340653	340753	340853	340953	
345054	XR	340154	340254	340354	340454	340554
		340654	340754	340854	340954	
345055	XR	340155	340255	340355	340455	340555
		340655	340755	340855	340955	
345056	XR	340156	340256	340356	340456	340556
		340656	340756	340856	340956	
345057	XR	340157	340257	340357	340457	340557
		340657	340757	340857	340957	
345058	XR	340158	340258	340358	340458	340558
		340658	340758	340858	340958	
345059	XR	340159	340259	340359	340459	340559
		340659	340759	340859	340959	

345 060	XR	340160	340260	340360	340460	340560
		340660	340760	340860	340960	
345 061	XR	340161	340261	340361	340461	340561
		340661	340761	340861	340961	
345 062	XR	340162	340262	340362	340462	340562
		340662	340762	340862	340962	
345 063	XR	340163	340263	340363	340463	340563
		340663	340763	340863	340963	
345 064	XR	340164	340264	340364	340464	340564
		340664	340764	340864	340964	
345 065	XR	340165	340265	340365	340465	340565
		340665	340765	340865	340965	
345 066	XR	340166	340266	340366	340466	340566
		340666	340766	340866	340966	

CLASS 350   DESIRO UK   SIEMENS

Outer suburban and long distance units.

Formation: DMCO–TCO–PTSO–DMCO.
Systems: 25 kV AC overhead (350/1s built with 750 V DC).
Construction: Welded aluminium.
Traction Motors: 4 Siemens 1TB2016-0GB02 asynchronous of 250 kW.
Wheel Arrangement: Bo-Bo + 2-2 + 2-2 + Bo-Bo.
Braking: Disc & regenerative.   **Dimensions:** 20.34 x 2.79 m.
Bogies: SGP SF5000.   **Couplers:** Dellner 12.
Gangways: Throughout.   **Control System:** IGBT Inverter.
Doors: Sliding plug.
Maximum Speed: 110 mph (350/1, 350/3 & 350/4) or 100 mph (350/2).
Heating & ventilation: Air conditioning.
Seating Layout: Various, see sub-class headings.
Multiple Working: Within class.

Class 350/1. Original-build units owned by Angel Trains. Formerly part of an aborted South West Trains 5-car Class 450/2 order. 2+2 seating.

Seating Layout: 1: 2+2 facing, 2: 2+2 facing/unidirectional.

Advertising livery: 350 110 Project 110 (silver centre cars).

DMSO(A). Siemens Krefeld 2004–05. –/60. 48.7 t.
TCO. Siemens Krefeld/Prague 2004–05. 24/32 1T. 36.2 t.
PTSO. Siemens Krefeld/Prague 2004–05. –/50(+9) 1TD 2W. 45.2 t.
DMSO(B). Siemens Krefeld 2004–05. –/60. 49.2 t.

350 101	**LM**	A	*LM*	NN	63761	66811	66861	63711
350 102	**LM**	A	*LM*	NN	63762	66812	66862	63712
350 103	**LM**	A	*LM*	NN	63765	66813	66863	63713
350 104	**LM**	A	*LM*	NN	63764	66814	66864	63714
350 105	**LM**	A	*LM*	NN	63763	66815	66868	63715
350 106	**LM**	A	*LM*	NN	63766	66816	66866	63716
350 107	**LM**	A	*LM*	NN	63767	66817	66867	63717
350 108	**LM**	A	*LM*	NN	63768	66818	66865	63718
350 109	**LM**	A	*LM*	NN	63769	66819	66869	63719

350 110	**AL**	A	*LM*	NN	63770	66820	66870	63720
350 111	**LM**	A	*LM*	NN	63771	66821	66871	63721
350 112	**LM**	A	*LM*	NN	63772	66822	66872	63722
350 113	**LM**	A	*LM*	NN	63773	66823	66873	63723
350 114	**LM**	A	*LM*	NN	63774	66824	66874	63724
350 115	**LM**	A	*LM*	NN	63775	66825	66875	63725
350 116	**LM**	A	*LM*	NN	63776	66826	66876	63726
350 117	**LM**	A	*LM*	NN	63777	66827	66877	63727
350 118	**LM**	A	*LM*	NN	63778	66828	66878	63728
350 119	**LM**	A	*LM*	NN	63779	66829	66879	63729
350 120	**LM**	A	*LM*	NN	63780	66830	66880	63730
350 121	**LM**	A	*LM*	NN	63781	66831	66881	63731
350 122	**LM**	A	*LM*	NN	63782	66832	66882	63732
350 123	**LM**	A	*LM*	NN	63783	66833	66883	63733
350 124	**LM**	A	*LM*	NN	63784	66834	66884	63734
350 125	**LM**	A	*LM*	NN	63785	66835	66885	63735
350 126	**LM**	A	*LM*	NN	63786	66836	66886	63736
350 127	**LM**	A	*LM*	NN	63787	66837	66887	63737
350 128	**LM**	A	*LM*	NN	63788	66838	66888	63738
350 129	**LM**	A	*LM*	NN	63789	66839	66889	63739
350 130	**LM**	A	*LM*	NN	63790	66840	66890	63740

Class 350/2. Owned by Porterbrook Leasing.

Seating Layout: 1: 2+2 facing, 2: 3+2 facing/unidirectional.

DMSO(A). Siemens Krefeld 2008–09. –/70. 43.7 t.
TCO. Siemens Prague 2008–09. 24/42 1T. 35.3 t.
PTSO. Siemens Prague 2008–09. –/61(+9) 1TD 2W. 42.9 t.
DMSO(B). Siemens Krefeld 2008–09. –/70. 44.2 t.

350 231	**LM**	P	*LM*	NN	61431	65231	67531	61531
350 232	**LM**	P	*LM*	NN	61432	65232	67532	61532
350 233	**LM**	P	*LM*	NN	61433	65233	67533	61533
350 234	**LM**	P	*LM*	NN	61434	65234	67534	61534
350 235	**LM**	P	*LM*	NN	61435	65235	67535	61535
350 236	**LM**	P	*LM*	NN	61436	65236	67536	61536
350 237	**LM**	P	*LM*	NN	61437	65237	67537	61537
350 238	**LM**	P	*LM*	NN	61438	65238	67538	61538
350 239	**LM**	P	*LM*	NN	61439	65239	67539	61539
350 240	**LM**	P	*LM*	NN	61440	65240	67540	61540
350 241	**LM**	P	*LM*	NN	61441	65241	67541	61541
350 242	**LM**	P	*LM*	NN	61442	65242	67542	61542
350 243	**LM**	P	*LM*	NN	61443	65243	67543	61543
350 244	**LM**	P	*LM*	NN	61444	65244	67544	61544
350 245	**LM**	P	*LM*	NN	61445	65245	67545	61545
350 246	**LM**	P	*LM*	NN	61446	65246	67546	61546
350 247	**LM**	P	*LM*	NN	61447	65247	67547	61547
350 248	**LM**	P	*LM*	NN	61448	65248	67548	61548
350 249	**LM**	P	*LM*	NN	61449	65249	67549	61549
350 250	**LM**	P	*LM*	NN	61450	65250	67550	61550
350 251	**LM**	P	*LM*	NN	61451	65251	67551	61551
350 252	**LM**	P	*LM*	NN	61452	65252	67552	61552

350253	LM	P	*LM*	NN	61453	65253	67553	61553
350254	LM	P	*LM*	NN	61454	65254	67554	61554
350255	LM	P	*LM*	NN	61455	65255	67555	61555
350256	LM	P	*LM*	NN	61456	65256	67556	61556
350257	LM	P	*LM*	NN	61457	65257	67557	61557
350258	LM	P	*LM*	NN	61458	65258	67558	61558
350259	LM	P	*LM*	NN	61459	65259	67559	61559
350260	LM	P	*LM*	NN	61460	65260	67560	61560
350261	LM	P	*LM*	NN	61461	65261	67561	61561
350262	LM	P	*LM*	NN	61462	65262	67562	61562
350263	LM	P	*LM*	NN	61463	65263	67563	61563
350264	LM	P	*LM*	NN	61464	65264	67564	61564
350265	LM	P	*LM*	NN	61465	65265	67565	61565
350266	LM	P	*LM*	NN	61466	65266	67566	61566
350267	LM	P	*LM*	NN	61467	65267	67567	61567

Name (carried on one side of PTSO): 350232   Chad Varah

Class 350/3. Owned by Angel Trains. London Midland units built for 110 mph operation.

Seating Layout: 1: 2+2 facing, 2: 2+2 facing/unidirectional.

DMSO(A). Siemens Krefeld 2014. –/60. 44.2 t.
TCO. Siemens Krefeld 2014. 24/36 1T. 36.3 t.
PTSO. Siemens Krefeld 2014. –/50(+9) 1TD 2W. 44.0 t.
DMSO(B). Siemens Krefeld 2014. –/60. 45.0 t.

350368	LM	A	*LM*	NN	60141	60511	60651	60151
350369	LM	A	*LM*	NN	60142	60512	60652	60152
350370	LM	A	*LM*	NN	60143	60513	60653	60153
350371	LM	A	*LM*	NN	60144	60514	60654	60154
350372	LM	A	*LM*	NN	60145	60515	60655	60155
350373	LM	A	*LM*	NN	60146	60516	60656	60156
350374	LM	A	*LM*	NN	60147	60517	60657	60157
350375	LM	A	*LM*	NN	60148	60518	60658	60158
350376	LM	A	*LM*	NN	60149	60519	60659	60159
350377	LM	A	*LM*	NN	60150	60520	60660	60160

Name: 350370   Lichfield Festival

Class 350/4. Owned by Angel Trains. TransPennine Express units used on the Manchester Airport–Edinburgh/Glasgow route.

Seating Layout: 1: 2+1 facing, 2: 2+2 facing/unidirectional.

DMSO(A). Siemens Krefeld 2013–14. –/56. 44.2 t.
TCO. Siemens Krefeld 2013–14. 19/24 1T. 36.2 t.
PTSO. Siemens Krefeld 2013–14. –/42 1TD 1T. 44.6 t.
DMSO(B). Siemens Krefeld 2013–14. –/56. 45.0 t.

350401	FT	A	*TP*	AK	60691	60901	60941	60671
350402	FT	A	*TP*	AK	60692	60902	60942	60672
350403	FT	A	*TP*	AK	60693	60903	60943	60673
350404	FT	A	*TP*	AK	60694	60904	60944	60674
350405	FT	A	*TP*	AK	60695	60905	60945	60675

350406	**FT**	A	*TP*	AK	60696	60906	60946	60676
350407	**FT**	A	*TP*	AK	60697	60907	60947	60677
350408	**FT**	A	*TP*	AK	60698	60908	60948	60678
350409	**FT**	A	*TP*	AK	60699	60909	60949	60679
350410	**FT**	A	*TP*	AK	60700	60910	60950	60680

CLASS 357 ELECTROSTAR
ADTRANZ/BOMBARDIER DERBY

Provision for 750 V DC supply if required.

Formation: DMSO–MSO–PTSO–DMSO.
Construction: Welded aluminium alloy underframe, sides and roof with steel ends. All sections bolted together.
Traction Motors: Two Adtranz asynchronous of 250 kW.
Wheel Arrangement: 2-Bo + 2-Bo + 2-2 + Bo-2.

Braking: Disc & regenerative.	**Dimensions:** 20.40/19.99 x 2.80 m.
Bogies: Adtranz P3-25/T3-25.	**Couplers:** Tightlock.
Gangways: Within unit.	**Control System:** IGBT Inverter.
Doors: Sliding plug.	**Maximum Speed:** 100 mph.
Heating & ventilation: Air conditioning.	
Seating Layout: 3+2 facing/unidirectional.	
Multiple Working: Within class.	

Class 357/0. Owned by Porterbrook Leasing.

DMSO(A). Adtranz Derby 1999–2001. –/71. 40.7 t.
MSO. Adtranz Derby 1999–2001. –/78. 36.7 t.
PTSO. Adtranz Derby 1999–2001. –/58(+4) 1TD 2W. 39.5 t.
DMSO(B). Adtranz Derby 1999–2001. –/71. 40.7 t.

357001	**C2**	P	*C2*	EM	67651	74151	74051	67751
357002	**C2**	P	*C2*	EM	67652	74152	74052	67752
357003	**C2**	P	*C2*	EM	67653	74153	74053	67753
357004	**C2**	P	*C2*	EM	67654	74154	74054	67754
357005	**C2**	P	*C2*	EM	67655	74155	74055	67755
357006	**C2**	P	*C2*	EM	67656	74156	74056	67756
357007	**C2**	P	*C2*	EM	67657	74157	74057	67757
357008	**C2**	P	*C2*	EM	67658	74158	74058	67758
357009	**C2**	P	*C2*	EM	67659	74159	74059	67759
357010	**C2**	P	*C2*	EM	67660	74160	74060	67760
357011	**C2**	P	*C2*	EM	67661	74161	74061	67761
357012	**C2**	P	*C2*	EM	67662	74162	74062	67762
357013	**C2**	P	*C2*	EM	67663	74163	74063	67763
357014	**C2**	P	*C2*	EM	67664	74164	74064	67764
357015	**C2**	P	*C2*	EM	67665	74165	74065	67765
357016	**C2**	P	*C2*	EM	67666	74166	74066	67766
357017	**C2**	P	*C2*	EM	67667	74167	74067	67767
357018	**C2**	P	*C2*	EM	67668	74168	74068	67768
357019	**C2**	P	*C2*	EM	67669	74169	74069	67769
357020	**C2**	P	*C2*	EM	67670	74170	74070	67770

357021	**C2**	P	*C2*	EM	67671	74171	74071	67771
357022	**C2**	P	*C2*	EM	67672	74172	74072	67772
357023	**C2**	P	*C2*	EM	67673	74173	74073	67773
357024	**C2**	P	*C2*	EM	67674	74174	74074	67774
357025	**C2**	P	*C2*	EM	67675	74175	74075	67775
357026	**C2**	P	*C2*	EM	67676	74176	74076	67776
357027	**C2**	P	*C2*	EM	67677	74177	74077	67777
357028	**C2**	P	*C2*	EM	67678	74178	74078	67778
357029	**C2**	P	*C2*	EM	67679	74179	74079	67779
357030	**C2**	P	*C2*	EM	67680	74180	74080	67780
357031	**C2**	P	*C2*	EM	67681	74181	74081	67781
357032	**C2**	P	*C2*	EM	67682	74182	74082	67782
357033	**C2**	P	*C2*	EM	67683	74183	74083	67783
357034	**C2**	P	*C2*	EM	67684	74184	74084	67784
357035	**C2**	P	*C2*	EM	67685	74185	74085	67785
357036	**C2**	P	*C2*	EM	67686	74186	74086	67786
357037	**C2**	P	*C2*	EM	67687	74187	74087	67787
357038	**C2**	P	*C2*	EM	67688	74188	74088	67788
357039	**C2**	P	*C2*	EM	67689	74189	74089	67789
357040	**C2**	P	*C2*	EM	67690	74190	74090	67790
357041	**C2**	P	*C2*	EM	67691	74191	74091	67791
357042	**C2**	P	*C2*	EM	67692	74192	74092	67792
357043	**C2**	P	*C2*	EM	67693	74193	74093	67793
357044	**C2**	P	*C2*	EM	67694	74194	74094	67794
357045	**C2**	P	*C2*	EM	67695	74195	74095	67795
357046	**C2**	P	*C2*	EM	67696	74196	74096	67796

Names (carried on DMSO(A) and DMSO(B) (one plate on each)):

357001 BARRY FLAXMAN
357002 ARTHUR LEWIS STRIDE 1841–1922
357003 SOUTHEND city.on.sea
357004 TONY AMOS
357005 SOUTHEND: 2017 Alternative City of Culture
357006 DIAMOND JUBILEE 1952–2012
357011 JOHN LOWING
357028 London, Tilbury & Southend Railway 1854–2004
357029 THOMAS WHITELEGG 1840–1922
357030 ROBERT HARBEN WHITELEGG 1871–1957

Class 357/2. Owned by Angel Trains.

DMSO(A). Bombardier Derby 2001–02. –/71. 40.7 t.
MSO. Bombardier Derby 2001–02. –/78. 36.7 t.
PTSO. Bombardier Derby 2001–02. –/58(+4) 1TD 2W. 39.5 t.
DMSO(B). Bombardier Derby 2001–02. –/71. 40.7 t.

357201	**C2**	A	*C2*	EM	68601	74701	74601	68701
357202	**C2**	A	*C2*	EM	68602	74702	74602	68702
357203	**C2**	A	*C2*	EM	68603	74703	74603	68703
357204	**C2**	A	*C2*	EM	68604	74704	74604	68704
357205	**C2**	A	*C2*	EM	68605	74705	74605	68705
357206	**C2**	A	*C2*	EM	68606	74706	74606	68706

357207	**C2**	A	*C2*	EM	68607	74707	74607	68707
357208	**C2**	A	*C2*	EM	68608	74708	74608	68708
357209	**C2**	A	*C2*	EM	68609	74709	74609	68709
357210	**C2**	A	*C2*	EM	68610	74710	74610	68710
357211	**C2**	A	*C2*	EM	68611	74711	74611	68711

Names (carried on DMSO(A) and DMSO(B) (one plate on each)):

357201	KEN BIRD	357206	MARTIN AUNGIER
357202	KENNY MITCHELL	357207	JOHN PAGE
357203	HENRY PUMFRETT	357208	DAVE DAVIS
357204	DEREK FOWERS	357209	JAMES SNELLING
357205	JOHN D'SILVA		

Class 357/3. Owned by Angel Trains. In 2015–16 17 Class 357/2s (357 212–228) were reconfigured as "high density" units 357 312–328 with fewer seats and more standing room for shorter distance workings.

Seating Layout: 2+2 facing/unidirectional.

DMSO(A). Bombardier Derby 2001–02. –/56. 40.7 t.
MSO. Bombardier Derby 2001–02. –/60. 36.7 t.
PTSO. Bombardier Derby 2001–02. –/50 1TD 2W. 39.5 t.
DMSO(B). Bombardier Derby 2001–02. –/56. 40.7 t.

357312	(357212)	**C2**	A	*C2*	EM	68612	74712	74612	68712
357313	(357213)	**C2**	A	*C2*	EM	68613	74713	74613	68713
357314	(357214)	**C2**	A	*C2*	EM	68614	74714	74614	68714
357315	(357215)	**C2**	A	*C2*	EM	68615	74715	74615	68715
357316	(357216)	**C2**	A	*C2*	EM	68616	74716	74616	68716
357317	(357217)	**C2**	A	*C2*	EM	68617	74717	74617	68717
357318	(357218)	**C2**	A	*C2*	EM	68618	74718	74618	68718
357319	(357219)	**C2**	A	*C2*	EM	68619	74719	74619	68719
357320	(357220)	**C2**	A	*C2*	EM	68620	74720	74620	68720
357321	(357221)	**C2**	A	*C2*	EM	68621	74721	74621	68721
357322	(357222)	**C2**	A	*C2*	EM	68622	74722	74622	68722
357323	(357223)	**C2**	A	*C2*	EM	68623	74723	74623	68723
357324	(357224)	**C2**	A	*C2*	EM	68624	74724	74624	68724
357325	(357225)	**C2**	A	*C2*	EM	68625	74725	74625	68725
357326	(357226)	**C2**	A	*C2*	EM	68626	74726	74626	68726
357327	(357227)	**C2**	A	*C2*	EM	68627	74727	74627	68727
357328	(357228)	**C2**	A	*C2*	EM	68628	74728	74628	68728

Names (carried on DMSO(A) and DMSO(B) (one plate on each)):

357313 UPMINSTER I.E.C.C.
357317 ALLAN BURNELL
357327 SOUTHEND UNITED

CLASS 360/0   DESIRO UK   SIEMENS

Outer suburban/express units.

Formation: DMCO–PTSO–TSO–DMCO.
Construction: Welded aluminium.
Traction Motors: Four Siemens 1TB2016-0GB02 asynchronous of 250 kW.
Wheel Arrangement: Bo-Bo + 2-2 + 2-2 + Bo-Bo.
Braking: Disc & regenerative.   **Dimensions:** 20.34 x 2.80 m.
Bogies: SGP SF5000.   **Couplers:** Dellner 12.
Gangways: Within unit.   **Control System:** IGBT Inverter.
Doors: Sliding plug.   **Maximum Speed:** 100 mph.
Heating & ventilation: Air conditioning.
Seating Layout: 1: 2+2 facing, 2: 3+2 facing/unidirectional.
Multiple Working: Within class.

DMCO(A). Siemens Krefeld 2002–03. 8/59. 45.0 t.
PTSO. Siemens Vienna 2002–03. –/60(+9) 1TD 2W. 43.0 t.
TSO. Siemens Vienna 2002–03. –/78. 35.0 t.
DMCO(B). Siemens Krefeld 2002–03. 8/59. 45.0 t.

360 101	**FB**	A	*GA*	IL	65551	72551	74551	68551
360 102	**FB**	A	*GA*	IL	65552	72552	74552	68552
360 103	**FB**	A	*GA*	IL	65553	72553	74553	68553
360 104	**FB**	A	*GA*	IL	65554	72554	74554	68554
360 105	**FB**	A	*GA*	IL	65555	72555	74555	68555
360 106	**FB**	A	*GA*	IL	65556	72556	74556	68556
360 107	**FB**	A	*GA*	IL	65557	72557	74557	68557
360 108	**FB**	A	*GA*	IL	65558	72558	74558	68558
360 109	**FB**	A	*GA*	IL	65559	72559	74559	68559
360 110	**FB**	A	*GA*	IL	65560	72560	74560	68560
360 111	**FB**	A	*GA*	IL	65561	72561	74561	68561
360 112	**FB**	A	*GA*	IL	65562	72562	74562	68562
360 113	**FB**	A	*GA*	IL	65563	72563	74563	68563
360 114	**FB**	A	*GA*	IL	65564	72564	74564	68564
360 115	**FB**	A	*GA*	IL	65565	72565	74565	68565
360 116	**FB**	A	*GA*	IL	65566	72566	74566	68566
360 117	**FB**	A	*GA*	IL	65567	72567	74567	68567
360 118	**FB**	A	*GA*	IL	65568	72568	74568	68568
360 119	**FB**	A	*GA*	IL	65569	72569	74569	68569
360 120	**FB**	A	*GA*	IL	65570	72570	74570	68570
360 121	**FB**	A	*GA*	IL	65571	72571	74571	68571

CLASS 360/2   DESIRO UK   SIEMENS

4-car Class 350 testbed units rebuilt for use by Heathrow Express on Paddington–Heathrow Airport stopping services ("Heathrow Connect").

Original 4-car sets 360201–204 were made up to 5-cars during 2007 using additional TSOs. A fifth unit (360205) was delivered in late 2005 as a 5-car set. This set is normally used on Terminals 1&3–Terminal 4 shuttle services.

Formation: DMSO–PTSO–TSO–TSO–DMSO.
Construction: Welded aluminium.
Traction Motors: Four Siemens 1TB2016-0GB02 asynchronous of 250 kW.
Wheel Arrangement: Bo-Bo + 2-2 + 2-2 + 2-2 + Bo-Bo.
Braking: Disc & regenerative.   **Dimensions:** 20.34 x 2.80 m.
Bogies: SGP SF5000.   **Couplers:** Dellner 12.
Gangways: Within unit.   **Control System:** IGBT Inverter.
Doors: Sliding plug.   **Maximum Speed:** 100 mph.
Heating & ventilation: Air conditioning.
Seating Layout: 3+2 (* 2+2) facing/unidirectional.
Multiple Working: Within class.

DMSO(A). Siemens Krefeld 2002–06. –/63 (* –/54). 44.8 t.
PTSO. Siemens Krefeld 2002–06. –/57(+9) 1TD 2W (* –/48(+9) 2W). 44.2 t.
TSO. Siemens Krefeld 2005–06. –/74 (* –/62). 35.3 t.
TSO. Siemens Krefeld 2002–06. –/74 (* –/62). 34.1 t.
DMSO(B). Siemens Krefeld 2002–06. –/63 (* –/54). 44.4 t.

360201		**HC**	HE	*HC*	OH	78431	63421	72431	72421	78441
360202		**HC**	HE	*HC*	OH	78432	63422	72432	72422	78442
360203		**HC**	HE	*HC*	OH	78433	63423	72433	72423	78443
360204		**HC**	HE	*HC*	OH	78434	63424	72434	72424	78444
360205	*	**HE**	HE	*HE*	OH	78435	63425	72435	72425	78445

CLASS 365   NETWORKER EXPRESS   ABB YORK

Outer suburban units. All now fitted with a new universal access toilet to comply with the 2020 accessibility regulations.

Formations: DMCO–TSO–PTSO–DMCO.
Systems: 25 kV AC overhead but with 750 V DC third rail capability (units 365501–516 were formerly used on DC lines in the South-East).
Construction: Welded aluminium alloy.
Traction Motors: Four GEC-Alsthom G354CX asynchronous of 157 kW.
Wheel Arrangement: Bo-Bo + 2-2 + 2-2 + Bo-Bo.
Braking: Disc & rheostatic.   **Dimensions:** 20.89/20.06 x 2.81 m.
Bogies: ABB P3-16/T3-16.   **Couplers:** Tightlock.
Gangways: Within unit.   **Control System:** GTO Inverter.
Doors: Sliding plug.   **Maximum Speed:** 100 mph.
Seating Layout: 1: 2+2 facing, 2: 2+2 facing.
Multiple Working: Within class only.

DMCO(A). Lot No. 31133 1994–95. 12/56. 41.7 t.
TSO. Lot No. 31134 1994–95. –/58 1TD 2W 32.9 t.
PTSO. Lot No. 31135 1994–95. –/70 1T. 35.2 t.
DMCO(B). Lot No. 31136 1994–95. 12/56. 41.7 t.

365 501	**TL**	E	*GN*	HE	65894	72241	72240	65935
365 502	**TL**	E	*GN*	HE	65895	72243	72242	65936
365 503	**TL**	E	*GN*	HE	65896	72245	72244	65937
365 504	**TL**	E	*GN*	HE	65897	72247	72246	65938
365 505	**TL**	E	*GN*	HE	65898	72249	72248	65939
365 506	**TL**	E	*GN*	HE	65899	72251	72250	65940
365 507	**TL**	E	*GN*	HE	65900	72253	72252	65941
365 508	**TL**	E	*GN*	HE	65901	72255	72254	65942
365 509	**TL**	E	*GN*	HE	65902	72257	72256	65943
365 510	**TL**	E	*GN*	HE	65903	72259	72258	65944
365 511	**TL**	E	*GN*	HE	65904	72261	72260	65945
365 512	**TL**	E	*GN*	HE	65905	72263	72262	65946
365 513	**TL**	E	*GN*	HE	65906	72265	72264	65947
365 514	**TL**	E	*GN*	HE	65907	72267	72266	65948
365 515	**TL**	E	*GN*	HE	65908	72269	72268	65949
365 516	**TL**	E	*GN*	HE	65909	72271	72270	65950
365 517	**TL**	E	*GN*	HE	65910	72273	72272	65951
365 518	**TL**	E	*GN*	HE	65911	72275	72274	65952
365 519	**TL**	E	*GN*	HE	65912	72277	72276	65953
365 520	**TL**	E	*GN*	HE	65913	72279	72278	65954
365 521	**TL**	E	*GN*	HE	65914	72281	72280	65955
365 522	**TL**	E	*GN*	HE	65915	72283	72282	65956
365 523	**TL**	E	*GN*	HE	65916	72285	72284	65957
365 524	**TL**	E	*GN*	HE	65917	72287	72286	65958
365 525	**TL**	E	*GN*	HE	65918	72289	72288	65959
365 527	**TL**	E	*GN*	HE	65920	72293	72292	65961
365 528	**TL**	E	*GN*	HE	65921	72295	72294	65962
365 529	**TL**	E	*GN*	HE	65922	72297	72296	65963
365 530	**TL**	E	*GN*	HE	65923	72299	72298	65964
365 531	**TL**	E	*GN*	HE	65924	72301	72300	65965
365 532	**TL**	E	*GN*	HE	65925	72303	72302	65966
365 533	**TL**	E	*GN*	HE	65926	72305	72304	65967
365 534	**TL**	E	*GN*	HE	65927	72307	72306	65968
365 535	**TL**	E	*GN*	HE	65928	72309	72308	65969
365 536	**TL**	E	*GN*	HE	65929	72311	72310	65970
365 537	**TL**	E	*GN*	HE	65930	72313	72312	65971
365 538	**TL**	E	*GN*	HE	65931	72315	72314	65972
365 539	**TL**	E	*GN*	HE	65932	72317	72316	65973
365 540	**TL**	E	*GN*	HE	65933	72319	72318	65974
365 541	**TL**	E	*GN*	HE	65934	72321	72320	65975

Names (carried on each DMCO):

365 517 Supporting Red Balloon
365 533 Max Appeal
365 537 Daniel Edwards (1974–2010) Cambridge Driver

CLASS 375 ELECTROSTAR
ADTRANZ/BOMBARDIER DERBY

Express and outer suburban units.

Formations: Various.
Systems: 25 kV AC overhead/750 V DC third rail (some third rail only with provision for retro-fitting of AC equipment).
Construction: Welded aluminium alloy underframe, sides and roof with steel ends. All sections bolted together.
Traction Motors: Two Adtranz asynchronous of 250 kW.
Wheel Arrangement: 2-Bo(+ 2-Bo) + 2-2 + Bo-2.
Braking: Disc & regenerative.   **Dimensions:** 20.40/19.99 x 2.80 m.
Bogies: Adtranz P3-25/T3-25.   **Couplers:** Dellner 12.
Gangways: Throughout.   **Control System:** IGBT Inverter.
Doors: Sliding plug.   **Maximum Speed:** 100 mph.
Heating & ventilation: Air conditioning.
Seating Layout: 1: 2+2 facing/unidirectional. 2: 2+2 facing/unidirectional (except 375/9 – 3+2 facing/unidirectional).
Multiple Working: Within class and with Classes 376, 377, 378 and 379.

Class 375/3. Express units. 750 V DC only. DMSO–TSO–DMCO.

DMSO. Bombardier Derby 2001–02. –/60. 43.8 t.
TSO. Bombardier Derby 2001–02. –/56 1TD 2W. 35.5 t.
DMCO. Bombardier Derby 2001–02. 12/48. 43.8 t.

375 301	**SB**	E	*SE*	RM	67921	74351	67931
375 302	**SB**	E	*SE*	RM	67922	74352	67932
375 303	**SB**	E	*SE*	RM	67923	74353	67933
375 304	**SB**	E	*SE*	RM	67924	74354	67934
375 305	**SB**	E	*SE*	RM	67925	74355	67935
375 306	**SB**	E	*SE*	RM	67926	74356	67936
375 307	**SB**	E	*SE*	RM	67927	74357	67937
375 308	**SB**	E	*SE*	RM	67928	74358	67938
375 309	**SB**	E	*SE*	RM	67929	74359	67939
375 310	**SB**	E	*SE*	RM	67930	74360	67940

Class 375/6. Express units. 25 kV AC/750 V DC. DMSO–MCO–PTSO–DMSO.

DMSO(A). Adtranz Derby 1999–2001. –/60. 46.2 t.
MCO. Adtranz Derby 1999–2001. 16/50 1T. 40.5 t.
PTSO. Adtranz Derby 1999–2001. –/56 1TD 2W. 40.7 t.
DMSO(B). Adtranz Derby 1999–2001. –/60. 46.2 t.

375 601	**SB**	E	*SE*	RM	67801	74251	74201	67851
375 602	**SB**	E	*SE*	RM	67802	74252	74202	67852
375 603	**SB**	E	*SE*	RM	67803	74253	74203	67853
375 604	**SB**	E	*SE*	RM	67804	74254	74204	67854
375 605	**SB**	E	*SE*	RM	67805	74255	74205	67855
375 606	**SB**	E	*SE*	RM	67806	74256	74206	67856
375 607	**SB**	E	*SE*	RM	67807	74257	74207	67857
375 608	**SB**	E	*SE*	RM	67808	74258	74208	67858

375 609	**SB**	E	*SE*	RM	67809	74259	74209	67859
375 610	**SB**	E	*SE*	RM	67810	74260	74210	67860
375 611	**SB**	E	*SE*	RM	67811	74261	74211	67861
375 612	**SB**	E	*SE*	RM	67812	74262	74212	67862
375 613	**SB**	E	*SE*	RM	67813	74263	74213	67863
375 614	**SB**	E	*SE*	RM	67814	74264	74214	67864
375 615	**SB**	E	*SE*	RM	67815	74265	74215	67865
375 616	**SB**	E	*SE*	RM	67816	74266	74216	67866
375 617	**SB**	E	*SE*	RM	67817	74267	74217	67867
375 618	**SB**	E	*SE*	RM	67818	74268	74218	67868
375 619	**SB**	E	*SE*	RM	67819	74269	74219	67869
375 620	**SB**	E	*SE*	RM	67820	74270	74220	67870
375 621	**SB**	E	*SE*	RM	67821	74271	74221	67871
375 622	**SB**	E	*SE*	RM	67822	74272	74222	67872
375 623	**SB**	E	*SE*	RM	67823	74273	74223	67873
375 624	**SB**	E	*SE*	RM	67824	74274	74224	67874
375 625	**SB**	E	*SE*	RM	67825	74275	74225	67875
375 626	**SB**	E	*SE*	RM	67826	74276	74226	67876
375 627	**SB**	E	*SE*	RM	67827	74277	74227	67877
375 628	**SB**	E	*SE*	RM	67828	74278	74228	67878
375 629	**SB**	E	*SE*	RM	67829	74279	74229	67879
375 630	**SB**	E	*SE*	RM	67830	74280	74230	67880

Class 375/7. Express units. 750 V DC only. DMCO–MSO–TSO–DMCO.

DMSO(A). Bombardier Derby 2001–02. –/60. 43.8 t.
MCO. Bombardier Derby 2001–02. 16/50 1T. 36.4 t.
TSO. Bombardier Derby 2001–02. –/56 1TD 2W. 34.1 t.
DMSO(B). Bombardier Derby 2001–02. –/60. 43.8 t.

375 701	**SB**	E	*SE*	RM	67831	74281	74231	67881
375 702	**SB**	E	*SE*	RM	67832	74282	74232	67882
375 703	**SB**	E	*SE*	RM	67833	74283	74233	67883
375 704	**SB**	E	*SE*	RM	67834	74284	74234	67884
375 705	**SB**	E	*SE*	RM	67835	74285	74235	67885
375 706	**SB**	E	*SE*	RM	67836	74286	74236	67886
375 707	**SB**	E	*SE*	RM	67837	74287	74237	67887
375 708	**SB**	E	*SE*	RM	67838	74288	74238	67888
375 709	**SB**	E	*SE*	RM	67839	74289	74239	67889
375 710	**SB**	E	*SE*	RM	67840	74290	74240	67890
375 711	**SB**	E	*SE*	RM	67841	74291	74241	67891
375 712	**SB**	E	*SE*	RM	67842	74292	74242	67892
375 713	**SB**	E	*SE*	RM	67843	74293	74243	67893
375 714	**SB**	E	*SE*	RM	67844	74294	74244	67894
375 715	**SB**	E	*SE*	RM	67845	74295	74245	67895

Names (carried on one side of each MSO or TSO):

375 701 Kent Air Ambulance Explorer
375 710 Rochester Castle
375 714 Rochester Cathedral

Class 375/8. Express units. 750 V DC only. DMCO–MSO–TSO–DMCO.

375 801–820 are fitted with de-icing equipment. TSO weighs 36.5 t.

DMCO(A). Bombardier Derby 2004. 12/48 († –/60). 43.3 t.
MSO. Bombardier Derby 2004. –/66 1T († 16/50 1T). 39.8 t.
TSO. Bombardier Derby 2004. –/52 1TD 2W. 35.9 t.
DMCO(B). Bombardier Derby 2004. 12/52 († –/64). 43.3 t.

375 801	†	**SB**	E	*SE*	RM	73301	79001	78201	73701
375 802	†	**SB**	E	*SE*	RM	73302	79002	78202	73702
375 803	†	**SB**	E	*SE*	RM	73303	79003	78203	73703
375 804	†	**SB**	E	*SE*	RM	73304	79004	78204	73704
375 805	†	**SB**	E	*SE*	RM	73305	79005	78205	73705
375 806	†	**SB**	E	*SE*	RM	73306	79006	78206	73706
375 807	†	**SB**	E	*SE*	RM	73307	79007	78207	73707
375 808		**CN**	E	*SE*	RM	73308	79008	78208	73708
375 809		**CN**	E	*SE*	RM	73309	79009	78209	73709
375 810		**CN**	E	*SE*	RM	73310	79010	78210	73710
375 811		**CN**	E	*SE*	RM	73311	79011	78211	73711
375 812		**CN**	E	*SE*	RM	73312	79012	78212	73712
375 813		**CN**	E	*SE*	RM	73313	79013	78213	73713
375 814		**CN**	E	*SE*	RM	73314	79014	78214	73714
375 815		**CN**	E	*SE*	RM	73315	79015	78215	73715
375 816		**CN**	E	*SE*	RM	73316	79016	78216	73716
375 817		**CN**	E	*SE*	RM	73317	79017	78217	73717
375 818		**CN**	E	*SE*	RM	73318	79018	78218	73718
375 819		**CN**	E	*SE*	RM	73319	79019	78219	73719
375 820		**CN**	E	*SE*	RM	73320	79020	78220	73720
375 821		**CN**	E	*SE*	RM	73321	79021	78221	73721
375 822		**CN**	E	*SE*	RM	73322	79022	78222	73722
375 823		**CN**	E	*SE*	RM	73323	79023	78223	73723
375 824		**CN**	E	*SE*	RM	73324	79024	78224	73724
375 825		**CN**	E	*SE*	RM	73325	79025	78225	73725
375 826		**CN**	E	*SE*	RM	73326	79026	78226	73726
375 827		**CN**	E	*SE*	RM	73327	79027	78227	73727
375 828		**CN**	E	*SE*	RM	73328	79028	78228	73728
375 829		**CN**	E	*SE*	RM	73329	79029	78229	73729
375 830		**CN**	E	*SE*	RM	73330	79030	78230	73730

Name (carried on one side of each MSO or TSO):

375 830 City of London

Class 375/9. Outer suburban units. 750 V DC only. DMCO–MSO–TSO–DMCO.

DMCO(A). Bombardier Derby 2003–04. 12/59. 43.4 t.
MSO. Bombardier Derby 2003–04. –/73 1T. 39.3 t.
TSO. Bombardier Derby 2003–04. –/62 1TD 2W. 35.6 t.
DMCO(B). Bombardier Derby 2003–04. 12/59. 43.4 t.

375 901		**CN**	E	*SE*	RM	73331	79031	79061	73731
375 902		**CN**	E	*SE*	RM	73332	79032	79062	73732
375 903		**CN**	E	*SE*	RM	73333	79033	79063	73733
375 904		**CN**	E	*SE*	RM	73334	79034	79064	73734

375905	CN	E	SE	RM	73335	79035	79065	73735
375906	SB	E	SE	RM	73336	79036	79066	73736
375907	SB	E	SE	RM	73337	79037	79067	73737
375908	SB	E	SE	RM	73338	79038	79068	73738
375909	SB	E	SE	RM	73339	79039	79069	73739
375910	CN	E	SE	RM	73340	79040	79070	73740
375911	CN	E	SE	RM	73341	79041	79071	73741
375912	CN	E	SE	RM	73342	79042	79072	73742
375913	CN	E	SE	RM	73343	79043	79073	73743
375914	CN	E	SE	RM	73344	79044	79074	73744
375915	CN	E	SE	RM	73345	79045	79075	73745
375916	CN	E	SE	RM	73346	79046	79076	73746
375917	CN	E	SE	RM	73347	79047	79077	73747
375918	SB	E	SE	RM	73348	79048	79078	73748
375919	CN	E	SE	RM	73349	79049	79079	73749
375920	CN	E	SE	RM	73350	79050	79080	73750
375921	CN	E	SE	RM	73351	79051	79081	73751
375922	CN	E	SE	RM	73352	79052	79082	73752
375923	CN	E	SE	RM	73353	79053	79083	73753
375924	SB	E	SE	RM	73354	79054	79084	73754
375925	CN	E	SE	RM	73355	79055	79085	73755
375926	CN	E	SE	RM	73356	79056	79086	73756
375927	CN	E	SE	RM	73357	79057	79087	73757

CLASS 376   ELECTROSTAR   BOMBARDIER DERBY

Inner suburban units.

Formation: DMSO–MSO–TSO–MSO–DMSO.
System: 750 V DC third rail.
Construction: Welded aluminium alloy underframe, sides and roof with steel ends. All sections bolted together.
Traction Motors: Two Bombardier asynchronous of 200 kW.
Wheel Arrangement: 2-Bo + 2-Bo + 2-2 + Bo-2 + Bo-2.
Braking: Disc & regenerative.   **Dimensions:** 20.40/19.99 x 2.80 m.
Bogies: Bombardier P3-25/T3-25.   **Couplers:** Dellner 12.
Gangways: Within unit.   **Control System:** IGBT Inverter.
Doors: Sliding.   **Maximum Speed:** 75 mph.
Heating & ventilation: Pressure heating and ventilation.
Seating Layout: 2+2 low density facing.
Multiple Working: Within class and with Classes 375, 377, 378 and 379.

DMSO(A). Bombardier Derby 2004–05. –/36(+6) 1W. 42.1 t.
MSO. Bombardier Derby 2004–05. –/48. 36.2 t.
TSO. Bombardier Derby 2004–05. –/48. 36.3 t.
DMSO(B). Bombardier Derby 2004–05. –/36(+6) 1W. 42.1 t.

376001	CN	E	SE	SG	61101	63301	64301	63501	61601
376002	CN	E	SE	SG	61102	63302	64302	63502	61602
376003	CN	E	SE	SG	61103	63303	64303	63503	61603
376004	CN	E	SE	SG	61104	63304	64304	63504	61604
376005	CN	E	SE	SG	61105	63305	64305	63505	61605

376 006	**CN**	E	*SE*	SG	61106	63306	64306	63506	61606
376 007	**CN**	E	*SE*	SG	61107	63307	64307	63507	61607
376 008	**CN**	E	*SE*	SG	61108	63308	64308	63508	61608
376 009	**CN**	E	*SE*	SG	61109	63309	64309	63509	61609
376 010	**CN**	E	*SE*	SG	61110	63310	64310	63510	61610
376 011	**CN**	E	*SE*	SG	61111	63311	64311	63511	61611
376 012	**CN**	E	*SE*	SG	61112	63312	64312	63512	61612
376 013	**CN**	E	*SE*	SG	61113	63313	64313	63513	61613
376 014	**CN**	E	*SE*	SG	61114	63314	64314	63514	61614
376 015	**CN**	E	*SE*	SG	61115	63315	64315	63515	61615
376 016	**CN**	E	*SE*	SG	61116	63316	64316	63516	61616
376 017	**CN**	E	*SE*	SG	61117	63317	64317	63517	61617
376 018	**CN**	E	*SE*	SG	61118	63318	64318	63518	61618
376 019	**CN**	E	*SE*	SG	61119	63319	64319	63519	61619
376 020	**CN**	E	*SE*	SG	61120	63320	64320	63520	61620
376 021	**CN**	E	*SE*	SG	61121	63321	64321	63521	61621
376 022	**CN**	E	*SE*	SG	61122	63322	64322	63522	61622
376 023	**CN**	E	*SE*	SG	61123	63323	64323	63523	61623
376 024	**CN**	E	*SE*	SG	61124	63324	64324	63524	61624
376 025	**CN**	E	*SE*	SG	61125	63325	64325	63525	61625
376 026	**CN**	E	*SE*	SG	61126	63326	64326	63526	61626
376 027	**CN**	E	*SE*	SG	61127	63327	64327	63527	61627
376 028	**CN**	E	*SE*	SG	61128	63328	64328	63528	61628
376 029	**CN**	E	*SE*	SG	61129	63329	64329	63529	61629
376 030	**CN**	E	*SE*	SG	61130	63330	64330	63530	61630
376 031	**CN**	E	*SE*	SG	61131	63331	64331	63531	61631
376 032	**CN**	E	*SE*	SG	61132	63332	64332	63532	61632
376 033	**CN**	E	*SE*	SG	61133	63333	64333	63533	61633
376 034	**CN**	E	*SE*	SG	61134	63334	64334	63534	61634
376 035	**CN**	E	*SE*	SG	61135	63335	64335	63535	61635
376 036	**CN**	E	*SE*	SG	61136	63336	64336	63536	61636

CLASS 377　ELECTROSTAR　BOMBARDIER DERBY

Express and outer suburban units.

Formations: Various.
Systems: 25 kV AC overhead/750 V DC third rail or third rail only with provision for retro-fitting of AC equipment.
Construction: Welded aluminium alloy underframe, sides and roof with steel ends. All sections bolted together.
Traction Motors: Two Bombardier asynchronous of 250 kW.
Wheel Arrangement: 2-Bo + 2-2 + Bo-2 or 2-Bo + 2-Bo + 2-2 + Bo-2 or 2-Bo + 2-Bo + 2-2 + Bo-2 + Bo-2.

Braking: Disc & regenerative.	**Dimensions:** 20.39/20.00 x 2.80 m.
Bogies: Bombardier P3-25/T3-25.	**Couplers:** Dellner 12.
Gangways: Throughout.	**Control System:** IGBT Inverter.
Doors: Sliding plug.	**Maximum Speed:** 100 mph.

Heating & ventilation: Air conditioning.
Seating Layout: Various, see sub-class headings.
Multiple Working: Within class and with Classes 375, 376, 378, 379 and 387.

Class 377/1. 750 V DC only. DMCO–MSO–TSO–DMCO.
Seating layout: 1: 2+2 facing/unidirectional, 2: 2+2 facing/unidirectional (377 101–119), 3+2/2+2 facing/unidirectional (377 120–139), 3+2 (middle cars and 2+2 (end cars) facing/unidirectional (377 140–164).

DMCO(A). Bombardier Derby 2002–03. 12/48 (s 12/56). 44.8 t.
MSO. Bombardier Derby 2002–03. –/62 (s –/70, t –/69). 1T. 39.0 t.
TSO. Bombardier Derby 2002–03. –/52 (s –/60, t –/57). 1TD 2W. 35.4 t.
DMCO(B). Bombardier Derby 2002–03. 12/48 (s 12/56). 43.4 t.

377 101		**SN**	P	*SN*	SU	78501	77101	78901	78701
377 102		**SN**	P	*SN*	SU	78502	77102	78902	78702
377 103		**SN**	P	*SN*	SU	78503	77103	78903	78703
377 104		**SN**	P	*SN*	SU	78504	77104	78904	78704
377 105		**SN**	P	*SN*	SU	78505	77105	78905	78705
377 106		**SN**	P	*SN*	SU	78506	77106	78906	78706
377 107		**SN**	P	*SN*	SU	78507	77107	78907	78707
377 108		**SN**	P	*SN*	SU	78508	77108	78908	78708
377 109		**SN**	P	*SN*	SU	78509	77109	78909	78709
377 110		**SN**	P	*SN*	SU	78510	77110	78910	78710
377 111		**SN**	P	*SN*	SU	78511	77111	78911	78711
377 112		**SN**	P	*SN*	SU	78512	77112	78912	78712
377 113		**SN**	P	*SN*	SU	78513	77113	78913	78713
377 114		**SN**	P	*SN*	SU	78514	77114	78914	78714
377 115		**SN**	P	*SN*	SU	78515	77115	78915	78715
377 116		**SN**	P	*SN*	SU	78516	77116	78916	78716
377 117		**SN**	P	*SN*	SU	78517	77117	78917	78717
377 118		**SN**	P	*SN*	SU	78518	77118	78918	78718
377 119		**SN**	P	*SN*	SU	78519	77119	78919	78719
377 120	s	**SN**	P	*SN*	SU	78520	77120	78920	78720
377 121	s	**SN**	P	*SN*	SU	78521	77121	78921	78721
377 122	s	**SN**	P	*SN*	SU	78522	77122	78922	78722
377 123	s	**SN**	P	*SN*	SU	78523	77123	78923	78723
377 124	s	**SN**	P	*SN*	SU	78524	77124	78924	78724
377 125	s	**SN**	P	*SN*	SU	78525	77125	78925	78725
377 126	s	**SN**	P	*SN*	SU	78526	77126	78926	78726
377 127	s	**SN**	P	*SN*	SU	78527	77127	78927	78727
377 128	s	**SN**	P	*SN*	SU	78528	77128	78928	78728
377 129	s	**SN**	P	*SN*	SU	78529	77129	78929	78729
377 130	s	**SN**	P	*SN*	SU	78530	77130	78930	78730
377 131	s	**SN**	P	*SN*	SU	78531	77131	78931	78731
377 132	s	**SN**	P	*SN*	SU	78532	77132	78932	78732
377 133	s	**SN**	P	*SN*	SU	78533	77133	78933	78733
377 134	s	**SN**	P	*SN*	SU	78534	77134	78934	78734
377 135	s	**SN**	P	*SN*	SU	78535	77135	78935	78735
377 136	s	**SN**	P	*SN*	SU	78536	77136	78936	78736
377 137	s	**SN**	P	*SN*	SU	78537	77137	78937	78737
377 138	s	**SN**	P	*SN*	SU	78538	77138	78938	78738
377 139	s	**SN**	P	*SN*	SU	78539	77139	78939	78739
377 140	t	**SN**	P	*SN*	SU	78540	77140	78940	78740
377 141	t	**SN**	P	*SN*	SU	78541	77141	78941	78741
377 142	t	**SN**	P	*SN*	SU	78542	77142	78942	78742

377 143	t	**SN**	P	*SN*	SU	78543	77143	78943	78743
377 144	t	**SN**	P	*SN*	SU	78544	77144	78944	78744
377 145	t	**SN**	P	*SN*	SU	78545	77145	78945	78745
377 146	t	**SN**	P	*SN*	SU	78546	77146	78946	78746
377 147	t	**SN**	P	*SN*	SU	78547	77147	78947	78747
377 148	t	**SN**	P	*SN*	SU	78548	77148	78948	78748
377 149	t	**SN**	P	*SN*	SU	78549	77149	78949	78749
377 150	t	**SN**	P	*SN*	SU	78550	77150	78950	78750
377 151	t	**SN**	P	*SN*	SU	78551	77151	78951	78751
377 152	t	**SN**	P	*SN*	SU	78552	77152	78952	78752
377 153	t	**SN**	P	*SN*	SU	78553	77153	78953	78753
377 154	t	**SN**	P	*SN*	SU	78554	77154	78954	78754
377 155	t	**SN**	P	*SN*	SU	78555	77155	78955	78755
377 156	t	**SN**	P	*SN*	SU	78556	77156	78956	78756
377 157	t	**SN**	P	*SN*	SU	78557	77157	78957	78757
377 158	t	**SN**	P	*SN*	SU	78558	77158	78958	78758
377 159	t	**SN**	P	*SN*	SU	78559	77159	78959	78759
377 160	t	**SN**	P	*SN*	SU	78560	77160	78960	78760
377 161	t	**SN**	P	*SN*	SU	78561	77161	78961	78761
377 162	t	**SN**	P	*SN*	SU	78562	77162	78962	78762
377 163	t	**SN**	P	*SN*	SU	78563	77163	78963	78763
377 164	t	**SN**	P	*SN*	SU	78564	77164	78964	78764

Class 377/2. 25 kV AC/750 V DC. DMCO–MSO–PTSO–DMCO. Dual-voltage units. **Seating layout:** 1: 2+2 facing/unidirectional, 2: 2+2 and 3+2 facing/ unidirectional (3+2 seating in middle cars only).

DMCO(A). Bombardier Derby 2003–04. 12/48. 44.2 t.
MSO. Bombardier Derby 2003–04. –/69 1T. 39.8 t.
PTSO. Bombardier Derby 2003–04. –/57 1TD 2W. 40.1 t.
DMCO(B). Bombardier Derby 2003–04. 12/48. 44.2 t.

377 201		**SN**	P	*SN*	SU	78571	77171	78971	78771
377 202		**SN**	P	*SN*	SU	78572	77172	78972	78772
377 203		**SN**	P	*SN*	SU	78573	77173	78973	78773
377 204		**SN**	P	*SN*	SU	78574	77174	78974	78774
377 205		**SN**	P	*SN*	SU	78575	77175	78975	78775
377 206		**SN**	P	*SN*	SU	78576	77176	78976	78776
377 207		**FU**	P	*TL*	BF	78577	77177	78977	78777
377 208		**SN**	P	*TL*	BF	78578	77178	78978	78778
377 209		**SN**	P	*TL*	BF	78579	77179	78979	78779
377 210		**SN**	P	*TL*	BF	78580	77180	78980	78780
377 211		**FU**	P	*TL*	BF	78581	77181	78981	78781
377 212		**FU**	P	*TL*	BF	78582	77182	78982	78782
377 213		**SN**	P	*TL*	BF	78583	77183	78983	78783
377 214		**SN**	P	*TL*	BF	78584	77184	78984	78784
377 215		**SN**	P	*TL*	BF	78585	77185	78985	78785

Class 377/3. 750 V DC only. DMCO–TSO–DMCO.
Seating Layout: 1: 2+2 facing/unidirectional, 2: 2+2 facing/unidirectional.

Units built as Class 375, but renumbered in the Class 377/3 range when fitted with Dellner couplers.

377342 was formerly 377442. It had been reformed as a 3-car unit owing to fire damage to MSO vehicle 78842 in November 2016.

DMCO(A). Bombardier Derby 2001–02. 12/48. 43.5 t.
TSO. Bombardier Derby 2001–02. –/56 1TD 2W. 35.4 t.
DMCO(B). Bombardier Derby 2001–02. 12/48. 43.5 t.

377301	(375311)	**SN**	P	*SN*	SU	68201	74801	68401
377302	(375312)	**SN**	P	*SN*	SU	68202	74802	68402
377303	(375313)	**SN**	P	*SN*	SU	68203	74803	68403
377304	(375314)	**SN**	P	*SN*	SU	68204	74804	68404
377305	(375315)	**SN**	P	*SN*	SU	68205	74805	68405
377306	(375316)	**SN**	P	*SN*	SU	68206	74806	68406
377307	(375317)	**SN**	P	*SN*	SU	68207	74807	68407
377308	(375318)	**SN**	P	*SN*	SU	68208	74808	68408
377309	(375319)	**SN**	P	*SN*	SU	68209	74809	68409
377310	(375320)	**SN**	P	*SN*	SU	68210	74810	68410
377311	(375321)	**SN**	P	*SN*	SU	68211	74811	68411
377312	(375322)	**SN**	P	*SN*	SU	68212	74812	68412
377313	(375323)	**SN**	P	*SN*	SU	68213	74813	68413
377314	(375324)	**SN**	P	*SN*	SU	68214	74814	68414
377315	(375325)	**SN**	P	*SN*	SU	68215	74815	68415
377316	(375326)	**SN**	P	*SN*	SU	68216	74816	68416
377317	(375327)	**SN**	P	*SN*	SU	68217	74817	68417
377318	(375328)	**SN**	P	*SN*	SU	68218	74818	68418
377319	(375329)	**SN**	P	*SN*	SU	68219	74819	68419
377320	(375330)	**SN**	P	*SN*	SU	68220	74820	68420
377321	(375331)	**SN**	P	*SN*	SU	68221	74821	68421
377322	(375332)	**SN**	P	*SN*	SU	68222	74822	68422
377323	(375333)	**SN**	P	*SN*	SU	68223	74823	68423
377324	(375334)	**SN**	P	*SN*	SU	68224	74824	68424
377325	(375335)	**SN**	P	*SN*	SU	68225	74825	68425
377326	(375336)	**SN**	P	*SN*	SU	68226	74826	68426
377327	(375337)	**SN**	P	*SN*	SU	68227	74827	68427
377328	(375338)	**SN**	P	*SN*	SU	68228	74828	68428
377328	(375338)	**SN**	P	*SN*	SU	68228	74828	68428
377342	(377442)	**SN**	P	*SN*	SU	73442	78642	73842

Class 377/4. 750 V DC only. DMCO–MSO–TSO–DMCO.
Seating Layout: 1: 2+2 facing/two seats longitudinal, 2: 2+2 and 3+2 facing/unidirectional (3+2 seating in middle cars only).

DMCO(A). Bombardier Derby 2004–05. 10/48. 43.1 t.
MSO. Bombardier Derby 2004–05. –/69 1T. 39.3 t.
TSO. Bombardier Derby 2004–05. –/56 1TD 2W. 35.3 t.
DMCO(B). Bombardier Derby 2004–05. 10/48. 43.2 t.

377401	**SN**	P	*SN*	SU	73401	78801	78601	73801
377402	**SN**	P	*SN*	SU	73402	78802	78602	73802
377403	**SN**	P	*SN*	SU	73403	78803	78603	73803
377404	**SN**	P	*SN*	SU	73404	78804	78604	73804
377405	**SN**	P	*SN*	SU	73405	78805	78605	73805
377406	**SN**	P	*SN*	SU	73406	78806	78606	73806

377 407	**SN**	P	*SN*	SU	73407	78807	78607	73807
377 408	**SN**	P	*SN*	SU	73408	78808	78608	73808
377 409	**SN**	P	*SN*	SU	73409	78809	78609	73809
377 410	**SN**	P	*SN*	SU	73410	78810	78610	73810
377 411	**SN**	P	*SN*	SU	73411	78811	78611	73811
377 412	**SN**	P	*SN*	SU	73412	78812	78612	73812
377 413	**SN**	P	*SN*	SU	73413	78813	78613	73813
377 414	**SN**	P	*SN*	SU	73414	78814	78614	73814
377 415	**SN**	P	*SN*	SU	73415	78815	78615	73815
377 416	**SN**	P	*SN*	SU	73416	78816	78616	73816
377 417	**SN**	P	*SN*	SU	73417	78817	78617	73817
377 418	**SN**	P	*SN*	SU	73418	78818	78618	73818
377 419	**SN**	P	*SN*	SU	73419	78819	78619	73819
377 420	**SN**	P	*SN*	SU	73420	78820	78620	73820
377 421	**SN**	P	*SN*	SU	73421	78821	78621	73821
377 422	**SN**	P	*SN*	SU	73422	78822	78622	73822
377 423	**SN**	P	*SN*	SU	73423	78823	78623	73823
377 424	**SN**	P	*SN*	SU	73424	78824	78624	73824
377 425	**SN**	P	*SN*	SU	73425	78825	78625	73825
377 426	**SN**	P	*SN*	SU	73426	78826	78626	73826
377 427	**SN**	P	*SN*	SU	73427	78827	78627	73827
377 428	**SN**	P	*SN*	SU	73428	78828	78628	73828
377 429	**SN**	P	*SN*	SU	73429	78829	78629	73829
377 430	**SN**	P	*SN*	SU	73430	78830	78630	73830
377 431	**SN**	P	*SN*	SU	73431	78831	78631	73831
377 432	**SN**	P	*SN*	SU	73432	78832	78632	73832
377 433	**SN**	P	*SN*	SU	73433	78833	78633	73833
377 434	**SN**	P	*SN*	SU	73434	78834	78634	73834
377 435	**SN**	P	*SN*	SU	73435	78835	78635	73835
377 436	**SN**	P	*SN*	SU	73436	78836	78636	73836
377 437	**SN**	P	*SN*	SU	73437	78837	78637	73837
377 438	**SN**	P	*SN*	SU	73438	78838	78638	73838
377 439	**SN**	P	*SN*	SU	73439	78839	78639	73839
377 440	**SN**	P	*SN*	SU	73440	78840	78640	73840
377 441	**SN**	P	*SN*	SU	73441	78841	78641	73841
377 443	**SN**	P	*SN*	SU	73443	78843	78643	73843
377 444	**SN**	P	*SN*	SU	73444	78844	78644	73844
377 445	**SN**	P	*SN*	SU	73445	78845	78645	73845
377 446	**SN**	P	*SN*	SU	73446	78846	78646	73846
377 447	**SN**	P	*SN*	SU	73447	78847	78647	73847
377 448	**SN**	P	*SN*	SU	73448	78848	78648	73848
377 449	**SN**	P	*SN*	SU	73449	78849	78649	73849
377 450	**SN**	P	*SN*	SU	73450	78850	78650	73850
377 451	**SN**	P	*SN*	SU	73451	78851	78651	73851
377 452	**SN**	P	*SN*	SU	73452	78852	78652	73852
377 453	**SN**	P	*SN*	SU	73453	78853	78653	73853
377 454	**SN**	P	*SN*	SU	73454	78854	78654	73854
377 455	**SN**	P	*SN*	SU	73455	78855	78655	73855
377 456	**SN**	P	*SN*	SU	73456	78856	78656	73856
377 457	**SN**	P	*SN*	SU	73457	78857	78657	73857
377 458	**SN**	P	*SN*	SU	73458	78858	78658	73858

377 459	**SN**	P	*SN*	SU	73459	78859	78659	73859
377 460	**SN**	P	*SN*	SU	73460	78860	78660	73860
377 461	**SN**	P	*SN*	SU	73461	78861	78661	73861
377 462	**SN**	P	*SN*	SU	73462	78862	78662	73862
377 463	**SN**	P	*SN*	SU	73463	78863	78663	73863
377 464	**SN**	P	*SN*	SU	73464	78864	78664	73864
377 465	**SN**	P	*SN*	SU	73465	78865	78665	73865
377 466	**SN**	P	*SN*	SU	73466	78866	78666	73866
377 467	**SN**	P	*SN*	SU	73467	78867	78667	73867
377 468	**SN**	P	*SN*	SU	73468	78868	78668	73868
377 469	**SN**	P	*SN*	SU	73469	78869	78669	73869
377 470	**SN**	P	*SN*	SU	73470	78870	78670	73870
377 471	**SN**	P	*SN*	SU	73471	78871	78671	73871
377 472	**SN**	P	*SN*	SU	73472	78872	78672	73872
377 473	**SN**	P	*SN*	SU	73473	78873	78673	73873
377 474	**SN**	P	*SN*	SU	73474	78874	78674	73874
377 475	**SN**	P	*SN*	SU	73475	78875	78675	73875
Spare	**SN**	P		ZN	78842			

Class 377/5. 25 kV AC/750 V DC. DMCO–MSO–PTSO–DMSO. Dual-voltage units. Details as Class 377/2 unless stated.

DMCO. Bombardier Derby 2008–09. 10/48. 43.1t.
MSO. Bombardier Derby 2008–09. –/69 1T. 40.3t.
PTSO. Bombardier Derby 2008–09. –/56 1TD 2W. 40.6 t.
DMSO. Bombardier Derby 2008–09. –/58. 44.9t.

377 501	**FB**	P	*SE*	SU	73501	75901	74901	73601
377 502	**FB**	P	*SE*	SU	73502	75902	74902	73602
377 503	**FB**	P	*SE*	SU	73503	75903	74903	73603
377 504	**FB**	P	*SE*	SU	73504	75904	74904	73604
377 505	**FB**	P	*SE*	SU	73505	75905	74905	73605
377 506	**FB**	P	*SE*	SU	73506	75906	74906	73606
377 507	**FB**	P	*SE*	SU	73507	75907	74907	73607
377 508	**FB**	P	*SE*	SU	73508	75908	74908	73608
377 509	**FB**	P	*TL*	SU	73509	75909	74909	73609
377 510	**FB**	P	*TL*	SU	73510	75910	74910	73610
377 511	**FB**	P	*TL*	SU	73511	75911	74911	73611
377 512	**FB**	P	*TL*	SU	73512	75912	74912	73612
377 513	**FB**	P	*TL*	SU	73513	75913	74913	73613
377 514	**FB**	P	*TL*	SU	73514	75914	74914	73614
377 515	**FB**	P	*TL*	SU	73515	75915	74915	73615
377 516	**FB**	P	*TL*	SU	73516	75916	74916	73616
377 517	**FB**	P	*TL*	SU	73517	75917	74917	73617
377 518	**FB**	P	*TL*	SU	73518	75918	74918	73618
377 519	**FB**	P	*TL*	SU	73519	75919	74919	73619
377 520	**FB**	P	*TL*	SU	73520	75920	74920	73620
377 521	**FB**	P	*TL*	SU	73521	75921	74921	73621
377 522	**FB**	P	*TL*	SU	73522	75922	74922	73622
377 523	**FB**	P	*TL*	SU	73523	75923	74923	73623

▲ Southern-liveried 313 204 leaves Lewes with the 14.17 Brighton–Seaford on 01/02/15. **Robert Pritchard**

▼ Still in Strathclyde PTE livery, 314 206 is seen on the outskirts of Neilston with the 12.30 Neilston–Glasgow Central on 10/05/16. **Stuart Fowler**

▲ London Overground-liveried 317 714 leads the 16.40 Chingford–London Liverpool Street through Hackney Central on 09/06/16. **Antony Guppy**

▼ Thameslink-liveried 319 444 arrives at Luton with the 16.37 from Sutton on 28/07/16. **Robert Pritchard**

▲ ScotRail Saltire-liveried 320 417 and 320 415 (both renumbered 321/4s) approach Lanark with the 16.50 from Glasgow Central on 26/08/16. **Robin Ralston**

▼ London Midland-liveried 323 243 calls at Tipton with the 12.20 Wolverhampton–Walsall on 14/03/16. **John Binch**

▲ Heathrow Express 332 008 stands at London Paddington with the 09.10 to Heathrow Airport on 06/08/16. **Alex Dasi-Sutton**

▼ ScotRail Saltire-liveried 334 033 and 334 001 pass Shettleston with the 10.23 Milngavie–Edinburgh Waverley on 11/09/15. **Robert Pritchard**

▲ Brand new Crossrail unit 345 001, in 7-car formation as the first 15 units will be delivered, is seen on the test track at Bombardier Derby on 19/07/16. These units will enter service between London Liverpool Street and Shenfield in May 2017. **Jonathan Webb**

▼ London Midland-liveried 350 376 leaves Stafford with the 15.04 Liverpool Lime Street–Birmingham New Street on 25/07/15. **Cliff Beeton**

▲ c2c-liveried 357 321 brings up the rear of the 17.53 London Liverpool Street–Shoeburyness (led by 357 315) at Stratford on 14/08/16.　　**Robert Pritchard**

▼ Heathrow Express-liveried 360 205 calls at Southall with the 10.21 Heathrow T4–London Paddington on 06/08/16. This unit normally works the Heathrow T1, 2 & 3–T4 shuttle service.　　**Chris Wilson**

▲ Thameslink-liveried 365 505 brings up the rear of the 10.22 London King's Cross–Peterborough, seen leaving King's Cross on 04/07/16.   **Robert Pritchard**

▼ Southeastern blue-liveried 375 704 and 375 707 trail the 15.30 London Charing Cross–Tunbridge Wells (led by white 375 802) at St Johns on 30/08/16.
Tony Christie

▲ Southeastern-liveried 376 010 and 376 028 arrive at Grove Park with the 17.06 Sevenoaks–London Charing Cross on 30/08/16. **Tony Christie**

▼ Southern-liveried 377 467 approaches Horley on 24/08/16. **Gavin Morrison**

▲ London Overground-liveried 378 229 calls at Acton Central with the 15.25 Stratford–Richmond on 15/06/16. **Robert Pritchard**

▼ In white livery with Stansted Express logos, 379 012 and 379 014 pass Silver Street with the diverted 16.15 Stansted Airport–London Liverpool Street on 14/08/16. **Robert Pritchard**

▲ ScotRail Saltire-liveried 380 105 is seen on the Lanark branch with the 09.21 Lanark–Glasgow Central on 27/04/16. **Robin Ralston**

▼ Two of the new Great Western Railway Class 387s, 387 132 and 387 133, pass Acton Mainline with a Heathrow Airport Junction–London Paddington test run on 24/08/16. **Alisdair Anderson**

▲ Virgin Trains-liveried 11-car Pendolino 390 141 passes Stafford on 25/07/15 with the 12.51 Edinburgh Waverley–London Euston. **Cliff Beeton**

▼ Southeastern blue-liveried 395 005 is seen on HS1 between Lenham and Harrietsham with the 17.00 Folkestone Central–London St Pancras on 16/06/16. **Robert Pritchard**

▲ Gatwick Express-liveried 442 417 and 442 404 are seen near Salfords with the 15.15 London Victoria–Gatwick Airport on 16/08/16.　　**Alex Dasi-Sutton**

▼ South West Trains white-liveried 444 023 arrives at Weymouth on 09/07/15 with the 14.05 from London Waterloo.　　**Stephen Ginn**

▲ Southern-liveried 455 804 arrives at Mitcham Junction with the 13.17 London Victoria–Epsom on 11/04/15.   **Robert Pritchard**

▼ South West Trains blue-liveried 458 506 and 458 528 arrive at Twickenham with the 10.08 Staines–London Waterloo on 09/04/16.   **Chris Wilson**

▲ Southeastern suburban-liveried 466 024 and 465 242 arrive at Waterloo East with the 11.02 London Charing Cross–Dartford on 12/07/16.   **Alex Dasi-Sutton**

▼ Island Line's ex-LUL 483 008 arrives at Sandown with the 16.49 Ryde Pier Head–Shanklin on 13/08/16.   **Nick Kelly**

▲ Merseyrail-liveried 508 114 arrives at Bache on 09/08/14 with the 14.30 Liverpool Central–Chester. **Cliff Beeton**

▼ Thameslink-liveried 700 112 arrives at Redhill with the 13.24 Bedford–Three Bridges on 15/08/16. **Alex Dasi-Sutton**

▲ Great Western Railway-liveried IEP 800 004 stands at London Paddington on 30/06/16 having just worked a special from Reading. **Robert Pritchard**

▼ Siemens Velaro e320 Eurostar 4006/05 is seen between Lenham and Harrietsham with the 16.13 Paris–London St Pancras on 16/06/16. **Robert Pritchard**

Class 377/6. 750 V DC. DMSO–MSO–TSO–MSO–DMSO. 5-car suburban units fitted with Fainsa seating. Technically the same as the 377/5s but using the slightly modified Class 379-style bodyshell.

Seating Layout: 2+2 facing/unidirectional.

DMSO. Bombardier Derby 2012–13. 24/36. 44.7 t.
MSO. Bombardier Derby 2012–13. –/64 1T. 38.8 t.
TSO. Bombardier Derby 2012–13. –/46(+2) 1TD 2W. 37.8 t.
MSO. Bombardier Derby 2012–13. –/66. 38.3 t.
DMSO. Bombardier Derby 2012–13. –/62. 44.7 t.

377 601	**SN**	P	*SN*	SU	70101	70201	70301	70401	70501
377 602	**SN**	P	*SN*	SU	70102	70202	70302	70402	70502
377 603	**SN**	P	*SN*	SU	70103	70203	70303	70403	70503
377 604	**SN**	P	*SN*	SU	70104	70204	70304	70404	70504
377 605	**SN**	P	*SN*	SU	70105	70205	70305	70405	70505
377 606	**SN**	P	*SN*	SU	70106	70206	70306	70406	70506
377 607	**SN**	P	*SN*	SU	70107	70207	70307	70407	70507
377 608	**SN**	P	*SN*	SU	70108	70208	70308	70408	70508
377 609	**SN**	P	*SN*	SU	70109	70209	70309	70409	70509
377 610	**SN**	P	*SN*	SU	70110	70210	70310	70410	70510
377 611	**SN**	P	*SN*	SU	70111	70211	70311	70411	70511
377 612	**SN**	P	*SN*	SU	70112	70212	70312	70412	70512
377 613	**SN**	P	*SN*	SU	70113	70213	70313	70413	70513
377 614	**SN**	P	*SN*	SU	70114	70214	70314	70414	70514
377 615	**SN**	P	*SN*	SU	70115	70215	70315	70415	70515
377 616	**SN**	P	*SN*	SU	70116	70216	70316	70416	70516
377 617	**SN**	P	*SN*	SU	70117	70217	70317	70417	70517
377 618	**SN**	P	*SN*	SU	70118	70218	70318	70418	70518
377 619	**SN**	P	*SN*	SU	70119	70219	70319	70419	70519
377 620	**SN**	P	*SN*	SU	70120	70220	70320	70420	70520
377 621	**SN**	P	*SN*	SU	70121	70221	70321	70421	70521
377 622	**SN**	P	*SN*	SU	70122	70222	70322	70422	70522
377 623	**SN**	P	*SN*	SU	70123	70223	70323	70423	70523
377 624	**SN**	P	*SN*	SU	70124	70224	70324	70424	70524
377 625	**SN**	P	*SN*	SU	70125	70225	70325	70425	70525
377 626	**SN**	P	*SN*	SU	70126	70226	70326	70426	70526

Class 377/7. 25kV AC/750 V DC. DMSO–MSO–TSO–MSO–DMSO. Dual-voltage units, used on both the South Croydon–Milton Keynes cross-London services and on suburban services alongside the Class 377/6s.

DMSO. Bombardier Derby 2013–14. 24/36. 45.6 t.
MSO. Bombardier Derby 2013–14. –/64 1T. 41.0 t.
PTSO. Bombardier Derby 2013–14. –/46(+2) 1TD 2W. 40.9 t.
MSO. Bombardier Derby 2013–14. –/66. 39.6 t.
DMSO. Bombardier Derby 2013–14. –/62. 45.2 t.

377 701	**SN**	P	*SN*	SU	65201	70601	65601	70701	65401
377 702	**SN**	P	*SN*	SU	65202	70602	65602	70702	65402
377 703	**SN**	P	*SN*	SU	65203	70603	65603	70703	65403
377 704	**SN**	P	*SN*	SU	65204	70604	65604	70704	65404
377 705	**SN**	P	*SN*	SU	65205	70605	65605	70705	65405

377706	**SN**	P	*SN*	SU	65206 70606 65606 70706 65406
377707	**SN**	P	*SN*	SU	65207 70607 65607 70707 65407
377708	**SN**	P	*SN*	SU	65208 70608 65608 70708 65408

CLASS 378   CAPITALSTAR   BOMBARDIER DERBY

These suburban Electrostars are designated Capitalstars by TfL.

Formation: DMSO–MSO–TSO–MSO–DMSO or DMSO–MSO–PTSO–MSO–DMSO.
System: Class 378/1 750 V DC third rail only. Class 378/2 25 kV AC overhead and 750 V DC third rail.
Construction: Welded aluminium alloy underframe, sides and roof with steel ends. All sections bolted together.
Traction Motors: Two Bombardier asynchronous of 200 kW.
Wheel Arrangement: 1A-Bo + 1A-Bo + 2-2 + Bo-1A + Bo-1A.
Braking: Disc & regenerative.   **Dimensions:** 20.46/20.14 x 2.80 m.
Bogies: Bombardier P3-25/T3-25.   **Couplers:** Dellner 12.
Gangways: Within unit + end doors.   **Control System:** IGBT Inverter.
Doors: Sliding.   **Maximum Speed:** 75 mph.
Heating & ventilation: Air conditioning.
Seating Layout: Longitudinal ("tube style") low density.
Multiple Working: Within class and with Classes 375, 376, 377 and 379.

57 extra MSOs (in the 384xx number series) were delivered 2014–15 to make all units up to 5-cars.

Class 378/1. 750 V DC. DMSO–MSO–TSO–MSO–DMSO. Third rail only units used on the East London Line. Provision for retro-fitting as dual voltage.

378 150–154 are fitted with de-icing equipment.

DMSO(A). Bombardier Derby 2009–10. –/36. 43.1 t.
MSO(A). Bombardier Derby 2009–10. –/40. 39.3 t.
TSO. Bombardier Derby 2009–10. –/34(+6) 2W. 34.3 t.
MSO(B). Bombardier Derby 2014–15. –/40. 40.2 t.
DMSO(B). Bombardier Derby 2009–10. –/36. 42.7 t.

378135	**LO**	QW	*LO*	NG	38035 38235 38335 38435 38135
378136	**LO**	QW	*LO*	NG	38036 38236 38336 38436 38136
378137	**LO**	QW	*LO*	NG	38037 38237 38337 38437 38137
378138	**LO**	QW	*LO*	NG	38038 38238 38338 38438 38138
378139	**LO**	QW	*LO*	NG	38039 38239 38339 38439 38139
378140	**LO**	QW	*LO*	NG	38040 38240 38340 38440 38140
378141	**LO**	QW	*LO*	NG	38041 38241 38341 38441 38141
378142	**LO**	QW	*LO*	NG	38042 38242 38342 38442 38142
378143	**LO**	QW	*LO*	NG	38043 38243 38343 38443 38143
378144	**LO**	QW	*LO*	NG	38044 38244 38344 38444 38144
378145	**LO**	QW	*LO*	NG	38045 38245 38345 38445 38145
378146	**LO**	QW	*LO*	NG	38046 38246 38346 38446 38146
378147	**LO**	QW	*LO*	NG	38047 38247 38347 38447 38147
378148	**LO**	QW	*LO*	NG	38048 38248 38348 38448 38148
378149	**LO**	QW	*LO*	NG	38049 38249 38349 38449 38149
378150	**LO**	QW	*LO*	NG	38050 38250 38350 38450 38150

378151	**LO**	QW	*LO*	NG	38051	38251	38351	38451	38151
378152	**LO**	QW	*LO*	NG	38052	38252	38352	38452	38152
378153	**LO**	QW	*LO*	NG	38053	38253	38353	38453	38153
378154	**LO**	QW	*LO*	NG	38054	38254	38354	38454	38154

Class 378/2. 25kV AC/750V DC. DMSO–MSO–PTSO–MSO–DMSO. Dual-voltage units mainly used on North London Railway services. 378201–224 were built as 3-car units 378001–024 and extended to 4-car units in 2010.

Fitted with tripcocks for operation on the tracks shared with London Underground between Queens Park and Harrow & Wealdstone.

378216–220 are fitted with de-icing equipment.

DMSO(A). Bombardier Derby 2008–11. –/36. 43.4 t.
MSO(A). Bombardier Derby 2008–11. –/40. 39.6 t.
PTSO. Bombardier Derby 2008–11. –/34(+6) 2W. 39.2t.
MSO(B). Bombardier Derby 2014–15. –/40. 40.4 t.
DMSO(B). Bombardier Derby 2008–11. –/36. 43.1 t.

378201	**LO**	QW	*LO*	NG	38001	38201	38301	38401	38101
378202	**LO**	QW	*LO*	NG	38002	38202	38302	38402	38102
378203	**LO**	QW	*LO*	NG	38003	38203	38303	38403	38103
378204	**LO**	QW	*LO*	NG	38004	38204	38304	38404	38104
378205	**LO**	QW	*LO*	NG	38005	38205	38305	38405	38105
378206	**LO**	QW	*LO*	NG	38006	38206	38306	38406	38106
378207	**LO**	QW	*LO*	NG	38007	38207	38307	38407	38107
378208	**LO**	QW	*LO*	NG	38008	38208	38308	38408	38108
378209	**LO**	QW	*LO*	NG	38009	38209	38309	38409	38109
378210	**LO**	QW	*LO*	NG	38010	38210	38310	38410	38110
378211	**LO**	QW	*LO*	NG	38011	38211	38311	38411	38111
378212	**LO**	QW	*LO*	NG	38012	38212	38312	38412	38112
378213	**LO**	QW	*LO*	NG	38013	38213	38313	38413	38113
378214	**LO**	QW	*LO*	NG	38014	38214	38314	38414	38114
378215	**LO**	QW	*LO*	NG	38015	38215	38315	38415	38115
378216	**LO**	QW	*LO*	NG	38016	38216	38316	38416	38116
378217	**LO**	QW	*LO*	NG	38017	38217	38317	38417	38117
378218	**LO**	QW	*LO*	NG	38018	38218	38318	38418	38118
378219	**LO**	QW	*LO*	NG	38019	38219	38319	38419	38119
378220	**LO**	QW	*LO*	NG	38020	38220	38320	38420	38120
378221	**LO**	QW	*LO*	NG	38021	38221	38321	38421	38121
378222	**LO**	QW	*LO*	NG	38022	38222	38322	38422	38122
378223	**LO**	QW	*LO*	NG	38023	38223	38323	38423	38123
378224	**LO**	QW	*LO*	NG	38024	38224	38324	38424	38124
378225	**LO**	QW	*LO*	NG	38025	38225	38325	38425	38125
378226	**LO**	QW	*LO*	NG	38026	38226	38326	38426	38126
378227	**LO**	QW	*LO*	NG	38027	38227	38327	38427	38127
378228	**LO**	QW	*LO*	NG	38028	38228	38328	38428	38128
378229	**LO**	QW	*LO*	NG	38029	38229	38329	38429	38129
378230	**LO**	QW	*LO*	NG	38030	38230	38330	38430	38130
378231	**LO**	QW	*LO*	NG	38031	38231	38331	38431	38131
378232	**LO**	QW	*LO*	NG	38032	38232	38332	38432	38132
378233	**LO**	QW	*LO*	NG	38033	38233	38333	38433	38133

| 378 234 | **LO** | QW *LO* | NG | 38034 38234 38334 38434 38134 |

378 255	**LO**	QW *LO*	NG	38055 38255 38355 38455 38155
378 256	**LO**	QW *LO*	NG	38056 38256 38356 38456 38156
378 257	**LO**	QW *LO*	NG	38057 38257 38357 38457 38157

Names (carried on DMSO(A)):

| 378 204 | Professor Sir Peter Hall | | 378 233 | Ian Brown CBE |

CLASS 379   ELECTROSTAR   BOMBARDIER DERBY

Express Electrostars used on Liverpool Street–Stansted Airport and Liverpool Street–Cambridge services.

Formation: DMSO–MSO–PTSO–DMCO.
System: 25 kV AC overhead.
Construction: Welded aluminium alloy underframe, sides and roof with steel ends. All sections bolted together.
Traction Motors: Two Bombardier asynchronous of 200 kW.
Wheel Arrangement: 2-Bo + 2-Bo + 2-2 + Bo-2.
Braking: Disc & regenerative.   **Dimensions:** 20.00 x 2.80 m.
Bogies: Bombardier P3-25/T3-25.   **Couplers:** Dellner 12.
Gangways: Throughout.   **Control System:** IGBT Inverter.
Doors: Sliding plug.   **Maximum Speed:** 100 mph.
Heating & ventilation: Air conditioning.
Seating Layout: 1: 2+1 facing. 2: 2+2 facing/unidirectional.
Multiple Working: Within class and with Classes 375, 376, 377 and 378.

DMSO. Bombardier Derby 2010–11. –/60. 42.1 t.
MSO. Bombardier Derby 2010–11. –/62 1T. 38.6 t.
PTSO. Bombardier Derby 2010–11. –/43(+2) 1TD 2W. 40.9 t.
DMCO. Bombardier Derby 2010–11. 20/24. 42.3 t.

379001	**NC**	MQ *GA*	IL	61201 61701 61901 62101
379002	**NC**	MQ *GA*	IL	61202 61702 61902 62102
379003	**NC**	MQ *GA*	IL	61203 61703 61903 62103
379004	**NC**	MQ *GA*	IL	61204 61704 61904 62104
379005	**NC**	MQ *GA*	IL	61205 61705 61905 62105
379006	**NC**	MQ *GA*	IL	61206 61706 61906 62106
379007	**NC**	MQ *GA*	IL	61207 61707 61907 62107
379008	**NC**	MQ *GA*	IL	61208 61708 61908 62108
379009	**NC**	MQ *GA*	IL	61209 61709 61909 62109
379010	**NC**	MQ *GA*	IL	61210 61710 61910 62110
379011	**NC**	MQ *GA*	IL	61211 61711 61911 62111
379012	**NC**	MQ *GA*	IL	61212 61712 61912 62112
379013	**NC**	MQ *GA*	IL	61213 61713 61913 62113
379014	**NC**	MQ *GA*	IL	61214 61714 61914 62114
379015	**NC**	MQ *GA*	IL	61215 61715 61915 62115
379016	**NC**	MQ *GA*	IL	61216 61716 61916 62116
379017	**NC**	MQ *GA*	IL	61217 61717 61917 62117
379018	**NC**	MQ *GA*	IL	61218 61718 61918 62118
379019	**NC**	MQ *GA*	IL	61219 61719 61919 62119
379020	**NC**	MQ *GA*	IL	61220 61720 61920 62120

379021	**NC**	MQ	*GA*	IL	61221	61721	61921	62121
379022	**NC**	MQ	*GA*	IL	61222	61722	61922	62122
379023	**NC**	MQ	*GA*	IL	61223	61723	61923	62123
379024	**NC**	MQ	*GA*	IL	61224	61724	61924	62124
379025	**NC**	MQ	*GA*	IL	61225	61725	61925	62125
379026	**NC**	MQ	*GA*	IL	61226	61726	61926	62126
379027	**NC**	MQ	*GA*	IL	61227	61727	61927	62127
379028	**NC**	MQ	*GA*	IL	61228	61728	61928	62128
379029	**NC**	MQ	*GA*	IL	61229	61729	61929	62129
379030	**NC**	MQ	*GA*	IL	61230	61730	61930	62130

Names (carried on end cars):

379005	Stansted Express	379015	City of Cambridge
379011	Ely Cathedral	379025	Go Discover
379012	The West Anglian		

CLASS 380   DESIRO UK   SIEMENS

Used on Strathclyde area services and between Glasgow/Edinburgh and North Berwick.

Formation: DMSO–PTSO–DMSO or DMSO–PTSO–TSO–DMSO.
System: 25 kV AC overhead.
Construction: Welded aluminium with steel ends.
Traction Motors: Four Siemens ITB2016-0GB02 asynchronous of 250 kW.
Wheel Arrangement: Bo-Bo + 2-2 (+2-2) + Bo-Bo
Braking: Disc & regenerative.
Bogies: SGP SF5000.
Gangways: Throughout.
Doors: Sliding plug.
Heating & ventilation: Air conditioning.
Multiple Working: Within class.
Dimensions: 23.78/23.57 x 2.80 m.
Couplers: Voith.
Control System: IGBT Inverter.
Maximum Speed: 100 mph.
Seating Layout: 2+2 facing/unidirectional.

DMSO(A). Siemens Krefeld 2009–10. –/70. 45.0 t.
PTSO. Siemens Krefeld 2009–10. –/57(+12) 1TD 2W. 42.7 t.
TSO. Siemens Krefeld 2009–10. –/74 1T. 34.8 t.
DMSO(B). Siemens Krefeld 2009–10. –/64(+5). 44.9 t.

Class 380/0. 3-car units. **Formation:** DMSO–PTSO–DMSO.

380001	**SR**	E	*SR*	GW	38501	38601	38701
380002	**SR**	E	*SR*	GW	38502	38602	38702
380003	**SR**	E	*SR*	GW	38503	38603	38703
380004	**SR**	E	*SR*	GW	38504	38604	38704
380005	**SR**	E	*SR*	GW	38505	38605	38705
380006	**SR**	E	*SR*	GW	38506	38606	38706
380007	**SR**	E	*SR*	GW	38507	38607	38707
380008	**SR**	E	*SR*	GW	38508	38608	38708
380009	**SR**	E	*SR*	GW	38509	38609	38709
380010	**SR**	E	*SR*	GW	38510	38610	38710
380011	**SR**	E	*SR*	GW	38511	38611	38711

380012	SR	E	*SR*	GW	38512	38612		38712
380013	SR	E	*SR*	GW	38513	38613		38713
380014	SR	E	*SR*	GW	38514	38614		38714
380015	SR	E	*SR*	GW	38515	38615		38715
380016	SR	E	*SR*	GW	38516	38616		38716
380017	SR	E	*SR*	GW	38517	38617		38717
380018	SR	E	*SR*	GW	38518	38618		38718
380019	SR	E	*SR*	GW	38519	38619		38719
380020	SR	E	*SR*	GW	38520	38620		38720
380021	SR	E	*SR*	GW	38521	38621		38721
380022	SR	E	*SR*	GW	38522	38622		38722

Class 380/1. 4-car units. **Formation:** DMSO–PTSO–TSO–DMSO.

380101	SR	E	*SR*	GW	38551	38651	38851	38751
380102	SR	E	*SR*	GW	38552	38652	38852	38752
380103	SR	E	*SR*	GW	38553	38653	38853	38753
380104	SR	E	*SR*	GW	38554	38654	38854	38754
380105	SR	E	*SR*	GW	38555	38655	38855	38755
380106	SR	E	*SR*	GW	38556	38656	38856	38756
380107	SR	E	*SR*	GW	38557	38657	38857	38757
380108	SR	E	*SR*	GW	38558	38658	38858	38758
380109	SR	E	*SR*	GW	38559	38659	38859	38759
380110	SR	E	*SR*	GW	38560	38660	38860	38760
380111	SR	E	*SR*	GW	38561	38661	38861	38761
380112	SR	E	*SR*	GW	38562	38662	38862	38762
380113	SR	E	*SR*	GW	38563	38663	38863	38763
380114	SR	E	*SR*	GW	38564	38664	38864	38764
380115	SR	E	*SR*	GW	38565	38665	38865	38765
380116	SR	E	*SR*	GW	38566	38666	38866	38766

CLASS 385   AT200   HITACHI

New 3- and 4-car units for ScotRail, due to enter service in autumn 2017 and financed by Caledonian Rail Leasing. There is an option for a further ten 3-car units. Full details awaited.

Formation: DMSO–PTSO–DMSO or DMCO–PTSO–TSO–DMSO.
System: 25 kV AC overhead.
Construction: Aluminium.
Traction Motors:
Wheel Arrangement:
Braking:
Dimensions: 23.0 x 2.74 m.
Bogies: Hitachi.
Gangways: Throughout.
Doors:
Couplers:
Control System: IGBT Inverter.
Maximum Speed: 100 mph.
Multiple Working: Within class only.
Heating & ventilation: Air conditioning.
Seating Layout: 1: 2+1 facing. 2: 2+2 facing/unidirectional.

Class 385/0. 3-car units. **Formation:** DMSO–PTSO–DMSO.

DMSO(A): Hitachi Newton Aycliffe/Kasado 2016–18.
PTSO: Hitachi Newton Aycliffe/Kasado 2016–18.
DMSO(B): Hitachi Newton Aycliffe/Kasado 2016–18.

385001	**SR**	CL	441001	442001	444001
385002	**SR**	CL	441002	442002	444002
385003	**SR**	CL	441003	442003	444003
385004	**SR**	CL	441004	442004	444004
385005	**SR**	CL	441005	442005	444005
385006	**SR**	CL	441006	442006	444006
385007	**SR**	CL	441007	442007	444007
385008	**SR**	CL	441008	442008	444008
385009	**SR**	CL	441009	442009	444009
385010	**SR**	CL	441010	442010	444010
385011	**SR**	CL	441011	442011	444011
385012	**SR**	CL	441012	442012	444012
385013	**SR**	CL	441013	442013	444013
385014	**SR**	CL	441014	442014	444014
385015	**SR**	CL	441015	442015	444015
385016	**SR**	CL	441016	442016	444016
385017	**SR**	CL	441017	442017	444017
385018	**SR**	CL	441018	442018	444018
385019	**SR**	CL	441019	442019	444019
385020	**SR**	CL	441020	442020	444020
385021	**SR**	CL	441021	442021	444021
385022	**SR**	CL	441022	442022	444022
385023	**SR**	CL	441023	442023	444023
385024	**SR**	CL	441024	442024	444024
385025	**SR**	CL	441025	442025	444025
385026	**SR**	CL	441026	442026	444026
385027	**SR**	CL	441027	442027	444027
385028	**SR**	CL	441028	442028	444028
385029	**SR**	CL	441029	442029	444029
385030	**SR**	CL	441030	442030	444030
385031	**SR**	CL	441031	442031	444031
385032	**SR**	CL	441032	442032	444032
385033	**SR**	CL	441033	442033	444033
385034	**SR**	CL	441034	442034	444034
385035	**SR**	CL	441035	442035	444035
385036	**SR**	CL	441036	442036	444036
385037	**SR**	CL	441037	442037	444037
385038	**SR**	CL	441038	442038	444038
385039	**SR**	CL	441039	442039	444039
385040	**SR**	CL	441040	442040	444040
385041	**SR**	CL	441041	442041	444041
385042	**SR**	CL	441042	442042	444042
385043	**SR**	CL	441043	442043	444043
385044	**SR**	CL	441044	442044	444044
385045	**SR**	CL	441045	442045	444045
385046	**SR**	CL	441046	442046	444046

Class 385/1. 4-car units. **Formation:** DMCO–PTSO–TSO–DMSO.

DMCO: Hitachi Newton Aycliffe/Kasado 2016–18.
PTSO: Hitachi Newton Aycliffe/Kasado 2016–18.
TSO: Hitachi Newton Aycliffe/Kasado 2016–18.
DMSO: Hitachi Newton Aycliffe/Kasado 2016–18.

385 101	**SR**	CL	441101	442101	443101	444101
385 102	**SR**	CL	441102	442102	443102	444102
385 103	**SR**	CL	441103	442103	443103	444103
385 104	**SR**	CL	441104	442104	443104	444104
385 105	**SR**	CL	441105	442105	443105	444105
385 106	**SR**	CL	441106	442106	443106	444106
385 107	**SR**	CL	441107	442107	443107	444107
385 108	**SR**	CL	441108	442108	443108	444108
385 109	**SR**	CL	441109	442109	443109	444109
385 110	**SR**	CL	441110	442110	443110	444110
385 111	**SR**	CL	441111	442111	443111	444111
385 112	**SR**	CL	441112	442112	443112	444112
385 113	**SR**	CL	441113	442113	443113	444113
385 114	**SR**	CL	441114	442114	443114	444114
385 115	**SR**	CL	441115	442115	443115	444115
385 116	**SR**	CL	441116	442116	443116	444116
385 117	**SR**	CL	441117	442117	443117	444117
385 118	**SR**	CL	441118	442118	443118	444118
385 119	**SR**	CL	441119	442119	443119	444119
385 120	**SR**	CL	441120	442120	443120	444120
385 121	**SR**	CL	441121	442121	443121	444121
385 122	**SR**	CL	441122	442122	443122	444122
385 123	**SR**	CL	441123	442123	443123	444123
385 124	**SR**	CL	441124	442124	443124	444124

CLASS 387   ELECTROSTAR   BOMBARDIER DERBY

The first 29 110 mph Class 387/1s were delivered in 2014–15 for Thameslink. During 2016–17 these are transfering to Great Northern for services from King's Cross to Cambridge/Kings Lynn and Peterborough. The 387/1s were the first units to feature 6-digit vehicle numbers.

A further 27 Class 387/2 units were delivered to Southern for Gatwick Express services in 2016.

Great Western Railway has 45 Class 387/1s on order for newly electrified routes from London Paddington.

Part of a speculative order by Porterbrook Leasing, c2c is took six Class 387/3s for 3 years from late 2016. Porterbrook had originally placed an order for 20 speculative units (387301–320), but the other 14 from this order will now form part of the GWR Class 387/1 fleet.

Formation: DMCO–MSO–PTSO–DMSO.
System: 25 kV AC overhead and 750 V DC third rail.
Construction: Welded aluminium alloy underframe, sides and roof with steel ends. All sections bolted together.
Traction Motors: Two Bombardier asynchronous of 250 kW.
Wheel Arrangement: 2-Bo + 2-Bo + 2-2 + Bo-2.

Braking: Disc & regenerative.	**Dimensions:** 20.39/20.00 x 2.80 m.
Bogies: Bombardier P3-25/T3-25.	**Couplers:** Dellner 12.
Gangways: Throughout.	**Control System:** IGBT Inverter.
Doors: Sliding plug.	**Maximum Speed:** 110 mph.

Heating & ventilation: Air conditioning.
Seating Layout: 2+2 facing/unidirectional.
Multiple Working: Within class and with Class 377.

Class 387/1. Units built for Thameslink, but transferring to Great Northern.

DMCO. Bombardier Derby 2014–15. 10/46. 46.0 t.
MSO. Bombardier Derby 2014–15. –/62 1T. 41.3 t.
PTSO. Bombardier Derby 2014–15. –/45(+2) 1TD 2W. 41.6 t.
DMSO. Bombardier Derby 2014–15. –/60. 45.9 t.

387 101	**TG**	P	*TL*	BI	421101	422101	423101	424101
387 102	**TG**	P	*GN*	HE	421102	422102	423102	424102
387 103	**TG**	P	*TL*	BI	421103	422103	423103	424103
387 104	**TG**	P	*GN*	HE	421104	422104	423104	424104
387 105	**TG**	P	*TL*	BI	421105	422105	423105	424105
387 106	**TG**	P	*GN*	HE	421106	422106	423106	424106
387 107	**TG**	P	*GN*	HE	421107	422107	423107	424107
387 108	**TG**	P	*GN*	HE	421108	422108	423108	424108
387 109	**TG**	P	*GN*	HE	421109	422109	423109	424109
387 110	**TG**	P	*GN*	HE	421110	422110	423110	424110
387 111	**TG**	P	*GN*	HE	421111	422111	423111	424111
387 112	**TG**	P	*GN*	HE	421112	422112	423112	424112
387 113	**TG**	P	*GN*	HE	421113	422113	423113	424113
387 114	**TG**	P	*GN*	HE	421114	422114	423114	424114
387 115	**TG**	P	*TL*	BI	421115	422115	423115	424115
387 116	**TG**	P	*GN*	HE	421116	422116	423116	424116
387 117	**TG**	P	*GN*	HE	421117	422117	423117	424117
387 118	**TG**	P	*TL*	BI	421118	422118	423118	424118
387 119	**TG**	P	*GN*	HE	421119	422119	423119	424119
387 120	**TG**	P	*GN*	HE	421120	422120	423120	424120
387 121	**TG**	P	*TL*	BI	421121	422121	423121	424121
387 122	**TG**	P	*TL*	BI	421122	422122	423122	424122
387 123	**TG**	P	*GN*	HE	421123	422123	423123	424123
387 124	**TG**	P	*TL*	BI	421124	422124	423124	424124
387 125	**TG**	P	*GN*	HE	421125	422125	423125	424125
387 126	**TG**	P	*GN*	HE	421126	422126	423126	424126
387 127	**TG**	P	*TL*	BI	421127	422127	423127	424127
387 128	**TG**	P	*GN*	HE	421128	422128	423128	424128
387 129	**TG**	P	*GN*	HE	421129	422129	423129	424129

Class 387/1. Units currently being delivered to Great Western Railway for services from London Paddington. Units are initially based at North Pole depot for day-to-day servicing, returning to Reading for exams.

DMCO. Bombardier Derby 2016–17. –/56. 46.0 t.
MSO. Bombardier Derby 2016–17. –/62 1T. 41.3 t.
PTSO. Bombardier Derby 2016–17. –/45(+2) 1TD 2W. 41.6 t.
DMSO. Bombardier Derby 2016–17. –/60. 45.9 t.

387 130	GW	P	*GW*	RG	421130	422130	423130	424130
387 131	GW	P	*GW*	RG	421131	422131	423131	424131
387 132	GW	P	*GW*	RG	421132	422132	423132	424132
387 133	GW	P	*GW*	RG	421133	422133	423133	424133
387 134	GW	P	*GW*	RG	421134	422134	423134	424134
387 135	GW	P	*GW*	RG	421135	422135	423135	424135
387 136	GW	P	*GW*	RG	421136	422136	423136	424136
387 137	GW	P	*GW*	RG	421137	422137	423137	424137
387 138	GW	P	*GW*	RG	421138	422138	423138	424138
387 139	GW	P	*GW*	RG	421139	422139	423139	424139
387 140	GW	P			421140	422140	423140	424140
387 141	GW	P			421141	422141	423141	424141
387 142	GW	P			421142	422142	423142	424142
387 143	GW	P			421143	422143	423143	424143
387 144	GW	P			421144	422144	423144	424144
387 145	GW	P			421145	422145	423145	424145
387 146	GW	P			421146	422146	423146	424146
387 147	GW	P			421147	422147	423147	424147
387 148	GW	P			421148	422148	423148	424148
387 149	GW	P			421149	422149	423149	424149
387 150	GW	P			421150	422150	423150	424150
387 151	GW	P			421151	422151	423151	424151
387 152	GW	P			421152	422152	423152	424152
387 153	GW	P			421153	422153	423153	424153
387 154	GW	P			421154	422154	423154	424154
387 155	GW	P			421155	422155	423155	424155
387 156	GW	P			421156	422156	423156	424156
387 157	GW	P			421157	422157	423157	424157
387 158	GW	P			421158	422158	423158	424158
387 159	GW	P			421159	422159	423159	424159
387 160	GW	P			421160	422160	423160	424160
387 161	GW	P			421161	422161	423161	424161
387 162	GW	P			421162	422162	423162	424162
387 163	GW	P			421163	422163	423163	424163
387 164	GW	P			421164	422164	423164	424164
387 165	GW	P			421165	422165	423165	424165
387 166	GW	P			421166	422166	423166	424166
387 167	GW	P			421167	422167	423167	424167
387 168	GW	P			421168	422168	423168	424168
387 169	GW	P			421169	422169	423169	424169
387 170	GW	P			421170	422170	423170	424170
387 171	GW	P			421171	422171	423171	424171
387 172	GW	P			421172	422172	423172	424172

| 387 173 | **GW** | P | | | 421173 | 422173 | 423173 | 424173 |
| 387 174 | **GW** | P | | | 421174 | 422174 | 423174 | 424174 |

Class 387/2. Southern units used on Gatwick Express-branded services on the London Victoria–Gatwick Airport–Brighton route.

DMCO. Bombardier Derby 2015–16. 22/34. 46.0 t.
MSO. Bombardier Derby 2015–16. –/60 1T. 41.3 t.
PTSO. Bombardier Derby 2015–16. –/45(+2) 1TD 2W. 41.6 t.
DMSO. Bombardier Derby 2015–16. –/60. 45.9 t.

387 201	**GX**	P	*SN*	SL	421201	422201	423201	424201
387 202	**GX**	P	*SN*	SL	421202	422202	423202	424202
387 203	**GX**	P	*SN*	SL	421203	422203	423203	424203
387 204	**GX**	P	*SN*	SL	421204	422204	423204	424204
387 205	**GX**	P	*SN*	SL	421205	422205	423205	424205
387 206	**GX**	P	*SN*	SL	421206	422206	423206	424206
387 207	**GX**	P	*SN*	SL	421207	422207	423207	424207
387 208	**GX**	P	*SN*	SL	421208	422208	423208	424208
387 209	**GX**	P	*SN*	SL	421209	422209	423209	424209
387 210	**GX**	P	*SN*	SL	421210	422210	423210	424210
387 211	**GX**	P	*SN*	SL	421211	422211	423211	424211
387 212	**GX**	P	*SN*	SL	421212	422212	423212	424212
387 213	**GX**	P	*SN*	SL	421213	422213	423213	424213
387 214	**GX**	P	*SN*	SL	421214	422214	423214	424214
387 215	**GX**	P	*SN*	SL	421215	422215	423215	424215
387 216	**GX**	P	*SN*	SL	421216	422216	423216	424216
387 217	**GX**	P	*SN*	SL	421217	422217	423217	424217
387 218	**GX**	P	*SN*	SL	421218	422218	423218	424218
387 219	**GX**	P	*SN*	SL	421219	422219	423219	424219
387 220	**GX**	P	*SN*	SL	421220	422220	423220	424220
387 221	**GX**	P	*SN*	SL	421221	422221	423221	424221
387 222	**GX**	P	*SN*	SL	421222	422222	423222	424222
387 223	**GX**	P	*SN*	SL	421223	422223	423223	424223
387 224	**GX**	P	*SN*	SL	421224	422224	423224	424224
387 225	**GX**	P	*SN*	SL	421225	422225	423225	424225
387 226	**GX**	P	*SN*	SL	421226	422226	423226	424226
387 227	**GX**	P	*SN*	SL	421227	422227	423227	424227

Class 387/3. c2c units, originally ordered speculatively by Porterbrook Leasing.

DMSO(A). Bombardier Derby 2016. –/56. 46.0 t.
MSO. Bombardier Derby 2016. –/62 1T. 41.3 t.
PTSO. Bombardier Derby 2016. –/45(+2) 1TD 2W. 41.6 t.
DMSO(B). Bombardier Derby 2016. –/60. 45.9 t.

387 301	**C2**	P	*C2*	EM	421301	422301	423301	424301
387 302	**C2**	P	*C2*	EM	421302	422302	423302	424302
387 303	**C2**	P	*C2*	EM	421303	422303	423303	424303
387 304	**C2**	P	*C2*	EM	421304	422304	423304	424304
387 305	**C2**	P	*C2*	EM	421305	422305	423305	424305
387 306	**C2**	P	*C2*	EM	421306	422306	423306	424306

CLASS 390   PENDOLINO   ALSTOM

Tilting units used on the West Coast Main Line.

Formations: As listed below.   **Construction:** Welded aluminium alloy.
Traction Motors: Two Alstom ONIX 800 of 425 kW.
Wheel Arrangement: 1A-A1 + 1A-A1 + 2-2 + 1A-A1 (+ 2-2 + 1A-A1) + 2-2 +
1A-A1 + 2-2 + 1A-A1 + 1A-A1.   **Braking:** Disc, rheostatic & regenerative.
Dimensions: 24.80/23.90 x 2.73 m.   **Couplers:** Dellner 12.
Bogies: Fiat-SIG.   **Control System:** IGBT Inverter.
Gangways: Within unit.   **Maximum Speed:** 125 mph.
Doors: Sliding plug.   **Heating & ventilation:** Air conditioning.
Seating Layout: 1: 2+1 facing/unidirectional, 2: 2+2 facing/unidirectional.
Multiple Working: Within class. Can also be controlled from Class 57/3 locos.

Units up to 390034 were delivered as 8-car sets, without the TSO (688xx).
During 2004–05 these units were increased to 9-cars.

62 extra vehicles were built 2010–12 to lengthen 31 sets to 11-cars. On
renumbering units were renumbered by adding 100 to the set number. Four
new complete 11-car units were also delivered. All these extra vehicles
were built at Savigliano in Italy (all original Pendolino vehicles were built
at Birmingham).

The 9-car units had their MFO(B) converted to an MSO in 2015 to give them
a better balance of Standard to First Class seating.

390033 was written off in the Lambrigg accident of February 2007.

Advertising livery: 390 104 – Black Alstom vinyls on Virgin silver livery.

DMRBFO: Alstom Birmingham/Savigliano 2001–05/2010–12. 18/–. 56.3 t.
MFO(A): Alstom Birmingham/Savigliano 2001–05/2010–12. 37/–(+2) 1TD 1W. 52.3 t.
PTFO: Alstom Birmingham/Savigliano 2001–05/2010–12. 44/– 1T. 51.2 t.
MFO(B: 11-car): Alstom Birmingham/Savigliano 2001–05/2010–12. 46/– 1T. 52.3 t.
MSO(C: 9-car): Alstom Birmingham/Savigliano 2001–05/2010–12. –/76 1T. 52.3 t.
(TSO: Alstom Savigliano 2010–12. –/74 1T. 49.2 t.)
(MSO: Alstom Savigliano 2010–12. –/76 1T. 52.2 t.)
TSO: Alstom Birmingham/Savigliano 2001–05/2010–12. –/76 1T. 45.5 t.
MSO(A): Alstom Birmingham/Savigliano 2001–05/2010–12. –/62(+4) 1TD 1W. 52.0 t.
PTSRMB: Alstom Birmingham/Savigliano 2001–05/2010–12. –/48. 53.2 t.
MSO(B): Alstom Birmingham/Savigliano 2001–05/2010–12. –/62(+2) 1TD 1W. 52.5 t.
DMSO: Alstom Birmingham/Savigliano 2001–05/2010–12. –/46 1T. 54.5 t.

Class 390/0. Original build 9-car units.
Formation: DMRFO–MFO–PTFO–MSO–TSO–MSO–PTSRMB–MSO–DMSO.

390 001	**VT**	A	*VW*	MA	69101	69401	69501	69601	68801
					69701	69801	69901	69201	
390 002	**VT**	A	*VW*	MA	69102	69402	69502	69602	68802
					69702	69802	69902	69202	
390 005	**VT**	A	*VW*	MA	69105	69405	69505	69605	68805
					69705	69805	69905	69205	
390 006	**VT**	A	*VW*	MA	69106	69406	69506	69606	68806
					69706	69806	69906	69206	

390008	**VT**	A	*VW* MA	69108 69408 69508 69608 68808
				69708 69808 69908 69208
390009	**VT**	A	*VW* MA	69109 69409 69509 69609 68809
				69709 69809 69909 69209
390010	**VT**	A	*VW* MA	69110 69410 69510 69610 68810
				69710 69810 69910 69210
390011	**VT**	A	*VW* MA	69111 69411 69511 69611 68811
				69711 69811 69911 69211
390013	**VT**	A	*VW* MA	69113 69413 69513 69613 68813
				69713 69813 69913 69213
390016	**VT**	A	*VW* MA	69116 69416 69516 69616 68816
				69716 69816 69916 69216
390020	**VT**	A	*VW* MA	69120 69420 69520 69620 68820
				69720 69820 69920 69220
390039	**VT**	A	*VW* MA	69139 69439 69539 69639 68839
				69739 69839 69939 69239
390040	**VT**	A	*VW* MA	69140 69440 69540 69640 68840
				69740 69840 69940 69240
390042	**VT**	A	*VW* MA	69142 69442 69542 69642 68842
				69742 69842 69942 69242
390043	**VT**	A	*VW* MA	69143 69443 69543 69643 68843
				69743 69843 69943 69243
390044	**VT**	A	*VW* MA	69144 69444 69544 69644 68844
				69744 69844 69944 69244
390045	**VT**	A	*VW* MA	69145 69445 69545 69645 68845
				69745 69845 69945 69245
390046	**VT**	A	*VW* MA	69146 69446 69546 69646 68846
				69746 69846 69946 69246
390047	**VT**	A	*VW* MA	69147 69447 69547 69647 68847
				69747 69847 69947 69247
390049	**VT**	A	*VW* MA	69149 69449 69549 69649 68849
				69749 69849 69949 69249
390050	**VT**	A	*VW* MA	69150 69450 69550 69650 68850
				69750 69850 69950 69250

Class 390/1. Original build 9-car units later extended to 11-cars, except 390 154–157 which were built new (in Italy) as 11-cars.
Formation: DMRFO–MFO–PTFO–MFO–TSO–MSO–TSO–MSO–PTSRMB–MSO–DMSO.

390103	**VT**	A	*VW* MA	69103 69403 69503 69603 65303 68903
				68803 69703 69803 69903 69203
390104	**AL**	A	*VW* MA	69104 69404 69504 69604 65304 68904
				68804 69704 69804 69904 69204
390107	**VT**	A	*VW* MA	69107 69407 69507 69607 65307 68907
				68807 69707 69807 69907 69207
390112	**VT**	A	*VW* MA	69112 69412 69512 69612 65312 68912
				68812 69712 69812 69912 69212
390114	**VT**	A	*VW* MA	69114 69414 69514 69614 65314 68914
				68814 69714 69814 69914 69214
390115	**VT**	A	*VW* MA	69115 69415 69515 69615 65315 68915
				68815 69715 69815 69915 69215

390 117	**VT**	A	*VW* MA	69117	69417	69517	69617	65317	68917
				68817	69717	69817	69917	69217	
390 118	**VT**	A	*VW* MA	69118	69418	69518	69618	65318	68918
				68818	69718	69818	69918	69218	
390 119	**VT**	A	*VW* MA	69119	69419	69519	69619	65319	68919
				68819	69719	69819	69919	69219	
390 121	**VT**	A	*VW* MA	69121	69421	69521	69621	65321	68921
				68821	69721	69821	69921	69221	
390 122	**VT**	A	*VW* MA	69122	69422	69522	69622	65322	68922
				68822	69722	69822	69922	69222	
390 123	**VT**	A	*VW* MA	69123	69423	69523	69623	65323	68923
				68823	69723	69823	69923	69223	
390 124	**VT**	A	*VW* MA	69124	69424	69524	69624	65324	68924
				68824	69724	69824	69924	69224	
390 125	**VT**	A	*VW* MA	69125	69425	69525	69625	65325	68925
				68825	69725	69825	69925	69225	
390 126	**VT**	A	*VW* MA	69126	69426	69526	69626	65326	68926
				68826	69726	69826	69926	69226	
390 127	**VT**	A	*VW* MA	69127	69427	69527	69627	65327	68927
				68827	69727	69827	69927	69227	
390 128	**VT**	A	*VW* MA	69128	69428	69528	69628	65328	68928
				68828	69728	69828	69928	69228	
390 129	**VT**	A	*VW* MA	69129	69429	69529	69629	65329	68929
				68829	69729	69829	69929	69229	
390 130	**VT**	A	*VW* MA	69130	69430	69530	69630	65330	68930
				68830	69730	69830	69930	69230	
390 131	**VT**	A	*VW* MA	69131	69431	69531	69631	65331	68931
				68831	69731	69831	69931	69231	
390 132	**VT**	A	*VW* MA	69132	69432	69532	69632	65332	68932
				68832	69732	69832	69932	69232	
390 134	**VT**	A	*VW* MA	69134	69434	69534	69634	65334	68934
				68834	69734	69834	69934	69234	
390 135	**VT**	A	*VW* MA	69135	69435	69535	69635	65335	68935
				68835	69735	69835	69935	69235	
390 136	**VT**	A	*VW* MA	69136	69436	69536	69636	65336	68936
				68836	69736	69836	69936	69236	
390 137	**VT**	A	*VW* MA	69137	69437	69537	69637	65337	68937
				68837	69737	69837	69937	69237	
390 138	**VT**	A	*VW* MA	69138	69438	69538	69638	65338	68938
				68838	69738	69838	69938	69238	
390 141	**VT**	A	*VW* MA	69141	69441	69541	69641	65341	68941
				68841	69741	69841	69941	69241	
390 148	**VT**	A	*VW* MA	69148	69448	69548	69648	65348	68948
				68848	69748	69848	69948	69248	
390 151	**VT**	A	*VW* MA	69151	69451	69551	69651	65351	68951
				68851	69751	69851	69951	69251	
390 152	**VT**	A	*VW* MA	69152	69452	69552	69652	65352	68952
				68852	69752	69852	69952	69252	
390 153	**VT**	A	*VW* MA	69153	69453	69553	69653	65353	68953
				68853	69753	69853	69953	69253	

390 154	**VT**	A	*VW* MA	69154 69454 69554 69654 65354 68954
				68854 69754 69854 69954 69254
390 155	**VT**	A	*VW* MA	69155 69455 69555 69655 65355 68955
				68855 69755 69855 69955 69255
390 156	**VT**	A	*VW* MA	69156 69456 69556 69656 65356 68956
				68856 69756 69856 69956 69256
390 157	**VT**	A	*VW* MA	69157 69457 69557 69657 65357 68957
				68857 69757 69857 69957 69257

Names (carried on MFO No. 696xx):

390 001	Virgin Pioneer	390 118	Virgin Princess
390 002	Stephen Sutton	390 119	Virgin Warrior
390 005	City of Wolverhampton	390 121	Virgin Dream
390 006	Tate Liverpool	390 122	Penny the Pendolino
390 008	Virgin King	390 123	Virgin Glory
390 009	Treaty of Union	390 124	Virgin Venturer
390 010	The Cumbrian Spirit	390 125	Virgin Stagecoach
390 011	City of Lichfield	390 126	Virgin Enterprise
390 013	Virgin Spirit	390 127	Virgin Buccaneer
390 016	Virgin Champion	390 128	City of Preston
390 020	Virgin Cavalier	390 129	City of Stoke-on-Trent
390 039	Virgin Quest	390 130	City of Edinburgh
390 040	Virgin Radio Star	390 131	City of Liverpool
390 042	City of Bangor/Dinas Bangor	390 132	City of Birmingham
390 043	Virgin Explorer	390 134	City of Carlisle
390 044	Virgin Lionheart	390 135	City of Lancaster
390 045	101 Squadron	390 136	City of Coventry
390 046	Virgin Soldiers	390 137	Virgin Difference
390 047	CLIC Sargent	390 138	City of London
390 049	Virgin Express	390 141	City of Chester
390 050	Virgin Invader	390 148	Virgin Harrier
390 103	Virgin Hero	390 151	Virgin Ambassador
390 104	Alstom Pendolino	390 152	Virgin Knight
390 107	Independence Day Resurgence	390 153	Mission Accomplished
390 112	Virgin Star	390 154	Matthew Flinders
390 114	City of Manchester	390 155	X-MEN Days of Future Past
390 115	Virgin Crusader	390 156	Stockport 170
390 117	Virgin Prince	390 157	Chad Varah

CLASS 395   JAVELIN   HITACHI JAPAN

6-car dual-voltage units used on Southeastern High Speed trains from London St Pancras.

Formation: PDTSO–MSO–MSO–MSO–MSO–PDTSO.
Systems: 25 kV AC overhead/750 V DC third rail.
Construction: Aluminium.
Traction Motors: Four Hitachi asynchronous of 210 kW.
Wheel Arrangement: 2-2 + Bo-Bo + Bo-Bo + Bo-Bo + Bo-Bo + 2-2.
Braking: Disc, rheostatic & regenerative.

Dimensions: 20.88/20.0 x 2.81 m.	**Couplers:** Scharfenberg.
Bogies: Hitachi.	**Control System:** IGBT Inverter.
Gangways: Within unit.	**Maximum Speed:** 140 mph.
Doors: Single-leaf sliding.	**Multiple Working:** Within class only.

Heating & ventilation: Air conditioning.
Seating Layout: 2+2 facing/unidirectional (mainly unidirectional).

PDTSO(A): Hitachi Kasado, Japan 2006–09. –/28(+12) 1TD 2W. 46.7 t.
MSO: Hitachi Kasado, Japan 2006–09. –/66. 45.0t–45.7 t.
PDTSO(B): Hitachi Kasado, Japan 2006–09. –/48 1T. 46.7 t.

395001	**SB**	E	*SE*	AD	39011	39012	39013	39014	39015	39016
395002	**SB**	E	*SE*	AD	39021	39022	39023	39024	39025	39026
395003	**SB**	E	*SE*	AD	39031	39032	39033	39034	39035	39036
395004	**SB**	E	*SE*	AD	39041	39042	39043	39044	39045	39046
395005	**SB**	E	*SE*	AD	39051	39052	39053	39054	39055	39056
395006	**SB**	E	*SE*	AD	39061	39062	39063	39064	39065	39066
395007	**SB**	E	*SE*	AD	39071	39072	39073	39074	39075	39076
395008	**SB**	E	*SE*	AD	39081	39082	39083	39084	39085	39086
395009	**SB**	E	*SE*	AD	39091	39092	39093	39094	39095	39096
395010	**SB**	E	*SE*	AD	39101	39102	39103	39104	39105	39106
395011	**SB**	E	*SE*	AD	39111	39112	39113	39114	39115	39116
395012	**SB**	E	*SE*	AD	39121	39122	39123	39124	39125	39126
395013	**SB**	E	*SE*	AD	39131	39132	39133	39134	39135	39136
395014	**SB**	E	*SE*	AD	39141	39142	39143	39144	39145	39146
395015	**SB**	E	*SE*	AD	39151	39152	39153	39154	39155	39156
395016	**SB**	E	*SE*	AD	39161	39162	39163	39164	39165	39166
395017	**SB**	E	*SE*	AD	39171	39172	39173	39174	39175	39176
395018	**SB**	E	*SE*	AD	39181	39182	39183	39184	39185	39186
395019	**SB**	E	*SE*	AD	39191	39192	39193	39194	39195	39196
395020	**SB**	E	*SE*	AD	39201	39202	39203	39204	39205	39206
395021	**SB**	E	*SE*	AD	39211	39212	39213	39214	39215	39216
395022	**SB**	E	*SE*	AD	39221	39222	39223	39224	39225	39226
395023	**SB**	E	*SE*	AD	39231	39232	39233	39234	39235	39236
395024	**SB**	E	*SE*	AD	39241	39242	39243	39244	39245	39246
395025	**SB**	E	*SE*	AD	39251	39252	39253	39254	39255	39256
395026	**SB**	E	*SE*	AD	39261	39262	39263	39264	39265	39266
395027	**SB**	E	*SE*	AD	39271	39272	39273	39274	39275	39276
395028	**SB**	E	*SE*	AD	39281	39282	39283	39284	39285	39286
395029	**SB**	E	*SE*	AD	39291	39292	39293	39294	39295	39296

Names (carried on end cars):

395 001 Dame Kelly Holmes	395 017 Dame Sarah Storey
395 002 Sebastian Coe	395 018 Mo Farah
395 003 Sir Steve Redgrave	395 019 Jessica Ennis
395 004 Sir Chris Hoy	395 020 Jason Kenny
395 005 Dame Tanni Grey-Thompson	395 021 Ed Clancy MBE
395 006 Daley Thompson	395 022 Alistair Brownlee
395 007 Steve Backley	395 023 Ellie Simmonds
395 008 Ben Ainslie	395 024 Jonnie Peacock
395 009 Rebecca Adlington	395 025 Victoria Pendleton
395 010 Duncan Goodhew	395 026 Marc Woods
395 011 Katherine Grainger	395 027 Hannah Cockcroft
395 015 LIVE ON	395 028 Laura Trott
395 016 SOMME 100	395 029 David Weir

CLASS 399   CITYLINK   VOSSLOH/STADLER

Tram-trains for the Sheffield–Rotherham Parkgate pilot tram-train project, being run jointly by South Yorkshire Passenger Transport Executive, Network Rail, Northern and Stagecoach Supertram. Dual-voltage 750 V DC/25 kV AC (although currently only planned to operate on 750 V DC). For operation on Network Rail lines EMU running numbers 399 201–207 are carried (as well as vehicle numbers in the 999xxx series), as well as Supertram fleet numbers 201–207. Due to enter service on the Supertram network in 2017 and on the national railway network as tram-trains in 2018.

Formation: DMSO–MSO–DMSO.
Systems: 750 V DC/25 kV AC overhead.
Construction: Steel.
Traction Motors: Six VEM of 145 kW.
Wheel Arrangement: Bo-2-Bo-Bo.
Braking: Disc, regenerative & emergency track.
Dimensions: 37.20 x 2.65 m (full set). **Couplers:** Albert (emergency use).
Bogies: Vossloh.   **Control System:** IGBT Inverter.
Gangways: Within unit.   **Maximum Speed:** 60 mph.
Doors: Sliding plug.   **Multiple Working:** Within class only.
Seating Layout: 2+2 facing/unidirectional.
Weight: 64 t.

DMSO(A): Vossloh, Valencia 2014–15. –/22(+4).
MSO: Vossloh, Valencia 2014–15. –/44.
DMSO(B): Vossloh, Valencia 2014–15. –/22(+4).

399 201	**SD**	SY	NU	999001	999101	999201
399 202	**SD**	SY	NU	999002	999102	999202
399 203	**SD**	SY	NU	999003	999103	999203
399 204	**SD**	SY	NU	999004	999104	999204
399 205	**SD**	SY	NU	999005	999105	999205
399 206	**SD**	SY	NU	999006	999106	999206
399 207	**SD**	SY	NU	999007	999107	999207

4.2. 750 V DC THIRD RAIL EMUs

These classes use the third rail system at 750 V DC (unless stated). Outer couplers are buckeyes on units built before 1982 with bar couplers within the units. Newer units generally have Dellner outer couplers.

CLASS 442   WESSEX EXPRESS   BREL DERBY

Units built for Waterloo–Bournemouth–Weymouth services. Previously used by South West Trains, used by Southern until 2016 when they were mostly replaced by Class 387/2s. From late 2016 Southern retained just six units for peak-hour London Bridge–Eastbourne trains.

Formation: DTSO(A)–TSO–MBC–TSO(W)–DTSO(B).
Construction: Steel.
Traction Motors: Four EE546 of 300 kW recovered from Class 432s.
Wheel Arrangement: 2-2 + 2-2 + Bo-Bo + 2-2 + 2-2.
Braking: Disc.   **Dimensions:** 23.15/23.00 x 2.74 m.
Bogies: Two BREL P7 motor bogies (MBSO). T3 bogies (trailer cars).
Couplers: Buckeye.   **Control System:** 1986-type.
Gangways: Throughout.   **Maximum Speed:** 100 mph.
Doors: Sliding plug.   **Heating & Ventilation:** Air conditioning.
Seating Layout: 1: 2+1 facing, 2: 2+2 mainly unidirectional.
Multiple Working: Within class and Class 33/1 & 73 locos in an emergency.

DTSO(A). Lot No. 31030 Derby 1988–89. –/74. 38.5 t.
TSO. Lot No. 31032 Derby 1988–89. –/76 2T. 37.5 t.
MBC. Lot No. 31034 Derby 1988–89. 24/28. 55.0 t.
TSO(W). Lot No. 31033 Derby 1988–89. –/66(+4) 1TD 1T 2W. 37.8 t.
DTSO(B). Lot No. 31031 Derby 1988–89. –/74. 37.3 t.

442 401	**GV**	A		EP	77382	71818	62937	71842	77414
442 402	**GV**	A	*SN*	SL	77383	71819	62938	71843	77407
442 403	**GV**	A		EP	77384	71820	62941	71844	77408
442 404	**GV**	A		EP	77385	71821	62939	71845	77409
442 405	**GV**	A		ZG	77386	71822	62944	71846	77410
442 406	**GV**	A	*SN*	SL	77389	71823	62942	71847	77411
442 407	**GV**	A		EP	77388	71824	62943	71848	77412
442 408	**GV**	A	*SN*	SL	77387	71825	62945	71849	77413
442 409	**GV**	A		EP	77390	71826	62946	71850	77406
442 410	**GV**	A	*SN*	SL	77391	71827	62948	71851	77415
442 411	**GV**	A		EP	77392	71828	62940	71858	77422
442 412	**GV**	A		EP	77393	71829	62947	71853	77417
442 413	**GV**	A	*SN*	SL	77394	71830	62949	71854	77418
442 414	**GV**	A		ZG	77395	71831	62950	71855	77419
442 415	**GV**	A		EP	77396	71832	62951	71856	77420
442 416	**GV**	A		EP	77397	71833	62952	71857	77421
442 417	**GV**	A		EP	77398	71834	62953	71852	77416
442 418	**GV**	A		EP	77399	71835	62954	71859	77423
442 419	**GV**	A	*SN*	SL	77400	71836	62955	71860	77424
442 420	**GV**	A		EP	77401	71837	62956	71861	77425

442 421	**GV**	A		EP	77402	71838	62957	71862	77426
442 422	**GV**	A		EP	77403	71839	62958	71863	77427
442 423	**GV**	A		EP	77404	71840	62959	71864	77428
442 424	**GV**	A		ZG	77405	71841	62960	71865	77429

CLASS 444   DESIRO UK   SIEMENS

Express units.

Formation: DMCO–TSO–TSO–TSORMB–DMSO.
Construction: Aluminium.
Traction Motors: 4 Siemens 1TB2016-0GB02 asynchronous of 250 kW.
Wheel Arrangement: Bo-Bo + 2-2 + 2-2 + 2-2 + Bo-Bo.
Braking: Disc, rheostatic & regenerative. **Dimensions:** 23.57 x 2.80 m.
Bogies: SGP SF5000. **Couplers:** Dellner 12.
Gangways: Throughout. **Control System:** IGBT Inverter.
Doors: Single-leaf sliding plug. **Maximum Speed:** 100 mph.
Heating & Ventilation: Air conditioning.
Seating Layout: 1: 2+1 facing/unidirectional, 2: 2+2 facing/unidirectional.
Multiple Working: Within class and with Class 450.

DMSO. Siemens Vienna/Krefeld 2003–04. –/76. 51.3t.
TSO 67101–145. Siemens Vienna/Krefeld 2003–04. –/76 1T. 40.3t.
TSO 67151–195. Siemens Vienna/Krefeld 2003–04. –/76 1T. 36.8t.
TSORMB. Siemens Vienna/Krefeld 2003–04. –/47 1T 1TD 2W. 42.1t.
DMCO. Siemens Vienna/Krefeld 2003–04. 35/24. 51.3t.

444 001	**ST**	A	*SW*	NT	63801	67101	67151	67201	63851
444 002	**ST**	A	*SW*	NT	63802	67102	67152	67202	63852
444 003	**ST**	A	*SW*	NT	63803	67103	67153	67203	63853
444 004	**ST**	A	*SW*	NT	63804	67104	67154	67204	63854
444 005	**ST**	A	*SW*	NT	63805	67105	67155	67205	63855
444 006	**ST**	A	*SW*	NT	63806	67106	67156	67206	63856
444 007	**ST**	A	*SW*	NT	63807	67107	67157	67207	63857
444 008	**ST**	A	*SW*	NT	63808	67108	67158	67208	63858
444 009	**ST**	A	*SW*	NT	63809	67109	67159	67209	63859
444 010	**ST**	A	*SW*	NT	63810	67110	67160	67210	63860
444 011	**ST**	A	*SW*	NT	63811	67111	67161	67211	63861
444 012	**ST**	A	*SW*	NT	63812	67112	67162	67212	63862
444 013	**ST**	A	*SW*	NT	63813	67113	67163	67213	63863
444 014	**ST**	A	*SW*	NT	63814	67114	67164	67214	63864
444 015	**ST**	A	*SW*	NT	63815	67115	67165	67215	63865
444 016	**ST**	A	*SW*	NT	63816	67116	67166	67216	63866
444 017	**ST**	A	*SW*	NT	63817	67117	67167	67217	63867
444 018	**ST**	A	*SW*	NT	63818	67118	67168	67218	63868
444 019	**ST**	A	*SW*	NT	63819	67119	67169	67219	63869
444 020	**ST**	A	*SW*	NT	63820	67120	67170	67220	63870
444 021	**ST**	A	*SW*	NT	63821	67121	67171	67221	63871
444 022	**ST**	A	*SW*	NT	63822	67122	67172	67222	63872
444 023	**ST**	A	*SW*	NT	63823	67123	67173	67223	63873
444 024	**ST**	A	*SW*	NT	63824	67124	67174	67224	63874
444 025	**ST**	A	*SW*	NT	63825	67125	67175	67225	63875

444 026	**ST**	A	*SW*	NT	63826 67126 67176 67226 63876
444 027	**ST**	A	*SW*	NT	63827 67127 67177 67227 63877
444 028	**ST**	A	*SW*	NT	63828 67128 67178 67228 63878
444 029	**ST**	A	*SW*	NT	63829 67129 67179 67229 63879
444 030	**ST**	A	*SW*	NT	63830 67130 67180 67230 63880
444 031	**ST**	A	*SW*	NT	63831 67131 67181 67231 63881
444 032	**ST**	A	*SW*	NT	63832 67132 67182 67232 63882
444 033	**ST**	A	*SW*	NT	63833 67133 67183 67233 63883
444 034	**ST**	A	*SW*	NT	63834 67134 67184 67234 63884
444 035	**ST**	A	*SW*	NT	63835 67135 67185 67235 63885
444 036	**ST**	A	*SW*	NT	63836 67136 67186 67236 63886
444 037	**ST**	A	*SW*	NT	63837 67137 67187 67237 63887
444 038	**ST**	A	*SW*	NT	63838 67138 67188 67238 63888
444 039	**ST**	A	*SW*	NT	63839 67139 67189 67239 63889
444 040	**ST**	A	*SW*	NT	63840 67140 67190 67240 63890
444 041	**ST**	A	*SW*	NT	63841 67141 67191 67241 63891
444 042	**ST**	A	*SW*	NT	63842 67142 67192 67242 63892
444 043	**ST**	A	*SW*	NT	63843 67143 67193 67243 63893
444 044	**ST**	A	*SW*	NT	63844 67144 67194 67244 63894
444 045	**ST**	A	*SW*	NT	63845 67145 67195 67245 63895

Names (carried on TSORMB):

444 001	NAOMI HOUSE	444 018	THE FAB 444
444 012	DESTINATION WEYMOUTH	444 038	SOUTH WESTERN RAILWAY

CLASS 450　　　　DESIRO UK　　　　SIEMENS

Outer suburban units.

Formation: DMSO–TCO–TSO–DMSO (DMSO–TSO–TCO–DMSO 450 111–127).
Construction: Aluminium.
Traction Motors: 4 Siemens 1TB2016-0GB02 asynchronous of 250 kW.
Wheel Arrangement: Bo-Bo + 2-2 + 2-2 + Bo-Bo.
Braking: Disc, rheostatic & regenerative. **Dimensions:** 20.34 x 2.79 m.
Bogies: SGP SF5000. **Couplers:** Dellner 12.
Gangways: Throughout. **Control System:** IGBT Inverter.
Doors: Sliding plug. **Maximum Speed:** 100 mph.
Heating & Ventilation: Air conditioning.
Seating Layout: 1: 2+2 facing/unidirectional, 2: 3+2 facing/unidirectional.
Multiple Working: Within class and with Class 444.

Class 450/0. Standard units.

DMSO(A). Siemens Krefeld/Vienna 2002–06. –/70. 48.0 t.
TCO. Siemens Krefeld/Vienna 2002–06. 24/32(+4) 1T. 35.8 t.
TSO. Siemens Krefeld/Vienna 2002–06. –/61(+9) 1TD 2W. 39.8 t.
DMSO(B). Siemens Krefeld/Vienna 2002–06. –/70. 48.6 t.

450 001	**SD**	A	*SW*	NT	63201 64201 68101 63601
450 002	**SD**	A	*SW*	NT	63202 64202 68102 63602
450 003	**SD**	A	*SW*	NT	63203 64203 68103 63603
450 004	**SD**	A	*SW*	NT	63204 64204 68104 63604
450 005	**SD**	A	*SW*	NT	63205 64205 68105 63605

450006	**SD**	A	*SW*	NT	63206	64206	68106	63606
450007	**SD**	A	*SW*	NT	63207	64207	68107	63607
450008	**SD**	A	*SW*	NT	63208	64208	68108	63608
450009	**SD**	A	*SW*	NT	63209	64209	68109	63609
450010	**SD**	A	*SW*	NT	63210	64210	68110	63610
450011	**SD**	A	*SW*	NT	63211	64211	68111	63611
450012	**SD**	A	*SW*	NT	63212	64212	68112	63612
450013	**SD**	A	*SW*	NT	63213	64213	68113	63613
450014	**SD**	A	*SW*	NT	63214	64214	68114	63614
450015	**SD**	A	*SW*	NT	63215	64215	68115	63615
450016	**SD**	A	*SW*	NT	63216	64216	68116	63616
450017	**SD**	A	*SW*	NT	63217	64217	68117	63617
450018	**SD**	A	*SW*	NT	63218	64218	68118	63618
450019	**SD**	A	*SW*	NT	63219	64219	68119	63619
450020	**SD**	A	*SW*	NT	63220	64220	68120	63620
450021	**SD**	A	*SW*	NT	63221	64221	68121	63621
450022	**SD**	A	*SW*	NT	63222	64222	68122	63622
450023	**SD**	A	*SW*	NT	63223	64223	68123	63623
450024	**SD**	A	*SW*	NT	63224	64224	68124	63624
450025	**SD**	A	*SW*	NT	63225	64225	68125	63625
450026	**SD**	A	*SW*	NT	63226	64226	68126	63626
450027	**SD**	A	*SW*	NT	63227	64227	68127	63627
450028	**SD**	A	*SW*	NT	63228	64228	68128	63628
450029	**SD**	A	*SW*	NT	63229	64229	68129	63629
450030	**SD**	A	*SW*	NT	63230	64230	68130	63630
450031	**SD**	A	*SW*	NT	63231	64231	68131	63631
450032	**SD**	A	*SW*	NT	63232	64232	68132	63632
450033	**SD**	A	*SW*	NT	63233	64233	68133	63633
450034	**SD**	A	*SW*	NT	63234	64234	68134	63634
450035	**SD**	A	*SW*	NT	63235	64235	68135	63635
450036	**SD**	A	*SW*	NT	63236	64236	68136	63636
450037	**SD**	A	*SW*	NT	63237	64237	68137	63637
450038	**SD**	A	*SW*	NT	63238	64238	68138	63638
450039	**SD**	A	*SW*	NT	63239	64239	68139	63639
450040	**SD**	A	*SW*	NT	63240	64240	68140	63640
450041	**SD**	A	*SW*	NT	63241	64241	68141	63641
450042	**SD**	A	*SW*	NT	63242	64242	68142	63642
450071	**SD**	A	*SW*	NT	63271	64271	68171	63671
450072	**SD**	A	*SW*	NT	63272	64272	68172	63672
450073	**SD**	A	*SW*	NT	63273	64273	68173	63673
450074	**SD**	A	*SW*	NT	63274	64274	68174	63674
450075	**SD**	A	*SW*	NT	63275	64275	68175	63675
450076	**SD**	A	*SW*	NT	63276	64276	68176	63676
450077	**SD**	A	*SW*	NT	63277	64277	68177	63677
450078	**SD**	A	*SW*	NT	63278	64278	68178	63678
450079	**SD**	A	*SW*	NT	63279	64279	68179	63679
450080	**SD**	A	*SW*	NT	63280	64280	68180	63680
450081	**SD**	A	*SW*	NT	63281	64281	68181	63681
450082	**SD**	A	*SW*	NT	63282	64282	68182	63682
450083	**SD**	A	*SW*	NT	63283	64283	68183	63683
450084	**SD**	A	*SW*	NT	63284	64284	68184	63684

450 085	**SD**	A	*SW*	NT	63285	64285	68185	63685
450 086	**SD**	A	*SW*	NT	63286	64286	68186	63686
450 087	**SD**	A	*SW*	NT	63287	64287	68187	63687
450 088	**SD**	A	*SW*	NT	63288	64288	68188	63688
450 089	**SD**	A	*SW*	NT	63289	64289	68189	63689
450 090	**SD**	A	*SW*	NT	63290	64290	68190	63690
450 091	**SD**	A	*SW*	NT	63291	64291	68191	63691
450 092	**SD**	A	*SW*	NT	63292	64292	68192	63692
450 093	**SD**	A	*SW*	NT	63293	64293	68193	63693
450 094	**SD**	A	*SW*	NT	63294	64294	68194	63694
450 095	**SD**	A	*SW*	NT	63295	64295	68195	63695
450 096	**SD**	A	*SW*	NT	63296	64296	68196	63696
450 097	**SD**	A	*SW*	NT	63297	64297	68197	63697
450 098	**SD**	A	*SW*	NT	63298	64298	68198	63698
450 099	**SD**	A	*SW*	NT	63299	64299	68199	63699
450 100	**SD**	A	*SW*	NT	63300	64300	68200	63700
450 101	**SD**	A	*SW*	NT	63701	66851	66801	63751
450 102	**SD**	A	*SW*	NT	63702	66852	66802	63752
450 103	**SD**	A	*SW*	NT	63703	66853	66803	63753
450 104	**SD**	A	*SW*	NT	63704	66854	66804	63754
450 105	**SD**	A	*SW*	NT	63705	66855	66805	63755
450 106	**SD**	A	*SW*	NT	63706	66856	66806	63756
450 107	**SD**	A	*SW*	NT	63707	66857	66807	63757
450 108	**SD**	A	*SW*	NT	63708	66858	66808	63758
450 109	**SD**	A	*SW*	NT	63709	66859	66809	63759
450 110	**SD**	A	*SW*	NT	63710	66860	66810	63760
450 111	**SD**	A	*SW*	NT	63901	66921	66901	63921
450 112	**SD**	A	*SW*	NT	63902	66922	66902	63922
450 113	**SD**	A	*SW*	NT	63903	66923	66903	63923
450 114	**SD**	A	*SW*	NT	63904	66924	66904	63924
450 115	**SD**	A	*SW*	NT	63905	66925	66905	63925
450 116	**SD**	A	*SW*	NT	63906	66926	66906	63926
450 117	**SD**	A	*SW*	NT	63907	66927	66907	63927
450 118	**SD**	A	*SW*	NT	63908	66928	66908	63928
450 119	**SD**	A	*SW*	NT	63909	66929	66909	63929
450 120	**SD**	A	*SW*	NT	63910	66930	66910	63930
450 121	**SD**	A	*SW*	NT	63911	66931	66911	63931
450 122	**SD**	A	*SW*	NT	63912	66932	66912	63932
450 123	**SD**	A	*SW*	NT	63913	66933	66913	63933
450 124	**SD**	A	*SW*	NT	63914	66934	66914	63934
450 125	**SD**	A	*SW*	NT	63915	66935	66915	63935
450 126	**SD**	A	*SW*	NT	63916	66936	66916	63936
450 127	**SD**	A	*SW*	NT	63917	66937	66917	63937

Names (carried on DMSO(B)):

450 015 DESIRO
450 042 TRELOAR COLLEGE

450 114 FAIRBRIDGE investing in the future

Class 450/5. 28 units converted 2007–08 with First Class removed and a modified seating layout with more standing room (some Standard Class seats were taken out). First Class was refitted in 2013 but the removed Standard Class seats were not refitted so the units have kept their 450 5xx series numbers.

DMSO(A). Siemens Krefeld/Vienna 2002–04. –/64. 48.0 t.
TCO. Siemens Krefeld/Vienna 2002–04. 24/30(+4) 1T. 35.5 t.
TSO. Siemens Krefeld/Vienna 2002–04. –/56(+9) 1TD 2W. 39.8 t.
DMSO(B). Siemens Krefeld/Vienna 2002–04. –/64. 48.0 t.

450543	(450043)	**SD**	A	*SW*	NT	63243	64243	68143	63643
450544	(450044)	**SD**	A	*SW*	NT	63244	64244	68144	63644
450545	(450045)	**SD**	A	*SW*	NT	63245	64245	68145	63645
450546	(450046)	**SD**	A	*SW*	NT	63246	64246	68146	63646
450547	(450047)	**SD**	A	*SW*	NT	63247	64247	68147	63647
450548	(450048)	**SD**	A	*SW*	NT	63248	64248	68148	63648
450549	(450049)	**SD**	A	*SW*	NT	63249	64249	68149	63649
450550	(450050)	**SD**	A	*SW*	NT	63250	64250	68150	63650
450551	(450051)	**SD**	A	*SW*	NT	63251	64251	68151	63651
450552	(450052)	**SD**	A	*SW*	NT	63252	64252	68152	63652
450553	(450053)	**SD**	A	*SW*	NT	63253	64253	68153	63653
450554	(450054)	**SD**	A	*SW*	NT	63254	64254	68154	63654
450555	(450055)	**SD**	A	*SW*	NT	63255	64255	68155	63655
450556	(450056)	**SD**	A	*SW*	NT	63256	64256	68156	63656
450557	(450057)	**SD**	A	*SW*	NT	63257	64257	68157	63657
450558	(450058)	**SD**	A	*SW*	NT	63258	64258	68158	63658
450559	(450059)	**SD**	A	*SW*	NT	63259	64259	68159	63659
450560	(450060)	**SD**	A	*SW*	NT	63260	64260	68160	63660
450561	(450061)	**SD**	A	*SW*	NT	63261	64261	68161	63661
450562	(450062)	**SD**	A	*SW*	NT	63262	64262	68162	63662
450563	(450063)	**SD**	A	*SW*	NT	63263	64263	68163	63663
450564	(450064)	**SD**	A	*SW*	NT	63264	64264	68164	63664
450565	(450065)	**SD**	A	*SW*	NT	63265	64265	68165	63665
450566	(450066)	**SD**	A	*SW*	NT	63266	64266	68166	63666
450567	(450067)	**SD**	A	*SW*	NT	63267	64267	68167	63667
450568	(450068)	**SD**	A	*SW*	NT	63268	64268	68168	63668
450569	(450069)	**SD**	A	*SW*	NT	63269	64269	68169	63669
450570	(450070)	**SD**	A	*SW*	NT	63270	64270	68170	63670

CLASS 455   BREL YORK

Inner suburban units. During 2016–17 the South West Trains fleet of 91 units are being fitted with new AC traction motors by Vossloh Kiepe.

Formation: DTSO–MSO–TSO–DTSO.
Construction: Steel. Class 455/7 TSO have a steel underframe and an aluminium alloy body & roof.
Traction Motors: Four GEC507-20J of 185 kW, some recovered from Class 405s (* Four TSA010163 AC motors of 240 kW).
Wheel Arrangement: 2-2 + Bo-Bo + 2-2 + 2-2.
Braking: Disc (* and regenerative).   **Dimensions:** 19.92/19.83 x 2.82 m.

Bogies: P7 (motor) and T3 (455/8 & 455/9) BX1 (455/7) trailer.
Gangways: Within unit + end doors (sealed on Southern units).
Couplers: Tightlock.   **Maximum Speed:** 75 mph.
Control System: 1982-type, camshaft (* IGBT Inverter).
Doors: Sliding.   **Heating & Ventilation:** Various.
Seating Layout: All units refurbished. SWT units: 2+2 high-back unidirectional/
facing seating. Southern units: 3+2 high back mainly facing seating.
Multiple Working: Within class and with Class 456.

Class 455/7. South West Trains units. Second series with TSOs originally in
Class 508s. Pressure heating & ventilation.

DTSO. Lot No. 30976 1984–85. –/50(+4) 1W. 30.8t.
MSO. Lot No. 30975 1984–85. –/68. 45.7t.
TSO. Lot No. 30944 1979–80. –/68. 26.1t.

5701	*	**SS**	P	*SW*	WD	77727	62783	71545	77728
5702		**SS**	P	*SW*	WD	77729	62784	71547	77730
5703		**SS**	P	*SW*	WD	77731	62785	71540	77732
5704		**SS**	P	*SW*	WD	77733	62786	71548	77734
5705	*	**SS**	P	*SW*	WD	77735	62787	71565	77736
5706		**SS**	P	*SW*	WD	77737	62788	71534	77738
5707	*	**SS**	P	*SW*	WD	77739	62789	71536	77740
5708		**SS**	P	*SW*	WD	77741	62790	71560	77742
5709	*	**SS**	P	*SW*	WD	77743	62791	71532	77744
5710	*	**SS**	P	*SW*	WD	77745	62792	71566	77746
5711	*	**SS**	P	*SW*	WD	77747	62793	71542	77748
5712		**SS**	P	*SW*	WD	77749	62794	71546	77750
5713	*	**SS**	P	*SW*	WD	77751	62795	71567	77752
5714	*	**SS**	P	*SW*	WD	77753	62796	71539	77754
5715	*	**SS**	P	*SW*	WD	77755	62797	71535	77756
5716	*	**SS**	P	*SW*	WD	77757	62798	71564	77758
5717		**SS**	P	*SW*	WD	77759	62799	71528	77760
5718		**SS**	P	*SW*	WD	77761	62800	71557	77762
5719	*	**SS**	P	*SW*	WD	77763	62801	71558	77764
5720	*	**SS**	P	*SW*	WD	77765	62802	71568	77766
5721	*	**SS**	P	*SW*	WD	77767	62803	71553	77768
5722		**SS**	P	*SW*	WD	77769	62804	71533	77770
5723		**SS**	P	*SW*	WD	77771	62805	71526	77772
5724	*	**SS**	P	*SW*	WD	77773	62806	71561	77774
5725	*	**SS**	P	*SW*	WD	77775	62807	71541	77776
5726	*	**SS**	P	*SW*	WD	77777	62808	71556	77778
5727	*	**SS**	P	*SW*	WD	77779	62809	71562	77780
5728	*	**SS**	P	*SW*	WD	77781	62810	71527	77782
5729	*	**SS**	P	*SW*	WD	77783	62811	71550	77784
5730	*	**SS**	P	*SW*	WD	77785	62812	71551	77786
5731	*	**SS**	P	*SW*	WD	77787	62813	71555	77788
5732	*	**SS**	P	*SW*	WD	77789	62814	71552	77790
5733	*	**SS**	P	*SW*	WD	77791	62815	71549	77792
5734	*	**SS**	P	*SW*	WD	77793	62816	71531	77794
5735	*	**SS**	P	*SW*	WD	77795	62817	71563	77796
5736	*	**SS**	P	*SW*	WD	77797	62818	71554	77798

5737	*	**SS**	P	*SW*	WD	77799	62819	71544	77800
5738	*	**SS**	P	*SW*	WD	77801	62820	71529	77802
5739	*	**SS**	P	*SW*	WD	77803	62821	71537	77804
5740	*	**SS**	P	*SW*	WD	77805	62822	71530	77806
5741	*	**SS**	P	*SW*	WD	77807	62823	71559	77808
5742	*	**SS**	P	*SW*	WD	77809	62824	71543	77810
5750	*	**SS**	P	*SW*	WD	77811	62825	71538	77812

Class 455/8. Southern units. First series. Pressure heating & ventilation. Fitted with in-cab air conditioning systems meaning that the end door has been sealed.

DTSO. Lot No. 30972 York 1982–84. –/74. 33.6 t.
MSO. Lot No. 30973 York 1982–84. –/84. 45.6 t.
TSO. Lot No. 30974 York 1982–84. –/75(+3) 2W. 34.0 t.

455801	**SN**	E	*SN*	SL	77627	62709	71657	77580
455802	**SN**	E	*SN*	SL	77581	62710	71664	77582
455803	**SN**	E	*SN*	SL	77583	62711	71639	77584
455804	**SN**	E	*SN*	SL	77585	62712	71640	77586
455805	**SN**	E	*SN*	SL	77587	62713	71641	77588
455806	**SN**	E	*SN*	SL	77589	62714	71642	77590
455807	**SN**	E	*SN*	SL	77591	62715	71643	77592
455808	**SN**	E	*SN*	SL	77637	62716	71644	77594
455809	**SN**	E	*SN*	SL	77623	62717	71648	77602
455810	**SN**	E	*SN*	SL	77597	62718	71646	77598
455811	**SN**	E	*SN*	SL	77599	62719	71647	77600
455812	**SN**	E	*SN*	SL	77595	62720	71645	77626
455813	**SN**	E	*SN*	SL	77603	62721	71649	77604
455814	**SN**	E	*SN*	SL	77605	62722	71650	77606
455815	**SN**	E	*SN*	SL	77607	62723	71651	77608
455816	**SN**	E	*SN*	SL	77609	62724	71652	77633
455817	**SN**	E	*SN*	SL	77611	62725	71653	77612
455818	**SN**	E	*SN*	SL	77613	62726	71654	77632
455819	**SN**	E	*SN*	SL	77615	62727	71637	77616
455820	**SN**	E	*SN*	SL	77617	62728	71656	77618
455821	**SN**	E	*SN*	SL	77619	62729	71655	77620
455822	**SN**	E	*SN*	SL	77621	62730	71658	77622
455823	**SN**	E	*SN*	SL	77601	62731	71659	77596
455824	**SN**	E	*SN*	SL	77593	62732	71660	77624
455825	**SN**	E	*SN*	SL	77579	62733	71661	77628
455826	**SN**	E	*SN*	SL	77630	62734	71662	77629
455827	**SN**	E	*SN*	SL	77610	62735	71663	77614
455828	**SN**	E	*SN*	SL	77631	62736	71638	77634
455829	**SN**	E	*SN*	SL	77635	62737	71665	77636
455830	**SN**	E	*SN*	SL	77625	62743	71666	77638
455831	**SN**	E	*SN*	SL	77639	62739	71667	77640
455832	**SN**	E	*SN*	SL	77641	62740	71668	77642
455833	**SN**	E	*SN*	SL	77643	62741	71669	77644
455834	**SN**	E	*SN*	SL	77645	62742	71670	77646
455835	**SN**	E	*SN*	SL	77647	62738	71671	77648
455836	**SN**	E	*SN*	SL	77649	62744	71672	77650

455837	**SN**	E	*SN*	SL	77651	62745	71673	77652
455838	**SN**	E	*SN*	SL	77653	62746	71674	77654
455839	**SN**	E	*SN*	SL	77655	62747	71675	77656
455840	**SN**	E	*SN*	SL	77657	62748	71676	77658
455841	**SN**	E	*SN*	SL	77659	62749	71677	77660
455842	**SN**	E	*SN*	SL	77661	62750	71678	77662
455843	**SN**	E	*SN*	SL	77663	62751	71679	77664
455844	**SN**	E	*SN*	SL	77665	62752	71680	77666
455845	**SN**	E	*SN*	SL	77667	62753	71681	77668
455846	**SN**	E	*SN*	SL	77669	62754	71682	77670

Class 455/8. South West Trains units. First series. Pressure heating & ventilation.

DTSO. Lot No. 30972 York 1982–84. –50(+4) 1W. 29.5 t.
MSO. Lot No. 30973 York 1982–84. –/68. 45.6 t.
TSO. Lot No. 30974 York 1982–84. –/68. 27.1 t.

5847		**SS**	P	*SW*	WD	77671	62755	71683	77672
5848		**SS**	P	*SW*	WD	77673	62756	71684	77674
5849		**SS**	P	*SW*	WD	77675	62757	71685	77676
5850		**SS**	P	*SW*	WD	77677	62758	71686	77678
5851		**SS**	P	*SW*	WD	77679	62759	71687	77680
5852		**SS**	P	*SW*	WD	77681	62760	71688	77682
5853		**SS**	P	*SW*	WD	77683	62761	71689	77684
5854		**SS**	P	*SW*	WD	77685	62762	71690	77686
5855		**SS**	P	*SW*	WD	77687	62763	71691	77688
5856		**SS**	P	*SW*	WD	77689	62764	71692	77690
5857		**SS**	P	*SW*	WD	77691	62765	71693	77692
5858		**SS**	P	*SW*	WD	77693	62766	71694	77694
5859		**SS**	P	*SW*	WD	77695	62767	71695	77696
5860		**SS**	P	*SW*	WD	77697	62768	71696	77698
5861		**SS**	P	*SW*	WD	77699	62769	71697	77700
5862		**SS**	P	*SW*	WD	77701	62770	71698	77702
5863		**SS**	P	*SW*	WD	77703	62771	71699	77704
5864		**SS**	P	*SW*	WD	77705	62772	71700	77706
5865		**SS**	P	*SW*	WD	77707	62773	71701	77708
5866		**SS**	P	*SW*	WD	77709	62774	71702	77710
5867		**SS**	P	*SW*	WD	77711	62775	71703	77712
5868		**SS**	P	*SW*	WD	77713	62776	71704	77714
5869		**SS**	P	*SW*	WD	77715	62777	71705	77716
5870	*	**SS**	P	*SW*	WD	77717	62778	71706	77718
5871		**SS**	P	*SW*	WD	77719	62779	71707	77720
5872		**SS**	P	*SW*	WD	77721	62780	71708	77722
5873		**SS**	P	*SW*	WD	77723	62781	71709	77724
5874		**SS**	P	*SW*	WD	77725	62782	71710	77726

Class 455/9. South West Trains units. Third series. Convection heating.
Dimensions: 19.96/20.18 x 2.82 m.

67301 and 67400 were converted from Class 210 DEMU vehicles to replace accident damaged cars.

DTSO. Lot No. 30991 York 1985. –/50(+4) 1W. 30.7 t.
MSO. Lot No. 30992 York 1985. –/68. 46.3 t.

MSO 67301. Lot No. 30932 Derby 1981. –/68.   t.
TSO. Lot No. 30993 York 1985. –/68. 28.3 t.
TSO 67400. Lot No. 30932 Derby 1981. –/68. 26.5 t.

5901		**SS**	P	*SW*	WD	77813	62826	71714	77814
5902		**SS**	P	*SW*	WD	77815	62827	71715	77816
5903		**SS**	P	*SW*	WD	77817	62828	71716	77818
5904		**SS**	P	*SW*	WD	77819	62829	71717	77820
5905		**SS**	P	*SW*	WD	77821	62830	71725	77822
5906		**SS**	P	*SW*	WD	77823	62831	71719	77824
5907		**SS**	P	*SW*	WD	77825	62832	71720	77826
5908		**SS**	P	*SW*	WD	77827	62833	71721	77828
5909		**SS**	P	*SW*	WD	77829	62834	71722	77830
5910		**SS**	P	*SW*	WD	77831	62835	71723	77832
5911		**SS**	P	*SW*	WD	77833	62836	71724	77834
5912		**SS**	P	*SW*	WD	77835	62837	67400	77836
5913		**SS**	P	*SW*	WD	77837	67301	71726	77838
5914		**SS**	P	*SW*	WD	77839	62839	71727	77840
5915		**SS**	P	*SW*	WD	77841	62840	71728	77842
5916	*	**SS**	P	*SW*	WD	77843	62841	71729	77844
5917		**SS**	P	*SW*	WD	77845	62842	71730	77846
5918		**SS**	P	*SW*	WD	77847	62843	71732	77848
5919		**SS**	P	*SW*	WD	77849	62844	71718	77850
5920		**SS**	P	*SW*	WD	77851	62845	71733	77852

CLASS 456   BREL YORK

Inner suburban units previously operated by Southern, but operated by South West Trains (following refurbishment) from 2014–15.

Formation: DMSO–DTSO.
Construction: Steel underframe, aluminium alloy body & roof.
Traction Motors: Two GEC507-21J of 185 kW, some recovered from Class 405s.
Wheel Arrangement: 2-Bo + 2-2.   **Dimensions:** 20.61 x 2.82 m.
Braking: Disc.   **Couplers:** Tightlock.
Bogies: P7 (motor) and T3 (trailer).   **Control System:** GTO Chopper.
Gangways: Within unit.   **Maximum Speed:** 75 mph.
Doors: Sliding.
Seating Layout: 2+2 facing/unidirectional.
Heating & Ventilation: Convection heating.
Multiple Working: Within class and with Class 455.

DMSO. Lot No. 31073 1990–91. –/59. 43.3 t.
DTSO. Lot No. 31074 1990–91. –/54(+5). 32.3 t.

456 001	**SS**	P	*SW*	WD	64735	78250
456 002	**SS**	P	*SW*	WD	64736	78251
456 003	**SS**	P	*SW*	WD	64737	78252
456 004	**SS**	P	*SW*	WD	64738	78253
456 005	**SS**	P	*SW*	WD	64739	78254
456 006	**SS**	P	*SW*	WD	64740	78255
456 007	**SS**	P	*SW*	WD	64741	78256

456008	**SS**	P	*SW*	WD	64742	78257
456009	**SS**	P	*SW*	WD	64743	78258
456010	**SS**	P	*SW*	WD	64744	78259
456011	**SS**	P	*SW*	WD	64745	78260
456012	**SS**	P	*SW*	WD	64746	78261
456013	**SS**	P	*SW*	WD	64747	78262
456014	**SS**	P	*SW*	WD	64748	78263
456015	**SS**	P	*SW*	WD	64749	78264
456016	**SS**	P	*SW*	WD	64750	78265
456017	**SS**	P	*SW*	WD	64751	78266
456018	**SS**	P	*SW*	WD	64752	78267
456019	**SS**	P	*SW*	WD	64753	78268
456020	**SS**	P	*SW*	WD	64754	78269
456021	**SS**	P	*SW*	WD	64755	78270
456022	**SS**	P	*SW*	WD	64756	78271
456023	**SS**	P	*SW*	WD	64757	78272
456024	**SS**	P	*SW*	WD	64758	78273

CLASS 458   JUNIPER   ALSTOM BIRMINGHAM

Outer suburban units. Between 2013 and 2016 the fleet of 30 4-car Class 458 units and the former Gatwick Express fleet of eight 8-car Class 460 units was combined to form a fleet of 36 5-car Standard Class only Class 458/5s. The work was carried out at Wabtec Doncaster and Brush Loughborough. Former Class 460 driving cars 67901/903/907/908 were not included in this programme and have been scrapped.

After lengthening each unit was renumbered into the 458 5xx series. All individual vehicles retained their original numbers.

Formation: DMSO–TSO*–TSO–MSO–DMSO (* ex-Class 460 in 458 501–530).
Construction: Steel.   **Dimensions:** 21.16 or 21.06 x 2.80 m.
Traction Motors: Two Alstom ONIX 800 asynchronous of 270 kW.
Wheel Arrangement: 2-Bo + 2-2 + 2-2 + Bo-2 + Bo-2.
Braking: Disc & regenerative.   **Control System:** IGBT Inverter.
Bogies: ACR.   **Doors:** Sliding plug.
Gangways: Throughout.
Couplers: Voith 136.
Maximum Speed: 75 mph.
Heating & Ventilation: Air conditioning. **Multiple Working:** Within class.
Seating Layout: 2+2 facing/unidirectional.

DMSO(A). Alstom 1998–2000. –/60. 45.7 t.
TSO. Alstom 1998–99. 458 501–530 –/56; 458 531–536 –/52 1T. 34.4 t.
TSO. Alstom 1998–2000. –/42 1TD 2W. 34.1 t.
MSO. Alstom 1998–2000. 458 501–530 –56 1T; 458 531–536 –/56. 40.1 t.
DMSO(B). Alstom 1998–2000. –/60. 44.9 t.

458501	**SD**	P	*SW*	WD	67601 74431 74001 74101 67701
458502	**SD**	P	*SW*	WD	67602 74421 74002 74102 67702
458503	**SD**	P	*SW*	WD	67603 74441 74003 74103 67703
458504	**SD**	P	*SW*	WD	67604 74451 74004 74104 67704

458 505	**SD**	P	*SW*	WD	67605	74425	74005	74105	67705
458 506	**SD**	P	*SW*	WD	67606	74436	74006	74106	67706
458 507	**SD**	P	*SW*	WD	67607	74428	74007	74107	67707
458 508	**SD**	P	*SW*	WD	67608	74433	74008	74108	67708
458 509	**SD**	P	*SW*	WD	67609	74452	74009	74109	67709
458 510	**SD**	P	*SW*	WD	67610	74405	74010	74110	67710
458 511	**SD**	P	*SW*	WD	67611	74435	74011	74111	67711
458 512	**SD**	P	*SW*	WD	67612	74427	74012	74112	67712
458 513	**SD**	P	*SW*	WD	67613	74437	74013	74113	67713
458 514	**SD**	P	*SW*	WD	67614	74407	74014	74114	67714
458 515	**SD**	P	*SW*	WD	67615	74404	74015	74115	67715
458 516	**SD**	P	*SW*	WD	67616	74406	74016	74116	67716
458 517	**SD**	P	*SW*	WD	67617	74426	74017	74117	67717
458 518	**SD**	P	*SW*	WD	67618	74432	74018	74118	67718
458 519	**SD**	P	*SW*	WD	67619	74403	74019	74119	67719
458 520	**SD**	P	*SW*	WD	67620	74401	74020	74120	67720
458 521	**SD**	P	*SW*	WD	67621	74438	74021	74121	67721
458 522	**SD**	P	*SW*	WD	67622	74424	74022	74122	67722
458 523	**SD**	P	*SW*	WD	67623	74434	74023	74123	67723
458 524	**SD**	P	*SW*	WD	67624	74402	74024	74124	67724
458 525	**SD**	P	*SW*	WD	67625	74422	74025	74125	67725
458 526	**SD**	P	*SW*	WD	67626	74442	74026	74126	67726
458 527	**SD**	P	*SW*	WD	67627	74412	74027	74127	67727
458 528	**SD**	P	*SW*	WD	67628	74408	74028	74128	67728
458 529	**SD**	P	*SW*	WD	67629	74423	74029	74129	67729
458 530	**SD**	P	*SW*	WD	67630	74401	74030	74130	67730

The following units were converted entirely from Class 460s.

458 531	**SD**	P	*SW*	WD	67913	74418	74446	74458	67912
458 532	**SD**	P	*SW*	WD	67904	74417	74447	74457	67905
458 533	**SD**	P	*SW*	WD	67917	74413	74443	74453	67916
458 534	**SD**	P	*SW*	WD	67914	74414	74444	74454	67918
458 535	**SD**	P	*SW*	WD	67915	74415	74445	74455	67911
458 536	**SD**	P	*SW*	WD	67906	74416	74448	74456	67902

CLASS 465   NETWORKER

Inner/outer suburban units.

Formation: DMSO–TSO–TSO–DMSO.
Construction: Welded aluminium alloy.
Traction Motors: Hitachi asynchronous of 280 kW (Classes 465/0 and 465/1) or GEC-Alsthom G352BY (Classes 465/2 and 465/9).
Wheel Arrangement: Bo-Bo + 2-2 + 2-2 + Bo-Bo.
Braking: Disc & rheostatic and regenerative (Classes 465/0 and 465/1 only).
Bogies: BREL P3/T3 (465/0 and 465/1), SRP BP62/BT52 (465/2 and 465/9).
Dimensions: 20.89/20.06 x 2.81 m.
Control System: IGBT Inverter (465/0 and 465/1) or 1992-type GTO Inverter.
Gangways: Within unit.   **Couplers:** Tightlock.
Doors: Sliding plug.   **Maximum Speed:** 75 mph.
Seating Layout: 3+2 facing/unidirectional.

Multiple Working: Within class and with Class 466.

64759–808. DMSO(A). Lot No. 31100 BREL York 1991–93. –/86. 39.2t.
64809–858. DMSO(B). Lot No. 31100 BREL York 1991–93. –/86. 39.2t.
65734–749. DMSO(A). Lot No. 31103 Metro-Cammell 1991–93. –/86. 39.2t.
65784–799. DMSO(B). Lot No. 31103 Metro-Cammell 1991–93. –/86. 39.2t.
65800–846. DMSO(A). Lot No. 31130 ABB York 1993–94. –/86. 39.2t.
65847–893. DMSO(B). Lot No. 31130 ABB York 1993–94. –/86. 39.2t.
72028–126 (even nos.) TSO. Lot No. 31102 BREL York 1991–93. –/90. 27.2t.
72029–127 (odd nos.) TSO. Lot No. 31101 BREL York 1991–93. –/86 1T. 28.0t.
72787–817 (odd nos.) TSO. Lot No. 31104 Metro-Cammell 1991–92. –/86 1T. 28.0t.
72788–818 (even nos.) TSO. Lot No. 31105 Metro-Cammell 1991–92. –/90. 27.2t.
72900–992 (even nos.) TSO. Lot No. 31102 ABB York 1993–94. –/90. 27.2t.
72901–993 (odd nos.) TSO. Lot No. 31101 ABB York 1993–94. –/86 1T. 28.0t.

Class 465/0. Built by BREL/ABB.

* Fitted with a universal access toilet to meet the 2020 accessibilty regulations. Full details awaited.

465001		**SE**	E	*SE*	SG	64759	72028	72029	64809
465002	*	**SE**	E	*SE*	SG	64760	72030	72031	64810
465003		**SE**	E	*SE*	SG	64761	72032	72033	64811
465004		**SE**	E	*SE*	SG	64762	72034	72035	64812
465005		**SE**	E	*SE*	SG	64763	72036	72037	64813
465006		**SE**	E	*SE*	SG	64764	72038	72039	64814
465007		**SE**	E	*SE*	SG	64765	72040	72041	64815
465008		**SE**	E	*SE*	SG	64766	72042	72043	64816
465009		**SE**	E	*SE*	SG	64767	72044	72045	64817
465010		**SE**	E	*SE*	SG	64768	72046	72047	64818
465011		**SE**	E	*SE*	SG	64769	72048	72049	64819
465012		**SE**	E	*SE*	SG	64770	72050	72051	64820
465013		**SE**	E	*SE*	SG	64771	72052	72053	64821
465014	*	**SE**	E	*SE*	SG	64772	72054	72055	64822
465015		**SE**	E	*SE*	SG	64773	72056	72057	64823
465016		**SE**	E	*SE*	SG	64774	72058	72059	64824
465017		**SE**	E	*SE*	SG	64775	72060	72061	64825
465018		**SE**	E	*SE*	SG	64776	72062	72063	64826
465019		**SE**	E	*SE*	SG	64777	72064	72065	64827
465020		**SE**	E	*SE*	SG	64778	72066	72067	64828
465021		**SE**	E	*SE*	SG	64779	72068	72069	64829
465022		**SE**	E	*SE*	SG	64780	72070	72071	64830
465023		**SE**	E	*SE*	SG	64781	72072	72073	64831
465024		**SE**	E	*SE*	SG	64782	72074	72075	64832
465025		**SE**	E	*SE*	SG	64783	72076	72077	64833
465026		**SE**	E	*SE*	SG	64784	72078	72079	64834
465027		**SE**	E	*SE*	SG	64785	72080	72081	64835
465028		**SE**	E	*SE*	SG	64786	72082	72083	64836
465029		**SE**	E	*SE*	SG	64787	72084	72085	64837
465030		**SE**	E	*SE*	SG	64788	72086	72087	64838
465031		**SE**	E	*SE*	SG	64789	72088	72089	64839
465032		**SE**	E	*SE*	SG	64790	72090	72091	64840
465033		**SE**	E	*SE*	SG	64791	72092	72093	64841

465 034		**SE**	E	*SE*	SG	64792	72094	72095	64842
465 035		**SE**	E	*SE*	SG	64793	72096	72097	64843
465 036		**SE**	E	*SE*	SG	64794	72098	72099	64844
465 037		**SE**	E	*SE*	SG	64795	72100	72101	64845
465 038		**SE**	E	*SE*	SG	64796	72102	72103	64846
465 039		**SE**	E	*SE*	SG	64797	72104	72105	64847
465 040		**SE**	E	*SE*	SG	64798	72106	72107	64848
465 041		**SE**	E	*SE*	SG	64799	72108	72109	64849
465 042		**SE**	E	*SE*	SG	64800	72110	72111	64850
465 043		**SE**	E	*SE*	SG	64801	72112	72113	64851
465 044		**SE**	E	*SE*	SG	64802	72114	72115	64852
465 045		**SE**	E	*SE*	SG	64803	72116	72117	64853
465 046		**SE**	E	*SE*	SG	64804	72118	72119	64854
465 047		**SE**	E	*SE*	SG	64805	72120	72121	64855
465 048		**SE**	E	*SE*	SG	64806	72122	72123	64856
465 049	*	**SE**	E	*SE*	SG	64807	72124	72125	64857
465 050		**SE**	E	*SE*	SG	64808	72126	72127	64858

Class 465/1. Built by BREL/ABB. Similar to Class 465/0 but with detail differences.

465 151	**SE**	E	*SE*	SG	65800	72900	72901	65847
465 152	**SE**	E	*SE*	SG	65801	72902	72903	65848
465 153	**SE**	E	*SE*	SG	65802	72904	72905	65849
465 154	**SE**	E	*SE*	SG	65803	72906	72907	65850
465 155	**SE**	E	*SE*	SG	65804	72908	72909	65851
465 156	**SE**	E	*SE*	SG	65805	72910	72911	65852
465 157	**SE**	E	*SE*	SG	65806	72912	72913	65853
465 158	**SE**	E	*SE*	SG	65807	72914	72915	65854
465 159	**SE**	E	*SE*	SG	65808	72916	72917	65855
465 160	**SE**	E	*SE*	SG	65809	72918	72919	65856
465 161	**SE**	E	*SE*	SG	65810	72920	72921	65857
465 162	**SE**	E	*SE*	SG	65811	72922	72923	65858
465 163	**SE**	E	*SE*	SG	65812	72924	72925	65859
465 164	**SE**	E	*SE*	SG	65813	72926	72927	65860
465 165	**SE**	E	*SE*	SG	65814	72928	72929	65861
465 166	**SE**	E	*SE*	SG	65815	72930	72931	65862
465 167	**SE**	E	*SE*	SG	65816	72932	72933	65863
465 168	**SE**	E	*SE*	SG	65817	72934	72935	65864
465 169	**SE**	E	*SE*	SG	65818	72936	72937	65865
465 170	**SE**	E	*SE*	SG	65819	72938	72939	65866
465 171	**SE**	E	*SE*	SG	65820	72940	72941	65867
465 172	**SE**	E	*SE*	SG	65821	72942	72943	65868
465 173	**SE**	E	*SE*	SG	65822	72944	72945	65869
465 174	**SE**	E	*SE*	SG	65823	72946	72947	65870
465 175	**SE**	E	*SE*	SG	65824	72948	72949	65871
465 176	**SE**	E	*SE*	SG	65825	72950	72951	65872
465 177	**SE**	E	*SE*	SG	65826	72952	72953	65873
465 178	**SE**	E	*SE*	SG	65827	72954	72955	65874
465 179	**SE**	E	*SE*	SG	65828	72956	72957	65875
465 180	**SE**	E	*SE*	SG	65829	72958	72959	65876
465 181	**SE**	E	*SE*	SG	65830	72960	72961	65877

465 182	**SE**	E	*SE*	SG	65831	72962	72963	65878
465 183	**SE**	E	*SE*	SG	65832	72964	72965	65879
465 184	**SE**	E	*SE*	SG	65833	72966	72967	65880
465 185	**SE**	E	*SE*	SG	65834	72968	72969	65881
465 186	**SE**	E	*SE*	SG	65835	72970	72971	65882
465 187	**SE**	E	*SE*	SG	65836	72972	72973	65883
465 188	**SE**	E	*SE*	SG	65837	72974	72975	65884
465 189	**SE**	E	*SE*	SG	65838	72976	72977	65885
465 190	**SE**	E	*SE*	SG	65839	72978	72979	65886
465 191	**SE**	E	*SE*	SG	65840	72980	72981	65887
465 192	**SE**	E	*SE*	SG	65841	72982	72983	65888
465 193	**SE**	E	*SE*	SG	65842	72984	72985	65889
465 194	**SE**	E	*SE*	SG	65843	72986	72987	65890
465 195	**SE**	E	*SE*	SG	65844	72988	72989	65891
465 196	**SE**	E	*SE*	SG	65845	72990	72991	65892
465 197	**SE**	E	*SE*	SG	65846	72992	72993	65893

Class 465/2. Built by Metro-Cammell. **Dimensions:** 20.80/20.15 x 2.81 m.

* Fitted with a universal access toilet to meet the 2020 accessibilty regulations. Full details awaited.

465 235		**SE**	A	*SE*	SG	65734	72787	72788	65784
465 236		**SE**	A	*SE*	SG	65735	72789	72790	65785
465 237		**SE**	A	*SE*	SG	65736	72791	72792	65786
465 238	*	**SE**	A	*SE*	SG	65737	72793	72794	65787
465 239		**SE**	A	*SE*	SG	65738	72795	72796	65788
465 240		**SE**	A	*SE*	SG	65739	72797	72798	65789
465 241		**SE**	A	*SE*	SG	65740	72799	72800	65790
465 242	*	**SE**	A	*SE*	SG	65741	72801	72802	65791
465 243		**SE**	A	*SE*	SG	65742	72803	72804	65792
465 244		**SE**	A	*SE*	SG	65743	72805	72806	65793
465 245		**SE**	A	*SE*	SG	65744	72807	72808	65794
465 246		**SE**	A	*SE*	SG	65745	72809	72810	65795
465 247		**SE**	A	*SE*	SG	65746	72811	72812	65796
465 248		**SE**	A	*SE*	SG	65747	72813	72814	65797
465 249		**SE**	A	*SE*	SG	65748	72815	72816	65798
465 250		**SE**	A	*SE*	SG	65749	72817	72818	65799

Class 465/9. Built by Metro-Cammell. Refurbished 2005 for longer distance services, with the addition of First Class. Details as Class 465/0 unless stated.
Formation: DMCO–TSO(A)–TSO(B)–DMCO.
Seating Layout: 1: 2+2 facing/unidirectional, 2: 3+2 facing/unidirectional.

* Fitted with a universal access toilet to meet the 2020 accessibilty regulations.

65700–733. DMCO(A). Lot No. 31103 Metro-Cammell 1991–93. 12/68. 39.2t.
72719–785 (odd nos.) TSO(A). Lot No. 31104 Metro-Cammell 1991–92. –/76 1T 2W (* –/65(+7) 1TD 2W). 30.3t.
72720–786 (even nos.) TSO(B). Lot No. 31105 Metro-Cammell 1991–92. –/90. 29.5t.
65750–783. DMCO(B). Lot No. 31103 Metro-Cammell 1991–93. 12/68. 39.2t.

| 465 901 | (465 201) | **SE** | A | *SE* | SG | 65700 72719 72720 65750 |

465 902	(465 202)		**SE**	A	*SE*	SG	65701	72721 72722	65751
465 903	(465 203)		**SE**	A	*SE*	SG	65702	72723 72724	65752
465 904	(465 204)		**SE**	A	*SE*	SG	65703	72725 72726	65753
465 905	(465 205)	*	**SE**	A	*SE*	SG	65704	72727 72728	65754
465 906	(465 206)	*	**SE**	A	*SE*	SG	65705	72729 72730	65755
465 907	(465 207)	*	**SE**	A	*SE*	SG	65706	72731 72732	65756
465 908	(465 208)	*	**SE**	A	*SE*	SG	65707	72733 72734	65757
465 909	(465 209)	*	**SE**	A	*SE*	SG	65708	72735 72736	65758
465 910	(465 210)	*	**SE**	A	*SE*	SG	65709	72737 72738	65759
465 911	(465 211)		**SE**	A	*SE*	SG	65710	72739 72740	65760
465 912	(465 212)		**SE**	A	*SE*	SG	65711	72741 72742	65761
465 913	(465 213)	*	**SE**	A	*SE*	SG	65712	72743 72744	65762
465 914	(465 214)	*	**SE**	A	*SE*	SG	65713	72745 72746	65763
465 915	(465 215)		**SE**	A	*SE*	SG	65714	72747 72748	65764
465 916	(465 216)	*	**SE**	A	*SE*	SG	65715	72749 72750	65765
465 917	(465 217)	*	**SE**	A	*SE*	SG	65716	72751 72752	65766
465 918	(465 218)		**SE**	A	*SE*	SG	65717	72753 72754	65767
465 919	(465 219)		**SE**	A	*SE*	SG	65718	72755 72756	65768
465 920	(465 220)		**SE**	A	*SE*	SG	65719	72757 72758	65769
465 921	(465 221)	*	**SE**	A	*SE*	SG	65720	72759 72760	65770
465 922	(465 222)		**SE**	A	*SE*	SG	65721	72761 72762	65771
465 923	(465 223)	*	**SE**	A	*SE*	SG	65722	72763 72764	65772
465 924	(465 224)	*	**SE**	A	*SE*	SG	65723	72765 72766	65773
465 925	(465 225)	*	**SE**	A	*SE*	SG	65724	72767 72768	65774
465 926	(465 226)		**SE**	A	*SE*	SG	65725	72769 72770	65775
465 927	(465 227)		**SE**	A	*SE*	SG	65726	72771 72772	65776
465 928	(465 228)	*	**SE**	A	*SE*	SG	65727	72773 72774	65777
465 929	(465 229)		**SE**	A	*SE*	SG	65728	72775 72776	65778
465 930	(465 230)		**SE**	A	*SE*	SG	65729	72777 72778	65779
465 931	(465 231)	*	**SE**	A	*SE*	SG	65730	72779 72780	65780
465 932	(465 232)		**SE**	A	*SE*	SG	65731	72781 72782	65781
465 933	(465 233)	*	**SE**	A	*SE*	SG	65732	72783 72784	65782
465 934	(465 234)	*	**SE**	A	*SE*	SG	65733	72785 72786	65783

CLASS 466   NETWORKER   GEC-ALSTHOM

Inner/outer suburban units.

Formation: DMSO–DTSO.
Construction: Welded aluminium alloy.
Traction Motors: Two GEC-Alsthom G352AY asynchronous of 280 kW.
Wheel Arrangement: Bo-Bo + 2-2.   **Couplers:** Tightlock.
Braking: Disc, rheostatic & regen.   **Control System:** 1992-type GTO Inverter.
Dimensions: 20.80 x 2.80 m.   **Maximum Speed:** 75 mph.
Bogies: BREL P3/T3.   **Doors:** Sliding plug.
Gangways: Within unit.   **Seating Layout:** 3+2 facing/unidirectional.
Multiple Working: Within class and with Class 465.

DMSO. Lot No. 31128 Birmingham 1993–94. –/86. 40.6 t.
DTSO. Lot No. 31129 Birmingham 1993–94. –/82 1T. 31.4 t.

466 001	**SE**	A	*SE*	SG	64860	78312
466 002	**SE**	A	*SE*	SG	64861	78313
466 003	**SE**	A	*SE*	SG	64862	78314
466 004	**SE**	A	*SE*	SG	64863	78315
466 005	**SE**	A	*SE*	SG	64864	78316
466 006	**SE**	A	*SE*	SG	64865	78317
466 007	**SE**	A	*SE*	SG	64866	78318
466 008	**SE**	A	*SE*	SG	64867	78319
466 009	**SE**	A	*SE*	SG	64868	78320
466 010	**SE**	A	*SE*	SG	64869	78321
466 011	**SE**	A	*SE*	SG	64870	78322
466 012	**SE**	A	*SE*	SG	64871	78323
466 013	**SE**	A	*SE*	SG	64872	78324
466 014	**SE**	A	*SE*	SG	64873	78325
466 015	**SE**	A	*SE*	SG	64874	78326
466 016	**SE**	A	*SE*	SG	64875	78327
466 017	**SE**	A	*SE*	SG	64876	78328
466 018	**SE**	A	*SE*	SG	64877	78329
466 019	**SE**	A	*SE*	SG	64878	78330
466 020	**SE**	A	*SE*	SG	64879	78331
466 021	**SE**	A	*SE*	SG	64880	78332
466 022	**SE**	A	*SE*	SG	64881	78333
466 023	**SE**	A	*SE*	SG	64882	78334
466 024	**SE**	A	*SE*	SG	64883	78335
466 025	**SE**	A	*SE*	SG	64884	78336
466 026	**SE**	A	*SE*	SG	64885	78337
466 027	**SE**	A	*SE*	SG	64886	78338
466 028	**SE**	A	*SE*	SG	64887	78339
466 029	**SE**	A	*SE*	SG	64888	78340
466 030	**SE**	A	*SE*	SG	64889	78341
466 031	**SE**	A	*SE*	SG	64890	78342
466 032	**SE**	A	*SE*	SG	64891	78343
466 033	**SE**	A	*SE*	SG	64892	78344
466 034	**SE**	A	*SE*	SG	64893	78345
466 035	**SE**	A	*SE*	SG	64894	78346
466 036	**SE**	A	*SE*	SG	64895	78347
466 037	**SE**	A	*SE*	SG	64896	78348
466 038	**SE**	A	*SE*	SG	64897	78349
466 039	**SE**	A	*SE*	SG	64898	78350
466 040	**SE**	A	*SE*	SG	64899	78351
466 041	**SE**	A	*SE*	SG	64900	78352
466 042	**SE**	A	*SE*	SG	64901	78353
466 043	**SE**	A	*SE*	SG	64902	78354

CLASS 483   METRO-CAMMELL

Built 1938 onwards for LTE. Converted 1989–90 for the Isle of Wight Line.

Formation: DMSO–DMSO.
System: 660 V DC third rail.
Construction: Steel.
Traction Motors: Two Crompton Parkinson/GEC/BTH LT100 of 125 kW.
Braking: Tread.   **Dimensions:** 16.15 x 2.69 m.
Bogies: LT design.   **Couplers:** Wedgelock.
Gangways: None. End doors.
Control System: Pneumatic Camshaft Motor (PCM).
Doors: Sliding.   **Maximum Speed:** 45 mph.
Seating Layout: Longitudinal or 2+2 facing/unidirectional.
Multiple Working: Within class.
The last three numbers of the unit number only are carried.

Former London Underground numbers are shown in parentheses.

DMSO (A). Lot No. 31071. –/40. 27.4 t.
DMSO (B). Lot No. 31072. –/42. 27.4 t.

483002	**LT**	SW		RY (S)	122	(10221)	225	(11142)	RAPTOR
483004	**LT**	SW	*SW*	RY	124	(10205)	224	(11205)	
483006	**LT**	SW	*SW*	RY	126	(10297)	226	(11297)	
483007	**LT**	SW	*SW*	RY	127	(10291)	227	(11291)	
483008	**LT**	SW	*SW*	RY	128	(10255)	228	(11255)	
483009	**LT**	SW	*SW*	RY	129	(10229)	229	(11229)	

CLASS 507   BREL YORK

Formation: BDMSO–TSO–DMSO.
Construction: Steel underframe, aluminium alloy body and roof.
Traction Motors: Four GEC G310AZ of 82.125 kW.
Wheel Arrangement: Bo-Bo + 2-2 + Bo-Bo.
Braking: Disc & rheostatic.   **Dimensions:** 20.18 x 2.82 m.
Bogies: BX1.   **Couplers:** Tightlock.
Gangways: Within unit + end doors.   **Control System:** Camshaft.
Doors: Sliding.   **Maximum Speed:** 75 mph.
Seating Layout: All refurbished with 2+2 high-back facing seating.
Multiple Working: Within class and with Class 508.

Fitted with tripcocks for operating on the Merseyrail Wirral Lines.

Advertising livery: 507 002 Liverpool Hope University (white).

BDMSO. Lot No. 30906 1978–80. –/56(+3) 1W. 37.0 t.
TSO. Lot No. 30907 1978–80. –/74. 25.5 t.
DMSO. Lot No. 30908 1978–80. –/56(+3) 1W. 35.5 t.

507001	**MY**	A	*ME*	BD	64367	71342	64405
507002	**AL**	A	*ME*	BD	64368	71343	64406
507003	**MY**	A	*ME*	BD	64369	71344	64407

507 004	**MY**	A	*ME*	BD	64388	71345	64408
507 005	**MY**	A	*ME*	BD	64371	71346	64409
507 006	**MY**	A	*ME*	BD	64372	71347	64410
507 007	**MY**	A	*ME*	BD	64373	71348	64411
507 008	**MY**	A	*ME*	BD	64374	71349	64412
507 009	**MY**	A	*ME*	BD	64375	71350	64413
507 010	**MY**	A	*ME*	BD	64376	71351	64414
507 011	**MY**	A	*ME*	BD	64377	71352	64415
507 012	**MY**	A	*ME*	BD	64378	71353	64416
507 013	**MY**	A	*ME*	BD	64379	71354	64417
507 014	**MY**	A	*ME*	BD	64380	71355	64418
507 015	**MY**	A	*ME*	BD	64381	71356	64419
507 016	**MY**	A	*ME*	BD	64382	71357	64420
507 017	**MY**	A	*ME*	BD	64383	71358	64421
507 018	**MY**	A	*ME*	BD	64384	71359	64422
507 019	**MY**	A	*ME*	BD	64385	71360	64423
507 020	**MY**	A	*ME*	BD	64386	71361	64424
507 021	**MY**	A	*ME*	BD	64387	71362	64425
507 023	**MY**	A	*ME*	BD	64389	71364	64427
507 024	**MY**	A	*ME*	BD	64390	71365	64428
507 025	**MY**	A	*ME*	BD	64391	71366	64429
507 026	**MY**	A	*ME*	BD	64392	71367	64430
507 027	**MY**	A	*ME*	BD	64393	71368	64431
507 028	**MY**	A	*ME*	BD	64394	71369	64432
507 029	**MY**	A	*ME*	BD	64395	71370	64433
507 030	**MY**	A	*ME*	BD	64396	71371	64434
507 031	**MY**	A	*ME*	BD	64397	71372	64435
507 032	**MY**	A	*ME*	BD	64398	71373	64436
507 033	**MY**	A	*ME*	BD	64399	71374	64437

Names:

507 004 Bob Paisley
507 008 Harold Wilson
507 009 Dixie Dean
507 016 Merseyrail – celebrating the first ten years (2003–2013)
507 020 John Peel
507 021 Red Rum
507 023 Operations Inspector Stuart Mason
507 026 Councillor George Howard
507 033 Councillor Jack Spriggs

CLASS 508   BREL YORK

Formation: DMSO–TSO–BDMSO.
Construction: Steel underframe, aluminium alloy body and roof.
Traction Motors: Four GEC G310AZ of 82.125 kW.
Wheel Arrangement: Bo-Bo + 2-2 + Bo-Bo.
Braking: Disc & rheostatic.   **Dimensions:** 20.18 x 2.82 m.
Bogies: BX1.   **Couplers:** Tightlock.
Gangways: Within unit + end doors.   **Control System:** Camshaft.
Doors: Sliding.   **Maximum Speed:** 75 mph.
Seating Layout: All refurbished with 2+2 high-back facing seating.
Multiple Working: Within class and with Class 507.

Fitted with tripcocks for operating on the Merseyrail Wirral Lines.

Advertising livery: 508 111 Beatles Story (blue).

DMSO. Lot No. 30979 1979–80. –/56(+3) 1W. 36.0 t.
TSO. Lot No. 30980 1979–80. –/74. 26.5 t.
BDMSO. Lot No. 30981 1979–80. –/56(+3) 1W. 36.5 t.

508 103	**MY**	A	*ME*	BD	64651	71485	64694
508 104	**MY**	A	*ME*	BD	64652	71486	64695
508 108	**MY**	A	*ME*	BD	64656	71490	64699
508 110	**MY**	A	*ME*	BD	64658	71492	64701
508 111	**AL**	A	*ME*	BD	64659	71493	64702
508 112	**MY**	A	*ME*	BD	64660	71494	64703
508 114	**MY**	A	*ME*	BD	64662	71496	64705
508 115	**MY**	A	*ME*	BD	64663	71497	64706
508 117	**MY**	A	*ME*	BD	64665	71499	64708
508 120	**MY**	A	*ME*	BD	64668	71502	64711
508 122	**MY**	A	*ME*	BD	64670	71504	64713
508 123	**MY**	A	*ME*	BD	64671	71505	64714
508 124	**MY**	A	*ME*	BD	64672	71506	64715
508 125	**MY**	A	*ME*	BD	64673	71507	64716
508 126	**MY**	A	*ME*	BD	64674	71508	64717
508 127	**MY**	A	*ME*	BD	64675	71509	64718
508 128	**MY**	A	*ME*	BD	64676	71510	64719
508 130	**MY**	A	*ME*	BD	64678	71512	64721
508 131	**MY**	A	*ME*	BD	64679	71513	64722
508 134	**MY**	A	*ME*	BD	64682	71516	64725
508 136	**MY**	A	*ME*	BD	64684	71518	64727
508 137	**MY**	A	*ME*	BD	64685	71519	64728
508 138	**MY**	A	*ME*	BD	64686	71520	64729
508 139	**MY**	A	*ME*	BD	64687	71521	64730
508 140	**MY**	A	*ME*	BD	64688	71522	64731
508 141	**MY**	A	*ME*	BD	64689	71523	64732
508 143	**MY**	A	*ME*	BD	64691	71525	64734

Names:

| 508 111 | The Beatles | | 508 136 | Wilfred Owen MC |
| 508 123 | William Roscoe | | | |

4.3. DUAL-VOLTAGE UNITS

Initially the Class 7xx EMU series was reserved for Siemens "Desiro City" units, but it later announced that the new Bombardier units for London Overground will be Class 710. The Class 7xx series is being used for EMUs as freight wagons take up many of the remaining potential Class 3xx series'.

CLASS 700   DESIRO CITY   SIEMENS

The Class 700s are a large fleet of EMUs currently entering service with Govia Thameslink. The first unit was delivered in summer 2015, the first entered traffic in spring 2016 and all units will be in traffic by the end of 2018. The units are financed by Cross London Trains (a consortium of Siemens Project Ventures, Innisfree Ltd and 3i Infrastructure Ltd).

Formations (8-car): DMCO–PTSO–MSO–TSO–TSO–MSO–PTSO–DMCO
or **(12-car):** DMCO–PTSO–MSO–MSO–TSO–TSO–TSO–TSO–MSO–MSO–PTSO–DMCO.
Systems: 25 kV AC overhead/750 V DC third rail.
Construction: Aluminium.
Traction Motors: 4 Siemens asynchronous of 200 kW.
Wheel Arrangement (8-car): Bo-Bo + 2-2 + Bo-Bo + 2-2 + 2-2 + Bo-Bo + 2-2 + Bo-Bo. **(12-car):** Bo-Bo + 2-2 + Bo-Bo + Bo-Bo + 2-2 + 2-2 + 2-2 + 2-2 + Bo-Bo + Bo-Bo + 2-2 + Bo-Bo.
Braking: Disc & regenerative   **Dimensions:** 20.52/20.16 m x 2.80 m.
Bogies: Siemens SF7000 inside-frame. **Couplers:** Dellner 12.
Gangways: Within unit.   **Control System:** IGBT Inverter.
Doors: Sliding plug.   **Maximum Speed:** 100 mph.
Heating & ventilation: Air conditioning.
Seating Layout: 2+2 facing/unidirectional.
Multiple Working: Within class and with Class 707.

Class 700/0. 8-car units.

DMCO(A). Siemens Krefeld 2014–18. 26/16(+3). 38.5 t.
PTSO. Siemens Krefeld 2014–18. –/54 1T. 33.1 t.
MSO. Siemens Krefeld 2014–18. –/64. 36.2 t.
TSO. Siemens Krefeld 2014–18. –/56(+3). 28.7 t.
TSO(W). Siemens Krefeld 2014–18. –/40(+8) 1TD 2W. 29.1 t.
MSO. Siemens Krefeld 2014–18. –/64. 36.2 t.
PTSO. Siemens Krefeld 2014–18. –/54 1T. 33.2 t.
DMCO(B). Siemens Krefeld 2014–18. 26/16(+3). 38.5 t.

700001	**TL**	CT			401001	402001	403001	406001
					407001	410001	411001	412001
700002	**TL**	CT	*TL*	TB	401002	402002	403002	406002
					407002	410002	411002	412002
700003	**TL**	CT	*TL*	TB	401003	402003	403003	406003
					407003	410003	411003	412003
700004	**TL**	CT	*TL*	TB	401004	402004	403004	406004
					407004	410004	411004	412004

700 005	**TL**	CT	*TL*	TB	401005	402005	403005	406005
					407005	410005	411005	412005
700 006	**TL**	CT	*TL*	TB	401006	402006	403006	406006
					407006	410006	411006	412006
700 007	**TL**	CT	*TL*	TB	401007	402007	403007	406007
					407007	410007	411007	412007
700 008	**TL**	CT	*TL*	TB	401008	402008	403008	406008
					407008	410008	411008	412008
700 009	**TL**	CT	*TL*	TB	401009	402009	403009	406009
					407009	410009	411009	412009
700 010	**TL**	CT	*TL*	TB	401010	402010	403010	406010
					407010	410010	411010	412010
700 011	**TL**	CT			401011	402011	403011	406011
					407011	410011	411011	412011
700 012	**TL**	CT		TB	401012	402012	403012	406012
					407012	410012	411012	412012
700 013	**TL**	CT			401013	402013	403013	406013
					407013	410013	411013	412013
700 014	**TL**	CT	*TL*	TB	401014	402014	403014	406014
					407014	410014	411014	412014
700 015	**TL**	CT	*TL*	TB	401015	402015	403015	406015
					407015	410015	411015	412015
700 016	**TL**	CT	*TL*	TB	401016	402016	403016	406016
					407016	410016	411016	412016
700 017	**TL**	CT	*TL*	TB	401017	402017	403017	406017
					407017	410017	411017	412017
700 018	**TL**	CT	*TL*	TB	401018	402018	403018	406018
					407018	410018	411018	412018
700 019	**TL**	CT	*TL*	TB	401019	402019	403019	406019
					407019	410019	411019	412019
700 020	**TL**	CT		TB	401020	402020	403020	406020
					407020	410020	411020	412020
700 021	**TL**	CT	*TL*	TB	401021	402021	403021	406021
					407021	410021	411021	412021
700 022	**TL**	CT			401022	402022	403022	406022
					407022	410022	411022	412022
700 023	**TL**	CT	*TL*	TB	401023	402023	403023	406023
					407023	410023	411023	412023
700 024	**TL**	CT		TB	401024	402024	403024	406024
					407024	410024	411024	412024
700 025	**TL**	CT			401025	402025	403025	406025
					407025	410025	411025	412025
700 026	**TL**	CT			401026	402026	403026	406026
					407026	410026	411026	412026
700 027	**TL**	CT		TB	401027	402027	403027	406027
					407027	410027	411027	412027
700 028	**TL**	CT		TB	401028	402028	403028	406028
					407028	410028	411028	412028
700 029	**TL**	CT		TB	401029	402029	403029	406029
					407029	410029	411029	412029

700 030	**TL**	CT	*TL*	TB	401030	402030	403030	406030				
					407030	410030	411030	412030				
700 031	**TL**	CT		TB	401031	402031	403031	406031				
					407031	410031	411031	412031				
700 032	**TL**	CT			401032	402032	403032	406032				
					407032	410032	411032	412032				
700 033	**TL**	CT			401033	402033	403033	406033				
					407033	410033	411033	412033				
700 034	**TL**	CT			401034	402034	403034	406034				
					407034	410034	411034	412034				
700 035	**TL**	CT			401035	402035	403035	406035				
					407035	410035	411035	412035				
700 036	**TL**	CT		TB	401036	402036	403036	406036				
					407036	410036	411036	412036				
700 037	**TL**	CT			401037	402037	403037	406037				
					407037	410037	411037	412037				
700 038	**TL**	CT			401038	402038	403038	406038				
					407038	410038	411038	412038				
700 039	**TL**	CT			401039	402039	403039	406039				
					407039	410039	411039	412039				
700 040	**TL**	CT			401040	402040	403040	406040				
					407040	410040	411040	412040				
700 041	**TL**	CT			401041	402041	403041	406041				
					407041	410041	411041	412041				
700 042	**TL**	CT			401042	402042	403042	406042				
					407042	410042	411042	412042				
700 043	**TL**	CT			401043	402043	403043	406043				
					407043	410043	411043	412043				
700 044	**TL**	CT			401044	402044	403044	406044				
					407044	410044	411044	412044				
700 045	**TL**	CT			401045	402045	403045	406045				
					407045	410045	411045	412045				
700 046	**TL**	CT			401046	402046	403046	406046				
					407046	410046	411046	412046				
700 047	**TL**	CT			401047	402047	403047	406047				
					407047	410047	411047	412047				
700 048	**TL**	CT			401048	402048	403048	406048				
					407048	410048	411048	412048				
700 049	**TL**	CT			401049	402049	403049	406049				
					407049	410049	411049	412049				
700 050	**TL**	CT			401050	402050	403050	406050				
					407050	410050	411050	412050				
700 051	**TL**	CT			401051	402051	403051	406051				
					407051	410051	411051	412051				
700 052	**TL**	CT			401052	402052	403052	406052				
					407052	410052	411052	412052				
700 053	**TL**	CT			401053	402053	403053	406053				
					407053	410053	411053	412053				
700 054	**TL**	CT			401054	402054	403054	406054				
					407054	410054	411054	412054				

700055	**TL** CT			401055	402055	403055	406055
				407055	410055	411055	412055
700056	**TL** CT			401056	402056	403056	406056
				407056	410056	411056	412056
700057	**TL** CT			401057	402057	403057	406057
				407057	410057	411057	412057
700058	**TL** CT			401058	402058	403058	406058
				407058	410058	411058	412058
700059	**TL** CT			401059	402059	403059	406059
				407059	410059	411059	412059
700060	**TL** CT			401060	402060	403060	406060
				407060	410060	411060	412060

Class 700/1. 12-car units.

DMCO(A). Siemens Krefeld 2013–18. 26/20. 38.2 t.
PTSO. Siemens Krefeld 2013–18. –/54 1T. 34.4 t.
MSO. Siemens Krefeld 2013–18. –/60(+3). 36.0 t.
MSO. Siemens Krefeld 2013–18. –/56 1T. 35.8 t.
TSO. Siemens Krefeld 2013–18. –/64. 26.8 t.
TSO. Siemens Krefeld 2013–18. –/56(+3). 28.3 t.
TSO(W). Siemens Krefeld 2013–18. –/38(+9) 1TD 2W. 28.7 t.
TSO. Siemens Krefeld 2013–18. –/64. 27.9 t.
MSO. Siemens Krefeld 2013–18. –/56 1T. 35.6 t.
MSO. Siemens Krefeld 2013–18. –/60(+3). 35.3 t.
PTSO. Siemens Krefeld 2013–18. –/54 1T. 34.4 t.
DMCO(B). Siemens Krefeld 2013–18. 26/20. 38.2 t.

700101	**TL** CT *TL*	TB	401101 402101 403101 404101 405101 406101
			407101 408101 409101 410101 411101 412101
700102	**TL** CT *TL*	TB	401102 402102 403102 404102 405102 406102
			407102 408102 409102 410102 411102 412102
700103	**TL** CT *TL*	TB	401103 402103 403103 404103 405103 406103
			407103 408103 409103 410103 411103 412103
700104	**TL** CT *TL*	TB	401104 402104 403104 404104 405104 406104
			407104 408104 409104 410104 411104 412104
700105	**TL** CT *TL*	TB	401105 402105 403105 404105 405105 406105
			407105 408105 409105 410105 411105 412105
700106	**TL** CT *TL*	TB	401106 402106 403106 404106 405106 406106
			407106 408106 409106 410106 411106 412106
700107	**TL** CT *TL*	TB	401107 402107 403107 404107 405107 406107
			407107 408107 409107 410107 411107 412107
700108	**TL** CT *TL*	TB	401108 402108 403108 404108 405108 406108
			407108 408108 409108 410108 411108 412108
700109	**TL** CT *TL*	TB	401109 402109 403109 404109 405109 406109
			407109 408109 409109 410109 411109 412109
700110	**TL** CT *TL*	TB	401110 402110 403110 404110 405110 406110
			407110 408110 409110 410110 411110 412110
700111	**TL** CT *TL*	TB	401111 402111 403111 404111 405111 406111
			407111 408111 409111 410111 411111 412111
700112	**TL** CT *TL*	TB	401112 402112 403112 404112 405112 406112
			407112 408112 409112 410112 411112 412112

700 113	**TL** CT *TL*	TB	401113	402113	403113	404113	405113	406113
			407113	408113	409113	410113	411113	412113
700 114	**TL** CT *TL*	TB	401114	402114	403114	404114	405114	406114
			407114	408114	409114	410114	411114	412114
700 115	**TL** CT *TL*	TB	401115	402115	403115	404115	405115	406115
			407115	408115	409115	410115	411115	412115
700 116	**TL** CT		401116	402116	403116	404116	405116	406116
			407116	408116	409116	410116	411116	412116
700 117	**TL** CT		401117	402117	403117	404117	405117	406117
			407117	408117	409117	410117	411117	412117
700 118	**TL** CT		401118	402118	403118	404118	405118	406118
			407118	408118	409118	410118	411118	412118
700 119	**TL** CT		401119	402119	403119	404119	405119	406119
			407119	408119	409119	410119	411119	412119
700 120	**TL** CT		401120	402120	403120	404120	405120	406120
			407120	408120	409120	410120	411120	412120
700 121	**TL** CT		401121	402121	403121	404121	405121	406121
			407121	408121	409121	410121	411121	412121
700 122	**TL** CT		401122	402122	403122	404122	405122	406122
			407122	408122	409122	410122	411122	412122
700 123	**TL** CT		401123	402123	403123	404123	405123	406123
			407123	408123	409123	410123	411123	412123
700 124	**TL** CT		401124	402124	403124	404124	405124	406124
			407124	408124	409124	410124	411124	412124
700 125	**TL** CT		401125	402125	403125	404125	405125	406125
			407125	408125	409125	410125	411125	412125
700 126	**TL** CT		401126	402126	403126	404126	405126	406126
			407126	408126	409126	410126	411126	412126
700 127	**TL** CT		401127	402127	403127	404127	405127	406127
			407127	408127	409127	410127	411127	412127
700 128	**TL** CT		401128	402128	403128	404128	405128	406128
			407128	408128	409128	410128	411128	412128
700 129	**TL** CT		401129	402129	403129	404129	405129	406129
			407129	408129	409129	410129	411129	412129
700 130	**TL** CT		401130	402130	403130	404130	405130	406130
			407130	408130	409130	410130	411130	412130
700 131	**TL** CT		401131	402131	403131	404131	405131	406131
			407131	408131	409131	410131	411131	412131
700 132	**TL** CT		401132	402132	403132	404132	405132	406132
			407132	408132	409132	410132	411132	412132
700 133	**TL** CT		401133	402133	403133	404133	405133	406133
			407133	408133	409133	410133	411133	412133
700 134	**TL** CT		401134	402134	403134	404134	405134	406134
			407134	408134	409134	410134	411134	412134
700 135	**TL** CT		401135	402135	403135	404135	405135	406135
			407135	408135	409135	410135	411135	412135
700 136	**TL** CT		401136	402136	403136	404136	405136	406136
			407136	408136	409136	410136	411136	412136
700 137	**TL** CT		401137	402137	403137	404137	405137	406137
			407137	408137	409137	410137	411137	412137

700 138	**TL** CT	401138 402138 403138 404138 405138 406138
		407138 408138 409138 410138 411138 412138
700 139	**TL** CT	401139 402139 403139 404139 405139 406139
		407139 408139 409139 410139 411139 412139
700 140	**TL** CT	401140 402140 403140 404140 405140 406140
		407140 408140 409140 410140 411140 412140
700 141	**TL** CT	401141 402141 403141 404141 405141 406141
		407141 408141 409141 410141 411141 412141
700 142	**TL** CT	401142 402142 403142 404142 405142 406142
		407142 408142 409142 410142 411142 412142
700 143	**TL** CT	401143 402143 403143 404143 405143 406143
		407143 408143 409143 410143 411143 412143
700 144	**TL** CT	401144 402144 403144 404144 405144 406144
		407144 408144 409144 410144 411144 412144
700 145	**TL** CT	401145 402145 403145 404145 405145 406145
		407145 408145 409145 410145 411145 412145
700 146	**TL** CT	401146 402146 403146 404146 405146 406146
		407146 408146 409146 410146 411146 412146
700 147	**TL** CT	401147 402147 403147 404147 405147 406147
		407147 408147 409147 410147 411147 412147
700 148	**TL** CT	401148 402148 403148 404148 405148 406148
		407148 408148 409148 410148 411148 412148
700 149	**TL** CT	401149 402149 403149 404149 405149 406149
		407149 408149 409149 410149 411149 412149
700 150	**TL** CT	401150 402150 403150 404150 405150 406150
		407150 408150 409150 410150 411150 412150
700 151	**TL** CT	401151 402151 403151 404151 405151 406151
		407151 408151 409151 410151 411151 412151
700 152	**TL** CT	401152 402152 403152 404152 405152 406152
		407152 408152 409152 410152 411152 412152
700 153	**TL** CT	401153 402153 403153 404153 405153 406153
		407153 408153 409153 410153 411153 412153
700 154	**TL** CT	401154 402154 403154 404154 405154 406154
		407154 408154 409154 410154 411154 412154
700 155	**TL** CT	401155 402155 403155 404155 405155 406155
		407155 408155 409155 410155 411155 412155

CLASS 707　　　　DESIRO CITY　　　　SIEMENS

These 30 5-car units are currently being delivered to South West Trains for suburban services, with the first unit due to enter traffic in April 2017. Built with the capability to be easily converted to dual voltage units.

Formation: DMSO–PTSO–TSO–TSO–DMSO.
Systems: 750 V DC third rail but with 25 kV AC overhead capability.
Construction: Aluminium.
Traction Motors: 4 Siemens asynchronous of 200 kW.
Wheel Arrangement: Bo-Bo + 2-2 + 2-2 + 2-2 + Bo-Bo.
Braking: Disc & regenerative　　　　**Dimensions:** 20.00/20.16 m x 2.80 m.
Bogies: Siemens SF7000 inside-frame. **Couplers:** Dellner 12.

Gangways: Within unit.   **Control System:** IGBT Inverter.
Doors: Sliding plug.   **Maximum Speed:** 100 mph.
Heating & ventilation: Air conditioning.
Seating Layout: 2+2/2+1 facing/unidirectional.
Multiple Working: Within class and with Class 700.

DMSO(A). Siemens Krefeld 2015–17. –/46.   t.
PTSO. Siemens Krefeld 2015–17. –/64.   t.
TSO. Siemens Krefeld 2015–17. –/53(+4) 2W.   t.
TSO. Siemens Krefeld 2015–17. –/62.   t.
DMSO(B). Siemens Krefeld 2015–17. –/46.   t.

707 001	**SS**	A		421001	422001	423001	424001	425001
707 002	**SS**	A		421002	422002	423002	424002	425002
707 003	**SS**	A		421003	422003	423003	424003	425003
707 004	**SS**	A		421004	422004	423004	424004	425004
707 005	**SS**	A		421005	422005	423005	424005	425005
707 006	**SS**	A		421006	422006	423006	424006	425006
707 007	**SS**	A		421007	422007	423007	424007	425007
707 008	**SS**	A		421008	422008	423008	424008	425008
707 009	**SS**	A		421009	422009	423009	424009	425009
707 010	**SS**	A		421010	422010	423010	424010	425010
707 011	**SS**	A		421011	422011	423011	424011	425011
707 012	**SS**	A		421012	422012	423012	424012	425012
707 013	**SS**	A		421013	422013	423013	424013	425013
707 014	**SS**	A		421014	422014	423014	424014	425014
707 015	**SS**	A		421015	422015	423015	424015	425015
707 016	**SS**	A		421016	422016	423016	424016	425016
707 017	**SS**	A		421017	422017	423017	424017	425017
707 018	**SS**	A		421018	422018	423018	424018	425018
707 019	**SS**	A		421019	422019	423019	424019	425019
707 020	**SS**	A		421020	422020	423020	424020	425020
707 021	**SS**	A		421021	422021	423021	424021	425021
707 022	**SS**	A		421022	422022	423022	424022	425022
707 023	**SS**	A		421023	422023	423023	424023	425023
707 024	**SS**	A		421024	422024	423024	424024	425024
707 025	**SS**	A		421025	422025	423025	424025	425025
707 026	**SS**	A		421026	422026	423026	424026	425026
707 027	**SS**	A		421027	422027	423027	424027	425027
707 028	**SS**	A		421028	422028	423028	424028	425028
707 029	**SS**	A		421029	422029	423029	424029	425029
707 030	**SS**	A		421030	422030	423030	424030	425030

CLASS 710   AVENTRA   BOMBARDIER DERBY

These 45 4-car units are under construction for London Overground for use on London Liverpool Street local services, Romford–Upminster, Gospel Oak–Barking and London Euston–Watford Junction. There are a mix of AC only and dual-voltage units. The first trains are due to enter service in early 2018. There are options for a further 249 Class 710 vehicles. Full details awaited.

Formation: DMSO–MSO–PMSO–DMSO.
Systems: Class 710/1 25 kV AC overhead only. Class 710/2 25 kV AC overhead and 750 V DC third rail.
Construction: Aluminium.
Traction Motors:
Wheel Arrangement:
Braking: Disc & regenerative   **Dimensions:**
Bogies: Inside-frame.   **Couplers:**
Gangways: Within unit.   **Control System:** IGBT Inverter.
Doors: Sliding plug.   **Maximum Speed:**
Heating & ventilation: Air conditioning.
Seating Layout:
Multiple Working:

DMSO(A). Bombardier Derby 2017–18.   t.
MSO. Bombardier Derby 2017–18.   t.
PMSO. Bombardier Derby 2017–18.   t.
DMSO(B). Bombardier Derby 2017–18.   t.

Class 710/1. 25 kV AC only units.

710101	431101	431401	431301	431501
710102	431102	431402	431302	431502
710103	431103	431403	431303	431503
710104	431104	431404	431304	431504
710105	431105	431405	431305	431505
710106	431106	431406	431306	431506
710107	431107	431407	431307	431507
710108	431108	431408	431308	431508
710109	431109	431409	431309	431509
710110	431110	431410	431310	431510
710111	431111	431411	431311	431511
710112	431112	431412	431312	431512
710113	431113	431413	431313	431513
710114	431114	431414	431314	431514
710115	431115	431415	431315	431515
710116	431116	431416	431316	431516
710117	431117	431417	431317	431517
710118	431118	431418	431318	431518
710119	431119	431419	431319	431519
710120	431120	431420	431320	431520
710121	431121	431421	431321	431521
710122	431122	431422	431322	431522
710123	431123	431423	431323	431523
710124	431124	431424	431324	431524
710125	431125	431425	431325	431525
710126	431126	431426	431326	431526
710127	431127	431427	431327	431527
710128	431128	431428	431328	431528
710129	431129	431429	431329	431529
710130	431130	431430	431330	431530
710131	431131	431431	431331	431531

Class 710/2. 25 kV AC/750 V DC units.

710 256	432156	432456	432356	432556
710 257	432157	432457	432357	432557
710 258	432158	432458	432358	432558
710 259	432159	432459	432359	432559
710 260	432160	432460	432360	432560
710 261	432161	432461	432361	432561
710 262	432162	432462	432362	432562
710 263	432163	432463	432363	432563
710 264	432164	432464	432364	432564
710 265	432165	432465	432365	432565
710 266	432166	432466	432366	432566
710 267	432167	432467	432367	432567
710 268	432168	432468	432368	432568
710 269	432169	432469	432369	432569

4.4. HITACHI IEP UNITS

CLASS 800 INTERCITY EXPRESS PROGRAMME
BI-MODE   HITACHI

In summer 2012 Agility Trains, a consortium of Hitachi and John Laing, signed a deal with the DfT to design, build, finance and maintain the next generation of InterCity rolling stock for the Great Western and East Coast Main Lines, principally to replace ageing High Speed Trains on these routes. A follow-on order in 2013 confirmed that a further 30 9-car trains would be ordered to replace the Class 91s and Mark 4 carriages on the ECML. This brought the total number of vehicles ordered to 866. Both Great Western Railway and Virgin Trains East Coast will have a mix of 5-car and 9-car units which will be bi-mode and straight electric trains, although the EMUs will also have one diesel engine fitted to each set. Engines are being supplied by MTU. Owing to delays with electrification works on the Great Western Main Line, in 2016 it was announced that the 21 9-car electric Class 801 units for GWR would be built as 21 9-car bi-mode units, numbered instead in the Class 800/3 series.

The units are broadly based on the Southeastern Class 395 EMUs, but have 26 m length bodyshells. They are numbered in the Class 800 (bi-mode) and Class 801 (EMU) number series'. 12 trains (76 vehicles) are being fully manufactured in Japan before the new Hitachi factory at Newton Aycliffe, County Durham is up and running. The remaining trains will be assembled at Newton Aycliffe. New maintenance depots are being constructed at Stoke Gifford (Bristol), Swansea and North Pole (London, the former Eurostar depot) for the GWR sets and at Doncaster for the VTEC sets.

The first trains arrived for testing in 2015. They will enter service on the Great Western Main Line from summer 2017 and on the East Coast Main Line from 2018.

In 2015 GWR ordered a further 22 5-car and seven 9-car IEPs, to be designated Class 802 (5-car) and Class 802/1 (9-car). These will be used on Paddington–West of England services. In 2016 GWR ordered a further seven 9-car Class 802s, TransPennine Express ordered 19 5-car Class 802s and Hull Trains ordered five 5-car Class 802s, for delivery 2019–20. As they will predominately operate on diesel power, on these units the engines will run at 700 kW at all times, rather than the Class 800s which will run at 560 kW in normal operation. They will also have larger fuel tanks. The GWR Class 802s will be constructed in Pistoia, Italy (the former AnsaldoBreda factory) and the TPE and Hull Trains Class 802s at Newton Aycliffe. The number series for the Class 802s has yet to be confirmed.

Formations: Various, see class headings for details.
Systems: Diesel/25 kV AC overhead electric.
Construction: Aluminium.
Engines: MTU 12V 1600 R80L of 700 kW (940 hp). Normally derated to 560 kW.
Traction Motors: Four Hitachi asynchronous of 226 kW.
Wheel Arrangement: 2-2 + Bo-Bo + Bo-Bo + Bo-Bo + 2-2 or
2-2 + Bo-Bo + Bo-Bo + 2-2 + Bo-Bo + Bo-Bo + Bo-Bo + 2-2.

Braking: Disc & regenerative.	**Dimensions:** 26.0 m x 2.7 m.
Bogies: Hitachi.	**Couplers:** Dellner 10.
Gangways: Within unit.	**Control System:** IGBT Inverter.
Doors: Single-leaf sliding.	**Maximum Speed:** 125 mph.

Heating & ventilation: Air conditioning.
Seating Layout: 1: 2+1 facing/unidirectional; 2+2 facing/unidirectional.
Multiple Working: Within class and with Class 801.

Class 800/0. 5-car units for Great Western Railway as replacements for HSTs. Full details awaited.

PDTSO. Hitachi Newton Aycliffe/Kasado 2013–18. –/56 1TD   t.
MSO. Hitachi Newton Aycliffe/Kasado 2013–18. –/88.   t.
MSO. Hitachi Newton Aycliffe/Kasado 2013–18. –/88 2T.   t.
MCO. Hitachi Newton Aycliffe/Kasado 2013–18. 18/58 1T.   t.
PDTRBFO. Hitachi Newton Aycliffe/Kasado 2013–18. 18/– 1TD 2W.   t.

800 001		NP	811001	812001	813001	814001	815001
800 002		NP	811002	812002	813002	814002	815002
800 003			811003	812003	813003	814003	815003
800 004	GW	NP	811004	812004	813004	814004	815004
800 005			811005	812005	813005	814005	815005
800 006			811006	812006	813006	814006	815006
800 007			811007	812007	813007	814007	815007
800 008			811008	812008	813008	814008	815008
800 009			811009	812009	813009	814009	815009
800 010			811010	812010	813010	814010	815010
800 011			811011	812011	813011	814011	815011
800 012			811012	812012	813012	814012	815012
800 013			811013	812013	813013	814013	815013
800 014			811014	812014	813014	814014	815014
800 015			811015	812015	813015	814015	815015
800 016			811016	812016	813016	814016	815016
800 017			811017	812017	813017	814017	815017

800018		811018	812018	813018	814018	815018
800019		811019	812019	813019	814019	815019
800020		811020	812020	813020	814020	815020
800021		811021	812021	813021	814021	815021
800022		811022	812022	813022	814022	815022
800023		811023	812023	813023	814023	815023
800024		811024	812024	813024	814024	815024
800025		811025	812025	813025	814025	815025
800026		811026	812026	813026	814026	815026
800027		811027	812027	813027	814027	815027
800028		811028	812028	813028	814028	815028
800029		811029	812029	813029	814029	815029
800030		811030	812030	813030	814030	815030
800031		811031	812031	813031	814031	815031
800032		811032	812032	813032	814032	815032
800033		811033	812033	813033	814033	815033
800034		811034	812034	813034	814034	815034
800035		811035	812035	813035	814035	815035
800036		811036	812036	813036	814036	815036

Name: 800 004   Isambard Kingdom Brunel/Sir Daniel Gooch (carried on alternative driving cars)

Class 800/1. 9-car units for Virgin Trains East Coast as replacements for HSTs. Full details awaited.

PDTRBFO. Hitachi Newton Aycliffe/Kasado 2013–18.   t.
MFO. Hitachi Newton Aycliffe/Kasado 2013–18.   t.
MCO. Hitachi Newton Aycliffe/Kasado 2013–18.   t.
TSO. Hitachi Newton Aycliffe/Kasado 2013–18.   t.
MSO. Hitachi Newton Aycliffe/Kasado 2013–18.   t.
TSO. Hitachi Newton Aycliffe/Kasado 2013–18.   t.
MSO. Hitachi Newton Aycliffe/Kasado 2013–18.   t.
MSO. Hitachi Newton Aycliffe/Kasado 2013–18.   t.
PDTSO. Hitachi Newton Aycliffe/Kasado 2013–18.   t.

800 101	NP	811101	812101	813101	814101	815101
		816101	817101	818101	819101	
800 102		811102	812102	813102	814102	815102
		816102	817102	818102	819102	
800 103		811103	812103	813103	814103	815103
		816103	817103	818103	819103	
800 104		811104	812104	813104	814104	815104
		816104	817104	818104	819104	
800 105		811105	812105	813105	814105	815105
		816105	817105	818105	819105	
800 106		811106	812106	813106	814106	815106
		816106	817106	818106	819106	
800 107		811107	812107	813107	814107	815107
		816107	817107	818107	819107	
800 108		811108	812108	813108	814108	815108
		816108	817108	818108	819108	

800 109		811109	812109	813109	814109	815109
		816109	817109	818109	819109	
800 110		811110	812110	813110	814110	815110
		816110	817110	818110	819110	
800 111		811111	812111	813111	814111	815111
		816111	817111	818111	819111	
800 112		811112	812112	813112	814112	815112
		816112	817112	818112	819112	
800 113		811113	812113	813113	814113	815113
		816113	817113	818113	819113	

Class 800/2. 5-car units for Virgin Trains East Coast as replacements for HSTs. Full details awaited.

PDTRBFO. Hitachi Newton Aycliffe/Kasado 2016–18. t.
MCO. Hitachi Newton Aycliffe/Kasado 2016–18. t.
MSO. Hitachi Newton Aycliffe/Kasado 2016–18. t.
MSO. Hitachi Newton Aycliffe/Kasado 2016–18. t.
PDTSO. Hitachi Newton Aycliffe/Kasado 2016–18. t.

800 201	811201	812201	813201	814201	815201
800 202	811202	812202	813202	814202	815202
800 203	811203	812203	813203	814203	815203
800 204	811204	812204	813204	814204	815204
800 205	811205	812205	813205	814205	815205
800 206	811206	812206	813206	814206	815206
800 207	811207	812207	813207	814207	815207
800 208	811208	812208	813208	814208	815208
800 209	811209	812209	813209	814209	815209
800 210	811210	812210	813210	814210	815210

Class 800/3. 9-car units for Great Western Railway as replacements for HSTs. Originally to be built as full electric trains and numbered in the Class 801/0 series. Full details awaited.

PDTRBFO. Hitachi Newton Aycliffe/Kasado 2016–18. 15/– 1TD 2W. t.
MFO. Hitachi Newton Aycliffe/Kasado 2016–18. 56/– 1T. t.
MSO. Hitachi Newton Aycliffe/Kasado 2016–18. –/88. t.
TSO. Hitachi Newton Aycliffe/Kasado 2016–18. –/88 2T. t.
MSO. Hitachi Newton Aycliffe/Kasado 2016–18. –/88 2T. t.
TSO. Hitachi Newton Aycliffe/Kasado 2016–18. –/88. t.
MSO. Hitachi Newton Aycliffe/Kasado 2016–18. –/88 2T. t.
MSO. Hitachi Newton Aycliffe/Kasado 2016–18. –/88 2T. t.
PDTSO. Hitachi Newton Aycliffe/Kasado 2016–18. –/48 1TD 2W. t.

800 301		821001	822001	823001	824001	825001
		826001	827001	828001	829001	
800 302		821002	822002	823002	824002	825002
		826002	827002	828002	829002	
800 303		821003	822003	823003	824003	825003
		826003	827003	828003	829003	
800 304		821004	822004	823004	824004	825004
		826004	827004	828004	829004	

800 305	821005	822005	823005	824005	825005
	826005	827005	828005	829005	
800 306	821006	822006	823006	824006	825006
	826006	827006	828006	829006	
800 307	821007	822007	823007	824007	825007
	826007	827007	828007	829007	
800 308	821008	822008	823008	824008	825008
	826008	827008	828008	829008	
800 309	821009	822009	823009	824009	825009
	826009	827009	828009	829009	
800 310	821010	822010	823010	824010	825010
	826010	827010	828010	829010	
800 311	821011	822011	823011	824011	825011
	826011	827011	828011	829011	
800 312	821012	822012	823012	824012	825012
	826012	827012	828012	829012	
800 313	821013	822013	823013	824013	825013
	826013	827013	828013	829013	
800 314	821014	822014	823014	824014	825014
	826014	827014	828014	829014	
800 315	821015	822015	823015	824015	825015
	826015	827015	828015	829015	
800 316	821016	822016	823016	824016	825016
	826016	827016	828016	829016	
800 317	821017	822017	823017	824017	825017
	826017	827017	828017	829017	
800 318	821018	822018	823018	824018	825018
	826018	827018	828018	829018	
800 319	821019	822019	823019	824019	825019
	826019	827019	828019	829019	
800 320	821020	822020	823020	824020	825020
	826020	827020	828020	829020	
800 321	821021	822021	823021	824021	825021
	826021	827021	828021	829021	

CLASS 801 INTERCITY EXPRESS PROGRAMME
ELECTRIC   HITACHI

The Class 801s are EMUs, but will still have one diesel engine fitted per unit
for emergency use.

Formations: Various, see class headings for details.
Systems: 25 kV AC overhead electric, plus one diesel engine per set.
Construction: Aluminium.
Engines: MTU 12V 1600 R80L of 700 kW (940 hp).
Traction Motors: Four Hitachi asynchronous of 226 kW.
Wheel Arrangement:
Braking: Disc & regenerative.   **Dimensions:** 26.0 m x 2.7 m.
Bogies: Hitachi.   **Couplers:** Dellner 10.
Gangways: Within unit.   **Control System:** IGBT Inverter.

Doors: Single-leaf sliding.   **Maximum Speed:** 125 mph.
Heating & ventilation: Air conditioning.
Seating Layout: 1: 2+1 facing/unidirectional; 2+2 facing/unidirectional.
Multiple Working: Within class and with Class 800.

Class 801/1. 5-car units for Virgin Trains East Coast as replacements for HSTs. Full details awaited.

PDTRBFO. Hitachi Newton Aycliffe/Kasado 2016–18.   t.
MCO. Hitachi Newton Aycliffe/Kasado 2016–18.   t.
MSO. Hitachi Newton Aycliffe/Kasado 2016–18.   t.
MSO. Hitachi Newton Aycliffe/Kasado 2016–18.   t.
PDTSO. Hitachi Newton Aycliffe/Kasado 2016–18.   t.

801 101	821101	822101	823101	824101	825101
801 102	821102	822102	823102	824102	825102
801 103	821103	822103	823103	824103	825103
801 104	821104	822104	823104	824104	825104
801 105	821105	822105	823105	824105	825105
801 106	821106	822106	823106	824106	825106
801 107	821107	822107	823107	824107	825107
801 108	821108	822108	823108	824108	825108
801 109	821109	822109	823109	824109	825109
801 110	821110	822110	823110	824110	825110
801 111	821111	822111	823111	824111	825111
801 112	821112	822112	823112	824112	825112

Class 801/2. 9-car units for Virgin Trains East Coast as replacements for locomotive-hauled Class 91+Mark 4 stock. Full details awaited.

PDTRBFO. Hitachi Newton Aycliffe 2017–19.   t.
MFO. Hitachi Newton Aycliffe 2017–19.   t.
MCO. Hitachi Newton Aycliffe 2017–19.   t.
TSO. Hitachi Newton Aycliffe 2017–19.   t.
MSO. Hitachi Newton Aycliffe 2017–19.   t.
TSO. Hitachi Newton Aycliffe 2017–19.   t.
MSO. Hitachi Newton Aycliffe 2017–19.   t.
MSO. Hitachi Newton Aycliffe 2017–19.   t.
PDTSO. Hitachi Newton Aycliffe 2017–19.   t.

801 201	821201	822201	823201	824201	825201
	826201	827201	828201	829201	
801 202	821202	822202	823202	824202	825202
	826202	827202	828202	829202	
801 203	821203	822203	823203	824203	825203
	826203	827203	828203	829203	
801 204	821204	822204	823204	824204	825204
	826204	827204	828204	829204	
801 205	821205	822205	823205	824205	825205
	826205	827205	828205	829205	
801 206	821206	822206	823206	824206	825206
	826206	827206	828206	829206	
801 207	821207	822207	823207	824207	825207
	826207	827207	828207	829207	

801208	821208	822208	823208	824208	825208
	826208	827208	828208	829208	
801209	821209	822209	823209	824209	825209
	826209	827209	828209	829209	
801210	821210	822210	823210	824210	825210
	826210	827210	828210	829210	
801211	821211	822211	823211	824211	825211
	826211	827211	828211	829211	
801212	821212	822212	823212	824212	825212
	826212	827212	828212	829212	
801213	821213	822213	823213	824213	825213
	826213	827213	828213	829213	
801214	821214	822214	823214	824214	825214
	826214	827214	828214	829214	
801215	821215	822215	823215	824215	825215
	826215	827215	828215	829215	
801216	821216	822216	823216	824216	825216
	826216	827216	828216	829216	
801217	821217	822217	823217	824217	825217
	826217	827217	828217	829217	
801218	821218	822218	823218	824218	825218
	826218	827218	828218	829218	
801219	821219	822219	823219	824219	825219
	826219	827219	828219	829219	
801220	821220	822220	823220	824220	825220
	826220	827220	828220	829220	
801221	821221	822221	823221	824221	825221
	826221	827221	828221	829221	
801222	821222	822222	823222	824222	825222
	826222	827222	828222	829222	
801223	821223	822223	823223	824223	825223
	826223	827223	828223	829223	
801224	821224	822224	823224	824224	825224
	826224	827224	828224	829224	
801225	821225	822225	823225	824225	825225
	826225	827225	828225	829225	
801226	821226	822226	823226	824226	825226
	826226	827226	828226	829226	
801227	821227	822227	823227	824227	825227
	826227	827227	828227	829227	
801228	821228	822228	823228	824228	825228
	826228	827228	828228	829228	
801229	821229	822229	823229	824229	825229
	826229	827229	828229	829229	
801230	821230	822230	823230	824230	825230
	826230	827230	828230	829230	

4.5. EUROSTAR UNITS

The original Eurostar Class 373 units were built for and are normally used on services between Britain and continental Europe via the Channel Tunnel. SNCF-owned units 3225/26 and 3227/28 have been removed from the Eurostar pool and withdrawn. As they are not now permitted through the Channel Tunnel they are not listed here. The trailers from SNCF set 3203/04 have now been refurbished to run with power cars 3211/12 (original power cars 3203/04 have been scrapped and 3211/12 renumbered 3203/04 to match the trailers).

Each Class 373 train consists of two 10-car units coupled, with a motor car at each driving end. All units are articulated with an extra motor bogie on the coach adjacent to the motor car.

All Class 373 sets can be used between London St Pancras and Paris, Brussels and Disneyland Paris. Certain sets (shown *) are equipped for 1500 V DC operation and are used for the winter service to Bourg Saint Maurice and the summer service to Avignon. All eight units being refurbished will be fitted for operation on 1500 V DC.

Seven 8-car Class 373 sets were built for Regional Eurostar services, but all except one power car (3308) and one half set were on long-term hire to SNCF for use on French internal services so are not listed here. They have now been taken out of traffic and will be scrapped in 2017. Power car 3308 has been preserved at the National Railway Museum, York.

The second generation Eurostar trains, the Siemens Class 374s, are currently being introduced and have already replaced most of the Class 373s, with withdrawn sets now being progressively moved to EMR Kingsbury for disposal. Eight sets are being fully refurbished and retained by Eurostar – 3007/08, 3015/16, 3205/06, 3209/10, 3211/12, 3219/20, 3221/22 and 3229/30.

CLASS 373   "THREE CAPITALS" EUROSTARS

10-car half-sets. Built for services starting from or terminating in London Waterloo (now St Pancras). Individual vehicles in each set are allocated numbers 373xxx0 + 373xxx1 + 373xxx2 + 373xxx3 + 373xxx4 + 373xxx5 + 373xxx6 + 373xxx7 + 373xxx8 + 373xxx9, where 3xxx denotes the set number.

Formation: DM–MSO–4TSO–RB–2TFO–TBFO. Gangwayed within pair of units. Air conditioned.
Construction: Steel.
Supply Systems: 25 kV AC 50 Hz overhead or 3000 V DC overhead (* also equipped for 1500 V DC overhead operation).
Control System: GTO–GTO Inverter on UK 750 V DC and 25 kV AC, GTO Chopper on SNCB 3000 V DC.
Continuous rating: 12 x 240 kW (25 kV AC); 5700 kW (1500 and 3000 V DC).
Wheel Arrangement: Bo-Bo + Bo–2–2–2–2–2–2–2–2–Bo.
Lengths: 22.15 m (DM), 21.85 m (MSO & TBFO), 18.70 m (other cars).
Couplers: Schaku 10S at outer ends, Schaku 10L at inner end of each DM and outer ends of each sub set.

Maximum Speed: 186 mph (300 km/h).
Built: 1992–93 by GEC-Alsthom/Brush/ANF/De Dietrich/BN Construction/ACEC.

DM vehicles carry the set numbers indicated below.

† Refurbished.
§ Originally numbered 3203/04.

373xxx0 series. DM. Lot No. 31118 1992–95. 68.5 t.
373xxx1 series. MSO. Lot No. 31119 1992–95. –/48 2T. 44.6 t.
373xxx2 series. TSO. Lot No. 31120 1992–95. –/56 1T. 28.1 t.
373xxx3 series. TSO. Lot No. 31121 1992–95. –/56 2T. 29.7 t.
373xxx4 series. TSO. Lot No. 31122 1992–95. –/56 1T. 28.3 t.
373xxx5 series. TSO. Lot No. 31123 1992–95. –/56 2T. 29.2 t.
373xxx6 series. RB. Lot No. 31124 1992–95. 31.1 t.
373xxx7 series. TFO. Lot No. 31125 1992–95. 39/– 1T. 29.6 t.
373xxx8 series. TFO. Lot No. 31126 1992–95. 39/– 1T. 32.2 t.
373xxx9 series. TBFO. Lot No. 31127 1992–95. 25/– 1TD. 39.4 t.

3001	**EU**	EU	EU	TI
3002	**EU**	EU	EU	TI
3007 *	**ER**	EU	EU	TI
3008 *	**ER**	EU	EU	TI
3009	**EU**	EU	EU	TI
3010	**EU**	EU	EU	TI
3011	**EU**	EU	EU	TI
3012	**EU**	EU	EU	TI
3013	**EU**	EU		TI (S)
3014	**EU**	EU		TI (S)
3015 †*	**ER**	EU	EU	TI
3016 †*	**ER**	EU	EU	TI
3017	**EU**	EU		TI (S)
3018	**EU**	EU		TI (S)
3021	**EU**	EU	EU	TI
3022	**EU**	EU	EU	TI
3101	**EU**	SB		TI (S)
3102	**EU**	SB		TI (S)
3103	**EU**	SB	EU	FF
3104	**EU**	SB	EU	FF
3105	**EU**	SB	EU	FF
3106	**EU**	SB	EU	FF
3107	**EU**	SB		FF (S)
3108	**EU**	SB		FF (S)
3201 *	**EU**	SF	EU	LY

3202 *	**EU**	SF	EU	LY
3205	**EU**	SF	EU	LY
3206	**EU**	SF	EU	LY
3208 *	**EU**	SF		LY (S)
3209 *	**EU**	SF	EU	LY
3210 *	**EU**	SF	EU	LY
3211 *§	**ER**	SF	EU	LY
3212 *§	**ER**	SF	EU	LY
3213 *	**EU**	SF	EU	LY
3214 *	**EU**	SF	EU	LY
3215 *	**EU**	SF	EU	LY
3216 *	**EU**	SF	EU	LY
3217	**EU**	SF	EU	LY
3218	**EU**	SF	EU	LY
3219	**ER**	SF	EU	LY
3220	**ER**	SF	EU	LY
3221	**EU**	SF	EU	LY
3222	**EU**	SF	EU	LY
3223 *	**EU**	SF	EU	LY
3224 *	**EU**	SF	EU	LY
3229 *	**EU**	SF	EU	LY
3230 *	**EU**	SF	EU	LY
3231	**EU**	SF	EU	LY
3232	**EU**	SF	EU	LY

Spare DM:

3999　　**ER**　EU　EU　TI

Names:

3001/02	Tread Lightly/Voyage Vert
3007/08	Waterloo Sunset
3009/10	REMEMBERING FROMELLES
3013/14	LONDON 2012
3209/10	THE DA VINCI CODE

CLASS 374   SIEMENS VELARO e320

8-car half-sets. Currently being delivered. These units are similar to the DB Class 407 ICE sets, with distributed power rather than a power car at either end like the Class 373s. The first sets entered service in November 2015, operating initially on the St Pancras–Paris route. They will also be used on the proposed St Pancras–Amsterdam service from December 2017.

The initial order was for ten units (4001–20) and this was then increased by another seven (4021–34) in 2014. An option exists for a further six units.

Formation: DMFO–TBFO–MFO–TSO–TSO–MSO–TSO–MSORB.
Gangwayed within pair of units. Air conditioned.
Construction: Aluminium.   **Control System:** IGBT Inverter.
Supply Systems: 25 kV AC 50 Hz overhead, 1500 V DC overhead and 3000 V DC overhead.
Continuous rating: 8000 kW (25 kV AC), 4200 kW (1500 and 3000 V DC).
Wheel Arrangement: Bo-Bo + 2-2 + Bo-Bo + 2-2 + 2-2 + Bo-Bo + 2-2 + Bo-Bo.
Lengths: 26.035 m (DMFO), 24.775 m (other cars).
Couplers: Dellner 12.   **Maximum Speed:** 200 mph (320 km/h).
Built: 2012–17 by Siemens, Krefeld, Germany.

DM vehicles carry the full 12-digit EVNs as indicated below. For example set 4001/02 carries the numbers 93 70 3740 011-9 + 93 70 3740 012-7 + 93 70 3740 013-5 + 93 70 3740 014-3 + 93 70 3740 015-0 + 93 70 3740 016-8 + 93 70 3740 017-6 + 93 70 3740 018-4 + 93 70 3740 028-3 + 93 70 3740 027-5 + 93 70 3740 026-7 + 93 70 3740 025-9 + 93 70 3740 024-2 + 93 70 3740 023-4 + 93 70 3740 022-6 + 93 70 3740 021-8.

93 70 3740 xx1-c series. DMFO. Siemens Krefeld 2012–17. 40/–. 58.0 t.
93 70 3740 xx2-c series. TBFO. Siemens Krefeld 2012–17. 36/– 2T. 59.0 t.
93 70 3740 xx3-c series. MFO. Siemens Krefeld 2012–17. 34/–(+2) 1TD 2W. 59.0 t.
93 70 3740 xx4-c series. TSO. Siemens Krefeld 2012–17. –/76 2T. 53.0 t.
93 70 3740 xx5-c series. TSO. Siemens Krefeld 2012–17. –/76 2T. 53.0 t.
93 70 3740 xx6-c series. MSO. Siemens Krefeld 2012–17. –/76 2T. 58.0 t.
93 70 3740 xx7-c series. TSO. Siemens Krefeld 2012–17. –/76 2T. 57.0 t.
93 70 3740 xx8-c series. MSORB. Siemens Krefeld 2012–17. –/32 2T. 58.0 t.

4001	**ER**	EU	*EU*	TI		4018	**ER**	EU	*EU*	TI
4002	**ER**	EU	*EU*	TI		4019	**ER**	EU	*EU*	TI
4003	**ER**	EU	*EU*	TI		4020	**ER**	EU	*EU*	TI
4004	**ER**	EU	*EU*	TI		4021	**ER**	EU	*EU*	TI
4005	**ER**	EU	*EU*	TI		4022	**ER**	EU	*EU*	TI
4006	**ER**	EU	*EU*	TI		4023	**ER**	EU	*EU*	TI
4007	**ER**	EU	*EU*	TI		4024	**ER**	EU	*EU*	TI
4008	**ER**	EU	*EU*	TI		4025	**ER**	EU		
4009	**ER**	EU	*EU*	TI		4026	**ER**	EU		
4010	**ER**	EU	*EU*	TI		4027	**ER**	EU		
4011	**ER**	EU	*EU*	TI		4028	**ER**	EU		
4012	**ER**	EU	*EU*	TI		4029	**ER**	EU		
4013	**ER**	EU	*EU*	TI		4030	**ER**	EU		
4014	**ER**	EU	*EU*	TI		4031	**ER**	EU		
4015	**ER**	EU	*EU*	TI		4032	**ER**	EU		
4016	**ER**	EU	*EU*	TI		4033	**ER**	EU		
4017	**ER**	EU	*EU*	TI		4034	**ER**	EU		

4.6. SERVICE EMUS

The following unit is used by Network Rail for ERTMS testing on the Hertford Loop. It has been heavily modified from its original condition, and now includes a toilet.

313 121 **Y** BN *GB* WN 62549 71233 62613

4.7. EMU VEHICLES IN INDUSTRIAL SERVICE

This list comprises EMU vehicles that have been withdrawn from active service but continue to be used in industrial service.

Cl. 390	69133	69833		Virgin Trains Training Centre, Westmere Drive, Crewe, Cheshire
Cl. 390	69633	69733		The Fire Service College, Moreton-in-Marsh, Gloucestershire
Cl. 390	69933			Safety & Accident Investigation Centre, Cranfield University, Cranfield, Bedfordshire
Cl. 508	64649	64712		Emergency Services Training Centre, Seacombe, Merseyside
Cl. 508	64681	71511	64724	The Fire Service College, Moreton-in-Marsh, Gloucestershire

4.8. EMUS AWAITING DISPOSAL

This list comprises vehicles awaiting disposal which are stored on the national railway network.

25 kV AC 50 Hz OVERHEAD UNITS:

| Cl. 309 | **RR** | WC | CS | 71758 |
| Cl. 365 | **N** | X | ZN | 65919 |

750 V DC THIRD RAIL UNITS:

| Cl. 508 | **CN** | A | ZG | 64680 | 64723 |

5. ON-TRACK MACHINES

These machines are used for maintaining, renewing and enhancing the infrastructure of the national railway network. With the exception of snowploughs all can be self-propelled, controlled either from a cab mounted on the machine or remotely. They are permitted to operate either under their own power or in train formations throughout the network both within and outside engineering possessions. Machines only permitted to be used within engineering possessions, referred to as On-Track Plant, are not included. Also not included are wagons included in OTM consists.

For each machine its Network Rail registered number, owner or responsible custodian and type is given, plus its name if carried. In addition, for snow clearance equipment the berthing location is given. Actual operation of each machine is undertaken by either the owner/responsible custodian or a contracted responsible custodian.

Machines were numbered by British Rail with either six-digit wagon series numbers or in the CEPS (Civil Engineers Plant System) series with five prefixed digits. Recently delivered machines have been numbered in the EVN series. Machines may also carry additional identifying numbers which are shown as "xxxx". Machines are listed here in CEPS/wagon series order. Those with EVN numbers are included where they would have been if allocated CEPS numbers.

(S) after the registered number designates a machine that is currently stored (the storage location of each is given at the end of this section).

DYNAMIC TRACK STABILISERS

| DR 72211 | BB | Plasser & Theurer DGS 62-N |
| DR 72213 | BB | Plasser & Theurer DGS 62-N |

TAMPERS

DR 73108	CS	Plasser & Theurer 09-32-RT	Tiger
DR 73109	SK	Plasser & Theurer 09-3X-RT	
DR 73110	SK	Plasser & Theurer 09-3X-RT	PETER WHITE
DR 73111	NR	Plasser & Theurer 09-3X-Dynamic	
DR 73113	NR	Plasser & Theurer 09-3X-Dynamic	
DR 73114	NR	Plasser & Theurer 09-3X-Dynamic	Ron Henderson
DR 73115	NR	Plasser & Theurer 09-3X-Dynamic	
DR 73116	NR	Plasser & Theurer 09-3X Dynamic	
DR 73117	NR	Plasser & Theurer 09-3X Dynamic	
DR 73118	NR	Plasser & Theurer 09-3X Dynamic	
99 70 9123 120-6	NR	Plasser & Theurer 09-3X Dynamic "DR 73120"	
99 70 9123 121-4	NR	Plasser & Theurer 09-2X Dynamic "DR 73121"	
99 70 9123 122-2	NR	Plasser & Theurer 09-2X Dynamic "DR 73122"	
DR 73803	SK	Plasser & Theurer 08-32U-RT	Alexander Graham Bell

DR 73804	SK	Plasser & Theurer 08-32U-RT	James Watt
DR 73805	CS	Plasser & Theurer 08-16/32U-RT	
DR 73806	CS	Plasser & Theurer 08-16/32U-RT	Karine
DR 73904	SK	Plasser & Theurer 08-4x4/4S-RT	Thomas Telford
DR 73905	CS	Plasser & Theurer 08-4x4/4S-RT	
DR 73906	CS	Plasser & Theurer 08-4x4/4S-RT	Panther
DR 73907	CS	Plasser & Theurer 08-4x4/4S-RT	
DR 73908	CS	Plasser & Theurer 08-4x4/4S-RT	
DR 73909	CS	Plasser & Theurer 08-4x4/4S-RT	Saturn
DR 73910	CS	Plasser & Theurer 08-4x4/4S-RT	Jupiter
DR 73911	CS	Plasser & Theurer 08-16/4x4C-RT	Puma
DR 73912	CS	Plasser & Theurer 08-16/4x4C-RT	Lynx
DR 73913	CS	Plasser & Theurer 08-12/4x4C-RT	
DR 73914	SK	Plasser & Theurer 08-4x4/4S-RT	Robert McAlpine
DR 73915	SK	Plasser & Theurer 08-16/4x4C-RT	William Arrol
DR 73916	SK	Plasser & Theurer 08-16/4x4C-RT	First Engineering
DR 73917	BB	Plasser & Theurer 08-4x4/4S-RT	
DR 73918	BB	Plasser & Theurer 08-4x4/4S-RT	
DR 73919	CS	Plasser & Theurer 08-16/4x4C100-RT	
DR 73920	CS	Plasser & Theurer 08-16/4x4C80-RT	
DR 73921	CS	Plasser & Theurer 08-16/4x4C80-RT	
DR 73922	CS	Plasser & Theurer 08-16/4x4C80-RT	John Snowdon
DR 73923	CS	Plasser & Theurer 08-4x4/4S-RT	Mercury
DR 73924	CS	Plasser & Theurer 08-16/4x4C100-RT	
DR 73925	CS	Plasser & Theurer 08-16/4x4C100-RT	Europa
DR 73926	BB	Plasser & Theurer 08-16/4x4C100-RT	Stephen Keith Blanchard
DR 73927	BB	Plasser & Theurer 08-16/4x4C100-RT	
DR 73928	BB	Plasser & Theurer 08-16/4x4C100-RT	
DR 73929	CS	Plasser & Theurer 08-4x4/4S-RT	
DR 73930	CS	Plasser & Theurer 08-4x4/4S-RT	
DR 73931	CS	Plasser & Theurer 08-16/4x4C100-RT	
DR 73932	SK	Plasser & Theurer 08-4x4/4S-RT	
DR 73933	SK	Plasser & Theurer 08-16/4x4/C100-RT	
DR 73934	SK	Plasser & Theurer 08-16/4x4/C100-RT	
DR 73935	CS	Plasser & Theurer 08-4x4/4S-RT	
DR 73936	CS	Plasser & Theurer 08-4x4/4S-RT	
DR 73937	BB	Plasser & Theurer 08-16/4x4C100-RT	
DR 73938	BB	Plasser & Theurer 08-16/4x4C100-RT	
DR 73939	BB	Plasser & Theurer 08-16/4x4C100-RT	Pat Best
DR 73940	SK	Plasser & Theurer 08-4x4/4S-RT	
DR 73941	SK	Plasser & Theurer 08-4x4/4S-RT	
DR 73942	CS	Plasser & Theurer 08-4x4/4S-RT	
DR 73943	BB	Plasser & Theurer 08-16/4x4C100-RT	
DR 73944	BB	Plasser & Theurer 08-16/4x4C100-RT	
DR 73945	BB	Plasser & Theurer 08-16/4x4C100-RT	
DR 73946	VO	Plasser & Theurer Euromat 08-4x4/4S	
DR 73947	CS	Plasser & Theurer 08-4x4/4S-RT	
DR 73948	CS	Plasser & Theurer 08-4x4/4S-RT	

99 70 9128 001-3 SK Plasser & Theurer Unimat 09-4x4/4S Dynamic "928001"
99 70 9128 002-1 SK Plasser & Theurer Unimat 09-4x4/4S Dynamic "DR 74002"

DR 75301	VO	Matisa B 45 UE	
DR 75302	VO	Matisa B 45 UE	
DR 75303	VO	Matisa B 45 UE	Gary Wright
DR 75401	VO	Matisa B 41 UE	
DR 75402	VO	Matisa B 41 UE	
DR 75403 (S)	VO	Matisa B 41 UE	
DR 75404	VO	Matisa B 41 UE	
DR 75405	VO	Matisa B 41 UE	
DR 75406	CS	Matisa B 41 UE	Eric Machell
DR 75407	CS	Matisa B 41 UE	
DR 75408	BB	Matisa B 41 UE	
DR 75409	BB	Matisa B 41 UE	
DR 75410	BB	Matisa B 41 UE	
DR 75411	BB	Matisa B 41 UE	
DR 75501	BB	Matisa B 66 UC	
DR 75502	BB	Matisa B 66 UC	

BALLAST CLEANERS

DR 76323	NR	Plasser & Theurer RM95-RT
DR 76324	NR	Plasser & Theurer RM95-RT
DR 76501	NR	Plasser & Theurer RM-900-RT
DR 76502	NR	Plasser & Theurer RM-900-RT
DR 76503	NR	Plasser & Theurer RM-900-RT

99 70 9314 504-0 NR   Plasser & Theurer RM-900   "DR 76504"

VACUUM PREPARATION MACHINES

DR 76701	NR	Plasser & Theurer VM80-NR
DR 76702	NR	Plasser & Theurer VM80-NR
DR 76703	NR	Plasser & Theurer VM80-NR
DR 76710 (S)	NR	Plasser & Theurer VM80-TRS
DR 76711 (S)	NR	Plasser & Theurer VM80-TRS

RAIL VACUUM MACHINES

99 70 9515 001-4	RC	Railcare 16000-480-UK RailVac OTM
99 70 9515 002-2	RC	Railcare 16000-480-UK RailVac OTM
99 70 9515 003-0	RC	Railcare 16000-480-UK RailVac OTM
99 70 9515 004-8	RC	Railcare 16000-480-UK RailVac OTM
99 70 9515 005-5	RC	Railcare 16000-480-UK RailVac OTM
99 70 9515 006-3	RC	Railcare 16000-480-UK RailVac OTM

BALLAST TRANSFER MACHINES

| DR 76750 | NR | Matisa D75 | *(works with DR 78802/DR 78812/ DR 78822/DR 78832)* |
| DR 76751 | NR | Matisa D75 | *(works with DR 78801/DR 78811/ DR 78821/DR 78831)* |

CONSOLIDATION MACHINES

DR 76801	NR	Plasser & Theurer 09-CM-NR
99 70 9320 802-0	NR	Plasser & Theurer 09-2X-CM "DR 76802"

FINISHING MACHINES & BALLAST REGULATORS

DR 77001	SK	Plasser & Theurer AFM 2000-RT Finishing Machine
DR 77002	SK	Plasser & Theurer AFM 2000-RT Finishing Machine

99 70 9125 010-7 NR　Plasser & Theurer USP 6000 Regulator "DR 77010"

DR 77315 (S)	BB	Plasser & Theurer USP 5000C Regulator
DR 77316 (S)	BB	Plasser & Theurer USP 5000C Regulator
DR 77322	BB	Plasser & Theurer USP 5000C Regulator
DR 77327	CS	Plasser & Theurer USP 5000C Regulator
DR 77336 (S)	BB	Plasser & Theurer USP 5000C Regulator
DR 77801	VO	Matisa R 24 S Regulator
DR 77802	VO	Matisa R 24 S Regulator
DR 77901	CS	Plasser & Theurer USP 5000-RT Regulator
DR 77903	NR	Plasser & Theurer USP 5000-RT Regulator
DR 77904	NR	Plasser & Theurer USP 5000-RT Regulator
DR 77905	NR	Plasser & Theurer USP 5000-RT Regulator
DR 77906	NR	Plasser & Theurer USP 5000-RT Regulator
DR 77907	NR	Plasser & Theurer USP 5000-RT Regulator
DR 77908	SK	Plasser & Theurer USP 5000-RT Regulator

99 70 9125 909-0 NR　Plasser & Theurer USP 5000 Regulator "DR 77909"

TWIN JIB TRACK RELAYERS

DRP 78213	VO	Plasser & Theurer Self-Propelled Heavy Duty
DRP 78215	SK	Plasser & Theurer Self-Propelled Heavy Duty
DRP 78216	BB	Plasser & Theurer Self-Propelled Heavy Duty
DRP 78217 (S)	SK	Plasser & Theurer Self-Propelled Heavy Duty
DRP 78218 (S)	BB	Plasser & Theurer Self-Propelled Heavy Duty
DRP 78219	SK	Plasser & Theurer Self-Propelled Heavy Duty
DRP 78221	BB	Plasser & Theurer Self-Propelled Heavy Duty
DRP 78222	BB	Plasser & Theurer Self-Propelled Heavy Duty
DRP 78223 (S)	BB	Plasser & Theurer Self-Propelled Heavy Duty
DRP 78224 (S)	BB	Plasser & Theurer Self-Propelled Heavy Duty
DRC 78226	CS	Cowans Sheldon Self-Propelled Heavy Duty
DRC 78229	NR	Cowans Sheldon Self-Propelled Heavy Duty
DRC 78231	NR	Cowans Sheldon Self-Propelled Heavy Duty
DRC 78234	NR	Cowans Sheldon Self-Propelled Heavy Duty
DRC 78235	CS	Cowans Sheldon Self-Propelled Heavy Duty
DRC 78237 (S)	NR	Cowans Sheldon Self-Propelled Heavy Duty

NEW TRACK CONSTRUCTION
TRAIN PROPULSION MACHINES

DR 78701	BB	Harsco Track Technologies NTC-PW
DR 78702	BB	Harsco Track Technologies NTC-PW

TRACK RENEWAL MACHINES

Matisa P95 Track Renewals Trains
DR 78801+DR 78811+DR 78821+DR 78831 NR *(works with DR 76751)*
DR 78802+DR 78812+DR 78822+DR 78832 NR *(works with DR 76750)*

RAIL GRINDING TRAINS

Loram SPML 15
DR 79200A + DR 79200B + DR 79200C   NR

Loram SPML 17
DR 79201A + DR 79201B   NR

Speno RPS-32
DR 79221 + DR 79222 + DR 79223 + DR 79224 + DR 79225 + DR 79226   SI

Loram C21
DR 79231 + DR 79232 + DR 79233 + DR 79234 + DR 79235 + DR 79236 + DR 79237   NR
DR 79241 + DR 79242 + DR 79243 + DR 79244 + DR 79245 + DR 79246 + DR 79247   NR
DR 79251 + DR 79252 + DR 79253 + DR 79254 + DR 79255 + DR 79256 + DR 79257   NR

Names: DR 79241/247   Roger South *(one plate on opposite sides of each)*
          DR 79251/257   Martin Elwood

Harsco Track Technologies RGH20C
DR 79261 + DR 79271   NR
DR 79262 + DR 79272   NR
DR 79263 + DR 79273   NR
DR 79264 + DR 79274   NR
DR 79265 (S)   NR   *spare vehicle*
DR 79267 + DR 79277   NR

Loram C44
99 70 9427 038-3 + 99 70 9427 039-1 + 99 70 9427 040-9 + 99 70 9427 041-7
                          NR   "DR 79301/302/303/304"

STONEBLOWERS

DR 80200 (S)	NR	Pandrol Jackson Plain Line
DR 80201	NR	Pandrol Jackson Plain Line
DR 80202 (S)	NR	Pandrol Jackson Plain Line
DR 80203 (S)	NR	Pandrol Jackson Plain Line
DR 80204 (S)	NR	Pandrol Jackson Plain Line
DR 80205	NR	Pandrol Jackson Plain Line
DR 80206	NR	Pandrol Jackson Plain Line
DR 80207 (S)	NR	Pandrol Jackson Plain Line
DR 80208	NR	Pandrol Jackson Plain Line
DR 80209	NR	Pandrol Jackson Plain Line
DR 80210	NR	Pandrol Jackson Plain Line
DR 80211	NR	Pandrol Jackson Plain Line
DR 80212 (S)	NR	Pandrol Jackson Plain Line
DR 80213	NR	Harsco Track Technologies Plain Line
DR 80214	NR	Harsco Track Technologies Plain Line
DR 80215	NR	Harsco Track Technologies Plain Line
DR 80216	NR	Harsco Track Technologies Plain Line
DR 80217	NR	Harsco Track Technologies Plain Line
DR 80301	NR	Harsco Track Technologies Multi-purpose Stephen Cornish
DR 80302	NR	Harsco Track Technologies Multi-purpose
DR 80303	NR	Harsco Track Technologies Multi-purpose

CRANES

DRP 81505	BB	Plasser & Theurer 12 tonne Heavy Duty Diesel Hydraulic
DRP 81507 (S)	BB	Plasser & Theurer 12 tonne Heavy Duty Diesel Hydraulic
DRP 81508	BB	Plasser & Theurer 12 tonne Heavy Duty Diesel Hydraulic
DRP 81511 (S)	BB	Plasser & Theurer 12 tonne Heavy Duty Diesel Hydraulic
DRP 81513	BB	Plasser & Theurer 12 tonne Heavy Duty Diesel Hydraulic
DRP 81517	BB	Plasser & Theurer 12 tonne Heavy Duty Diesel Hydraulic
DRP 81519 (S)	BB	Plasser & Theurer 12 tonne Heavy Duty Diesel Hydraulic
DRP 81522	BB	Plasser & Theurer 12 tonne Heavy Duty Diesel Hydraulic
DRP 81525	BB	Plasser & Theurer 12 tonne Heavy Duty Diesel Hydraulic
DRP 81532	BB	Plasser & Theurer 12 tonne Heavy Duty Diesel Hydraulic
DRK 81601	VO	Kirow KRC 810UK 100 tonne Heavy Duty Diesel Hydraulic
DRK 81602	BB	Kirow KRC 810UK 100 tonne Heavy Duty Diesel Hydraulic
DRK 81611	BB	Kirow KRC 1200UK 125 tonne Heavy Duty Diesel Hydraulic
DRK 81612	CS	Kirow KRC 1200UK 125 tonne Heavy Duty Diesel Hydraulic
DRK 81613	VO	Kirow KRC 1200UK 125 tonne Heavy Duty Diesel Hydraulic
DRK 81621	VO	Kirow KRC 250UK 25 tonne Diesel Hydraulic
DRK 81622	VO	Kirow KRC 250UK 25 tonne Diesel Hydraulic
DRK 81623	SK	Kirow KRC 250UK 25 tonne Diesel Hydraulic
DRK 81624	SK	Kirow KRC 250UK 25 tonne Diesel Hydraulic
DRK 81625	SK	Kirow KRC 250UK 25 tonne Diesel Hydraulic

99 70 9319 012-9 SK Kirow KRC 250S 25 tonne Diesel Hydraulic "DRK 81626"
99 70 9319 013-7 NR Kirow KRC 1200UK 125 tonne Heavy Duty Diesel Hydraulic

Names:

DRK 81601   Nigel Chester | DRK 81611   Malcolm L. Pearce

LONG WELDED RAIL TRAIN PROPULSION MACHINES

DR 89005	NR	Cowans Boyd PW
DR 89006 (S)	NR	Cowans Boyd PW
DR 89007	NR	Cowans Boyd PW
DR 89008	NR	Cowans Boyd PW
DR 89009 (S)	NR	Cowans Boyd PW

BALLAST SYSTEM PROPULSION MACHINES

DR 92263 (S)	NR	Plasser & Theurer MFS-PW	
DR 92264	NR	Plasser & Theurer NB-PW	
DR 92285	NR	Plasser & Theurer PW-RT	
DR 92286	NR	Plasser & Theurer NPW-RT	
DR 92331	NR	Plasser & Theurer PW-RT	
DR 92332	NR	Plasser & Theurer NPW-RT	
DR 92431	NR	Plasser & Theurer PW-RT	
DR 92432	NR	Plasser & Theurer NPW-RT	
99 70 9310 477-3	NR	Plasser & Theurer PW	"DR 92477"
99 70 9310 478-1	NR	Plasser & Theurer NPW	"DR 92478"

BREAKDOWN CRANES

ADRC 96710 (S)	NR	Cowans Sheldon 75 tonne Diesel Hydraulic
ADRC 96713 (S)	NR	Cowans Sheldon 75 tonne Diesel Hydraulic
ADRC 96714 (S)	NR	Cowans Sheldon 75 tonne Diesel Hydraulic
ADRC 96715 (S)	NR	Cowans Sheldon 75 tonne Diesel Hydraulic

GENERAL PURPOSE VEHICLES

DR 97001	H1	Eiv de Brieve DU94BA TRAMM with Crane "DU 94 B 001 URS"
DR 97011	H1	Windhoff MPV (Modular)
DR 97012	H1	Windhoff MPV (Modular)
DR 97013	H1	Windhoff MPV (Modular)
DR 97014	H1	Windhoff MPV (Modular)
DR 98215A + DR 98215B	BB	Plasser & Theurer GP-TRAMM with Trailer
DR 98216A + DR 98216B	BB	Plasser & Theurer GP-TRAMM with Trailer
DR 98217A + DR 98217B	BB	Plasser & Theurer GP-TRAMM with Trailer
DR 98218A + DR 98218B	BB	Plasser & Theurer GP-TRAMM with Trailer
DR 98219A + DR 98219B	BB	Plasser & Theurer GP-TRAMM with Trailer
DR 98220A + DR 98220B	BB	Plasser & Theurer GP-TRAMM with Trailer
DR 98305 (S)	NR	Geismar GP-TRAMM VMT 860 PL/UM
DR 98306 (S)	NR	Geismar GP-TRAMM VMT 860 PL/UM

INFRASTRUCTURE MONITORING VEHICLES

Note: "950 001" is a purpose-built Track Assessment Unit based on the BREL Class 150/1 design.

DR 98008	NR	Windhoff MPV Twin-cab with surveying equipment
999600+999601	NR	BREL York Track Assessment Unit "950 001"
999800 (S)	NR	Plasser & Theurer EM-SAT 100/RT Track Survey Car
999801 (S)	NR	Plasser & Theurer EM-SAT 100/RT Track Survey Car

Name:

999800   Richard Spoors

SNOWPLOUGHS

ADB 965203	NR	Independent Drift Plough	Carlisle Kingmoor Depot
ADB 965206	NR	Independent Drift Plough	York Parcels Sidings
ADB 965208	NR	Independent Drift Plough	Motherwell Depot
ADB 965209	NR	Independent Drift Plough	Taunton Fairwater Yard
ADB 965210	NR	Independent Drift Plough	Tonbridge West Yard
ADB 965211	NR	Independent Drift Plough	March Depot
ADB 965217	NR	Independent Drift Plough	Edinburgh Slateford Depot
ADB 965219	NR	Independent Drift Plough	Edinburgh Slateford Depot
ADB 965223	NR	Independent Drift Plough	Cardiff Canton Depot
ADB 965224	NR	Independent Drift Plough	Carlisle Kingmoor Depot
ADB 965230	NR	Independent Drift Plough	Carlisle Kingmoor Depot
ADB 965231	NR	Independent Drift Plough	Taunton Tamper Sidings
ADB 965234	NR	Independent Drift Plough	Inverness Millburn Yard
ADB 965235	NR	Independent Drift Plough	Cardiff Taff Vale Sidings
ADB 965236	NR	Independent Drift Plough	Tonbridge West Yard
ADB 965237	NR	Independent Drift Plough	March Depot
ADB 965240	NR	Independent Drift Plough	Motherwell Depot
ADB 965241	NR	Independent Drift Plough	York Turntable Sidings
ADB 965242	NR	Independent Drift Plough	Carlisle High Wapping Sidings
ADB 965243	NR	Independent Drift Plough	Inverness Millburn Yard
ADB 965576	NR	Beilhack Type PB600 Plough	Doncaster West Yard
ADB 965577	NR	Beilhack Type PB600 Plough	Doncaster West Yard
ADB 965578	NR	Beilhack Type PB600 Plough	Carlisle Kingmoor Yard
ADB 965579	NR	Beilhack Type PB600 Plough	Carlisle Kingmoor Yard
ADB 965580	NR	Beilhack Type PB600 Plough	Crewe Gresty Bridge Depot
ADB 965581	NR	Beilhack Type PB600 Plough	Crewe Gresty Bridge Depot
ADB 966098	NR	Beilhack Type PB600 Plough	Doncaster West Yard
ADB 966099	NR	Beilhack Type PB600 Plough	Doncaster West Yard

SNOWBLOWERS

ADB 968500	NR	Beilhack Self-Propelled Rotary	Edinburgh Slateford Depot
ADB 968501	NR	Beilhack Self-Propelled Rotary	Edinburgh Slateford Depot